W9-AMA-462

THIRD EDITION

Java Cookbook

Ian F. Darwin

Beijing · Cambridge · Farnham · Köln · Sebastopol · Tokyo   

Java Cookbook, Third Edition

by Ian F. Darwin

Copyright © 2014 RejmiNet Group, Inc.. All rights reserved.

Printed in the United States of America.

Published by O'Reilly Media, Inc., 1005 Gravenstein Highway North, Sebastopol, CA 95472.

O'Reilly books may be purchased for educational, business, or sales promotional use. Online editions are also available for most titles (*http://my.safaribooksonline.com*). For more information, contact our corporate/institutional sales department: 800-998-9938 or *corporate@oreilly.com*.

Editors: Mike Loukides and Meghan Blanchette	**Indexer:** Lucie Haskins
Production Editor: Melanie Yarbrough	**Cover Designer:** Randy Comer
Copyeditor: Kim Cofer	**Interior Designer:** David Futato
Proofreader: Jasmine Kwityn	**Illustrator:** Rebecca Demarest

June 2014:   Third Edition

Revision History for the Third Edition:

2014-06-20:   First release

See *http://oreilly.com/catalog/errata.csp?isbn=9781449337049* for release details.

Nutshell Handbook, the Nutshell Handbook logo, and the O'Reilly logo are registered trademarks of O'Reilly Media, Inc. *Java Cookbook*, the cover image of a domestic chicken, and related trade dress are trademarks of O'Reilly Media, Inc.

Many of the designations used by manufacturers and sellers to distinguish their products are claimed as trademarks. Where those designations appear in this book, and O'Reilly Media, Inc. was aware of a trademark claim, the designations have been printed in caps or initial caps.

While every precaution has been taken in the preparation of this book, the publisher and author assume no responsibility for errors or omissions, or for damages resulting from the use of the information contained herein.

ISBN: 978-1-449-33704-9

[LSI]

Table of Contents

Preface

Preface to the Third Edition

Java 8 is the new kid on the block. Java 7 was a significant but incremental improvement over its predecessors. So much has changed since the previous edition of this book! What was "new in Java 5" has become ubiquitous in Java: annotations, generic types, concurrency utilities, and more. APIs have come and gone across the entire tableau of Java: JavaME is pretty much dead now that BlackBerry has abandoned it; JSF is (slowly) replacing JSP in parts of Enterprise Java; and Spring continues to expand its reach. Many people seem to think that "desktop Java" is dead or even that "Java is dying," but it is definitely not rolling over yet; Swing, JavaFX, Java Enterprise, and (despite a major lawsuit by Oracle) Android are keeping the Java language very much alive. Additionally, a renewed interest in other "JVM languages" such as Groovy, JRuby, Jython, Scala, and Clojure is keeping the platform in the forefront of the development world.

Indeed, the main challenge in preparing this third edition has been narrowing down the popular APIs, keeping my own excitement and biases in check, to make a book that will fit into the size constraints established by the O'Reilly *Cookbook* series and my own previous editions. The book has to remain around 900 pages in length, and it certainly would not were I to try to fit in "all that glistens."

I've also removed certain APIs that were in the previous editions. Most notable is the chapter on serial and parallel ports (pared down to one recipe in Chapter 10); computers generally don't ship with these anymore, and hardly anybody is using them: the main attention has moved to USB, and there doesn't seem to be a standard API for Java yet (nor, frankly, much real interest among developers).

Preface to Previous Editions

If you know a little Java, great. If you know more Java, even better! This book is ideal for anyone who knows some Java and wants to learn more. If you don't know *any* Java yet, you should start with one of the more introductory books, such as *Head First*

Java (O'Reilly) or *Learning Java* (O'Reilly) if you're new to this family of languages, or *Java in a Nutshell* (O'Reilly) if you're an experienced C programmer.

I started programming in C in 1980 while working at the University of Toronto, and C served me quite well through the 1980s and into the 1990s. In 1995, as the nascent language Oak was being renamed Java, I had the good fortune of being told about it by my colleague J. Greg Davidson. I sent an email to the address Greg provided, and got this mail back from James Gosling, Java's inventor, in March 1995:

```
| Hi. A friend told me about WebRunner(?), your extensible network
| browser. It and Oak(?) its extension language, sounded neat. Can
| you please tell me if it's available for play yet, and/or if any
| papers on it are available for FTP?

Check out http://java.sun.com
(oak got renamed to java and webrunner got renamed to
 hotjava to keep the lawyers happy)
```

So Oak became Java[1] before I could get started with it. I downloaded HotJava and began to play with it. At first I wasn't sure about this newfangled language, which looked like a mangled C/C++. I wrote test and demo programs, sticking them a few at a time into a directory that I called *javasrc* to keep it separate from my C source (because often the programs would have the same name). And as I learned more about Java, I began to see its advantages for many kinds of work, such as the automatic memory reclaim ("garbage collection") and the elimination of pointer calculations. The *javasrc* directory kept growing. I wrote a Java course for Learning Tree,[2] and the directory grew faster, reaching the point where it needed subdirectories. Even then, it became increasingly difficult to find things, and it soon became evident that some kind of documentation was needed.

In a sense, this book is the result of a high-speed collision between my *javasrc* directory and a documentation framework established for another newcomer language. In O'Reilly's *Perl Cookbook*, Tom Christiansen and Nathan Torkington worked out a very successful design, presenting the material in small, focused articles called "recipes," for the then-new Perl language. The original model for such a book is, of course, the familiar kitchen cookbook. Using the term "cookbook" to refer to an enumeration of how-to recipes relating to computers has a long history. On the software side, Donald Knuth applied the "cookbook" analogy to his book *The Art of Computer Programming* (Addison-Wesley), first published in 1968. On the hardware side, Don Lancaster wrote *The TTL Cookbook* (Sams). (Transistor-transistor logic, or TTL, was the small-scale building block of electronic circuits at the time.) Tom and Nathan worked out a

---

1. Editor's note: the "other Oak" that triggered this renaming was not a computer language, as is sometimes supposed, but Oak Technology, makers of video cards and the *cdrom.sys* file that was on every DOS/Windows PC at one point.

2. One of the world's leading high-tech, vendor-independent training companies; see *http://www.learning tree.com/*.

successful variation on this, and I recommend their book for anyone who wishes to, as they put it, "learn more Perl." Indeed, the work you are now reading strives to be the book for the person who wishes to "learn more Java."

The code in each recipe is intended to be largely self-contained; feel free to borrow bits and pieces of any of it for use in your own projects. The code is distributed with a Berkeley-style copyright, just to discourage wholesale reproduction.

Who This Book Is For

I'm going to assume that you know the basics of Java. I won't tell you how to `println` a string and a number at the same time, or how to write a class that extends `JFrame` and prints your name in the window. I'll presume you've taken a Java course or studied an introductory book such as *Head First Java*, *Learning Java*, or *Java in a Nutshell* (O'Reilly). However, Chapter 1 covers some techniques that you might not know very well and that are necessary to understand some of the later material. Feel free to skip around! Both the printed version of the book and the electronic copy are heavily cross-referenced.

What's in This Book?

Unlike my Perl colleagues Tom and Nathan, I don't have to spend as much time on the oddities and idioms of the language; Java is refreshingly free of strange quirks.[3] But that doesn't mean it's trivial to learn well! If it were, there'd be no need for this book. My main approach, then, is to concentrate on the Java APIs. I'll teach you by example what the important APIs are and what they are good for.

Like Perl, Java is a language that grows on you and with you. And, I confess, I use Java most of the time nowadays. Things I once did in C—except for device drivers and legacy systems—I now do in Java.

Java is suited to a different range of tasks than Perl, however. Perl (and other scripting languages, such as awk and Python) is particularly suited to the "one-liner" utility task. As Tom and Nathan show, Perl excels at things like printing the 42nd line from a file. Although Java can certainly do these things, it seems more suited to "development in the large," or enterprise applications development, because it is a compiled, object-oriented language. Indeed, much of the API material added in Java 2 was aimed at this type of development. However, I will necessarily illustrate many techniques with shorter examples and even code fragments. Be assured that every fragment of code you see here (except for some one- or two-liners) has been compiled and run.

---

3. Well, not completely. See the *Java Puzzlers* books (*http://javapuzzlers.com*) by Joshua Bloch and Neal Gafter for the actual quirks.

Some of the longer examples in this book are tools that I originally wrote to automate some mundane task or another. For example, a tool called MkIndex (in the *javasrc* repository) reads the top-level directory of the place where I keep all my Java example source code and builds a browser-friendly *index.html* file for that directory. For another example, the body of the first edition was partly composed in XML (see Chapter 20); I used XML to type in and mark up the original text of some of the chapters of this book, and text was then converted to the publishing software format by the XmlForm program. This program also handled—by use of another program, GetMark—full and partial code insertions from the *javasrc* directory into the book manuscript. XmlForm is discussed in Chapter 20.

Organization of This Book

Let's go over the organization of this book. I start off Chapter 1, *Getting Started: Compiling, Running, and Debugging* by describing some methods of compiling your program on different platforms, running them in different environments (browser, command line, windowed desktop), and debugging.

Chapter 2, *Interacting with the Environment* moves from compiling and running your program to getting it to adapt to the surrounding countryside—the other programs that live in your computer.

The next few chapters deal with basic APIs. Chapter 3, *Strings and Things* concentrates on one of the most basic but powerful data types in Java, showing you how to assemble, dissect, compare, and rearrange what you might otherwise think of as ordinary text.

Chapter 4, *Pattern Matching with Regular Expressions* teaches you how to use the powerful regular expressions technology from Unix in many string-matching and pattern-matching problem domains. "Regex" processing has been standard in Java for years, but if you don't know how to use it, you may be "reinventing the flat tire."

Chapter 5, *Numbers* deals both with built-in numeric types such as int and double, as well as the corresponding API classes (Integer, Double, etc.) and the conversion and testing facilities they offer. There is also brief mention of the "big number" classes. Because Java programmers often need to deal in dates and times, both locally and internationally, Chapter 6, *Dates and Times—New API* covers this important topic.

The next two chapters cover data processing. As in most languages, *arrays* in Java are linear, indexed collections of similar-kind objects, as discussed in Chapter 7, *Structuring Data with Java*. This chapter goes on to deal with the many "Collections" classes: powerful ways of storing quantities of objects in the java.util package, including use of "Java Generics."

Despite some syntactic resemblance to procedural languages such as C, Java is at heart an object-oriented programming (OOP) language. Chapter 8, *Object-Oriented Techniques* discusses some of the key notions of OOP as it applies to Java, including the commonly overridden methods of `java.lang.Object` and the important issue of design patterns.

Java is not, and never will be, a pure "functional programming" (FP) language. However, it is possible to use some aspects of FP, increasingly so with Java 8 and its support of "lambda expressions" (a.k.a. "closures"). This is discussed in Chapter 9, *Functional Programming Techniques: Functional Interfaces, Streams, Parallel Collections*.

The next few chapters deal with aspects of traditional input and output. Chapter 10, *Input and Output* details the rules for reading and writing files (don't skip this if you think files are boring; you'll need some of this information in later chapters: you'll read and write on serial or parallel ports in this chapter, and on a socket-based network connection in Chapter 13, *Network Clients*!). Chapter 11, *Directory and Filesystem Operations* shows you everything else about files—such as finding their size and last-modified time—and about reading and modifying directories, creating temporary files, and renaming files on disk.

Chapter 12, *Media: Graphics, Audio, Video* leads us into the GUI development side of things. This chapter is a mix of the lower-level details (such as drawing graphics and setting fonts and colors), and very high-level activities (such as controlling a video clip or movie). In Chapter 14, *Graphical User Interfaces*, I cover the higher-level aspects of a GUI, such as buttons, labels, menus, and the like—the GUI's predefined components. Once you have a GUI (really, before you actually write it), you'll want to read Chapter 15, *Internationalization and Localization* so your programs can work as well in Akbar, Afghanistan, Algiers, Amsterdam, and Angleterre as they do in Alberta, Arkansas, and Alabama.

Because Java was originally promulgated as "the programming language for the Internet," it's only fair that we spend some of our time on networking in Java. Chapter 13, *Network Clients* covers the basics of network programming from the client side, focusing on sockets. For the third edition, Chapter 13, *Network Clients* has been refocused from applets and web clients to emphasize web service clients instead. Today so many applications need to access a web service, primarily RESTful web services, that this seemed to be necessary. We'll then move to the server side in Chapter 16, *Server-Side Java*, wherein you'll learn some server-side programming techniques.

Programs on the Net often need to generate or process electronic mail, so Chapter 17, *Java and Electronic Mail* covers this topic.

Chapter 18, *Database Access* covers the essentials of the higher-level database access (JPA and Hibernate) and the lower-level Java Database Connectivity (JDBC), showing how to connect to local or remote relational databases, store and retrieve data, and find out information about query results or about the database.

One simple text-based representation for data interchange is JSON, the JavaScript Object Notation. Chapter 19, *Processing JSON Data* describes the format and some of the many APIs that have emerged to deal with it.

Another textual form of storing and exchanging data is XML. Chapter 20, *Processing XML* discusses XML's formats and some operations you can apply using SAX and DOM, two standard Java APIs.

Chapter 21, *Packages and Packaging* shows how to create packages of classes that work together. This chapter also talks about "deploying" or distributing and installing your software.

Chapter 22, *Threaded Java* tells you how to write classes that appear to do more than one thing at a time and let you take advantage of powerful multiprocessor hardware.

Chapter 23, *Reflection, or "A Class Named Class"* lets you in on such secrets as how to write API cross-reference documents mechanically ("become a famous Java book author in your spare time!") and how web servers are able to load any old Servlet—never having seen that particular class before—and run it.

Sometimes you already have code written and working in another language that can do part of your work for you, or you want to use Java as part of a larger package. Chapter 24, *Using Java with Other Languages* shows you how to run an external program (compiled or script) and also interact directly with "native code" in C/C++ or other languages.

There isn't room in an 800-page book for everything I'd like to tell you about Java. The Afterword presents some closing thoughts and a link to my online summary of Java APIs that every Java developer should know about.

Finally, Appendix A gives the storied history of Java in a release-by-release timeline, so whatever version of Java you learned, you can jump in here and get up to date quickly.

No two programmers or writers will agree on the best order for presenting all the Java topics. To help you find your way around, I've included extensive cross-references, mostly by recipe number.

Platform Notes

Java has gone through many major versions as discussed in Appendix A. This book is aimed at the Java 7 and 8 platforms. By the time of publication, I expect that all Java projects in development will be using Java 6 or 7, with a few stragglers wedded to earlier versions for historical reasons (note that Java 6 has been in "end of life" status for about a year prior to this edition's publication). I have compiled all the code in the *javasrc* archive on several combinations of operating systems and Java versions to test this code for portability.

The Java API consists of two parts: core APIs and noncore APIs. The core is, by definition, what's included in the JDK that you download free from the Java website (*http://java.com*). Noncore is everything else. But even this "core" is far from tiny: it weighs in at around 50 packages and well over 3,000 public classes, averaging around a dozen public methods each. Programs that stick to this core API are reasonably assured of portability to any standard Java platform.

Java's noncore APIs are further divided into standard extensions and nonstandard extensions. All standard extensions have package names beginning with `javax`. But note that not all packages named `javax` are extensions: `javax.swing` and its subpackages—the Swing GUI packages—used to be extensions, but are now core. A Java licensee (such as Apple or IBM) is not required to implement every standard extension, but if it does, the interface of the standard extension should be adhered to. This book calls your attention to any code that depends on a standard extension. Little code here depends on nonstandard extensions, other than code listed in the book itself. My own package, `com.darwinsys`, contains some utility classes used here and there; you will see an import for this at the top of any file that uses classes from it.

In addition, two other *platforms*, Java ME and Java EE, are standardized. Java Micro Edition (Java ME) is concerned with small devices such as handhelds, cell phones, fax machines, and the like. Within Java ME are various "profiles" for different classes of devices. At the other end, the Java Enterprise Edition (Java EE) is concerned with building large, scalable, distributed applications. Servlets, JavaServer Pages, JavaServer Faces, CORBA, RMI, JavaMail, Enterprise JavaBeans (EJBs), Transactions, and other APIs are part of Java EE. Java ME and Java EE packages normally begin with "javax" because they are not core packages. This book does not cover these at all, but includes a few of the EE APIs that are also useful on the client side, such as JavaMail. As mentioned earlier, coverage of Servlets and JSPs from the first edition of this book has been removed because there is now a *Java Servlet and JSP Cookbook*.

Speaking of cell phones and mobile devices, you probably know that Android uses Java as its language. What is comforting to Java developers is that Android also uses most of the core Java API, except for Swing and AWT, for which it provides Android-specific replacements. The Java developer who wants to learn Android may consider looking at my *Android Cookbook*, or the book's website (*http://androidcookbook.com*).

Java Books

A lot of useful information is packed into this book. However, due to the breadth of topics, it is not possible to give book-length treatment to any one topic. Because of this, the book also contains references to many websites and other books. This is in keeping with my target audience: the person who wants to learn more about Java.

O'Reilly publishes, in my opinion, the best selection of Java books on the market. As the API continues to expand, so does the coverage. Check out the latest versions and ordering information from O'Reilly's collection of Java books (*http://oreil.ly/1j2WBGC*); you can buy them at most bookstores, both physical and virtual. You can also read them online through Safari (*http://safari.oreilly.com*), a paid subscription service. And, of course, most are now available in ebook format; O'Reilly eBooks are DRM free so you don't have to worry about their copy-protection scheme locking you into a particular device or system, as you do with certain other publishers. Though many books are mentioned at appropriate spots in the book, a few deserve special mention here.

First and foremost, David Flanagan's *Java in a Nutshell* (O'Reilly) offers a brief overview of the language and API and a detailed reference to the most essential packages. This is handy to keep beside your computer. *Head First Java* offers a much more whimsical introduction to the language and is recommended for the less experienced developer.

A definitive (and monumental) description of programming the Swing GUI is *Java Swing* by Marc Loy, Robert Eckstein, Dave Wood, James Elliott, and Brian Cole (O'Reilly).

Java Virtual Machine, by Jon Meyer and Troy Downing (O'Reilly), will intrigue the person who wants to know more about what's under the hood. This book is out of print but can be found used and in libraries.

Java Network Programming and *Java I/O*, both by Elliotte Rusty Harold (O'Reilly), are also useful references.

For Java Database work, *Database Programming with JDBC and Java* by George Reese, and *Pro JPA 2: Mastering the Java Persistence API* by Mike Keith and Merrick Schincariol (Apress), are recommended.

Although this book doesn't have much coverage of the Java EE, I'd like to mention two books on that topic:

- Arun Gupta's *Java EE 7 Essentials* covers the latest incarnation of the Enterprise Edition.
- Adam Bien's *Real World Java EE Patterns: Rethinking Best Practices* (*http://amzn.to/1gKnQFf*) offers useful insights in designing and implementing an Enterprise application.

You can find many more at the O'Reilly website (*http://oreilly.com*).

Before building and releasing a GUI application you should read Sun's official *Java Look and Feel Design Guidelines* (*http://bit.ly/1poMpke*) (Addison-Wesley). This work presents the views of the human factors and user-interface experts at Sun (before the

Oracle takeover) who worked with the Swing GUI package since its inception; they tell you how to make it work well.

Finally, although it's not a book, Oracle has a great deal of Java information (*http://bit.ly/1njtSRO*) on the Web. Part of this web page is a large diagram showing all the components of Java in a "conceptual diagram." An early version of this is shown in Figure P-1; each colored box is a clickable link to details on that particular technology. Note the useful "Java SE API" link at the right, which takes you to the javadoc pages for the entire Java SE API.

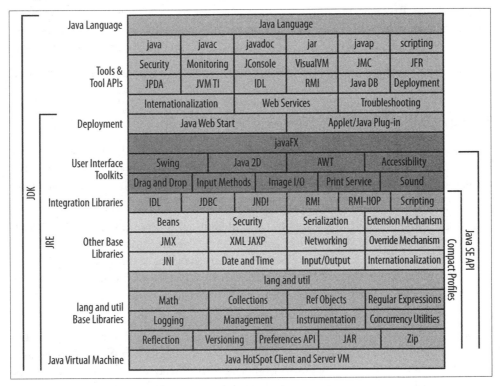

Figure P-1. Java conceptual diagram—Oracle Web

General Programming Books

Donald E. Knuth's *The Art of Computer Programming* has been a source of inspiration to generations of computing students since its first publication by Addison-Wesley in 1968. Volume 1 covers *Fundamental Algorithms*, Volume 2 is *Seminumerical Algorithms*, and Volume 3 is *Sorting and Searching*. The remaining four volumes in the projected series are still not completed. Although his examples are far from Java (he invented a hypothetical assembly language for his examples), many of his discussions of algorithms—of how computers ought to be used to solve real problems—are as relevant today as they were years ago.[4]

Though its code examples are quite dated now, the book *The Elements of Programming Style*, by Kernighan and Plauger, set the style (literally) for a generation of programmers with examples from various structured programming languages. Kernighan and Plauger also wrote a pair of books, *Software Tools* and *Software Tools in Pascal*, which demonstrated so much good advice on programming that I used to advise all programmers to read them. However, these three books are dated now; many times I wanted to write a follow-on book in a more modern language, but instead defer to *The Practice of Programming*, Brian's follow-on—cowritten with Rob Pike—to the *Software Tools* series. This book continues the Bell Labs (now part of Lucent) tradition of excellence in software textbooks. In Recipe 3.13, I have even adapted one bit of code from their book.

See also *The Pragmatic Programmer* by Andrew Hunt and David Thomas (Addison-Wesley).

Design Books

Peter Coad's *Java Design* (PTR-PH/Yourdon Press) discusses the issues of object-oriented analysis and design specifically for Java. Coad is somewhat critical of Java's implementation of the observable-observer paradigm and offers his own replacement for it.

One of the most famous books on object-oriented design in recent years is *Design Patterns* (*http://amzn.to/1eGbWw7*), by Gamma, Helm, Johnson, and Vlissides (Addison-Wesley). These authors are often collectively called "the gang of four," resulting in their book sometimes being referred to as "the GoF book." One of my colleagues called it "the best book on object-oriented design ever," and I agree; at the very least, it's among the best.

Refactoring, by Martin Fowler, covers a lot of "coding cleanups" that can be applied to code to improve readability and maintainability. Just as the GoF book introduced new terminology that helps developers and others communicate about how code is to be designed, Fowler's book provided a vocabulary for discussing how it is to be improved. But this book may be less useful than others; many of the "refactorings" now appear in the Refactoring Menu of the Eclipse IDE (see Recipe 1.3).

Two important streams of methodology theories are currently in circulation. The first is collectively known as Agile Methods, and its best-known members are Scrum (*http://bit.ly/1mNMszR*) and Extreme Programming (XP). XP (the methodology, not last year's flavor of Microsoft's OS) is presented in a series of small, short, readable texts led by its

---

4. With apologies for algorithm decisions that are less relevant today given the massive changes in computing power now available.

designer, Kent Beck. The first book in the XP series is *Extreme Programming Explained*. A good overview of all the Agile methods is Highsmith's *Agile Software Development Ecosystems*.

Another group of important books on methodology, covering the more traditional object-oriented design, is the UML series led by "the Three Amigos" (Booch, Jacobson, and Rumbaugh). Their major works are the UML *User Guide*, *UML Process*, and others. A smaller and more approachable book in the same series is Martin Fowler's *UML Distilled*.

Conventions Used in This Book

This book uses the following conventions.

Programming Conventions

I use the following terminology in this book. A program means any unit of code that can be run: an applet, a servlet, or an application. An applet is a Java program for use in a browser. A servlet is a Java component for use in a server, normally via HTTP. An application is any other type of program. A desktop application (a.k.a. client) interacts with the user. A server program deals with a client indirectly, usually via a network connection (and usually HTTP/HTTPS these days).

The examples shown are in two varieties. Those that begin with zero or more import statements, a javadoc comment, and a `public class` statement are complete examples. Those that begin with a declaration or executable statement, of course, are excerpts. However, the full versions of these excerpts have been compiled and run, and the online source includes the full versions.

Recipes are numbered by chapter and number, so, for example, Recipe 8.5 refers to the fifth recipe in Chapter 8.

Typesetting Conventions

The following typographic conventions are used in this book:

Italic
> Used for commands, filenames, and example URLs. It is also used to define new terms when they first appear in the text.

`Constant width`
> Used in code examples to show partial or complete Java source code program listings. It is also used for class names, method names, variable names, and other fragments of Java code.

Constant width bold

Used for user input, such as commands that you type on the command line.

Constant width italic

Shows text that should be replaced with user-supplied values or by values determined by context.

 This element signifies a tip or suggestion.

 This element signifies a general note.

 This icon indicates a warning or caution.

This icon indicates by its single digit the minimum Java platform required to use the API discussed in a given recipe (you may need Java 7 to compile the example code, even if it's not marked with a 7 icon). Only Java 6, 7, and 8 APIs are so denoted; anything earlier is assumed to work on any JVM that is still being used to develop code. Nobody should be using Java 5 (or anything before it!) for anything, and nobody should be doing new development in Java 6. If you are: it's time to move on!

Code Examples

Many programs are accompanied by an example showing them in action, run from the command line. These will usually show a prompt ending in either $ for Unix or > for Windows, depending on what type of computer I was using that day. Text before this prompt character can be ignored; it may be a pathname or a hostname, again depending on the system.

These will usually also show the full package name of the class because Java requires this when starting a program from the command line. This has the side effect of reminding you which subdirectory of the source repository to find the source code in, so this will not be pointed out explicitly very often.

We appreciate, but do not require, attribution. An attribution usually includes the title, author, publisher, and ISBN. For example: "*Java Cookbook* by Ian F. Darwin (O'Reilly). Copyright 2014 RejmiNet Group, Inc., 978-1-449-33704-9."

If you feel your use of code examples falls outside fair use or the permission given above, feel free to contact us at *permissions@oreilly.com*.

Safari® Books Online

 *Safari Books Online* is an on-demand digital library that delivers expert content in both book and video form from the world's leading authors in technology and business.

Technology professionals, software developers, web designers, and business and creative professionals use Safari Books Online as their primary resource for research, problem solving, learning, and certification training.

Safari Books Online offers a range of product mixes and pricing programs for organizations, government agencies, and individuals. Subscribers have access to thousands of books, training videos, and prepublication manuscripts in one fully searchable database from publishers like O'Reilly Media, Prentice Hall Professional, Addison-Wesley Professional, Microsoft Press, Sams, Que, Peachpit Press, Focal Press, Cisco Press, John Wiley & Sons, Syngress, Morgan Kaufmann, IBM Redbooks, Packt, Adobe Press, FT Press, Apress, Manning, New Riders, McGraw-Hill, Jones & Bartlett, Course Technology, and dozens more. For more information about Safari Books Online, please visit us online.

Comments and Questions

As mentioned earlier, I've tested all the code on at least one of the reference platforms, and most on several. Still, there may be platform dependencies, or even bugs, in my code or in some important Java implementation. Please report any errors you find, as well as your suggestions for future editions, by writing to:

O'Reilly Media, Inc.
1005 Gravenstein Highway North
Sebastopol, CA 95472
800-998-9938 (in the United States or Canada)
707-829-0515 (international or local)
707-829-0104 (fax)

We have a web page for this book, where we list errata, examples, and any additional information. You can access this page at *http://bit.ly/java-cookbook-3e*.

To comment or ask technical questions about this book, send email to *bookques tions@oreilly.com*.

For more information about our books, courses, conferences, and news, see our website at *http://www.oreilly.com*.

Find us on Facebook: *http://facebook.com/oreilly*

Follow us on Twitter: *http://twitter.com/oreillymedia*

Watch us on YouTube: *http://www.youtube.com/oreillymedia*

The O'Reilly site lists errata. You'll also find the source code for all the Java code examples to download; *please* don't waste your time typing them again! For specific instructions, see Recipe 1.5.

Acknowledgments

I wrote in the Afterword to the first edition that "writing this book has been a humbling experience." I should add that maintaining it has been humbling, too. While many reviewers and writers have been lavish with their praise—one very kind reviewer called it "arguably the best book ever written on the Java programming language"—I have been humbled by the number of errors and omissions in the first edition. In preparing this edition, I have endeavored to correct these.

My life has been touched many times by the flow of the fates bringing me into contact with the right person to show me the right thing at the right time. Steve Munro (*http://bit.ly/1qcUuXk*), with whom I've long since lost touch, introduced me to computers—in particular an IBM 360/30 at the Toronto Board of Education that was bigger than a living room, had 32 or 64*K* (not *M* or *G*!) of memory, and had perhaps the power of a PC/XT. Herb Kugel took me under his wing at the University of Toronto while I was learning about the larger IBM mainframes that came later. Terry Wood and Dennis Smith at the University of Toronto introduced me to mini- and micro-computers before there was an IBM PC. On evenings and weekends, the Toronto Business Club of Toastmasters International (*http://www.toastmasters.org*) and Al Lambert's Canada SCUBA School allowed me to develop my public speaking and instructional abilities. Several people at the University of Toronto, but especially Geoffrey Collyer (*http://bit.ly/1pfGwm1*), taught me the features and benefits of the Unix operating system at a time when I was ready to learn it.

Greg Davidson of UCSD taught the first Learning Tree course I attended and welcomed me as a Learning Tree instructor. Years later, when the Oak language was about to be released on Sun's website, Greg encouraged me to write to James Gosling and find out about it. James' reply (cited near the beginning of this Preface) that the lawyers had made them rename the language to Java and that it was "just now" available for download, is the prized first entry in my saved Java mailbox. Mike Rozek took me on as a Learning Tree course author for a Unix course and two Java courses. After Mike's departure from the company, Francesco Zamboni, Julane Marx, and Jennifer Urick in turn provided product management of these courses. When that effort ran out of steam, Jennifer also arranged permission for me to "reuse some code" in this book that had previously been used in my Java course notes. Finally, thanks to the many Learning Tree instructors and students who showed me ways of improving my presentations. I still teach for "The Tree" and recommend their courses for the busy developer who wants to zero in on one topic in detail over four days. You can also visit their website (*http://www.learningtree.com*).

Closer to this project, Tim O'Reilly believed in "the little Lint book" when it was just a sample chapter, enabling my early entry into the rarefied circle of O'Reilly authors. Years later, Mike Loukides encouraged me to keep trying to find a Java book idea that both he and I could work with. And he stuck by me when I kept falling behind the deadlines. Mike also read the entire manuscript and made many sensible comments, some of which brought flights of fancy down to earth. Jessamyn Read turned many faxed and emailed scratchings of dubious legibility into the quality illustrations you see in this book. And many, many other talented people at O'Reilly helped put this book into the form in which you now see it.

Third Edition

As always, this book would be nowhere without the wonderful support of so many people at O'Reilly. Meghan Blanchette, Sarah Schneider, Adam Witwer, Melanie Yarbrough, and the many production people listed on the copyright page all played a part in getting this book ready for you to read. The code examples are now dynamically included (so updates get done faster) rather than pasted in; my son and Haskell developer Benjamin Darwin, helped meet the deadline by converting almost the entire code base to O'Reilly's newest "include" mechanism, and by resolving a couple of other non-Java presentation issues; he also helped make Chapter 9 clearer and more functional. My reviewer, Alex Stangl, read the manuscript and went far above the call of duty, making innumerable helpful suggestions, even finding typos that had been present in previous editions! Helpful suggestions on particular sections were made by Benjamin Darwin, Mark Finkov, Igor Savin, and anyone I've forgotten to mention: I thank you all!

And again a thanks to all the readers who found errata and suggested improvements. Every new edition is better for the efforts of folks like you, who take the time and trouble to report that which needs reporting!

Second Edition

I wish to express my heartfelt thanks to all who sent in both comments and criticisms of the book after the first English edition was in print. Special mention must be made of one of the book's German translators,[5] Gisbert Selke, who read the first edition cover to cover during its translation and clarified my English. Gisbert did it all over again for the second edition and provided many code refactorings, which have made this a far better book than it would be otherwise. Going beyond the call of duty, Gisbert even contributed one recipe (Recipe 24.5) and revised some of the other recipes in the same chapter. Thank you, Gisbert! The second edition also benefited from comments by Jim Burgess, who read large parts of the book. Comments on individual chapters were received from Jonathan Fuerth, Kim Fowler, Marc Loy, and Mike McCloskey. My wife, Betty, and teenaged children each proofread several chapters as well.

The following people contributed significant bug reports or suggested improvements from the first edition: Rex Bosma, Rod Buchanan, John Chamberlain, Keith Goldman, Gilles-Philippe Gregoire, B. S. Hughes, Jeff Johnston, Rob Konigsberg, Tom Murtagh, Jonathan O'Connor, Mark Petrovic, Steve Reisman, Bruce X. Smith, and Patrick Wohlwend. My thanks to all of them, and my apologies to anybody I've missed.

My thanks to the good guys behind the O'Reilly "bookquestions" list for fielding so many questions. Thanks to Mike Loukides, Deb Cameron, and Marlowe Shaeffer for editorial and production work on the second edition.

First Edition

I also must thank my first-rate reviewers for the first edition, first and foremost my dear wife, Betty Cerar, who still knows more about the caffeinated beverage that I drink while programming than the programming language I use, but whose passion for clear expression and correct grammar has benefited so much of my writing during our life together. Jonathan Knudsen, Andy Oram, and David Flanagan commented on the out-

---

5. The first edition is available today in English, German, French, Polish, Russian, Korean, Traditional Chinese, and Simplified Chinese. My thanks to all the translators for their efforts in making the book available to a wider audience.

line when it was little more than a list of chapters and recipes, and yet were able to see the kind of book it could become, and to suggest ways to make it better. Learning Tree instructor Jim Burgess read most of the first edition with a very critical eye on locution, formulation, and code. Bil Lewis and Mike Slinn (*mslinn@mslinn.com*) made helpful comments on multiple drafts of the book. Ron Hitchens (*ron@ronsoft.com*) and Marc Loy carefully read the entire final draft of the first edition. I am grateful to Mike Loukides for his encouragement and support throughout the process. Editor Sue Miller helped shepherd the manuscript through the somewhat energetic final phases of production. Sarah Slocombe read the XML chapter in its entirety and made many lucid suggestions; unfortunately, time did not permit me to include all of them in the first edition. Each of these people made this book better in many ways, particularly by suggesting additional recipes or revising existing ones. The faults that remain are my own.

No book on Java would be complete without a quadrium[6] of thanks to James Gosling for inventing the first Unix Emacs, the *sc* spreadsheet, the NeWS window system, and Java. Thanks also to his employer Sun Microsystems (before they were taken over by Oracle) for creating not only the Java language but an incredible array of Java tools and API libraries freely available over the Internet.

Thanks to Tom and Nathan for the *Perl Cookbook*. Without them I might never have come up with the format for this book.

Willi Powell of Apple Canada provided Mac OS X access in the early days of OS X; I have since worn out an Apple notebook or two of my own. Thanks also to Apple for basing OS X on BSD Unix, making Apple the world's largest-volume commercial Unix company in the desktop environment (Google's Android is way larger than OS X in terms of unit shipments, but it's based on Linux and isn't a big player in the desktop).

To each and every one of you, my sincere thanks.

Book Production Software

I used a variety of tools and operating systems in preparing, compiling, and testing the first edition. The developers of OpenBSD (*http://www.openbsd.org*), "the proactively secure Unix-like system," deserve thanks for making a stable and secure Unix clone that is also closer to traditional Unix than other freeware systems. I used the *vi* editor (*vi* on OpenBSD and *vim* on Windows) while inputting the original manuscript in XML, and Adobe FrameMaker to format the documents. Each of these is an excellent tool in its own way, but I must add a caveat about FrameMaker. Adobe had four years from the release of OS X until I started the next revision cycle of this book, during which it could have produced a current Macintosh version of FrameMaker. It chose not do so, requiring

---

6. It's a good thing he only invented four major technologies, not five, or I'd have to rephrase that to avoid infringing on an Intel trademark.

me to do that revision in the increasingly ancient Classic environment. Strangely enough, its Mac sales of FrameMaker dropped steadily during this period, until, during the final production of the second edition, Adobe officially announced that it would no longer be producing any Macintosh versions of this excellent publishing software, ever. I do not know if I can ever forgive Adobe for destroying what was arguably the world's best documentation system.

Because of this, the crowd-sourced *Android Cookbook* that I edited was not prepared with Adobe's FrameMaker, but instead used XML DocBook (generated from Wiki markup on a Java-powered website that I wrote for the purpose) and a number of custom tools provided by O'Reilly's tools group.

The third edition of *Java Cookbook* was formatted in AsciiDoc (*http://asciidoc.org*) and the newer, faster AsciiDoctor (*http://asciidoctor.org*), and brought to life on the publishing interface of O'Reilly's Atlas (*http://atlas.oreilly.com*).

## CHAPTER 1

Getting Started: Compiling, Running, and Debugging

1.0. Introduction

This chapter covers some entry-level tasks that you need to know how to do before you can go on—it is said you must crawl before you can walk, and walk before you can ride a bicycle. Before you can try out anything in this book, you need to be able to compile and run your Java code, so I start there, showing several ways: the JDK way, the Integrated Development Environment (IDE) way, and the build tools (Ant, Maven, etc.) way. Another issue people run into is setting CLASSPATH correctly, so that's dealt with next. Deprecation warnings follow after that, because you're likely to encounter them in maintaining "old" Java code. The chapter ends with some general information about conditional compilation, unit testing, assertions, and debugging.

If you don't already have Java installed, you'll need to download it. Be aware that there are several different downloads. The JRE (Java Runtime Environment) is a smaller download for end users. The JDK or Java SDK download is the full development environment, which you'll want if you're going to be developing Java software.

Standard downloads for the current release of Java are available at Oracle's website (*http://bit.ly/TEA7iC*).

You can sometimes find prerelease builds of the next major Java version on *http://java.net*. For example, while this book's third edition was being written, Java 8 was not yet released, but JDK 8 builds could be obtained from the OpenJDK project (*https://jdk8.java.net/download.html*). The entire (almost) JDK is maintained as an open source project, and the OpenJDK source tree is used (with changes and additions) to build the commercial and supported Oracle JDKs.

If you're already happy with your IDE, you may wish to skip some or all of this material. It's here to ensure that everybody can compile and debug their programs before we move on.

1.1. Compiling and Running Java: JDK

Problem

You need to compile and run your Java program.

Solution

This is one of the few areas where your computer's operating system impinges on Java's portability, so let's get it out of the way first.

JDK

Using the command-line Java Development Kit (JDK) may be the best way to keep up with the very latest improvements in Java. Assuming you have the standard JDK installed in the standard location and/or have set its location in your PATH, you should be able to run the command-line JDK tools. Use the commands *javac* to compile and *java* to run your program (and, on Windows only, *javaw* to run a program without a console window). For example:

```
C:\javasrc>javac HelloWorld.java

C:\javasrc>java HelloWorld
Hello, World

C:\javasrc>
```

As you can see from the compiler's (lack of) output, this compiler works on the Unix "no news is good news" philosophy: if a program was able to do what you asked it to, it shouldn't bother nattering at you to say that it did so. Many people use this compiler or one of its clones.

There is an optional setting called CLASSPATH, discussed in Recipe 1.4, that controls where Java looks for classes. CLASSPATH, if set, is used by both `javac` and `java`. In older versions of Java, you had to set your CLASSPATH to include ".", even to run a simple program from the current directory; this is no longer true on current Java implementations.

Sun/Oracle's *javac* compiler is the official reference implementation. There were several alternative open source command-line compilers, including Jikes (*http://bit.ly/1l5jP5I*) and Kaffe (*http://www.kaffe.org*) but they are, for the most part, no longer actively maintained.

There have also been some Java runtime clones, including Apache Harmony (*http://harmony.apache.org*), Japhar (*http://bit.ly/1n72D0b*), the IBM Jikes Runtime (from the same site as Jikes), and even JNODE (*http://www.jnode.org*), a complete, standalone operating system written in Java, but since the Sun/Oracle JVM has been open-sourced (GPL), most of these projects have become unmaintained. Harmony was retired by Apache in November 2011, although parts of it are still in use (e.g., parts of Harmony's JavaSE runtime library are used in the popular Android mobile operating system (*http://android.com*)).

Mac OS X

The JDK is pure command line. At the other end of the spectrum in terms of keyboard-versus-visual, we have the Apple Macintosh. Books have been written about how great the Mac user interface is, and I won't step into that debate. Mac OS X (Release 10.x of Mac OS) is built upon a BSD Unix (and "Mach") base. As such, it has a regular command line (the Terminal application, hidden away under */Applications/Utilities*), as well as all the traditional Mac tools. Java SE 6 was provided by Apple and available through Software Update. Effective with Java 7, Apple has devolved this support to Oracle (*http://bit.ly/1gxfRvJ*) to make the distributions, which are now available for download (*http://bit.ly/TEA7iC*) (avoid the JRE-only downloads (*http://java.com*)). More information on Oracle Java for OS X is available (*http://bit.ly/TOEeQY*).

Mac OS X users can use the command-line JDK tools as above or Ant (see Recipe 1.6). Compiled classes can be packaged into "clickable applications" using the Jar Packager discussed in Recipe 21.5. Alternatively, Mac fans can use one of the many full IDE tools discussed in Recipe 1.3.

1.2. Editing and Compiling with a Syntax-Highlighting Editor

Problem

You are tired of command-line tools, but not ready for an IDE.

Solution

Use a syntax-highlighting editor.

Discussion

It's less than an IDE (see the next recipe), but more than a command line. What is it? It's an editor with Java support. Tools such as TextPad (*http://www.textpad.com*), Visual SlickEdit, and others are free or low-cost windowed editors (many primarily for Microsoft Windows) that have some amount of Java recognition built in, and the ability to compile from within the editor. TextPad recognizes quite a number of file types, including batch files and shell scripts, C, C++, Java, JSP, JavaScript, and many others. For each of these, it uses syntax highlighting to denote keywords, comments, string literals, etc., usually by using one color for keywords, another for class variables, another for locals, etc. This is very useful in spotting when part of your code has been swallowed up by an unterminated /* comment or a missing quote.

Though this isn't the same as the deep understanding of Java that a full IDE might possess, experience has shown that it definitely aids programmer productivity. TextPad also has a "compile Java" command and a "run external program" command. Both of these have the advantage of capturing the entire command output into a window, which may be easier to scroll than a command-line window on some platforms. On the other hand, you don't see the command results until the program terminates, which can be most uncomfortable if your GUI application throws an exception before it puts up its main window. Despite this minor drawback, TextPad is a very useful tool. Other editors that include color highlighting include *vim* (an enhanced version of the Unix tool *vi*, available for Windows and Unix platforms from *http://www.vim.org*), the ever-popular Emacs editor, and more.

And speaking of Emacs (*http://bit.ly/TOEr6E*), because it is so extensible, it's natural that people have built enhanced Java capabilities for it. One example is Java Development Environment for Emacs (*http://jdee.sourceforge.net*) (JDEE), an Emacs "major mode" (jde-mode, based on c-mode) with a set of menu items such as Generate Getters/Setters. You could say that JDEE is in between using a Color-Highlighting Editor and an IDE.

Even without JDEE, Emacs features dabbrev-expand, which does class and method name completion. It is, however, based on what's in your current edit buffers, so it doesn't know about classes in the standard API or in external JARs. For that level of functionality, you have to turn to a full-blown IDE, such as those discussed in Recipe 1.3.

1.3. Compiling, Running, and Testing with an IDE

Problem

It is cumbersome to use several tools for the various development tasks.

Solution

Use an integrated development environment (IDE), which combines editing, testing, compiling, running, debugging, and package management.

Discussion

Many programmers find that using a handful of separate tools—a text editor, a compiler, and a runner program, not to mention a debugger (see Recipe 1.12)—is too many. An IDE *integrates* all of these into a single toolset with a graphical user interface. Many IDEs are available, ranging all the way up to fully integrated tools with their own compilers and virtual machines. Class browsers and other features of IDEs round out the ease-of-use feature sets of these tools. It has been argued many times whether an IDE really makes you more productive or if you just have more fun doing the same thing. However, today most developers use an IDE because of the productivity gains. Although I started as a command-line junkie, I do find that the following IDE benefits make me more productive:

Code completion
> *Ian's Rule* here is that I never type more than three characters of any name that is known to the IDE; let the computer do the typing!

"Incremental compiling" features
> Note and report compilation errors as you type, instead of waiting until you are finished typing.

Refactoring
> The ability to make far-reaching yet behavior-preserving changes to a code base without having to manually edit dozens of individual files.

Beyond that, I don't plan to debate the IDE versus the command-line process; I use both modes at different times and on different projects. I'm just going to show a few examples of using a couple of the Java-based IDEs.

The three most popular Java IDEs, which run on all mainstream platforms and quite a few niche ones, are *Eclipse*, *NetBeans*, and *IntelliJ IDEA*. Eclipse is the most widely used, but the others each have a special place in the hearts and minds of some developers. If you develop for Android, the ADT has traditionally been developed for Eclipse, but it is in the process of moving to IntelliJ as the basis for "Android Studio," which is in early access as this book goes to press.

Let's look first at NetBeans. Originally created by NetBeans.com and called Forte, this IDE was so good that Sun bought the company, and Oracle now distributes NetBeans as a free, open source tool for Java developers. There is a plug-in API; and quite a few plug-ins available. You can download the free version and extension modules (*http://www.netbeans.org*). If you want support for it, the Oracle "Java Development Tools Support" offering (*http://bit.ly/1hRIURc*) covers NetBeans, Oracle JDeveloper, and Oracle Enterprise Pack for Eclipse—see the "Pro Support." For convenience to those getting started with Java, you can download a single bundle that includes both the JDK and NetBeans, from the Oracle download site (*http://bit.ly/TEA7iC*).

NetBeans comes with a variety of templates. In Figure 1-1, I have opted for the plain Java template.

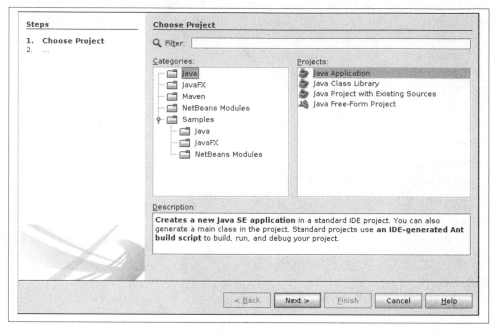

Figure 1-1. NetBeans: New Class Wizard

In Figure 1-2, NetBeans lets me specify a project name and package name for the new program I am building, and optionally to create a new class, by giving its full class name.

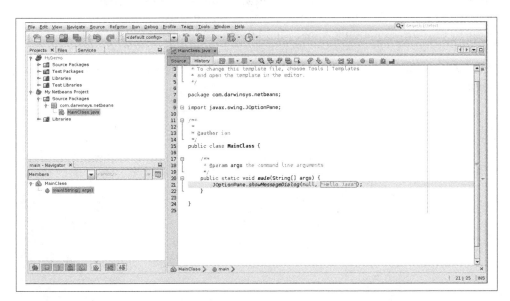

Figure 1-2. NetBeans: Name that class

In Figure 1-3, we have the opportunity to type in the main class.

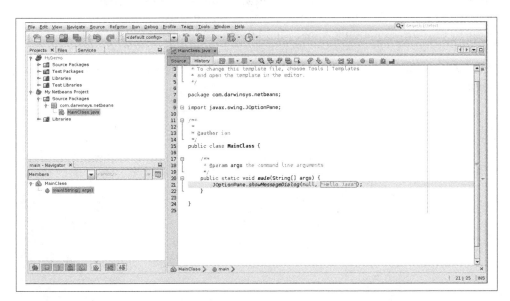

Figure 1-3. NetBeans: Entering main class code

In Figure 1-4, we run the main class.

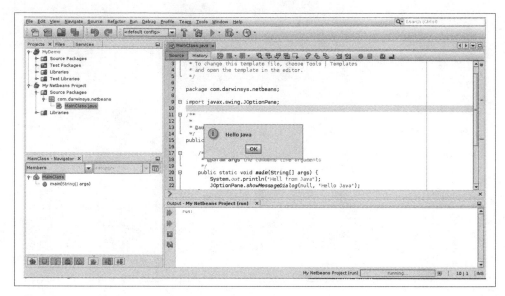

Figure 1-4. NetBeans: Running the application

Perhaps the most popular cross-platform, open source IDE for Java is Eclipse, originally from IBM and now shepherded by the Eclipse Foundation (*http://eclipse.org*), now the home of many software projects. Just as NetBeans is the basis of Sun Studio, so Eclipse is the basis of IBM's Rational Application Developer (RAD). All IDEs do basically the same thing for you when getting started; see, for example, the Eclipse New Java Class Wizard shown in Figure 1-5. It also features a number of refactoring capabilities, shown in Figure 1-6.

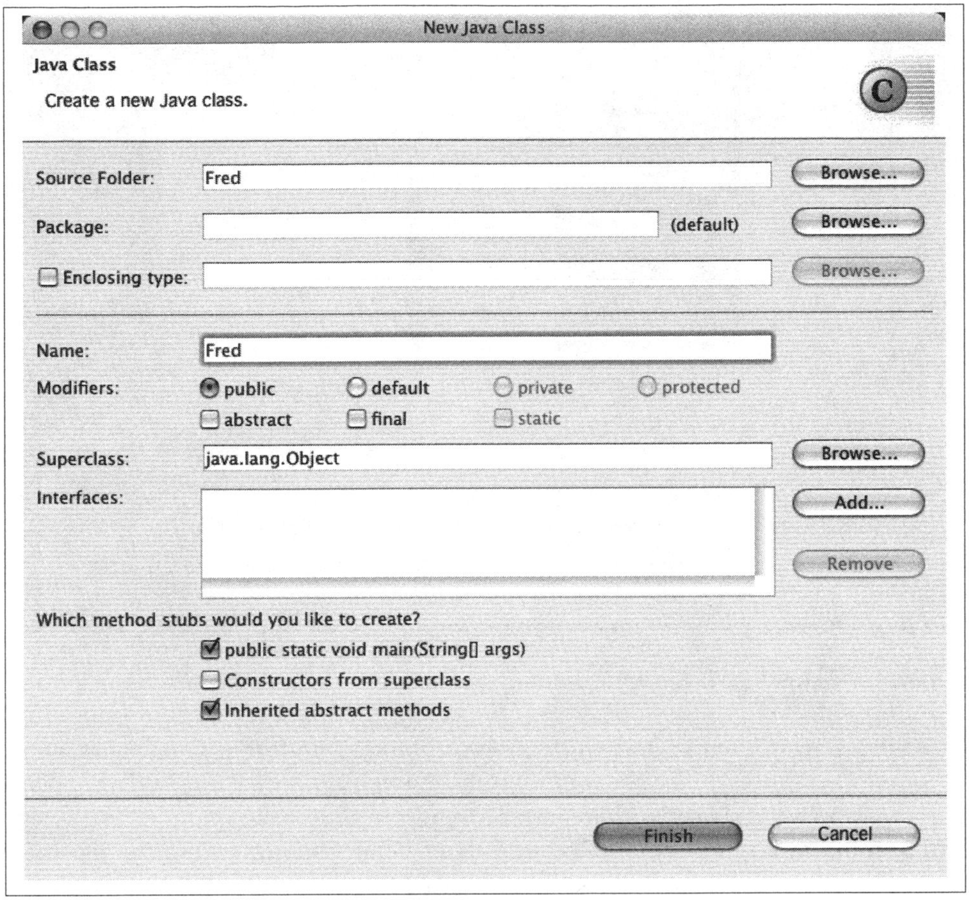

Figure 1-5. Eclipse: New Java Class Wizard

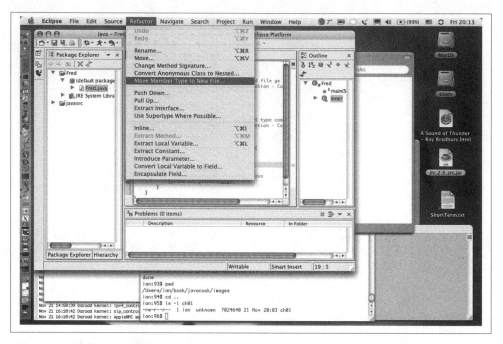

Figure 1-6. Eclipse: Refactoring

The third IDE is IntelliJ IDEA (*http://www.jetbrains.com/idea*). This also has a free version (open source) and a commercial version. IntelliJ supports a wide range of languages via optional plug-ins (I have installed Android and Haskell plug-ins on the system used in these screenshots). You can start by defining a new project, as shown in Figure 1-7.

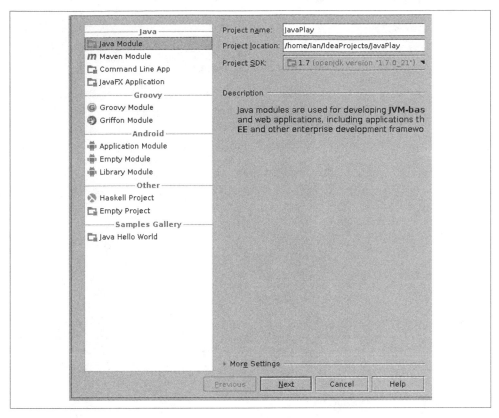

Figure 1-7. IntelliJ New Project Wizard

To create a new class, right-click the source folder and select New→Class. Pick a name and package for your class, as shown in Figure 1-8.

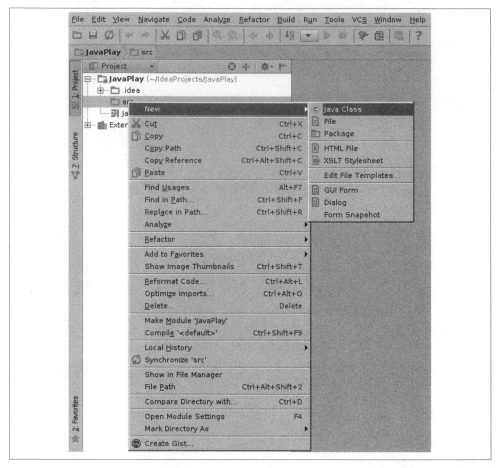

Figure 1-8. IntelliJ New Class Wizard

You will start with a blank class. Type some code into it, such as the canonical "Hello World" app, as shown in Figure 1-9.

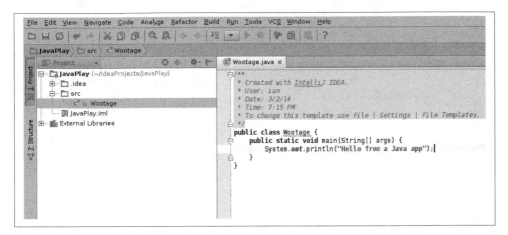

Figure 1-9. IntelliJ class typed in

Finally, you can click the green Run button, or context-click in the source window and select Run, and have your program executed. As you can see in Figure 1-10, the output will appear in a console window, as in the other IDEs.

Mac OS X includes Apple's Developer Tools. The main IDE is Xcode. Unfortunately, current versions of Xcode do not really support Java development, so there is little to recommend it for our purposes; it is primarily for those building non-portable (iOS-only or OS X–only) applications in the Objective-C programming language. So even if you are on OS X, to do Java development you should use one of the three Java IDEs.

How do you choose an IDE? Given that all three major IDEs (Eclipse, NetBeans, IntelliJ) can be downloaded free, why not try them all and see which one best fits the kind of development you do? Regardless of what platform you use to develop Java, if you have a Java runtime, you should have plenty of IDEs from which to choose.

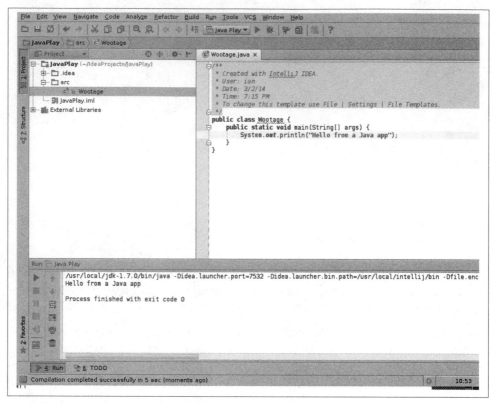

Figure 1-10. IntelliJ program output

See Also

Each IDE's site maintains an up-to-date list of resources, including books.

All major IDEs are extensible; see their documentation for a list of the many, many plug-ins available. Most of them now allow you to find and install plug-ins from within the IDE, though they vary in how convenient they make this process. As a last resort, if you need/want to write a plug-in that extends the functionality of your IDE, you can do that too, in Java.

1.4. Using CLASSPATH Effectively

Problem

You need to keep your class files in a common directory, or you're wrestling with CLASSPATH.

Solution

Set CLASSPATH to the list of directories and/or JAR files that contain the classes you want.

Discussion

CLASSPATH is one of the more "interesting" aspects of using Java. You can store your class files in any of a number of directories, JAR files, or ZIP files. Just like the PATH your system uses for finding programs, the CLASSPATH is used by the Java runtime to find classes. Even when you type something as simple as *java HelloWorld*, the Java interpreter looks in each of the places named in your CLASSPATH until it finds a match. Let's work through an example.

The CLASSPATH can be set as an environment variable on systems that support this (Microsoft Windows and Unix, including Mac OS X). You set it the same way you set other environment variables, such as your PATH environment variable.

Alternatively, you can specify the CLASSPATH for a given command on the command line:

```
C:\> java -classpath c:\ian\classes MyProg
```

Suppose your CLASSPATH were set to *C:\classes;.* on Windows or *~/classes:.* on Unix (on the Mac, you can set the CLASSPATH with JBindery). Suppose you had just compiled a file named *HelloWorld.java* into *HelloWorld.class* and tried to run it. On Unix, if you run one of the kernel tracing tools (`trace`, `strace`, `truss`, `ktrace`), you would probably see the `Java` program `open` (or `stat`, or `access`) the following files:

- Some file(s) in the JDK directory
- Then *~/classes/HelloWorld.class*, which it probably wouldn't find
- Finally, *./HelloWorld.class*, which it would find, open, and read into memory

The vague "some file(s) in the JDK directory" is release-dependent. You should not mess with the JDK files, but if you're curious, you can find them in the System Properties under `sun.boot.class.path` (see Recipe 2.2 for System Properties information).

Suppose you had also installed the JAR file containing the supporting classes for programs from this book, *darwinsys-api.jar* (the actual filename if you download it may have a version number as part of the filename). You might then set your CLASSPATH to *C:\classes;C:\classes\darwinsys-api.jar;.* on Windows or *~/classes:~/classes/darwinsys-api.jar:.* on Unix. Notice that you *do* need to list the JAR file explicitly. Unlike a single class file, placing a JAR file into a directory listed in your CLASSPATH does not suffice to make it available.

Note that certain specialized programs (such as a web server running a Java EE Servlet container) may not use either bootpath or CLASSPATH as shown; these application servers typically provide their own `ClassLoader` (see Recipe 23.5 for information on class loaders). EE Web containers, for example, set your web app classpath to include the directory *WEB-INF/classes* and all the JAR files found under *WEB-INF/lib*.

How can you easily generate class files into a directory in your CLASSPATH? The *javac* command has a -d dir option, which specifies where the compiler output should go. For example, using -d to put the *HelloWorld* class file into my *$HOME/classes* directory, I just type the following (note that from here on I will be using the package name in addition to the class name, like a good kid):

```
javac -d $HOME/classes HelloWorld.java
java -cp $HOME/classes starting.HelloWorld
Hello, world!
```

As long as this directory remains in my CLASSPATH, I can access the class file regardless of my current directory. That's one of the key benefits of using CLASSPATH.

Managing CLASSPATH can be tricky, particularly when you alternate among several JVMs (as I do) or when you have multiple directories in which to look for JAR files. Some Linux distributions have an "alternatives" mechanism for managing this. Otherwise you may want to use some sort of batch file or shell script to control this. The following is part of the shell script that I have used—it was written for the standard shell on Unix (should work on Bash, Ksh, etc.), but similar scripts could be written in other shells or as a DOS batch file:

```
# These guys must be present in my classpath...
export CLASSPATH=/home/ian/classes/darwinsys-api.jar:

# Now a for loop, testing for .jar/.zip or [ -d ... ]
OPT_JARS="$HOME/classes $HOME/classes/*.jar
    ${JAVAHOME}/jre/lib/ext/*.jar
    /usr/local/jars/antlr-3.2.0"

for thing in $OPT_JARS
do
    if [ -f $thing ]; then        //must be either a file...
        CLASSPATH="$CLASSPATH:$thing"
    else if [ -d $thing ]; then        //or a directory
        CLASSPATH="$CLASSPATH:$thing"
    fi
done
CLASSPATH="$CLASSPATH:."
```

This builds a minimum CLASSPATH out of *darwinsys-api.jar*, then goes through a list of other files and directories to check that each is present on this system (I use this script on several machines on a network), and ends up adding a dot (.) to the end of the CLASSPATH.

Note that, on Unix, a shell script executed normally can change environment variables like CLASSPATH only for itself; the "parent" shell (the one running commands in your terminal or window) is not affected. Changes that are meant to be permanent need to be stored in your startup files (*.profile*, *.bashrc*, or whatever you normally use).

1.5. Downloading and Using the Code Examples

Problem

You want to try out my example code and/or use my utility classes.

Solution

Download the latest archive of the book source files, unpack it, and run Maven (see Recipe 1.7) to compile the files.

Discussion

The source code used as examples in this book is drawn from several source code repositories that have been in continuous development since 1995. These are listed in Table 1-1.

Table 1-1. The main source repositories

Repository name	Github.com URL	Package description	Approx. size
javasrc	*http://github.com/IanDarwin/javasrc*	Java classes from all APIs	1,200 classes
darwinsys-api	*http://github.com/Iandarwin/darwinsys-api*	A published API	250 classes

A small number of examples are drawn from the older *javasrcee* (Java EE) examples, which I split off from javasrc due to the overall size; this is also on GitHub (*https://github.com/IanDarwin/javasrcee*).

You can download these repositories from the GitHub URLs shown in Table 1-1. GitHub allows you to download, by use of `git clone`, a ZIP file of the entire repository's current state, or to view individual files on the web interface. Downloading with `git clone` instead of as an archive is preferred because you can then update at any time with a simple `git pull` command. And with the amount of updating this has undergone for Java 8, you are sure to find changes after the book is published.

If you are not familiar with Git, see "CVS, Subversion, Git, Oh My!" on page 21.

javasrc

This is the largest repo, and consists primarily of code written to show a particular feature or API. The files are organized into subdirectories by topic, many of which correspond more or less to book chapters—for example, a directory for *strings* examples (Chapter 3), *regex* for regular expressions (Chapter 4), *numbers* (Chapter 5), and so on. The archive also contains the index by name and index by chapter files from the download site, so you can easily find the files you need.

There are about 80 subdirectories in javasrc (under *src/main/java*), too many to list here. They are listed in the file *src/main/java/index-of-directories.txt*.

darwinsys-api

I have built up a collection of useful stuff, partly by moving some reusable classes from *javasrc* into my own API, which I use in my own Java projects. I use example code from it in this book, and I import classes from it into many of the other examples. So, if you're going to be downloading and compiling the examples *individually*, you should first download the file *darwinsys-api-1.x.jar* (for the latest value of *x*) and include it in your CLASSPATH. Note that if you are going to build the *javasrc* code with Eclipse or Maven, you can skip this download because the top-level Maven script starts off by including the JAR file for this API.

This is the only one of the repos that appears in Maven Central (*http://bit.ly/1kRi0bB*); find it by searching for *darwinsys*. The current Maven artifact is:

```
<dependency>
    <groupId>com.darwinsys</groupId>
    <artifactId>darwinsys-api</artifactId>
    <version>1.0.3</version>
</dependency>
```

This API consists of about two dozen `com.darwinsys` packages, listed in Table 1-2. You will notice that the structure vaguely parallels the standard Java API; this is intentional. These packages now include more than 200 classes and interfaces. Most of them have javadoc documentation that can be viewed with the source download.

Table 1-2. The com.darwinsys packages

Package name	Package description
`com.darwinsys.ant`	A demonstration Ant task
`com.darwinsys.csv`	Classes for comma-separated values files
`com.darwinsys.database`	Classes for dealing with databases in a general way
`com.darwinsys.diff`	Comparison utilities
`com.darwinsys.genericui`	Generic GUI stuff
`com.darwinsys.geo`	Classes relating to country codes, provinces/states, and so on
`com.darwinsys.graphics`	Graphics

Package name	Package description
`com.darwinsys.html`	Classes (only one so far) for dealing with HTML
`com.darwinsys.io`	Classes for input and output operations, using Java's underlying I/O classes
`com.darwinsys.jsptags`	Java EE JSP tags
`com.darwinsys.lang`	Classes for dealing with standard features of Java
`com.darwinsys.locks`	Pessimistic locking API
`com.darwinsys.mail`	Classes for dealing with email, mainly a convenience class for sending mail
`com.darwinsys.model`	Modeling
`com.darwinsys.net`	Networking
`com.darwinsys.preso`	Presentations
`com.darwinsys.reflection`	Reflection
`com.darwinsys.regex`	Regular expression stuff: an REDemo program, a Grep variant, and so on
`com.darwinsys.security`	Security
`com.darwinsys.servlet`	Servlet API helpers
`com.darwinsys.sql`	Classes for dealing with SQL databases
`com.darwinsys.swingui`	Classes for helping construct and use Swing GUIs
`com.darwinsys.swingui.layout`	A few interesting LayoutManager implementations
`com.darwinsys.testdata`	Test data generators
`com.darwinsys.testing`	Testing tools
`com.darwinsys.unix`	Unix helpers
`com.darwinsys.util`	A few miscellaneous utility classes
`com.darwinsys.xml`	XML utilities

Many of these classes are used as examples in this book; just look for files whose first line *begins*:

```
package com.darwinsys;
```

You'll also find that many of the other examples have imports from the `com.darwinsys` packages.

General notes

If you are short on time, the majority of the examples are in *javasrc*, so cloning or downloading that repo will get you most of the code from the book. Also, its Maven script refers to a copy of the *darwinsys-api* that is in Maven Central, so you could get 90% of the code with one *git clone*, for *javasrc*. Your best bet is to use *git clone* to download a copy of all three, and do *git pull* every few months to get updates.

Alternatively, you can download a single intersection set of all three that is made up almost exclusively of files actually used in the book, from this book's catalog page (*http://*

oreil.ly/java-cookbook-3e). This archive is made from the sources that are dynamically included into the book at formatting time, so it should reflect exactly the examples you see in the book. But it will not include as many examples as the three individual archives.

You can find links to all of these from my own website for this book (*http://java cook.darwinsys.com*); just follow the Downloads link.

The three separate repositories are each self-contained projects with support for building both with Eclipse (Recipe 1.3) and with Maven (Recipe 1.7). Note that Maven will automatically fetch a vast array of prerequisite libraries when first invoked on a given project, so be sure you're online on a high-speed Internet link. However, Maven will ensure that all prerequisites are installed before building. If you choose to build pieces individually, look in the file *pom.xml* for the list of dependencies. Unfortunately, I will probably not be able to help you if you are not using either Eclipse or Maven with the control files included in the download.

If you have Java 7 instead of the current Java 8, a few files will not compile. You can make up "exclusion elements" for the files that are known not to compile.

All my code in the three projects is released under the least-restrictive credit-only license, the two-clause BSD license. If you find it useful, incorporate it into your own software. There is no need to write to ask me for permission; just use it, with credit.

 Most of the command-line examples refer to source files, assuming you are in *src/main/java*, and runnable classes, assuming you are in (or have added to your classpath) the build directory (e.g., for Maven this is *target/classes*, and for Eclipse it is *build*). This will not be mentioned with each example, because it would waste a lot of paper.

Caveat Lector

The repos have been in development since 1995. This means that you will find some code that is not up to date, or that no longer reflects best practices. This is not surprising: any body of code will grow old if any part of it is not actively maintained. (Thus, at this point, I invoke Culture Club's, "Do You Really Want to Hurt Me?": "Give me time to realize my crimes.") Where advice in the book disagrees with some code you found in the repo, keep this in mind. One of the practices of Extreme Programming is Continuous Refactoring—the ability to improve any part of the code base at any time. Don't be surprised if the code in the online source directory differs from what appears in the book; it is a rare week that I don't make some improvement to the code, and the results are committed and pushed quite often. So if there are differences between what's printed in the book and what you get from GitHub, be glad, not sad, for you'll have received the benefit of hindsight. Also, people can contribute easily on GitHub via "pull request"; that's what makes it interesting. If you find a bug or an improvement, do send me a pull request!

The consolidated archive on *oreilly.com* will not be updated as frequently.

CVS, Subversion, Git, Oh My!

Many distributed version control systems or source code management systems are available. The ones that have been widely used in open source in recent years include:

- Concurrent Versions System (CVS) (*http://bit.ly/1a1nZCI*)
- Apache Subversion (*http://subversion.apache.org*)
- Git (*http://git-scm.com*)
- As well as others that are used in particular niches (e.g., Mercurial)

Although each has its advantages and disadvantages, the use of Git in the Linux build process (and projects based on Linux, such as the Android mobile environment), as well as the availability of sites like *github.com* and *gitorious.org*, give Git a massive momentum over the others. I don't have statistics, but I suspect the number of projects in Git repositories probably exceeds the others combined. Several well-known organizations using Git are listed on the Git home page.

For this reason, I have been moving my projects to GitHub; see *http://github.com/IanDarwin/*. To download the projects and be able to get updates applied automatically, use Git to download them. Options include:

- The command-line Git client (*http://git-scm.com*). If you are on any modern Unix or Linux system, Git is either included or available in your ports or packaging or "developer tools," but can also be downloaded for MS Windows, Mac, Linux, and Solaris from the home page under Downloads.
- Eclipse release Kepler bundles Egit 3.x, or you can install the Egit plug-in from an update site (*http://www.eclipse.org/egit/download*)
- NetBeans has Git support built in on current releases
- IntelliJ IDEA has Git support built in on current releases (see the VCS menu)
- Similar support for most other IDEs
- Numerous standalone GUI clients (*http://git-scm.com/downloads/guis*)
- Even Continuous Integration servers such as Jenkins/Hudson (see Recipe 1.14) have plug-ins available for updating a project with Git (and other popular SCMs) before building them

You will want to have one or more of these Git clients at your disposal to download my code examples. You can download them as ZIP or TAR archive files from the GitHub page, but then you won't get updates. You can also view or download individual files from the GitHub page via a web browser.

1.6. Automating Compilation with Apache Ant

Problem

You get tired of typing *javac* and *java* commands.

Solution

Use the Ant program to direct your compilations.

Discussion

Ant is a pure Java solution for automating the build process. Ant is free software; it is available in source form or ready-to-run from the Apache Foundation's Ant website (*http://ant.apache.org*). Like *make*, Ant uses a file or files—Ant's are written in XML—listing what to do and, if necessary, how to do it. These rules are intended to be platform-independent, though you can of course write platform-specific recipes if necessary.

To use Ant, you must create a file specifying various options. This file should be called *build.xml*; if you call it anything else, you'll have to give a special command-line argument every time you run Ant. Example 1-1 shows the build script used to build the files in the *starting* directory. See Chapter 20 for a discussion of the syntax of XML. For now, note that the <!-- begins an XML comment, which extends to the -->.

Example 1-1. Ant example file (build.xml)

```
<project name="Java Cookbook Examples" default="compile" basedir=".">

  <!-- Set global properties for this build -->
  <property name="src" value="."/>
  <property name="build" value="build"/>
  <!-- Specify the compiler to use. -->
  <property name="build.compiler" value="modern"/>

  <target name="init">
    <!-- Create the time stamp -->
    <tstamp/>
    <!-- Create the build directory structure used by compile -->
    <mkdir dir="${build}"/>
  </target>

  <!-- Specify what to compile. This builds everything -->
  <target name="compile" depends="init">

    <!-- Compile the java code from ${src} into ${build} -->
    <javac srcdir="${src}" destdir="${build}"
           classpath="../darwinsys-api.jar"/>
  </target>
```

```
</project>
```

When you run Ant, it produces a reasonable amount of notification as it goes:

```
$ ant compile
Buildfile: build.xml
Project base dir set to: /home/ian/javasrc/starting
Executing Target: init
Executing Target: compile
Compiling 19 source files to /home/ian/javasrc/starting/build
Performing a Modern Compile
Copying 22 support files to /home/ian/javasrc/starting/build
Completed in 8 seconds
$
```

See Also

The following sidebar and *Ant: The Definitive Guide* by Steve Holzner (O'Reilly).

---

make Versus Java Build Tools

make is the original build tool from the 1970s, used in Unix and C/C++ development. *make* and the Java-based tools each have advantages; I'll try to compare them without too much bias.

The Java build tools work the same on all platforms, as much as possible. `make` is rather platform-dependent; there is GNU `make`, BSD `make`, Xcode `make`, Visual Studio `make`, and several others, each with slightly different syntax.

That said, there are many Java build tools to choose from, including:

- Apache Ant
- Apache Maven
- Gradle
- Apache Buildr

Makefiles and `Buildr/Gradle` build files are the shortest. Make just lets you list the commands you want run and their dependencies. `Buildr` and `Gradle` each have their own language (based on Ruby and Groovy, respectively), instead of using XML, so can be a lot more terse. Maven uses XML, but with a lot of sensible defaults and a standard, default workflow. Ant also uses XML, but makes you specify each task you want performed.

make runs faster for single tasks; it's written in C. However, the Java tools can run many Java tasks in a single JVM—such as the built-in Java compiler, *jar/war/tar/zip* files, and many more—to the extent that it may be more efficient to run several Java compilations

---

in one JVM process than to run the same compilations using *make*. In other words, once the JVM that is running Ant/Maven/Gradle itself is up and running, it doesn't take long at all to run the Java compiler and run the compiled class. This is Java as it was meant to be!

Java build tool files can do more for you. The *javac* task in Ant, for example, automatically finds all the **.java* files in subdirectories. Maven's built-in *compile* goal does this too, and knows to look in the "src" folder by default. With *make*, you have to spell such things out.

Ant has special knowledge of CLASSPATH, making it easy to set a CLASSPATH in various ways for compile time. See the CLASSPATH setting in Example 1-1. You may have to duplicate this in other ways—shell scripts or batch files—for using *make* or for manually running or testing your application.

Maven and Gradle take Ant one step further, and handle dependency management. You simply list the API and version that you want, and the tool finds it, downloads it, and adds it to your classpath at the right time—all without writing any rules.

Gradle goes further yet, and allows scripting logic in its configuration file (strictly speaking, Ant and Maven do as well, but Gradle's is much easier to use).

make is simpler to extend, but harder to do so portably. You can write a one-line *make* rule for getting a CVS archive from a remote site, but you may run into incompatibilities between GNU *make*, BSD *make*, Microsoft *make*, and so on. There is a built-in Ant task for getting an archive from CVS using Ant; it was written as a Java source file instead of just a series of command-line commands.

make has been around much longer. There are probably millions (literally) more *Make-files* than Ant files. Non-Java developers have typically not heard of Ant; they almost all use *make*. Most non-Java open source projects use *make*, except for programming languages that provide their own build tool (e.g., Ruby provides Rake and Thor, Haskell provides Cabal, …).

The advantages of the Java tools make more sense on larger projects. Primarily, *make* has been used on the really large projects. For example, *make* is used for telephone switch source code, which consists of hundreds of thousands of source files totalling tens or hundreds of millions of lines of source code. By contrast, Tomcat is about 500,000 lines of code, and the JBoss Java EE server "WildFly" is about 800,000 lines. Use of the Java tools is growing steadily, particularly now that most of the widely used Java IDEs (JBuilder, Eclipse, NetBeans, etc.) have interfaces to Ant, Maven, and/or Gradle. Effectively all Java open source projects use Ant (or its larger and stronger sibling, Maven) or the newest kid on that block, Gradle.

make is included with most Unix and Unix-like systems and shipped with many Windows IDEs. Ant and Maven are not included with any operating system distribution that I know of, but can be installed as packages on almost all, and both are available direct from Apache. The same is true for Gradle, but it installs from *http://gradle.org*, and Buildr from the Apache website (*http://buildr.apache.org*).

To sum up, although *make* and the Java tools are good, new Java projects should use one of the newer Java-based tools such as Maven or Gradle.

1.7. Automating Dependencies, Compilation, Testing, and Deployment with Apache Maven

Problem

You tried Ant and liked it, but want a tool that does more automatically.

Solution

Use Maven.

Discussion

Maven is a tool one level up from Ant. Although Ant is good for managing compilation, Maven includes a sophisticated, distributed dependency management system that also gives it rules for building application packages such as JAR, WAR, and EAR files and deploying them to an array of different targets. Whereas Ant build files focus on the *how*, Maven files focus on the *what*, specifying what you want done.

Maven is controlled by a file called *pom.xml* (for Project Object Model). A sample *pom.xml* might look like this:

```
<project xmlns="http://maven.apache.org/POM/4.0.0"
  xmlns:xsi="http://www.w3.org/2001/XMLSchema-instance"
  xsi:schemaLocation="http://maven.apache.org/POM/4.0.0
                      http://maven.apache.org/xsd/maven-4.0.0.xsd">
<modelVersion>4.0.0</modelVersion>

<groupId>com.example</groupId>
<artifactId>my-se-project</artifactId>
<version>1.0-SNAPSHOT</version>
<packaging>jar</packaging>

<name>my-se-project</name>
<url>http://com.example/</url>

<properties>
  <project.build.sourceEncoding>UTF-8</project.build.sourceEncoding>
</properties>

<dependencies>
```

```
<dependency>
  <groupId>junit</groupId>
  <artifactId>junit</artifactId>
  <version>4.8.1</version>
  <scope>test</scope>
</dependency>
  </dependencies>
</project>
```

This specifies a project called "my-se-project" (my standard-edition project) that will be packaged into a JAR file; it depends on the JUnit 4.x framework for unit testing (see Recipe 1.13), but only needs it for compiling and running tests. If I type *mvn install* in the directory with this POM, Maven will ensure that it has a copy of the given version of JUnit (and anything that JUnit depends on), then compile everything (setting CLASSPATH and other options for the compiler), run any and all unit tests, and if they all pass, generate a JAR file for the program; it will then install it in my personal Maven repo (under *~/.m2/repository*) so that other Maven projects can depend on my new project JAR file. Note that I haven't had to tell Maven where the source files live, nor how to compile them—this is all handled by sensible defaults, based on a well-defined project structure. The program source is expected to be found in *src/main/java*, and the tests in *src/test/java*; if it's a web application, the web root is expected to be in *src/main/webapp* by default. Of course, you can override these.

Note that even the preceding config file does not have to be, and was not, written by hand; Maven's "archteype generation rules" let it build the starting version of any of several hundred types of projects. Here is how the file was created:

```
$ mvn archetype:generate \
        -DarchetypeGroupId=org.apache.maven.archetypes \
        -DarchetypeArtifactId=maven-archetype-quickstart \
        -DgroupId=com.example -DartifactId=my-se-project

\[INFO] Scanning for projects...
Downloading: http://repo1.maven.org/maven2/org/apache/maven/plugins/
    maven-deploy-plugin/2.5/maven-deploy-plugin-2.5.pom
\[several dozen or hundred lines of downloading POM files and Jar files...]
\[INFO] Generating project in Interactive mode
\[INFO] Archetype [org.apache.maven.archetypes:maven-archetype-quickstart:1.1]
    found in catalog remote
\[INFO] Using property: groupId = com.example
\[INFO] Using property: artifactId = my-se-project
Define value for property 'version':  1.0-SNAPSHOT: :
\[INFO] Using property: package = com.example
Confirm properties configuration:
groupId: com.example
artifactId: my-se-project
version: 1.0-SNAPSHOT
package: com.example
 Y: : y
\[INFO] ------------------------------------------------------------------------
```

```
\[INFO] Using following parameters for creating project from Old (1.x) Archetype:
    maven-archetype-quickstart:1.1
\[INFO] ------------------------------------------------------------------------
\[INFO] Parameter: groupId, Value: com.example
\[INFO] Parameter: packageName, Value: com.example
\[INFO] Parameter: package, Value: com.example
\[INFO] Parameter: artifactId, Value: my-se-project
\[INFO] Parameter: basedir, Value: /private/tmp
\[INFO] Parameter: version, Value: 1.0-SNAPSHOT
\[INFO] project created from Old (1.x) Archetype in dir: /private/tmp/
    my-se-project
\[INFO] ------------------------------------------------------------------------
\[INFO] BUILD SUCCESS
\[INFO] ------------------------------------------------------------------------
\[INFO] Total time: 6:38.051s
\[INFO] Finished at: Sun Jan 06 19:19:18 EST 2013
\[INFO] Final Memory: 7M/81M
\[INFO] ------------------------------------------------------------------------
```

The IDEs (see Recipe 1.3) have support for Maven. For example, if you use Eclipse, M2Eclipse (m2e) is an Eclipse plug-in that will build your Eclipse project dependencies from your POM file; this plug-in ships by default with current (Kepler) Java Developer builds of Eclipse, is tested with previous (Juno) releases, and is also available for some older releases; see the Eclipse website (*http://eclipse.org/m2e*) for plug-in details.

A POM file can redefine any of the standard "goals." Common Maven goals (predefined by default to do something sensible) include:

clean
> Removes all generated artifacts

compile
> Compiles all source files

test
> Compiles and runs all unit tests

package
> Builds the package

install
> Installs the *pom.xml* and package into your local Maven repository for use by your other projects

deploy
> Tries to install the package (e.g., on an application server)

Most of the steps implicitly invoke the previous ones—e.g., package will compile any missing *.class* files, and run the tests if that hasn't already been done in this run.

Typically there are application-server–specific targets provided; as a single example, with the JBoss Application Server "WildFly" (formerly known as JBoss AS), you would install some additional plug-in(s) as per their documentation, and then deploy to the app server using:

```
mvn jboss-as:deploy
```

instead of the regular deploy.

Maven pros and cons

Maven can handle complex projects and is very configurable. I built the *darwinsys-api* and *javasrc* projects with Maven and let it handle finding dependencies, making the download of the project source code smaller (actually, moving the download overhead to the servers of the projects themselves). The only real downsides to Maven is that it takes a bit longer to get fully up to speed with it, and the fact that it can be a bit hard to diagnose when things go wrong. A good web search engine is your friend when things fail.

One issue I fear is that a hacker could gain access to a project's site and modify, or install a new version of, a POM. Maven automatically fetches updated POM versions. Although the same issue could affect you if you manage your dependencies manually, it is more likely that the problem would be detected before you manually fetched the infected version. I am not aware of this having happened, but it still worries me.

See Also

Start at *http://maven.apache.org*.

Maven Central: Mapping the World of Java Software

There is an immense collection of software freely available to Maven users just for adding a <dependency> element or "Maven Artifact" into your *pom.xml*. You can search this repository at *http://search.maven.org/* or *https://repository.sonatype.org/index.html*.

Figure 1-11 shows a search for my *darwinsys-api* project, and the information it reveals. Note that the *dependency* information listed there is all you need to have the library added to your Maven project; just copy the Dependency Information section and paste it into the <dependencies> of your POM, and you're done! Because Maven Central has become the definitive place to look for software, many other Java build tools piggyback on Maven Central. To serve these users, in turn, Maven Central offers to serve up the dependency information in a form that half a dozen other build tools can directly use in the same copy-and-paste fashion.

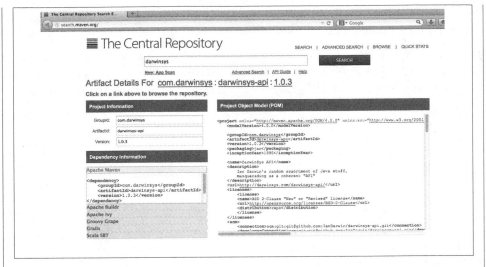

Figure 1-11. Maven Central search results

When you get to the stage of having a useful open source project that others can build upon, you may, in turn, want to share it on Maven Central. The process is longer than building for yourself but not onerous. Refer to this Maven guide (*http://bit.ly/1n8FfPQ*) or Sonatype OSS Maven Repository Usage Guide (*http://bit.ly/163Hb0y*).

1.8. Automating Dependencies, Compilation, Testing, and Deployment with Gradle

Problem

You want a build tool that doesn't make you use a lot of XML in your configuration file.

Solution

Use Gradle's simple build file with "strong, yet flexible conventions."

Discussion

Gradle is the latest in the succession of build tools (make, ant, and Maven). Gradle bills itself as "the enterprise automation tool," and has integration with the other build tools and IDEs.

Unlike the other Java-based tools, Gradle doesn't use XML as its scripting language, but rather a domain-specific language (DSL) based on the JVM-based and Java-based scripting language Groovy (*http://groovy.codehaus.org*).

You can install Gradle by downloading from the Gradle website (*http://gradle.org*), unpacking the ZIP, and adding its *bin* subdirectory to your path.

Then you can begin to use Gradle. Assuming you use the "standard" source directory (*src/main/java*, *src/main/test*) that is shared by Maven and Gradle among other tools, the example *build.gradle* file in Example 1-2 will build your app and run your unit tests.

Example 1-2. Example build.gradle file

```
# Simple Gradle Build for the Java-based DataVis project
apply plugin: 'java'
# Set up mappings for Eclipse project too
apply plugin: 'eclipse'

# The version of Java to use
sourceCompatibility = 1.7
# The version of my project
version = '1.0.3'
# Configure JAR file packaging
jar {
    manifest {
        attributes 'Main-class': 'com.somedomainnamehere.data.DataVis',
                'Implementation-Version': version
    }
}

# optional feature: like -Dtesting=true but only when running tests ("test task")
test {
    systemProperties 'testing': 'true'
}
```

You can bootstrap the industry's vast investment in Maven infrastructure by adding lines like these into your *build.gradle*:

```
# Tell it to look in Maven Central
repositories {
    mavenCentral()
}

# We need darwinsys-api for compiling as well as JUnit for testing
dependencies {
    compile group: 'com.darwinsys', name: 'darwinsys-api', version: '1.0.3+'
    testCompile group: 'junit', name: 'junit', version: '4.+'
}
```

See Also

There is much more functionality in Gradle. Start at Gradle's website (*http://www.gradle.org*), and see the documentation (*http://www.gradle.org/docs*).

1.9. Dealing with Deprecation Warnings

Problem

Your code used to compile cleanly, but now it gives deprecation warnings.

Solution

You must have blinked. Either live—dangerously—with the warnings, or revise your code to eliminate them.

Discussion

Each new release of Java includes a lot of powerful new functionality, but at a price: during the evolution of this new stuff, Java's maintainers find some old stuff that wasn't done right and shouldn't be used anymore because they can't really fix it. In the first major revision, for example, they realized that the `java.util.Date` class had some serious limitations with regard to internationalization. Accordingly, many of the `Date` class methods and constructors are marked "deprecated." According to the *American Heritage Dictionary*, to deprecate something means to "express disapproval of; deplore." Java's developers are therefore disapproving of the old way of doing things. Try compiling this code:

```
import java.util.Date;

/** Demonstrate deprecation warning */
public class Deprec {

    public static void main(String[] av) {

        // Create a Date object for May 5, 1986
        Date d =
            new Date(86, 04, 05);    // EXPECT DEPRECATION WARNING
        System.out.println("Date is " + d);
    }
}
```

What happened? When I compile it, I get this warning:

```
C:\javasrc>javac Deprec.java
Note: Deprec.java uses or overrides a deprecated API.  Recompile with
"-deprecation" for details.
1 warning
C:\javasrc>
```

So, we follow orders. For details, recompile with `-deprecation` (if using Ant, use `<javac deprecation= `*true...*`>`):

```
C:\javasrc>javac -deprecation Deprec.java
Deprec.java:10: warning: constructor Date(int,int,int) in class java.util.Date
has been deprecated
                Date d = new Date(86, 04, 05);              // May 5, 1986
                         ^
1 warning

C:\javasrc>
```

The warning is simple: the Date constructor that takes three integer arguments has been deprecated. How do you fix it? The answer is, as in most questions of usage, to refer to the javadoc documentation for the class. The introduction to the Date page says, in part:

> The class Date represents a specific instant in time, with millisecond precision.
>
> Prior to JDK 1.1, the class Date had two additional functions. It allowed the interpretation of dates as year, month, day, hour, minute, and second values. It also allowed the formatting and parsing of date strings. Unfortunately, the API for these functions was not amenable to internationalization. As of JDK 1.1, the Calendar class should be used to convert between dates and time fields and the DateFormat class should be used to format and parse date strings. The corresponding methods in Date are deprecated.

And more specifically, in the description of the three-integer constructor, the Date javadoc says:

Date(int year, int month, int date)

> Deprecated. As of JDK version 1.1, replaced by Calendar.set(year + 1900, month, date) or GregorianCalendar(year + 1900, month, date).

As a general rule, when something has been deprecated, you should not use it in any new code and, when maintaining code, strive to eliminate the deprecation warnings.

In addition to Date (Java 8 includes a whole new Date and Time API; see Chapter 6), the main areas of deprecation warnings in the standard API are the really ancient "event handling" and some methods (a few of them important) in the Thread class.

You can also deprecate your own code, when you come up with a better way of doing things. Put an @Deprecated annotation immediately before the class or method you wish to deprecate and/or use a @deprecated tag in a javadoc comment (see Recipe 21.2). The javadoc comment allows you to explain the deprecation, whereas the annotation is easier for some tools to recognize because it is present at runtime (so you can use Reflection (see Chapter 23).

See Also

Numerous other tools perform extra checking on your Java code. See my book *Checking Java Programs with Open Source Tools* (O'Reilly).

1.10. Conditional Debugging Without #ifdef

Problem

You want conditional compilation and Java doesn't seem to provide it.

Solution

Use constants, command-line arguments, or assertions (see Recipe 1.11), depending upon the goal.

Discussion

Some older languages such as C, PL/I, and C++ provide a feature known as conditional compilation. Conditional compilation means that parts of the program can be included or excluded at compile time based upon some condition. One thing it's often used for is to include or exclude debugging print statements. When the program appears to be working, the developer is struck by a fit of hubris and removes all the error checking. A more common rationale is that the developer wants to make the finished program smaller—a worthy goal—or make it run faster by removing conditional statements.

Conditional compilation?

Although Java lacks any explicit conditional compilation, a kind of conditional compilation is implicit in the language. All Java compilers must do flow analysis to ensure that all paths to a local variable's usage pass through a statement that assigns it a value first, that all returns from a function pass out via someplace that provides a return value, and so on. Imagine what the compiler will do when it finds an `if` statement whose value is known to be false at compile time. Why should it even generate code for the condition? True, you say, but how can the results of an `if` statement be known at compile time? Simple: through `final boolean` variables. Further, if the value of the `if` condition is known to be false, the body of the `if` statement should not be emitted by the compiler either. Presto—instant conditional compilation!

This is shown in the following code:

```
// IfDef.java
final boolean DEBUG = false;
System.out.println("Hello, World ");
if (DEBUG) {
        System.out.println("Life is a voyage, not a destination");
}
```

Compilation of this program and examination of the resulting class file reveals that the string "Hello" does appear, but the conditionally printed epigram does not. The entire `println` has been omitted from the class file. So Java does have its own conditional compilation mechanism:

```
darian$ jr IfDef
 javac IfDef.java
 java IfDef
Hello, World
darian$ strings IfDef.class | grep Life # not found!
darian$ javac IfDef.java # try another compiler
darian$ strings IfDef.class | grep Life # still not found!
darian$
```

What if we want to use debugging code similar to this but have the condition applied at runtime? We can use `System.properties` (see Recipe 2.2) to fetch a variable. Instead of using this conditional compilation mechanism, you may want to leave your debugging statements in the code but enable them only at runtime when a problem surfaces. This is a good technique for all but the most compute-intensive applications, because the overhead of a simple `if` statement is not all that great. Let's combine the flexibility of runtime checking with the simple `if` statement to debug a hypothetical `fetch()` method (part of *Fetch.java*):

```
String name = "poem";
if (System.getProperty("debug.fetch") != null) {
    System.err.println("Fetching " + name);
}
value = fetch(name);
```

Then, we can compile and run this normally and the debugging statement is omitted. But if we run it with a `-D` argument to enable `debug.fetch`, the printout occurs:

```
> java starting.Fetch# See? No output
> java -Ddebug.fetch starting.Fetch
Fetching poem
>
```

Of course this kind of `if` statement is tedious to write in large quantities. I originally encapsulated it into a `Debug` class, which remains part of my `com.darwinsys.util` package. However, I currently advise the use of a full-function logging package such as `java.util.logging` (see Recipe 16.10), Log4J (see Recipe 16.9), or similar.

This is as good a place as any to interject about another feature—inline code generation. The C/C++ world has a language keyword `inline`, which is a hint to the compiler that the function (method) is not needed outside the current source file. Therefore, when the C compiler is generating machine code, a call to the function marked with `inline` can be replaced by the actual method body, eliminating the overhead of pushing arguments onto a stack, passing control, retrieving parameters, and returning values. In Java, making a method `final` enables the compiler to know that it can be inlined, or emitted in line. This is an optional optimization that the compiler is not obliged to perform, but may for efficiency.

See Also

Recipe 1.11.

"Conditional compilation" is used in some languages to enable or disable the printing or "logging" of a large number of debug or informational statements. In Java, this is normally the function of a "logger" package. Some of the common logging mechanisms —including ones that can log across a network connection—are covered in Recipes 16.7, 16.9, and 16.10.

1.11. Maintaining Program Correctness with Assertions

Problem

You want to leave tests in your code but not have runtime checking overhead until you need it.

Solution

Use the Java `assertion` mechanism.

Discussion

The Java language `assert` keyword takes two arguments separated by a colon (by analogy with the conditional operator): an expression that is asserted by the developer to be true, and a message to be included in the exception that is thrown if the expression is false. Normally, assertions are meant to be left in place (unlike quick-and-dirty print statements, which are often put in during one test and then removed). To reduce runtime overhead, assertion checking is not enabled by default; it must be enabled explicitly with the `-enableassertions` (or `-ea`) command-line flag. Here is a simple demo program that shows the use of the assertion mechanism:

testing/AssertDemo.java

```
public class AssertDemo {
    public static void main(String[] args) {
        int i = 4;
        if (args.length == 1) {
            i = Integer.parseInt(args[0]);
        }
        assert i > 0 : "i is non-positive";
        System.out.println("Hello after an assertion");
    }
}
$ javac -d . testing/AssertDemo.java
$ java testing.AssertDemo -1
Hello after an assertion
```

```
$ java -ea testing.AssertDemo -1
Exception in thread "main" java.lang.AssertionError: i is non-positive
        at AssertDemo.main(AssertDemo.java:15)
$
```

1.12. Debugging with JDB

Problem

The use of debugging printouts and assertions in your code is still not enough.

Solution

Use a debugger, preferably the one that comes with your IDE.

Discussion

The JDK includes a command-line–based debugger, *jdb*, and all mainstream IDEs include their own debugging tools. If you've focused on one IDE, learn to use the debugger that it provides. If you're a command-line junkie, you may want to learn at least the basic operations of *jdb*.

Here is a buggy program. It intentionally has bugs introduced so that you can see their effects in a debugger:

starting/Buggy.java

```
/** This program exhibits some bugs, so we can use a debugger */
public class Buggy {
    static String name;

    public static void main(String[] args) {
        int n = name.length();    // bug # 1
        System.out.println(n);

        name += "; The end.";    // bug #2
        System.out.println(name); // #3
    }
}
```

Here is a session using *jdb* to find these bugs:

```
$ java starting.Buggy
Exception in thread "main" java.lang.NullPointerException
        at Buggy.main(Compiled Code)
$ jdb starting/Buggy
Initializing jdb...
0xb2:class(Buggy)
> run
run Buggy
```

```
running ...
main[1]
Uncaught exception: java.lang.NullPointerException
        at Buggy.main(Buggy.java:6)
        at sun.tools.agent.MainThread.runMain(Native Method)
        at sun.tools.agent.MainThread.run(MainThread.java:49)

main[1] list
2          public class Buggy {
3                  static String name;
4
5                  public static void main(String[] args) {
6     =>                 int n = name.length( );   // bug # 1
7
8                          System.out.println(n);
9
10                         name += "; The end.";    // bug #2
main[1] print Buggy.name
Buggy.name = null
main[1] help
** command list **
threads [threadgroup]      -- list threads
thread <thread id>         -- set default thread
suspend [thread id(s)]     -- suspend threads (default: all)
resume [thread id(s)]      -- resume threads (default: all)
where [thread id] | all    -- dump a thread's stack
wherei [thread id] | all   -- dump a thread's stack, with pc info
threadgroups               -- list threadgroups
threadgroup <name>         -- set current threadgroup

print <id> [id(s)]         -- print object or field
dump <id> [id(s)]          -- print all object information

locals                     -- print all local variables in current stack frame

classes                    -- list currently known classes
methods <class id>         -- list a class's methods

stop in <class id>.<method>[(argument_type,...)] -- set a breakpoint in a method
stop at <class id>:<line> -- set a breakpoint at a line
up [n frames]              -- move up a thread's stack
down [n frames]            -- move down a thread's stack
clear <class id>.<method>[(argument_type,...)]  -- clear a breakpoint in a method
clear <class id>:<line>    -- clear a breakpoint at a line
step                       -- execute current line
step up                    -- execute until current method returns to its caller
stepi                      -- execute current instruction
next                       -- step one line (step OVER calls)
cont                       -- continue execution from breakpoint

catch <class id>           -- break for the specified exception
ignore <class id>          -- ignore when the specified exception
```

```
list [line number|method] -- print source code
use [source file path]    -- display or change the source path

memory                    -- report memory usage
gc                        -- free unused objects

load classname            -- load Java class to be debugged
run <class> [args]        -- start execution of a loaded Java class
!!                        -- repeat last command
help (or ?)               -- list commands
exit (or quit)            -- exit debugger
main[1] exit
$
```

Other debuggers are available; some of them can even work remotely because the Java Debugger API (which the debuggers use) is network based. Most IDEs feature their own debugging tools; you may want to spend some time becoming familiar with the tools in your chosen IDE.

1.13. Avoiding the Need for Debuggers with Unit Testing

Problem

You don't want to have to debug your code.

Solution

Use unit testing to validate each class as you develop it.

Discussion

Stopping to use a debugger is time consuming; it's better to test beforehand. The methodology of unit testing has been around for a long time; it is a tried-and-true means of getting your code tested in small blocks. Typically, in an OO language like Java, unit testing is applied to individual classes, in contrast to "system" or "integration" testing where the entire application is tested.

I have long been an advocate of this very basic testing methodology. Indeed, developers of the software methodology known as Extreme Programming (*http://www.extreme programming.org*) (XP for short) advocate "Test Driven Development" (TDD): writing the unit tests *before* you write the code. They also advocate running your tests almost every time you build your application. And they ask one good question: *If you don't have a test, how do you know your code (still) works?* This group of unit-testing advocates has some well-known leaders, including Erich Gamma of *Design Patterns* book fame and Kent Beck of *eXtreme Programming* book fame. I definitely go along with their advocacy of unit testing.

Indeed, many of my classes used to come with a "built-in" unit test. Classes that are not main programs in their own right would often include a main method that just tests out the functionality of the class. What surprised me is that, before encountering XP, I used to think I did this often, but an actual inspection of two projects indicated that only about a third of my classes had test cases, either internally or externally. Clearly what is needed is a uniform methodology. That is provided by JUnit.

JUnit is a Java-centric methodology for providing test cases that you can download for free (*http://www.junit.org*). JUnit is a very simple but useful testing tool. It is easy to use—you just write a test class that has a series of methods and annotate them with @Test (the older JUnit 3.8 required you to have test methods' names begin with test). JUnit uses introspection (see Chapter 23) to find all these methods, and then runs them for you. Extensions to JUnit handle tasks as diverse as load testing and testing enterprise components; the JUnit website provides links to these extensions. All modern IDEs provide built-in support for generating and running JUnit tests.

How do you get started using JUnit? All that's necessary is to write a test. Here I have written a simple test of my Person class and placed it into a class called PersonTest (note the obvious naming pattern):

```
public class PersonTest {

    @Test
    public void testNameConcat() {
        Person p = new Person("Ian", "Darwin");
        String f = p.getFullName();
        assertEquals("Name concatenation", "Ian Darwin", f);
    }
}
```

To run it manually, I compile the test and invoke the command-line test harness TestRunner:

```
$ javac PersonTest.java
$ java -classpath junit4.x.x.jar junit.textui.TestRunner testing.PersonTest
.
Time: 0.188

OK (1 tests)

$
```

In fact, running that is tedious, so I usually have a *regress* target in my Ant scripts. There is a `junit` task in Ant's "Optional Tasks" package.[1] Using it is easy:

```
<target  name="regress" depends="build">
    <junit>
            <test name="PersonTest" />
    </junit>
</target>
```

In fact, even *that* is tedious, so nowadays I just put my tests in the "standard directory structure" (i.e., *src/test/java/*) with the same package as the code being tested, and run Maven (see Recipe 1.7), which will automatically compile and run all the unit tests, and halt the build if any test fails.

The *Hamcrest matchers* allow you to write more expressive tests, at the cost of an additional download. Support for them is built into JUnit 4 with the `assertThat` static method, but you need to download the matchers from Hamcrest (*http://hamcrest.org*) or via the Maven artifact.

Here's an example of using the Hamcrest Matchers:

```
public class HamcrestDemo {

    @Test
    public void testNameConcat() {
        Person p = new Person("Ian", "Darwin");
        String f = p.getFullName();
        assertThat(f, containsString("Ian"));
        assertThat(f, equalTo("Ian Darwin"));
        assertThat(f, not(containsString("/"))); // contrived, to show syntax
    }
}
```

See Also

If you prefer flashier GUI output, several JUnit variants (built using Swing and AWT; see Chapter 14) will run the tests with a GUI. More importantly, all modern IDEs provide built-in support for running tests; in Eclipse, you can right-click a project in the Package Explorer and select Run As→Unit Test to have it find and run all the JUnit tests in the entire project.

JUnit offers considerable documentation of its own; download it from the website listed earlier.

Also, for *manual testing* of graphical components, I have developed a simple component tester, described in Recipe 12.2.

---

1. In some versions of Ant, you may need an additional download for this to function.

An alternative Unit Test framework for Java is *TestNG*; it got some early traction by adopting Java annotations before `JUnit` did, but since `JUnit` got with the annotations program, `JUnit` has remained the dominant package for Java Unit Testing.

Remember: *Test early and often!*

1.14. Maintaining Your Code with Continuous Integration

Problem

You want to be sure that your entire code base compiles and passes its tests periodically.

Solution

Use a Continuous Integration server such as Jenkins/Hudson.

Discussion

If you haven't previously used continuous integration, you are going to wonder how you got along without it. CI is simply the practice of having all developers on a project periodically integrate their changes into a single master copy of the project's "source." This might be a few times a day, or every few days, but should not be more than that, else the integration will likely run into larger hurdles where multiple developers have modified the same file.

But it's not just big projects that benefit from CI. Even on a one-person project, it's great to have a single button you can click that will check out the latest version of everything, compile it, link or package it, run all the automated tests, and give a red or green pass/ fail indicator.

And it's not just code-based projects that benefit from CI. If you have a number of small websites, putting them all under CI control is one of several important steps toward developing an automated, "dev-ops" culture around website deployment and management.

If you are new to the idea of CI, I can do no better than to plead with you to read Martin Fowler's insightful (as ever) paper on the topic (*http://martinfowler.com/articles/contin uousIntegration.html*). One of the key points is to automate both the *management* of the code *and* all the other artifacts needed to build your project, and to automate the actual process of *building* it, possibly using one of the build tools discussed earlier in this chapter.[2]

---

2. If the deployment or build includes a step like "Get Smith to process file X on his desktop and copy to the server," you aren't automated.

There are many CI servers, both free and commercial. In the open source world, CruiseControl and Jenkins/Hudson are among the best known. Jenkins (*http://jenkins-ci.org*)/Hudson (*http://hudson-ci.org*) began as Hudson, largely written by Kohsuke Kawaguchi, while working for Sun Microsystems. Unsurprising, then, that he wrote it in Java. Not too surprising, either, that when Oracle took over Sun, there were some cultural clashes over this project, like many other open source projects,[3] with the key players (includine Kohsuke) packing up and moving on, creating a new "fork" or split of the project. Kohsuke works on the half now known as Jenkins (for a long time, each project regarded itself as the real project and the other as the fork). Hereafter, I'll just use the name Jenkins, because that's the one I use, and because it takes too long to say "Jenkins/Hudson" all the time. But almost everything here applies to Hudson as well.

Jenkins is a web application; once it's started, you can use any standard web browser as its user interface. Installing and starting Jenkins can be as simple as unpacking a distribution and invoking it as follows:

```
java -jar jenkins.war
```

If you do that, be sure to enable security if your machine is on the Internet! This will start up its own tiny web server. Many people find it more secure to run Jenkins in a full-function Java EE or Java web server; anything from Tomcat to JBoss to WebSphere or Weblogic will do the job, and let you impose additional security constraints.

Once Jenkins is up and running and you have enabled security and are logged in on an account with sufficient privilege, you can create "jobs." A job usually corresponds to one project, both in terms of origin (one source code checkout) and in terms of results (one war file, one executable, one library, one whatever). Setting up a project is as simple as clicking the "New Job" button at the top-left of the dashboard, as shown in Figure 1-12.

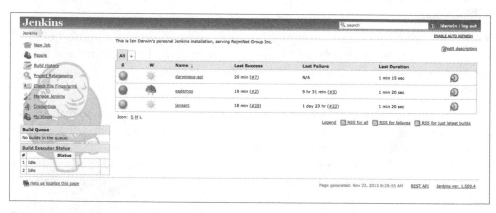

Figure 1-12. Jenkins: Dashboard

---

3. See also Open Office/Libre Office and MySql/mariadb, both involving Oracle.

You can fill in the first few pieces of information: the project's name and a brief description. Note that each and every input field has a "?" Help icon beside it, which will give you hints as you go along. Don't be afraid to peek at these hints! Figure 1-13 shows the first few steps of setting up a new job.

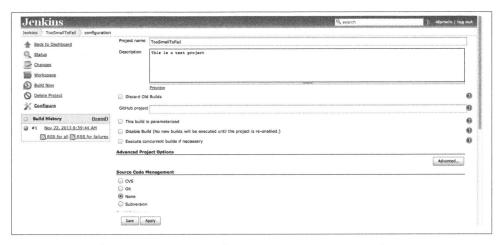

Figure 1-13. Jenkins: Starting a new job

In the next few sections of the form, Jenkins uses dynamic HTML to make entry fields appear based on what you've checked. My demo project "TooSmallToFail" starts off with no source code management (SCM) repository, but your real project is probably already in Git, Subversion, or maybe even CVS or some other SCM. Don't worry if yours is not listed; there are hundreds of plug-ins to handle almost any SCM. Once you've chosen your SCM, you will enter the parameters to fetch the project's source from that SCM repository, using text fields that ask for the specifics needed for that SCM: a URL for Git, a CVSROOT for CVS, and so on.

You also have to tell Jenkins *when* and *how* to build (and package, test, deploy…) your project. For the *when*, you have several choices such as building it after another Jenkins project, building it every so often based on a cron-like schedule, or based on polling the SCM to see if anything has changed (using the same cron-like scheduler). If your project is at GitHub (not just a local Git server), or some other SCMs, you can have the project built whenever somebody pushes changes up to the repository. It's all a matter of finding the right plug-ins and following the documentation for them.

Then the *how*, or the build process. Again, a few build types are included with Jenkins, and many more are available as plug-ins: I've used Apache Ant, Apache Maven, Gradle, the traditional Unix make tool, and even shell or command lines. As before, text fields specific to your chosen tool will appear once you select the tool. In the toy example, TooSmallToFail, I just use the shell command /bin/false (which should be present on any Unix or Linux system) to ensure that the project does, in fact, fail to build, just so you can see what that looks like.

You can have zero or more build steps; just keep clicking the Add button and add additional ones, as shown in Figure 1-14.

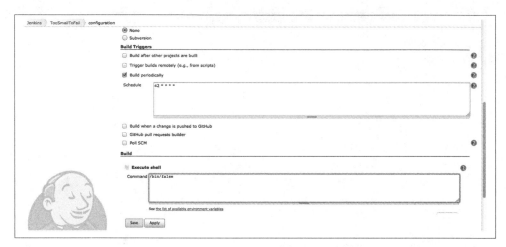

Figure 1-14. Jenkins: Dynamic web page for SCM and adding build steps

Once you think you've entered all the necessary information, click the Save button at the bottom of the page, and you'll go back to the project's main page. Here you can click the funny little "build now" icon at the far left to initiate a build right away. Or if you have set up build triggers, you could wait until they kick in, but then again, wouldn't you rather know right away whether you've got it just right? Figure 1-15 shows the build starting.

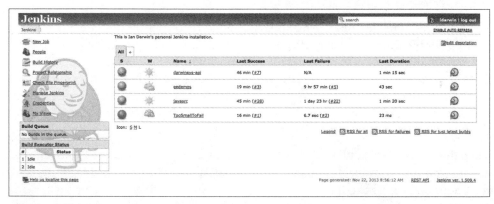

Figure 1-15. Jenkins: After a new job is added

Should a job fail to build, you get a red ball instead of a green one. Actually, success shows a blue ball by default, but most people here prefer green for success, so the optional "Green Ball" plug-in is usually one of the first to be added to a new installation.

Beside the red or green ball, you will see a "weather report" ranging from sunny (the last several builds have succeeded), cloudy, rainy, or stormy (no recent builds have succeeded).

Click the link to the project that failed, and then the link to Console Output, and figure out what went wrong. The usual workflow is then to make changes to the project, commit/push them to the source code repository, and run the Jenkins build again.

As mentioned, there are hundreds of optional plug-ins for Jenkins. To make your life easier, almost all of them can be installed by clicking the Manage Jenkins link and then going to Manage Plug-ins. The Available tab lists all the ones that are available from Jenkins.org; you just need to click the checkbox beside the ones you want, and click Apply. You can also find updates here. If your plug-in addtion or upgrade requires a restart, you'll see a yellow ball and words to that effect; otherwise you should see a green (or blue) ball indicating plug-in success. You can also see the list of plug-ins directly on the Web (*https://wiki.jenkins-ci.org/display/JENKINS/Plugins*).

I mentioned that Jenkins began life under the name Hudson. The Hudson project still exists, and is hosted at the Eclipse website. Last I checked, both projects had maintained plug-in compatibility, so many or most plug-ins from one can be used with the other. In fact, the most popular plug-ins appear in the Available tab of both, and most of what's said in this recipe about Jenkins applies equally to Hudson. If you use a different CI system, you'll need to check that system's documentation, but the concepts and the benefits will be similar.

1.15. Getting Readable Tracebacks

Problem

You're getting an exception stack trace at runtime, but most of the important parts don't have line numbers.

Solution

Be sure you have compiled with debugging enabled. On older systems, disable JIT and run it again, or use the current HotSpot runtime.

Discussion

When a Java program throws an exception, the exception propagates up the call stack until there is a catch clause that matches it. If none is found, the Java interpreter program that invoked your `main()` method catches the exception and prints a stack traceback showing all the method calls that got from the top of the program to the place where the exception was thrown. You can print this traceback yourself in any `catch` clause: the `Throwable` class has several methods called `printStackTrace()`.

The traceback includes line numbers only if they were compiled in. When using `javac`, this is the default. When using Ant's `javac` task, this is not the default; you must be sure you have used `<javac debug="true" …>` in your *build.xml* file if you want line numbers.

1.16. Finding More Java Source Code: Programs, Frameworks, Libraries

Problem

You want to build a large application and need to minimize coding, avoiding the "Not Invented Here" syndrome.

Solution

Use the Source, Luke. There are thousands of Java apps, frameworks, and libraries available in open source.

Discussion

Java source code is everywhere. As mentioned in the Preface, all the code examples from this book can be downloaded from the book's catalog page (*http://bit.ly/java-cookbook-3e*).

Another valuable resource is the source code for the Java API. You may not have realized it, but the source code for all the public parts of the Java API are included with each release of the Java Development Kit. Want to know how `java.util.ArrayList` actually works? You have the source code. Got a problem making a `JTable` behave? The standard JDK includes the source for all the public classes! Look for a file called *src.zip* or *src.jar*; some versions unzip this and some do not.

If that's not enough, you can get the source for the whole JDK for free over the Internet, just by committing to the Sun Java Community Source License and downloading a large file. This includes the source for the public and nonpublic parts of the API, as well as the compiler (written in Java) and a large body of code written in C/C++ (the runtime itself and the interfaces to the native library). For example, `java.io.Reader` has a method called `read()`, which reads bytes of data from a file or network connection. This is written in C because it actually calls the `read()` system call for Unix, Windows, Mac OS, BeOS, or whatever. The JDK source kit includes the source for all this stuff.

And ever since the early days of Java, a number of websites have been set up to distribute free software or open source Java, just as with most other modern "evangelized" languages, such as Perl, Python, Tk/Tcl, and others. (In fact, if you need native code to deal with some oddball filesystem mechanism in a portable way, beyond the material in Chapter 11, the source code for these runtime systems might be a good place to look.)

Although most of this book is about writing Java code, this recipe is about *not* writing code, but about using code written by others. There are hundreds of good frameworks to add to your Java application—why reinvent the flat tire when you can buy a perfectly round one? Many of these frameworks have been around for years and have become well rounded by feedback from users.

What, though, is the difference between a library and a framework? It's sometimes a bit vague, but in general, a framework is "a program with holes that you fill in," whereas a library is code you call. It is roughly the difference between building a car by buying a car almost complete but with no engine, and building a car by buying all the pieces and bolting them together yourself.

When considering using a third-party framework, there are many choices and issues to consider. One is cost, which gets into the issue of open source versus closed source. Most "open source" tools can be downloaded for free and used, either without any conditions or with conditions that you must comply with. There is not the space here to discuss these licensing issues, so I will refer you to *Understanding Open Source and Free Software Licensing* (O'Reilly).

Some well-known collections of open source frameworks and libraries for Java are listed in Table 1-3. Most of the projects on these sites are "curated"—that is, judged and found worthy—by some sort of community process.

Table 1-3. Reputable open source Java collections

Organization	URL	Notes
Apache Software Foundation	http://projects.apache.org	Not just a web server!
Spring framework	http://spring.io/projects	
JBoss community	http://www.jboss.org/projects	Not just a Java EE app server!

There are also a variety of open source code repositories, which are not curated—anybody who signs up can create a project there, regardless of the existing community size (if any). Sites like this that are successful accumulate too many projects to have a single page listing them—you have to search. Most are not specific to Java. Table 1-4 shows some of the open source code repos.

Table 1-4. Open source code repositories

Name	URL	Notes
Sourceforge.net	*http://sourceforge.net/*	One of the oldest
GitHub	*http://github.com/*	"Social Coding"
Google Code	*http://code.google.com/p*	
java.net	*http://dev.java.net/*	Java-specific; sponsored by Sun, now Oracle

That is not to disparage these—indeed, the collection of demo programs for this book is hosted on GitHub—but only to say that you have to know what you're looking for, and exercise a bit more care before deciding on a framework. Is there a community around it, or is it a dead end?

Finally, the author of this book maintains a small Java site (*http://www.darwinsys.com/java*), which may be of value. It includes a listing of Java resources and material related to this book.

For the Java enterprise or web tier, there are two main frameworks that also provide "dependency injection": JavaServer Faces (JSF) and CDI, and the Spring Framework "SpringMVC" package. JSF and the built-in CDI (Contexts and Dependency Injection) provides DI as well as some additional Contexts, such as a very useful Web Conversation context that holds objects across multiple web page interactions. The Spring Framework provides dependency injection and the SpringMVC web-tier helper classes. Table 1-5 shows some web tier resources.

Table 1-5. Web tier resources

Name	URL	Notes
Ians List of 100 Java Web Frameworks	*http://darwinsys.com/jwf/*	
JSF	*http://bit.ly/1ICLULS*	Java EE new standard technology for web pages

Because JSF is a component-based framework, there are many add-on components that will make your JSF-based website much more capable (and better looking) than the default JSF components. Table 1-6 shows some of the JSF add-on libraries.

Table 1-6. JSF add-on libraries

Name	URL	Notes
PrimeFaces	*http://primefaces.org/*	Rich components library
RichFaces	*http://richfaces.org/*	Rich components library
OpenFaces	*http://openfaces.org/*	Rich components library
IceFaces	*http://icefaces.org/*	Rich components library
Apache Deltaspike	*http://deltaspike.apache.org/*	Numerous code add-ons for JSF
JSFUnit	*http://www.jboss.org/jsfunit/*	JUnit Testing for JSFUnit

There are frameworks and libraries for almost everything these days. If my lists don't lead you to what you need, a web search probably will. Try not to reinvent the flat tire!

As with all free software, be sure that you understand the ramifications of the various licensing schemes. Code covered by the GPL, for example, automatically transfers the GPL to any code that uses even a small part of it. Consult a lawyer. Your mileage may vary. Despite these caveats, the source code is an invaluable resource to the person who wants to learn more Java.

## CHAPTER 2

Interacting with the Environment

2.0. Introduction

This chapter describes how your Java program can deal with its immediate surroundings, with what we call the runtime environment. In one sense, everything you do in a Java program using almost any Java API involves the environment. Here we focus more narrowly on things that directly surround your program. Along the way we'll be introduced to the System class, which knows a lot about your particular system.

Two other runtime classes deserve brief mention. The first, java.lang.Runtime, lies behind many of the methods in the System class. System.exit(), for example, just calls Runtime.exit(). Runtime is technically part of "the environment," but the only time we use it directly is to run other programs, which is covered in Recipe 24.1. The java.awt.Toolkit object is also part of the environment and is discussed in Chapter 12.

2.1. Getting Environment Variables

Problem

You want to get the value of "environment variables" from within your Java program.

Solution

Use System.getenv().

Discussion

The seventh edition of Unix, released in 1979, had a new feature known as environment variables. Environment variables are in all modern Unix systems (including Mac OS X) and in most later command-line systems, such as the "DOS" or Command Prompt in

Windows, but are not in some older platforms or other Java runtimes. Environment variables are commonly used for customizing an individual computer user's runtime environment, hence the name. To take one familiar example, on Unix or DOS the environment variable PATH determines where the system looks for executable programs. So of course the question comes up: "How do I get at environment variables from my Java program?"

The answer is that you can do this in all modern versions of Java, but you should exercise caution in depending on being able to specify environment variables because some rare operating systems may not provide them. That said, it's unlikely you'll run into such a system because all "standard" desktop systems provide them at present.

In some very ancient versions of Java, `System.getenv()` was deprecated and/or just didn't work. Nowadays the `getenv()` method is no longer deprecated, though it still carries the warning that System Properties (see Recipe 2.2) should be used instead. Even among systems that support them, environment variable names are case sensitive on some platforms and case insensitive on others. The code in Example 2-1 is a short program that uses the `getenv()` method.

Example 2-1. environ/GetEnv.java

```java
public class GetEnv {
    public static void main(String[] argv) {
        System.out.println("System.getenv(\"PATH\") = " + System.getenv("PATH"));
    }
}
```

Running this code will produce output similar to the following:

```
C:\javasrc>java environ.GetEnv
System.getenv("PATH") = C:\windows\bin;c:\jdk1.8\bin;c:\documents
    and settings\ian\bin
C:\javasrc>
```

The no-argument form of the method `System.getenv()` returns *all* the environment variables, in the form of an immutable `String Map`. You can iterate through this map and access all the user's settings or retrieve multiple environment settings.

Both forms of `getenv()` require you to have permissions to access the environment, so they typically do not work in restricted environments such as applets.

2.2. Getting Information from System Properties

Problem

You need to get information from the system properties.

Solution

Use `System.getProperty()` or `System.getProperties()`.

Discussion

What is a *property* anyway? A property is just a name and value pair stored in a `java.util.Properties` object, which we discuss more fully in Recipe 7.12.

The `System.Properties` object controls and describes the Java runtime. The `System` class has a static `Properties` member whose content is the merger of operating system specifics (`os.name`, for example), system and user tailoring (`java.class.path`), and properties defined on the command line (as we'll see in a moment). Note that the use of periods in these names (like `os.arch`, `os.version`, `java.class.path`, and `java.lang.version`) makes it look as though there is a hierarchical relationship similar to that for class names. The `Properties` class, however, imposes no such relationships: each key is just a string, and dots are not special.

To retrieve one system-provided property, use `System.getProperty()`. If you want them all, use `System.getProperties()`. Accordingly, if I wanted to find out if the `System Properties` had a property named `"pencil_color"`, I could say:

```
String sysColor = System.getProperty("pencil_color");
```

But what does that return? Surely Java isn't clever enough to know about everybody's favorite pencil color? Right you are! But we can easily tell Java about our pencil color (or anything else we want to tell it) using the `-D` argument.

The `-D` option argument is used to predefine a value in the system properties object. It must have a name, an equals sign, and a value, which are parsed the same way as in a properties file (see Recipe 7.12). You can have more than one `-D` definition between the java command and your class name on the command line. At the Unix or Windows command line, type:

```
java -D"pencil_color=Deep Sea Green" environ.SysPropDemo
```

When running this under an IDE, put the variable's name and value in the appropriate dialog box, typically in the IDE's "Run Configuration" dialog.

The `SysPropDemo` program has code to extract just one or a few properties, so you can run it like:

```
$ java environ.SysPropDemo os.arch
os.arch = x86
```

Which reminds me—this is a good time to mention system-dependent code. Recipe 2.3 talks about release-dependent code, and Recipe 2.4 talks about OS-dependent code.

See Also

Recipe 7.12 lists more details on using and naming your own `Properties` files. The javadoc page for `java.util.Properties` lists the exact rules used in the `load()` method, as well as other details.

2.3. Learning About the Current JDK Release

Problem

You need to write code that looks at the current JDK release (e.g., to see what release of Java you are running under).

Solution

Use `System.getProperty()` with an argument of `java.specification.version`.

Discussion

Although Java is meant to be portable, Java runtimes have some significant variations. Sometimes you need to work around a feature that may be missing in older runtimes, but you want to use it if it's present. So one of the first things you want to know is how to find out the JDK release corresponding to the Java runtime. This is easily obtained with `System.getProperty()`:

```
System.out.println(System.getProperty("java.specification.version"));
```

Alternatively, and with greater generality, you may want to test for the presence or absence of particular classes. One way to do this is with `Class.forName("class")` (see Chapter 23), which throws an exception if the class cannot be loaded—a good indication that it's not present in the runtime's library. Here is code for this, from an application wanting to find out whether the common Swing UI components are available (they normally would be in any modern standard Java SE implementation, but not, for example, in the pre–museum-piece JDK 1.1, nor in the Java-based Android runtime). The javadoc for the standard classes reports the version of the JDK in which this class first appeared, under the heading "Since." If there is no such heading, it normally means that the class has been present since the beginnings of Java:

starting/CheckForSwing.java

```
public class CheckForSwing {
    public static void main(String[] args) {
        try {
            Class.forName("javax.swing.JButton");
        } catch (ClassNotFoundException e) {
            String failure =
                "Sorry, but this version of MyApp needs \n" +
```

```
                        "a Java Runtime with JFC/Swing components\n" +
                        "having the final names (javax.swing.*)";
                // Better to make something appear in the GUI. Either a
                // JOptionPane, or: myPanel.add(new Label(failure));
                System.err.println(failure);
            }
            // No need to print anything here - the GUI should work...
        }
    }
```

It's important to distinguish between testing this at compile time and at runtime. In both cases, this code must be compiled on a system that includes the classes you are testing for—JDK >= 1.1 and Swing, respectively. These tests are only attempts to help the poor backwater Java runtime user trying to run your up-to-date application. The goal is to provide this user with a message more meaningful than the simple "class not found" error that the runtime gives. It's also important to note that this test becomes unreachable if you write it inside any code that depends on the code you are testing for. The check for Swing won't ever see the light of day on a JDK 1.0 system if you write it in the constructor of a JPanel subclass (think about it). Put the test early in the main flow of your application, before any GUI objects are constructed. Otherwise the code just sits there wasting space on newer runtimes and never gets run on Java 1.0 systems. Obviously this is a very early example, but you can use the same technique to test for any runtime feature added at any stage of Java's evolution (see Appendix A for an outline of the features added in each release of Java). You can also use this technique to determine whether a needed third-party library has been successfully added to your classpath.

As for what the class Class actually does, we'll defer that until Chapter 23.

2.4. Dealing with Operating System–Dependent Variations

Problem

You need to write code that adapts to the underlying operating system.

Solution

You can use System.Properties to find out the operating system, and various features in the File class to find out some platform-dependent features.

Discussion

Though Java is designed to be portable, some things aren't. These include such variables as the filename separator. Everybody on Unix knows that the filename separator is a slash character (/) and that a backward slash, or backslash (\), is an escape character.

Back in the late 1970s, a group at Microsoft was actually working on Unix—their version was called Xenix, later taken over by SCO—and the people working on DOS saw and liked the Unix filesystem model. The earliest versions of MS-DOS didn't have directories, it just had "user numbers" like the system it was a clone of, Digital Research CP/M (itself a clone of various other systems). So the Microsoft developers set out to clone the Unix filesystem organization. Unfortunately, they had already committed the slash character for use as an option delimiter, for which Unix had used a dash (-); and the PATH separator (:) was also used as a "drive letter" delimiter, as in C: or A:. So we now have commands like those shown in Table 2-1.

Table 2-1. Directory listing commands

System	Directory list command	Meaning	Example PATH setting
Unix	*ls -R /*	Recursive listing of /, the top-level directory	*PATH=/bin:/usr/bin*
DOS	*dir/s *	Directory with subdirectories option (i.e., recursive) of \, the top-level directory (but only of the current drive)	*PATH=C:\windows;D:\mybin*

Where does this get us? If we are going to generate filenames in Java, we may need to know whether to put a / or a \ or some other character. Java has two solutions to this. First, when moving between Unix and Microsoft systems, at least, it is *permissive*: either / or \ can be used,[1] and the code that deals with the operating system sorts it out. Second, and more generally, Java makes the platform-specific information available in a platform-independent way. First, for the file separator (and also the PATH separator), the `java.io.File` class (see Chapter 11) makes available some static variables containing this information. Because the `File` class is platform dependent, it makes sense to anchor this information here. The variables are shown in Table 2-2.

Table 2-2. File properties

Name	Type	Meaning
`separator`	`static String`	The system-dependent filename separator character (e.g., / or \).
`separatorChar`	`static char`	The system-dependent filename separator character (e.g., / or \).
`pathSeparator`	`static String`	The system-dependent path separator character, represented as a string for convenience.
`pathSeparatorChar`	`static char`	The system-dependent path separator character.

Both filename and path separators are normally characters, but they are also available in `String` form for convenience.

---

1. When compiling strings for use on Windows, remember to double them because \ is an escape character in most places other than the MS-DOS command line: `String rootDir = "C:\\";`.

A second, more general, mechanism is the system *Properties* object mentioned in Recipe 2.2. You can use this to determine the operating system you are running on. Here is code that simply lists the system properties; it can be informative to run this on several different implementations:

```
public class SysPropDemo {
    public static void main(String[] argv) throws IOException {
        if (argv.length == 0)
            System.getProperties().list(System.out);
        else {
            for (String s : argv) {
                System.out.println(s + " = " +
                    System.getProperty(s));
            }
        }
    }
}
```

Some OSes, for example, provide a mechanism called "the null device" that can be used to discard output (typically used for timing purposes). Here is code that asks the system properties for the "os.name" and uses it to make up a name that can be used for discarding data (if no null device is known for the given platform, we return the name *junk*, which means that on such platforms, we'll occasionally create, well, junk files; I just remove these files when I stumble across them):

```
package com.darwinsys.lang;

import java.io.File;

/** Some things that are System Dependent.
 * All methods are static.
 * @author Ian Darwin
 */
public class SysDep {

    final static String UNIX_NULL_DEV = "/dev/null";
    final static String WINDOWS_NULL_DEV = "NUL:";
    final static String FAKE_NULL_DEV = "jnk";

    /** Return the name of the "Null Device" on platforms which support it,
     * or "jnk" (to create an obviously well-named temp file) otherwise.
     */
    public static String getDevNull() {

        if (new File(UNIX_NULL_DEV).exists()) {          ❶
            return UNIX_NULL_DEV;
        }

        String sys = System.getProperty("os.name");      ❷
        if (sys==null) {                                 ❸
            return FAKE_NULL_DEV;
```

```
        }
        if (sys.startsWith("Windows")) {          ❹
            return WINDOWS_NULL_DEV;
        }
        return FAKE_NULL_DEV;                      ❺
    }
}
```

❶   If /dev/null exists, use it.

❷   If not, ask System.properties if it knows the OS name.

❸   Nope, so give up, return jnk.

❹   We know it's Microsoft Windows, so use NUL:.

❺   All else fails, go with jnk.

In one case you do need to check for the OS. Mac OS X has a number of GUI goodies that can be used only on that OS and yet should be used to make your GUI application look more like a "native" Mac application. Recipe 14.18 explores this issue in more detail. In brief, Apple says to look for the string mrj.version to determine whether you are running on OS X:

```
boolean isMacOS = System.getProperty("mrj.version") != null;
```

2.5. Using Extensions or Other Packaged APIs

Problem

You have a JAR file of classes you want to use.

Solution

Simply add the JAR to your CLASSPATH.

Discussion

As you build more sophisticated applications, you will need to use more and more third-party libraries. You can add these to your CLASSPATH.

It used to be recommended that you could drop these JAR files into the Java Extensions Mechanism directory, typically something like \jdk1.x\jre\lib\ext., instead of listing each JAR file in your CLASSPATH variable. However, this is no longer generally recommended.

The benefit of using CLASSPATH rather than the extensions directory is that it is more clear what your application depends on. Programs like Ant (see Recipe 1.6) or Maven (see Recipe 1.7) as well as IDEs can simplify or even automate the addition of JAR files to your classpath.

A further drawback to the use of the extensions directory is that it requires modifying the installed JDK or JRE, which can lead to maintenance issues, or problems when a new JDK or JRE is used.

It is anticipated that Java 9 will provide a new mechanism for program modularization, so you may not want to invest too heavily in anything complicated here. Use the existing tools mentioned earlier.

2.6. Parsing Command-Line Arguments

Problem

You need to parse command-line options. Java doesn't provide an API for it.

Solution

Look in the `args` array passed as an argument to `main`. Or use my `GetOpt` class.

Discussion

The Unix folks have had to deal with this longer than anybody, and they came up with a C-library function called `getopt`.[2] `getopt` processes your command-line arguments and looks for single-character options set off with dashes and optional arguments. For example, the command:

```
sort -n -o outfile myfile1 yourfile2
```

runs the Unix/Linux/Mac system-provided *sort* program. The `-n` tells it that the records are numeric rather than textual, and the `-o outfile` tells it to write its output into a file named *outfile*. The remaining words, *myfile1* and *yourfile2*, are treated as the input files to be sorted. On Windows, command arguments are sometimes set off with slashes (/). We use the Unix form—a dash—in our API, but feel free to change the code to use slashes.

Each `GetOpt` parser instance is constructed to recognize a particular set of arguments, because a given program normally has a fixed set of arguments that it accepts. You can construct an array of `GetOptDesc` objects that represent the allowable arguments. For the sort program shown previously, you might use:

---

2. The Unix world has several variations on `getopt`; mine emulates the original AT&T version fairly closely, with some frills such as long-name arguments.

```
GetOptDesc[] options = {
    new GetOptDesc('n', "numeric", false),
    new GetOptDesc('o', "output-file", true),
};
Map optionsFound = new GetOpt(options).parseArguments(argv);
if (optionsFound.get("n") != null) {
    System.out.println("sortType = NUMERIC;")
}
String outputFile = null;
if ((outputFile = optionsFound.get("o") != null) {
    System.out.println("output file specified as " + outputFile)
} else {
    System.out.println("Output to System.out");
}
```

The simple way of using GetOpt is to call its parseArguments method.

For backward compatibility with people who learned to use the Unix version in C, the getopt() method can be used normally in a while loop. It returns once for each valid option found, returning the value of the character that was found or the constant DONE when all options (if any) have been processed.

Here is a complete program that uses my GetOpt class just to see if there is a -h (for help) argument on the command line:

```java
public class GetOptSimple {
    public static void main(String[] args) {
        GetOpt go = new GetOpt("h");
        char c;
        while ((c = go.getopt(args)) != 0) {
            switch(c) {
            case 'h':
                helpAndExit(0);
                break;
            default:
                System.err.println("Unknown option in " +
                    args[go.getOptInd()-1]);
                helpAndExit(1);
            }
        }
        System.out.println();
    }

    /** Stub for providing help on usage
     * You can write a longer help than this, certainly.
     */
    static void helpAndExit(int returnValue) {
        System.err.println("This would tell you how to use this program");
        System.exit(returnValue);
    }
}
```

This longer demo program has several options:

```java
public class GetOptDemoNew {
    public static void main(String[] argv) {
        boolean numeric_option = false;
        boolean errs = false;
        String outputFileName = null;

        GetOptDesc[] options = {
            new GetOptDesc('n', "numeric", false),
            new GetOptDesc('o', "output-file", true),
        };
        GetOpt parser = new GetOpt(options);
        Map<String,String> optionsFound = parser.parseArguments(argv);
        for (String key : optionsFound.keySet()) {
            char c = key.charAt(0);
            switch (c) {
                case 'n':
                    numeric_option = true;
                    break;
                case 'o':
                    outputFileName = (String)optionsFound.get(key);
                    break;
                case '?':
                    errs = true;
                    break;
                default:
                    throw new IllegalStateException(
                    "Unexpected option character: " + c);
            }
        }
        if (errs) {
            System.err.println("Usage: GetOptDemo [-n][-o file][file...]");
        }
        System.out.print("Options: ");
        System.out.print("Numeric: " + numeric_option + ' ');
        System.out.print("Output: " + outputFileName + "; ");
        System.out.print("Input files: ");
        for (String fileName : parser.getFilenameList()) {
            System.out.print(fileName);
            System.out.print(' ');
        }
        System.out.println();
    }
}
```

If we invoke it several times with different options, including both single-argument and
long-name options, here's how it behaves:

```
> java environ.GetOptDemoNew
Options: Numeric: false Output: null; Inputs:
> java environ.GetOptDemoNew -M
Options: Numeric: false Output: null; Inputs: -M
```

```
> java environ.GetOptDemoNew -n a b c
Options: Numeric: true Output: null; Inputs: a b c
> java environ.GetOptDemoNew -numeric a b c
Options: Numeric: true Output: null; Inputs: a b c
> java environ.GetOptDemoNew -numeric -output-file /tmp/foo a b c
Options: Numeric: true Output: /tmp/foo; Inputs: a b c
```

You can find a longer example exercising all the ins and outs of this version of GetOpt in the online *darwinsys-api* repo under *src/main/test/lang/*. The source code for GetOpt itself lives in *darwinsys-api* under *src/main/java/com/darwinsys/lang/GetOpt.java*, and is shown in Example 2-2.

Example 2-2. Source code for GetOpt

```java
// package com.darwinsys.lang;
public class GetOpt {
    /** The List of File Names found after args */
    protected List<String> fileNameArguments;
    /** The set of characters to look for */
    protected final GetOptDesc[] options;
    /** Where we are in the options */
    protected int optind = 0;
    /** Public constant for "no more options" */
    public static final int DONE = 0;
    /** Internal flag - whether we are done all the options */
    protected boolean done = false;
    /** The current option argument. */
    protected String optarg;

    /** Retrieve the current option argument; UNIX variant spelling. */
    public String optarg() {
        return optarg;
    }
    /** Retrieve the current option argument; Java variant spelling. */
    public String optArg() {
        return optarg;
    }

    /** Construct a GetOpt parser, given the option specifications
     * in an array of GetOptDesc objects. This is the preferred constructor.
     */
    public GetOpt(final GetOptDesc[] opt) {
        this.options = opt.clone();
    }

    /** Construct a GetOpt parser, storing the set of option characters.
     * This is a legacy constructor for backward compatibility.
     * That said, it is easier to use if you don't need long-name options,
     * so it has not been and will not be marked "deprecated".
     */
    public GetOpt(final String patt) {
        if (patt == null) {
```

```
            throw new IllegalArgumentException("Pattern may not be null");
    }
    if (patt.charAt(0) == ':') {
        throw new IllegalArgumentException(
            "Pattern incorrect, may not begin with ':'");
    }

    // Pass One: just count the option letters in the pattern
    int n = 0;
    for (char ch : patt.toCharArray()) {
        if (ch != ':')
            ++n;
    }
    if (n == 0) {
        throw new IllegalArgumentException(
            "No option letters found in " + patt);
    }

    // Pass Two: construct an array of GetOptDesc objects.
    options = new GetOptDesc[n];
    for (int i = 0, ix = 0; i<patt.length(); i++) {
        final char c = patt.charAt(i);
        boolean argTakesValue = false;
        if (i < patt.length() - 1 && patt.charAt(i+1) == ':') {
            argTakesValue = true;
            ++i;
        }
        Debug.println("getopt",
            "CONSTR: options[" + ix + "] = " + c + ", " + argTakesValue);
        options[ix++] = new GetOptDesc(c, null, argTakesValue);
    }
}

/** Reset this GetOpt parser */
public void rewind() {
    fileNameArguments = null;
    done = false;
    optind = 0;
    optarg = null;
}

/**
 * Modern way of using GetOpt: call this once and get all options.
 * <p>
 * This parses the options, returns a Map whose keys are the found options.
 * Normally followed by a call to getFilenameList().
 * <br>Side effect: sets "fileNameArguments" to a new List
 * @return a Map whose keys are Strings of length 1 (containing the char
 * from the option that was matched) and whose value is a String
 * containing the value, or null for a non-option argument.
 */
public Map<String,String> parseArguments(String[] argv) {
```

```
            Map<String, String> optionsValueMap = new HashMap<String, String>();
            fileNameArguments = new ArrayList<String>();
            for (int i = 0; i < argv.length; i++) {     // Cannot use foreach, need i
                Debug.println("getopt", "parseArg: i=" + i + ": arg " + argv[i]);
                char c = getopt(argv);     // sets global "optarg"
                if (c == DONE) {
                    fileNameArguments.add(argv[i]);
                } else {
                    optionsValueMap.put(Character.toString(c), optarg);
                    // If this arg takes an option, must arrange here to skip it.
                    if (optarg != null) {
                        i++;
                    }
                }
            }
        }
        return optionsValueMap;
    }

    /** Get the list of filename-like arguments after options;
     * only for use if you called parseArguments.
     */
    public List<String> getFilenameList() {
        if (fileNameArguments == null) {
            throw new IllegalArgumentException(
                "Illegal call to getFilenameList() before parseOptions()");
        }
        return fileNameArguments;
    }

    /** The true heart of getopt, whether used old way or new way:
     * returns one argument; call repeatedly until it returns DONE.
     * Side-effect: sets globals optarg, optind
     */
    public char getopt(String argv[]) {
        Debug.println("getopt",
            "optind=" + optind + ", argv.length="+argv.length);

        if (optind >= (argv.length) || !argv[optind].startsWith("-")) {
            done = true;
        }

        // If we are finished (either now OR from before), bail.
        // Do not collapse this into the "if" above
        if (done) {
            return DONE;
        }

        optarg = null;

        // XXX TODO - two-pass, 1st check long args, 2nd check for
        // char, to allow advanced usage like "-no outfile" == "-n -o outfile".
```

```
            // Pick off next command line argument, if it starts "-",
            // then look it up in the list of valid args.
            String thisArg = argv[optind];

            if (thisArg.startsWith("-")) {
                for (GetOptDesc option : options) {
                    if ((thisArg.length() == 2 &&
                            option.getArgLetter() == thisArg.charAt(1)) ||
                        (option.getArgName() != null &&
                        option.getArgName().equals(thisArg.substring(1)))) { // found it
                        // If it needs an option argument, get it.
                        if (option.takesArgument()) {
                            if (optind < argv.length-1) {
                                optarg = argv[++optind];
                            } else {
                                throw new IllegalArgumentException(
                                    "Option " + option.getArgLetter() +
                                    " needs value but found end of arg list");
                            }
                        }
                        ++optind;
                        return option.getArgLetter();
                    }
                }
                // Began with "-" but not matched, so must be error.
                ++optind;
                return '?';
            } else {
                // Found non-argument non-option word in argv: end of options.
                ++optind;
                done = true;
                return DONE;
            }


        }

        /** Return optind, the index into args of the last option we looked at */
        public int getOptInd() {
            return optind;
        }
    }
}
```

See Also

GetOpt is an adequate tool for processing command-line options. You may come up with something better and contribute it to the Java world; this is left as an exercise for the reader.

For another way of dealing with command lines, see the Apache Commons Command Line Interface (*http://bit.ly/1v50F1A*).

## CHAPTER 3

Strings and Things

3.0. Introduction

Character strings are an inevitable part of just about any programming task. We use them for printing messages for the user; for referring to files on disk or other external media; and for people's names, addresses, and affiliations. The uses of strings are many, almost without number (actually, if you need numbers, we'll get to them in Chapter 5).

If you're coming from a programming language like C, you'll need to remember that `String` is a defined type (class) in Java—that is, a string is an object and therefore has methods. It is not an array of characters (though it contains one) and should not be thought of as an array. Operations like `fileName.endsWith(".gif")` and `exten- sion.equals(".gif")` (and the equivalent `".gif".equals(extension)`) are common- place.foonote:[They are "equivalent" with the exception that the first can throw a `Null- PointerException` while the second cannot.]

Notice that a given `String` object, once constructed, is immutable. In other words, once I have said `String s = "Hello" + yourName;`, the contents of the particular object that reference variable s refers to can never be changed. You can assign s to refer to a different string, even one derived from the original, as in `s = s.trim()`. And you can retrieve characters from the original string using `charAt()`, but it isn't called `getCharAt()` because there is not, and never will be, a `setCharAt()` method. Even methods like `toUpperCase()` don't change the `String`; they return a new `String` object containing the translated characters. If you need to change characters within a `String`, you should instead create a `StringBuilder` (possibly initialized to the starting value of the

String), manipulate the StringBuilder to your heart's content, and then convert that to String at the end, using the ubiquitous toString() method.[1]

How can I be so sure they won't add a setCharAt() method in the next release? Because the immutability of strings is one of the fundamentals of the Java Virtual Machine. Immutable objects are generally good for software reliability (some languages do not allow mutable objects). Immutability avoids conflicts, particularly where multiple threads are involved, or where software from multiple organizations has to work together; for example, you can safely pass immutable objects to a third-party library and expect that the objects will not be modifed.

Of course, it may be possible to tinker with the String's internal data structures using the Reflection API, as shown in Recipe 23.3, but then all bets are off. Secured environments, of course, do not permit access to the Reflection API.

Remember also that the String is a fundamental type in Java. Unlike most of the other classes in the core API, the behavior of strings is not changeable; the class is marked final so it cannot be subclassed. So you can't declare your own String subclass. Think if you could—you could masquerade as a String but provide a setCharAt() method! Again, they thought of that. If you don't believe me, try it out:

```
public class WolfInStringsClothing
    extends java.lang.String {//EXPECT COMPILE ERROR

    public void setCharAt(int index, char newChar) {
        // The implementation of this method
        // would be left as an exercise for the reader.
        // Hint: compile this code exactly as is before bothering!
    }
}
```

Got it? They thought of that!

Of course you do need to be able to modify strings. Some methods extract part of a String; these are covered in the first few recipes in this chapter. And StringBuilder is an important set of classes that deals in characters and strings and has many methods for changing the contents, including, of course, a toString() method. Reformed C programmers should note that Java strings are not arrays of chars as in C, so you must use methods for such operations as processing a string one character at a time; see Recipe 3.4. Figure 3-1 shows an overview of String, StringBuilder, and C-language strings.

---

1. StringBuilder was added in Java 5. It is functionally equivalent to the older StringBuffer. We will delve into the details in Recipe 3.3.

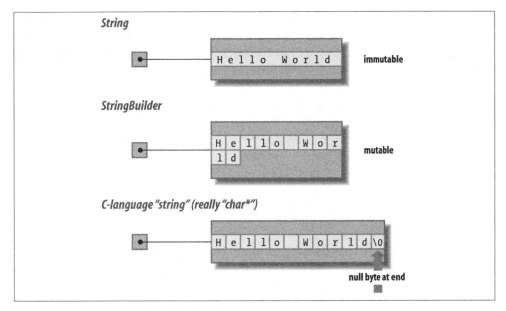

Figure 3-1. String, StringBuilder, and C-language strings

Although we haven't discussed the details of the `java.io` package yet (we will, in Chapter 10), you need to be able to read text files for some of these programs. Even if you're not familiar with `java.io`, you can probably see from the examples that read text files that a `BufferedReader` allows you to read "chunks" of data, and that this class has a very convenient `readLine()` method.

I won't show you how to sort an array of strings here; the more general notion of sorting a collection of objects is discussed in Recipe 7.13.

3.1. Taking Strings Apart with Substrings

Problem

You want to break a string apart into substrings by position.

Solution

Use the `String` object's `substring()` method.

Discussion

The `substring()` method constructs a new `String` object made up of a run of characters contained somewhere in the original string, the one whose `substring()` you called. The substring method is overloaded: both forms require a starting index (which is always *zero-based*). The one-argument form returns from startIndex to the end. The two-argument form takes an ending index (not a length, as in some languages), so that an index can be generated by the String methods indexOf() or lastIndexOf().

 Note that the end index is one beyond the last character! Java adopts this "half open interval" (or inclusive start, exclusive end) policy fairly consistently; there are good practical reasons for adopting this approach, and some other languages do likewise.

```
public class SubStringDemo {
    public static void main(String[] av) {
        String a = "Java is great.";
        System.out.println(a);
        String b = a.substring(5);     // b is the String "is great."
        System.out.println(b);
        String c = a.substring(5,7);// c is the String "is"
        System.out.println(c);
        String d = a.substring(5,a.length());// d is "is great."
        System.out.println(d);
    }
}
```

When run, this prints the following:

```
C:> java strings.SubStringDemo
Java is great.
is great.
is
is great.
C:>
```

3.2. Breaking Strings Into Words

Problem

You need to take a string apart into words or tokens.

Solution

To accomplish this, construct a StringTokenizer around your string and call its methods hasMoreTokens() and nextToken().

Or, use regular expressions (see Chapter 4).

Discussion

The easiest way is to use a regular expression; we'll discuss these in Chapter 4, but for now, a string containing a space is a valid regular expression to match space characters, so you can most easily split a string into words like this:

```
for (String word : some_input_string.split(" ")) {
    System.out.println(word);
}
```

If you need to match multiple spaces, or spaces and tabs, use the string `"\s+"`.

Another method is to use `StringTokenizer`. The `StringTokenizer` methods implement the `Iterator` interface and design pattern (see Recipe 7.9):

StrTokDemo.java

```
StringTokenizer st = new StringTokenizer("Hello World of Java");

while (st.hasMoreTokens( ))
    System.out.println("Token: " + st.nextToken( ));
```

`StringTokenizer` also implements the `Enumeration` interface directly (also in Recipe 7.9), but if you use the methods thereof you need to cast the results to `String`.

A `StringTokenizer` normally breaks the `String` into tokens at what we would think of as "word boundaries" in European languages. Sometimes you want to break at some other character. No problem. When you construct your `StringTokenizer`, in addition to passing in the string to be tokenized, pass in a second string that lists the "break characters." For example:

StrTokDemo2.java

```
StringTokenizer st = new StringTokenizer("Hello, World|of|Java", ", |");

while (st.hasMoreElements( ))
    System.out.println("Token: " + st.nextElement( ));
```

It outputs the four words, each on a line by itself, with no punctuation.

But wait, there's more! What if you are reading lines like:

```
FirstName|LastName|Company|PhoneNumber
```

and your dear old Aunt Begonia hasn't been employed for the last 38 years? Her "Company" field will in all probability be blank.[2] If you look very closely at the previous code example, you'll see that it has two delimiters together (the comma and the space), but if you run it, there are no "extra" tokens—that is, the `StringTokenizer` normally discards adjacent consecutive delimiters. For cases like the phone list, where you need to

---

2. Unless, perhaps, you're as slow at updating personal records as I am.

preserve null fields, there is good news and bad news. The good news is that you can do it: you simply add a second argument of true when constructing the StringTokenizer, meaning that you wish to see the delimiters as tokens. The bad news is that you now get to see the delimiters as tokens, so you have to do the arithmetic yourself. Want to see it? Run this program:

StrTokDemo3.java

```
StringTokenizer st =
    new StringTokenizer("Hello, World|of|Java", ", |", true);

while (st.hasMoreElements( ))
    System.out.println("Token: " + st.nextElement( ));
```

and you get this output:

```
C:\>java strings.StrTokDemo3
Token: Hello
Token: ,
Token:
Token: World
Token: |
Token: of
Token: |
Token: Java
C:\>
```

This isn't how you'd like StringTokenizer to behave, ideally, but it is serviceable enough most of the time. Example 3-1 processes and ignores consecutive tokens, returning the results as an array of Strings.

Example 3-1. StrTokDemo4.java (StringTokenizer)

```
public class StrTokDemo4 {
    public final static int MAXFIELDS = 5;
    public final static String DELIM = "|";

    /** Processes one String, returns it as an array of Strings */
    public static String[] process(String line) {
        String[] results = new String[MAXFIELDS];

        // Unless you ask StringTokenizer to give you the tokens,
        // it silently discards multiple null tokens.
        StringTokenizer st = new StringTokenizer(line, DELIM, true);

        int i = 0;
        // stuff each token into the current slot in the array.
        while (st.hasMoreTokens()) {
            String s = st.nextToken();
            if (s.equals(DELIM)) {
                if (i++>=MAXFIELDS)
                    // This is messy: See StrTokDemo4b which uses
```

```
                // a List to allow any number of fields.
                throw new IllegalArgumentException("Input line " +
                    line + " has too many fields");
            continue;
        }
        results[i] = s;
    }
    return results;
}

public static void printResults(String input, String[] outputs) {
    System.out.println("Input: " + input);
    for (String s : outputs)
        System.out.println("Output " + s + " was: " + s);
}

// Should be a JUnit test but is referred to in the book text,
// so I can't move it to "tests" until the next edit.
public static void main(String[] a) {
    printResults("A|B|C|D", process("A|B|C|D"));
    printResults("A||C|D", process("A||C|D"));
    printResults("A|||D|E", process("A|||D|E"));
}
}
```

When you run this, you will see that A is always in Field 1, B (if present) is in Field 2, and so on. In other words, the null fields are being handled properly:

```
Input: A|B|C|D
Output 0 was: A
Output 1 was: B
Output 2 was: C
Output 3 was: D
Output 4 was: null
Input: A||C|D
Output 0 was: A
Output 1 was: null
Output 2 was: C
Output 3 was: D
Output 4 was: null
Input: A|||D|E
Output 0 was: A
Output 1 was: null
Output 2 was: null
Output 3 was: D
Output 4 was: E
```

See Also

Many occurrences of `StringTokenizer` may be replaced with regular expressions (see Chapter 4) with considerably more flexibility. For example, to extract all the numbers from a `String`, you can use this code:

```
Matcher toke = Pattern.compile("\\d+").matcher(inputString);
while (toke.find( )) {
        String courseString = toke.group(0);
        int courseNumber = Integer.parseInt(courseString);
        ...
```

This allows user input to be more flexible than you could easily handle with a `String-Tokenizer`. Assuming that the numbers represent course numbers at some educational institution, the inputs "471,472,570" or "Courses 471 and 472, 570" or just "471 472 570" should all give the same results.

3.3. Putting Strings Together with StringBuilder

Problem

You need to put some `String` pieces (back) together.

Solution

Use string concatenation: the + operator. The compiler implicitly constructs a `String-Builder` for you and uses its `append( )` methods (unless all the string parts are known at compile time). Better yet, construct and use it yourself.

Discussion

An object of one of the `StringBuilder` classes basically represents a collection of characters. It is similar to a `String` object, but, as mentioned, `Strings` are immutable. `StringBuilders` are mutable and designed for, well, building `Strings`. You typically construct a `StringBuilder`, invoke the methods needed to get the character sequence just the way you want it, and then call `toString( )` to generate a `String` representing the same character sequence for use in most of the Java API, which deals in `Strings`.

`StringBuffer` is historical—it's been around since the beginning of time. Some of its methods are synchronized (see Recipe 22.5), which involves unneeded overhead in a single-threaded context. In Java 5, this class was "split" into `StringBuffer` (which is synchronized) and `StringBuilder` (which is not synchronized); thus, it is faster and preferable for single-threaded use. Another new class, `AbstractStringBuilder`, is the parent of both. In the following discussion, I'll use "the `StringBuilder` classes" to refer to all three because they mostly have the same methods.

The book's example code provides a `StringBuilderDemo` and a `StringBufferDemo`. Except for the fact that `StringBuilder` is not threadsafe, these API classes are identical and can be used interchangeably, so my two demo programs are almost identical except that each one uses the appropriate builder class.

The `StringBuilder` classes have a variety of methods for inserting, replacing, and otherwise modifying a given `StringBuilder`. Conveniently, the `append()` methods return a reference to the `StringBuilder` itself, so statements like `.append(…).append(…)` are fairly common. You might even see this third way in a `toString()` method. Example 3-2 shows three ways of concatenating strings.

Example 3-2. StringBuilderDemo.java

```java
public class StringBuilderDemo {

    public static void main(String[] argv) {

        String s1 = "Hello" + ", " + "World";
        System.out.println(s1);

        // Build a StringBuilder, and append some things to it.
        StringBuilder sb2 = new StringBuilder();
        sb2.append("Hello");
        sb2.append(',');
        sb2.append(' ');
        sb2.append("World");

        // Get the StringBuilder's value as a String, and print it.
        String s2 = sb2.toString();
        System.out.println(s2);

        // Now do the above all over again, but in a more
        // concise (and typical "real-world" Java) fashion.

        System.out.println(
          new StringBuilder()
            .append("Hello")
            .append(',')
            .append(' ')
            .append("World"));
    }
}
```

In fact, all the methods that modify more than one character of a `StringBuilder`'s contents (i.e., `append()`, `delete()`, `deleteCharAt()`, `insert()`, `replace()`, and `reverse()`) return a reference to the builder object to facilitate this "fluent API" style of coding.

As another example of using a `StringBuilder`, consider the need to convert a list of items into a comma-separated list, while avoiding getting an extra comma after the last element of the list. Code for this is shown in Example 3-3.

Example 3-3. StringBuilderCommaList.java

```
// Method using regexp split
StringBuilder sb1 = new StringBuilder();
for (String word : SAMPLE_STRING.split(" ")) {
    if (sb1.length() > 0) {
        sb1.append(", ");
    }
    sb1.append(word);
}
System.out.println(sb1);

// Method using a StringTokenizer
StringTokenizer st = new StringTokenizer(SAMPLE_STRING);
StringBuilder sb2 = new StringBuilder();
while (st.hasMoreElements()) {
    sb2.append(st.nextToken());
    if (st.hasMoreElements()) {
        sb2.append(", ");
    }
}
System.out.println(sb2);
```

The first method uses the `StringBuilder.length()` method, so it will only work correctly when you are starting with an empty `StringBuilder`. The second method relies on calling the informational method `hasMoreElements()` in the `Enumeration` (or `hasNext()` in an `Iterator`, as discussed in Recipe 7.9) more than once on each element. An alternative method, particularly when you aren't starting with an empty builder, would be to use a `boolean` flag variable to track whether you're at the beginning of the list.

3.4. Processing a String One Character at a Time

Problem

You want to process the contents of a string, one character at a time.

Solution

Use a `for` loop and the `String`'s `charAt()` method. Or a "for each" loop and the `String`'s `toCharArray` method.

Discussion

A string's `charAt()` method retrieves a given character by index number (starting at zero) from within the `String` object. To process all the characters in a `String`, one after another, use a `for` loop ranging from zero to `String.length()-1`. Here we process all the characters in a `String`:

strings/StrCharAt.java

```
public class StrCharAt {
    public static void main(String[] av) {
        String a = "A quick bronze fox lept a lazy bovine";
        for (int i=0; i < a.length(); i++) // Don't use foreach
            System.out.println("Char " + i + " is " + a.charAt(i));
    }
}
```

Given that the "for each" loop has been in the language for ages, you might be excused for expecting to be able to write something like `for (char ch : myString) {…}`. Unfortunately, this does not work. But you can use `myString.toCharArray()` as in the following:

```
public class ForEachChar {
    public static void main(String[] args) {
        String s = "Hello world";
        // for (char ch : s) {...} Does not work, in Java 7
        for (char ch : s.toCharArray()) {
            System.out.println(ch);
        }
    }
}
```

A "checksum" is a numeric quantity representing and confirming the contents of a file. If you transmit the checksum of a file separately from the contents, a recipient can checksum the file—assuming the algorithm is known—and verify that the file was received intact. Example 3-4 shows the simplest possible checksum, computed just by adding the numeric values of each character. Note that on files, it does not include the values of the newline characters; in order to fix this, retrieve `System.getProperty("line.separator")`; and add its character value(s) into the sum at the end of each line. Or give up on line mode and read the file a character at a time.

Example 3-4. CheckSum.java

```
/** CheckSum one text file, given an open BufferedReader.
 * Checksumm does not include line endings, so will give the
 * same value for given text on any platform. Do not use
 * on binary files!
 */
public static int process(BufferedReader is) {
    int sum = 0;
```

```
        try {
            String inputLine;

            while ((inputLine = is.readLine()) != null) {
                int i;
                for (i=0; i<inputLine.length(); i++) {
                    sum += inputLine.charAt(i);
                }
            }
        } catch (IOException e) {
            throw new RuntimeException("IOException: " + e);
        }
        return sum;
    }
```

3.5. Aligning Strings

Problem

You want to align strings to the left, right, or center.

Solution

Do the math yourself, and use `substring` (see Recipe 3.1) and a `StringBuilder` (see Recipe 3.3). Or, use my `StringAlign` class, which is based on the `java.text.Format` class. For left or right alignment, use `String.format()`.

Discussion

Centering and aligning text comes up fairly often. Suppose you want to print a simple report with centered page numbers. There doesn't seem to be anything in the standard API that will do the job fully for you. But I have written a class called `StringAlign` that will. Here's how you might use it:

```
public class StringAlignSimple {

    public static void main(String[] args) {
        // Construct a "formatter" to center strings.
        StringAlign formatter = new StringAlign(70, StringAlign.Justify.CENTER);
        // Try it out, for page "i"
        System.out.println(formatter.format("- i -"));
        // Try it out, for page 4. Since this formatter is
        // optimized for Strings, not specifically for page numbers,
        // we have to convert the number to a String
        System.out.println(formatter.format(Integer.toString(4)));
    }
}
```

If you compile and run this class, it prints the two demonstration line numbers centered, as shown:

```
> javac -d . StringAlignSimple.java
> java strings.StringAlignSimple
                            - i -
                             4
>
```

Example 3-5 is the code for the StringAlign class. Note that this class extends the class Format in the package java.text. There is a series of Format classes that all have at least one method called format(). It is thus in a family with numerous other formatters, such as DateFormat, NumberFormat, and others, that we'll take a look at in upcoming chapters.

Example 3-5. StringAlign.java

```java
public class StringAlign extends Format {

    private static final long serialVersionUID = 1L;

    public enum Justify {
        /* Constant for left justification. */
        LEFT,
        /* Constant for centering. */
        CENTER,
        /** Constant for right-justified Strings. */
        RIGHT,
    }

    /** Current justification */
    private Justify just;
    /** Current max length */
    private int maxChars;

    /** Construct a StringAlign formatter; length and alignment are
     * passed to the Constructor instead of each format() call as the
     * expected common use is in repetitive formatting e.g., page numbers.
     * @param maxChars - the maximum length of the output
     * @param just - one of the enum values LEFT, CENTER or RIGHT
     */
    public StringAlign(int maxChars, Justify just) {
        switch(just) {
        case LEFT:
        case CENTER:
        case RIGHT:
            this.just = just;
            break;
        default:
            throw new IllegalArgumentException("invalid justification arg.");
        }
        if (maxChars < 0) {
            throw new IllegalArgumentException("maxChars must be positive.");
```

```java
        }
        this.maxChars = maxChars;
    }

    /** Format a String.
     * @param input - the string to be aligned.
     * @parm where - the StringBuffer to append it to.
     * @param ignore - a FieldPosition (may be null, not used but
     * specified by the general contract of Format).
     */
    public StringBuffer format(
        Object input, StringBuffer where, FieldPosition ignore)  {

        String s = input.toString();
        String wanted = s.substring(0, Math.min(s.length(), maxChars));

        // Get the spaces in the right place.
        switch (just) {
            case RIGHT:
                pad(where, maxChars - wanted.length());
                where.append(wanted);
                break;
            case CENTER:
                int toAdd = maxChars - wanted.length();
                pad(where, toAdd/2);
                where.append(wanted);
                pad(where, toAdd - toAdd/2);
                break;
            case LEFT:
                where.append(wanted);
                pad(where, maxChars - wanted.length());
                break;
        }
        return where;
    }

    protected final void pad(StringBuffer to, int howMany) {
        for (int i=0; i<howMany; i++)
            to.append(' ');
    }

    /** Convenience Routine */
    String format(String s) {
        return format(s, new StringBuffer(), null).toString();
    }

    /** ParseObject is required, but not useful here. */
    public Object parseObject (String source, ParsePosition pos)  {
        return source;
    }
}
```

See Also

The alignment of numeric columns is considered in Chapter 5.

3.6. Converting Between Unicode Characters and Strings

Problem

You want to convert between Unicode characters and `Strings`.

Solution

Unicode is an international standard that aims to represent all known characters used by people in their various languages. Though the original ASCII character set is a subset, Unicode is huge. At the time Java was created, Unicode was a 16-bit character set, so it seemed natural to make Java `char` values be 16 bits in width, and for years a `char` could hold any Unicode character. However, over time, Unicode has grown, to the point that it now includes over a million "code points" or characters, more than the 65,525 that could be represented in 16 bits.[3] Not all possible 16-bit values were defined as characters in UCS-2, the 16-bit version of Unicode originally used in Java. A few were reserved as "escape characters," which allows for multicharacter-length mappings to less common characters. Fortunately, there is a go-between standard, called UTF-16 (16-bit Unicode Transformation Format). As the `String` class documentation puts it:

> A String represents a string in the UTF-16 format in which supplementary characters are represented by surrogate pairs (see the section Unicode Character Representations in the Character class for more information). Index values refer to char code units, so a supplementary character uses two positions in a String.
>
> The String class provides methods for dealing with Unicode code points (i.e., characters), in addition to those for dealing with Unicode code units (i.e., char values).

The `charAt()` method of `String` returns the `char` value for the character at the specified offset. The `StringBuilder append()` method has a form that accepts a `char`. Because `char` is an integer type, you can even do arithmetic on `chars`, though this is not needed as frequently as in, say, C. Nor is it often recommended, because the `Character` class provides the methods for which these operations were normally used in languages such as C. Here is a program that uses arithmetic on `chars` to control a loop, and also appends the characters into a `StringBuilder` (see Recipe 3.3):

```
// UnicodeChars.java
StringBuffer b = new StringBuffer();
```

---

3. Indeed, there are so many characters in Unicode that a fad has emerged of displaying your name upside down using characters that approximate upside-down versions of the Latin alphabet. Do a web search for "upside down unicode."

```
for (char c = 'a'; c<'d'; c++) {
    b.append(c);
}
b.append('\u00a5');     // Japanese Yen symbol
b.append('\u01FC');     // Roman AE with acute accent
b.append('\u0391');     // GREEK Capital Alpha
b.append('\u03A9');     // GREEK Capital Omega

for (int i=0; i<b.length(); i++) {
    System.out.printf(
        "Character #%d (%04x) is %c%n",
        i, (int)b.charAt(i), b.charAt(i));
}
System.out.println("Accumulated characters are " + b);
```

When you run it, the expected results are printed for the ASCII characters. On my Unix system, the default fonts don't include all the additional characters, so they are either omitted or mapped to irregular characters (Recipe 12.3 shows how to draw text in other fonts):

```
C:\javasrc\strings>java strings.UnicodeChars
Character #0 is a
Character #1 is b
Character #2 is c
Character #3 is %
Character #4 is |
Character #5 is
Character #6 is )
Accumulated characters are abc%|)
```

The Windows system used to try this doesn't have most of those characters either, but at least it prints the ones it knows are lacking as question marks (Windows system fonts are more homogenous than those of the various Unix systems, so it is easier to know what won't work). On the other hand, it tries to print the Yen sign as a Spanish capital Enye (N with a ~ over it). Amusingly, if I capture the console log under Windows into a file and display it under Unix, the Yen symbol now appears:

```
Character #0 is a
Character #1 is b
Character #2 is c
Character #3 is ¥
Character #4 is ?
Character #5 is ?
Character #6 is ?
Accumulated characters are abc¥___
```

where the "_" characters are unprintable characters, which may appear as a question mark ("?").

On a Mac OS X using the standard Terminal application and default fonts, it looks a bit better:

```
$ java -cp build strings.UnicodeChars
Character #0 is a
Character #1 is b
Character #2 is c
Character #3 is ¥
Character #4 is ǽ
Character #5 is A
Character #6 is Ω
Accumulated characters are abc¥ǽAΩ
```

See Also

The `Unicode` program in this book's online source displays any 256-character section of the Unicode character set. You can download documentation listing every character in the Unicode character set from the Unicode Consortium (*http://www.unicode.org*).

3.7. Reversing a String by Word or by Character

Problem

You wish to reverse a string, a character, or a word at a time.

Solution

You can reverse a string by character easily, using a `StringBuilder`. There are several ways to reverse a string a word at a time. One natural way is to use a `StringTokenizer` and a stack. `Stack` is a class (defined in `java.util`; see Recipe 7.18) that implements an easy-to-use last-in, first-out (LIFO) stack of objects.

Discussion

To reverse the characters in a string, use the `StringBuilder reverse()` method:

StringRevChar.java

```
String sh = "FCGDAEB";
System.out.println(sh + " -> " + new StringBuilder(sh).reverse( ));
```

The letters in this example list the order of the sharps in the key signatures of Western music; in reverse, it lists the order of flats. Alternatively, of course, you could reverse the characters yourself, using character-at-a-time mode (see Recipe 3.4).

A popular mnemonic, or memory aid, for the order of sharps and flats consists of one word for each sharp instead of just one letter, so we need to reverse this one word at a time. Example 3-6 adds each one to a `Stack` (see Recipe 7.18), then processes the whole lot in LIFO order, which reverses the order.

Example 3-6. StringReverse.java

```
String s = "Father Charles Goes Down And Ends Battle";

// Put it in the stack frontwards
Stack<String> myStack = new Stack<>();
StringTokenizer st = new StringTokenizer(s);
while (st.hasMoreTokens()) {
    myStack.push(st.nextToken());
}

// Print the stack backwards
System.out.print('"' + s + '"' + " backwards by word is:\n\t\"");
while (!myStack.empty()) {
    System.out.print(myStack.pop());
    System.out.print(' ');
}
System.out.println('"');
```

3.8. Expanding and Compressing Tabs

Problem

You need to convert space characters to tab characters in a file, or vice versa. You might want to replace spaces with tabs to save space on disk, or go the other way to deal with a device or program that can't handle tabs.

Solution

Use my Tabs class or its subclass EnTab.

Discussion

Example 3-7 is a listing of EnTab, complete with a sample main program. The program works a line at a time. For each character on the line, if the character is a space, we see if we can coalesce it with previous spaces to output a single tab character. This program depends on the Tabs class, which we'll come to shortly. The Tabs class is used to decide which column positions represent tab stops and which do not. The code also has several Debug printouts; these are controlled by an environment setting (see the online code in the com.darwinsys.util.Debug class).

Example 3-7. Entab.java

```
public class EnTab {
    /** The Tabs (tab logic handler) */
    protected Tabs tabs;

    /**
```

```
     * Delegate tab spacing information to tabs.
     */
    public int getTabSpacing() {
        return tabs.getTabSpacing();
    }

    /**
     * Main program: just create an EnTab object, and pass the standard input
     * or the named file(s) through it.
     */
    public static void main(String[] argv) throws IOException {
        EnTab et = new EnTab(8);
        if (argv.length == 0) // do standard input
            et.entab(
                new BufferedReader(new InputStreamReader(System.in)),
                System.out);
        else
            for (String fileName : argv) { // do each file
                et.entab(
                    new BufferedReader(new FileReader(fileName)),
                    System.out);
            }
    }

    /**
     * Constructor: just save the tab values.
     *
     * @param n
     *              The number of spaces each tab is to replace.
     */
    public EnTab(int n) {
        tabs = new Tabs(n);
    }

    public EnTab() {
        tabs = new Tabs();
    }

    /**
     * entab: process one file, replacing blanks with tabs.
     *
     * @param is A BufferedReader opened to the file to be read.
     * @param out a PrintWriter to send the output to.
     */
    public void entab(BufferedReader is, PrintWriter out) throws IOException {
        String line;

        // main loop: process entire file one line at a time.
        while ((line = is.readLine()) != null) {
            out.println(entabLine(line));
        }
    }
```

```java
/**
 * entab: process one file, replacing blanks with tabs.
 *
 * @param is A BufferedReader opened to the file to be read.
 * @param out A PrintStream to write the output to.
 */
public void entab(BufferedReader is, PrintStream out) throws IOException {
    entab(is, new PrintWriter(out));
}

/**
 * entabLine: process one line, replacing blanks with tabs.
 *
 * @param line -
 *              the string to be processed
 */
public String entabLine(String line) {
    int N = line.length(), outCol = 0;
    StringBuffer sb = new StringBuffer();
    char ch;
    int consumedSpaces = 0;

    for (int inCol = 0; inCol < N; inCol++) {
        ch = line.charAt(inCol);
        // If we get a space, consume it, don't output it.
        // If this takes us to a tab stop, output a tab character.
        if (ch == ' ') {
            Debug.println("space", "Got space at " + inCol);
            if (!tabs.isTabStop(inCol)) {
                consumedSpaces++;
            } else {
                Debug.println("tab", "Got a Tab Stop " + inCol);
                sb.append('\t');
                outCol += consumedSpaces;
                consumedSpaces = 0;
            }
            continue;
        }

        // We're at a non-space; if we're just past a tab stop, we need
        // to put the "leftover" spaces back out, since we consumed
        // them above.
        while (inCol-1 > outCol) {
            Debug.println("pad", "Padding space at " + inCol);
            sb.append(' ');
            outCol++;
        }

        // Now we have a plain character to output.
        sb.append(ch);
        outCol++;
```

```
    }
    // If line ended with trailing (or only!) spaces, preserve them.
    for (int i = 0; i < consumedSpaces; i++) {
        Debug.println("trail", "Padding space at end # " + i);
        sb.append(' ');
    }
    return sb.toString();
    }
}
```

This code was patterned after a program in Kernighan and Plauger's classic work, *Software Tools*. While their version was in a language called RatFor (Rational Fortran), my version has since been through several translations. Their version actually worked one character at a time, and for a long time I tried to preserve this overall structure. Eventually, I rewrote it to be a line-at-a-time program.

The program that goes in the opposite direction—putting tabs in rather than taking them out—is the DeTab class shown in Example 3-8; only the core methods are shown.

Example 3-8. DeTab.java

```
public class DeTab {
    Tabs ts;

    public static void main(String[] argv) throws IOException {
        DeTab dt = new DeTab(8);
        dt.detab(new BufferedReader(new InputStreamReader(System.in)),
                new PrintWriter(System.out));
    }

    public DeTab(int n) {
        ts = new Tabs(n);
    }
    public DeTab() {
        ts = new Tabs();
    }

    /** detab one file (replace tabs with spaces)
     * @param is - the file to be processed
     * @param out - the updated file
     */
    public void detab(BufferedReader is, PrintWriter out) throws IOException {
        String line;
        while ((line = is.readLine()) != null) {
            out.println(detabLine(line));
        }
    }

    /** detab one line (replace tabs with spaces)
     * @param line - the line to be processed
     * @return the updated line
     */
```

```java
public String detabLine(String line) {
    char c;
    int col;
    StringBuffer sb = new StringBuffer();
    col = 0;
    for (int i = 0; i < line.length(); i++) {
        // Either ordinary character or tab.
        if ((c = line.charAt(i)) != '\t') {
            sb.append(c); // Ordinary
            ++col;
            continue;
        }
        do { // Tab, expand it, must put >=1 space
            sb.append(' ');
        } while (!ts.isTabStop(++col));
    }
    return sb.toString();
}
}
```

The Tabs class provides two methods: settabpos() and istabstop(). Example 3-9 is the source for the Tabs class.

Example 3-9. Tabs.java

```java
public class Tabs {
    /** tabs every so often */
    public final static int DEFTABSPACE =    8;
    /** the current tab stop setting. */
    protected int tabSpace = DEFTABSPACE;
    /** The longest line that we initially set tabs for. */
    public final static int MAXLINE  = 255;

    /** Construct a Tabs object with a given tab stop settings */
    public Tabs(int n) {
        if (n <= 0) {
            n = 1;
        }
        tabSpace = n;
    }

    /** Construct a Tabs object with a default tab stop settings */
    public Tabs() {
        this(DEFTABSPACE);
    }

    /**
     * @return Returns the tabSpace.
     */
    public int getTabSpacing() {
        return tabSpace;
    }
```

```
/** isTabStop - returns true if given column is a tab stop.
 * @param col - the current column number
 */
public boolean isTabStop(int col) {
    if (col <= 0)
        return false;
    return (col+1) % tabSpace == 0;
}
}
```

3.9. Controlling Case

Problem

You need to convert strings to uppercase or lowercase, or to compare strings without regard for case.

Solution

The String class has a number of methods for dealing with documents in a particular case. toUpperCase() and toLowerCase() each return a new string that is a copy of the current string, but converted as the name implies. Each can be called either with no arguments or with a Locale argument specifying the conversion rules; this is necessary because of internationalization. Java provides significantly more internationalization and localization features than ordinary languages, a feature that is covered in Chapter 15. Whereas the equals() method tells you if another string is exactly the same, equalsIgnoreCase() tells you if all characters are the same regardless of case. Here, you can't specify an alternative locale; the system's default locale is used:

```
String name = "Java Cookbook";
System.out.println("Normal:\t" + name);
System.out.println("Upper:\t" + name.toUpperCase());
System.out.println("Lower:\t" + name.toLowerCase());
String javaName = "java cookBook"; // If it were Java identifiers :-)
if (!name.equals(javaName))
    System.err.println("equals() correctly reports false");
else
    System.err.println("equals() incorrectly reports true");
if (name.equalsIgnoreCase(javaName))
    System.err.println("equalsIgnoreCase() correctly reports true");
else
    System.err.println("equalsIgnoreCase() incorrectly reports false");
```

If you run this, it prints the first name changed to uppercase and lowercase, then it reports that both methods work as expected:

```
C:\javasrc\strings>java strings.Case
Normal: Java Cookbook
```

```
Upper:  JAVA COOKBOOK
Lower:  java cookbook
equals( ) correctly reports false
equalsIgnoreCase( ) correctly reports true
```

See Also

Regular expressions make it simpler to ignore case in string searching (see Chapter 4).

3.10. Indenting Text Documents

Problem

You need to indent (or "undent" or "dedent") a text document.

Solution

To indent, either generate a fixed-length string and prepend it to each output line, or use a for loop and print the right number of spaces:

```
while ((inputLine = is.readLine()) != null) {
    for (int i=0; i<nSpaces; i++) System.out.print(' ');
    System.out.println(inputLine);
}
```

A more efficient approach to generating the spaces might be to construct a long string of spaces and use substring( ) to get the number of spaces you need.

To undent, use substring to generate a string that does not include the leading spaces. Be careful of inputs that are shorter than the amount you are removing! By popular demand, I'll give you this one, too. First, though, here's a demonstration of an Undent object created with an undent value of 5, meaning remove up to five spaces (but don't lose other characters in the first five positions):

```
$ java strings.Undent
Hello World
Hello World
 Hello
Hello
     Hello
Hello
      Hello
 Hello

^C
$
```

I test it by entering the usual test string "Hello World," which prints fine. Then "Hello" with one space, and the space is deleted. With five spaces, exactly the five spaces go.

With six or more spaces, only five spaces go. A blank line comes out as a blank line (i.e., without throwing an Exception or otherwise going berserk). I think it works!

```
while ((inputLine = is.readLine()) != null) {
    int toRemove = 0;
    for (int i=0; i<nSpaces && i < inputLine.length() &&
    Character.isWhitespace(inputLine.charAt(i)); i++)
        ++toRemove;
    System.out.println(inputLine.substring(toRemove));
}
```

3.11. Entering Nonprintable Characters

Problem

You need to put nonprintable characters into strings.

Solution

Use the backslash character and one of the Java string escapes.

Discussion

The Java string escapes are listed in Table 3-1.

Table 3-1. String escapes

To get:	Use:	Notes
Tab	\t	
Linefeed (Unix newline)	\n	The call System.getProperty("line.separator") will give you the platform's line end.
Carriage return	\r	
Form feed	\f	
Backspace	\b	
Single quote	\'	
Double quote	\"	
Unicode character	\u *NNNN*	Four hexadecimal digits (no \x as in C/C++). See *http://www.unicode.org* for codes.
Octal(!) character	\ *NNN*	Who uses octal (base 8) these days?
Backslash	\\	

Here is a code example that shows most of these in action:

```
public class StringEscapes {
    public static void main(String[] argv) {
        System.out.println("Java Strings in action:");
        // System.out.println("An alarm or alert: \a");    // not supported
```

```
        System.out.println("An alarm entered in Octal: \007");
        System.out.println("A tab key: \t(what comes after)");
        System.out.println("A newline: \n(what comes after)");
        System.out.println("A UniCode character: \u0207");
        System.out.println("A backslash character: \\");
    }
}
```

If you have a lot of non-ASCII characters to enter, you may wish to consider using Java's input methods, discussed briefly in the JDK online documentation.

3.12. Trimming Blanks from the End of a String

Problem

You need to work on a string without regard for extra leading or trailing spaces a user may have typed.

Solution

Use the String class trim( ) method.

Discussion

Example 3-10 uses trim( ) to strip an arbitrary number of leading spaces and/or tabs from lines of Java source code in order to look for the characters //+ and //-. These strings are special Java comments I use to mark the parts of the programs in this book that I want to include in the printed copy.

Example 3-10. GetMark.java (trimming and comparing strings)

```
public class GetMark {
    /** the default starting mark. */
    public final String START_MARK = "//+";
    /** the default ending mark. */
    public final String END_MARK = "//-";
    /** Set this to TRUE for running in "exclude" mode (e.g., for
     * building exercises from solutions) and to FALSE for running
     * in "extract" mode (e.g., writing a book and omitting the
     * imports and "public class" stuff).
     */
    public final static boolean START = true;
    /** True if we are currently inside marks. */
    protected boolean printing = START;
    /** True if you want line numbers */
    protected final boolean number = false;

    /** Get Marked parts of one file, given an open LineNumberReader.
     * This is the main operation of this class, and can be used
```

```
    * inside other programs or from the main() wrapper.
    */
public void process(String fileName,
    LineNumberReader is,
    PrintStream out) {
    int nLines = 0;
    try {
        String inputLine;

        while ((inputLine = is.readLine()) != null) {
            if (inputLine.trim().equals(START_MARK)) {
                if (printing)
                    // These go to stderr, so you can redirect the output
                    System.err.println("ERROR: START INSIDE START, " +
                        fileName + ':' + is.getLineNumber());
                printing = true;
            } else if (inputLine.trim().equals(END_MARK)) {
                if (!printing)
                    System.err.println("ERROR: STOP WHILE STOPPED, " +
                        fileName + ':' + is.getLineNumber());
                printing = false;
            } else if (printing) {
                if (number) {
                    out.print(nLines);
                    out.print(": ");
                }
                out.println(inputLine);
                ++nLines;
            }
        }
        is.close();
        out.flush(); // Must not close - caller may still need it.
        if (nLines == 0)
            System.err.println("ERROR: No marks in " + fileName +
                "; no output generated!");
    } catch (IOException e) {
        System.out.println("IOException: " + e);
    }
}
```

3.13. Parsing Comma-Separated Data

Problem

You have a string or a file of lines containing comma-separated values (CSV) that you
need to read. Many Windows-based spreadsheets and some databases use CSV to export
data.

Solution

Use my CSV class or a regular expression (see Chapter 4).

Discussion

CSV is deceptive. It looks simple at first glance, but the values may be quoted or unquoted. If quoted, they may further contain escaped quotes. This far exceeds the capabilities of the StringTokenizer class (see Recipe 3.2). Either considerable Java coding or the use of regular expressions is required. I'll show both ways.

First, a Java program. Assume for now that we have a class called CSV that has a no-argument constructor and a method called parse() that takes a string representing one line of the input file. The parse() method returns a list of fields. For flexibility, the fields are returned as a List, which you can process in any way you like:

CSVSimple.java

```java
package com.darwinsys.csv;

import java.util.List;

/* Simple demo of CSV parser class. */
public class CSVSimple {
    public static void main(String[] args) {
        CSVImport parser = new CSVImport();
        List<String> list = parser.parse(
            "\"LU\",86.25,\"11/4/1998\",\"2:19PM\",+4.0625");
        for (String word : list) {
            System.out.println(word);
        }

        // Now try with a non-default separator
        parser = new CSVImport('|');
        list = parser.parse(
            "\"LU\"|86.25|\"11/4/1998\"|\"2:19PM\"|+4.0625");
        for (String word : list) {
            System.out.println(word);
        }
    }
}
```

After the quotes are escaped, the string being parsed is actually the following:

```
"LU",86.25,"11/4/1998","2:19PM",+4.0625
```

Running CSVSimple yields the following output:

```
> java csv.CSVSimple
LU
86.25
11/4/1998
```

```
2:19PM
+4.0625
>
```

But what about the CSV class itself? The code in Example 3-11 started as a translation of a CSV program written in C++ by Brian W. Kernighan and Rob Pike that appeared in their book *The Practice of Programming* (Addison-Wesley). Their version commingled the input processing with the parsing; my CSV class does only the parsing because the input could be coming from any of a variety of sources. And it has been substantially rewritten over time. The main work is done in `parse()`, which delegates handling of individual fields to `advquoted()` in cases where the field begins with a quote; otherwise, to `advplain()`.

Example 3-11. CSV.java

```java
// package com.darwinsys.csv;

public class CSVImport implements CSVParser {

    public static final char DEFAULT_SEP = ',';

    /** Construct a CSV parser, with the default separator (`,'). */
    public CSVImport() {
        this(DEFAULT_SEP);
    }

    /** Construct a CSV parser with a given separator.
     * @param sep The single char for the separator (not a list of
     * separator characters)
     */
    public CSVImport(char sep) {
        fieldSep = sep;
    }

    /** The fields in the current String */
    protected List<String> list = new ArrayList<>();

    /** the separator char for this parser */
    protected char fieldSep;

    /** parse: break the input String into fields
     * @return java.util.Iterator containing each field
     * from the original as a String, in order.
     */
    public List<String> parse(String line) {
        StringBuffer sb = new StringBuffer();
        list.clear();             // recycle to initial state
        int i = 0;

        if (line.length() == 0) {
            list.add(line);
```

```
            return list;
        }

        do {
            sb.setLength(0);
            if (i < line.length() && line.charAt(i) == '"')
                i = advQuoted(line, sb, ++i);    // skip quote
            else
                i = advPlain(line, sb, i);
            list.add(sb.toString());
            Debug.println("csv", sb.toString());
            i++;
        } while (i < line.length());

        return list;
    }

    /** advQuoted: quoted field; return index of next separator */
    protected int advQuoted(String s, StringBuffer sb, int i)
    {
        int j;
        int len= s.length();
        for (j=i; j<len; j++) {
            if (s.charAt(j) == '"' && j+1 < len) {
                if (s.charAt(j+1) == '"') {
                    j++; // skip escape char
                } else if (s.charAt(j+1) == fieldSep) { //next delimeter
                    j++; // skip end quotes
                    break;
                }
            } else if (s.charAt(j) == '"' && j+1 == len) { // end quote @ line end
                break; //done
            }
            sb.append(s.charAt(j));    // regular character.
        }
        return j;
    }

    /** advPlain: unquoted field; return index of next separator */
    protected int advPlain(String s, StringBuffer sb, int i)
    {
        int j;

        j = s.indexOf(fieldSep, i); // look for separator
        Debug.println("csv", "i = " + i + ", j = " + j);
        if (j == -1) {                    // none found
            sb.append(s.substring(i));
            return s.length();
        } else {
            sb.append(s.substring(i, j));
            return j;
        }
    }
```

```
        }
}
```

In the online source directory, you'll find *CSVFile.java*, which reads a text file and runs it through `parse()`. You'll also find Kernighan and Pike's original C++ program.

We haven't discussed regular expressions yet (we will in Chapter 4). However, many readers are familiar with regexes in a general way, so the following example demonstrates the power of regexes, as well as providing code for you to reuse. Note that the following program replaces *all* the code in both *CSV.java* and *CSVFile.java* (the key to understanding regexes is that a little specification can match a lot of data):[4]

```
// package com.darwinsys.csv;
public class CSVRE implements CSVParser {
    /** The rather involved pattern used to match CSV's consists of three
     * alternations: the first matches a quoted field, the second unquoted,
     * the third a null field.
     */
    public static final String CSV_PATTERN =
        "\"([^\"]+?)\",?|([^,]+),?|,";

    private final static Pattern csvRE = Pattern.compile(CSV_PATTERN);

    public static void main(final String[] argv) throws IOException {
        System.out.println(CSV_PATTERN);
        new CSVRE().process(
            new BufferedReader(new InputStreamReader(System.in)));
    }

    /** Process one file. Delegates to parse() a line at a time */
    public void process(final BufferedReader input) throws IOException {
        String line;

        // For each line...
        while ((line = input.readLine()) != null) {
            System.out.println("line = `" + line + "'");
            final List<String> list = parse(line);
            System.out.println("Found " + list.size() + " items.");
            for (String str : list) {
                System.out.print(str + ",");
            }
            System.out.println();
        }
    }

    /** Parse one line.
     * @return List of Strings, minus their double quotes
```

---

4. With the caveat that it doesn't handle different delimiters; this could be added using `GetOpt` and constructing the pattern around the delimiter.

```
    */
    public List<String> parse(final String line) {
        final List<String> list = new ArrayList<>();
        final Matcher m = csvRE.matcher(line);
        // For each field
        while (m.find()) {
            String match = m.group();
            if (match == null) {
                break;
            }
            if (match.endsWith(",")) {    // trim trailing ,
                match = match.substring(0, match.length() - 1);
            }
            if (match.startsWith("\"")) { // must also end with \"
                if (!match.endsWith("\"")) {
                    throw new IllegalArgumentException(
                        "Quoted column missing end quote: " + line);
                }
                match = match.substring(1, match.length() - 1);
            }
            if (match.length() == 0) {
                match = "";
            }
            list.add(match);
        }
        return list;
    }
}
```

It is sometimes "downright scary" how much mundane code you can eliminate with a single, well-formulated regular expression.

3.14. Program: A Simple Text Formatter

This program is a very primitive text formatter, representative of what people used on most computing platforms before the rise of standalone graphics-based word processors, laser printers, and, eventually, desktop publishing and desktop office suites. It simply reads words from a file—previously created with a text editor—and outputs them until it reaches the right margin, when it calls `println()` to append a line ending. For example, here is an input file:

```
It's a nice
day, isn't it, Mr. Mxyzzptllxy?
I think we should
go for a walk.
```

Given the preceding as its input, the Fmt program prints the lines formatted neatly:

```
It's a nice day, isn't it, Mr. Mxyzzptllxy? I think we should go for a
walk.
```

As you can see, it fits the text we gave it to the margin and discards all the line breaks present in the original. Here's the code:

```java
public class Fmt {
    /** The maximum column width */
    public static final int COLWIDTH=72;
    /** The file that we read and format */
    final BufferedReader in;
    /** Where the output goes */
    PrintWriter out;

    /** If files present, format each, else format the standard input. */
    public static void main(String[] av) throws IOException {
        if (av.length == 0)
            new Fmt(System.in).format();
        else for (String name : av) {
            new Fmt(name).format();
        }
    }

    public Fmt(BufferedReader inFile, PrintWriter outFile) {
        this.in = inFile;
        this.out = outFile;
    }

    public Fmt(PrintWriter out) {
        this(new BufferedReader(new InputStreamReader(System.in)), out);
    }

    /** Construct a Formatter given an open Reader */
    public Fmt(BufferedReader file) throws IOException {
        this(file, new PrintWriter(System.out));
    }

    /** Construct a Formatter given a filename */
    public Fmt(String fname) throws IOException {
        this(new BufferedReader(new FileReader(fname)));
    }

    /** Construct a Formatter given an open Stream */
    public Fmt(InputStream file) throws IOException {
        this(new BufferedReader(new InputStreamReader(file)));
    }

    /** Format the File contained in a constructed Fmt object */
    public void format() throws IOException {
        String line;
        StringBuilder outBuf = new StringBuilder();
        while ((line = in.readLine()) != null) {
            if (line.length() == 0) {        // null line
                out.println(outBuf);      // end current line
                out.println();      // output blank line
```

```
                        outBuf.setLength(0);
                    } else {
                        // otherwise it's text, so format it.
                        StringTokenizer st = new StringTokenizer(line);
                        while (st.hasMoreTokens()) {
                            String word = st.nextToken();

                            // If this word would go past the margin,
                            // first dump out anything previous.
                            if (outBuf.length() + word.length() > COLWIDTH) {
                                out.println(outBuf);
                                outBuf.setLength(0);
                            }
                            outBuf.append(word).append(' ');
                        }
                    }
                }
                if (outBuf.length() > 0) {
                    out.println(outBuf);
                } else {
                    out.println();
                }
            }
        }
    }
```

A slightly fancier version of this program, Fmt2, is in the online source for this book. It uses "dot commands"—lines beginning with periods—to give limited control over the formatting. A family of "dot command" formatters includes Unix's *roff, nroff, troff,* and *groff,* which are in the same family with programs called *runoff* on Digital Equipment systems. The original for this is J. Saltzer's *runoff,* which first appeared on Multics and from there made its way into various OSes. To save trees, I did not include Fmt2 here; it subclasses Fmt and overrides the format() method to include additional functionality (the source code is in the full *javasrc* repository for the book).

3.15. Program: Soundex Name Comparisons

The difficulties in comparing (American-style) names inspired the U.S. Census Bureau to develop the Soundex algorithm in the early 1900s. Each of a given set of consonants maps to a particular number, the effect being to map similar-sounding names together, on the grounds that in those days many people were illiterate and could not spell their family names consistently. But it is still useful today—for example, in a company-wide telephone book application. The names Darwin and Derwin, for example, map to D650, and Darwent maps to D653, which puts it adjacent to D650. All of these are believed to be historical variants of the same name. Suppose we needed to sort lines containing these names together: if we could output the Soundex numbers at the beginning of each line, this would be easy. Here is a simple demonstration of the Soundex class:

```
public class SoundexSimple {

    /** main */
    public static void main(String[] args) {
        String[] names = {
            "Darwin, Ian",
            "Davidson, Greg",
            "Darwent, William",
            "Derwin, Daemon"
        };
        for (String name : names) {
            System.out.println(Soundex.soundex(name) + ' ' + name);
        }
    }
}
```

Let's run it:

```
> javac -d . SoundexSimple.java
> java strings.SoundexSimple | sort
D132 Davidson, Greg
D650 Darwin, Ian
D650 Derwin, Daemon
D653 Darwent, William
>
```

As you can see, the Darwin-variant names (including Daemon Derwin[5]) all sort together and are distinct from the Davidson (and Davis, Davies, etc.) names that normally appear between Darwin and Derwin when using a simple alphabetic sort. The Soundex algorithm has done its work.

Here is the Soundex class itself—it uses Strings and StringBuilders to convert names into Soundex codes:

```
public class Soundex {

    static boolean debug = false;

    /* Implements the mapping
     * from: AEHIOUWYBFPVCGJKQSXZDTLMNR
     * to:   000000000111112222222222334556
     */
    public static final char[] MAP = {
        //A  B   C   D   E   F   G   H   I   J   K   L   M
        '0','1','2','3','0','1','2','0','0','2','2','4','5',
        //N  O   P   W   R   S   T   U   V   W   X   Y   Z
        '5','0','1','2','6','2','3','0','1','0','2','0','2'
    };
};
```

---

5. In Unix terminology, a "daemon" is a server. The old English word has nothing to do with satanic "demons" but refers to a helper or assistant. Derwin Daemon was actually a character in Susannah Coleman's "Source Wars" online comic strip, which long ago was online at a now-departed site called *darby.daemonnews.org*.

```
/** Convert the given String to its Soundex code.
 * @return null If the given string can't be mapped to Soundex.
 */
public static String soundex(String s) {

    // Algorithm works on uppercase (mainframe era).
    String t = s.toUpperCase();

    StringBuffer res = new StringBuffer();
    char c, prev = '?', prevOutput = '?';

    // Main loop: find up to 4 chars that map.
    for (int i=0; i<t.length() && res.length() < 4 &&
        (c = t.charAt(i)) != ','; i++) {

        // Check to see if the given character is alphabetic.
        // Text is already converted to uppercase. Algorithm
        // only handles ASCII letters, do NOT use Character.isLetter()!
        // Also, skip double letters.
        if (c>='A' && c<='Z' && c != prev) {
            prev = c;

            // First char is installed unchanged, for sorting.
            if (i==0) {
                res.append(c);
            } else {
                char m = MAP[c-'A'];
                if (debug) {
                    System.out.println(c + " --> " + m);
                }
                if (m != '0' && m != prevOutput) {
                    res.append(m);
                    prevOutput = m;
                }
            }
        }
    }
    if (res.length() == 0)
        return null;
    for (int i=res.length(); i<4; i++)
        res.append('0');
    return res.toString();
}
```

There are apparently some nuances of the full Soundex algorithm that are not implemented by this application. A more complete test using JUnit (see Recipe 1.13) is also online as *SoundexTest.java*, in the *src/tests/java/strings* directory. The dedicated reader may use this to provoke failures of such nuances, and send a pull request with updated versions of the test and the code.

See Also

The Levenshtein string edit distance algorithm can be used for doing approximate string comparisons in a different fashion. You can find this in Apache Commons StringUtils (*http://bit.ly/1poDJuf*). I show a non-Java (Perl) implementation of this alrorithm in Recipe 24.5.

## CHAPTER 4

Pattern Matching with Regular Expressions

4.0. Introduction

Suppose you have been on the Internet for a few years and have been very faithful about saving all your correspondence, just in case you (or your lawyers, or the prosecution) need a copy. The result is that you have a 5 GB disk partition dedicated to saved mail. And let's further suppose that you remember that somewhere in there is an email message from someone named Angie or Anjie. Or was it Angy? But you don't remember what you called it or where you stored it. Obviously, you have to look for it.

But while some of you go and try to open up all 15,000,000 documents in a word processor, I'll just find it with one simple command. Any system that provides regular expression support allows me to search for the pattern in several ways. The simplest to understand is:

```
Angie|Anjie|Angy
```

which you can probably guess means just to search for any of the variations. A more concise form ("more thinking, less typing") is:

```
An[^ dn]
```

The syntax will become clear as we go through this chapter. Briefly, the "A" and the "n" match themselves, in effect finding words that begin with "An", while the cryptic [^ dn] requires the "An" to be followed by a character other than (^ means *not* in this context) a space (to eliminate the very common English word "an" at the start of a sentence) or "d" (to eliminate the common word "and") or "n" (to eliminate Anne, Announcing, etc.). Has your word processor gotten past its splash screen yet? Well, it doesn't matter, because I've already found the missing file. To find the answer, I just typed the command:

```
grep 'An[^ dn]' *
```

Regular expressions, or regexes for short, provide a concise and precise specification of patterns to be matched in text.

As another example of the power of regular expressions, consider the problem of bulk-updating hundreds of files. When I started with Java, the syntax for declaring array references was `baseType arrayVariableName[]`. For example, a method with an array argument, such as every program's main method, was commonly written as:

```
public static void main(String args[]) {
```

But as time went by, it became clear to the stewards of the Java language that it would be better to write it as `baseType[] arrayVariableName`. For example:

```
public static void main(String[] args) {
```

This is better Java style because it associates the "array-ness" of the type with the type itself, rather than with the local argument name, and the compiler now accepts both modes. I wanted to change all occurrences of `main` written the old way to the new way. I used the pattern *main(String [a-z]* with the *grep* utility described earlier to find the names of all the files containing old-style main declarations (i.e., `main(String` followed by a space and a name character rather than an open square bracket). I then used another regex-based Unix tool, the stream editor *sed*, in a little shell script to change all occurrences in those files from *main(String *([a-z][a-z]*)[]* to *main(String[] $1* (the syntax used here is discussed later in this chapter). Again, the regex-based approach was orders of magnitude faster than doing it interactively, even using a reasonably powerful editor such as `vi` or `emacs`, let alone trying to use a graphical word processor.

Historically, the syntax of regexes has changed as they get incorporated into more tools and more languages, so the exact syntax in the previous examples is not exactly what you'd use in Java, but it does convey the conciseness and power of the regex mechanism.
[1]

As a third example, consider parsing an Apache web server logfile, where some fields are delimited with quotes, others with square brackets, and others with spaces. Writing *ad-hoc* code to parse this is messy in any language, but a well-crafted regex can break the line into all its constituent fields in one operation (this example is developed in Recipe 4.10).

These same time gains can be had by Java developers. Regular expression support has been in the standard Java runtime for ages and is well integrated (e.g., there are regex

---

1. Non-Unix fans fear not, for you can use tools like `grep` on Windows systems using one of several packages. One is an open source package alternately called CygWin (after Cygnus Software) or GnuWin32 (*http://sources.redhat.com/cygwin*). Another is Microsoft's `findstr` command for Windows. Or you can use my Grep program in Recipe 4.6 if you don't have grep on your system. Incidentally, the name *grep* comes from an ancient Unix line editor command g/RE/p, the command to find the regex globally in all lines in the edit buffer and print the lines that match—just what the `grep` program does to lines in files.

methods in the standard class `java.lang.String` and in the "new I/O" package). There are a few other regex packages for Java, and you may occasionally encounter code using them, but pretty well all code from this century can be expected to use the built-in package. The syntax of Java regexes themselves is discussed in Recipe 4.1, and the syntax of the Java API for using regexes is described in Recipe 4.2. The remaining recipes show some applications of regex technology in Java.

See Also

Mastering Regular Expressions by Jeffrey Friedl (O'Reilly) is the definitive guide to all the details of regular expressions. Most introductory books on Unix and Perl include some discussion of regexes; *Unix Power Tools* devotes a chapter to them.

4.1. Regular Expression Syntax

Problem

You need to learn the syntax of Java regular expressions.

Solution

Consult Table 4-1 for a list of the regular expression characters.

Discussion

These pattern characters let you specify regexes of considerable power. In building patterns, you can use any combination of ordinary text and the *metacharacters*, or special characters, in Table 4-1. These can all be used in any combination that makes sense. For example, `a+` means any number of occurrences of the letter `a`, from one up to a million or a gazillion. The pattern `Mrs?\.` matches `Mr.` or `Mrs.` And `.*` means "any character, any number of times," and is similar in meaning to most command-line interpreters' meaning of the `\*` alone. The pattern `\d+` means any number of numeric digits. `\d{2,3}` means a two- or three-digit number.

Table 4-1. Regular expression metacharacter syntax

Subexpression	Matches	Notes
General		
\^	Start of line/string	
$	End of line/string	
\b	Word boundary	
\B	Not a word boundary	
\A	Beginning of entire string	

Subexpression	Matches	Notes
\z	End of entire string	
\Z	End of entire string (except allowable final line terminator)	See Recipe 4.9
.	Any one character (except line terminator)	
[...]	"Character class"; any one character from those listed	
[\^...]	Any one character not from those listed	See Recipe 4.2
Alternation and Grouping		
(...)	Grouping (capture groups)	See Recipe 4.3
|	Alternation	
(?:_re_)	Noncapturing parenthesis	
\G	End of the previous match	
\ *n*	Back-reference to capture group number "*n*"	
Normal (greedy) quantifiers		
{ *m,n* }	Quantifier for "from *m* to *n* repetitions"	See Recipe 4.4
{ *m* ,}	Quantifier for "*m* or more repetitions"	
{ *m* }	Quantifier for "exactly *m* repetitions"	See Recipe 4.10
{,*n* }	Quantifier for 0 up to *n* repetitions	
*	Quantifier for 0 or more repetitions	Short for {0,}
+	Quantifier for 1 or more repetitions	Short for {1,}; see Recipe 4.2
?	Quantifier for 0 or 1 repetitions (i.e., present exactly once, or not at all)	Short for {0,1}
Reluctant (non-greedy) quantifiers		
{ *m,n* }?	Reluctant quantifier for "from *m* to *n* repetitions"	
{ *m* ,}?	Reluctant quantifier for "*m* or more repetitions"	
{,*n* }?	Reluctant quantifier for 0 up to *n* repetitions	
*?	Reluctant quantifier: 0 or more	
+?	Reluctant quantifier: 1 or more	See Recipe 4.10
??	Reluctant quantifier: 0 or 1 times	
Possessive (very greedy) quantifiers		
{ *m,n* }+	Possessive quantifier for "from *m* to *n* repetitions"	
{ *m* ,}+	Possessive quantifier for "*m* or more repetitions"	
{,*n* }+	Possessive quantifier for 0 up to *n* repetitions	
*+	Possessive quantifier: 0 or more	
++	Possessive quantifier: 1 or more	

Subexpression	Matches	Notes
?+	Possessive quantifier: 0 or 1 times	
Escapes and shorthands		
\	Escape (quote) character: turns most metacharacters off; turns subsequent alphabetic into metacharacters	
\Q	Escape (quote) all characters up to \E	
\E	Ends quoting begun with \Q	
\t	Tab character	
\r	Return (carriage return) character	
\n	Newline character	See Recipe 4.9
\f	Form feed	
\w	Character in a word	Use \w+ for a word; see Recipe 4.10
\W	A nonword character	
\d	Numeric digit	Use \d+ for an integer; see Recipe 4.2
\D	A nondigit character	
\s	Whitespace	Space, tab, etc., as determined by java.lang.Character.isWhitespace()
\S	A nonwhitespace character	See Recipe 4.10
Unicode blocks (representative samples)		
\p{InGreek}	A character in the Greek block	(Simple block)
\P{InGreek}	Any character not in the Greek block	
\p{Lu}	An uppercase letter	(Simple category)
\p{Sc}	A currency symbol	
POSIX-style character classes (defined only for US-ASCII)		
\p{Alnum}	Alphanumeric characters	[A-Za-z0-9]
\p{Alpha}	Alphabetic characters	[A-Za-z]
\p{ASCII}	Any ASCII character	[\x00-\x7F]
\p{Blank}	Space and tab characters	
\p{Space}	Space characters	[\t\n\x0B\f\r]
\p{Cntrl}	Control characters	[\x00-\x1F\x7F]
\p{Digit}	Numeric digit characters	[0-9]
\p{Graph}	Printable and visible characters (not spaces or control characters)	
\p{Print}	Printable characters	

Subexpression	Matches	Notes
\p{Punct}	Punctuation characters	One of ! "#$%&'()* +,-./:;<=>?@[]\^_`{|} \~
\p{Lower}	Lowercase characters	[a-z]
\p{Upper}	Uppercase characters	[A-Z]
\p{XDigit}	Hexadecimal digit characters	[0-9a-fA-F]

Regexes match anyplace possible in the string. Patterns followed by greedy quantifiers (the only type that existed in traditional Unix regexes) consume (match) as much as possible without compromising any subexpressions that follow; patterns followed by possessive quantifiers match as much as possible without regard to following subexpressions; patterns followed by reluctant quantifiers consume as few characters as possible to still get a match.

Also, unlike regex packages in some other languages, the Java regex package was designed to handle Unicode characters from the beginning. And the standard Java escape sequence \u *nnnn* is used to specify a Unicode character in the pattern. We use methods of java.lang.Character to determine Unicode character properties, such as whether a given character is a space. Again, note that the backslash must be doubled if this is in a Java string that is being compiled because the compiler would otherwise parse this as "backslash-u" followed by some numbers.

To help you learn how regexes work, I provide a little program called REDemo.[2] The code for REDemo is too long to include in the book; in the online directory *regex* of the *darwinsys-api* repo, you will find REDemo.java, which you can run to explore how regexes work.

In the uppermost text box (see Figure 4-1), type the regex pattern you want to test. Note that as you type each character, the regex is checked for syntax; if the syntax is OK, you see a checkmark beside it. You can then select Match, Find, or Find All. Match means that the entire string must match the regex, and Find means the regex must be found somewhere in the string (Find All counts the number of occurrences that are found). Below that, you type a string that the regex is to match against. Experiment to your heart's content. When you have the regex the way you want it, you can paste it into your Java program. You'll need to escape (backslash) any characters that are treated specially by both the Java compiler and the Java regex package, such as the backslash itself, double quotes, and others (see the following sidebar). Once you get a regex the way you want it, there is a "Copy" button (not shown in these screenshots) to export the regex to the clipboard, with or without backslash doubling depending on how you want to use it.

---

2. REDemo was inspired by (but does not use any code from) a similar program provided with the now-retired Apache Jakarta Regular Expressions package.

Remember This!

Remember that because a regex compiles strings that are also compiled by *javac*, you usually need two levels of escaping for any special characters, including backslash, double quotes, and so on. For example, the regex:

```
"You said it\."
```

has to be typed like this to be a valid compile-time Java language `String`:

```
"\"You said it\\.\""
```

I can't tell you how many times I've made the mistake of forgetting the extra backslash in \d+, \w+, and their kin!

In Figure 4-1, I typed qu into the REDemo program's Pattern box, which is a syntactically valid regex pattern: any ordinary characters stand as regexes for themselves, so this looks for the letter q followed by u. In the top version, I typed only a q into the string, which is not matched. In the second, I have typed quack and the q of a second quack. Because I have selected Find All, the count shows one match. As soon as I type the second u, the count is updated to two, as shown in the third version.

Regexes can do far more than just character matching. For example, the two-character regex ^T would match beginning of line (^) immediately followed by a capital T—that is, any line beginning with a capital T. It doesn't matter whether the line begins with *Tiny trumpets*, *Titanic tubas*, or *Triumphant twisted trombones*, as long as the capital T is present in the first position.

But here we're not very far ahead. Have we really invested all this effort in regex technology just to be able to do what we could already do with the `java.lang.String` method `startsWith()`? Hmmm, I can hear some of you getting a bit restless. Stay in your seats! What if you wanted to match not only a letter T in the first position, but also a vowel (a, e, i, o, or u) immediately after it, followed by any number of letters in a word, followed by an exclamation point? Surely you could do this in Java by checking `starts-With("T")` and `charAt(1) == 'a' || charAt(1) == 'e'`, and so on? Yes, but by the time you did that, you'd have written a lot of very highly specialized code that you couldn't use in any other application. With regular expressions, you can just give the pattern ^T[aeiou]\w*!. That is, ^ and T as before, followed by a character class listing the vowels, followed by any number of word characters (\w*), followed by the exclamation point.

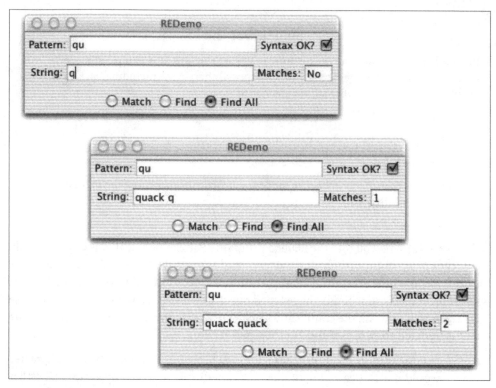

Figure 4-1. REDemo with simple examples

"But wait, there's more!" as my late, great boss Yuri Rubinsky used to say. What if you want to be able to change the pattern you're looking for *at runtime*? Remember all that Java code you just wrote to match T in column 1, plus a vowel, some word characters, and an exclamation point? Well, it's time to throw it out. Because this morning we need to match Q, followed by a letter other than u, followed by a number of digits, followed by a period. While some of you start writing a new function to do that, the rest of us will just saunter over to the RegEx Bar & Grille, order a ^Q[^u]\d+\.. from the bartender, and be on our way.

OK, the [^u] means *match any one character that is not the character u*. The \d+ means one or more numeric digits. The + is a quantifier meaning one or more occurrences of what it follows, and \d is any one numeric digit. So \d+ means a number with one, two, or more digits. Finally, the \.? Well, . by itself is a metacharacter. Most single meta-characters are switched off by preceding them with an escape character. Not the Esc key on your keyboard, of course. The regex "escape" character is the backslash. Preceding a metacharacter like . with this escape turns off its special meaning, so we look for a literal period rather than "any character." Preceding a few selected alphabetic characters (e.g., n, r, t, s, w) with escape turns them into metacharacters. Figure 4-2 shows the Q[^u]

\d\..+ regex in action. In the first frame, I have typed part of the regex as ^Q[^u and because there is an unclosed square bracket, the Syntax OK flag is turned off; when I complete the regex, it will be turned back on. In the second frame, I have finished typing the regex, and typed the data string as QA577 (which you should expect to match the ^Q[^u]\d+, but not the period since I haven't typed it). In the third frame, I've typed the period so the Matches flag is set to Yes.

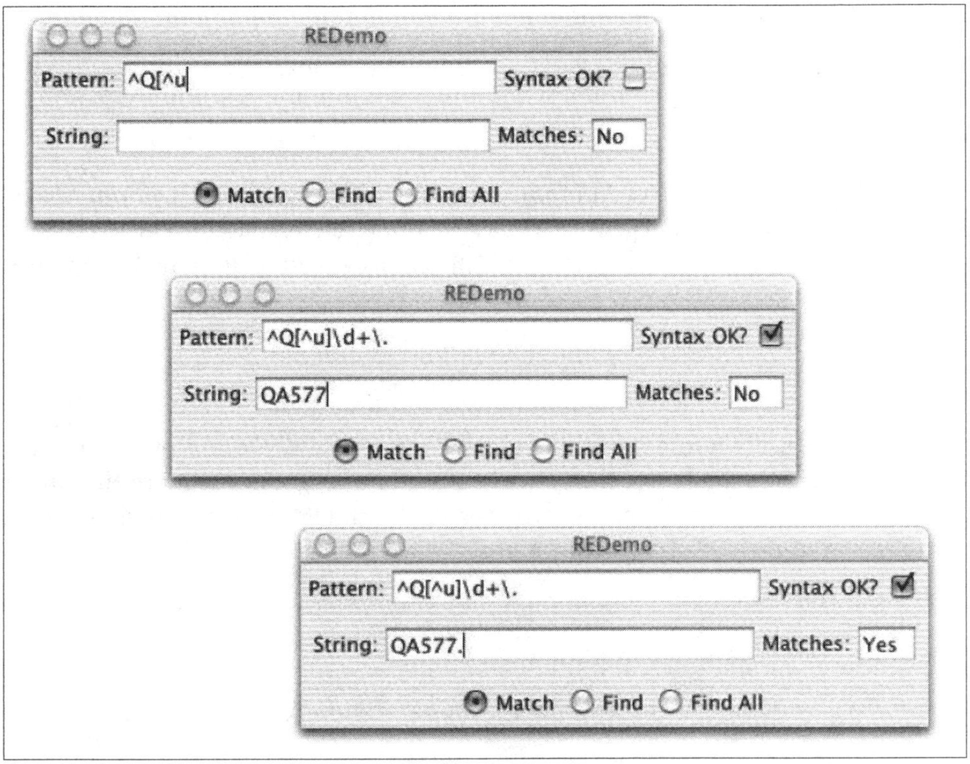

Figure 4-2. REDemo with "Q not followed by u" example

One good way to think of regular expressions is as a "little language" for matching patterns of characters in text contained in strings. Give yourself extra points if you've already recognized this as the design pattern known as Interpreter. A regular expression API is an interpreter for matching regular expressions.

So now you should have at least a basic grasp of how regexes work in practice. The rest of this chapter gives more examples and explains some of the more powerful topics, such as capture groups. As for how regexes work in theory—and there are a lot of theoretical details and differences among regex flavors—the interested reader is referred to in *Mastering Regular Expressions*. Meanwhile, let's start learning how to write Java programs that use regular expressions.

4.2. Using regexes in Java: Test for a Pattern

Problem

You're ready to get started using regular expression processing to beef up your Java code by testing to see if a given pattern can match in a given string.

Solution

Use the Java Regular Expressions Package, `java.util.regex`.

Discussion

The good news is that the Java API for regexes is actually easy to use. If all you need is to find out whether a given regex matches a string, you can use the convenient `boolean matches()` method of the `String` class, which accepts a regex pattern in `String` form as its argument:

```
if (inputString.matches(stringRegexPattern)) {
    // it matched... do something with it...
}
```

This is, however, a convenience routine, and convenience always comes at a price. If the regex is going to be used more than once or twice in a program, it is more efficient to construct and use a `Pattern` and its `Matcher(s)`. A complete program constructing a `Pattern` and using it to `match` is shown here:

```
public class RESimple {
    public static void main(String[] argv) {
        String pattern = "^Q[^u]\\d+\\.";
        String[] input = {
            "QA777. is the next flight. It is on time.",
            "Quack, Quack, Quack!"
        };

        Pattern p = Pattern.compile(pattern);

        for (String in : input) {
            boolean found = p.matcher(in).lookingAt();

            System.out.println("'" + pattern + "'" +
            (found ? " matches '" : " doesn't match '") + in + "'");
        }
    }
}
```

The `java.util.regex` package consists of two classes, `Pattern` and `Matcher`, which provide the public API shown in Example 4-1.

Example 4-1. Regex public API

```java
/** The main public API of the java.util.regex package.
 * Prepared by javap and Ian Darwin.
 */

package java.util.regex;

public final class Pattern {
    // Flags values ('or' together)
    public static final int
        UNIX_LINES, CASE_INSENSITIVE, COMMENTS, MULTILINE,
        DOTALL, UNICODE_CASE, CANON_EQ;
    // No public constructors; use these Factory methods
    public static Pattern compile(String patt);
    public static Pattern compile(String patt, int flags);
    // Method to get a Matcher for this Pattern
    public Matcher matcher(CharSequence input);
    // Information methods
    public String pattern();
    public int flags();
    // Convenience methods
    public static boolean matches(String pattern, CharSequence input);
    public String[] split(CharSequence input);
    public String[] split(CharSequence input, int max);
}

public final class Matcher {
    // Action: find or match methods
    public boolean matches();
    public boolean find();
    public boolean find(int start);
    public boolean lookingAt();
    // "Information about the previous match" methods
    public int start();
    public int start(int whichGroup);
    public int end();
    public int end(int whichGroup);
    public int groupCount();
    public String group();
    public String group(int whichGroup);
    // Reset methods
    public Matcher reset();
    public Matcher reset(CharSequence newInput);
    // Replacement methods
    public Matcher appendReplacement(StringBuffer where, String newText);
    public StringBuffer appendTail(StringBuffer where);
    public String replaceAll(String newText);
    public String replaceFirst(String newText);
    // information methods
    public Pattern pattern();
}
```

```
/* String, showing only the RE-related methods */
public final class String {
    public boolean matches(String regex);
    public String replaceFirst(String regex, String newStr);
    public String replaceAll(String regex, String newStr);
    public String[] split(String regex);
    public String[] split(String regex, int max);
}
```

This API is large enough to require some explanation. The normal steps for regex matching in a production program are:

1. Create a `Pattern` by calling the static method `Pattern.compile()`.

2. Request a `Matcher` from the pattern by calling `pattern.matcher(CharSequence)` for each `String` (or other `CharSequence`) you wish to look through.

3. Call (once or more) one of the finder methods (discussed later in this section) in the resulting `Matcher`.

The `java.lang.CharSequence` interface provides simple read-only access to objects containing a collection of characters. The standard implementations are `String` and `StringBuffer`/`StringBuilder` (described in Chapter 3), and the "new I/O" class `java.nio.CharBuffer`.

Of course, you can perform regex matching in other ways, such as using the convenience methods in `Pattern` or even in `java.lang.String`. For example:

```
public class StringConvenience {
    public static void main(String[] argv) {

        String pattern = ".*Q[^u]\\d+\\..*";
        String line = "Order QT300. Now!";
        if (line.matches(pattern)) {
            System.out.println(line + " matches \"" + pattern + "\"");
        } else {
            System.out.println("NO MATCH");
        }
    }
}
```

But the three-step list just described is the "standard" pattern for matching. You'd likely use the `String` convenience routine in a program that only used the regex once; if the regex were being used more than once, it is worth taking the time to "compile" it because the compiled version runs faster.

In addition, the `Matcher` has several finder methods, which provide more flexibility than the `String` convenience routine `match()`. The `Matcher` methods are:

`match()`

> Used a to compare the entire string against the pattern; this is the same as the routine in `java.lang.String`. Because it matches the entire `String`, I had to put `.*` before and after the pattern.

`lookingAt()`

> Used to match the pattern only at the beginning of the string.

`find()`

> Used to match the pattern in the string (not necessarily at the first character of the string), starting at the beginning of the string or, if the method was previously called and succeeded, at the first character not matched by the previous match.

Each of these methods returns `boolean`, with `true` meaning a match and `false` meaning no match. To check whether a given string matches a given pattern, you need only type something like the following:

```
Matcher m = Pattern.compile(patt).matcher(line);
if (m.find( )) {
    System.out.println(line + " matches " + patt)
}
```

But you may also want to extract the text that matched, which is the subject of the next recipe.

The following recipes cover uses of this API. Initially, the examples just use arguments of type `String` as the input source. Use of other `CharSequence` types is covered in Recipe 4.5.

4.3. Finding the Matching Text

Problem

You need to find the text that the regex matched.

Solution

Sometimes you need to know more than just whether a regex matched a string. In editors and many other tools, you want to know exactly what characters were matched. Remember that with quantifiers such as *, the length of the text that was matched may have no relationship to the length of the pattern that matched it. Do not underestimate the mighty `.*`, which happily matches thousands or millions of characters if allowed to. As you saw in the previous recipe, you can find out whether a given match succeeds just by using `find()` or `matches()`. But in other applications, you will want to get the characters that the pattern matched.

After a successful call to one of the preceding methods, you can use these "information" methods to get information on the match:

start(), end()
> Returns the character position in the string of the starting and ending characters that matched.

groupCount()
> Returns the number of parenthesized capture groups, if any; returns 0 if no groups were used.

group(int i)
> Returns the characters matched by group i of the current match, if i is greater than or equal to zero and less than or equal to the return value of groupCount(). Group 0 is the entire match, so group(0) (or just group()) returns the entire portion of the input that matched.

The notion of parentheses or "capture groups" is central to regex processing. Regexes may be nested to any level of complexity. The group(int) method lets you retrieve the characters that matched a given parenthesis group. If you haven't used any explicit parens, you can just treat whatever matched as "level zero." Example 4-2 shows part of *REMatch.java*.

Example 4-2. Part of REMatch.java

```java
public class REmatch {
    public static void main(String[] argv) {

        String patt = "Q[^u]\\d+\\.";
        Pattern r = Pattern.compile(patt);
        String line = "Order QT300. Now!";
        Matcher m = r.matcher(line);
        if (m.find()) {
            System.out.println(patt + " matches \"" +
                m.group(0) +
                "\" in \"" + line + "\"");
        } else {
            System.out.println("NO MATCH");
        }
    }
}
```

When run, this prints:

```
Q[\^u]\d+\. matches "QT300." in "Order QT300. Now!"
```

An extended version of the REDemo program presented in Recipe 4.2, called REDemo2, provides a display of all the capture groups in a given regex; one example is shown in Figure 4-3.

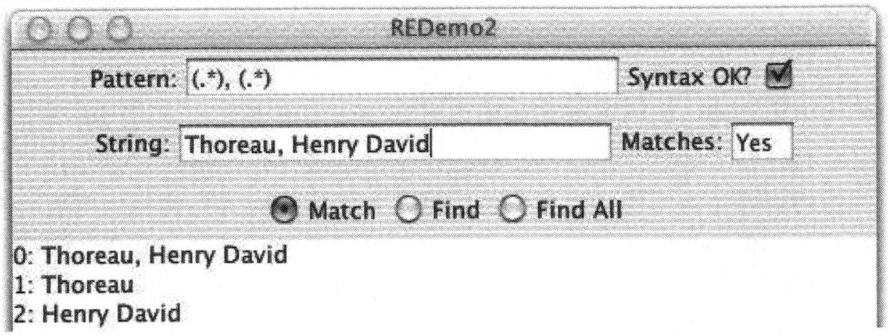

Figure 4-3. REDemo2 in action

It is also possible to get the starting and ending indices and the length of the text that the pattern matched (remember that terms with quantifiers, such as the \d+ in this example, can match an arbitrary number of characters in the string). You can use these in conjunction with the String.substring() methods as follows:

```
String patt = "Q[^u]\\d+\\.";
Pattern r = Pattern.compile(patt);
String line = "Order QT300. Now!";
Matcher m = r.matcher(line);
if (m.find()) {
    System.out.println(patt + " matches \"" +
        line.substring(m.start(0), m.end(0)) +
        "\" in \"" + line + "\"");
} else {
    System.out.println("NO MATCH");
}
```

Suppose you need to extract several items from a string. If the input is:

```
Smith, John
Adams, John Quincy
```

and you want to get out:

```
John Smith
John Quincy Adams
```

just use:

```
public class REmatchTwoFields {
    public static void main(String[] args) {
        String inputLine = "Adams, John Quincy";
        // Construct an RE with parens to "grab" both field1 and field2
        Pattern r = Pattern.compile("(.*), (.*)");
        Matcher m = r.matcher(inputLine);
        if (!m.matches())
            throw new IllegalArgumentException("Bad input");
        System.out.println(m.group(2) + ' ' + m.group(1));
```

```
        }
    }
```

4.4. Replacing the Matched Text

As we saw in the previous recipe, regex patterns involving quantifiers can match a lot of characters with very few metacharacters. We need a way to replace the text that the regex matched without changing other text before or after it. We could do this manually using the String method substring(). However, because it's such a common requirement, the Java Regular Expression API provides some substitution methods. In all these methods, you pass in the replacement text or "righthand side" of the substitution (this term is historical: in a command-line text editor's substitute command, the lefthand side is the pattern and the righthand side is the replacement text). The replacement methods are:

replaceAll(newString)
> Replaces all occurrences that matched with the new string.

appendReplacement(StringBuffer, newString)
> Copies up to before the first match, plus the given newString.

appendTail(StringBuffer)
> Appends text after the last match (normally used after appendReplacement).

Example 4-3 shows use of these three methods.

Example 4-3. ReplaceDemo.java

```java
/**
 * Quick demo of RE substitution: correct U.S. 'favor'
 * to Canadian/British 'favour', but not in "favorite"
 * @author Ian F. Darwin, http://www.darwinsys.com/
 */
public class ReplaceDemo {
    public static void main(String[] argv) {

        // Make an RE pattern to match as a word only (\b=word boundary)
        String patt = "\\bfavor\\b";

        // A test input.
        String input = "Do me a favor? Fetch my favorite.";
        System.out.println("Input: " + input);

        // Run it from a RE instance and see that it works
        Pattern r = Pattern.compile(patt);
        Matcher m = r.matcher(input);
        System.out.println("ReplaceAll: " + m.replaceAll("favour"));

        // Show the appendReplacement method
        m.reset();
```

```
        StringBuffer sb = new StringBuffer();
        System.out.print("Append methods: ");
        while (m.find()) {
            // Copy to before first match,
            // plus the word "favor"
            m.appendReplacement(sb, "favour");
        }
        m.appendTail(sb);           // copy remainder
        System.out.println(sb.toString());
    }
}
```

Sure enough, when you run it, it does what we expect:

```
Input: Do me a favor? Fetch my favorite.
ReplaceAll: Do me a favour? Fetch my favorite.
Append methods: Do me a favour? Fetch my favorite.
```

4.5. Printing All Occurrences of a Pattern

Problem

You need to find all the strings that match a given regex in one or more files or other sources.

Solution

This example reads through a file one line at a time. Whenever a match is found, I extract it from the line and print it.

This code takes the group() methods from Recipe 4.3, the substring method from the CharacterIterator interface, and the match() method from the regex and simply puts them all together. I coded it to extract all the "names" from a given file; in running the program through itself, it prints the words import, java, until, regex, and so on, each on its own line:

```
C:\\> javac -d . ReaderIter.java
C:\\> java regex.ReaderIter ReaderIter.java
import
java
util
regex
import
java
io
Print
all
the
strings
```

```
that
match
given
pattern
from
file
public
...
C:\\>
```

I interrupted it here to save paper. This can be written two ways: a traditional "line at a time" pattern shown in Example 4-4 and a more compact form using "new I/O" shown in Example 4-5 (the "new I/O" package is described in Chapter 10).

Example 4-4. ReaderIter.java

```java
public class ReaderIter {
    public static void main(String[] args) throws IOException {
        // The RE pattern
        Pattern patt = Pattern.compile("[A-Za-z][a-z]+");
        // A FileReader (see the I/O chapter)
        BufferedReader r = new BufferedReader(new FileReader(args[0]));

        // For each line of input, try matching in it.
        String line;
        while ((line = r.readLine()) != null) {
            // For each match in the line, extract and print it.
            Matcher m = patt.matcher(line);
            while (m.find()) {
                // Simplest method:
                // System.out.println(m.group(0));

                // Get the starting position of the text
                int start = m.start(0);
                // Get ending position
                int end = m.end(0);
                // Print whatever matched.
                // Use CharacterIterator.substring(offset, end);
                System.out.println(line.substring(start, end));
            }
        }
    }
}
```

Example 4-5. GrepNIO.java

```java
public class GrepNIO {
    public static void main(String[] args) throws IOException {

        if (args.length < 2) {
            System.err.println("Usage: GrepNIO patt file [...]");
            System.exit(1);
        }
```

```
        Pattern p=Pattern.compile(args[0]);
        for (int i=1; i<args.length; i++)
            process(p, args[i]);
    }

    static void process(Pattern pattern, String fileName) throws IOException {

        // Get a FileChannel from the given file.
        FileChannel fc = new FileInputStream(fileName).getChannel();

        // Map the file's content
        ByteBuffer buf = fc.map(FileChannel.MapMode.READ_ONLY, 0, fc.size());

        // Decode ByteBuffer into CharBuffer
        CharBuffer cbuf =
            Charset.forName("ISO-8859-1").newDecoder().decode(buf);

        Matcher m = pattern.matcher(cbuf);
        while (m.find()) {
            System.out.println(m.group(0));
        }
    }
}
```

The NIO version shown in Example 4-5 relies on the fact that an NIO `Buffer` can be used as a `CharSequence`. This program is more general in that the pattern argument is taken from the command-line argument. It prints the same output as the previous example if invoked with the pattern argument from the previous program on the command line:

```
java regex.GrepNIO "[A-Za-z][a-z]+"  ReaderIter.java
```

You might think of using \w+ as the pattern; the only difference is that my pattern looks for well-formed capitalized words, whereas \w+ would include Java-centric oddities like theVariableName, which have capitals in nonstandard positions.

Also note that the NIO version will probably be more efficient because it doesn't reset the `Matcher` to a new input source on each line of input as `ReaderIter` does.

4.6. Printing Lines Containing a Pattern

Problem

You need to look for lines matching a given regex in one or more files.

Solution

Write a simple *grep*-like program.

Discussion

As I've mentioned, once you have a regex package, you can write a *grep*-like program. I gave an example of the Unix *grep* program earlier. *grep* is called with some optional arguments, followed by one required regular expression pattern, followed by an arbitrary number of filenames. It prints any line that contains the pattern, differing from Recipe 4.5, which prints only the matching text itself. For example:

```
grep "[dD]arwin" *.txt
```

The preceding code searches for lines containing either darwin or Darwin in every line of every file whose name ends in *.txt*.[3] Example 4-6 is the source for the first version of a program to do this, called Grep0. It reads lines from the standard input and doesn't take any optional arguments, but it handles the full set of regular expressions that the Pattern class implements (it is, therefore, not identical to the Unix programs of the same name). We haven't covered the java.io package for input and output yet (see Chapter 10), but our use of it here is simple enough that you can probably intuit it. The online source includes Grep1, which does the same thing but is better structured (and therefore longer). Later in this chapter, Recipe 4.12 presents a JGrep program that uses my GetOpt (see Recipe 2.6) to parse command-line options.

Example 4-6. Grep0.java

```
public class Grep0 {
    public static void main(String[] args) throws IOException {
        BufferedReader is =
            new BufferedReader(new InputStreamReader(System.in));
        if (args.length != 1) {
            System.err.println("Usage: MatchLines pattern");
            System.exit(1);
        }
        Pattern patt = Pattern.compile(args[0]);
        Matcher matcher = patt.matcher("");
        String line = null;
        while ((line = is.readLine()) != null) {
            matcher.reset(line);
            if (matcher.find()) {
                System.out.println("MATCH: " + line);
            }
        }
    }
}
```

---

3. On Unix, the shell or command-line interpreter expands *.txt to all the matching filenames before running the program, but the normal Java interpreter does this for you on systems where the shell isn't energetic or bright enough to do it.

4.7. Controlling Case in Regular Expressions

Problem

You want to find text regardless of case.

Solution

Compile the `Pattern` passing in the `flags` argument `Pattern.CASE_INSENSITIVE` to indicate that matching should be case-independent ("fold" or ignore differences in case). If your code might run in different locales (see Chapter 15) then you should add `Pattern.UNICODE_CASE`. Without these flags, the default is normal, case-sensitive matching behavior. This flag (and others) are passed to the `Pattern.compile()` method, as in:

```
// CaseMatch.java
Pattern  reCaseInsens = Pattern.compile(pattern, Pattern.CASE_INSENSITIVE |
    Pattern.UNICODE_CASE);
reCaseInsens.matches(input);          // will match case-insensitively
```

This flag must be passed when you create the `Pattern`; because `Pattern` objects are immutable, they cannot be changed once constructed.

The full source code for this example is online as *CaseMatch.java*.

Pattern.compile() Flags

Half a dozen flags can be passed as the second argument to `Pattern.compile()`. If more than one value is needed, they can be or'd together using the bitwise or operator |. In alphabetical order, the flags are:

CANON_EQ
> Enables so-called "canonical equivalence." In other words, characters are matched by their base character, so that the character e followed by the "combining character mark" for the acute accent (´) can be matched either by the composite character é or the letter e followed by the character mark for the accent (see Recipe 4.8).

CASE_INSENSITIVE
> Turns on case-insensitive matching (see Recipe 4.7).

COMMENTS
> Causes whitespace and comments (from # to end-of-line) to be ignored in the pattern.

DOTALL
> Allows dot (.) to match any regular character or the newline, not just any regular character other than newline (see Recipe 4.9).

MULTILINE

    Specifies multiline mode (see Recipe 4.9).

UNICODE_CASE

    Enables Unicode-aware case folding (see Recipe 4.7).

UNIX_LINES

    Makes \n the only valid "newline" sequence for MULTILINE mode (see Recipe 4.9).

4.8. Matching "Accented" or Composite Characters

Problem

You want characters to match regardless of the form in which they are entered.

Solution

Compile the Pattern with the flags argument Pattern.CANON_EQ for "canonical equality."

Discussion

Composite characters can be entered in various forms. Consider, as a single example, the letter e with an acute accent. This character may be found in various forms in Unicode text, such as the single character é (Unicode character \u00e9) or as the two-character sequence eʹ (e followed by the Unicode combining acute accent, \u0301). To allow you to match such characters regardless of which of possibly multiple "fully decomposed" forms are used to enter them, the regex package has an option for "canonical matching," which treats any of the forms as equivalent. This option is enabled by passing CANON_EQ as (one of) the flags in the second argument to Pattern.compile(). This program shows CANON_EQ being used to match several forms:

```
public class CanonEqDemo {
    public static void main(String[] args) {
        String pattStr = "\u00e9gal"; // egal
        String[] input = {
                "\u00e9gal", // egal - this one had better match :-)
                "e\u0301gal", // e + "Combining acute accent"
                "e\u02cagal", // e + "modifier letter acute accent"
                "e'gal", // e + single quote
                "e\u00b4gal", // e + Latin-1 "acute"
        };
        Pattern pattern = Pattern.compile(pattStr, Pattern.CANON_EQ);
        for (int i = 0; i < input.length; i++) {
            if (pattern.matcher(input[i]).matches()) {
                System.out.println(
```

```
                        pattStr + " matches input " + input[i]);
            } else {
                System.out.println(
                    pattStr + " does not match input " + input[i]);
            }
        }
    }
}
```

This program correctly matches the "combining accent" and rejects the other characters, some of which, unfortunately, look like the accent on a printer, but are not considered "combining accent" characters:

```
égal matches input égal
égal matches input e?gal
égal does not match input e?gal
égal does not match input e'gal
égal does not match input e´gal
```

For more details, see the character charts (*http://www.unicode.org*).

4.9. Matching Newlines in Text

Problem

You need to match newlines in text.

Solution

Use \n or \r.

See also the flags constant `Pattern.MULTILINE`, which makes newlines match as beginning-of-line and end-of-line (\^ and $).

Discussion

Though line-oriented tools from Unix such as *sed* and *grep* match regular expressions one line at a time, not all tools do. The *sam* text editor from Bell Laboratories was the first interactive tool I know of to allow multiline regular expressions; the Perl scripting language followed shortly after. In the Java API, the newline character by default has no special significance. The `BufferedReader` method `readLine()` normally strips out whichever newline characters it finds. If you read in gobs of characters using some method other than `readLine()`, you may have some number of \n, \r, or \r\n sequences in your text string.[4] Normally all of these are treated as equivalent to \n. If you want only \n to match, use the UNIX_LINES flag to the Pattern.compile() method.

In Unix, ^ and $ are commonly used to match the beginning or end of a line, respectively. In this API, the regex metacharacters \^ and $ ignore line terminators and only match at the beginning and the end, respectively, of the entire string. However, if you pass the MULTILINE flag into Pattern.compile(), these expressions match just after or just before, respectively, a line terminator; $ also matches the very end of the string. Because the line ending is just an ordinary character, you can match it with . or similar expressions, and, if you want to know exactly where it is, \n or \r in the pattern match it as well. In other words, to this API, a newline character is just another character with no special significance. See the sidebar "Pattern.compile() Flags" on page 125. An example of newline matching is shown in Example 4-7.

Example 4-7. NLMatch.java

```java
public class NLMatch {
    public static void main(String[] argv) {

        String input = "I dream of engines\nmore engines, all day long";
        System.out.println("INPUT: " + input);
        System.out.println();

        String[] patt = {
            "engines.more engines",
            "ines\nmore",
            "engines$"
        };

        for (int i = 0; i < patt.length; i++) {
            System.out.println("PATTERN " + patt[i]);

            boolean found;
            Pattern p1l = Pattern.compile(patt[i]);
            found = p1l.matcher(input).find();
            System.out.println("DEFAULT match " + found);

            Pattern pml = Pattern.compile(patt[i],
                Pattern.DOTALL|Pattern.MULTILINE);
            found = pml.matcher(input).find();
            System.out.println("MultiLine match " + found);
            System.out.println();
        }
    }
}
```

4. Or a few related Unicode characters, including the next-line (\u0085), line-separator (\u2028), and paragraph-separator (\u2029) characters.

If you run this code, the first pattern (with the wildcard character .) always matches, whereas the second pattern (with $) matches only when MATCH_MULTILINE is set:

```
> java regex.NLMatch
INPUT: I dream of engines
more engines, all day long

PATTERN engines
more engines
DEFAULT match true
MULTILINE match: true

PATTERN engines$
DEFAULT match false
MULTILINE match: true
```

4.10. Program: Apache Logfile Parsing

The Apache web server is the world's leading web server and has been for most of the Web's history. It is one of the world's best-known open source projects, and the first of many fostered by the Apache Foundation. But the name Apache is often claimed to be a pun on the origins of the server; its developers began with the free NCSA server and kept hacking at it or "patching" it until it did what they wanted. When it was sufficiently different from the original, a new name was needed. Because it was now "a patchy server," the name Apache was chosen. Officialdom denies the story, but it's cute anyway. One place actual patchiness does show through is in the logfile format. Consider Example 4-8.

Example 4-8. Apache log file excerpt

```
123.45.67.89 - - [27/Oct/2000:09:27:09 -0400] "GET /java/javaResources.html
HTTP/1.0" 200 10450 "-" "Mozilla/4.6 [en] (X11; U; OpenBSD 2.8 i386; Nav)"
```

The file format was obviously designed for human inspection but not for easy parsing. The problem is that different delimiters are used: square brackets for the date, quotes for the request line, and spaces sprinkled all through. Consider trying to use a String-Tokenizer; you might be able to get it working, but you'd spend a lot of time fiddling with it. However, this somewhat contorted regular expression[5] makes it easy to parse:

```
\^([\d.]+) (\S+) (\S+) \[([\w:/]+\s[+\-]\d{4})\] "(.+?)" (\d{3}) (\d+) "([\^"]+)"
"([\^"]+)"
```

You may find it informative to refer back to Table 4-1 and review the full syntax used here. Note in particular the use of the nongreedy quantifier +? in \"(.+?)\" to match a

---

5. You might think this would hold some kind of world record for complexity in regex competitions, but I'm sure it's been outdone many times.

quoted string; you can't just use .+ because that would match too much (up to the quote at the end of the line). Code to extract the various fields such as IP address, request, referrer URL, and browser version is shown in Example 4-9.

Example 4-9. LogRegExp.java

```java
public class LogRegExp  {

    public static void main(String argv[]) {

        String logEntryPattern =
            "^([\\d.]+) (\\S+) (\\S+) \\[([\\w:/]+\\s[+-]\\d{4})\\] " +
            "\"(.+?)\" (\\d{3}) (\\d+) \"([^\"]+)\" \"([^\"]+)\"";

        System.out.println("RE Pattern:");
        System.out.println(logEntryPattern);

        System.out.println("Input line is:");
        String logEntryLine = LogExample.logEntryLine;
        System.out.println(logEntryLine);

        Pattern p = Pattern.compile(logEntryPattern);
        Matcher matcher = p.matcher(logEntryLine);
        if (!matcher.matches() ||
            LogExample.NUM_FIELDS != matcher.groupCount()) {
            System.err.println("Bad log entry (or problem with regex):");
            System.err.println(logEntryLine);
            return;
        }
        System.out.println("IP Address: " + matcher.group(1));
        System.out.println("UserName: " + matcher.group(3));
        System.out.println("Date/Time: " + matcher.group(4));
        System.out.println("Request: " + matcher.group(5));
        System.out.println("Response: " + matcher.group(6));
        System.out.println("Bytes Sent: " + matcher.group(7));
        if (!matcher.group(8).equals("-"))
            System.out.println("Referer: " + matcher.group(8));
        System.out.println("User-Agent: " + matcher.group(9));
    }
}
```

The implements clause is for an interface that just defines the input string; it was used in a demonstration to compare the regular expression mode with the use of a String-Tokenizer. The source for both versions is in the online source for this chapter. Running the program against the sample input from Example 4-8 gives this output:

```
Using regex Pattern:
\^([\d.]+) (\S+) (\S+) \[([\w:/]+\s[+\-]\d{4})\] "(.+?)" (\d{3}) (\d+) "([\^"]+)"
"([\^"]+)"
Input line is:
123.45.67.89 - - [27/Oct/2000:09:27:09 -0400] "GET /java/javaResources.html
```

```
HTTP/1.0" 200 10450 "-" "Mozilla/4.6 [en] (X11; U; OpenBSD 2.8 i386; Nav)"
IP Address: 123.45.67.89
Date&Time: 27/Oct/2000:09:27:09 -0400
Request: GET /java/javaResources.html HTTP/1.0
Response: 200
Bytes Sent: 10450
Browser: Mozilla/4.6 [en] (X11; U; OpenBSD 2.8 i386; Nav)
```

The program successfully parsed the entire logfile format with one call to `matcher.matches()`.

4.11. Program: Data Mining

Suppose that I, as a published author, want to track how my book is selling in comparison to others. I can obtain this information for free just by clicking the page for my book on any of the major bookseller sites, reading the sales rank number off the screen, and typing the number into a file—but that's too tedious. As I wrote in the book that this example looks for, "computers get paid to extract relevant information from files; people should not have to do such mundane tasks." This program uses the Regular Expressions API and, in particular, newline matching to extract a value from an HTML page on the hypothetical *QuickBookShops.web* website. It also reads from a URL object (see Recipe 13.10). The pattern to look for is something like this (bear in mind that the HTML may change at any time, so I want to keep the pattern fairly general):

```
<b>QuickBookShop.web Sales Rank: </b>
26,252
</font><br>
```

Because the pattern may extend over more than one line, I read the entire web page from the URL into a single long string using my `FileIO.readerToString()` method (see Recipe 10.10) instead of the more traditional line-at-a-time paradigm. I then plot a graph using an external program (see Recipe 24.1); this could (and should) be changed to use a Java graphics program (see Recipe 12.14 for some leads). The complete program is shown in Example 4-10.

Example 4-10. BookRank.java

```java
public class BookRank {
    public final static String DATA_FILE = "book.sales";
    public final static String GRAPH_FILE = "book.png";
    public final static String PLOTTER_PROG = "/usr/local/bin/gnuplot";

    final static String isbn = "0596007019";
    final static String title = "Java Cookbook";

    /** Grab the sales rank off the web page and log it. */
    public static void main(String[] args) throws Exception {

        Properties p = new Properties();
```

```
        p.load(new FileInputStream(
            args.length == 0 ? "bookrank.properties" : args[1]));
        String title = p.getProperty("title", "NO TITLE IN PROPERTIES");
        // The url must have the "isbn=" at the very end, or otherwise
        // be amenable to being string-catted to, like the default.
        String url = p.getProperty("url", "http://test.ing/test.cgi?isbn=");
        // The 10-digit ISBN for the book.
        String isbn  = p.getProperty("isbn", "0000000000");
        // The RE pattern (MUST have ONE capture group for the number)
        String pattern = p.getProperty("pattern", "Rank: (\\d+)");

        int rank = getBookRank(isbn);

        System.out.println("Rank is " + rank);

        // Now try to draw the graph, using external
        // plotting program against all historical data.
        // Could use gnuplot, R, any other math/graph program.
        // Better yet: use one of the Java plotting APIs.

        PrintWriter pw = new PrintWriter(
            new FileWriter(DATA_FILE, true));
        String date = new SimpleDateFormat("MM dd hh mm ss yyyy ").
            format(new Date());
        pw.println(date + " " + rank);
        pw.close();

        String gnuplot_cmd =
            "set term png\n" +
            "set output \"" + GRAPH_FILE + "\"\n" +
            "set xdata time\n" +
            "set ylabel \"Book sales rank\"\n" +
            "set bmargin 3\n" +
            "set logscale y\n" +
            "set yrange [1:60000] reverse\n" +
            "set timefmt \"%m %d %H %M %S %Y\"\n" +
            "plot \"" + DATA_FILE +
                "\" using 1:7 title \"" + title + "\" with lines\n"
        ;

        if (!new File(PLOTTER_PROG).exists()) {
            System.out.println("Plotting software not installed");
            return;
        }
        Process proc = Runtime.getRuntime().exec(PLOTTER_PROG);
        PrintWriter gp = new PrintWriter(proc.getOutputStream());
        gp.print(gnuplot_cmd);
        gp.close();
    }

    /**
     * Look for something like this in the HTML input:
```

```
 *      <b>Sales Rank:</b>
 *      #26,252
 *      </font><br>
 * @throws IOException
 * @throws IOException
 */
public static int getBookRank(String isbn) throws IOException {

    // The RE pattern - digits and commas allowed
    final String pattern = "Rank:</b> #([\\d,]+)";
    final Pattern r = Pattern.compile(pattern);

    // The url -- must have the "isbn=" at the very end, or otherwise
    // be amenable to being appended to.
    final String url = "http://www.amazon.com/exec/obidos/ASIN/" + isbn;

    // Open the URL and get a Reader from it.
    final BufferedReader is = new BufferedReader(new InputStreamReader(
        new URL(url).openStream()));

    // Read the URL looking for the rank information, as
    // a single long string, so can match RE across multi-lines.
    final String input = readerToString(is);

    // If found, append to sales data file.
    Matcher m = r.matcher(input);
    if (m.find()) {
        // Paren 1 is the digits (and maybe ','s) that matched; remove comma
        return Integer.parseInt(m.group(1).replace(",",""));
    } else {
        throw new RuntimeException(
            "Pattern not matched in `" + url + "'!");
    }
}

private static String readerToString(BufferedReader is) throws IOException {
    StringBuilder sb = new StringBuilder();
    String line;
    while ((line = is.readLine()) != null) {
        sb.append(line);
    }
    return sb.toString();
}
}
```

4.12. Program: Full Grep

Now that we've seen how the regular expressions package works, it's time to write
JGrep, a full-blown version of the line-matching program with option parsing. Table 4-2
lists some typical command-line options that a Unix implementation of *grep* might
include.

Table 4-2. Grep command-line options

Option	Meaning
-c	Count only: don't print lines, just count them
-C	Context; print some lines above and below each line that matches (not implemented in this version; left as an exercise for the reader)
-f pattern	Take pattern from file named after -f instead of from command line
-h	Suppress printing filename ahead of lines
-i	Ignore case
-l	List filenames only: don't print lines, just the names they're found in
-n	Print line numbers before matching lines
-s	Suppress printing certain error messages
-v	Invert: print only lines that do NOT match the pattern

We discussed the GetOpt class in Recipe 2.6. Here we use it to control the operation of an application program. As usual, because main() runs in a static context but our application main line does not, we could wind up passing a lot of information into the constructor. To save space, this version just uses global variables to track the settings from the command line. Unlike the Unix grep tool, this one does not yet handle "combined options," so -l -r -i is OK, but -lri will fail, due to a limitation in the GetOpt parser used.

The program basically just reads lines, matches the pattern in them, and, if a match is found (or not found, with -v), prints the line (and optionally some other stuff, too). Having said all that, the code is shown in Example 4-11.

Example 4-11. JGrep.java

```
/** A command-line grep-like program. Accepts some command-line options,
 * and takes a pattern and a list of text files.
 * N.B. The current implementation of GetOpt does not allow combining short
 * arguments, so put spaces e.g., "JGrep -l -r -i pattern file..." is OK, but
 * "JGrep -lri pattern file..." will fail. Getopt will hopefully be fixed soon.
 */
public class JGrep {
    private static final String USAGE =
        "Usage: JGrep pattern [-chilrsnv][-f pattfile][filename...]";
    /** The pattern we're looking for */
    protected Pattern pattern;
    /** The matcher for this pattern */
    protected Matcher matcher;
    private boolean debug;
    /** Are we to only count lines, instead of printing? */
    protected static boolean countOnly = false;
    /** Are we to ignore case? */
    protected static boolean ignoreCase = false;
    /** Are we to suppress printing of filenames? */
```

```
protected static boolean dontPrintFileName = false;
/** Are we to only list names of files that match? */
protected static boolean listOnly = false;
/** are we to print line numbers? */
protected static boolean numbered = false;
/** Are we to be silent about errors? */
protected static boolean silent = false;
/** are we to print only lines that DONT match? */
protected static boolean inVert = false;
/** Are we to process arguments recursively if directories? */
protected static boolean recursive = false;

/** Construct a Grep object for the pattern, and run it
 * on all input files listed in argv.
 * Be aware that a few of the command-line options are not
 * acted upon in this version - left as an exercise for the reader!
 */
public static void main(String[] argv) {

    if (argv.length < 1) {
        System.err.println(USAGE);
        System.exit(1);
    }
    String patt = null;

    GetOpt go = new GetOpt("cf:hilnrRsv");

    char c;
    while ((c = go.getopt(argv)) != 0) {
        switch(c) {
            case 'c':
                countOnly = true;
                break;
            case 'f':    /* External file contains the pattern */
                try (BufferedReader b =
                    new BufferedReader(new FileReader(go.optarg()))) {
                    patt = b.readLine();
                } catch (IOException e) {
                    System.err.println(
                        "Can't read pattern file " + go.optarg());
                    System.exit(1);
                }
                break;
            case 'h':
                dontPrintFileName = true;
                break;
            case 'i':
                ignoreCase = true;
                break;
            case 'l':
                listOnly = true;
                break;
```

```
                case 'n':
                    numbered = true;
                    break;
                case 'r':
                case 'R':
                    recursive = true;
                    break;
                case 's':
                    silent = true;
                    break;
                case 'v':
                    inVert = true;
                    break;
                case '?':
                    System.err.println("Getopts was not happy!");
                    System.err.println(USAGE);
                    break;
            }
        }

        int ix = go.getOptInd();

        if (patt == null)
            patt = argv[ix++];

        JGrep prog = null;
        try {
            prog = new JGrep(patt);
        } catch (PatternSyntaxException ex) {
            System.err.println("RE Syntax error in " + patt);
            return;
        }

        if (argv.length == ix) {
            dontPrintFileName = true; // Don't print filenames if stdin
            if (recursive) {
                System.err.println("Warning: recursive search of stdin!");
            }
            prog.process(new InputStreamReader(System.in), null);
        } else {
            if (!dontPrintFileName)
                dontPrintFileName = ix == argv.length - 1; // Nor if only one file.
            if (recursive)
                dontPrintFileName = false;                  // unless a directory!

            for (int i=ix; i<argv.length; i++) { // note starting index
                try {
                    prog.process(new File(argv[i]));
                } catch(Exception e) {
                    System.err.println(e);
                }
            }
```

```
        }
    }

    /** Construct a JGrep object.
     * @param patt The pattern to look for
     * @param args the command-line options.
     */
    public JGrep(String patt) throws PatternSyntaxException {
        if (debug) {
            System.err.printf("JGrep.JGrep(%s)%n", patt);
        }
        // compile the regular expression
        int caseMode = ignoreCase ?
            Pattern.UNICODE_CASE | Pattern.CASE_INSENSITIVE :
            0;
        pattern = Pattern.compile(patt, caseMode);
        matcher = pattern.matcher("");
    }

    /** Process one command line argument (file or directory)
     * @throws FileNotFoundException
     */
    public void process(File file) throws FileNotFoundException {
        if (!file.exists() || !file.canRead()) {
            System.err.println(
                "ERROR: can't read file " + file.getAbsolutePath());
            return;
        }
        if (file.isFile()) {
            process(new BufferedReader(new FileReader(file)),
                file.getAbsolutePath());
            return;
        }
        if (file.isDirectory()) {
            if (!recursive) {
                System.err.println(
                    "ERROR: -r not specified but directory given " +
                    file.getAbsolutePath());
                return;
            }
            for (File nf : file.listFiles()) {
                process(nf);    // "Recursion, n.: See Recursion."
            }
            return;
        }
        System.err.println(
            "WEIRDNESS: neither file nor directory: " + file.getAbsolutePath());
    }

    /** Do the work of scanning one file
     * @param      ifile    Reader     Reader object already open
     * @param      fileName String     Name of the input file
```

```
        */
    public void process(Reader ifile, String fileName) {

        String inputLine;
        int matches = 0;

        try (BufferedReader reader = new BufferedReader(ifile)) {

            while ((inputLine = reader.readLine()) != null) {
                matcher.reset(inputLine);
                if (matcher.find()) {
                    if (listOnly) {
                        // -l, print filename on first match, and we're done
                        System.out.println(fileName);
                        return;
                    }
                    if (countOnly) {
                        matches++;
                    } else {
                        if (!dontPrintFileName) {
                            System.out.print(fileName + ": ");
                        }
                        System.out.println(inputLine);
                    }
                } else if (inVert) {
                    System.out.println(inputLine);
                }
            }
            if (countOnly)
                System.out.println(matches + " matches in " + fileName);
        } catch (IOException e) {
            System.err.println(e);
        }
    }
}
```

## CHAPTER 5

Numbers

5.0. Introduction

Numbers are basic to just about any computation. They're used for array indices, temperatures, salaries, ratings, and an infinite variety of things. Yet they're not as simple as they seem. With floating-point numbers, how accurate is accurate? With random numbers, how random is random? With strings that should contain a number, what actually constitutes a number?

Java has several built-in or "primitive" types that can be used to represent numbers, summarized in Table 5-1 with their "wrapper" (object) types, as well as some numeric types that do not represent primitive types. Note that unlike languages such as C or Perl, which don't specify the size or precision of numeric types, Java—with its goal of portability—specifies these exactly and states that they are the same on all platforms.

Table 5-1. Numeric types

Built-in type	Object wrapper	Size of built-in (bits)	Contents
byte	Byte	8	Signed integer
short	Short	16	Signed integer
int	Integer	32	Signed integer
long	Long	64	Signed integer
float	Float	32	IEEE-754 floating point
double	Double	64	IEEE-754 floating point
char	Character	16	Unsigned Unicode character
n/a	BigInteger	unlimited	Arbitrary-size immutable integer value
n/a	BigDecimal	unlimited	Arbitrary-size-and-precision immutable floating-point value

As you can see, Java provides a numeric type for just about any purpose. There are four sizes of signed integers for representing various sizes of whole numbers. There are two sizes of floating-point numbers to approximate real numbers. There is also a type specifically designed to represent and allow operations on Unicode characters. The primitive numeric types are discussed here. The "Big" value types are described in Recipe 5.18.

When you read a string representing a number from user input or a text file, you need to convert it to the appropriate type. The object wrapper classes in the second column have several functions, one of which is to provide this basic conversion functionality—replacing the C programmer's *atoi*/*atof* family of functions and the numeric arguments to *scanf*.

Going the other way, you can convert any number (indeed, anything at all in Java) to a string just by using string concatenation. If you want a little bit of control over numeric formatting, Recipe 5.8 shows you how to use some of the object wrappers' conversion routines. And if you want full control, that recipe also shows the use of `NumberFormat` and its related classes to provide full control of formatting.

As the name *object wrapper* implies, these classes are also used to "wrap" a number in a Java object, as many parts of the standard API are defined in terms of objects. Later on, Recipe 10.18 shows using an `Integer` object to save an `int`'s value to a file using object serialization, and retrieving the value later.

But I haven't yet mentioned the issues of floating point. Real numbers, you may recall, are numbers with a fractional part. There is an infinite number of real numbers. A floating-point number—what a computer uses to approximate a real number—is not the same as a real number. The number of floating-point numbers is finite, with only 2^{32} different bit patterns for `floats`, and $2\backslash{}^{64}$ for `doubles`. Thus, most real values have only an approximate correspondence to floating point. The result of printing the real number 0.3 works correctly, as in:

```
// RealValues.java
System.out.println("The real value 0.3 is " + 0.3);
```

results in this printout:

```
The real value 0.3 is 0.3
```

But the difference between a real value and its floating-point approximation can accumulate if the value is used in a computation; this is often called a *rounding error*. Continuing the previous example, the real 0.3 multiplied by 3 yields:

```
The real 0.3 times 3 is 0.89999999999999991
```

Surprised? Not only is it off by a bit from what you might expect, you will of course get the same output on any conforming Java implementation. I ran it on machines as disparate as an AMD/Intel PC with OpenBSD, a PC with Windows and the standard JDK, and on Mac OS X. Always the same answer.

And what about random numbers? How random are they? You have probably heard the expression "pseudorandom number generator, or PRNG." All conventional random number generators, whether written in Fortran, C, or Java, generate pseudo-random numbers. That is, they're not truly random! True randomness comes only from specially built hardware: an analog source of Brownian noise connected to an analog-to-digital converter, for example.[1] Your average PC of today may have some good sources of entropy, or even hardware-based sources of randomness (which have not been widely used or tested yet). However, pseudorandom number generators are good enough for most purposes, so we use them. Java provides one random generator in the base library `java.lang.Math`, and several others; we'll examine these in Recipe 5.13.

The class `java.lang.Math` contains an entire "math library" in one class, including trigonometry, conversions (including degrees to radians and back), rounding, truncating, square root, minimum, and maximum. It's all there. Check the javadoc for `java.lang.Math`.

The package `java.Math` contains support for "big numbers"—those larger than the normal built-in long integers, for example. See Recipe 5.18.

Java works hard to ensure that your programs are reliable. The usual ways you'd notice this are in the common requirement to catch potential exceptions—all through the Java API—and in the need to "cast" or convert when storing a value that might or might not fit into the variable you're trying to store it in. I'll show examples of these.

Overall, Java's handling of numeric data fits well with the ideals of portability, reliability, and ease of programming.

See Also

The Java Language Specification. The javadoc page for `java.lang.Math`.

5.1. Checking Whether a String Is a Valid Number

Problem

You need to check whether a given string contains a valid number, and, if so, convert it to binary (internal) form.

---

1. For a low-cost source of randomness, check out the now-defunct Lavarand (*http://en.wikipedia.org/wiki/Lavarand*). The process used digitized video of 1970s "lava lamps" to provide "hardware-based" randomness. Fun!

Solution

To accomplish this, use the appropriate wrapper class's conversion routine and catch the NumberFormatException. This code converts a string to a double :

```
public static void main(String[] argv) {
    String aNumber = argv[0];    // not argv[1]
    double result;
    try {
        result = Double.parseDouble(aNumber);
        System.out.println("Number is " + result);
    } catch(NumberFormatException exc) {
        System.out.println("Invalid number " + aNumber);
        return;
    }
}
```

Discussion

Of course, that lets you validate only numbers in the format that the designers of the wrapper classes expected. If you need to accept a different definition of numbers, you could use regular expressions (see Chapter 4) to make the determination.

There may also be times when you want to tell if a given number is an integer number or a floating-point number. One way is to check for the characters ., d, e, or f in the input; if one of these characters is present, convert the number as a double. Otherwise, convert it as an int:

```
public class GetNumber extends Frame {

    /** The input textField */
    private TextField textField;
    /** The results area */
    private TextField statusLabel;

    /** Constructor: set up the GUI */
    public GetNumber() {
        Panel p = new Panel();
        p.add(new Label("Number:"));
        p.add(textField = new TextField(10));
        add(BorderLayout.NORTH, p);
        textField.addActionListener(new ActionListener() {
            public void actionPerformed(ActionEvent ev) {
                String s = textField.getText();
                statusLabel.setText(process(s).toString());
            }
        });
        add(BorderLayout.SOUTH, statusLabel = new TextField(10));
        pack();
    }
```

```
    private static Number NAN = new Double(Double.NaN);

    /* Process one String, returning it as a Number subclass
     * Does not require the GUI.
     */
    public static Number process(String s) {
        if (s.matches("[+-]*\\d*\\.\\d+[dDeEfF]*")) {
            try {
                double dValue = Double.parseDouble(s);
                System.out.println("It's a double: " + dValue);
                return Double.valueOf(dValue);
            } catch (NumberFormatException e) {
                System.out.println("Invalid double: " + s);
                return NAN;
            }
        } else // did not contain . d e or f, so try as int.
            try {
                int iValue = Integer.parseInt(s);
                System.out.println("It's an int: " + iValue);
                return Integer.valueOf(iValue);
            } catch (NumberFormatException e2) {
                System.out.println("Not a number: " + s);
                return NAN;
            }
    }

    public static void main(String[] ap) {
        new GetNumber().setVisible(true);
    }
}
```

See Also

A more involved form of parsing is offered by the DecimalFormat class, discussed in Recipe 5.8.

There is also the Scanner class; see Recipe 10.6.

5.2. Storing a Larger Number in a Smaller Number

Problem

You have a number of a larger type and you want to store it in a variable of a smaller type.

Solution

Cast the number to the smaller type. (A *cast* is a type listed in parentheses before a value that causes the value to be treated as though it were of the listed type.)

For example, to cast a long to an int, you need a cast. To cast a double to a float, you also need a cast.

Discussion

This causes newcomers some grief because the default type for a number with a decimal point is double, not float. So code like:

```
float f = 3.0;
```

won't even compile! It's as if you had written:

```
double tmp = 3.0;
float f = tmp;
```

You can fix it in one of several ways:

- By making the 3.0 a float (probably the best solution)
- By making f a double
- By putting in a cast
- By assigning an integer value of 3, which will get "promoted" (e.g., float f = 3)

```
float f = 3.0f; // or just 3f
double f = 3.0;
float f = (float)3.0;
float f = 3;
```

The same applies when storing an int into a short, char, or byte:

```
public static void main(String[] argv) {
    int i;
    double j = 2.75;
    i = j;              // EXPECT COMPILE ERROR
    i = (int)j;         // with cast; i gets 2
    System.out.println("i =" + i);
    byte b;
    b = i;              // EXPECT COMPILE ERROR
    b = (byte)i;        // with cast, i gets 2
    System.out.println("b =" + b);
}
```

The lines marked EXPECT COMPILE ERROR do not compile unless either commented out or changed to be correct. The lines marked "with cast" show the correct forms.

5.3. Converting Numbers to Objects and Vice Versa

Problem

You need to convert numbers to objects and objects to numbers.

Solution

Use the Object Wrapper classes listed in Table 5-1 at the beginning of this chapter.

Discussion

Often you have a primitive number and you need to pass it into a method where an `Object` is required, or vice versa. Long ago you had to invoke the conversion routines that are part of the `wrapper` classes, but now you can generally use automatic conversion (called "autoboxing"/"autounboxing"). See Example 5-1 for examples of both.

Example 5-1. AutoboxDemo.java

```java
public class AutoboxDemo {

    /** Shows autoboxing (in the call to foo(i), i is wrapped automatically)
     * and auto-unboxing (the return value is automatically unwrapped).
     */
    public static void main(String[] args) {
        int i = 42;
        int result = foo(i);              ❶
        System.out.println(result);
    }

    public static Integer foo(Integer i) {
        System.out.println("Object = " + i);
        return Integer.valueOf(123);      ❷
    }
}
```

❶ Autoboxing: `int 42` is converted to `Integer(42)`. Also auto-unboxing: the `Integer` returned from `foo()` is auto-unboxed to assign to `int result`.

❷ No Auto-boxing: `valueOf()` returns `Integer`. If the line said `return Integer.intValueOf(123)` then it would be a second example of auto-boxing because the method return value is `Integer`.

To explicitly convert between an `int` and an `Integer` object, or vice versa, you can use the `wrapper` class methods:

```java
public class IntObject {
    public static void main(String[] args) {
        // int to Integer
        Integer i1 = Integer.valueOf(42);
        System.out.println(i1.toString());      // or just i1

        // Integer to int
        int i2 = i1.intValue();
        System.out.println(i2);
```

```
        }
    }
```

5.4. Taking a Fraction of an Integer Without Using Floating Point

Problem

You want to multiply an integer by a fraction without converting the fraction to a floating-point number.

Solution

Multiply the integer by the numerator and divide by the denominator.

This technique should be used only when efficiency is more important than clarity because it tends to detract from the readability—and therefore the maintainability—of your code.

Discussion

Because integers and floating-point numbers are stored differently, it may sometimes be desirable and feasible, for efficiency purposes, to multiply an integer by a fractional value without converting the values to floating point and back, and without requiring a "cast":

```
public class FractMult {
    public static void main(String[] u) {

        double d1 = 0.666 * 5;   // fast but obscure and inaccurate: convert
        System.out.println(d1); // 2/3 to 0.666 in programmer's head

        double d2 = 2/3 * 5;     // wrong answer - 2/3 == 0, 0*5 = 0
        System.out.println(d2);

        double d3 = 2d/3d * 5;   // "normal"
        System.out.println(d3);

        double d4 = (2*5)/3d;    // one step done as integers, almost same answer
        System.out.println(d4);

        int i5 = 2*5/3;          // fast, approximate integer answer
        System.out.println(i5);
    }
}
```

Running it looks like this:

```
$ java numbers.FractMult
3.33
0.0
3.333333333333333
3.3333333333333335
3
$
```

You should also beware of the possibility of numeric overflow, and avoid this optimization if you cannot guarantee that the multiplication by the numerator will not overflow.

5.5. Ensuring the Accuracy of Floating-Point Numbers

Problem

You want to know if a floating-point computation generated a sensible result.

Solution

Compare with the INFINITY constants, and use isNaN() to check for "not a number."

Fixed-point operations that can do things like divide by zero result in Java notifying you abruptly by throwing an exception. This is because integer division by zero is considered a *logic error*.

Floating-point operations, however, do not throw an exception because they are defined over an (almost) infinite range of values. Instead, they signal errors by producing the constant POSITIVE_INFINITY if you divide a positive floating-point number by zero, the constant NEGATIVE_INFINITY if you divide a negative floating-point value by zero, and NaN (Not a Number) if you otherwise generate an invalid result. Values for these three public constants are defined in both the Float and the Double wrapper classes. The value NaN has the unusual property that it is not equal to itself (i.e., NaN != NaN). Thus, it would hardly make sense to compare a (possibly suspect) number against NaN, because the following expression can never be true:

```
x == NaN
```

can never be true. Instead, the methods Float.isNaN(float) and Double.isNaN(double) must be used:

```
public static void main(String[] argv) {
    double d = 123;
    double e = 0;
    if (d/e == Double.POSITIVE_INFINITY)
        System.out.println("Check for POSITIVE_INFINITY works");
    double s = Math.sqrt(-1);
    if (s == Double.NaN)
```

```
        System.out.println("Comparison with NaN incorrectly returns true");
    if (Double.isNaN(s))
        System.out.println("Double.isNaN() correctly returns true");
}
```

Note that this, by itself, is not sufficient to ensure that floating-point calculations have been done with adequate accuracy. For example, the following program demonstrates a contrived calculation—Heron's formula for the area of a triangle—both in float and in double. The double values are correct, but the floating-point value comes out as zero due to rounding errors. This happens because, in Java, operations involving only float values are performed as 32-bit calculations. Related languages such as C automatically promote these to double during the computation, which can eliminate some loss of accuracy. Let's take a look:

```
public class Heron {
    public static void main(String[] args) {
        // Sides for triangle in float
        float af, bf, cf;
        float sf, areaf;

        // Ditto in double
        double ad, bd, cd;
        double sd, aread;

        // Area of triangle in float
        af = 12345679.0f;
        bf = 12345678.0f;
        cf = 1.01233995f;

        sf = (af+bf+cf)/2.0f;
        areaf = (float)Math.sqrt(sf * (sf - af) * (sf - bf) * (sf - cf));
        System.out.println("Single precision: " + areaf);

        // Area of triangle in double
        ad = 12345679.0;
        bd = 12345678.0;
        cd = 1.01233995;

        sd = (ad+bd+cd)/2.0d;
        aread =        Math.sqrt(sd * (sd - ad) * (sd - bd) * (sd - cd));
        System.out.println("Double precision: " + aread);
    }
}
```

Now let's run it. To ensure that the rounding is not an implementation artifact, I'll try it both with Sun's JDK and with an ancient implementation of Kaffe (once an alternative Java SE implementation):

```
$ java numbers.Heron
Single precision: 0.0
Double precision: 972730.0557076167
```

```
$ kaffe Heron
Single precision: 0.0
Double precision: 972730.05570761673
```

If in doubt, use double!

To ensure consistency of very large magnitude double computations on different Java implementations, Java provides the keyword strictfp, which can apply to classes, interfaces, or methods within a class.[2] If a computation is Strict-FP, then it must always, for example, return the value INFINITY if a calculation would overflow the value of Double.MAX_VALUE (or underflow the value Double.MIN_VALUE). Non-Strict-FP calculations—the default—are allowed to perform calculations on a greater range and can return a valid final result that is in range even if the interim product was out of range. This is pretty esoteric and affects only computations that approach the bounds of what fits into a double.

5.6. Comparing Floating-Point Numbers

Problem

You want to compare two floating-point numbers for equality.

Solution

Based on what we've just discussed, you probably won't just go comparing two floats or doubles for equality. You might expect the floating-point wrapper classes, Float and Double, to override the equals() method, which they do. The equals() method returns true if the two values are the same bit for bit (i.e., if and only if the numbers are the same or are both NaN). It returns false otherwise, including if the argument passed in is null, or if one object is +0.0 and the other is –0.0.

If this sounds weird, remember that the complexity comes partly from the nature of doing real number computations in the less-precise floating-point hardware, and partly from the details of the IEEE Standard 754, which specifies the floating-point functionality that Java tries to adhere to, so that underlying floating-point processor hardware can be used even when Java programs are being interpreted.

To actually compare floating-point numbers for equality, it is generally desirable to compare them within some tiny range of allowable differences; this range is often regarded as a tolerance or as *epsilon*. Example 5-2 shows an equals() method you can

---

2. Note that an expression consisting entirely of compile-time constants, like Math.PI * 2.1e17, is also considered to be Strict-FP.

use to do this comparison, as well as comparisons on values of NaN. When run, it prints that the first two numbers are equal within epsilon:

```
$ java numbers.FloatCmp
True within epsilon 1.0E-7
$
```

Example 5-2. FloatCmp.java

```java
public class FloatCmp {

    final static double EPSILON = 0.0000001;

    public static void main(String[] argv) {
        double da = 3 * .3333333333;
        double db = 0.99999992857;

        // Compare two numbers that are expected to be close.
        if (da == db) {
            System.out.println("Java considers " + da + "==" + db);
        // else compare with our own equals overload
        } else if (equals(da, db, 0.0000001)) {
            System.out.println("Equal within epsilon " + EPSILON);
        } else {
            System.out.println(da + " != " + db);
        }

        System.out.println("NaN prints as " + Double.NaN);

        // Show that comparing two NaNs is not a good idea:
        double nan1 = Double.NaN;
        double nan2 = Double.NaN;
        if (nan1 == nan2)
            System.out.println("Comparing two NaNs incorrectly returns true.");
        else
            System.out.println("Comparing two NaNs correctly reports false.");

        if (new Double(nan1).equals(new Double(nan2)))
            System.out.println("Double(NaN).equals(NaN) correctly returns true.");
        else
            System.out.println("Double(NaN).equals(NaN) incorrectly returns false.");
    }

    /** Compare two doubles within a given epsilon */
    public static boolean equals(double a, double b, double eps) {
        if (a==b) return true;
        // If the difference is less than epsilon, treat as equal.
        return Math.abs(a - b) < eps;
    }

    /** Compare two doubles, using default epsilon */
    public static boolean equals(double a, double b) {
        return equals(a, b, EPSILON);
```

```
        }
}
```

Note that neither of the `System.err` messages about "incorrect returns" prints. The point of this example with NaNs is that you should always make sure values are not NaN before entrusting them to `Double.equals()`.

5.7. Rounding Floating-Point Numbers

Problem

You need to round floating-point numbers to integers or to a particular precision.

Solution

If you simply cast a floating value to an integer value, Java truncates the value. A value like 3.999999 cast to an `int` or `long` becomes 3, not 4. To round floating-point numbers properly, use `Math.round()`. It has two overloads: if you give it a `double`, you get a `long` result; if you give it a `float`, you get an `int`.

What if you don't like the rounding rules used by `round`? If, for some bizarre reason, you wanted to round numbers greater than 0.54 instead of the normal 0.5, you could write your own version of `round()`:

```
public class Round {
    /** We round a number up if its fraction exceeds this threshold. */
    public static final double THRESHOLD = 0.54;

    /*
     * Round floating values to integers.
     * @return the closest int to the argument.
     * @param d A non-negative values to be rounded.
     */
    public static int round(double d) {
        return (int)Math.floor(d + 1.0 - THRESHOLD);
    }

    public static void main(String[] argv) {
        for (double d = 0.1; d<=1.0; d+=0.05) {
            System.out.println("My way:   " + d + "-> " + round(d));
            System.out.println("Math way:" + d + "-> " + Math.round(d));
        }
    }
}
```

If, on the other hand, you simply want to display a number with less precision than it normally gets, you probably want to use a `DecimalFormat` object or a `Formatter` object, which we look at in Recipe 5.8.

5.8. Formatting Numbers

Problem

You need to format numbers.

Solution

Use a NumberFormat subclass.

Java did not originally provide C-style *printf/scanf* functions because they tend to mix together formatting and input/output in a very inflexible way. Programs using *printf/scanf* can be hard to internationalize, for example. Of course, "by popular demand," Java did eventually introduce printf(), which along with String.format() is now standard in Java; see Recipe 10.4.

Java has an entire package, java.text, full of formatting routines as general and flexible as anything you might imagine. As with *printf*, it has an involved formatting language, described in the javadoc page. Consider the presentation of long numbers. In North America, the number one thousand twenty-four and a quarter is written 1,024.25, in most of Europe it is 1 024,25, and in some other part of the world it might be written 1.024,25. Not to mention how currencies and percentages are formatted! Trying to keep track of this yourself would drive the average small software shop around the bend rather quickly.

Fortunately, the java.text package includes a Locale class, and, furthermore, the Java runtime automatically sets a default Locale object based on the user's environment; (on the Macintosh and Windows, the user's preferences, and on Unix, the user's environment variables). (To provide a nondefault locale, see Recipe 15.8.) To provide formatters customized for numbers, currencies, and percentages, the NumberFormat class has static *factory methods* that normally return a DecimalFormat with the correct pattern already instantiated. A DecimalFormat object appropriate to the user's locale can be obtained from the factory method NumberFormat.getInstance() and manipulated using set methods. Surprisingly, the method setMinimumIntegerDigits() turns out to be the easy way to generate a number format with leading zeros. Here is an example:

```
public class NumFormat2 {
    /** A number to format */
    public static final double data[] = {
        0, 1, 22d/7, 100.2345678
    };

    /** The main (and only) method in this class. */
    public static void main(String[] av) {
        // Get a format instance
        NumberFormat form = NumberFormat.getInstance();
```

```
            // Set it to look like 999.99[99]
            form.setMinimumIntegerDigits(3);
            form.setMinimumFractionDigits(2);
            form.setMaximumFractionDigits(4);

            // Now print using it.
            for (int i=0; i<data.length; i++)
                System.out.println(data[i] + "\tformats as " +
                    form.format(data[i]));
        }
    }
```

This prints the contents of the array using the `NumberFormat` instance `form`:

```
$ java numbers.NumFormat2
0.0      formats as 000.00
1.0      formats as 001.00
3.142857142857143        formats as 003.1429
100.2345678      formats as 100.2346
$
```

You can also construct a `DecimalFormat` with a particular pattern or change the pattern dynamically using `applyPattern()`. Some of the more common pattern characters are shown in Table 5-2.

Table 5-2. DecimalFormat pattern characters

Character	Meaning
#	Numeric digit (leading zeros suppressed)
0	Numeric digit (leading zeros provided)
.	Locale-specific decimal separator (decimal point)
,	Locale-specific grouping separator (comma in English)
-	Locale-specific negative indicator (minus sign)
%	Shows the value as a percentage
;	Separates two formats: the first for positive and the second for negative values
'	Escapes one of the above characters so it appears
Anything else	Appears as itself

The `NumFormatDemo` program uses one `DecimalFormat` to print a number with only two decimal places and a second to format the number according to the default locale:

```
/** A number to format */
public static final double intlNumber = 1024.25;
/** Another number to format */
public static final double ourNumber = 100.2345678;

    NumberFormat defForm = NumberFormat.getInstance();
    NumberFormat ourForm = new DecimalFormat("##0.##");
```

```
        // toPattern() will reveal the combination of #0., etc
        // that this particular Locale uses to format with!
        System.out.println("defForm's pattern is " +
            ((DecimalFormat)defForm).toPattern());
        System.out.println(intlNumber + " formats as " +
            defForm.format(intlNumber));
        System.out.println(ourNumber + " formats as " +
            ourForm.format(ourNumber));
        System.out.println(ourNumber + " formats as " +
            defForm.format(ourNumber) + " using the default format");
```

This program prints the given pattern and then formats the same number using several formats:

```
$ java numbers.NumFormatDemo
defForm's pattern is #,##0.###
1024.25 formats as 1,024.25
100.2345678 formats as 100.23
100.2345678 formats as 100.235 using the default format
$
```

See Also

Chapter 16; *Java I/O* by Elliotte Rusty Harold (O'Reilly) provides good coverage of "java.io" but has not been updated for "NIO."

5.9. Converting Between Binary, Octal, Decimal, and Hexadecimal

Problem

You want to display an integer as a series of bits—for example, when interacting with certain hardware devices—or in some alternative number base (binary is base 2, octal is base 8, decimal is 10, hexadecimal is 16). You want to convert a binary number or a hexadecimal value into an integer.

Solution

The class `java.lang.Integer` provides the solutions. Most of the time you can use `Integer.parseInt(String input, int radix)` to convert from any type of number to an `Integer`, and `Integer.toString(int input, int radix)` to go the other way. Example 5-3 shows some examples of using the `Integer` class.

Example 5-3. IntegerBinOctHexEtc.java

```
        String input = "101010";
        for (int radix : new int[] { 2, 8, 10, 16, 36 }) {
            System.out.print(input + " in base " + radix + " is "
```

```
                + Integer.valueOf(input, radix) + "; ");
        int i = 42;
        System.out.println(i + " formatted in base " + radix + " is "
                + Integer.toString(i, radix));
    }
```

This program prints the binary string as an integer in various bases, and the integer 42 in those same number bases:

```
$ java numbers.IntegerBinOctHexEtc
101010 in base 2 is 42; 42 formatted in base 2 is 101010
101010 in base 8 is 33288; 42 formatted in base 8 is 52
101010 in base 10 is 101010; 42 formatted in base 10 is 42
101010 in base 16 is 1052688; 42 formatted in base 16 is 2a
101010 in base 36 is 60512868; 42 formatted in base 36 is 16
$
```

Discussion

There are also specialized versions of toString(int) that don't require you to specify the radix; for example, toBinaryString() to convert an integer to binary, toHex-String() for hexadecimal, and so on. The javadoc page for the Integer class is your friend here.

Going the other way, the Integer class includes toBinaryString(), toOctal-String(), and toHexString().

The String class itself includes a series of static methods—valueOf(int), val-ueOf(double), and so on—that also provide default formatting. That is, they return the given numeric value formatted as a string.

5.10. Operating on a Series of Integers

Problem

You need to work on a range of integers.

Solution

For a contiguous set, use a for loop.

Discussion

To process a contiguous set of integers, Java provides a for loop.[3] Loop control for the for loop is in three parts: initialize, test, and change. If the test part is initially false, the loop will never be executed, not even once.

For discontinuous ranges of numbers, use a java.util.BitSet.

The following program demonstrates all of these techniques:

```java
public class NumSeries {
    public static void main(String[] args) {

        // When you want an ordinal list of numbers, use a for loop
        // starting at 1.
        for (int i = 1; i <= months.length; i++)
            System.out.println("Month # " + i);

        // When you want a set of array indices, use a for loop
        // starting at 0.
        for (int i = 0; i < months.length; i++)
            System.out.println("Month " + months[i]);

        // For e.g., counting by 3 from 11 to 27, use a for loop
        for (int i = 11; i <= 27; i += 3) {
            System.out.println("i = " + i);
        }


        // A discontiguous set of integers, using a BitSet

        // Create a BitSet and turn on a couple of bits.
        BitSet b = new BitSet();
        b.set(0);     // January
        b.set(3);     // April
        b.set(8);     // September

        // Presumably this would be somewhere else in the code.
        for (int i = 0; i<months.length; i++) {
            if (b.get(i))
                System.out.println("Month " + months[i]);
        }

        // Same example but shorter:
        // a discontiguous set of integers, using an array
        int[] numbers = {0, 3, 8};

        // Presumably this would be somewhere else in the code.
```

---

3. If the set of numbers is in an array or collection (see Chapter 7), use a "foreach" loop (see "Java 5 foreach loop" on page 833).

```
    for (int n : numbers) {
        System.out.println("Month: " + months[n]);
    }
}
/** The names of the months. See Dates/Times chapter for a better way */
protected static String months[] = {
    "January", "February", "March", "April",
    "May", "June", "July", "August",
    "September", "October", "November", "December"
};
}
```

5.11. Working with Roman Numerals

Problem

You need to format numbers as Roman numerals. Perhaps you've just written the next *Titanic* or *Star Wars* episode and you need to get the copyright date correct on the script. Or, on a more mundane level, you need to format page numbers in the front matter of a book.

Solution

Use my RomanNumberFormat class:

```
RomanNumberFormat nf = new RomanNumberFormat();
int year = LocalDate.now().getYear();
System.out.println(year + " -> " + nf.format(year));
```

Running RomanNumberSimple produces this output:

```
2014 -> MMXIV
```

Discussion

Nothing in the standard API formats Roman numerals. But the java.text.Format class is designed to be subclassed for precisely such unanticipated purposes, so I have done just that and developed a class to format numbers as Roman numerals. Here is a better and complete example program of using it to format the current year. I can pass a number of arguments on the command line, including a "-" where I want the year to appear (note that these arguments are normally not quoted; the "-" must be an argument all by itself, just to keep the program simple). I use it as follows:

```
$ java numbers.RomanYear Copyright (c) - Ian Darwin
Copyright (c) MMXIV Ian Darwin
$
```

The code for the RomanYear program is simple, yet it correctly puts spaces around the arguments:

```
public class RomanYear {

    public static void main(String[] argv) {

        RomanNumberFormat rf = new RomanNumberFormat();
        Calendar cal = Calendar.getInstance();
        int year = cal.get(Calendar.YEAR);

        // If no arguments, just print the year.
        if (argv.length == 0) {
            System.out.println(rf.format(year));
            return;
        }

        // Else a micro-formatter: replace "-" arg with year, else print.
        for (int i=0; i<argv.length; i++) {
            if (argv[i].equals("-"))
                System.out.print(rf.format(year));
            else
                System.out.print(argv[i]);      // e.g., "Copyright"
            System.out.print(' ');
        }
        System.out.println();
    }
}
```

Now here's the code for the `RomanNumberFormat` class. I did sneak in one additional class, `java.text.FieldPosition`. A `FieldPosition` simply represents the position of one numeric field in a string that has been formatted using a variant of `NumberFormat.format()`. You construct it to represent either the integer part or the fraction part (of course, Roman numerals don't have fractional parts). The `FieldPosition` methods `getBeginIndex()` and `getEndIndex()` indicate where in the resulting string the given field wound up.

Example 5-4 is the class that implements Roman number formatting. As the comments indicate, the one limitation is that the input number must be less than 4,000.

Example 5-4. RomanNumberFormat.java

```
public class RomanNumberFormat extends Format {

    private static final long serialVersionUID = -23038093319102357783L;

    /** Characters used in "Arabic to Roman", that is, format() methods. */
    final static char A2R[][] = {
            { 0, 'M' },
            { 0, 'C', 'D', 'M' },
            { 0, 'X', 'L', 'C' },
            { 0, 'I', 'V', 'X' },
    };
```

```
static class R2A {
    char ch;
    public R2A(char ch, int amount) {
        super();
        this.ch = ch;
        this.amount = amount;
    }
    int amount;
}

final static R2A[] R2A = {
    new R2A('M', 1000),
    new R2A('D', 500),
    new R2A('C', 100),
    new R2A('L', 50),
    new R2A('X', 10),
    new R2A('V', 5),
    new R2A('I', 1),
};

/** Format a given double as a Roman Numeral; just truncate to a
 * long, and call format(long).
 */
public String format(double n) {
    return format((long)n);
}

/** Format a given long as a Roman Numeral. Just call the
 * three-argument form.
 */
public String format(long n) {
    if (n <= 0 || n >= 4000)
        throw new NumberFormatException(n + " must be > 0 && < 4000");
    StringBuffer sb = new StringBuffer();
    format(Integer.valueOf((int)n), sb,
        new FieldPosition(NumberFormat.INTEGER_FIELD));
    return sb.toString();
}

/* Format the given Number as a Roman Numeral, returning the
 * Stringbuffer (updated), and updating the FieldPosition.
 * This method is the REAL FORMATTING ENGINE.
 * Method signature is overkill, but required as a subclass of Format.
 */
public StringBuffer format(Object on, StringBuffer sb, FieldPosition fp) {
    if (!(on instanceof Number))
        throw new IllegalArgumentException(on + " must be a Number object");
    if (fp.getField() != NumberFormat.INTEGER_FIELD)
        throw new IllegalArgumentException(
        fp + " must be FieldPosition(NumberFormat.INTEGER_FIELD");
    int n = ((Number)on).intValue();    // TODO: check in range.
```

```
        // First, put the digits on a tiny stack. Must be 4 digits.
        for (int i=0; i<4; i++) {
            int d=n%10;
            push(d);
            // System.out.println("Pushed " + d);
            n=n/10;
        }

        // Now pop and convert.
        for (int i=0; i<4; i++) {
            int ch = pop();
            // System.out.println("Popped " + ch);
            if (ch==0)
                continue;
            else if (ch <= 3) {
                for(int k=1; k<=ch; k++)
                    sb.append(A2R[i][1]); // I
            }
            else if (ch == 4) {
                sb.append(A2R[i][1]);     // I
                sb.append(A2R[i][2]);     // V
            }
            else if (ch == 5) {
                sb.append(A2R[i][2]);     // V
            }
            else if (ch <= 8) {
                sb.append(A2R[i][2]);     // V
                for (int k=6; k<=ch; k++)
                    sb.append(A2R[i][1]);    // I
            }
            else { // 9
                sb.append(A2R[i][1]);
                sb.append(A2R[i][3]);
            }
        }
        // fp.setBeginIndex(0);
        // fp.setEndIndex(3);
        return sb;
    }

    /** Parse a generic object, returning an Object */
    public Object parseObject(String what, ParsePosition where) {
        int n = 0;
        for (char ch : what.toUpperCase().toCharArray()) {
            for (R2A r : R2A) {
                if (r.ch == ch) {
                    n += r.amount;
                    break;
                }
            }
        }
        return new Long(n);
```

```
    }

    /* Implement a toy stack */
    protected int stack[] = new int[10];
    protected int depth = 0;

    /* Implement a toy stack */
    protected void push(int n) {
        stack[depth++] = n;
    }
    /* Implement a toy stack */
    protected int pop() {
        return stack[--depth];
    }
}
```

Several of the public methods are required because I wanted it to be a subclass of `Format`, which is abstract. This accounts for some of the complexity, like having three different format methods.

Note that the `parseObject( )` method is also required, but we don't actually implement parsing in this version. This is left as an exercise for the reader.

See Also

Java I/O (O'Reilly) includes an entire chapter on `NumberFormat` and develops the subclass `ExponentialNumberFormat`.

The online source for this book has `ScaledNumberFormat`, which prints numbers with a maximum of four digits and a computerish scale factor (B for bytes, K for kilo-, M for mega-, and so on).

5.12. Formatting with Correct Plurals

Problem

You're printing something like `"We used " + n + " items"`, but in English, "We used 1 items" is ungrammatical. You want "We used 1 item."

Solution

Use a `ChoiceFormat` or a conditional statement.

Use Java's ternary operator (`cond ? trueval:falseval`) in a string concatenation. Both zero and plurals get an "s" appended to the noun in English ("no books, one book, two books"), so we test for n==1:

```
public class FormatPlurals {
    public static void main(String[] argv) {
        report(0);
        report(1);
        report(2);
    }

    /** report -- using conditional operator */
    public static void report(int n) {
        System.out.println("We used " + n + " item" + (n==1?"":"s"));
    }
}
```

Does it work?

```
$ java numbers.FormatPlurals
We used 0 items
We used 1 item
We used 2 items
$
```

The final `println` statement is effectively equivalent to:

```
if (n==1)
    System.out.println("We used " + n + " item");
else
    System.out.println("We used " + n + " items");
```

This is a lot longer, in fact, so the ternary conditional operator is worth learning.

The `ChoiceFormat` is ideal for this. It is actually capable of much more, but here I'll show only this simplest use. I specify the values 0, 1, and 2 (or more), and the string values to print corresponding to each number. The numbers are then formatted according to the range they fall into:

```
public class FormatPluralsChoice extends FormatPlurals {

    // ChoiceFormat to just give pluralized word
    static double[] limits = { 0, 1, 2 };
    static String[] formats = { "reviews", "review", "reviews"};
    static ChoiceFormat pluralizedFormat = new ChoiceFormat(limits, formats);

    // ChoiceFormat to give English text version, quantified
    static ChoiceFormat quantizedFormat = new ChoiceFormat(
        "0#no reviews|1#one review|1<many reviews");

    // Test data
    static int[] data = { -1, 0, 1, 2, 3 };

    public static void main(String[] argv) {
        System.out.println("Pluralized Format");
        for (int i : data) {
            System.out.println("Found " + i + " " + pluralizedFormat.format(i));
```

```
    }

    System.out.println("Quantized Format");
    for (int i : data) {
        System.out.println("Found " + quantizedFormat.format(i));
    }
  }
}
```

This generates the same output as the basic version. It is slightly longer, but more general, and lends itself better to internationalization.

See Also

In addition to `ChoiceFormat`, the same result can be achieved with a `MessageFormat`, discussed in Chapter 15.

5.13. Generating Random Numbers

Problem

You need to generate random numbers in a hurry.

Solution

Use `java.lang.Math.random()` to generate random numbers. There is no claim that the random values it returns are very *good* random numbers, however. This code exercises the `random()` method:

```
// Random1.java
// java.lang.Math.random( ) is static, don't need any constructor calls
System.out.println("A random from java.lang.Math is " + Math.random( ));
```

Note that this method only generates double values. If you need integers, construct a `java.util.Random` object and call its `nextInt()` method; if you pass it an integer value, this will become the upper bound. Here I generate integers from 1 to 10:

```
public class RandomInt {
    public static void main(String[] a) {
        Random r = new Random();
        for (int i=0; i<1000; i++)
            // nextInt(10) goes from 0-9; add 1 for 1-10;
            System.out.println(1+r.nextInt(10));
    }
}
```

To see if my `RandomInt` demo was really working well, I used the Unix tools *sort* and *uniq*, which together give a count of how many times each value was chosen. For 1,000 integers, each of 10 values should be chosen about 100 times. I ran it twice to get a better idea of the distribution.

```
$ java numbers.RandomInt | sort | uniq -c | sort -k 2 -n
  96 1
 107 2
 102 3
 122 4
  99 5
 105 6
  97 7
  96 8
  79 9
  97 10
$ java -cp build numbers.RandomInt | sort | uniq -c | sort -k 2 -n
  86 1
  88 2
 110 3
  97 4
  99 5
 109 6
  82 7
 116 8
  99 9
 114 10
$
```

The next step is to run these through a statistical program to see how really random they are; we'll return to this in a minute.

In general, to generate random numbers, you need to construct a `java.util.Random` object (not just any old random object) and call its `next*()` methods. These methods include `nextBoolean()`, `nextBytes()` (which fills the given array of bytes with random values), `nextDouble()`, `nextFloat()`, `nextInt()`, and `nextLong()`. Don't be confused by the capitalization of `Float`, `Double`, etc. They return the primitive types `boolean`, `float`, `double`, etc., not the capitalized wrapper objects. Clear enough? Maybe an example will help:

```
// java.util.Random methods are non-static, so need to construct
Random r = new Random();
for (int i=0; i<10; i++)
System.out.println("A double from java.util.Random is " + r.nextDouble());
for (int i=0; i<10; i++)
System.out.println("An integer from java.util.Random is " + r.nextInt());
```

You can also use the `java.util.Random` `nextGaussian()` method, as shown next. The `nextDouble()` methods try to give a "flat" distribution between 0 and 1.0, in which each value has an equal chance of being selected. A Gaussian or normal distribution is a bell-curve of values from negative infinity to positive infinity, with the majority of the values around zero (0.0).

```
// Random3.java
Random r = new Random();
for (int i = 0; i < 10; i++)
    System.out.println("A gaussian random double is " + r.nextGaussian());
```

To illustrate the different distributions, I generated 10,000 numbers using `nextRan-dom()` first and then using `nextGaussian()`. The code for this is in *Random4.java* (not shown here) and is a combination of the previous programs with code to print the results into files. I then plotted histograms using the R statistics package (see *http://www.r-project.org*; the R script used to generate the graph is in *javasrc* under *src/main/resources*). The results are shown in Figure 5-1.

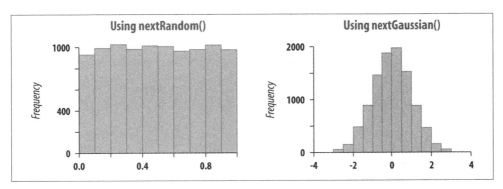

Figure 5-1. Flat (left) and Gaussian (right) distributions

See Also

The javadoc documentation for `java.util.Random`, and the warning in Recipe 5.0 about pseudorandomness versus real randomness.

For cryptographic use, see class `java.security.SecureRandom`, which provides cryptographically strong pseudorandom number generators (PRNG).

5.14. Calculating Trigonometric Functions

Problem

You need to compute sine, cosine, and other trigonometric functions.

Solution

Use the trig functions in `java.lang.Math`. Like `java.lang.Math.random()`, all the methods of the `Math` class are static, so no `Math` instance is necessary. This makes sense because none of these computations maintains any state. Note that the arguments for trigonometric functions are in radians, not in degrees. Here is a program that computes one trigonometric value and displays the values of e and PI that are available in the math library:

```
// Trig.java
System.out.println("The cosine of 1.1418 is " + Math.cos(1.1418));
System.out.println("Java's PI is " + Math.PI);
System.out.println("Java's e is " + Math.E);
```

The java.lang.StrictMath class is intended to perform the same operations as java.lang.Math but with greater cross-platform repeatability.

5.15. Taking Logarithms

Problem

You need to take the logarithm of a number.

Solution

For logarithms to base e, use java.lang.Math's log() function:

```
// Logarithm.java
double someValue;
// compute someValue...
double log_e = Math.log(someValue);
```

For logarithms to other bases, use the identity that:

$$\log_n (x) = \frac{\log_e (x)}{\log_e (n)}$$

where x is the number whose logarithm you want, n is any desired base, and e is the natural logarithm base. I have a simple LogBase class containing code that implements this functionality:

```
// LogBase.java
public static double log_base(double base, double value) {
    return Math.log(value) / Math.log(base);
}
```

Discussion

My log_base function allows you to compute logs to any positive base. If you have to perform a lot of logs to the same base, it is more efficient to rewrite the code to cache the log(base) once. Here is an example of using log_base:

```
// LogBaseUse.java
public static void main(String argv[]) {
```

```
        double d = LogBase.log_base(10, 10000);
        System.out.println("log10(10000) = " + d);
    }
C:> java numbers.LogBaseUse
log10(10000) = 4.0
```

5.16. Multiplying Matrices

Problem

You need to multiply a pair of two-dimensional arrays, as is common in mathematical and engineering applications.

Solution

Use the following code as a model.

Discussion

It is straightforward to multiply an array of a numeric type. The code in Example 5-5 implements matrix multiplication.

Example 5-5. Matrix.java

```java
public class Matrix {

    /* Matrix-multiply two arrays together.
     * The arrays MUST be rectangular.
     * @author Tom Christiansen & Nathan Torkington, Perl Cookbook version.
     */
    public static int[][] multiply(int[][] m1, int[][] m2) {
        int m1rows = m1.length;
        int m1cols = m1[0].length;
        int m2rows = m2.length;
        int m2cols = m2[0].length;
        if (m1cols != m2rows)
            throw new IllegalArgumentException(
                "matrices don't match: " + m1cols + " != " + m2rows);
        int[][] result = new int[m1rows][m2cols];

        // multiply
        for (int i=0; i<m1rows; i++) {
            for (int j=0; j<m2cols; j++) {
                for (int k=0; k<m1cols; k++) {
                    result[i][j] += m1[i][k] * m2[k][j];
                }
            }
        }

        return result;
```

```
    }

    /** Matrix print.
     */
    public static void mprint(int[][] a) {
        int rows = a.length;
        int cols = a[0].length;
        System.out.println("array["+rows+"]["+cols+"] = {");
        for (int i=0; i<rows; i++) {
            System.out.print("{");
            for (int j=0; j<cols; j++)
                System.out.print(" " + a[i][j] + ",");
            System.out.println("},");
        }
        System.out.println("};");
    }
}
```

Here is a program that uses the Matrix class to multiply two arrays of ints:

```
int x[][] = {
    { 3, 2, 3 },
    { 5, 9, 8 },
};
int y[][] = {
    { 4, 7 },
    { 9, 3 },
    { 8, 1 },
};
int z[][] = Matrix.multiply(x, y);
Matrix.mprint(x);
Matrix.mprint(y);
Matrix.mprint(z);
```

See Also

Consult a book on numerical methods for more things to do with matrices; one of our reviewers recommends *Numerical Recipes in Fortran* by Teukolsky, Flannery, et al., available as a PDF (*http://bit.ly/U3Dwzq*) and for online viewing (*http://bit.ly/1juEIlm*). The example recipes in that book have been translated into Java but are only available in this form to licensed purchasers of the software (*http://bit.ly/1p9MhDF*).

Commercial software packages can do some of these calculations for you; for one example, see the numeric libraries available from Rogue Wave Software (*http://www.rogue wave.com*).

5.17. Using Complex Numbers

Problem

You need to manipulate complex numbers, as is common in mathematical, scientific, or engineering applications.

Solution

Java does not provide any explicit support for dealing with complex numbers. You could keep track of the real and imaginary parts and do the computations yourself, but that is not a very well-structured solution.

A better solution, of course, is to use a class that implements complex numbers. I provide just such a class. First, an example of using it:

```java
public class ComplexDemo {
    /** The program */
    public static void main(String[] args) {
        Complex c = new Complex(3,  5);
        Complex d = new Complex(2, -2);
        System.out.println(c);
        System.out.println(c + ".getReal() = " + c.getReal());
        System.out.println(c + " + " + d + " = " + c.add(d));
        System.out.println(c + " + " + d + " = " + Complex.add(c, d));
        System.out.println(c + " * " + d + " = " + c.multiply(d));
        System.out.println(Complex.divide(c, d));
    }
}
```

Example 5-6 is the complete source for the `Complex` class and shouldn't require much explanation.

To keep the API general, I provide—for each of add, subtract, and multiply—both a static method that works on two complex objects and a nonstatic method that applies the operation to the given object and one other object.

Example 5-6. Complex.java

```java
public class Complex {
    /** The real part */
    private double r;
    /** The imaginary part */
    private double i;

    /** Construct a Complex */
    Complex(double rr, double ii) {
        r = rr;
        i = ii;
    }
```

```java
/** Display the current Complex as a String, for use in
 * println() and elsewhere.
 */
public String toString() {
    StringBuffer sb = new StringBuffer().append(r);
    if (i>0)
        sb.append('+');        // else append(i) appends - sign
    return sb.append(i).append('i').toString();
}

/** Return just the Real part */
public double getReal() {
    return r;
}
/** Return just the Real part */
public double getImaginary() {
    return i;
}
/** Return the magnitude of a complex number */
public double magnitude() {
    return Math.sqrt(r*r + i*i);
}

/** Add another Complex to this one
 */
public Complex add(Complex other) {
    return add(this, other);
}

/** Add two Complexes
 */
public static Complex add(Complex c1, Complex c2) {
    return new Complex(c1.r+c2.r, c1.i+c2.i);
}

/** Subtract another Complex from this one
 */
public Complex subtract(Complex other) {
    return subtract(this, other);
}

/** Subtract two Complexes
 */
public static Complex subtract(Complex c1, Complex c2) {
    return new Complex(c1.r-c2.r, c1.i-c2.i);
}

/** Multiply this Complex times another one
 */
public Complex multiply(Complex other) {
    return multiply(this, other);
```

```
        }

        /** Multiply two Complexes
         */
        public static Complex multiply(Complex c1, Complex c2) {
            return new Complex(c1.r*c2.r - c1.i*c2.i, c1.r*c2.i + c1.i*c2.r);
        }

        /** Divide c1 by c2.
         * @author Gisbert Selke.
         */
        public static Complex divide(Complex c1, Complex c2) {
            return new Complex(
                (c1.r*c2.r+c1.i*c2.i)/(c2.r*c2.r+c2.i*c2.i),
                (c1.i*c2.r-c1.r*c2.i)/(c2.r*c2.r+c2.i*c2.i));
        }

        /* Compare this Complex number with another
         */
        public boolean equals(Object o) {
            if (o.getClass() != Complex.class) {
                throw new IllegalArgumentException(
                        "Complex.equals argument must be a Complex");
            }
            Complex other = (Complex)o;
            return r == other.r && i == other.i;
        }

        /* Generate a hashCode; not sure how well distributed these are.
         */
        public int hashCode() {
            return (int)(r) |  (int)i;
        }
}
```

5.18. Handling Very Large Numbers

Problem

You need to handle integer numbers larger than Long.MAX_VALUE or floating-point values larger than Double.MAX_VALUE.

Solution

Use the BigInteger or BigDecimal values in package java.math, as shown in Example 5-7.

Example 5-7. BigNums.java

```
    System.out.println("Here's Long.MAX_VALUE: " + Long.MAX_VALUE);
    BigInteger bInt = new BigInteger("341922922333720368547758807");
    System.out.println("Here's a bigger number: " + bInt);
    System.out.println("Here it is as a double: " + bInt.doubleValue());
```

Note that the constructor takes the number as a string. Obviously you couldn't just type the numeric digits because, by definition, these classes are designed to represent numbers larger than will fit in a Java long.

Discussion

Both BigInteger and BigDecimal objects are immutable; that is, once constructed, they always represent a given number. That said, a number of methods return new objects that are mutations of the original, such as negate(), which returns the negative of the given BigInteger or BigDecimal. There are also methods corresponding to most of the Java language built-in operators defined on the base types int/long and float/double. The division method makes you specify the rounding method; consult a book on numerical analysis for details. Example 5-8 is a simple stack-based calculator using BigDecimal as its numeric data type.

Example 5-8. BigNumCalc

```
public class BigNumCalc {

    /** an array of Objects, simulating user input */
    public static Object[] testInput = {
        new BigDecimal("341922922333720368547758807.23343"),
        new BigDecimal("2.0"),
        "*",
    };

    public static void main(String[] args) {
        BigNumCalc calc = new BigNumCalc();
        System.out.println(calc.calculate(testInput));
    }

    /**
     * Stack of numbers being used in the calculator.
     */
    Stack<BigDecimal> stack = new Stack<>();

    /**
     * Calculate a set of operands; the input is an Object array containing
     * either BigDecimal objects (which may be pushed onto the Stack) and
     * operators (which are operated on immediately).
     * @param input
     * @return
     */
```

```java
public BigDecimal calculate(Object[] input) {
    BigDecimal tmp;
    for (int i = 0; i < input.length; i++) {
        Object o = input[i];
        if (o instanceof BigDecimal) {
            stack.push((BigDecimal) o);
        } else if (o instanceof String) {
            switch (((String)o).charAt(0)) {
            // + and * are commutative, order doesn't matter
            case '+':
                stack.push((stack.pop()).add(stack.pop()));
                break;
            case '*':
                stack.push((stack.pop()).multiply(stack.pop()));
                break;
            // - and /, order *does* matter
            case '-':
                tmp = (BigDecimal)stack.pop();
                stack.push((stack.pop()).subtract(tmp));
                break;
            case '/':
                tmp = stack.pop();
                stack.push((stack.pop()).divide(tmp,
                    BigDecimal.ROUND_HALF_UP));
                break;
            default:
                throw new IllegalStateException("Unknown OPERATOR popped");
            }
        } else {
            throw new IllegalArgumentException("Syntax error in input");
        }
    }
    return stack.pop();
}
}
```

Running this produces the expected (very large) value:

```
> javac -d . numbers/BigNumCalc.java
> java numbers.BigNumCalc
6838458446744073709551614.466860
>
```

The current version has its inputs hardcoded, as does the JUnit test program, but in real life you can use regular expressions to extract words or operators from an input stream (as in Recipe 4.5), or you can use the StreamTokenizer approach of the simple calculator (see Recipe 10.5). The stack of numbers is maintained using a java.util.Stack (see Recipe 7.18).

BigInteger is mainly useful in cryptographic and security applications. Its method isProbablyPrime() can create prime pairs for public key cryptography. BigDecimal might also be useful in computing the size of the universe.

5.19. Program: TempConverter

The program shown in Example 5-9 prints a table of Fahrenheit temperatures (still used in daily weather reporting in the United States) and the corresponding Celsius temperatures (used in science everywhere, and in daily life in most of the world).

Example 5-9. TempConverter.java

```
public class TempConverter {

    public static void main(String[] args) {
        TempConverter t = new TempConverter();
        t.start();
        t.data();
        t.end();
    }

    protected void start() {
    }

    protected void data() {
        for (int i=-40; i<=120; i+=10) {
            float c = (i-32)*(5f/9);
            print(i, c);
        }
    }

    protected void print(float f, float c) {
        System.out.println(f + " " + c);
    }

    protected void end() {
    }
}
```

This works, but these numbers print with about 15 digits of (useless) decimal fractions! The second version of this program subclasses the first and uses printf (see Recipe 10.4) to control the formatting of the converted temperatures (see Example 5-10). It will now look right, assuming you're printing in a monospaced font.

Example 5-10. TempConverter2.java

```
public class TempConverter2 extends TempConverter {

    public static void main(String[] args) {
        TempConverter t = new TempConverter2();
```

```
        t.start();
        t.data();
        t.end();
    }

    protected void print(float f, float c) {
        System.out.printf("%6.2f %6.2f%n", f, c);
    }

    protected void start() {
        System.out.println("Fahr    Centigrade");
    }

    protected void end() {
        System.out.println("------------------");
    }
}

C:\javasrc\numbers>java numbers.TempConverter2
Fahr    Centigrade
-40.00 -40.00
-30.00 -34.44
-20.00 -28.89
-10.00 -23.33
  0.00 -17.78
 10.00 -12.22
 20.00  -6.67
 30.00  -1.11
 40.00   4.44
 50.00  10.00
 60.00  15.56
 70.00  21.11
 80.00  26.67
 90.00  32.22
100.00  37.78
110.00  43.33
120.00  48.89
```

5.20. Program: Number Palindromes

My wife, Betty, recently reminded me of a theorem that I must have studied in high school but whose name I have long since forgotten: that any positive integer number can be used to generate a palindrome by adding to it the number comprised of its digits in reverse order. Palindromes are sequences that read the same in either direction, such as the name "Anna" or the phrase "Madam, I'm Adam" (ignoring spaces and punctuation). We normally think of palindromes as composed of text, but the concept can be applied to numbers: 13531 is a palindrome. Start with the number 72, for example, and add to it the number 27. The results of this addition is 99, which is a (short) palindrome. Starting with 142, add 241, and you get 383. Some numbers take more than one try to generate a palindrome. 1951 + 1591 yields 3542, which is not palindromic. The second round, however, 3542 + 2453, yields 5995, which is. The number 17,892, which my son Benjamin picked out of the air, requires 12 rounds to generate a palindrome, but it does terminate:

```
C:\javasrc\numbers>java  numbers.Palindrome 72 142 1951 17892
Trying 72
72->99
Trying 142
142->383
Trying 1951
Trying 3542
1951->5995
Trying 17892
Trying 47763
Trying 84537
Trying 158085
Trying 738936
Trying 1378773
Trying 5157504
Trying 9215019
Trying 18320148
Trying 102422529
Trying 1027646730
Trying 1404113931
17892->2797227972

C:\javasrc\numbers>
```

If this sounds to you like a natural candidate for recursion, you are correct. *Recursion* involves dividing a problem into simple and identical steps, which can be implemented by a function that calls itself and provides a way of termination. Our basic approach, as shown in method findPalindrome, is:

```
long findPalindrome(long num) {
    if (isPalindrome(num))
        return num;
    return findPalindrome(num + reverseNumber(num));
}
```

That is, if the starting number is already a palindromic number, return it; otherwise, add it to its reverse, and try again. The version of the code shown here handles simple cases directly (single digits are always palindromic, for example). We won't think about negative numbers because these have a character at the front that loses its meaning if placed at the end, and hence are not strictly palindromic. Further, palindromic forms of certain numbers are too long to fit in Java's 64-bit long integer. These cause underflow, which is trapped. As a result, an error message like "too big" is reported.[4] Having said all that, Example 5-11 shows the code.

Example 5-11. Palindrome.java

```java
public class Palindrome {

    public static boolean verbose = true;

    public static void main(String[] argv) {
        for (int i=0; i<argv.length; i++)
            try {
                long l = Long.parseLong(argv[i]);
                if (l < 0) {
                    System.err.println(argv[i] + " -> TOO SMALL");
                    continue;
                }
                System.out.println(argv[i] + "->" + findPalindrome(l));
            } catch (NumberFormatException e) {
                System.err.println(argv[i] + "-> INVALID");
            } catch (IllegalStateException e) {
                System.err.println(argv[i] + "-> " + e);
            }
    }

    /** find a palindromic number given a starting point, by
     * calling ourself until we get a number that is palindromic.
     */
    static long findPalindrome(long num) {
        if (num < 0)
            throw new IllegalStateException("negative");
        if (isPalindrome(num))
            return num;
        if (verbose)
            System.out.println("Trying " + num);
        return findPalindrome(num + reverseNumber(num));
    }

    /** The number of digits in Long.MAX_VALUE */
    protected static final int MAX_DIGITS = 19;

    // digits array is shared by isPalindrome and reverseNumber,
    // which cannot both be running at the same time.

    /* Statically allocated array to avoid new-ing each time. */
    static long[] digits = new long[MAX_DIGITS];

    /** Check if a number is palindromic. */
```

---

4. Certain values do not work; for example, Ashish Batia reported that this version gets an exception on the value 8989 (which it does).

```
    static boolean isPalindrome(long num) {
        // Consider any single digit to be as palindromic as can be
        if (num >= 0 && num <= 9)
            return true;

        int nDigits = 0;
        while (num > 0) {
            digits[nDigits++] = num % 10;
            num /= 10;
        }
        for (int i=0; i<nDigits/2; i++)
            if (digits[i] != digits[nDigits - i - 1])
                return false;
        return true;
    }

    static long reverseNumber(long num) {
        int nDigits = 0;
        while (num > 0) {
            digits[nDigits++] = num % 10;
            num /= 10;
        }
        long ret = 0;
        for (int i=0; i<nDigits; i++) {
            ret *= 10;
            ret += digits[i];
        }
        return ret;
    }
}
```

See Also

People using Java in scientific or large-scale numeric computing may wish to check out the historical archive of the Java Grande Forum (*http://www.javagrande.org*), which was once a working group aiming to ensure Java's usability in these realms.

## CHAPTER 6

Dates and Times—New API

6.0. Introduction

Developers suffered for a decade and a half under the inconsistencies and ambiguities of the `Date` class from Java 1.0 and its replacement-wannabe, the `Calendar` class from Java 1.1. Several alternative "`Date` replacement" packages emerged, including the simple and sensible Date4J (*http://date4j.net*) and the more comprehensive Joda-Time package (*http://bit.ly/1lCZLGH*). Java 8 introduced a new, consistent, and well-thought-out package for date and time handling, under the aegis of the Java Community Process, JSR-310, shepherded by Stephen Colbourne, based on his earlier package Joda-Time, but with several important design changes.[1] This package is biased toward "ISO 8601" dates; the default format is, for example, 2015-10-23T10:22:45. But it can, of course, work with other calendar schemes.

One of the key benefits of the new API is that it provides *useful operations* such as adding/subtracting dates/times. Much time was wasted by developers using the previous APIs re-implementing these over and over. That said, millions of lines of code are based on the old APIs, so we review them briefly, and consider interfacing the new API to legacy code, in the final recipe of this chapter, Recipe 6.7.

Another advantage of the new API is that almost all objects are immutable, and thus thread-safe. This can be of considerable benefit as we move headlong into the massively parallel era.

Because there are no `set` methods, and thus the "get" method paradigm doesn't always make sense, the API provides a series of new methods to replace such methods, listed in Table 6-1.

---

1. For those with an interest in historical arcana, the differences are documented on his blog (*http://bit.ly/1imu8iT*).

Table 6-1. New Date/Time API: Common methods

Name	Description
at	Combines with another object
format	Use provided formatter to produce a formatted string
from	Factory: Convert input parameters to instance of target
get	Retrieve one field from the instance
is	Examine the state of the given object
minus	Return a copy with the given amount subtracted
of	Factory: Create new method by parsing inputs
parse	Factory: Parse single input string to produce instance of target
plus	Return a copy with the given amount added
to	Convert this object to another type
with	Return a copy with the given field changed; replaces set methods

The JSR 310 API specifies a dozen or so main classes. Those representing times are either "continuous" or "human" time. Continuous time is based on Unix time—a deeper truth from the dawn of (computer) time, and is represented as a single monotonically increasing number. The "time" value of 0 in Unix represented the first second of January 1, 1970 UTC—about the time Unix was invented. Each unit of increment there represented one second of time. This has been used as a time base in most operating systems developed since. However, a 32-bit integer representing the number of seconds since 1970 runs out fairly soon—in the year 2038 AD. Most Unix systems have, in the aftermath of the Y2K frenzy, quietly and well in advance headed off a possible Y2038 frenzy by converting the time value from a 32-bit quantity to a 64-bit quantity. Java also used this time base, but based its time in milliseconds, because a 64-bit time in milliseconds since 1970 will not overlow until "quite a few" years into the future (keep this date open in your calendar—August 17, 292,278,994 CE).

```
Date endOfTime = new Date(Long.MAX_VALUE);
System.out.println("Java8 time overflows on " + endOfTime);
```

The new API is in five packages, as shown in Table 6-2; as usual, the top-level one contains the most commonly used pieces.

Table 6-2. New Date/Time API: Packages

Name	Description
java.time	Common classes for dates, times, instants, and durations
java.time.chrono	API for non-ISO calendar systems
java.time.format	Formatting classes (see Recipe 6.2)
java.time.temporal	Date and time access using fields, units, adjusters
java.time.zone	Support for time zones and their rules

The basic `java.time` package contains a dozen or so classes, as well as a couple of enums and one general-purpose exception (shown in Tables 6-3, 6-4, and 6-5).

Table 6-3. New Date/Time API: Basics

Class	Description
Instant	A point in time since January 1st, 1970, expressed in nanoseconds
Duration	A length of time, also expressed in nanoseconds

Human time represents times and dates as we use them in our everyday life. These classes are listed in Table 6-4.

Table 6-4. New Date/Time API: Human time

Class	Description
Calendrical	Connects to the low-level API
DateTimeFields	Stores a map of field-value pairs, which are not required to be consistent
DayOfWeek	A day of the week (e.g., Tuesday)
LocalDate	A bare date (day, month, and year) with no adjustments
LocalTime	A bare time (hour, minute, seconds) with no adjustments
LocalDateTime	The combination of the above
MonthDay	Month and day
OffsetTime	A time of day with a time zone offset like −04:00, with no date or zone
OffsetDateTime	A date and time with a time zone offset like −04:00 with no time zone
Period	A descriptive amount of time, such as "2 months and 3 days"
ZonedDateTime	The date and time with a time zone and an offset
Year	A year by itself
YearMonth	A year and month

Almost all the top-level classes directly extend `java.lang.Object` and are held to consistency by a variety of interfaces, which are declared in the subpackages. The date and time classes mostly implement `Comparable`, which makes sense.

Table 6-5 shows the two time zone–specific classes, used with `ZonedDateTime`, `OffsetDateTime`, and `OffsetTime`.

Table 6-5. New Date/Time API: Support

Class	Description
ZoneOffset	A time offset from UTC (hours, minutes, seconds)
ZoneId	Defines a time zone such as *Canada/Eastern*, and its conversion rules

The new API is a "fluent" API, in which most operations return the object they have operated upon, so that you can chain multiple calls without the need for tedious and annoying temporary variables:

```
LocalTime time = LocalTime.now().minusHours(5); // the time 5 hours ago
```

This results in a more natural and convenient coding style, in my opinion. You can always write code with lots of temporary variables if you want; you're the one who will have to read through it later.

6.1. Finding Today's Date

Problem

You want to find today's date and/or time.

Solution

Construct a LocalDate, LocalTime, or LocalDateTime object and call its to-String( ) method.

Discussion

Each of these classes is abstract, so you will need to call one of its factory methods to get an instance. They all provide a now( ) method, which does what its name implies. The CurrentDateTime demo program shows simple use of all three:

```
public class CurrentDateTime {
    public static void main(String[] args) {
        LocalDate dNow = LocalDate.now();
        System.out.println(dNow);
        LocalTime tNow = LocalTime.now();
        System.out.println(tNow);
        LocalDateTime now = LocalDateTime.now();
        System.out.println(now);
    }
}
```

Running it produces this output:

```
2013-10-28
22:23:55.641
2013-10-28T22:23:55.642
```

The formatting is nothing spectacular, but it's adequate. We'll deal with fancier formatting in the next recipe, Recipe 6.2.

6.2. Formatting Dates and Times

Problem

You want to provide better formatting for date and time objects.

Solution

Use `java.time.format.DateTimeFormatter`.

Discussion

The `DateTimeFormatter` class provides an amazing number of possible formatting styles. If you don't want to use one of the provided 20 or so predefined formats, you can define your own using `DateTimeFormatter.ofPattern(String pattern)`. The "pattern" string can contain any characters, but almost every letter of the alphabet has been defined to mean something, in addition to the obvious Y, M, D, h, m, and s. In addition, the quote character and square bracket characters are defined, and the sharp sign (#) and curly braces are "reserved for future use."

As is common with date formatting languages, the number of repetitions of a letter in the pattern gives a clue to its intended length of detail. Thus, for example, "MMM" gives "Jan," whereas "MMMM" gives "January."

Table 6-6 is an attempt at a complete list of the formatting characters, adapted from the javadoc for JSR-310.

Table 6-6. DateFormatter format characters

Symbol	Meaning	Presentation	Examples
G	Era	Text	AD; Anno Domini
y	Year-of-era	Year	2004; 04
u	Year-of-era	Year	See note.
D	Day-of-year	Number	189
M/L	Month-of-year	Number/text	7; 07; Jul; July; J
d	Day-of-month	Number	10
Q/q	Quarter-of-year	Number/text	3; 03; Q3, 3rd quarter
Y	Week-based-year	Year	1996; 96
w	Week-of-week-based year	Number	27
W	Week-of-month	Number	4
e/c	Localized day-of-week	Number/text	2; 02; Tue; Tuesday; T
E	Day-of-week	Text	Tue; Tuesday; T
F	Week-of-month	Number	3

Symbol	Meaning	Presentation	Examples
a	am-pm-of-day	Text	PM
h	Clock-hour-of-am-pm (1-12)	Number	12
K	Hour-of-am-pm (0-11)	Number	0
k	Clock-hour-of-am-pm (1-24)	Number	0
H	Hour-of-day (0-23)	Number	0
m	Minute-of-hour	Number	30
s	Second-of-minute	Number	55
S	Fraction-of-second	Fraction	978
A	Milli-of-day	Number	1234
n	Nano-of-second	Number	987654321
N	Nano-of-day	Number	1234000000
V	Time-zone ID	Zone-id	America/Los_Angeles; Z; −08:30
z	Time-zone name	Zone-name	Pacific Standard Time; PST
X	Zone-offset Z for zero	Offset-X	Z; −08; −0830; −08:30; −083015; −08:30:15;
x	Zone-offset	Offset-x	+0000; −08; −0830; −08:30; −083015; −08:30:15;
Z	Zone-offset	Offset-Z	+0000; −0800; −08:00;
O	Localized zone-offset	Offset-O	GMT+8; GMT+08:00; UTC−08:00;
p	Pad next	Pad modifier	1

 y and *u* work the same for A.D. years; however, for a year of 3 B.C., y pattern returns 3, whereas u pattern returns −2 (aka proleptic year).

Example 6-1 contains some examples of converting in both directions between strings and dates.

Example 6-1. DateFormatter.java—Example date formatting and parsing

```java
public class DateFormatter {
    public static void main(String[] args) {

        // Format a date ISO8601-like but with slashes instead of dashes
        DateTimeFormatter df = DateTimeFormatter.ofPattern("yyyy/LL/dd");
        System.out.println(df.format(LocalDate.now()));

        // Parse a String to a date using the same formatter
        System.out.println(LocalDate.parse("2014/04/01", df));

        // Format a Date and Time without timezone information
        DateTimeFormatter nTZ =
```

```
          DateTimeFormatter.ofPattern("d MMMM, yyyy h:mm a");
      System.out.println(ZonedDateTime.now().format(nTZ));
  }
}
```

6.3. Converting Among Dates/Times, YMDHMS, and Epoch Seconds

Problem

You need to convert among dates/times, YMDHMS, Epoch seconds, or some other numeric value.

Solution

Use the appropriate Date/Time factory or retrieval methods.

Discussion

"The Epoch" is the beginning of time as far as modern operating systems go. Unix time, and some versions of Windows time, count off inexorably the seconds since the Epoch. When Ken Thompson and Dennis Ritchie came up with this format in 1970, seconds seemed like a fine measure, and 32 bits' worth of seconds seemed nearly infinite. On systems that store this in a 32-bit integer, however, time is running out. Older versions of most operating systems stored this as a 32-bit signed integer, which unfortunately will overflow in the year 2038.

When Java first came out, it featured a method called System.currentTimeMillis(), presenting Epoch seconds with millisecond accuracy. The new Java API uses "epoch nanoseconds," which are still on the same time base.

Any of these epoch-related numbers can be converted into, or obtained from, a local date/time. Other numbers can also be used, such as integer years, months, and days. As usual, there are factory methods that create new objects where a change is requested. Here is a program that shows some of these conversions in action:

DateConversions.java

```
// Convert a number of Seconds since the Epoch, to a local date/time
Instant epochSec = Instant.ofEpochSecond(1000000000L);
ZoneId zId = ZoneId.systemDefault();
ZonedDateTime then = ZonedDateTime.ofInstant(epochSec, zId);
System.out.println("The epoch was a billion seconds old on " + then);

// Convert a date/time to Epoch seconds
long epochSecond = ZonedDateTime.now().toInstant().getEpochSecond();
System.out.println("Current epoch seconds = " + epochSecond);
```

```
LocalDateTime now = LocalDateTime.now();
ZonedDateTime there = now.atZone(ZoneId.of("Canada/Pacific"));
System.out.printf("When it's %s here, it's %s in Vancouver%n",
    now, there);
```

6.4. Parsing Strings into Dates

Problem

You need to convert user input into `java.time` objects.

Solution

Use a `parse()` method.

Discussion

Many of the date/time classes have a `parse()` factory method, which tries to parse a string into an object of that class. For example, `LocalDate.parse(String)` returns a `LocalDate` object for the date given in the input `String`:

```
/** Show some date parses */
public class DateParse {
    public static void main(String[] args) {

        String armisticeDate = "1914-11-11";
        LocalDate aLD = LocalDate.parse(armisticeDate);
        System.out.println("Date: " + aLD);

        String armisticeDateTime = "1914-11-11T11:11";
        LocalDateTime aLDT = LocalDateTime.parse(armisticeDateTime);
        System.out.println("Date/Time: " + aLDT);
```

As you probably expect by now, the default format is the ISO8601 date format. However, we often have to deal with dates in other formats. For this, the `DateTimeFormatter` allows you to specify a particular pattern. For example, "dd MMM uuuu" represents the day of the month (two digits), three letters of the name of the month (Jan, Feb, Mar, …), and a four-digit year:

```
DateTimeFormatter df = DateTimeFormatter.ofPattern("dd MMM uuuu");
String anotherDate = "27 Jan 2011";
LocalDate random = LocalDate.parse(anotherDate, df);
System.out.println(anotherDate + " parses as " + random);
```

As its name implies, the `DateTimeFormatter` object is bidirectional; it can both parse input and format output. We could add this line to the `DateParse` example:

```
System.out.println(aLD + " formats as " + df.format(aLD));
```

When we run the program, we see the output as follows:

```
Date: 1914-11-11
Date/Time: 1914-11-11T11:11
27 Jan 2011 parses as 2011-01-27
1914-11-11 formats as 11 Nov 1914
```

6.5. Difference Between Two Dates

Problem

You need to compute the difference between two dates.

Solution

Use the static method `Period.between()` to find the difference between two `Local-Dates`.

Discussion

Given two `LocalDate` objects, you can find the difference between them, as a `Period`, simply using the static `Period.between()` method. You can `toString()` the `Period` or, if its default format isn't good enough, format the result yourself:

```java
import java.time.LocalDate;
import java.time.Period;

public class DateDiff {

    public static void main(String[] args) {
        /** The date at the end of the last century */
        LocalDate endofCentury = LocalDate.of(2000, 12, 31);
        LocalDate now = LocalDate.now();

        Period diff = Period.between(endofCentury, now);

        System.out.printf("The 21st century (up to %s) is %s old%n", now, diff);
        System.out.printf(
                "The 21st century is %d years, %d months and %d days old",
                diff.getYears(), diff.getMonths(), diff.getDays());
    }
}
```

I'm editing this recipe at the end of October 2013; the 20th century A.D. ended at the end of 2000, so the value should be about $12 \, {}^{10}/_{12}$ years, and it is:

```
$ java datetime.DateDiff
The 21st century (up to 2013-10-28) is P12Y9M28D old
The 21st century is 12 years, 9 months and 28 days old
```

Because of the API's regularity, you can use the same technique with `LocalTime` or `LocalDateTime`.

See Also

A higher-level way of formatting date/time values is discussed in Recipe 6.2.

6.6. Adding to or Subtracting from a Date or Calendar

Problem

You need to add or subtract a fixed period to or from a date.

Solution

Create a past or future date by using a locution such as `LocalDate.plus(Period.of-Days(N));`.

Discussion

`java.time` offers a `Period` class to represent a length of time, such as a number of days, or hours and minutes. `LocalDate` and friends offer `plus()` and `minus()` methods to add or subtract a `Period` or other time-related object. `Period` offers factory methods such as `ofDays()`. The following code computes what the date will be 700 days from now:

```
import java.time.LocalDate;
import java.time.Period;

/** DateAdd -- compute the difference between two dates
 * (e.g., today and 700 days from now).
 */
public class DateAdd {
    public static void main(String[] av) {
        /** Today's date */
        LocalDate now =  LocalDate.now();

        Period p = Period.ofDays(700);
        LocalDate then = now.plus(p);

        System.out.printf("Seven hundred days from %s is %s%n", now, then);
    }
}
```

Running this program reports the current date and time, and what the date and time will be seven hundred days from now. For example:

```
Seven hundred days from 2013-11-09 is 2015-10-10
```

6.7. Interfacing with Legacy Date and Calendar Classes

Problem

You need to deal with the old Date and Calendar classes.

Solution

Assuming you have code using the original java.util.Date and java.util.Calendar, you can convert values as needed using conversion methods.

Discussion

All the classes and interfaces in the new API were chosen to avoid conflicting with the traditional API. It is thus possible, and will be common for a while, to have imports from both packages into the same code.

To keep the new API clean, most of the necessary conversion routines were added *to the old API*. Table 6-7 summarizes these conversion routines; note that the methods are static if they are shown being invoked with a capitalized class name, else they are instance methods.

Table 6-7. Legacy Date/Time interchange

Legacy Class	Convert to legacy	Convert to modern
java.util.Date	date.from(Instant)	Date.toInstant()
java.util.Calendar	calendar.toInstant()	-
java.util.GregorianCalendar	GregorianCalendar.from(ZonedDateTime)	calendar.toZonedDateTime()
java.util.TimeZone	-	timeZone.toZoneId()
java.time.DateTimeFormatter	-	dateTimeFormatter.toFormat()

The following code shows some of these APIs in action:

```
public class LegacyDates {
    public static void main(String[] args) {

        // There and back again, via Date
        Date legacyDate = new Date();
        System.out.println(legacyDate);

        LocalDateTime newDate =
            LocalDateTime.ofInstant(legacyDate.toInstant(),
            ZoneId.systemDefault());
        System.out.println(newDate);
```

```
        // And via Calendar
        Calendar c = Calendar.getInstance();
        System.out.println(c);
        LocalDateTime newCal =
            LocalDateTime.ofInstant(c.toInstant(),
            ZoneId.systemDefault());
        System.out.println(newCal);
    }
}
```

Of course you do not have to use these legacy converters; you are free to write your own. The file *LegacyDatesDIY.java* in the *javasrc* repository explores this option in the unlikely event you wish to pursue it.

Given the amount of code written before Java 8, it is likely that the legacy Date and Calendar will be around until the end of Java time.

The new Date/Time API has many capabilities that we have not explored. Almost enough for a small book on the subject, in fact. Meanwhile, you can study the API details at Oracle (*http://bit.ly/TPaYtk*).

## CHAPTER 7

Structuring Data with Java

7.0. Introduction

Almost every application beyond "Hello World" needs to keep track of some structured data. A simple numeric problem might work with three or four numbers only, but most applications have groups of similar data items. A GUI-based application may need to keep track of a number of dialog windows. A personal information manager, or PIM, needs to keep track of a number of, well, persons. An operating system needs to keep track of who is allowed to log in, who is currently logged in, and what those users are doing. A library needs to keep track of who has books checked out and when they're due. A network server may need to keep track of its active clients. A pattern emerges here, and it revolves around variations of what has traditionally been called *data structuring*.

There are data structures in the memory of a running program; there is structure in the data in a file on disk, and there is structure in the information stored in a database. In this chapter, we concentrate on the first aspect: in-memory data. We'll cover the second aspect in Chapter 10 and the third in Chapter 18.

If you had to think about in-memory data, you might want to compare it to a collection of index cards in a filing box, or to a treasure hunt where each clue leads to the next. Or you might think of it like my desk—apparently scattered, but actually a very powerful collection filled with meaningful information. Each of these is a good analogy for a type of data structuring that Java provides. An array is a fixed-length linear collection of data items, like the card filing box: it can only hold so much, then it overflows. The treasure hunt is like a data structure called a *linked list*. The first releases of Java had no standard linked list class, but you could write your own "traditional data structure" classes (and still can; you see a DIY Linked List implementation in Recipe 7.10). The complex collection represents Java's `Collection` classes. A document entitled *Collections Framework Overview*, distributed with the Java Development Kit documentation (and stored therein as file *…/docs/guide/collections/overview.html* and online (*http://bit.ly/1m8Wlu1*)), provides a detailed discussion of the Collections Framework. The framework aspects of Java collections are summarized in Recipe 7.3.

Beware of some typographic issues. The word `Arrays` (in constant width font) is short for the class `java.util.Arrays`, but in the normal typeface, the word "arrays" is simply the plural of "array" (and will be found capitalized at the beginning of a sentence). Also, note that `HashMap` and `HashSet` follow the rule of having a "midcapital" at each word boundary, whereas the older `Hashtable` does not (the "t" is not capitalized).

The `java.util` package has become something of a catch-all over the years. Besides the legacy Date/Time API covered in Recipe 6.7, several other classes from `java.util` are not covered in this chapter. All the classes whose names begin with `Abstract` are, in fact, abstract, and we discuss their nonabstract subclasses. The `StringTokenizer` class is covered in Recipe 3.2. `BitSet` is used less frequently than some of the classes discussed here and is simple enough to learn on your own; I have examples of it in Recipes 2.6 and 5.10. `BitSet` stores the bits very compactly in memory, but because it predates the Collection API and wasn't retrofitted, it doesn't implement any of the standard collection interfaces. Also here are `EnumSet` and `EnumMap`, specialized for efficient storage/retrieval of enums. These are newer than `BitSet` and *do* implement the modern collection interfaces.

We start our discussion of data structuring techniques with one of the oldest structures, the array. We discuss the overall structure of `java.util`'s Collections Framework. Then we'll go through a variety of structuring techniques using classes from `java.util`.

7.1. Using Arrays for Data Structuring

Problem

You need to keep track of a fixed amount of information and retrieve it (usually) sequentially.

Solution

Use an array.

Discussion

Arrays can be used to hold any linear collection of data. The items in an array must all be of the same type. You can make an array of any primitive type or any object type. For *arrays of primitive types*, such as `ints`, `booleans`, etc., the data is stored in the array. For *arrays of objects*, a reference is stored in the array, so the normal rules of reference variables and casting apply. Note in particular that if the array is declared as `Object[]`,

object references of any type can be stored in it without casting, although a valid cast is required to take an `Object` reference out and use it as its original type. I'll say a bit more on two-dimensional arrays in Recipe 7.19; otherwise, you should treat this as a review example:

```
public class Array1  {
    @SuppressWarnings("unused")
    public static void main(String[] argv) {
        int[] monthLen1;              // declare a reference
        monthLen1 = new int[12];         // construct it
        int[] monthLen2 = new int[12];    // short form
        // even shorter is this initializer form:
        int[] monthLen3 = {
                31, 28, 31, 30,
                31, 30, 31, 31,
                30, 31, 30, 31,
        };

        final int MAX = 10;
        Calendar[] days = new Calendar[MAX];
        for (int i=0; i<MAX; i++) {
            // Note that this actually stores GregorianCalendar
            // etc. instances into a Calendar Array
            days[i] = Calendar.getInstance();
        }

        // Two-Dimensional Arrays
        // Want a 10-by-24 array
        int[][] me = new int[10][];
        for (int i=0; i<10; i++)
            me[i] = new int[24];

        // Remember that an array has a ".length" attribute
        System.out.println(me.length);
        System.out.println(me[0].length);

    }
}
```

Arrays in Java work nicely. The type checking provides reasonable integrity, and array bounds are always checked by the runtime system, further contributing to reliability.

The only problem with arrays is: what if the array fills up and you still have data coming in? See Recipe 7.2.

7.2. Resizing an Array

Problem

The array filled up, and you got an `ArrayIndexOutOfBoundsException`.

Solution

Make the array bigger. Or, use an `ArrayList`.

Discussion

One approach is to allocate the array at a reasonable size to begin with, but if you find yourself with more data than will fit, reallocate a new, bigger array and copy the elements into it.[1] Here is code that does so:

```java
public class Array2  {
    public final static int INITIAL = 10,     ❶
        GROW_FACTOR = 2;                       ❷

    public static void main(String[] argv) {
        int nDates = 0;
        Date[] dates = new Date[INITIAL];
        StructureDemo source = new StructureDemo(21);
        Date c;
        while ((c=(Date)(source.getDate())) != null) {

            // if (nDates >= dates.length) {
            //     System.err.println("Too Many Dates! Simplify your life!!");
            //     System.exit(1);  // wimp out
            // }

            // better: reallocate, making data structure dynamic
            if (nDates >= dates.length) {
                Date[] tmp = new Date[dates.length * GROW_FACTOR];
                System.arraycopy(dates, 0, tmp, 0, dates.length);
                dates = tmp;     // copies the array reference
                // old array will be garbage collected soon...
            }
            dates[nDates++] = c;
        }
        System.out.println("Final array size = " + dates.length);
    }
}
```

❶ A good guess is necessary; know your data!

❷ The growth factor is arbitary; 2 is a good value here but will continue to double exponentially. If Java did type inference, it would not be inconvenient to use a factor like 1.5, which would mean more allocations at the low end but less explosive growth. You need to manage this somehow!

---

1. You could copy it yourself using a `for` loop if you wish, but `System.arrayCopy( )` is likely to be faster because it's implemented in native code.

This technique works reasonably well for simple or relatively small linear collections of data. For data with a more variable structure, you probably want to use a more dynamic approach, as in Recipe 7.4.

7.3. The Collections Framework

Problem

You're having trouble keeping track of all these lists, sets, and iterators.

Solution

There's a pattern to it. See Figure 7-1 and Table 7-1.

Discussion

`List`, `Set`, and `Map` are the three fundamental data structures of the Collections Framework. `List` and `Set` are both sequences, with the difference that `List` preserves order and allows duplicate entries, whereas `Set`, true to the mathematical concept behind it, does not. `Map` is a key/value store, also known as a "hash," a "dictionary," or an "associative store."

Figure 7-1, in the fashion of the package-level class diagrams in the O'Reilly classic *Java in a Nutshell*, shows the collection-based classes from package `java.util`.

See Also

The javadoc documentation on `Collections`, `Arrays`, `List`, `Set`, and the classes that implement them provides more details than there's room for here. Table 7-1 may further help you to absorb the regularity of the Collections Framework.

Table 7-1. Java collections

Interfaces	Resizable array	Hashed table	Linked list	Balanced tree
Set		HashSet		TreeSet
List	ArrayList, Vector		LinkList	
Map		HashMap, HashTable		TreeMap

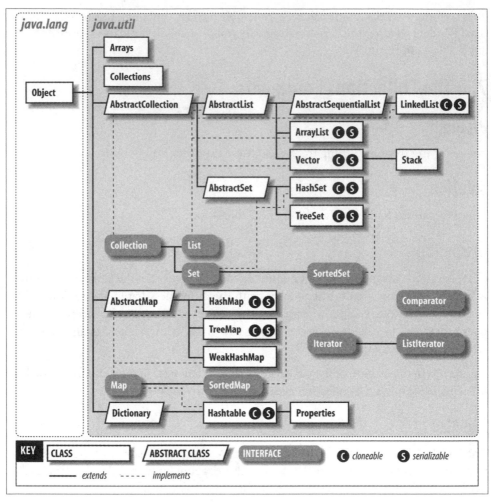

Figure 7-1. The Collections Framework

7.4. Like an Array, but More Dynamic

Problem

You don't want to worry about storage reallocation; you want a standard class to handle it for you.

Solution

Use an ArrayList.

Discussion

The first of the `Collections` classes we will discuss, `ArrayList` is a standard class from `java.util` that encapsulates the functionality of an array but allows it to expand automatically. You can just keep on adding things to it, and each addition behaves the same. If you watch *really* closely, you might notice a brief extra pause once in a while when adding objects as the `ArrayList` reallocates and copies. But you don't have to think about it.

However, because `ArrayList` is a class and isn't part of the syntax of Java, you can't use Java's array syntax; you must use methods to access the `ArrayList`'s data. It has methods to add objects, retrieve objects, find objects, and tell you how big the `List` is and how big it can become without having to reallocate (note that the `ArrayList` class is but one implementation of the `List` interface; more on that later). Like the other collection classes in `java.util`, `ArrayList`'s storing and retrieval methods were originally defined to have parameters and return values of `java.lang.Object`. Because `Object` is the ancestor of every defined type, you can store objects of any type in a `List` (or any collection) and cast it when retrieving it. If you need to store a small number of built-ins (like `int`, `float`, etc.) into a collection containing other data, use the appropriate wrapper class (see the Introduction to Chapter 5). To store `booleans`, either store them directly in a `java.util.BitSet` (see the online documentation) or store them in a `List` using the `Boolean` wrapper class.

Because `Object` is usually too general for accurate work, all modern versions of Java provide the "generic types" mechanism described in Recipe 7.5. So nowadays, you declare an `ArrayList` (or other collection) with a "type parameter" in angle brackets, and the parameters and returns are treated as being of that type, ensuring that objects of the wrong type don't make it into your collections, and avoiding the need to write casts when retrieving objects.

Table 7-2 shows some of the most important methods of `ArrayList`. Equally important, those listed are also methods of the `List` interface, which we'll discuss shortly. This means that the same methods can be used with the older `Vector` class and several other classes.

Table 7-2. List access methods

Method signature	Usage
add(Object o)	Add the given element at the end
add(int i, Object o)	Insert the given element at the specified position
clear( )	Remove all element references from the `Collection`
contains(Object o)	True if the `List` contains the given `Object`
get(int i)	Return the object reference at the specified position

Method signature	Usage
indexOf(Object o)	Return the index where the given object is found, or −1
remove(Object o)remove(int i)	Remove an object by reference or by position
toArray( )	Return an array containing the objects in the Collection

ArrayListDemo stores data in an ArrayList and retrieves it for processing:

```
public class ArrayListDemo {
    public static void main(String[] argv) {
        ArrayList<Date> al = new ArrayList<>();

        // Create a source of Objects
        StructureDemo source = new StructureDemo(15);

        // Add lots of elements to the ArrayList...
        al.add(source.getDate());
        al.add(source.getDate());
        al.add(source.getDate());

        // Print them out using old-style for loop to index number.
        System.out.println("Retrieving by index:");
        for (int i = 0; i<al.size(); i++) {
            System.out.println("Element " + i + " = " + al.get(i));
        }
    }
}
```

The older Vector and Hashtable classes predate the Collections framework, so they provide additional methods with different names: Vector provides addElement() and elementAt(). You will see these in legacy code, but you should use the Collections methods add() and get() instead. Another difference is that the methods of Vector are synchronized, meaning that they can be accessed from multiple threads (see Recipe 22.5). This does mean more overhead, though, so in a single-threaded application it is usually faster to use an ArrayList (see timing results in Recipe 7.20).

There are various conversion methods. Table 7-2 mentions toArray(), which will expose the contents of a List as an array. The java.util.Arrays class features an asList() method, which converts in the other direction, from an array to a List. With the Variable Arguments feature of modern Java (described in "Variable argument lists" on page 835), you can create and populate a list in one call to Arrays.asList(). For example:

```
// ArraysAsListDemo.java
List<String> firstNames = Arrays.asList("Robin", "Jaime", "Joey");
```

In days of yore, you needed to be more explicit, like so:

```
List<String> lastNames =
Arrays.asList(new String[]{"Smith", "Jones", "MacKenzie"});
```

Java does indeed get less verbose as time goes by!

7.5. Using Generic Collections

Problem

You want to store your data in one of the Collection classes defined in Chapter 7 with type safety, and without having to write downcasts when retrieving data from the collection.

Solution

Use Java's Generic Types mechanism, and declare the Collection with a "type parameter" of the correct type. The type parameter name appears in angle brackets after the declaration and instantiation. For example, to declare an ArrayList for holding String object references:

```
List<String> myList = new ArrayList<String>();
```

Discussion

When you instantiate a Collection (or any other class using Generic Types), the class appears to be instantiated with the type given in angle brackets becoming the type of arguments passed in, values returned, and so on. Recipe 7.6 provides some details on the implementation. As an example, consider the code in Example 7-1, which creates and uses an ArrayList specialized to contain String objects.

Example 7-1. ArrayListGenericDemo.java

```java
public class ArrayListGenericDemo {
    public static void main(String[] args) {
        ArrayList<String> data = new ArrayList<>();
        data.add("hello");
        data.add("goodbye");

        // data.add(new Date()); This won't compile!

        data.forEach(s -> System.out.println(s));
    }
}
```

As you know from the ArrayList example in Recipe 7.4, prior to Generics, the references obtained from a Collection or Iterator would have to be downcasted to their specific type, often after testing with the instanceof operator. A key benefit of Generic Types is that they obviate this testing and downcasting by doing more work at compile time. The casting is still done at runtime, but it disappears from your attention.

You can still instantiate classes such as `ArrayList` without using a specific type. In this case, they behave as in the old days—that is, the objects returned from a `Collection` or `Iterator` are treated as of type `java.lang.Object` and must be downcast before you can call any application-specific methods or use them in any application-specific method calls.

As a further example, consider the `Map` interface mentioned in Chapter 7. A `Map` requires a key and a value in its `put()` method. A `Map`, therefore, has two parameterized types. To set up a `Map` whose keys are `Person` objects and whose values are `Address` objects (assuming these two classes exist in your application), you could define it as:

```
Map<Person, Address> addressMap = new HashMap<>( );
```

This `Map` expects a `Person` as its key and an `Address` as its value in the `put()` method; the `get()` method returns an `Address` object, the `keySet()` method returns `Set<Person>` (i.e., a `Set` specialized for `Person` objects), and so on.

See Also

Although the generics avoid your having to write downcasts, the casts still occur at runtime; they are just provided by the compiler. The compiler techniques used in compiling these new constructs in a backward-compatible way include *erasure* and *bridging*, topics discussed in an article (*https://today.java.net/pub/a/today/2003/12/02/explorations.html*) by O'Reilly author William Grosso.

7.6. Avoid Casting by Using Generics

Problem

You wish to define your own container classes using the Generic Type mechanism to avoid needless casting.

Solution

Define a class using < *TypeName* > where the container type is declared, and *TypeName* where it is used.

Discussion

Consider the very simple `Stack` class in Example 7-2. (We discuss the nature and uses of stack classes in Recipe 7.18).

This version has been parameterized to take a type whose local name is `T`. This type `T` will be the type of the argument of the `push()` method, the return type of the `pop()` method, and so on. Because of this return type—more specific than the `Object` return type of the original Collections—the return value from `pop()` does not need to be downcasted. All containers in the Collections Framework (`java.util`) are parameterized similarly.

Example 7-2. MyStack.java

```java
public class MyStack<T> implements SimpleStack<T> {

    private int depth = 0;
    public static final int DEFAULT_INITIAL = 10;
    private T[] stack;

    public MyStack() {
        this(DEFAULT_INITIAL);
    }

    public MyStack(int howBig) {
        if (howBig <= 0) {
            throw new IllegalArgumentException(
            howBig + " must be positive, but was " + howBig);
        }
        stack = (T[])new Object[howBig];
    }

    @Override
    public boolean empty() {
        return depth == 0;
    }

    /** push - add an element onto the stack */
    @Override
    public void push(T obj) {
        // Could check capacity and expand
        stack[depth++] = obj;
    }

    /* pop - return and remove the top element */
    @Override
    public T pop() {
        --depth;
        T tmp = stack[depth];
        stack[depth] = null;
        return tmp;
    }

    /** peek - return the top element but don't remove it */
    @Override
    public T peek() {
        if (depth == 0) {
            return null;
        }
        return stack[depth-1];
```

```
        }

    public boolean hasNext() {
        return depth > 0;
    }

    public boolean hasRoom() {
        return depth < stack.length;
    }

    public int getStackDepth() {
        return depth;
    }
}
```

The association of a particular type is done at the time the class is instantiated. For example, to instantiate a MyStack specialized for holding BankAccount objects, you would need to code only the following:

```
MyStack<BankAccount> theAccounts = new MyStack<>( );
```

The "<>" is called the "diamond operator." Prior to Java 7, the compiler was not smart enough to apply the type parameter (BankAccount) from the declaration to the definition; you had to repeat the (redundant) statement of the type:

```
MyStack<BankAccount> theAccounts = new MyStack<BankAccount>( );
```

Note that if you do not provide a specific type, this class defaults to the most general behavior (i.e., type T is treated as java.lang.Object). So this little collection, like the real ones in java.util, will behave as they did in the days before Generic Collections —accepting input arguments of any type, returning java.lang.Object from getter methods, and requiring downcasting—as their default, backward-compatible behavior. Example 7-3 shows a program that creates two instances of MyStack, one specialized for Strings and one left general. The general one, called ms2, is loaded up with the same two String objects as ms1 but also includes a Date object. The printing code is now "broken," because it will throw a ClassCastException: a Date is not a String. I handle this case specially for pedantic purposes: it is illustrative of the kinds of errors you can get into when using nonparameterized container classes.

Example 7-3. MyStackDemo.java

```
public class MyStackDemo {
    public static void main(String[] args) {
        MyStack<String> ms1 = new MyStack<>();
        ms1.push("billg");
        ms1.push("scottm");

        while (ms1.hasNext()) {
            String name = ms1.pop();
            System.out.println(name);
```

```
        }

        // Old way of using Collections: not type safe.
        // DO NOT GENERICIZE THIS
        MyStack ms2 = new MyStack();
        ms2.push("billg");                // EXPECT WARNING
        ms2.push("scottm");               // EXPECT WARNING
        ms2.push(new java.util.Date());   // EXPECT WARNING

        // Show that it is broken
        try {
            String bad = (String)ms2.pop();
            System.err.println("Didn't get expected exception, popped " + bad);
        } catch (ClassCastException ex) {
            System.out.println("Did get expected exception.");
        }

        // Removed the brokenness, print rest of it.
        while (ms2.hasNext()) {
            String name = (String)ms2.pop();
            System.out.println(name);
        }
    }
}
```

Because of this potential for error, the compiler warns that you have unchecked raw types. Like the deprecation warnings discussed in Recipe 1.9, by default, these warnings are not printed in detail by the javac compiler (they will appear in most IDEs). You ask for them, with the rather lengthy option -Xlint:unchecked:

```
C:> javac -source 1.5 structure/MyStackDemo.java
Note: MyStackDemo.java uses unchecked or unsafe operations.
Note: Recompile with -Xlint:unchecked for details.
C:> javac -source 1.5 -Xlint:unchecked structure/MyStackDemo.java
MyStackDemo.java:14: warning: unchecked call to push(T) as a member of the raw
type MyStack
                ms2.push("billg");
                   ^
MyStackDemo.java:15: warning: unchecked call to push(T) as a member of the raw
type MyStack
                ms2.push("scottm");
                   ^
MyStackDemo.java:16: warning: unchecked call to push(T) as a member of the raw
type MyStack
                ms2.push(new java.util.Date( ));
                   ^
3 warnings
C:>
```

I say more about the development and evolution of MyStack in Recipe 7.18.

7.7. How Shall I Iterate Thee? Let Me Enumerate the Ways

Problem

You need to iterate over some structured data.

Solution

Java provides many ways to iterate over collections of data. In newest-first order:

- `Iterable.forEach` method (Java 8)
- Java "foreach" loop (Java 5)
- `java.util.Iterator` (Java 2)
- Three-part `for` loop
- "while" loop
- Enumeration

Pick one and use it. Or learn them all and save!

Discussion

A few words on each of the iteration methods are given here.

Iterable.forEach method (Java 8)

The most recent iteration technique is the `Iterable.forEach()` method, added in Java 8. This method can be called on any `Iterable` (unfortunately, the array class does not yet implement `Iterable`), and takes one argument implementing the *functional interface* `java.util.function.Consumer`. Functional Interfaces are discussed in Chapter 9, but here is one example:

```
public class IterableForEach {

    public static void main(String[] args) {
        Collection<String> c =                      ❶
                Arrays.asList("One", "Two", "Three");  ❷
        c.forEach(s -> System.out.println(s));      ❸
    }
}
```

❶ Declare a `Collection` (a `Collection` is an `Iterable`).

❷ Populate it with `Arrays.asList`, passing a literal array into the `asList()` method (see "Variable argument lists" on page 835 for how this arbitrary argument list becomes an array).

❸ Invoke the collection's forEach() method, passing a lambda expression (see Chapter 9 for a discussion of how s→System.out.println(s) gets mapped to a Consumer interface implementation without your even having to import this interface).

This style of iteration—sometimes called "internal iteration"—inverts the control from the traditional for loop; the collection is in charge of when and how the iteration works.

Java "foreach" loop (Java 5)

The "foreach" loop syntax is:

```
for (Type var : Iterable<Type>) {
        // do something with "var"
}
```

This is probably the most common style of loop in modern Java code. The Iterable can be an array, or anything that implements Iterable (the Collection implementations are included in this).

This style is used throughout the book, and is discussed a bit more in "Java 5 foreach loop" on page 833.

java.util.Iterator (Java 2)

The older Iterator is discussed in Recipe 7.9.

Three-part for loop

This is the standard for loop invented in the early 1970s in the C language. The syntax is:

```
for (init; test; change) {
        // do something
}
```

Its most common form is with an int "index variable" or "loop variable":

```
MyDataType[] data = ...
for (int i = 0; i < data.length; i++)
        MyDataType d = data[i];
        // do something with it
}
```

while loop

A while loop executes its loop body as long as ("while") the test condition is true. Commonly used in conjunction with the Enumeration or Iterator, as in

```
Iterator<MyData> iterator = ...
while (iterator.hasNext()) {
```

```
        MyData md = iterator.next();
        //
    }
```

Enumeration

An `Enumeration` is like an `Iterator` (shown earlier and discussed in Recipe 7.9), but it lacks the `remove()` method, and the control methods have longer names—for example, `hasMoreElements()` and `nextElement()`.

7.8. Eschewing Duplicates with a Set

Problem

You want a structure that will avoid storing duplicates.

Solution

Use a `Set` implementation instead of a `List` (e.g., `Set<String> myNames = new Hash-Set<>()`).

Discussion

The `Set` interface is similar to the `List` interface,[2] with methods like `add()`, `remove()`, `contains()`, `size()`, `isEmpty()`, and the like. The differences are that it does not preserve order; instead, it enforces uniqueness—if you add the "same" item (as considered by its `equals()` method) twice or more, it will only be present once in the set. For this reason, the index-based methods such as `add(int, Object)` and `get(int)`, are missing from the `Set` implementation: you might "know" that you've added seven objects but only five of those were unique, so calling `get()` to retrieve the sixth one would have to throw an `ArrayIndexOutOfBoundsException`! Better that you don't think of a `Set` as being indexed.

 As the Java 7 `Set` document states: "Note: Great care must be exercised if mutable objects are used as set elements. The behavior of a set is not specified if the value of an object is changed in a manner that affects equals comparisons while the object is an element in the set. A special case of this prohibition is that it is not permissible for a set to contain itself as an element."

2. Both `List` and `Set` extend `Collection`.

This code shows a duplicate entry being made to a Set, which will contain only one copy of the strong "One":.

```
Set<String> hashSet = new HashSet<>();
hashSet.add("One");
hashSet.add("Two");
hashSet.add("One"); // DUPLICATE
hashSet.add("Three");
hashSet.forEach(s -> System.out.println(s));
```

Not surprisingly, only the three distinct values are printed.

If you need a sorted Set, there is in fact a SortedSet interface, of which the most common implementation is a TreeSet; see a TreeSet example in Recipe 7.14.

7.9. Using Iterators or Enumerations for Data-Independent Access

Problem

You want to write your code so that users don't have to know whether you store it in an array, a Vector, an ArrayList, or even a doubly linked list of your own choosing.

Solution

Use the Iterator interface.

Discussion

If you are making collections of data available to other classes, you may not want the other classes to depend on how you have stored the data so that you can revise your class easily at a later time. Yet you need to publish a method that gives these classes access your data. It is for this very purpose that the Enumeration and Iterator interfaces were included in the java.util package. These provide a pair of methods that allow you to iterate, or step through, all the elements of a data structure without knowing or caring how the data is stored. The newer Iterator interface also allows deletions, though classes that implement the interface are free either to implement the use of deletions or to throw an UnsupportedOperationException.

Here is IteratorDemo, the previous ArrayList demo rewritten to use an Iterator to access the elements of the data structure:

```
public class IteratorDemo {

    public static void main(String[] argv) {

        List<Date> l = new ArrayList<>();
```

```
StructureDemo source = new StructureDemo(15);

// Add lots of elements to the list...
l.add(source.getDate());
l.add(source.getDate());
l.add(source.getDate());

int i = 0;

Iterator it = l.iterator();

// Process the data structure using an iterator.
// This part of the code does not know or care
// if the data is an an array, a List, a Vector, or whatever.
while (it.hasNext()) {
    Object o = it.next();
    System.out.println("Element " + i++ + " = " + o);
}
    }
}
```

To demystify the Iterator and show that it's actually easy to build, you create your own Iterator in Recipe 7.17.

7.10. Structuring Data in a Linked List

Problem

Your data isn't suitable for use in an array.

Solution

Write your own data structure(s).

Discussion

Anybody who's taken Computer Science 101 (or any computer science course) should be familiar with data structuring, such as linked lists, binary trees, and the like. Though this is not the place to discuss the details of such things, I'll give a brief illustration of the common linked list. A linked list is commonly used when you have an unpredictably large number of data items, you wish to allocate just the right amount of storage, and usually want to access them in the same order that you created them. Figure 7-2 is a diagram showing the normal arrangement.

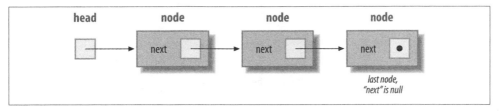

Figure 7-2. Linked list structure

Of course, the Collections API provides a `LinkedList` class; here is a simple program that uses it:

```
public class LinkedListDemo {
    public static void main(String[] argv) {
        System.out.println("Here is a demo of Java's LinkedList class");
        LinkedList<String> l = new LinkedList<>();
        l.add(new Object().toString());
        l.add("Hello");
        l.add("end of the list");

        System.out.println("Here is a list of all the elements");
        ListIterator li = l.listIterator(0);
        while (li.hasNext())
            System.out.println("Next to: " + li.next());

        if (l.indexOf("Hello") < 0)
            System.err.println("Lookup does not work");
        else
            System.err.println("Lookup works");

        // Now, for added fun, let's walk the linked list backwards.
        while (li.hasPrevious()) {
            System.out.println("Back to: " + li.previous());
        }
    }
}
```

The `ListIterator` used here is a subinterface of `Iterator`, which was discussed in Recipe 7.9.

Here is code that shows *part of the implemention* of a simple linked list:

```
public class LinkList<T> implements List<T> {

    /* A TNode stores one node or item in a Linked List */
    private static class TNode<T> {
        TNode<T> next;
        T data;
        TNode(T o) {
            data = o;
            next = null;
```

```java
        }
    }

    private boolean DIAGNOSTIC = true;

    /** The root or first TNode in the list. */
    protected TNode<T> first;
    /** The last TNode in the list */
    protected TNode<T> last;

    /** Construct a LinkList: initialize the first and last nodes */
    public LinkList() {
        clear();
    }

    /** Construct a LinkList given another Collection.
     * This method is recommended by the general contract of List.
     */
    public LinkList(Collection<T> c) {
        this();
        addAll(c);
    }

    /** Set the List (back) to its initial state.
     * Any references held will be discarded.
     */
    public void clear() {
        first = new TNode<T>(null);
        last = first;
    }

    /** Add one object to the end of the list. Update the "next"
     * reference in the previous end, to refer to the new node.
     * Update "last" to refer to the new node.
     */
    public boolean add(T o) {
        last.next = new TNode<T>(o);
        last = last.next;
        return true;
    }

    public void add(int where, T o) {
        TNode<T> t = first;
        for (int i=0; i<=where; i++) {
            t = t.next;
            if (t == null) {
                throw new IndexOutOfBoundsException(
                    "'add(n,T) went off end of list");
            }
            if (DIAGNOSTIC) {
                System.out.printf("add(int,T): i = %d, t = %s%n", i, t);
            }
```

```
    }
    TNode<T> t2 = t;
    t.next = new TNode<T>(o);
    t.next = t2;
}

public int size() {
    TNode<T> t = first;
    int i;
    for (i=0; ; i++) {
        if (t == null)
            break;
        t = t.next;
    }
    return i - 1;    // subtract one for mandatory head node.
}

public boolean isEmpty() {
    return first == last;
}

public T get(int where) {
    TNode<T> t = first;
    int i=0;
    // If we get to the end of list before 'where', error out
    while (i<=where) {
        i++;
        if ((t = t.next) == null) {
            throw new IndexOutOfBoundsException();
        }
    }
    return t.data;
}

public T set(int i, T o) {
    return null;
}

public boolean contains(Object o) {
        TNode<T> t = first;
    while ((t = t.next) != null) {
        if (t.data.equals(o)) {
            return true;
        }
    }
    return false;
}
public boolean addAll(Collection<? extends T> c) {
    c.forEach(o -> add((T) o));
    return false;
}
```

```java
public ListIterator<T> listIterator() {
    throw new UnsupportedOperationException("listIterator");
}

public Iterator<T> iterator() {
    return new Iterator<T>() {
        TNode<T> t = first.next;
        public boolean hasNext() {
            return t != last;
        }
        public T next() {
            if (t == last)
                throw new IndexOutOfBoundsException();
            return (T) (t = t.next);
        }
        public void remove() {
            throw new UnsupportedOperationException("remove");
        }
    };
}
```

 This is just to show how the implementation of a linked list might work. Do not use the simple LinkList class shown here; use the real one, java.util.LinkedList, shown in action in the first example.

7.11. Mapping with Hashtable and HashMap

Problem

You need a one-way mapping from one data item to another.

Solution

Use a HashMap or the older Hashtable.

Discussion

HashMap and the older Hashtable provide a one-way mapping from one set of object references to another. They are completely general purpose. I've used them to map Swing push buttons (see Recipe 14.5) to the URL to jump to when the button is pushed, to map names to addresses, and to implement a simple in-memory cache in a web server. You can map from anything to anything. In the following example, we map from company names to addresses; the addresses here are String objects, but in real life they'd probably be Address objects:

```
public class HashMapDemo {

    public static void main(String[] argv) {

        // Construct and load the hash. This simulates loading a
        // database or reading from a file, or wherever the data is.

        Map<String,String> map = new HashMap<String,String>();

        // The hash maps from company name to address.
        // In real life this might map to an Address object...
        map.put("Adobe", "Mountain View, CA");
        map.put("IBM", "White Plains, NY");
        map.put("Learning Tree", "Los Angeles, CA");
        map.put("Microsoft", "Redmond, WA");
        map.put("Netscape", "Mountain View, CA");
        map.put("O'Reilly", "Sebastopol, CA");
        map.put("Sun", "Mountain View, CA");

        // Two versions of the "retrieval" phase.
        // Version 1: get one pair's value given its key
        // (presumably the key would really come from user input):
        String queryString = "O'Reilly";
        System.out.println("You asked about " + queryString + ".");
        String resultString = map.get(queryString);
        System.out.println("They are located in: " + resultString);
        System.out.println();

        // Version 2: get ALL the keys and values
        // (maybe to print a report, or to save to disk)
        for( String key : map.keySet()) {
            System.out.println("Key " + key +
                "; Value " + map.get(key));
        }

        // Version 3: Same but using a Map.Entry lambda
        map.entrySet().forEach(mE ->
            System.out.println("Key + " + mE.getKey()+
                "; Value " +mE.getValue()));
    }
}
```

For this version we used both a Java 5 for loop and a Java 8 forEach() loop; the latter uses the return from entrySet(), a set of Map.Entry, each of which contains one key and one value (this may be faster on large maps because it avoids going back into the map to get the value each time through the loop). If you are modifying the list as you are going through it (e.g., removing elements), either inside the loop or in another thread, then these forms will fail with a ConcurrentModificationException; you need to use an Iterator to control the loop:

```
// Version 2: get ALL the keys and values
// with concurrent modification
Iterator<String> it = map.keySet( ).iterator( );
while (it.hasNext( )) {
    String key = it.next( );
    if (key.equals("Sun")) {
        it.remove();
        continue;
    }
    System.out.println("Company " + key + "; " +
        "Address " + map.get(key));
}
```

 The Hashtable methods are synchronized, for use with multiple threads. They are therefore slower, and unless you need the synchronization, use the newer HashMap.

7.12. Storing Strings in Properties and Preferences

Problem

You need to store keys and values that are both strings, possibly with persistence across runs of a program—for example, program customization.

Solution

Use a `java.util.prefs.Preferences` object or a `java.util.Properties` object.

Discussion

Here are three approaches to customization based on the user's environment. Java offers `Preferences` and `Properties` for cross-platform customizations.

Preferences

The `Preferences` class `java.util.prefs.Preferences` provides an easy-to-use mechanism for storing user customizations in a system-dependent way (which might mean dot files on Unix, a preferences file on the Mac, or the registry on Windows systems). This class provides a hierarchical set of nodes representing a user's preferences. Data is stored in the system-dependent storage format but can also be exported to or imported from an XML format. Here is a simple demonstration of `Preferences`:

```
public class PrefsDemo {

    public static void main(String[] args) throws Exception {
```

```
        // Setup the Preferences for this application, by class.
        Preferences prefs = Preferences.userNodeForPackage(PrefsDemo.class);

        // Retrieve some preferences previously stored, with defaults in case
        // this is the first run.
        String text    = prefs.get("textFontName", "lucida-bright");
        String display = prefs.get("displayFontName", "lucida-blackletter");
        System.out.println(text);
        System.out.println(display);

        // Assume the user chose new preference values: Store them back.
        prefs.put("textFontName", "times-roman");
        prefs.put("displayFontName", "helvetica");

        // Toss in a couple more values for the curious who want to look
        // at how Preferences values are actually stored.
        Preferences child = prefs.node("a/b");
        child.putInt("meaning", 42);
        child.putDouble("pi", Math.PI);

        // And dump the subtree from our first node on down, in XML.
        prefs.exportSubtree(System.out);
    }
}
```

When you run the `PrefsDemo` program the first time, of course, it doesn't find any settings, so the calls to `preferences.get( )` return the default values:

```
> javac -d . structure/PrefsDemo.java
> java structure.PrefsDemo
lucida-bright
lucida-blackletter
<preferences EXTERNAL_XML_VERSION="1.0">>
<root type="user">>
<map/>>
<node name="structure">>
<map>>
<entry key="displayFontName" value="helvetica"/>>
<entry key="textFontName" value="times-roman"/>>
</map>>
<node name="a">>
<map/>>
<node name="b">>
<map>>
<entry key="meaning" value="42"/>>
<entry key="pi" value="3.141592653589793"/>>
</map>>
</node>>
</node>>
</node>>
</root>>
</preferences>
```

On subsequent runs, it finds and returns the "user provided" settings (I've elided the XML output from the second run, because most of the XML output is the same):

```
> java structure.PrefsDemo
times-roman
helvetica
...
>
```

Properties

The `Properties` class is similar to a `HashMap` or `Hashtable` (it extends the latter), but with methods defined specifically for string storage and retrieval and for loading/saving. `Properties` objects are used throughout Java, for everything from setting the platform font names to customizing user applications into different `Locale` settings as part of internationalization and localization. When stored on disk, a `Properties` object looks just like a series of `name=value` assignments, with optional comments. Comments are added when you edit a Properties file by hand, ignored when the `Properties` object reads itself, and lost when you ask the `Properties` object to save itself to disk. Here is an example of a Properties file that could be used to internationalize the menus in a GUI-based program:

```
# Default properties for MenuIntl
program.title=Demonstrate I18N (MenuIntl)
program.message=Welcome to an English-localized Java Program
#
# The File Menu
#
file.label=File Menu
file.new.label=New File
file.new.key=N
file.open.label=Open...
file.open.key=O
file.save.label=Save
file.save.key=S
file.exit.label=Exit
file.exit.key=Q
```

Here is another example, showing some personalization properties:

```
name=Ian Darwin
favorite_popsicle=cherry
favorite_rock group=Fleetwood Mac
favorite_programming_language=Java
pencil_color=green
```

A `Properties` object can be loaded from a file. The rules are flexible: either =, :, or spaces can be used after a key name and its values. Spaces after a nonspace character are ignored in the key. A backslash can be used to continue lines or to escape other characters.

Comment lines may begin with either # or !. Thus, a Properties file containing the previous items, if prepared by hand, could look like this:

```
# Here is a list of properties
! first, my name
name Ian Darwin
favorite_popsicle = cherry
favorite_rock\ group \
 Fleetwood Mac
favorite_programming_language=Java
pencil_color green
```

Fortunately, when a `Properties` object writes itself to a file, it uses the simple format:

```
key=value
```

Here is an example of a program that creates a `Properties` object and adds into it the list of companies and their locations from Recipe 7.11. It then loads additional properties from disk. To simplify the I/O processing, the program assumes that the Properties file to be loaded is contained in the standard input, as would be done using a command-line redirection on either Unix or DOS:

```java
public class PropsCompanies {

    public static void main(String[] argv) throws java.io.IOException {

        Properties props = new Properties();

        // Get my data
        props.put("Adobe", "Mountain View, CA");
        props.put("IBM", "White Plains, NY");
        props.put("Learning Tree", "Los Angeles, CA");
        props.put("Microsoft", "Redmond, WA");
        props.put("Netscape", "Mountain View, CA");
        props.put("O'Reilly", "Sebastopol, CA");
        props.put("Sun", "Mountain View, CA");

        // Now load additional properties
        props.load(System.in);

        // List merged properties, using System.out
        props.list(System.out);
    }
}
```

Running it as:

```
java structure.PropsCompanies < PropsDemo.out
```

produces the following output in the file *PropsDemo.out*:

```
-- listing properties --
Sony=Japan
Sun=Mountain View, CA
```

```
IBM=White Plains, NY
Netscape=Mountain View, CA
Nippon_Kogaku=Japan
Acorn=United Kingdom
Adobe=Mountain View, CA
Ericsson=Sweden
O'Reilly & Associates=Sebastopol, CA
Learning Tree=Los Angeles, CA
```

In case you didn't notice in either the HashMap or the Properties examples, the order in which the outputs appear in these examples is neither sorted nor in the same order we put them in. The hashing classes and the Properties subclass make no claim about the order in which objects are retrieved. If you need them sorted, see Recipe 7.13.

As a convenient shortcut, my FileProperties class includes a constructor that takes a filename, as in:

```
import com.darwinsys.util.FileProperties;
...
Properties p = new FileProperties("PropsDemo.dat");
```

Note that constructing a FileProperties object causes it to be loaded, and therefore the constructor may throw a checked exception of class IOException.

7.13. Sorting a Collection

Problem

You put your data into a collection in random order or used a Properties object that doesn't preserve the order, and now you want it sorted.

Solution

Use the static method Arrays.sort() or Collections.sort(), optionally providing a Comparator.

Discussion

If your data is in an array, then you can sort it using the static sort() method of the Arrays utility class. If it is in a Collection, you can use the static sort() method of the Collections class. Here is a set of strings being sorted in-place in an Array:

```
public class SortArray {
    public static void main(String[] unused) {
        String[] strings = {
            "painful",
            "mainly",
            "gaining",
```

```
        "raindrops"
    };
    Arrays.sort(strings);
    for (int i=0; i<strings.length; i++) {
        System.out.println(strings[i]);
    }
  }
}
```

What if the default sort order isn't what you want? Well, you can create an object that implements the Comparator<T> interface and pass that as the second argument to sort. Fortunately, for the most common ordering next to the default, you don't have to: a public constant String.CASE_INSENSITIVE_ORDER can be passed as this second argument. The String class defines it as "a Comparator<String> that orders String objects as by compareToIgnoreCase." But if you need something fancier, you probably need to write a Comparator<T>. Suppose that, for some strange reason, you need to sort strings using all but the first character of the string. One way to do this would be to write this Comparator<String>:

```
/** Comparator for comparing strings ignoring first character.
 */
public class SubstringComparator implements Comparator<String> {
    @Override
    public int compare(String s1, String s2) {
        s1 = s1.substring(1);
        s2 = s2.substring(1);
        return s1.compareTo(s2);
        // or, more concisely:
        // return s1.substring(1).compareTo(s2.substring(1));
    }
}
```

Using it is just a matter of passing it as the Comparator argument to the correct form of sort(), as shown here:

```
public class SubstrCompDemo {
    public static void main(String[] unused) {
        String[] strings = {
            "painful",
            "mainly",
            "gaining",
            "raindrops"
        };
        Arrays.sort(strings);
        dump(strings, "Using Default Sort");
        Arrays.sort(strings, new SubstringComparator());
        dump(strings, "Using SubstringComparator");

    }
    static void dump(String[] args, String title) {
        System.out.println(title);
```

```
        for (int i=0; i<args.length; i++)
            System.out.println(args[i]);
    }
}
```

Here is the output of running it:

```
$ java structure.SubstrCompDemo
Using Default Sort
gaining
mainly
painful
raindrops
Using SubstringComparator
raindrops
painful
gaining
mainly
```

And this is all as it should be.

On the other hand, you may be writing a class and want to build in the comparison functionality so that you don't always have to remember to pass the Comparator with it. In this case, you can directly implement the java.lang.Comparable interface. The String class; the wrapper classes Byte, Character, Double, Float, Long, Short, and Integer, BigInteger, and BigDecimal from java.math; File from java.io; java.util.Date; and java.text.CollationKey all implement this interface, so arrays or Collections of these types can be sorted without providing a Comparator. Classes that implement Comparable are said to have a "natural" ordering. The documentation strongly recommends that a class's natural ordering be consistent with its equals() method, and it is consistent with equals() if and only if e1.compareTo((Object)e2)==0 has the same Boolean value as e1.equals((Object)e2) for every instance, e1 and e2 of the given class. This means that if you implement Comparable, you should also implement equals(), and the logic of equals() should be consistent with the logic of the compareTo() method. Here, for example, is part of the appointment class Appt from a hypothetical scheduling program:

```
// public class Appt implements Comparable {
    // Much code and variables omitted - see online version
    //----------------------------------------------------------------
    //     METHODS - COMPARISON
    //----------------------------------------------------------------
    /** compareTo method, from Comparable interface.
     * Compare this Appointment against another, for purposes of sorting.
     * <P>Only text, and date and time participate, not repetition!
     * (Repetition has to do with recurring events, e.g.,
     *   "Meeting every Tuesday at 9").
     * This methods is consistent with equals().
     * @return -1 if this<a2, +1 if this>a2, else 0.
     */
```

```
@Override
public int compareTo(Appt a2) {
    if (year < a2.year)
        return -1;
    if (year > a2.year)
        return +1;
    if (month < a2.month)
        return -1;
    if (month > a2.month)
        return +1;
    if (day < a2.day)
        return -1;
    if (day > a2.day)
        return +1;
    if (hour < a2.hour)
        return -1;
    if (hour > a2.hour)
        return +1;
    if (minute < a2.minute)
        return -1;
    if (minute > a2.minute)
        return +1;
    return text.compareTo(a2.text);
}

/** Compare this appointment against another, for equality.
 * Consistent with compareTo(). For this reason, only
 * text, date & time participate, not repetition.
 * @returns true if the objects are equal, false if not.
 */
@Override
public boolean equals(Object o2) {
    Appt a2 = (Appt) o2;
    if (year != a2.year ||
        month != a2.month ||
        day != a2.day ||
        hour != a2.hour ||
        minute != a2.minute)
        return false;
    return text.equals(a2.text);
}
```

If you're still confused between Comparable and Comparator, you're probably not alone. Table 7-3 summarizes the two "comparison" interfaces.

Table 7-3. Comparable compared with Comparator

Interface name	Description	Method(s)
`java.lang.Comparable<T>`	Provides a natural order to objects. Written in the class whose objects are being sorted.	`int compareTo(T o);`
`java.util.Comparator<T>`	Provides total control over sorting objects of another class. Standalone; pass to `sort()` method or `Collection` constructor. Implements Strategy Design Pattern.	`int compare(T o1, T o2); boolean equals(T c2)`

7.14. Avoiding the Urge to Sort

Problem

Your data needs to be sorted, but you don't want to stop and sort it periodically.

Solution

Not everything that requires order requires an explicit *sort* operation. Just keep the data sorted at all times.

Discussion

You can avoid the overhead and elapsed time of an explicit sorting operation by ensuring that the data is in the correct order at all times, though this may or may not be faster overall, depending on your data and how you choose to keep it sorted. You can keep it sorted either manually or by using a `TreeSet` or a `TreeMap`. First, here is some code from a call tracking program that I first wrote on the very first public release of Java (the code has been modernized slightly!) to keep track of people I had extended contact with. Far less functional than a Rolodex, my `CallTrack` program maintained a list of people sorted by last name and first name. It also had the city, phone number, and email address of each person. Here is a very small portion of the code surrounding the event handling for the New User push button:

```
public class CallTrack {

    /** The list of Person objects. */
    protected List<Person> usrList = new ArrayList<>();

    /** The scrolling list */
    protected java.awt.List visList = new java.awt.List();

    /** Add one (new) Person to the list, keeping the list sorted. */
    protected void add(Person p) {
        String lastName = p.getLastName();
        int i;
        // Find in "i" the position in the list where to insert this person
```

```
        for (i=0; i<usrList.size(); i++)
            if (lastName.compareTo((usrList.get(i)).getLastName()) <= 0)
                break; // If we don't break, will insert at end of list.
        usrList.add(i, p);

        // Now insert them in the scrolling list, in the same position.
        visList.add(p.getName(), i);
        visList.select(i);        // ensure current
    }

}
```

This code uses the `String` class `compareTo(String)` routine.

This code uses a linear search, which was fine for the original application, but could get very slow on large lists (it is *O(n)*). You'd need to use hashing or a binary search to find where to put the values on large lists.

If I were writing this code today, I might well use a `TreeSet` (which keeps objects in order) or a `TreeMap` (which keeps the keys in order and maps from keys to values; the keys would be the name and the values would be the `Person` objects). Both insert the objects into a tree in the correct order, so an `Iterator` that traverses the tree always returns the objects in sorted order. In addition, they have methods such as `headSet()` and `headMap()`, which give a new `Set` or `Map` of objects of the same class, containing the objects lexically before a given value. The `tailSet()` and `tailMap()` methods, similarly, return objects greater than a given value, and `subSet()` and `subMap()` return a range. The `first()` and `last()` methods retrieve the obvious components from the collection. The following program uses a `TreeSet` to sort some names:

```
// A TreeSet keeps objects in sorted order. Use a Comparator
// published by String for case-insensitive sorting order.
TreeSet<String> theSet = new TreeSet<>(String.CASE_INSENSITIVE_ORDER);
theSet.add("Gosling");
theSet.add("da Vinci");
theSet.add("van Gogh");
theSet.add("Java To Go");
theSet.add("Vanguard");
theSet.add("Darwin");
theSet.add("Darwin");      // TreeSet is Set, ignores duplicates.

System.out.printf("Our set contains %d elements", theSet.size());

// Since it is sorted we can easily get various subsets
System.out.println("Lowest (alphabetically) is " + theSet.first());

// Print how many elements are greater than "k"
// Should be 2 - "van Gogh" and "Vanguard"
```

```
System.out.println(theSet.tailSet("k").toArray().length +
    " elements higher than \"k\"");

// Print the whole list in sorted order
System.out.println("Sorted list:");
theSet.forEach(name -> System.out.println(name));
```

One last point to note is that if you have a `Hashtable` or `HashMap`, you can convert it to a `TreeMap`, and therefore get it sorted, just by passing it to the `TreeMap` constructor:

```
TreeMap sorted = new TreeMap(unsortedHashMap);
```

7.15. Finding an Object in a Collection

Problem

You need to see whether a given collection contains a particular value.

Solution

Ask the collection if it contains an object of the given value.

Discussion

If you have created the contents of a collection, you probably know what is in it and what is not. But if the collection is prepared by another part of a large application, or even if you've just been putting objects into it and now need to find out if a given value was found, this recipe's for you. There is quite a variety of methods, depending on which collection class you have. The methods in Table 7-4 can be used.

Table 7-4. Finding objects in a collection

Method(s)	Meaning	Implementing classes
`binarySearch()`	Fairly fast search	`Arrays`, `Collections`
`contains( )`	Search	`ArrayList`, `HashSet`, `Hashtable`, `Link-List`, `Properties`, `Vector`
`containsKey( )`, `containsValue( )`	Checks if the collection contains the object as a Key or as a Value	`HashMap`, `Hashtable`, `Properties`, `Tree-Map`
`indexOf( )`	Returns location where object is found	`ArrayList`, `LinkedList`, `List`, `Stack`, `Vector`
`search( )`	Search	`Stack`

The methods whose names start with `contains` will use a linear search if the collection is a collection (`List`, `Set`), but will be quite fast if the collection is hashed (`HashSet`, `HashMap`). So you do have to know what implementation is being used to think about performance, particularly when the collection is (or is likely to grow) large.

The next example plays a little game of "find the hidden number" (or "needle in a haystack"): the numbers to look through are stored in an array. As games go, it's fairly pathetic: the computer plays against itself, so you probably know who's going to win. I wrote it that way so I would know that the data array contains valid numbers. The interesting part is not the generation of the random numbers (discussed in Recipe 5.13). The array to be used with Arrays.binarySearch() must be in sorted order, but because we just filled it with random numbers, it isn't initially sorted. Hence, we call Arrays.sort() on the array. Then we are in a position to call Arrays.binary-Search(), passing in the array and the value to look for. If you run the program with a number, it runs that many games and reports on how it fared overall. If you don't bother, it plays only one game:

```java
public class ArrayHunt  {
    /** the maximum (and actual) number of random ints to allocate */
    protected final static int MAX    = 4000;
    /** the value to look for */
    protected final static int NEEDLE = 1999;
    int[] haystack;
    Random r;

    public static void main(String[] argv) {
        ArrayHunt h = new ArrayHunt();
        if (argv.length == 0)
            h.play();
        else {
            int won = 0;
            int games = Integer.parseInt(argv[0]);
            for (int i=0; i<games; i++)
                if (h.play())
                    ++won;
            System.out.println("Computer won " + won +
                " out of " + games + ".");
        }
    }

    /** Construct the hunting ground */
    public ArrayHunt() {
        haystack = new int[MAX];
        r = new Random();
    }

    /** Play one game. */
    public boolean play() {
        int i;

        // Fill the array with random data (hay?)
        for (i=0; i<MAX; i++) {
            haystack[i] = (int)(r.nextFloat() * MAX);
        }
```

```
        // Precondition for binary search is that data be sorted!
        Arrays.sort(haystack);

        // Look for needle in haystack
        i = Arrays.binarySearch(haystack, NEEDLE);

        if (i >= 0) {            // Found it, we win.
            System.out.println("Value " + NEEDLE +
                " occurs at haystack[" + i + "]");
            return true;
        } else {            // Not found, we lose.
            System.out.println("Value " + NEEDLE +
                " does not occur in haystack; nearest value is " +
                haystack[-(i+2)] + " (found at " + -(i+2) + ")");
            return false;
        }
    }
}
```

The `Collections.binarySearch()` works almost exactly the same way, except it looks in a `Collection`, which must be sorted (presumably using `Collections.sort`, as discussed in Recipe 7.13).

7.16. Converting a Collection to an Array

Problem

You have a `Collection` but you need a Java language array.

Solution

Use the `Collection` method `toArray()`.

Discussion

If you have an `ArrayList` or other `Collection` and you need an array, you can get it just by calling the `Collection`'s `toArray()` method. With no arguments, you get an array whose type is `Object[]`. You can optionally provide an array argument, which is used for two purposes:

- The type of the array argument determines the type of array returned.
- If the array is big enough (and you can ensure that it is by allocating the array based on the `Collection`'s `size()` method), then this array is filled and returned. If the array is not big enough, a new array is allocated instead. If you provide an array and

objects in the `Collection` cannot be cast to this type, then you will get an `ArrayS-toreException`.

Example 7-4 shows code for converting an `ArrayList` to an array of type `Object`.

Example 7-4. structure/ToArray.java

```java
List<String> list = new ArrayList<>();
list.add("Blobbo");
list.add("Cracked");
list.add("Dumbo");

// Convert a collection to Object[], which can store objects
// of any type.
Object[] ol = list.toArray();
System.out.println("Array of Object has length " + ol.length);

String[] sl = (String[]) list.toArray(new String[0]);
System.out.println("Array of String has length " + sl.length);
```

7.17. Rolling Your Own Iterator

Problem

You have your own data structure, but you want to publish the data as an `Iterator` to provide generic access to it.

Solution

Write your own `Iterator`. Just implement (or provide an inner class that implements) the `Iterator` (or `Enumeration`) interface. For extra points, implement `Iterable` and your objects can be iterated with a "foreach" loop.

Discussion

To make data from one part of your program available in a storage-independent way to other parts of the code, generate an `Iterator`. Here is a short program that constructs, upon request, an `Iterator` for some data that it is storing—in this case, in an array. The `Iterator` interface has only three methods—`hasNext()`, `next()`, and `remove()`:

```java
package com.darwinsys.util;

import java.util.Iterator;
import java.util.NoSuchElementException;

/** Demonstrate the Iterator and Iterable interfaces, showing how
 * to write a simple Iterator for an Array of Objects.
 * @author    Ian Darwin, http://www.darwinsys.com/
```

```java
 */
public class ArrayIterator<T> implements Iterable<T>, Iterator<T> {
    /** The data to be iterated over. */
    protected T[] data;

    protected int index = 0;

    /** Construct an ArrayIterator object.
     * @param d The array of objects to be iterated over.
     */
    public ArrayIterator(final T[] d) {
        setData(d);
    }

    /** (Re)set the data array to the given array, and reset the iterator.
     * @param d The array of objects to be iterated over.
     */
    public void setData(final T[] d) {
        this.data = d;
        index = 0;
    }

    // -------------------
    // Methods of Iterable
    // -------------------

    @Override
    public Iterator<T> iterator() {
        index = 0;
        return this;     // since main class implements both interfaces
    }

    // -------------------
    // Methods of Iterator
    // -------------------


    /**
     * Tell if there are any more elements.
     * @return true if not at the end, i.e., if next() will succeed.
     * @return false if next() will throw an exception.
     */
    @Override
    public boolean hasNext() {
        return (index < data.length);
    }

    /** Returns the next element from the data */
    @Override
    public T next() {
        if (hasNext()) {
            return data[index++];
```

```
        }
        throw new NoSuchElementException("only " + data.length + " elements");
    }

    /** Remove the object that next() just returned.
     * An Iterator is not required to support this interface,
     * and we don't.
     * @throws UnsupportedOperationException unconditionally
     */
    @Override
    public void remove() {
        throw new UnsupportedOperationException(
            "This demo Iterator does not implement the remove method");
    }
}
```

The comments on the remove() method remind me of an interesting point. This interface introduces java.util's attempt at something Java doesn't really have, the "optional method." Because there is no syntax for this, and they didn't want to introduce any new syntax, the developers of the Collections Framework decided on an implementation using existing syntax. If they are not implemented, the optional methods are required to throw an UnsupportedOperationException if they ever get called. My remove( ) method does this. Note that UnsupportedOperationException is subclassed from RuntimeException, so it is not required to be declared or caught.

This code is unrealistic in several ways, but it does show the syntax and demonstrates how the Iterator interface works. In real code, the Iterator and the data are usually separate objects (the Iterator might be an inner class from the data store class). Also, you don't even need to write this code for an array; you can just construct an Array-List object, copy the array elements into it, and ask it to provide the Iterator. However, I believe it's worth showing this simple example of the internals of an Iterator so that you can understand both how it works and how you could provide one for a more sophisticated data structure, should the need arise.

The Iterable interface has only one nondefault method, iterator(), which must provide an Iterator for objects of the given type. Because the ArrayIterator class implements this as well, we can use an object of type ArrayIterator in a "foreach" loop:

structure/ArrayIteratorDemo.java

```
package structure;

import com.darwinsys.util.ArrayIterator;

public class ArrayIteratorDemo {

    private final static String[] names = {
        "rose", "petunia", "tulip"
    };
```

```
    public static void main(String[] args) {
        ArrayIterator<String> arrayIterator = new ArrayIterator<>(names);

        // Java 5, 6 way
        for (String s : arrayIterator) {
            System.out.println(s);
        }

        // Java 8 way
        arrayIterator.forEach(s->System.out.println(s));
    }
}
```

Java 8 Iterable.foreach

Java 8 adds foreach to the Iterable interface, a *default method* (discussed in Recipe 9.5) that you don't have to write. Thus, without changing the ArrayIterator, after moving to Java 8 we can use the newest-style loop, Iterator.foreach(Consumer), with a lambda expression (see Chapter 9) to print each element (see Figure 7-2).

7.18. Stack

Problem

You need to process data in "last-in, first-out" (LIFO) or "most recently added" order.

Solution

Write your own code for creating a stack; it's easy. Or, use a java.util.Stack.

Discussion

You need to put things into a holding area quickly and retrieve them in last-in, first-out order. This is a common data structuring operation and is often used to reverse the order of objects. The basic operations of any stack are push() (add to stack), pop() (remove from stack), and peek() (examine top element without removing). ToyStack in Example 7-5 is a simple class for stacking only ints. If you want to stack user-defined objects, see Example 7-6.

Example 7-5. ToyStack

```java
public class ToyStack {

    /** The maximum stack depth */
    protected int MAX_DEPTH = 10;
    /** The current stack depth */
    protected int depth = 0;
    /* The actual stack */
    protected int[] stack = new int[MAX_DEPTH];

    /** push - add an element onto the stack */
    protected void push(int n) {
        stack[depth++] = n;
    }
    /** pop - return and remove the top element */
    protected int pop() {
        return stack[--depth];
    }
    /** peek - return the top element but don't remove it */
    protected int peek() {
        return stack[depth-1];
    }
}
```

If you are not familiar with the basic idea of a stack, you should work through the code here; if you are familiar with it, you can skip ahead. While looking at it, of course, think about what happens if pop() or peek() is called when push() has never been called, or if push() is called to stack more data than will fit.

A second version of this code, ToyStack2, has been changed to implement my Simple-Stack interface and parameterized, so that we can use it with objects of any type. There is a tiny performance hit here; the previous version dealt with primitive ints rather than objects. However, the generality gain is probably more significant: we can use any kind of values in this stack:

Example 7-6. ToyStack2

```java
/** Toy Stack, converted to SimpleStack interface.
 */
public class ToyStack2 implements SimpleStack<Integer> {

    /** The maximum stack depth */
    protected int MAX_DEPTH = 10;
    /** The current stack depth */
    protected int depth = 0;
    /* The actual stack */
    protected int[] stack = new int[MAX_DEPTH];

    @Override
    public boolean empty() {
```

```
        return depth == 0;
    }

    @Override
    public void push(Integer n) {
        stack[depth++] = n;
    }

    @Override
    public Integer pop() {
        return stack[--depth];
    }

    @Override
    public Integer peek() {
        return stack[depth-1];
    }
}
```

While working on ToyStack2, I extracted its interface into SimpleStack, which just lists
the operations. At the same time I added the empty() method for some compatibility
with the "standard" java.util.Stack API:

```
public interface SimpleStack<T> {

    /** empty - return true if the stack is empty */
    abstract boolean empty();

    /** push - add an element onto the stack */
    abstract void push(T n);

    /** pop - return and remove the top element */
    abstract T pop();

    /** peek - return the top element but don't remove it */
    abstract T peek();
}
```

I then made another of my demo stack classes, MyStack, implement the same interface:

```
public class MyStack<T> implements SimpleStack<T> {

    private int depth = 0;
    public static final int DEFAULT_INITIAL = 10;
    private T[] stack;

    public MyStack() {
        this(DEFAULT_INITIAL);
    }

    public MyStack(int howBig) {
        if (howBig <= 0) {
```

```
            throw new IllegalArgumentException(
                howBig + " must be positive, but was " + howBig);
        }
        stack = (T[])new Object[howBig];
    }

    @Override
    public boolean empty() {
        return depth == 0;
    }

    /** push - add an element onto the stack */
    @Override
    public void push(T obj) {
        // Could check capacity and expand
        stack[depth++] = obj;
    }

    /* pop - return and remove the top element */
    @Override
    public T pop() {
        --depth;
        T tmp = stack[depth];
        stack[depth] = null;
        return tmp;
    }

    /** peek - return the top element but don't remove it */
    @Override
    public T peek() {
        if (depth == 0) {
            return null;
        }
        return stack[depth-1];
    }

    public boolean hasNext() {
        return depth > 0;
    }

    public boolean hasRoom() {
        return depth < stack.length;
    }

    public int getStackDepth() {
        return depth;
    }
}
```

This version has a lot more error checking (and a unit test, in the *src/test/java/struc-ture* folder), as well as some additional methods not in the original (e.g., hasRoom()—

unlike the full-blown `java.util.Stack`, this one does not expand beyond its original size, so we need a way to see if it is full without throwing an exception).

For an example of the "real" `java.util.Stack` in operation, Recipe 5.18 provides a simple stack-based numeric calculator.

7.19. Multidimensional Structures

Problem

You need a two-, three-, or more dimensional array or `ArrayList`.

Solution

No problem. Java supports this.

Discussion

As mentioned back in Recipe 7.1, Java arrays can hold any reference type. Because an array is a reference type, it follows that you can have arrays of arrays or, in other terminology, *multidimensional* arrays. Further, because each array has its own length attribute, the columns of a two-dimensional array, for example, do not all have to be the same length (see Figure 7-3).

Here is code to allocate a couple of two-dimensional arrays, one using a loop and the other using an initializer. Both are selectively printed:

```
public class ArrayTwoDObjects {

    /** Return list of subscript names (unrealistic; just for demo). */
    public static String[][] getArrayInfo() {
        String info[][];
        info = new String[10][10];
        for (int i=0; i < info.length; i++) {
            for (int j = 0; j < info[i].length; j++) {
                info[i][j] = "String[" + i + "," + j + "]";
            }
        }
        return info;
    }

    /** Return list of allowable parameters (Applet method). */
    public static String[][] getParameterInfo() {
        String param_info[][] = {
            {"fontsize",    "9-18",     "Size of font"},
            {"URL",      "-",      "Where to download"},
        };
        return param_info;
```

```
    }

    /** Run both initialization methods and print part of the results */
    public static void main(String[] args) {
        print("from getArrayInfo", getArrayInfo());
        print("from getParameterInfo", getParameterInfo());
    }

    /** Print selected elements from the 2D array */
    public static void print(String tag, String[][] array) {
        System.out.println("Array " + tag + " is " + array.length + " x " +
            array[0].length);
        System.out.println("Array[0][0] = " + array[0][0]);
        System.out.println("Array[0][1] = " + array[0][1]);
        System.out.println("Array[1][0] = " + array[1][0]);
        System.out.println("Array[0][0] = " + array[0][0]);
        System.out.println("Array[1][1] = " + array[1][1]);
    }
}
```

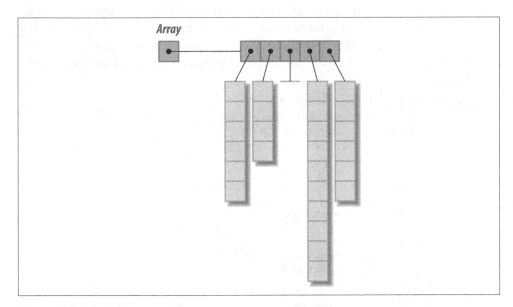

Figure 7-3. Multidimensional arrays

Running it produces this output:

```
> java structure.ArrayTwoDObjects
Array from getArrayInfo is 10 x 10
Array[0][0] = String[0,0]
Array[0][1] = String[0,1]
Array[1][0] = String[1,0]
Array[0][0] = String[0,0]
Array[1][1] = String[1,1]
```

```
Array from getParameterInfo is 2 x 3
Array[0][0] = fontsize
Array[0][1] = 9-18
Array[1][0] = URL
Array[0][0] = fontsize
Array[1][1] = -
>
```

The same kind of logic can be applied to any of the Collections. You could have an ArrayList of ArrayLists, or a Vector of linked lists, or whatever your little heart desires.

As Figure 7-3 shows, it is not necessary for the array to be "regular" (i.e., it's possible for each column of the 2D array to have a different height). That is why I used array[0].length for the length of the first column in the code example.

7.20. Program: Timing Comparisons

New developers sometimes worry about the overhead of these collections and think they should use arrays instead of data structures. To investigate, I wrote a program that creates and accesses 250,000 objects, once through a Java array and again through an ArrayList. This is a lot more objects than most programs use. First the code for the Array version:

```
public class Array {
    public static final int MAX = 250000;
    public static void main(String[] args) {
        System.out.println(new Array().run());
    }
    public int run() {
        MutableInteger list[] = new MutableInteger[MAX];
        for (int i=0; i<list.length; i++) {
            list[i] = new MutableInteger(i);
        }
        int sum = 0;
        for (int i=0; i<list.length; i++) {
            sum += list[i].getValue();
        }
        return sum;
    }
}
```

And the ArrayList version:

```
public class ArrayLst {
    public static final int MAX = 250000;
    public static void main(String[] args) {
        System.out.println(new ArrayLst().run());
    }
    public int run() {
```

```
        ArrayList<MutableInteger> list = new ArrayList<>();
        for (int i=0; i<MAX; i++) {
            list.add(new MutableInteger(i));
        }
        int sum = 0;
        for (int i=0; i<MAX; i++) {
            sum += ((MutableInteger)list.get(i)).getValue();
        }
        return sum;
    }
}
```

The `Vector`-based version, `ArrayVec`, is sufficiently similar that I don't feel the need to kill a tree reprinting its code—it's online.

How can we time this? As covered in Recipe 23.6, you can either use the operating system's *time* command, if available, or just use a bit of Java that times a run of your main program. To be portable, I chose to use the latter on an older, slower machine. Its exact speed doesn't matter because the important thing is to compare only versions of this program running on the same machine.

Finally (drum roll, please), the results:

```
$ java performance.Time Array
Starting class class Array
1185103928
runTime=4.310
$ java performance.Time ArrayLst
Starting class class ArrayLst
1185103928
runTime=5.626
$ java performance.Time ArrayVec
Starting class class ArrayVec
1185103928
runTime=6.699
$
```

Notice that I have ignored one oft-quoted bit of advice that recommends giving a good initial estimate on the size of the `ArrayList`. I did time it that way as well; in this example, it made a difference of less than 4% in the total runtime.

The bottom line is that the efficiency of `ArrayList` is not totally awful compared to arrays. Obviously there is more overhead in calling a "get" method than in retrieving an element from an array. The overhead of objects whose methods actually do some computation probably outweighs the overhead of fetching and storing objects in an `ArrayList` rather than in an `Array`. Unless you are dealing with large numbers of objects, you may not need to worry about it. `Vector` is slightly slower but still only about two-thirds the speed of the original array version. If you are concerned about the time, once the "finished" size of the `ArrayList` is known, you can convert the `ArrayList` to an array (see Recipe 7.16).

## CHAPTER 8

Object-Oriented Techniques

8.0. Introduction

Java is an object-oriented (OO) language in the tradition of Simula-67, SmallTalk, and C++. It borrows syntax from C++ and ideas from SmallTalk. The Java API has been designed and built on the OO model. Design Patterns (see the book of the same name), such as Factory and Delegate, are used throughout; an understanding of these patterns will help you better understand the use of the API and improve the design of your own classes.

Advice, or Mantras

There are any number of short bits of advice that I could give. A few recurring themes arise when learning the basics of Java, and then when learning more Java.

Use the API

I can't say this often enough. A lot of the things you need to do have already been done by the good folks who develop the standard Java library (and third-party libraries). And this grows with every release. Learning the API well is a good grounds for avoiding that deadly "reinventing the flat tire" syndrome—coming up with a second-rate equivalent of a first-rate product that was available to you the whole time. In fact, part of this book's mission is to prevent you from reinventing what's already there. One example of this is the Collections API in `java.util`, discussed in Chapter 7. The Collections API has a high degree of generality and regularity, so there is often no need to invent your own data structuring code.

Exceptions to the rule

There is one exception to the "use the API" rule: the `clone()` method in `java.lang.Object` should generally *not* be used. If you need to copy an object, just write a copy method, or a "copy constructor." Joshua Bloch's arguments against the clone() method in the book *Effective Java* (Addison-Wesley) are persuasive, and should be read by any dedicated Java programmer. While you're at it, read that whole book.

Another exception is the finalize() method in java.lang.Object(). Don't use it. It isn't guaranteed to be invoked, but because it might get invoked, it will cause your dead objects not to be garbage collected, resulting in a memory leak. If you need some kind of cleanup, you must take responsibility for defining a method and invoking it before you let any object of that class go out of reference. You might call such a method cleanUp(). For application-level cleanup, see Recipe 8.3.

Generalize

There is a trade-off between generality (and the resulting reusability), which is emphasized here, and the convenience of application specificity. If you're writing one small part of a very large application designed according to OO design techniques, you'll have in mind a specific set of use cases. On the other hand, if you're writing "toolkit-style" code, you should write classes with few assumptions about how they'll be used. Making code easy to use from a variety of programs is the route to writing reusable code.

Read and write javadoc

You've no doubt looked at the Java online documentation in a browser, in part because I just told you to learn the API well. Do you think Sun/Oracle hired millions of tech writers to produce all that documentation? No. That documentation exists because the developers of the API took the time to write javadoc comments, those funny /** comments you've seen in code. So, one more bit of advice: use javadoc. The standard JDK provides a good, standard mechanism for API documentation. And use it as you write the code—don't think you'll come back and write it in later. That kind of tomorrow never comes.

See Recipe 21.2 for details on using javadoc.

Use subclassing and delegation

Use subclassing. But don't overuse subclassing. It is one of the best ways not only for avoiding code duplication, but for developing software that works. See any number of good books on the topic of object-oriented design and programming for more details.

There are several alternatives. One alternative to subclassing is delegation. Think about "is-a" versus "has-a." For example, instead of subclassing NameAndAddress to make Supplier and Customer, make Supplier and Customer have instances of NameAndAddress. That is a clearer structure; having a supplier *be a* NameAndAddress just because a supplier *has a* name and address would not make sense. And delegation also makes it easier for a Customer to have both a billing address and a shipping address. Another alternative is aspect-oriented programming (AOP), which allows you to "bolt on" extra functionality from the outside of your classes. AOP is provided by the Java EE using EJB Interception, and by the Spring Framework AOP mechanism.

Use Design Patterns

In the Preface, I mentioned *Design Patterns* (Addison-Wesley) as one of the Very Important Books on object-oriented programming. Often called the "Gang of Four" (GoF) book for its four authors, it provides a powerful catalog of things that programmers often reinvent. A Design Pattern provides a statement of a problem and its solution(s), rather like the present book, but generally at a higher level of abstraction. It is as important for giving a standard vocabulary of design as it is for its clear explanations of how the basic patterns work and how they can be implemented.

Table 8-1 shows some example uses of Design Patterns in the standard API.

Table 8-1. Design Patterns in the JavaSE API

Pattern name	Meaning	Examples in Java API
Command	Encapsulate requests, allowing queues of requests, undoable operations, etc.	`javax.swing.Action`; `javax.swing.undo.UndoableEdit`
Decorator	One class "decorates" another	Swing Borders
Factory Method	One class makes up instances for you, controlled by subclasses	`getInstance` (in `Calendar`, `Format`, `Locale`...); socket constructor; RMI `InitialContext`
Iterator	Loop over all elements in a collection, visiting each exactly once	`Iterator`; older `Enumeration`; `java.sql.ResultSet`
Model-View-Controller	Model represents data; View is what the user sees; Controller responds to user requests	`ActionListener` and friends; `Observer`/`Observable`; used internally by all visible Swing components
Proxy	One object stands in for another	RMI, AOP, Dynamic Proxy
Singleton	Only one instance may exist	`java.lang.Runtime`, `java.awt.Toolkit`

8.1. Formatting Objects for Printing with toString()

Problem

You want your objects to have a useful default format.

Solution

Override the `toString()` method inherited from `java.lang.Object`.

Discussion

Whenever you pass an object to `System.out.println()` or any equivalent method, or involve it in string concatenation, Java automatically calls its `toString()` method. Java "knows" that every object has a `toString()` method because `java.lang.Object` has one and all classes are ultimately subclasses of `Object`. The default implementation, in `java.lang.Object`, is neither pretty nor interesting: it just prints the class name, an @ sign, and the object's `hashCode()` value (see Recipe 8.2). For example, if you run this code:

```
public class ToStringWithout {
    int x, y;

    /** Simple constructor */
    public ToStringWithout(int anX, int aY) {
        x = anX; y = aY;
    }

    /** Main just creates and prints an object */
    public static void main(String[] args) {
        System.out.println(new ToStringWithout(42, 86));
    }
}
```

you might see this uninformative output:

```
ToStringWithout@990c747b
```

To make it print better, you should provide an implementation of `toString()` that prints the class name and some of the important states in all but the most trivial classes. This gives you formatting control in `println()`, in debuggers, and anywhere your objects get referred to in a `String` context. Here is the previous program rewritten with a `toString()` method:

```
public class ToStringWith {
    int x, y;

    /** Simple constructor */
    public ToStringWith(int anX, int aY) {
        x = anX; y = aY;
    }

    @Override
    public String toString() {
        return "ToStringWith[" + x + "," + y + "]";
    }

    /** Main just creates and prints an object */
    public static void main(String[] args) {
        System.out.println(new ToStringWith(42, 86));
```

```
        }
    }
```

This version produces the more useful output:

```
ToStringWith[42,86]
```

See Also

This example uses `String` concatenation, but you may also want to use `String.format()` or `StringBuilder`; see Chapter 3.

To avoid having to write all the code in a `toString` method, have a look at the Apache Commons `ToStringBuilder` (*http://bit.ly/1f2rnyF*).

8.2. Overriding the equals() and hashCode() Methods

Problem

You want to be able to compare objects of your class and/or use these objects reliably in `Maps` and other `Collections`.

Solution

Outfit your class with an `equals()` and `hashCode()` method.

Discussion

How do you determine equality? For arithmetic or Boolean operands, the answer is simple: you test with the equals operator (`==`). For object references, though, Java provides both `==` and the `equals()` method inherited from `java.lang.Object`. The `equals` operator can be confusing because it simply compares two object references to see if they refer to the same object. This is not the same as comparing the objects themselves.

The inherited `equals()` method is also not as useful as you might imagine. Some people seem to start their lives as Java developers thinking that the default `equals()` magically does some kind of detailed, field-by-field or even binary comparison of objects. But it does *not* compare fields! It just does the simplest possible thing: it returns the value of an `==` comparison on the two objects involved! So, for any *value classes* you write, you probably have to write an `equals` method.[1] Note that both the `equals` and `hashCode` methods are used by `Maps` or hashes (`Hashtable`, `HashMap`; see Recipe 7.11). So if you think somebody using your class might want to create instances and put them into a

---

1. A value class is one used mainly to hold state, rather than logic: a `Person` is a value class, whereas `java.lang.Math` is not. Many classes are somewhere in between.

Map, or even compare your objects, you owe it to them (and to yourself!) to implement both `equals()` and `hashCode()`, and to implement them properly. The Eclipse IDE (see Recipe 1.3) offers a `Source` menu item "Generate hashCode() and equals()"—it will only do both at the same time, not let you generate `equals()` without `hashCode()` nor vice versa.

equals()

Here are the rules for a correct `equals()` method:

It is reflexive
> `x.equals(x)` must be true.

It is symmetrical
> `x.equals(y)` must be true if and only if `y.equals(x)` is also true.

It is transitive
> If `x.equals(y)` is true and `y.equals(z)` is true, then `x.equals(z)` must also be true.

It is repeatable
> Multiple calls on `x.equals(y)` return the same value (unless state values used in the comparison are changed, as by calling a set method).

It is cautious
> `x.equals(null)` must return false rather than accidentally throwing a `NullPointerException`.

In addition, beware of one common mistake: the argument to `equals()` must be declared as `java.lang.Object`, not the class it is in; this is so that polymorphism will work correctly (some classes may not have an `equals()` method of their own). To prevent this mistake, the `@Override` annotation was designed, as mentioned in Recipe 21.3.

Here is a class that endeavors to implement these rules:

```java
public class EqualsDemo {
    private int int1;
    private SomeClass obj1;

    /** Constructor */
    public EqualsDemo(int i, SomeClass o) {
        int1 = i;
        if (o == null) {
            throw new IllegalArgumentException("Data Object may not be null");
        }
        obj1 = o;
    }

    /** Default Constructor */
```

```
    public EqualsDemo() {
        this(0, new SomeClass());
    }

    /** Demonstration "equals" method */
    @Override
    public boolean equals(Object o) {
        if (o == this)                    // ❶ optimization
            return true;

        if (o == null)                    // ❷ No object ever equals null
            return false;

        // Of the correct class?
        if (o.getClass() != EqualsDemo.class)   ❸
            return false;

        EqualsDemo other = (EqualsDemo)o; // OK, cast to this class

        // compare field-by-field        ❹
        if (int1 != other.int1)           // compare primitives directly
            return false;
        if (!obj1.equals(other.obj1))     // compare objects using their equals
            return false;
        return true;
    }
}
```

❶   Optimization: if same object, true by definition. Some say this is a premature optimization.

❷   If other object null, false by definition.

❸   Compare class descriptors using ==; see following paragraph.

❹   Optimization: compare primitives first. May or may not be worthwhile; may be better to order by those most likely to differ—depends on the data and the usage.

Another common mistake to avoid: note the use of class descriptor equality (i.e., o.getClass() != EqualsDemo.class) to ensure the correct class, rather than via in-stanceof, as is sometimes erroneously done. The reflexive requirement of the equals() method contract pretty much makes it impossible to compare a subclass with a super-class correctly, so we now use class equality (see Chapter 23, *Reflection, or "A Class Named Class"* for details on the class descriptor).

Here is a basic JUnit test (see Recipe 1.13) for the EqualsDemo class:

```
/** Some JUnit test cases for EqualsDemo.
 * Writing a full set is left as "an exercise for the reader".
 */
public class EqualsDemoTest {
```

```
/** an object being tested */
EqualsDemo d1;
/** another object being tested */
EqualsDemo d2;

/** Method to be invoked before each test method */
@Before
public void setUp() {
    d1 = new EqualsDemo();
    d2 = new EqualsDemo();
}

@Test
public void testSymmetry() {
    assertTrue(d1.equals(d1));
}

@Test
public void testSymmetric() {
    assertTrue(d1.equals(d2) && d2.equals(d1));
}

@Test
public void testCaution() {
    assertTrue(!d1.equals(null));
}
}
```

With all that testing, what could go wrong? Well, some things still need care. What if the object is a *subclass* of EqualsDemo? We should test that it returns false in this case.

What else could go wrong? Well, what if either obj1 or other.obj1 is null? You might have just earned a nice shiny new NullPointerException. So you also need to test for any possible null values. Good constructors can avoid these NullPointerExceptions, as I've tried to do in EqualsDemo, or else test for them explicitly.

hashCode()

The hashCode() method is supposed to return an int that should uniquely identify different objects.

A properly written hashCode() method will follow these rules:

It is repeatable.
    hashCode(x) must return the same int when called repeatedly, unless set methods have been called.

It is consistent with equality.
    If x.equals(y), then x.hashCode() must == y.hashCode().

Distinct objects should produce distinct hashCodes

If `!x.equals(y)`, it is not required that `x.hashCode() != y.hashCode()`, but doing so may improve performance of hash tables (i.e., hashes may call `hashCode()` before `equals()`).

The default `hashCode()` on the standard JDK returns a machine address, which conforms to the first rule. Conformance to the second and third rules depends, in part, on your `equals()` method. Here is a program that prints the hashcodes of a small handful of objects:

```
public class PrintHashCodes {

    /** Some objects to hashCode() on */
    protected static Object[] data = {
        new PrintHashCodes(),
        new java.awt.Color(0x44, 0x88, 0xcc),
        new SomeClass()
    };

    public static void main(String[] args) {
        System.out.println("About to hashCode " + data.length + " objects.");
        for (int i=0; i<data.length; i++) {
            System.out.println(data[i].toString() + " --> " +
                data[i].hashCode());
        }
        System.out.println("All done.");
    }
}
```

What does it print?

```
> javac -d . oo/PrintHashCodes.java
> java oo.PrintHashCodes
About to hashCode 3 objects.
PrintHashCodes@982741a0 --> -1742257760
java.awt.Color[r=68,g=136,b=204] --> -12285748
SomeClass@860b41ad --> -2046082643
All done.
>
```

The hashcode value for the `Color` object is interesting. It is actually computed as something like:

```
alpha<<24 + r<<16 + g<<8 + b
```

In this formula, r, g, and b are the red, green, and blue components, respectively, and alpha is the transparency. Each of these quantities is stored in 8 bits of a 32-bit integer. If the alpha value is greater than 128, the "high bit" in this word—having been set by shifting into the sign bit of the word—causes the integer value to appear negative when printed as a signed integer. Hashcode values are of type `int`, so they are allowed to be negative.

Difficulties and Alternatives to Clone

The `java.util.Observable` class (designed to implement the Model-View-Controller pattern with AWT or Swing applications) contains a private `Vector` but no clone method to deep-clone it. Thus, `Observable` objects cannot safely be cloned, ever!

This and several other issues around `clone()`—such as the uncertainty of whether a given `clone()` implementation is deep or shallow—suggest that `clone()` was not as well thought out as might be. An alternative is simply to provide a "copy constructor" or similar method:

```
public class CopyConstructorDemo {
    public static void main(String[] args) {
        CopyConstructorDemo object1 = new CopyConstructorDemo(123, "Hello");
        CopyConstructorDemo object2 = new CopyConstructorDemo(object1);
        if (!object1.equals(object2)) {
            System.out.println("Something is terribly wrong...");
        }
        System.out.println("All done.");
    }

    private int number;
    private String name;

    /** Default constructor */
    public CopyConstructorDemo()  {
    }

    /** Normal constructor */
    public CopyConstructorDemo(int number, String name)  {
        this.number = number;
        this.name = name;
    }

    /** Copy Constructor */
    public CopyConstructorDemo(CopyConstructorDemo other)  {
        this.number = other.number;
        this.name = other.name;
    }
    // hashCode() and equals() not shown
```

8.3. Using Shutdown Hooks for Application Cleanup

Problem

You want some cleanup performed when your application shuts down.

Solution

Use the shutdown hook.

Discussion

One way of performing application-level cleanup is the runtime method addShutdown-Hook(), to which you pass a nonstarted Thread subclass object. *If the virtual machine has a chance*, it runs your shutdown hook code as part of JVM termination. This normally works, but won't happen if the VM was terminated abruptly as by a kill signal on Unix or a KillProcess on Win32, or the VM aborts due to detecting internal corruption of its data structures.

Program ShutdownDemo shown in Example 8-1 contains both a finalize() method (I told you not to use those earlier in this chapter) and a shutdown hook. The program normally exits while holding a reference to the object with the finalize() method. If run with -f as an argument, it "frees" the object and "forces" a GC run by calling System.gc(); only in this case does the finalize() method run. The shutdown hook is run in every case.

Example 8-1. ShutdownDemo

```java
public class ShutdownDemo {
    public static void main(String[] args) throws Exception {

        // Create an Object with a finalize() method - Bad idea!
        Object f = new Object() {
            public void finalize() throws Throwable {
                System.out.println( "Running finalize()");
                super.finalize();
            }
        };

        // Add a shutdownHook to the JVM
        Runtime.getRuntime().addShutdownHook(new Thread() {
            public void run() {
                System.out.println("Running Shutdown Hook");
            }
        });

        // Unless the user puts -f (this-program-specific argument for "free") on
        // the command line, call System.exit while holding a reference to
        // Object f, which can therefore not be finalized().

        if (args.length == 1 && args[0].equals("-f")) {
            f = null;
            System.gc();
        }

        System.out.println("Calling System.exit(), with f = " + f);
```

```
        System.exit(0);
    }
}
```

The bottom line? There's no guarantee at all on finalizers, but shutdown hooks have pretty good odds of being run, at least in a standalone application (this will not work in a web application, for example). But if you want to be sure, just write a method of your own and call it!

8.4. Using Inner Classes

Problem

You need to write a private class, or a class to be used in one other class at most.

Solution

Use a nonpublic class or an inner class.

Discussion

A nonpublic class can be written as part of another class's source file, but not inside that class. An inner class is Java terminology for a class defined inside another class. Inner classes were first popularized with early Java for use as event handlers for GUI applications (see Recipe 14.5), but they have a much wider application.

Inner classes can, in fact, be constructed in several contexts. An inner class defined as a member of a class can be instantiated anywhere in that class. An inner class defined inside a method can be referred to later only in the same method. Inner classes can also be named or anonymous. A named inner class has a full name that is compiler-dependent; the standard JVM uses a name like MainClass$InnerClass for the resulting file. An anonymous inner class, similarly, has a compiler-dependent name; the JVM uses MainClass$1, MainClass$2, and so on.

These classes cannot be instantiated in any other context; any explicit attempt to refer to, say, OtherMainClass$InnerClass, is caught at compile time:

oo/AllClasses.java

```
public class AllClasses {
    public class Data {        ❶
        int x;
        int y;
    }
    public void getResults() {
        JButton b = new JButton("Press me");
        b.addActionListener(new ActionListener() {    ❷
```

```
        public void actionPerformed(ActionEvent evt) {
            Data loc = new Data();
            loc.x = ((Component)evt.getSource()).getX();
            loc.x = ((Component)evt.getSource()).getY();
            System.out.println("Thanks for pressing me");
        }
    });
    }
}

/** Class contained in same file as AllClasses, but can be used
 * (with a warning) in other contexts.
 */
class AnotherClass {                    ❸
    // methods and fields here...
    AnotherClass() {
        // Inner class from above cannot be used here, of course
        // Data d = new Data();    // EXPECT COMPILE ERROR
    }
}
```

❶ Inner class, can be used anywhere in class `AllClasses`.

❷ Anonymous inner class syntax, using new with a type followed by (){, a class body, and }. Compiler will assign a name; class will extend or implement the given type, as appropriate.

❸ Nonpublic class; can be used in the main class, and (with warning) in other classes.

One issue is that the inner class retains a reference to the outer class. If you want to avoid memory leaks if the inner class will be held for a longer time than the outer, you can make it a `static` inner class.

Inner classes implementing a single-method interface can be written in a much more concise fashion as lambda expressions (see Chapter 9).

8.5. Providing Callbacks via Interfaces

Problem

You want to provide callbacks—that is, have unrelated classes call back into your code.

Solution

One way is to use a Java interface.

Discussion

An interface is a class-like entity that can contain only abstract methods and final fields. As we've seen, interfaces are used a lot in Java! In the standard API, the following are a few of the commonly used interfaces:

- Runnable, Comparable, and Cloneable (in java.lang)
- List, Set, Map, and Enumeration/Iterator (in the Collections API; see Chapter 7)
- ActionListener, WindowListener, and others (in the GUI layer; see Recipe 14.5)
- Driver, Connection, Statement, and ResultSet (in JDBC; see Recipe 18.2)
- The "remote interface"—the contact between the client and the server—is specified as an Interface (in RMI, CORBA, and EJB)

Subclass, Abstract Class, or Interface?

There is usually more than one way to solve a problem. Some problems can be solved by subclassing, by use of abstract classes, or by interfaces. The following general guidelines may help:

- *Use an abstract class* when you want to provide a template for a series of subclasses, all of which may inherit some of their functionality from the parent class but are required to implement some of it themselves. (Any subclass of a geometric Shapes class might have to provide a computeArea() method; because the top-level Shapes class cannot do this, it would be abstract. This is implemented in Recipe 8.6.)
- *Subclass* when you need to extend a class and add some functionality to it, whether the parent class is abstract or not. See the standard Java APIs and the examples in Recipes 1.13, 5.11, 8.12, 10.12, and others throughout this book.
- *Subclass* when you are required to extend a given class. Some APIs such as *servlets* use subclassing to ensure "base" functionality in classes that are dynamically loaded (see Recipe 23.4).
- *Define an interface* when there is no common parent class with the desired functionality and when you want only certain unrelated classes to have that functionality (see the PowerSwitchable interface in Recipe 8.5). You should also choose this option if you know that you'll need (or think there is even a chance you might later need) to be able to pass in unrelated classes for testing purposes. "Mock object" is a very common strategy in unit testing. Some say that interfaces should be your first choice at least as often as subclassing.
- *Use interfaces as "markers"* to indicate something about a class. The standard API, for example, uses Serializable (see Recipe 10.20) as a "marker interface."

Suppose we are generating a building management system. To be energy efficient, we want to be able to remotely turn off (at night and on weekends) such things as room lights and computer monitors, which use a lot of energy. Assume we have some kind of "remote control" technology. It could be a commercial version of BSR's house-light control technology X10, it could be Bluetooth or 802.11—it doesn't matter. What matters is that we have to be very careful what we turn off. It would cause great ire if we turned off computer processors automatically—people often leave things running overnight. It would be a matter of public safety if we ever turned off the building emergency lighting.[2]

So we've come up with the design shown in Figure 8-1.

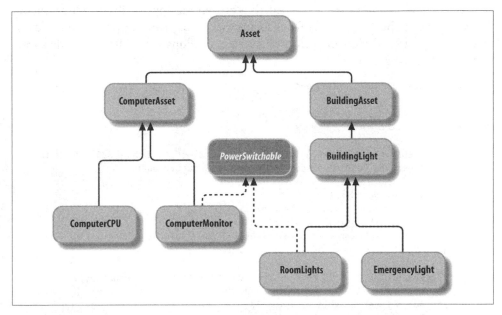

Figure 8-1. Classes for a building management system

The code for these data classes is not shown (it's pretty trivial) but it's in the *oo/interfaces* directory of the online source. The top-level classes (i.e., BuildingLight and Asset) are abstract classes. You can't instantiate them, because they don't have any specific functionality. To ensure—both at compile time and at runtime—that we can never switch off the emergency lighting, we need only ensure that the class representing it, EmergencyLight, does not implement the PowerSwitchable interface.

---

2. Of course these lights wouldn't have remote power-off. But the computers might, for maintenance purposes.

Note that we can't very well use direct inheritance here. No common ancestor class includes both ComputerMonitor and RoomLights that doesn't also include Computer-CPU and EmergencyLight. Use interfaces to define functionality in unrelated classes.

How we use these is demonstrated by the BuildingManagement class; this class is not part of the hierarchy shown in Figure 8-1, but *uses* an array of Asset objects from that hierarchy.

Items that can't be switched must nonetheless be in the database, for various purposes (auditing, insurance, etc.). In the method that turns things off, the code is careful to check whether each object in the database is an instance of the PowerSwitchable interface. If so, the object is casted to PowerSwitchable so that its powerDown() method can be called. If not, the object is skipped, thus preventing any possibility of turning out the emergency lights or shutting off a machine that is busy running *Seti@Home*, downloading a big MP3 playlist, or performing system backups. The following code shows this set of classes in action:

```
public class BuildingManagement {

    Asset things[] = new Asset[24];
    int numItems = 0;

    /** Scenario: goodNight() is called from a timer Thread at 2200, or when
     * we get the "shutdown" command from the security guard.
     */
    public void goodNight() {
        for (int i=0; i<things.length; i++)
            if (things[i] instanceof PowerSwitchable)
                ((PowerSwitchable)things[i]).powerDown();
    }

    // goodMorning() would be the same, but call each one's powerUp().

    /** Add a Asset to this building */
    public void add(Asset thing) {
        System.out.println("Adding " + thing);
        things[numItems++] = thing;
    }

    /** The main program */
    public static void main(String[] av) {
        BuildingManagement b1 = new BuildingManagement();
        b1.add(new RoomLights(101));     // control lights in room 101
        b1.add(new EmergencyLight(101));    // and emerg. lights.
        // add the computer on desk#4 in room 101
        b1.add(new ComputerCPU(10104));
        // and its monitor
        b1.add(new ComputerMonitor(10104));

        // time passes, and the sun sets...
```

```
        b1.goodNight();
    }
}
```

When you run this program, it shows all the items being added, but only the `Power-Switchable` ones being switched off:

```
> java oo.interfaces.BuildingManagement
Adding RoomLights@2dc77f32
Adding EmergencyLight@2e3b7f32
Adding ComputerCPU@2e637f32
Adding ComputerMonitor@2f1f7f32
Dousing lights in room 101
Dousing monitor at desk 10104
>
```

8.6. Polymorphism/Abstract Methods

Problem

You want each of a number of subclasses to provide its own version of one or more methods.

Solution

Make the method abstract in the parent class; this makes the compiler ensure that each subclass implements it.

Discussion

A hypothetical drawing program uses a Shape subclass for anything that is drawn. Shape has an abstract method called computeArea() that computes the exact area of the given shape:

```
public abstract class Shape {
    protected int x, y;
    public abstract double computeArea( );
}
```

A Rectangle subclass, for example, has a computeArea() that multiplies width times height and returns the result:

```
public class Rectangle extends Shape {
    double width, height;
    public double computeArea( ) {
        return width * height;
    }
}
```

A Circle subclass returns πr^2:

```
public class Circle extends Shape {
    double radius;
    public double computeArea( ) {
        return Math.PI * radius * radius;
    }
}
```

This system has a high degree of generality. In the main program, we can iterate over a collection of Shape objects and—here's the real beauty—call computeArea() on any Shape subclass object without having to worry about what kind of shape it is. Java's polymorphic methods automatically call the correct computeArea( ) method in the class of which the object was originally constructed:

oo/shapes/ShapeDriver.java

```
/** Part of a main program using Shape objects */
public class ShapeDriver {

    Collection<Shape> allShapes;     // created in a Constructor, not shown

    /** Iterate over all the Shapes, getting their areas;
     * this cannot use the Java 8 Collection.forEach because the
     * variable total would have to be final, which would defeat the purpose :-)
     */
    public double totalAreas() {
        double total = 0.0;
        for (Shape s : allShapes) {
            total += s.computeArea();
        }
        return total;
    }
}
```

Polymorphism is a great boon for software maintenance: if a new subclass is added, the code in the main program does not change. Further, all the code that is specific to, say, polygon handling, is all in one place: in the source file for the Polygon class. This is a big improvement over older languages, where type fields in a structure or record were used with case or switch statements scattered all across the software. Java makes software more reliable and maintainable with the use of polymorphism.

8.7. Passing Values

Problem

You need to pass a number like an int into a routine and get back the routine's updated version of that value in addition to the routine's return value.

This often comes up in working through strings; the routine may need to return a boolean, say, or the number of characters transferred, but also needs to increment an integer array or string index in the calling class.

It is also useful in constructors, which can't return a value but may need to indicate that they have "consumed" or processed a certain number of characters from within a string, such as when the string will be further processed in a subsequent call.

Solution

Use a specialized class such as the MutableInteger class presented here.

Discussion

The Integer class is one of Java's predefined Number subclasses, mentioned in the Introduction to Chapter 5. It serves as a wrapper for an int value and also has static methods for parsing and formatting integers.

It's fine as it is, but you may want something simpler.

Here is a class I wrote, called MutableInteger, that is like an Integer but specialized by omitting the overhead of Number and providing only the set, get, and incr operations. The latter is overloaded to provide a no-argument version that performs the increment (++) operator on its value, and also a one-integer version that adds that increment into the value (analogous to the += operator). Because Java doesn't support operator overloading, the calling class has to call these methods instead of invoking the operations syntactically, as you would on an int. For applications that need this functionality, the advantages outweigh this minor syntactic restriction. First, let's look at an example of how it might be used. Assume you need to call a scanner function called, say, parse() and get back both a Boolean (indicating whether a value was found) and an integer value indicating where it was found:

```
public class StringParse {
    /** This is the function that has a return value of true but
     * also "passes back" the offset into the String where a
     * value was found. Contrived example!
     */
    public static boolean parse(String in, char lookFor,
        MutableInteger whereFound) {

        int i = in.indexOf(lookFor);
        if (i == -1)
            return false;      // not found
        whereFound.setValue(i);      // say where found
        return true;            // say that it was found
    }

    public static void main(String[] args) {
        MutableInteger mi = new MutableInteger();
        String text = "Hello, World";
        char c = 'W';
        if (parse(text, c, mi)) {
```

```
            System.out.println("Character " + c + " found at offset " +
                mi + " in " + text);
        } else {
            System.out.println("Not found");
        }
    }
}
```

Now many OO purists argue—convincingly—that you shouldn't do this, and that you can always rewrite it so there is only one return value. Either return and have the caller interpret a single value (in this case, return the offset in the return statement, and let the user know that -1 indicates not found), or define a trivial wrapper class containing both the integer and the Boolean. However, there is precedent in the standard API: this code is remarkably similar to how the ParsePosition class is used. Anyway, this functionality is requested often enough that I feel justified in showing how to do it, accompanied by this disclaimer: try to avoid doing it this way in new code!

Having said all that, here is the MutableInteger class:

com/darwinsys/lang/MutableInteger.java

```
package com.darwinsys.lang;

/** A MutableInteger is like an Integer but mutable, to avoid the
 * excess object creation involved in
 * c = new Integer(c.getInt()+1)
 * which can get expensive if done a lot.
 * Not subclassed from Integer, since Integer is final (for performance :-))
 */
public class MutableInteger {
    private int value = 0;

    public MutableInteger(int i) {
        value = i;
    }

    public MutableInteger() {
        this(0);
    }

    public int incr() {
        value++;
        return value;
    }

    public int incr(int amt) {
        value += amt;
        return value;
    }

    public int decr() {
```

```
        value--;
        return value;
    }

    public int setValue(int i) {
        value = i;
        return value;
    }

    public int getValue() {
        return value;
    }

    public String toString() {
        return Integer.toString(value);
    }

    public static String toString(int val) {
        return Integer.toString(val);
    }

    public static int parseInt(String str) {
        return Integer.parseInt(str);
    }
}
```

See Also

As mentioned, this use of my `MutableInteger` class could be replaced with the standard class `ParsePosition`. However, `MutableInteger` has other uses: it makes a fine in-memory counter in a servlet or other application. For immutable argument passing, one solution is to use Java's typesafe enumeration pattern (`enums`, which have been in the language for a decade; see Recipe 8.8).

8.8. Using Typesafe Enumerations

Problem

You need to manage a small list of discrete values within a program.

Solution

Use the Java `enum` mechanism.

Discussion

To enumerate means to list all the values. You often know that a small list of possible values is all that's wanted in a variable, such as the months of the year, the suits or ranks in a deck of cards, the primary and secondary colors, and so on. The C programming language provided an `enum` keyword:

```
enum  { BLACK, RED, ORANGE} color;
```

Java was criticized in its early years for its lack of enumerations, which many developers have wished for. Many have had to develop custom classes to implement the "typesafe enumeration pattern."

But C enumerations are not "typesafe"; they simply define constants that can be used in any integer context. For example, this code compiles without warning, even on *gcc* 3 with -`Wall` (all warnings), whereas a C++ compiler catches the error:[3]

```
enum { BLACK, RED, ORANGE} color;
enum { READ, UNREAD } state;

/*ARGSUSED*/
int main(int argc, char *argv[]) {
        color = RED;
        color = READ; // In C this will compile, give bad results
        return 0;
}
```

To replicate this mistake in Java, one needs only to define a series of `final int` values; it will still not be typesafe. By typesafe I mean that you cannot accidentally use values other than those defined for the given enumeration. The definitive statement on the "typesafe enumeration pattern" is probably the version defined in Item 21 of Joshua Bloch's book *Effective Java* (Addison-Wesley). All modern Java versions include enumerations in the language; it is no longer necessary to use the code from Bloch's book. Bloch was one of the authors of the Typesafe Enumeration specification (`enum` keyword), so you can be sure that Java now does a good job of implementing his pattern. These `enums` are implemented as classes, subclassed (transparently, by the compiler) from the class `java.lang.Enum`. Unlike C, and unlike the "series of final int" implementation, Java typesafe enumerations:

- Are printable (they print as the name, not as an underlying `int` implementation).
- Are almost as fast as `int` constants, but the code is more readable.
- Can be easily iterated over.
- Utilize a separate namespace for each `enum` type, so you don't have to prefix each with some sort of constant name, like ACCOUNT_SAVINGS, ACCOUNT_CHECKING, etc.

---

3. For Java folks not that familiar with C/C++, C is the older, non-OO language; C++ is an OO derivative of C; and Java is in part a portable, more strongly typesafe derivative of C++.

Enum constants are not compiled into clients, giving you the freedom to reorder the constants within your enum without recompiling the client classes. That does not mean you should, however; think about the case where objects that use them have been persisted, and the person designing the database mapping used the numeric values of the enums. Bad idea to reorder then!

Additionally, an enum type is a class, so it can, for example, implement arbitrary interfaces, and you can add constructors, fields, and methods to an enum class.

Compared to Bloch's Typesafe Enum pattern in the book:

- Java enums are simpler to use and more readable (those in the book require a lot of methods, making them cumbersome to write).
- Enums can be used in switch statements.

So there are many benefits and few pitfalls.

The enum keyword is at the same level as the keyword class in declarations. That is, an enum may be declared in its own file with public or default access. It may also be declared inside classes, much like nested or inner classes (see Recipe 8.4). *Media.java*, shown in Example 8-2, is a code sample showing the definition of a typesafe enum.

Example 8-2. structure/Media.java

```
public enum Media {
    BOOK, MUSIC_CD, MUSIC_VINYL, MOVIE_VHS, MOVIE_DVD;
}
```

Notice that an enum is a class; see what *javap* thinks of the Media class:

```
C:> javap Media
Compiled from "Media.java"
public class Media extends java.lang.Enum{
    public static final Media BOOK;
    public static final Media MUSIC_CD;
    public static final Media MUSIC_VINYL;
    public static final Media MOVIE_VHS;
    public static final Media MOVIE_DVD;
    public static final Media[] values( );
    public static Media valueOf(java.lang.String);
    public Media(java.lang.String, int);
    public int compareTo(java.lang.Enum);
    public int compareTo(java.lang.Object);
    static {};
}
C:>
```

Product.java, shown in Example 8-3, is a code sample that uses the Media enum.

Example 8-3. structure/Product.java

```java
public class Product {
    String title;
    String artist;
    Media  media;

    public Product(String artist, String title, Media media) {
        this.title = title;
        this.artist = artist;
        this.media = media;
    }

    @Override
    public String toString() {
        switch (media) {
        case BOOK:
            return title + " is a book";
        case MUSIC_CD:
            return title + " is a CD";
        case MUSIC_VINYL:
            return title + " is a relic of the age of vinyl";
        case MOVIE_VHS:
            return title + " is on old video tape";
        case MOVIE_DVD:
            return title + " is on DVD";
        default:
            return title + ": Unknown media " + media;
        }
    }
}
```

In Example 8-4, MediaFancy shows how operations (methods) can be added to enumerations; the toString() method is overridden for the "book" value of this enum.

Example 8-4. structure/MediaFancy.java

```java
/** An example of an enum with method overriding */
public enum MediaFancy {
    /** The enum constant for a book, with a method override */
    BOOK {
        public String toString() { return "Book"; }
    },
    /** The enum constant for a Music CD */
    MUSIC_CD,
    /** ... */
    MUSIC_VINYL,
    MOVIE_VHS,
    MOVIE_DVD;

    /** It is generally disparaged to have a main() in an enum;
     * please forgive this tiny demo class for doing so.
     */
```

```
        public static void main(String[] args) {
            MediaFancy[] data =  { BOOK, MOVIE_DVD, MUSIC_VINYL };
            for (MediaFancy mf : data) {
                System.out.println(mf);
            }
        }
    }
}
```

Running the MediaFancy program produces this output:

```
Book
MOVIE_DVD
MUSIC_VINYL
```

That is, the Book values print in a "user-friendly" way compared to the default way the other values print. In real life you'd want to extend this to all the values in the enum.

Finally, EnumList, in Example 8-5, shows how to list all the possible values that a given enum can take on; simply iterate over the array returned by the enum class's inherited values() method.

Example 8-5. structure/EnumList.java

```
public class EnumList {
    enum State {
        ON, OFF, UNKNOWN
    }
    public static void main(String[] args) {
        for (State i : State.values()) {
            System.out.println(i);
        }
    }
}
```

The output of the EnumList program is, of course:

```
ON
OFF
UNKNOWN
```

8.9. Enforcing the Singleton Pattern

Problem

You want to be sure there is only one instance of your class in a given Java Virtual Machine.

Solution

Make your class enforce the Singleton Pattern (see page 127 of the book *Design Patterns*), primarily by having only a private constructor(s).

Discussion

It is often useful to ensure that only one instance of a class gets created, usually to funnel all requests for some resource through a single point. An example of a Singleton from the standard API is `java.lang.Runtime`; you cannot create instances of Runtime, you simply ask for a reference by calling the static method `Runtime.getRuntime()`. Singleton is also an example of a design pattern that can be easily implemented.

The easiest implementation consists of a private constructor and a field to hold its result, and a static accessor method with a name like `getInstance()`.

The private field can be assigned from within a static initializer block or, more simply, using an initializer. The `getInstance()` method (which must be public) then simply returns this instance:

```
public class Singleton {

    private static Singleton instance;

    /** A private Constructor prevents any other class from instantiating. */
    private Singleton() {
        // nothing to do this time
    }

    /** The Static initializer constructs the instance at class loading time;
     * this is to simulate a more involved construction process (it it
     * were really simple, you'd just use an initializer)
     */
    static {
        instance = new Singleton();
    }

    /** Static 'instance' method */
    public static Singleton getInstance() {
        return instance;
    }

    // other methods protected by singleton-ness would be here...

    /** A simple demo method */
    public String demoMethod() {
        return "demo";
    }
}
```

Note that the method of using "lazy evaluation" in the `getInstance()` method (which is advocated in *Design Patterns*), is not necessary in Java because Java already uses "lazy loading." Your `Singleton` class will probably not get loaded unless its `getInstance()` is called, so there is no point in trying to defer the singleton construction until it's needed by having `getInstance()` test the singleton variable for null and creating the singleton there.

Using this class is equally simple: simply get and retain the reference, and invoke methods on it:

```java
public class SingletonDemo {
    public static void main(String[] args) {
        Singleton tmp = Singleton.getInstance( );
        tmp.demoMethod( );
    }
}
```

Some commentators believe that a Singleton should also provide a `public final clone()` method that just throws an exception, to avoid subclasses that "cheat" and `clone()` the singleton. However, it is clear that a class with only a private constructor cannot be subclassed, so this paranoia does not appear to be necessary.

Variation

One variation is to make all methods static (as `java.lang.Math` does), but this works only if methods do not need to share state. You also lose the scalability that is inherent in the Singleton pattern: if you later need, say, two or three instances, you could easily change the `getInstance()` method to give out references to one of several, but you can't do that if all the methods are static.

See Also

The `Collections` class in `java.util` has methods `singletonList()`, `singleton-Map()`, and `singletonSet()`, which give out an immutable `List`, `Map`, or `Set`, respectively, containing only the one object that is passed to the method. This does not, of course, convert the object into a Singleton in the sense of preventing that object from being cloned or other instances from being constructed, but it does qualify by providing a single access point that always returns the same instance.

Many frameworks including Spring and EJB3 (Recipe 8.11) provide mechanisms for Singleton-style instantiation of plain classes.

8.10. Roll Your Own Exceptions

Problem

You'd like to use an application-specific exception class or two.

Solution

Go ahead and subclass `Exception` or `RuntimeException`.

Discussion

In theory, you could subclass `Throwable` directly, but that's considered rude. You normally subclass `Exception` (if you want a checked exception) or `RuntimeException` (if you want an unchecked exception). Checked exceptions are those that an application developer is required to catch or "throw upward" by listing them in the `throws` clause of the invoking method.

When subclassing either of these, it is customary to provide at least these constructors:

- A no-argument constructor
- A one-string argument constructor
- A two argument constructor—a string message and a `Throwable` "cause"

The "cause" will appear if the code receiving the exception performs a stack trace operation on it, with the prefix "Root Cause is" or similar. Example 8-6 shows these three constructors for an application-defined exception, `ChessMoveException:`.

Example 8-6. oo/ChessMoveException.java

```
/** A ChessMoveException is thrown  when the user makes an illegal move. */
public class ChessMoveException extends Exception {

    private static final long serialVersionUID = 802911736988179079L;

    public ChessMoveException () {
        super();
    }

    public ChessMoveException (String msg) {
        super(msg);
    }

    public ChessMoveException(String msg, Exception cause) {
        super(msg, cause);
    }
}
```

See Also

The javadoc documentation for `Exception` lists a large number of subclasses; you might look there first to see if there is one you can use.

8.11. Using Dependency Injection

Problem

You want to avoid excessive coupling between classes, and you want to avoid excessive code dedicated to object creation/lookup.

Solution

Use a Dependency Injection Framework.

Discussion

A Dependency Injection Framework allows you to have objects "passed in" to your code instead of making you either create them explicitly (which ties your code to the implementing class name, since you're calling the constructor) or looking for them (which requires use of a possibly cumbersome lookup API, such as JNDI, the Java Naming and Directory Interface).

Three of the best-known Dependency Injection Frameworks are the Spring Framework (*http://springframework.org*), the Java Enterprise Edition's Context and Depency Injection (CDI) (*http://docs.oracle.com/javaee/6/tutorial/doc/giwhl.html*), and Google Guice (*http://code.google.com/p/google-guice*). Suppose we have three classes, a Model, a View, and a Controller, implementing the traditional MVC pattern. Given that we may want to have different versions of some of these, especially the View, we'll define Java interfaces for simple versions of the Model and View, shown in the following code:

Example 8-7. MVC Model Interface

```
public interface Model {
        String getMessage();
}
```

MVC View Interface

```
    public interface View {

        void displayMessage();

    }
```

The implementations of these are not shown, because they're so trivial, but they are online. The Controller in this example is a main program, no interface needed. First, a version of the main program *not* using Dependency Injection. Obviously the View requires the Model, to get the data to display:

ControllerTightlyCoupled.java

```
public class ControllerTightlyCoupled {

    public static void main(String[] args) {
        Model m = new SimpleModel();
        View v = new ConsoleViewer();
        ((ConsoleViewer)v).setModel(m);
        v.displayMessage();
    }
}
```

Here we have four tasks to undertake:

1. Create the Model.
2. Create the View.
3. Tie the Model into the View.
4. Ask the View to display some data.

Now a version using Dependency Injection:

Spring Controller.java

```
public class Controller {

    public static void main(String[] args) {
        ApplicationContext ctx =
            new AnnotationConfigApplicationContext( "di.spring");
        View v = ctx.getBean("myView", View.class);
        v.displayMessage();
    }
}
```

In this version, we have only three tasks:

1. Set up the Spring "context," which provides the dependency injection framework.
2. Get the View from the context; it already has the Model set into it!
3. Ask the View to display some data.

Furthermore, we don't depend on particular implementations of the interface.

How does Spring know to "inject" or provide a Model to the View? And how does it know what code to use for the View? There might be multiple implementations of the

View interface. Of course we have to tell it these things, which we'll do here with annotations:

Spring ConsoleViewer.java

```java
@Component("myView")
public class ConsoleViewer implements View {

    Model messageProvider;

    @Override
    public void displayMessage() {
        System.out.println(messageProvider.getMessage());
    }

    @Resource(name="myModel")
    public void setModel(Model messageProvider) {
        this.messageProvider = messageProvider;
    }

}
```

Note that whereas the @Component annotation is from Spring, the @Resource annotation is a standard part of Java, in package javax.annotation.

Due to the persistence of information on the Web, if you do a web search for Spring Injection, you will probably find zillions of articles that refer to the older Spring 2.x way of doing things, which is to use an XML configuration file. You can still use this, but modern Spring practice is to use Java annotations to configure the dependencies.

Annotations are also used in the Java Enterprise Edition Contexts and Dependency Injection (CDI). Although this is most widely used in web applications, we'll reuse the same example, using the open source "Weld" implementation of CDI. CDI is quite a bit more powerful than Spring's DI; because in CDI we don't even need to know the class from which a resource is being injected, we don't even need the interfaces from the Spring example! First, the "Controller" or main program, which requires a Weld-specific import or two because CDI was originally designed for use in enterprise applications:

CDI ConsoleViewer.java

```java
public class ConsoleViewer implements View {
    @Inject @MyModel
    private String message;

    @Override
    public void displayMessage() {
        System.out.println(message);
    }
}
```

The View interface is shared between both implementations. The ConsoleViewer implementation is similar too, except it isn't coupled to the Model; it just asks to have a String injected. In this simple example there is only one String in the application; in a larger app you would need one additional annotation to specify which string to inject:

CDI ConsoleViewer.java

```
public class ConsoleViewer implements View {
    @Inject @MyModel
    private String message;

    @Override
    public void displayMessage() {
        System.out.println(message);
    }
}
```

Where does the injected String come from? From the Model, as before:

CDI Model.java

```
public class Model {

    public @Produces @MyModel String getModelData(InjectionPoint ip)
        throws IOException {

        ResourceBundle props = ResourceBundle.getBundle("messages");
        return props.getString(
            ip.getMember().getDeclaringClass().getSimpleName() + "." +
            ip.getMember().getName());
    }
}
```

See Also

Spring DI, Java EE CDI, and Guice all provide powerful "dependency injection." Spring's is more widely used; Java EE's is more powerful. All work standalone and inside web applications, with minor variations; in the EE, Spring provides special support for web apps, and in EE containers, CDI is already set up so the first statement in the CDIMain statement is not needed in an EE app. There are many books on Spring. One book specifically treats Weld: *JBoss Weld CDI for Java Platform* by Ken Finnegan (O'Reilly).

8.12. Program: Plotter

Not because it is very sophisticated, but because it is simple, this program serves as an example of some of the things we've covered in this chapter, and also, in its subclasses, provides a springboard for other discussions. This class describes a series of old-fashioned (i.e., common in the 1970s and 1980s) pen plotters. A pen plotter, in case you've never seen one, is a device that moves a pen around a piece of paper and draws things. It can lift the pen off the paper or lower it, and it can draw lines, letters, and so on. Before the rise of laser printers and ink-jet printers, pen plotters were the dominant means of preparing charts of all sorts, as well as presentation slides (this was, ah, well before the rise of programs like Harvard Presents and Microsoft PowerPoint). Today, few, if any, companies still manufacture pen plotters, but I use them here because they are simple enough to be well understood from this brief description. Today's "3-D Printers" may be thought of as representing a resurgence of the pen plotter with just one additional axis of motion. And a fancier pen.

I'll present a high-level class that abstracts the key characteristics of a series of such plotters made by different vendors. It would be used, for example, in an analytical or data-exploration program to draw colorful charts showing the relationships found in data. But I don't want my main program to worry about the gory details of any particular brand of plotter, so I'll abstract into a Plotter class, whose source is as follows:

plotter/Plotter.java

```java
/**
 * Plotter abstract class. Must be subclassed
 * for X, DOS, Penman, HP plotter, etc.
 *
 * Coordinate space: X = 0 at left, increases to right.
 *         Y = 0 at top, increases downward (same as AWT).
 *
 * @author    Ian F. Darwin
 */
public abstract class Plotter {
    public final int MAXX = 800;
    public final int MAXY = 600;
    /** Current X co-ordinate (same reference frame as AWT!) */
    protected int curx;
    /** Current Y co-ordinate (same reference frame as AWT!) */
    protected int cury;
    /** The current state: up or down */
    protected boolean penIsUp;
    /** The current color */
    protected int penColor;

    Plotter() {
        penIsUp = true;
        curx = 0; cury = 0;
    }
    abstract void rmoveTo(int incrx, int incry);
    abstract void moveTo(int absx, int absy);
    abstract void penUp();
    abstract void penDown();
    abstract void penColor(int c);

    abstract void setFont(String fName, int fSize);
    abstract void drawString(String s);
```

```
/* Concrete methods */

/** Draw a box of width w and height h */
public void drawBox(int w, int h) {
    penDown();
    rmoveTo(w, 0);
    rmoveTo(0, h);
    rmoveTo(-w, 0);
    rmoveTo(0, -h);
    penUp();
}

/** Draw a box given an AWT Dimension for its size */
public void drawBox(java.awt.Dimension d) {
    drawBox(d.width, d.height);
}

/** Draw a box given an AWT Rectangle for its location and size */
public void drawBox(java.awt.Rectangle r) {
    moveTo(r.x, r.y);
    drawBox(r.width, r.height);
}

/** Show the current location; useful for
 * testing, if nothing else.
 */
public Point getLocation() {
    return new Point(curx, cury);
}
}
```

Note the variety of abstract methods. Those related to motion, pen control, or drawing are left abstract, due to the number of different methods for dealing with them. However, the method for drawing a rectangle (drawBox) has a default implementation, which simply puts the currently selected pen onto the paper at the last-moved-to location, draws the four sides, and raises the pen. Subclasses for "smarter" plotters will likely override this method, but subclasses for less-evolved plotters will probably use the default version. This method also has two overloaded convenience methods for cases where the client has an AWT Dimension for the size or an AWT Rectangle for the location and size.

To demonstrate one of the subclasses of this program, consider the following simple "driver" program. This is intended to simulate a larger graphics application such as GnuPlot. The Class.forName() near the beginning of main is discussed in Recipe 23.2; for now, you can take my word that it simply creates an instance of the given subclass, which we store in a Plotter reference named "r" and use to draw the plot:

plotter/PlotDriver.java

```java
public class PlotDriver {

    /** Construct a Plotter driver, and try it out. */
    public static void main(String[] argv) {
        Plotter r ;
        if (argv.length != 1) {
            System.err.println("Usage: PlotDriver driverclass");
            return;
        }
        try {
            Class<?> c = Class.forName(argv[0]);
            Object o = c.newInstance();
            if (!(o instanceof Plotter))
                throw new ClassNotFoundException("Not instanceof Plotter");
            r = (Plotter)o;
        } catch (ClassNotFoundException e) {
            System.err.println("Sorry, class " + argv[0] +
                    " not a plotter class");
            return;
        } catch (Exception e) {
            e.printStackTrace();
            return;
        }
        r.penDown();
        r.penColor(1);
        r.moveTo(200, 200);
        r.penColor(2);
        r.drawBox(123, 200);
        r.rmoveTo(10, 20);
        r.penColor(3);
        r.drawBox(123, 200);
        r.penUp();
        r.moveTo(300, 100);
        r.penDown();
        r.setFont("Helvetica", 14);
        r.drawString("Hello World");
        r.penColor(4);
        r.drawBox(10, 10);
    }
}
```

We'll see example subclasses of this Plotter class in upcoming chapters.

## CHAPTER 9

Functional Programming Techniques: Functional Interfaces, Streams, Parallel Collections

9.0. Introduction

Java is an object-oriented (OO) language. You know what that is. Functional Programming (FP) has been attracting attention lately. There may not be quite as many definitions of FP as there are FP languages, but it's close. Wikipedia's definition of Functional Programming is …

> "… a programming paradigm, a style of building the structure and elements of computer programs, that treats computation as the evaluation of mathematical functions and avoids state and mutable data. Functional programming emphasizes functions that produce results that depend only on their inputs and not on the program state - i.e. pure mathematical functions. It is a declarative programming paradigm, which means programming is done with expressions. In functional code, the output value of a function depends only on the arguments that are input to the function, so calling a function f twice with the same value for an argument x will produce the same result f(x) both times. Eliminating side effects, i.e. changes in state that don't depend on the function inputs, can make it much easier to understand and predict the behavior of a program, which is one of the key motivations for the development of functional programming…"
>
> — *http://bit.ly/1eUS2QP*
> *viewed December 2013*

How can we benefit from the FP paradigm? One way would be to switch to using an FP language; some of the leading ones are Haskell, Ocaml, Erlang, and the LISP family. But most of those would require walking away from the Java ecosystem. You could consider using Scala (*http://bit.ly/16miGQf*) or Clojure (*http://clojure.org*), JVM-based languages that provide functional programming support in the context of an OO language.

But this is the *Java Cookbook*, so you can imagine we're going to try to get some of the benefits of functional programming while remaining in the Java language. Some features of FP include:

- Pure functions; having no side-effects and whose results depend only on their inputs and not on mutable state elsewhere in the program
- First-class functions (e.g., functions as data)
- Immutable data
- Extensive use of recursion and lazy evaluation

Pure functions are completely self-contained; their operation depends only on the input parameters and internal logic, not on any variable "state" in other parts of the program —indeed, there are no "global variables," only global *constants*. Although this can be hard to accept for those schooled in imperative languages like Java, it does make it much easier to test and ensure program correctness! It means that, no matter what else is going on in the program (even with multiple threads), a method call like `computeValue(27)` will always, unconditionally, return the same value every time (with exceptions, of course, for things like the current time, random seeds, etc., which are global state).

We'll use the terms *function* and *method* interchangeably in this chapter, although it's not strictly correct. FP people use the term "function" in the mathematical function sense, whereas "methods" in Java just mean "some code you can call" (a Java "method call" is also referred to as a *message* being *sent* to an object, in the OO view of things).

"Functions as data" means that you can create an object that is a function, pass it into another function, write a function that returns another function, and so on—with no special syntax, because, well, functions *are* data.

One of Java 8's approach to FP is the definition of "functional interfaces." A *functional interface* in Java is one that has only one method, such as the widely used `Runnable`, whose only method is `run()`, or the common Swing "action handler" `ActionListener`, whose only method is `actionPerformed(ActionEvent)`. Actually, also new in Java 8, interfaces can have methods annotated with the new-in-this-context `default` keyword. A `default` method in an interface becomes available for use in any class that `implements` the interface; if you think about it, you'll see that such methods cannot depend on instance state in a particular class because they would have no way of referring to it at compile time.

So a functional interface is more precisely defined as one that has a single nondefault method. You can do functional-style programming in Java if you use functional interfaces and if you restrict code in your methods to not depending on any nonfinal instance or class fields; using default methods is one way of achieving this. The first few recipes in this chapter discuss functional interfaces.

Another Java 8 approach to this is "lambda expressions." A lambda is an expression of a functional interface, and can be used as data (i.e., assigned, returned, etc.). Just to give a couple of short examples for now:

```
ActionListener x = (e -> System.out.println("You activated " + e.getSource()));

public class RunnableLambda {
    public static void main(String[] args) {
        new Thread(() -> System.out.println("Hello from a thread")).start();
    }
}
```

Also new in Java 8 is the notion of `Stream` classes. A `Stream` is like a pipeline that you can feed into, fan out, collect down—like a cross between the Unix notion of pipelines and Google's distributed programming concept of Map-Reduce, as exemplified in Hadoop (*http://hadoop.apache.org*), but running in a single VM, a single program. Streams can be sequential or parallel; the latter are designed to take advantage of the massive parallelism that is happening in hardware design (particularly servers, where 12- and 16-core processors are popular). We discuss `Streams` in several recipes in this chapter.

Tied in with `Streams` is the notion of a `Spliterator`, a derivative (logically, not by inheritance) of the familiar `Iterator`, but designed for use in parallel processing. *Most users will not be expected to develop their own Spliterator and will likely not even call its methods directly very often*, so we do not discuss them in detail.

See Also

For general information on Functional Programming, see the new book *Functional Thinking*.

There is an entire book dedicated to lambda expressions and related tools, Richard Warburton's *Java 8 Lambdas* (O'Reilly).

9.1. Using Lambdas/Closures Instead of Inner Classes

Problem

You want to avoid all the typing that even the anonymous style of inner class requires.

Solution

Use Java's lambda expressions.

Discussion

The symbol lambda (λ) is the 11th letter of the Greek alphabet, and thus as old as Western society. The Lambda Calculus (*http://en.wikipedia.org/wiki/Lambda_calculus*) is about as old as our notions of computing. In this context, Lambda expressions are *small units of calculation that can be referred to*. They are "functions as data." In that sense, they are a lot like anonymous inner classes, though it's probably better to think of them as *anonymous methods*. They are essentially used to replace inner classes for a *functional interface*—that is, an interface with one abstract method ("function") in it. A very common example is the AWT *ActionListener* interface, widely used in GUI code, whose only method is:

```
public void actionPerformed(ActionEvent);
```

We'll see examples of using lambdas for GUI action listeners in Chapter 14. Here's one single example to whet your appetite:

```
quitButton.addActionListener(e -> System.exit(0));
```

Because not everybody writes GUI applications these days, let's start with an example that doesn't require GUI programming. Suppose we have a collection of camera model descriptor objects that has *already been loaded from a database into memory*, and we want to write a general-purpose API for searching them, for use by other parts of our application.

The first thought might be along the following lines:

```
public interface CameraInfo {
    public List<Camera> findByMake();
    public List<Camera> findByModel();
```

```
    ...
}
```

Perhaps you can already see the problem. You will also need to write a `findBy-Price()`, `findByMakeAndModel()`, `findByYearIntroduced()`, and so on, as your application grows in complexity.

You could consider implementing a "query by example" method, where you pass in a `Camera` object and all its nonnull fields are used in the comparison. But then how would you implement finding cameras with interchangeable lenses *under $500*?[1]

So a better approach is probably to use a "callback function" to do the comparison. Then you can provide an anonymous inner class to do any kind of searching you need. You'd want to be able to write callback methods like this:

```
public boolean choose(Camera c) {
    return c.isIlc() && c.getPrice() < 500;
}
```

Accordingly, we'll build that into an interface:[2]

```
/** An Acceptor accepts some elements from a Collection */
public interface CameraAcceptor {
    boolean choose(Camera c);
}
```

Now the search application provides a method:

```
public List<Camera> search(CameraAcceptor acc);
```

which we can call with code like this (assuming you're comfortable with anonymous inner classes):

```
results = searchApp.search(new CameraAcceptor() {
    public boolean choose(Camera c) {
        return c.isIlc() && c.getPrice() < 500;
    }
}
```

Or, if you were not comfortable with anonymous inner classes, you might have to type

---

1. If you ever have to do this kind of thing where the data is stored in a relational database using the Java Persistence API (see Recipe 18.1), you should check out Apache DeltaSpike Data (*http://bit.ly/TOPpJt*), which allows you to define an interface with method names like `findCameraByInterchangeableTrueAndPrice-LessThan(double price)` and have DeltaSpike Data *implement these methods for you*. There are also template projects for CDI+DeltaSpike on GitHub: Java SE (*http://bit.ly/1krOO5Z*) and Java Web (*http://bit.ly/1kRmuyP*).

2. If you're just not that into cameras, the description "Interchangeable Lens Camera (ILC)" includes two categories of what you might find in a camera store in 2014: traditional DSLR (digital single lens reflex) cameras, and the newer category of "Compact System Cameras" like the Nikon 1, Sony ILCE (formerly known as NEX), and the Canon EOS-M, all of which are smaller and lighter than the older DSLRs.

```
class MyIlcPriceAcceptor implements CameraAcceptor {
    public boolean choose(Camera c) {
        return c.isIlc() && c.getPrice() < 500;
    }
}
CameraAcceptor myIlcPriceAcceptor = nwq MyIlcPriceAcceptor();
results = searchApp.search(myIlcPriceAcceptor);
```

That's really a great deal of typing just to get one method packaged up for sending into the search engine. Java's support for lambda expressions or Closures was argued about for many years (literally) before the experts agreed on how to do it. And the result is staggeringly simple. One way to think of Java lambda expressions is that each one is just *a method that implements a functional interface*. With lambda expressions, you can rewrite the preceding as just:

```
results = searchApp.search(c -> c.isIlc() && c.getPrice() < 500);
```

The arrow notation -> indicates the code to execute. If it's a simple expression as here, you just write it as shown. If there is conditional logic or other statements, you have to use a block, as is usual in Java.

Here I just rewrite the search example to show it as a block:

```
results = searchApp.search(c -> {
    if (c.isIlc() && c.getPrice() < 500)
        return true;
    else
        return false;
});
```

The first c inside the parenthesis corresponds to Camera c in the explicitly implemented choose() method: you can omit the type because the compiler knows it! If there is more than one argument to the method, you must parenthesize them. Suppose we had a compare method that takes two cameras and returns a quantitative value (oh, and good luck trying to get two photographers to agree on *that* algorithm!):

```
double goodness = searchApp.compare((c1, c2) -> {
    // write some amazing code here
});
```

This notion of *lambdas* seems pretty potent, and it is! You will see much more of this in Java as Java 8 moves into the mainstream of computing.

Up to here, we still have to write an interface for each type of method that we want to be able to lambda-ize. The next recipe shows some predefined interfaces that you can use to further simplify (or at least shorten) your code.

And, of course, there are many existing interfaces that are "functional," such as the ActionListener interface from GUI applications. Interestingly, the IntelliJ IDE (see Recipe 1.3) automatically recognizes inner class definitions that are replaceable by lambdas and, when using "code folding" (the IDE feature of representing an entire method definition with a single line), replaces the inner class with the corresponding lambda! Figures 9-1 and 9-2 show a before-and-after picture of this code folding.

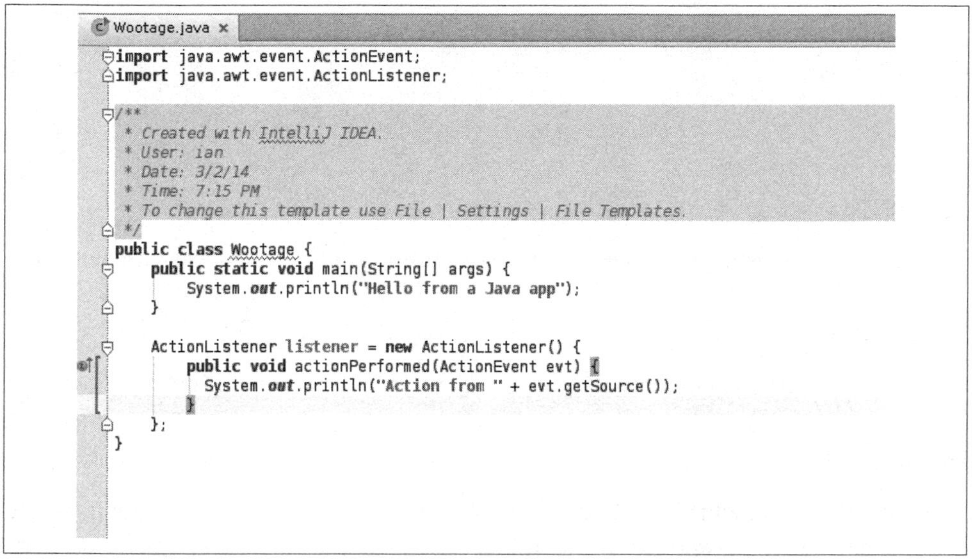

Figure 9-1. IntelliJ code unfolded

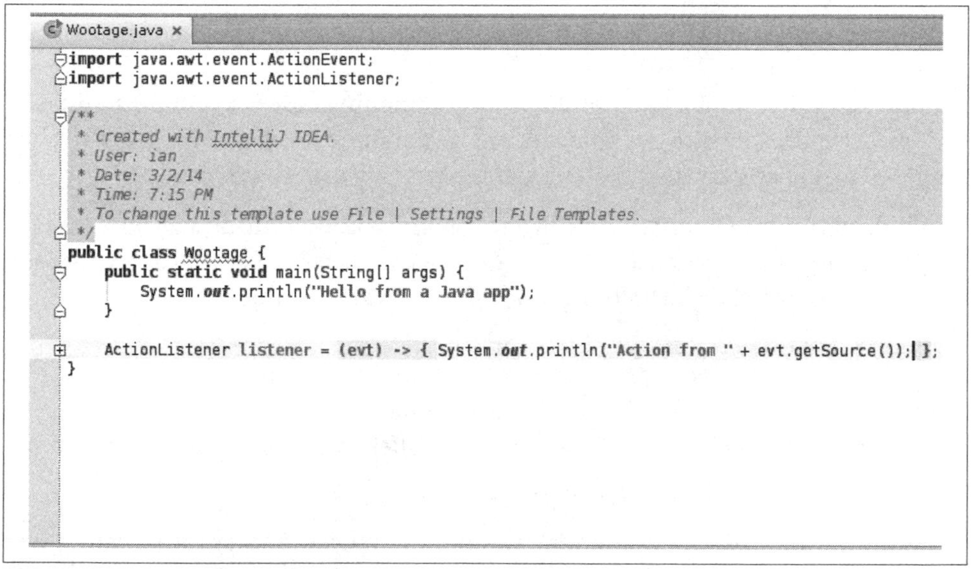

Figure 9-2. IntelliJ code folded

9.2. Using Lambda Predefined Interfaces Instead of Your Own

Problem

You want to use existing interfaces, instead of defining your own, for use with Lambdas.

Solution

Use the Java 8 lambda Functional interfaces from `java.util.function`.

Discussion

In Recipe 9.1, we used the interface method `acceptCamera()` defined in the interface `CameraAcceptor`. Acceptor-type methods are quite common, so the package `java.util.function` includes the `Predicate<T>` interface, which we can use instead of `CameraAcceptor`. This interface has only one method—`boolean test(T t)`:

```
interface Predicate<T> {
    boolean test(T t);
}
```

This package includes about 50 of the most commonly needed functional interfaces, such as `IntUnaryOperator`, which takes one `int` argument and returns an `int` value; `LongPredicate`, which takes one `long` and returns `boolean`; and so on.

To use the `Predicate` interface, as with any generic type, we provide an actual type for the parameter `Camera`, giving us (in this case) the parameterized type `Predicate<Camera>`, which is the following (although we don't have to write this out):

```
interface Predicate<Camera> {
    boolean test(Camera c);
}
```

So now our search application will be changed to offer us the following search method:

```
public List<Camera> search(Predicate p);
```

Conveniently, this has the same "signature" as our own `CameraAcceptor` *from the point of view of the anonymous methods that lambdas implement,* so the rest of our code doesn't have to change! This is still a valid call to the `search()` method:

```
results = searchApp.search(c -> c.isIlc() && c.getPrice() < 500);
```

Here is the implementation of the search method:

functional/CameraSearchPredicate.java

```java
public List<Camera> search(Predicate<Camera> tester) {
    List<Camera> results = new ArrayList<>();
    privateListOfCameras.forEach(c -> {
        if (tester.test(c))
            results.add(c);
    });
    return results;
}
```

Suppose we only need the list to do one operation on each element, and then we'll discard it. Upon reflection, we don't actually need to get the list back, but merely to get our hooks on each element that matches our Predicate in turn.

9.3. Simplifying Processing with Streams

Problem

You want to process some data through a pipeline-like mechanism.

Solution

Use a Stream class and its operations.

Discussion

Streams are a new mechanism introduced with Java 8 to allow a collection to send its values out one at a time through a pipeline-like mechanism where they can be processed in various ways, with varying degrees of parallelism. There are three types of methods involved with Streams:

- Stream-producing methods (see Recipe 7.3)
- Stream-passing methods, which operate on a Stream and return a reference to it, to allow for "fluent programming" (chained methods calls); examples include dis-tinct(), filter(), limit(), map(), peek(), sorted(), unsorted(), and more

- Stream-terminating methods, which conclude a streaming operation; examples include count(), findFirst(), max(), min(), reduce(), sum(), among others

In Example 9-1, we have a list of Hero objects representing superheroes through the ages. We use the Stream mechanism to filter just the adult heros, and sum their ages. We then use it again to sort the heros' names alphabetically.

In both operations we start with a stream generator (Arrays.stream()), run it through several steps, one of which involves a mapping operation (don't confuse with java.util.Map!) that causes a different value to be sent along the pipeline, followed by a terminating operation. The map and filter operations almost invariably are controlled by a lambda expression (inner classes would be too tedious to use in this style of programming!).

Example 9-1. SimpleStreamDemo.java

```
static Hero[] heroes = {
    new Hero("Grelber", 21),
    new Hero("Roderick", 12),
    new Hero("Francisco", 35),
    new Hero("Superman", 65),
    new Hero("Jumbletron", 22),
    new Hero("Mavericks", 1),
    new Hero("Palladin", 50),
    new Hero("Athena", 50) };

public static void main(String[] args) {

    long adultYearsExperience = Arrays.stream(heroes)
            .filter(b -> b.age >= 18)
            .mapToInt(b -> b.age).sum();
    System.out.println("We're in good hands! The adult superheros have " +
            adultYearsExperience + " years of experience");

    List<Object> sorted = Arrays.stream(heroes)
            .sorted((h1, h2) -> h1.name.compareTo(h2.name))
            .map(h -> h.name)
            .collect(Collectors.toList());
    System.out.println("Heroes by name: " + sorted);
}
```

And let's run it to be sure it works:

```
We're in good hands! The adult superheros have 243 years of experience
Heroes by name: [Athena, Francisco, Grelber, Jumbletron, Mavericks, Palladin,
            Roderick, Superman]
```

See the javadoc for the java.util.stream.Stream interface for a complete list of the operations.

9.4. Improving Throughput with Parallel Streams and Collections

Problem

You want to combine `Streams` with parallelism, and still be able to use the nonthread-safe Collections API.

Solution

Use a parallel stream.

Discussion

The standard Collections classes such as most `List`, `Set`, and `Map` implementations are not thread-safe for update; if you add or remove objects from one in one thread while another thread is accessing the objects stored in the collection, failure will result. Multiple threads reading from the same collection with no modification is OK. We discuss multithreading in Chapter 22.

The Collections Framework does provide "synchronized wrappers," which provide automatic synchronization but at the cost of adding thread contention, which reduces parallelism. To enable efficient operations, *parallel streams* let you use the nonthread-safe collections safely, as long as you *do not modify the collection while you are operating on it*.

To use a parallel stream, you just ask the collection for it, using `parallelStream()` instead of the `stream()` method we used in Recipe 9.3.

For example, suppose that our camera business takes off, and we need to find cameras by type and price range *quickly* (and with less code than we used before):

```
public static void main(String[] args) {
    for (Object camera : privateListOfCameras.parallelStream().    ❶
            filter(c -> c.isIlc() && c.getPrice() < 500).           ❷
            toArray()) {                                            ❸
        System.out.println(camera);                                ❹
    }
}
```

❶ Create a parallel stream from the List of Camera objects. The end result of the stream will be iterated over by the foreach loop.

❷ Filter the cameras on price, using the same Predicate lambda that we used in Recipe 9.1.

❸ Terminate the Stream by converting it to an array.

❹ The body of the foreach loop: print one Camera from the stream.

 This is only reliable as long as no thread is modifying the data at the same time as the searching is going on. See the thread interlocking mechanisms in Chapter 22 to see how to ensure this.

9.5. Creating Your Own Functional Interfaces

Problem

You want to create functional interfaces for use within lambda expressions.

Solution

Create an interface with one abstract method; optionally annotate it with @Functiona-lInterface.

Discussion

As mentioned previously, a functional interface is one with a single abstract method. Some well-known functional interfaces are java.lang.Runnable, java.util.Observer, and java.awt.event.ActionListener. Some "nonfunctional" (in this sense) interfaces include java.util.Observable and java.awt.event.WindowListener, each of which has more than one method.

You can create your own functional interface easily. However, before you do so, consider that a large selection of these is already available in the JDK! As discussed in Recipe 9.2, you should check the documentation for the package `java.util.function`, which provides lots of predefined general-purpose functional interfaces, including `Predicate`, which we've already used.

So, you still want to do it yourself? A simple example of a functional interface would be:

```
public interface MyFunctionalInterface {
    int compute(int x);
}
```

This could be used to process an array of integers as:

```
public class ProcessIntsFunctional {
    static int[] integers = { 0, 1, 2, 3, 4, 5 };

    /** Function to be called with an int and a Function;
     * just apply the function to the int and return the result
     */
    static int doTheMath(int n, Function<Integer,Integer> func) {
        return func.apply(n);
    }

    public static void main(String[] args) {

        int total = 0;
        for (int i : integers) {
            // Call doTheMath with 'i' and a Lambda for n^2 +1
            total += doTheMath(i, k -> k * k + 1 );
        }
        System.out.println(total);
    }
}
```

If `compute` were a nonfunctional interface—having multiple abstract methods—you would not be able to use it in this fashion.

To ensure that a given interface is and remains functional, there is a `@FunctionalInterface` annotation, whose use is analogous to `@Override` (both annotations are in `java.lang`). It is always optional, and is always used to ensure that a given interface conforms to the contract of being a functional interface. Our preceding interface could sport the annotation like so:

```
@FunctionalInterface
public interface MyFunctionalInterface {
    int compute(int x);
}
```

If somebody later working on the code were to add an additional method:

```
int recompute(int x);
```

the interface would cease to be functional, but the compiler or IDE would detect that fact as soon as you saved or compiled the interface, saving you from puzzling out why the lambda expression was invalid. Javac will complain as follows:

```
C:\javasrc>javac -d build src/lang/MyFunctionalInterface.java
src\lang\MyFunctionalInterface.java:3: error: Unexpected @FunctionalInterface
annotation
@FunctionalInterface
^
  MyFunctionalInterface is not a functional interface
    multiple non-overriding abstract methods found in
    interface MyFunctionalInterface

1 error

C:\javasrc>
```

Sometimes, of course, you really do need an interface to have more than one method. In that case, the illusion (or the effect) of functionality can sometimes be preserved by denoting all but one of the methods with the "default" keyword—the nondefault method will still be usable in lambdas. A default method has a method body:

```
public interface ThisIsStillFunctional {
    default int compute(int ix) { return ix * ix + 1 };
    int anotherMethod(int y);
}
```

Only default methods may contain executable statements, and there may only be one nondefault method per functional interface.

Oh, and of course, our `MyFunctionalInterface` given earlier can be totally replaced by `java.util.function.IntUnaryOperator`, changing the method name `apply()` to `applyAsInt()`. There is a version of the `ProcessInts` program under the name `ProcessIntsIntUnaryOperator` in the *javasrc* repository.

See Also

Default methods in interfaces can be used to produce "mixins," as described in Recipe 9.7.

9.6. Using Existing Code as Functional with Method References

Problem

You have existing code that matches a functional interface and want to use it without renaming methods to match the interface name.

Solution

Use function references such as `MyClass::myFunc` or `someObj::someFunc`.

Discussion

The word "reference" is almost as overloaded in Java as the word "Session." Consider:

- Ordinary objects are usually accessed with references.
- Reference Types such as `WeakReference` have defined semantics for garbage collection.
- And now, for something completely different, Java 8 lets you reference an individual method.
- You can even reference "an Instance Method of an Arbitrary Object of a Particular Type."

The new syntax consists of an object or class name, two colons, and the name of a method that can be invoked in the context of the object or class name (as per the usual rules of Java, a class name can refer to static methods and an instance can refer to an instance method). To refer to a constructor as the method, you can use `new`—for example, `MyClass::new`. The reference creates a lambda that can be invoked, stored in a variable of a functional interface type, and so on.

In Example 9-2, we create a `Runnable` reference that holds, not the usual `run` method, but a method with the same type and arguments but with the name `walk`. Note the use of `this` as the object part of the method reference. We then pass this `Runnable` into a `Thread` constructor and start the thread, with the result that `walk` is invoked where `run` would normally be.

Example 9-2. ReferencesDemo.java

```java
/** "Walk, don't run" */
public class ReferencesDemo {

    // Assume this is an existing method we don't want to rename
    public void walk() {
        System.out.println("ReferencesDemo.walk(): Stand-in run method called");
    }

    // This is our main processing method; it runs "walk" in a Thread
    public void doIt() {
        Runnable r = this::walk;
        new Thread(r).start();
    }

    // The usual simple main method to start things off
    public static void main(String[] args) {
        new ReferencesDemo().doIt();
    }
}
```

The output is as follows:

```
ReferencesDemo.walk(): Stand-in run method called
```

Example 9-3 creates an `AutoCloseable` for use in a try-with-resource (see "Try With Resources" on page 840). The normal `AutoCloseable` method is `close()`, but ours is named `cloz()`. The `AutoCloseable` reference variable `autoCloseable` is created inside the `try` statement, so its close–like method will be called when the body completes. In this example, we are in a static `main` method wherein we have a reference `rnd2` to an instance of the class, so we use this in referring to the `AutoCloseable`-compatible method.

Example 9-3. ReferencesDemo2.java

```java
public class ReferencesDemo2 {
    void cloz() {
        System.out.println("Stand-in close() method called");
    }

    public static void main(String[] args) throws Exception {
        ReferencesDemo2 rd2 = new ReferencesDemo2();

        // Use a method reference to assign the AutoCloseable interface
        // variable "ac" to the matching method signature "c" (obviously
        // short for close, but just to she the method name isn't what matters).
        try (AutoCloseable autoCloseable = rd2::cloz) {
            System.out.println("Some action happening here.");
        }
    }
}
```

The output is as follows:

```
Some action happening here.
Stand-in close() method called
```

It is, of course, possible to use this with your own functional interfaces, defined as in Recipe 9.5. You're also probably at least vaguely aware that any normal Java object reference can be passed to System.out.println() and you'll get some description of the referenced object. Example 9-4 explores these two themes. We define a functional interface imaginatively known as FunInterface with a method with a bunch of arguments (merely to avoid it being mistaken for any existing functional interface). The method name is process, but as you now know the name is not important; our implementation method goes by the name work. The work method is static, so we could not state that the class implements FunInterface (even if the method names were the same; a static method may not hide an inherited instance method), but we can nonetheless create a lambda reference to the work method. We then print this out to show that it has a valid structure as a Java object.

Example 9-4. ReferencesDemo3.java

```
public class ReferencesDemo3 {

    interface FunInterface {
        void process(int i, String j, char c, double d);
    }

    public static void work(int i, String j, char c, double d){
        System.out.println("Moo");
    }

    public static void main(String[] args) {
        FunInterface sample = ReferencesDemo3::work;
        System.out.println("My process method is " + sample);
    }
}
```

This generates the following output:

```
My process method is functional.ReferencesDemo3$$Lambda$1/713338599@4a574795
```

The Lambda$1 in the name is structurally similar to the "$1" used in anonymous inner classes.

The fourth way, what Oracle documentation calls "an Instance Method of an Arbitrary Object of a Particular Type," may be the most esoteric thing in all of Java 8. It allows you to declare a reference to an instance method, but without specifying which instance. Because there is no particualr instance in mind, you again use the class name. This means you can use it with any instance of the given class! In Example 9-5, we have an array of Strings to sort. Because the names in this array can begin with a lowercase letter, we want to sort them using the String method compareToIgnoreCase(), which nicely ignores case differences for us.

Because I want to show the sorting several different ways, I set up two array referencess, the original, unsorted one, and a working one that is re-created, sorted, and printed using a simple dump routine, which isn't shown (it's just a for loop printing the strings from the passed array).

Example 9-5. ReferencesDemo4.java

```java
import java.util.Arrays;
import java.util.Comparator;

public class ReferencesDemo4 {

    static final String[] unsortedNames = {
        "Gosling", "de Raadt", "Torvalds", "Ritchie", "Hopper"
    };

    public static void main(String[] args) {
        String[] names;

        // Sort using
        // "an Instance Method of an Arbitrary Object of a Particular Type"
        names = unsortedNames.clone();
        Arrays.sort(names, String::compareToIgnoreCase);           ❶
        dump(names);

        // Equivalent Lambda:
        names = unsortedNames.clone();
        Arrays.sort(names, (str1, str2) -> str1.compareToIgnoreCase(str2));  ❷
        dump(names);

        // Equivalent old way:
        names = unsortedNames.clone();
        Arrays.sort(names, new Comparator<String>() {               ❸
            @Override
            public int compare(String str1, String str2) {
                return str1.compareToIgnoreCase(str2);
            }
        });
        dump(names);

        // Simpest way, using existing comparator
        names = unsortedNames.clone();
        Arrays.sort(names, String.CASE_INSENSITIVE_ORDER);          ❹
        dump(names);
    }
```

- ① Using "an Instance Method of an Arbitrary Object of a Particular Type," declares a reference to the compareToIgnoreCase method of any String used in the invocation.
- ② Shows the equivalent lambda expression.
- ③ Shows "Your grandparents' Java" way of doing things.
- ④ Using the exported Comparator directly, just to show that there is always more than one way to do things.

Just to be safe, I ran the demo, and got the expected output:

```
de Raadt Gosling Hopper Ritchie Torvalds
de Raadt Gosling Hopper Ritchie Torvalds
de Raadt Gosling Hopper Ritchie Torvalds
de Raadt Gosling Hopper Ritchie Torvalds
```

9.7. Java Mixins: Mixing in Methods

Problem

You've heard about "mixins" and want to apply them in Java.

Solution

Use static imports. Or, declare one or more functional interfaces with a "default" method containing the code to execute, and simply implement it.

Discussion

Developers from other languages sometimes deride Java for its inability to handle "mixins," the ability to "mix in" bits of code from other classes.

One way to implement mixins is with the "static import" feature, which has been in the language for a decade. This is often done in Unit Testing (see Recipe 1.13). A limitation of this approach is that, as the name implies, the methods must be static methods, not instance methods.

A newer mechanism depends on an interesting bit of fallout from the Java 8 language changes in support of lambdas: you can now "mix in" code from unrelated places into one class. Has Java finally abandoned its staunch opposition to multiple inheritance? It may seem that way when you first hear it, but relax: you can only pull methods from multiple interfaces, not from multiple classes. If you didn't know that you could have methods defined (rather than merely declared) in interfaces, see Recipe 9.5. Consider the following example:

lang/MixinsDemo.java

```
interface Bar {
    default String filter(String s) {
        return "Filtered " + s;
    }
}

interface Foo {
    default String convolve(String s) {
        return "Convolved " + s;
    }
}

public class MixinsDemo implements Foo, Bar{

    public static void main(String[] args) {
        String input = args.length > 0 ? args[0] : "Hello";
        String output = new MixinsDemo().process(input);
        System.out.println(output);
    }

    private String process(String s) {
        return filter(convolve(s)); // methods mixed in!
    }
}
```

If we run this, we see the expected results:

```
C:\javasrc>javac -d build lang/MixinsDemo.java
C:\javasrc>java -cp build lang.MixinsDemo
Filtered Convolved Hello

C:\javasrc>
```

Presto—Java now supports mixins!

Does this mean you should go crazy trying to build interfaces with code in them? No. Remember this was designed to provide the notion of "functional interfaces" for use in lambda calculations. Used sparingly, it can provide the ability to "mixin" code to build up applications in another way than direct inheritance, aggregation, or AOP. Overused, it can make your code heavy, drive pre–Java 8 developers crazy, and lead to chaos.

CHAPTER 10
Input and Output

10.0. Introduction

Most programs need to interact with the outside world, and one common way of doing so is by reading and writing files. Files are normally on some persistent medium such as a disk drive, and, for the most part, we shall happily ignore the differences between files on a hard disk (and all the operating system-dependent filesystem types), a USB drive or SD card, a DVD-ROM, and others. For now, they're just files. And, like most other languages and OSes, Java extends the "reading and writing" model to network (socket) communications, which we'll touch on in Chapters 13 and 16.

Java provides many classes for input and output; they are summarized in Figure 10-1. This chapter covers all the normal input/output operations such as opening/closing and reading/writing files. Files are assumed to reside on some kind of file store or permanent storage. Distributed filesystems such as Sun's Network File System (NFS, common on Unix and available for Windows), SMB (the Windows network filesystem, available for Unix via the open source Samba program), and FUSE (Filesystem in User SpacE, implementations for most Unix/Linux systems) are assumed to work "just like" disk filesystems, except where noted.

The `Formatter` and `Scanner` classes provide formatting and scanning, of course. `Formatter` allows many formatting tasks to be performed either into a `String` or to almost any output destination. `Scanner` parses many kinds of objects, again either from a `String` or from almost any input source. These are new and very powerful; each is given its own recipe in this chapter.

Finally, this chapter provides only minimal coverage of the moribund Java Communications API, designed to read and write on serial and parallel ports. Previous editions of this book contained full coverage of this API, but it is little used now, and even less maintained.

Streams and Readers/Writers

Java provides two sets of classes for reading and writing. The Stream section of package java.io (see Figure 10-1) is for reading or writing bytes of data. Older languages tended to assume that a byte (which is a machine-specific collection of bits, usually eight bits on modern computers) is exactly the same thing as a "character"—a letter, digit, or other linguistic element. However, Java is designed to be used internationally, and eight bits is simply not enough to handle the many different character sets used around the world. Script-based languages like Arabic and Indian languages, and pictographic languages like Chinese and Japanese, each have many more than 256 characters, the maximum that can be represented in an eight-bit byte. The unification of these many character code sets is called, not surprisingly, Unicode. Both Java and XML use Unicode as their character sets, allowing you to read and write text in any of these human languages. But you should use Readers and Writers, not Streams, for textual data.

Unicode itself doesn't solve the entire problem. Many of these human languages were used on computers long before Unicode was invented, and they didn't all pick the same representation as Unicode. And they all have zillions of files encoded in a particular representation that isn't Unicode. So routines are needed when reading and writing to convert between Unicode String objects used inside the Java machine and the particular external representation in which a user's files are written. These converters are packaged inside a powerful set of classes called Readers and Writers. Readers and Writers should always be used instead of InputStreams and OutputStreams when you want to deal with characters instead of bytes. We'll see more on this conversion, and how to specify which conversion, a little later in this chapter.

See Also

One topic *not* addressed in depth here is the Java New I/O package (a poor choice of name: it was "new" in Java SE 1.4). NIO is more complex to use, and the benefits accrue primarily in large-scale server-side processing. Recipe 4.5 provides one example of using NIO. The NIO package is given full coverage in the book *Java NIO* by Ron Hitchens (O'Reilly).

Another issue not addressed here is hardcopy printing. Java's scheme for printing onto paper uses the same graphics model as is used in AWT, the basic Window System package. For this reason, I defer discussion of printing to Chapter 12.

Another topic not covered here is that of having the read or write occur concurrently with other program activity. This requires the use of threads, or multiple flows of control within a single program. Threaded I/O is a necessity in many programs: those reading from slow devices such as tape drives, those reading from or writing to network connections, and those with a GUI. For this reason, the topic is given considerable attention, in the context of multithreaded applications, in Chapter 22.

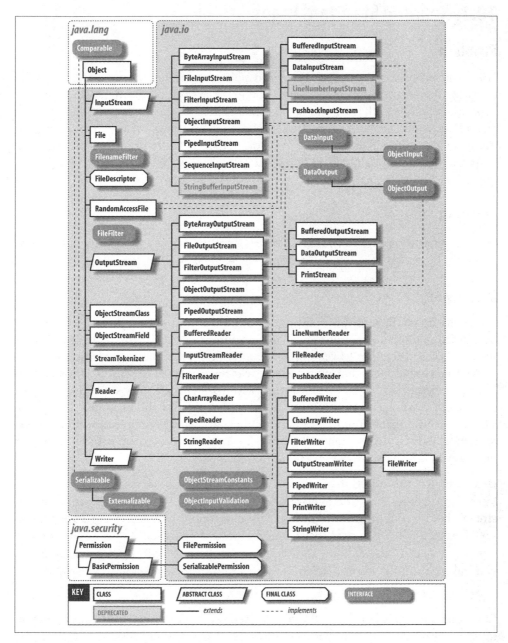

Figure 10-1. java.io classes

10.1. Reading Standard Input

Problem

You really do need to read from the standard input, or console. One reason is that simple test programs are often console-driven. Another is that some programs naturally require a lot of interaction with the user and you want something faster than a GUI (consider an interactive mathematics or statistical exploration program). Yet another is piping the output of one program directly to the input of another, a very common operation among Unix users and quite valuable on other platforms, such as Windows, that support this operation.

Solution

To read bytes, wrap a `BufferedInputStream()` around `System.in`. For the more common case of reading text, use an `InputStreamReader` and a `BufferedReader`.

Discussion

Most desktop platforms support the notion of standard input (a keyboard, a file, or the output from another program) and standard output (a terminal window, a printer, a file on disk, or the input to yet another program). Most such systems also support a standard error output so that error messages can be seen by the user even if the standard output is being redirected. When programs on these platforms start up, the three streams are preassigned to particular platform-dependent handles, or *file descriptors*. The net result is that ordinary programs on these operating systems can read the standard input or write to the standard output or standard error stream without having to open any files or make any other special arrangements.

Java continues this tradition and enshrines it in the `System` class. The static variables `System.in`, `System.out`, and `System.err` are connected to the three operating system streams before your program begins execution (an application is free to reassign these; see "Discussion"). So, to read the standard input, you need only refer to the variable `System.in` and call its methods. For example, to read one byte from the standard input, you call the read method of `System.in`, which returns the byte in an `int` variable:

```
int b = System.in.read( );
```

But is that enough? No, because the `read()` method can throw an `IOException`. So you must either declare that your program throws an `IOException`, as in:

```
public static void main(String ap[]) throws IOException {
...
}
```

or you can put a `try/catch` block around the `read()` method:

```
    int b = 0;
    try {
        b = System.in.read();
        System.out.println("Read this data: " + (char)b);
    } catch (Exception e) {
        System.out.println("Caught " + e);
    }
```

In this case, it makes sense to print the results inside the try/catch block because there's no point in trying to print the value you read, if the read() threw an IOException. Note that I cavalierly convert the byte to a char for printing, assuming that you've typed a valid character in the terminal window.

Well, that certainly works and gives you the ability to read a byte at a time from the standard input. But most applications are designed in terms of larger units, such as integers, or a line of text. To read a value of a known type, such as int, from the standard input, you can use the Scanner class (covered in more detail in Recipe 10.6):

```
// part of ReadStdinInt15.java
Scanner sc = Scanner.create(System.in);
int i = sc.nextInt( );
```

For reading characters of text with an input character converter so that your program will work with multiple input encodings around the world, use a Reader class. The particular subclass that allows you to read lines of characters is a BufferedReader. But there's a hitch. Remember I mentioned those two categories of input classes, Streams and Readers? But I also said that System.in is a Stream, and you want a Reader. How do you get from a Stream to a Reader? A "crossover" class called InputStreamReader is tailor-made for this purpose. Just pass your Stream (like System.in) to the Input-StreamReader constructor and you get back a Reader, which you in turn pass to the BufferedReader constructor. The usual idiom for writing this in Java is to nest the constructor calls:

```
BufferedReader is = new BufferedReader(new InputStreamReader(System.in));
```

You can then read lines of text from the standard input using the readLine() method. This method takes no argument and returns a String that is made up for you by readLine() containing the characters (converted to Unicode) from the next line of text in the file. If there are no more lines of text, the constant null is returned:

```
public class CatStdin {

    public static void main(String[] av) {
        try {
            BufferedReader is =
                new BufferedReader(new InputStreamReader(System.in));
            String inputLine;

            while ((inputLine = is.readLine()) != null) {
```

```
            System.out.println(inputLine);
        }
        is.close();
    } catch (IOException e) {
        System.out.println("IOException: " + e);
    }
    }
}
```

Now that we've covered the InputStreamReader, and because it's something that people have asked me several times, I'll show how to read an Integer from the standard input:

```
public class ReadStdinInt {
    public static void main(String[] ap) {
        String line = null;
        int val = 0;
        try {
            BufferedReader is = new BufferedReader(
                new InputStreamReader(System.in));
            line = is.readLine();
            val = Integer.parseInt(line);
            System.out.println("I read this number: " + val);
        } catch (NumberFormatException ex) {
            System.err.println("Not a valid number: " + line);
        } catch (IOException e) {
            System.err.println("Unexpected IO ERROR: " + e);
        }
    }
}
```

There are many other things you might want to do with lines of text read from a Reader. In the demo program shown in this recipe, I just printed them. In the demo program in Recipe 10.8, I convert them to integer values using Integer.parseInt() (also see Recipe 5.1) or using a DecimalFormat (see Recipe 5.8). You can interpret them as dates (Chapter 6), or break them into words with a StringTokenizer (see Recipe 3.2). You can also process the lines as you read them; several methods for doing so are listed in Recipe 10.5.

10.2. Reading from the Console or Controlling Terminal; Reading Passwords Without Echoing

Problem

You want to read directly from the program's controlling terminal or console terminal.

Solution

Use the Java 6 `System.console()` method to obtain a `Console` object, and use its methods.

Discussion

The `Console` class is intended for reading directly from a program's controlling terminal. When you run an application from a "terminal window" or "command prompt window" on most systems, its console and its standard input are both connected to the terminal, by default. However, the standard input can be changed by piping or redirection on most OSes. If you really want to read from "wherever the user is sitting," bypassing any indirections, then the `Console` class is usually your friend.

You cannot instantiate `Console` yourself; you must get an instance from the `System` class's `console()` method. You can then call methods such as `readLine()`, which behaves largely like the method of the same name in the `BufferedReader` class used in the previous recipe.

The following code shows an example of prompting for a name and reading it from the console:

src/main/java/io/ConsoleRead.java

```java
public class ConsoleRead {
    public static void main(String[] args) {
        String name = System.console().readLine("What is your name?");
        System.out.println("Hello, " + name.toUpperCase());
    }
}
```

One complication is that the `System.console()` method can return `null` if the console isn't connected. Annoyingly, some IDEs including Eclipse don't manage to set up a controlling terminal when you use the Run As→Java Application mechanism. So production-quality code should always check for `null` before trying to use the Console. If you do get `null`, you can fall back to using the code in Recipe 10.1.

One facility the `Console` class is quite useful for is reading a password without having it echo. This has been a standard facility of command-line applications for decades, as the most obvious way of preventing "shoulder surfing"—looking over your shoulder to see your password. Nonecho password reading is now supported in Java: the `Console` class has a `readPassword()` method that takes a *prompt* argument, intended to be used like: `cons.readPassword("Password:")`. This method returns an array of bytes, which can be used directly in some encryption and security APIs, or can easily be converted into a String. It is generally advised to overwrite the byte array after use to prevent security leaks when other code can access the stack, although the benefits of this are probably reduced when you've constructed a String as we do in the simple example shown in Example 10-1.

Example 10-1. src/main/java/io/ReadPassword.java

```java
public class ReadPassword {
    public static void main(String[] args) {
        Console cons;
        if ((cons = System.console()) != null) {
            char[] passwd = null;
            try {
                passwd = cons.readPassword("Password:");
                // In real life you would send the password into authentication code
                System.out.println("Your password was: " + new String(passwd));
            } finally {
                // Shred this in-memory copy for security reasons
                if (passwd != null) {
                    java.util.Arrays.fill(passwd, ' ');
                }
            }
        } else {
            throw new RuntimeException("No console, can't get password");
        }
    }
}
```

10.3. Writing Standard Output or Standard Error

Problem

You want your program to write to the standard output or the standard error stream.

Solution

Use System.out or System.err as appropriate.

Discussion

In certain circumstances (such as a server program with no connection back to the user's terminal), System.out and System.err can become very important debugging tools (assuming that you can find out what file the server program has redirected standard output into; see "Discussion").

`System.out` is a `PrintStream` connected to the "standard output"—whatever that is on your operating system and your runtime environment—so in every introductory text you see a program containing this line, or one like it:[1]

```
System.out.println("Hello World of Java");
```

The `println` method is polymorphic; it has several forms for `Object` (which obviously calls the given object's `toString( )` method), for `String`, and for each of the primitive types (`int`, `float`, `boolean`, etc.). Each takes only one argument, so it is common to use string concatenation:

```
System.out.println("The answer is " + myAnswer + " at this time.");
```

Remember that string concatenation is also polymorphic: you can "add" anything at all to a string, and the result is a string.

`System.err` is a `PrintStream` connected to "the standard error output"—again, whatever that means in your environment. In a lot of cases, it makes no difference which of the two outputs you use. But using `System.err` sends a clear signal that the output you are conveying has some importance as an indication of failure. On a dumb terminal output, these streams will be indistinguishable. However, most IDEs will use color highlighting in the Console view when you run an application. For example, Eclipse (see Recipe 1.3) will show the standard output in black or blue, but the standard error stream in red; this makes it easy to find actual errors when there is a lot of nonerror output.

Up to here I have been using a `Stream`, `System.out`, or `System.err`. What if you want to use a `Writer`? The `PrintWriter` class has all the same methods as `PrintStream` and a constructor that takes a `Stream`, so you can just say:

```
PrintWriter pw = new PrintWriter(System.out);
pw.println("The answer is " + myAnswer + " at this time.");
```

One caveat with this string concatenation is that if you are appending a bunch of things, and a number and a character come together at the front, they are added before concatenation due to the precedence rules. So don't do this:

```
int i = ...;
System.out.println(i + '=' + " the answer.");
```

Given that `i` is an integer, then `i + '='` (`i` added to the equals sign, which is of the numeric type `char`) is a valid *numeric* expression, which will result in a single value of type `int`. If the variable `i` has the value 42, and the character = in a Unicode (or ASCII) code chart has the value 61, this prints:

```
103 the answer.
```

---

1. All the examples in this recipe are found in one file, *PrintStandardOutput.java*.

The wrong value and no equals sign! Safer approaches include using parentheses, using double quotes around the equals sign, using a StringBuilder (see Recipe 3.3) or a MessageFormat (see Recipe 15.10), or using String.format() (see Recipe 10.4). Of course in this simple example you could just move the = to be part of the string literal, but the example was chosen to illustrate the problem of arithmetic on char values being confused with string contatenation.

10.4. Printing with Formatter and printf

Problem

You want the ease of use that the java.util.Formatter class brings to simple printing tasks.

Solution

Use Formatter for printing values with fine-grained control over the formatting.

Discussion

The Formatter class is patterned after C's printf routines. In fact, PrintStream and PrintWriter have convenience routines named printf() that simply delegate to the stream or writer's format() method, which uses a default Formatter instance. Unlike in C, however, Java is a strongly typed language, so invalid arguments will throw an exception rather than generating gibberish.

The underlying Formatter class in java.util works on a String containing format codes. For each item that you want to format, you put a format code. The format code consists of a percent sign (%), optionally an argument number followed by a dollar sign ($), optionally a field width or precision, and a format type (d for decimal integer, that is, an integer with no decimal point, f for floating point, and so on). A simple use might look like the following:

```
System.out.printf("%04d - the year of %f%n", 1956, Math.PI);
```

As shown in Figure 10-2, the "%04d" controls formatting of the year and the "%2$f" controls formatting of the value of PI.[2]

---

2. The central character in Yann Martel's novel *Life of Pi* would have been born in 1956, according to information in Wikipedia (*http://en.wikipedia.org/wiki/Life_of_pi*).

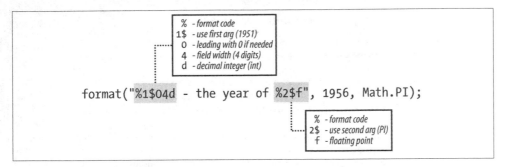

Figure 10-2. Format codes examined

Many format codes are available; Table 10-1 lists some of the more common ones. For a complete description, refer to the javadoc for `java.util.Formatter`.

Table 10-1. Formatter format codes

Code	Meaning
c	Character (argument must be `char` or integral type containing valid character value).
d	"decimal int"—integer to be printed as a decimal (radix 10) with no decimal point (argument must be integral type).
f	Floating-point value with decimal fraction (must be numeric); field width may be followed by decimal point and fractional digit field width; e.g., 7.2f.
e	Floating-point value in scientific notation.
g	Floating-point value, as per f or e, depending on magnitude.
s	General format; if value is null, prints "null," else if arg implements `Formattable`, format as per `arg.format-To()`; else format as per `arg.toString()`.
t	Date codes; follow with secondary code. Common date codes are shown in Table 10-2. Argument must be `long`, `Long`, `Calendar`, or `Date`.
n	Newline; insert the platform-dependent line ending character.
%	Insert a literal % character.

Note also that you may, but are not required to, put a "parameter order" number between the % and the format code. For example, in "%2$04d", the "2$" means to format the *second* parameter, regardless of the order of the parameters. This is primarily useful with dates (see the following example, where you need to format several different portions of the same `Date` or `Calendar`, or any time you want to format the same object more than once) and in internationalization, where different languages may require words to be in a different order within a sentence.

Some examples of using a `Formatter` are shown in Example 10-2.

Example 10-2. src/main/java/io/FormatterDemo.java

```java
public class FormatterDemo {
    public static void main(String[] args) {

        // The arguments to all these format methods consist of
        // a format code String and 1 or more arguments.
        // Each format code consists of the following:
        // % - code lead-in
        // N$ - which parameter number (1-based) after the code - OPTIONAL
        // N - field width
        // L - format letter (d: decimal(int); f: float; s: general; many more)
        // For the full(!) story, see javadoc for java.util.Formatter.

        // Most general (cumbersome) way of proceding.
        Formatter fmtr = new Formatter();
        Object result = fmtr.format("%1$04d - the year of %2$f", 1956, Math.PI);
        System.out.println(result);

        // Shorter way using static String.format(), and
        // default parameter numbering.
        Object stringResult = String.format("%04d - the year of %f", 1956, Math.PI);
        System.out.println(stringResult);

        // A shorter way using PrintStream/PrintWriter.format, more in line with
        // other languages. But this way you must provide the newline delimiter
        // using %n (do NOT use \n as that is platform-dependent!).
        System.out.printf("%04d - the year of %f%n", 1956, Math.PI);

        // Format doubles with more control
        System.out.printf("PI is approximately %4.2f%n", Math.PI);
    }
}
```

Running `FormatterDemo` produces this:

```
C:> javac FormatterDates.java
C:> java io.FormatterDates
1956 - The year of 3.141593
1956 - The year of 3.141593
1956 - The year of 3.141593
PI is about 3.14
```

For formatting legacy `java.util` date and time objects, a large variety of format codes are available—about 40 in all. For formatting `java.time` date and time objects, a similarly large API is available, discussed in Chapter 6.

Table 10-2 shows the more common date/time format codes. Each must be preceded by a t, so to format the first argument as a year, you would use %1$tY.

Table 10-2. Formatting codes for dates and times

Format code	Meaning
Y	Year (at least four digits)
m	Month as 2-digit (leading zeros) number
B	Locale-specific month name (b for abbreviated)
d	Day of month (2 digits, leading zeros)
e	Day of month (1 or 2 digits)
A	Locale-specific day of week (a for abbreviated)
H or I	Hour in 24-hour (H) or 12-hour (I) format (2 digits, leading zeros)
M	Minute (2 digits)
S	Second (2 digits)
P/p	Locale-specific AM or PM in uppercase (P) or lowercase (p)
R or T	24-hour time combination: %tH:%tM ® or %tH:%tM:%tS (T)
D	Date formatted as "%tm/%td/%ty"

In my opinion, embedding these directly in applications that you distribute or make available as web applications is often a bad idea, because any direct use of them assumes that you know the correct order to print these fields in all locales around the world. Trust me, you don't. Instead of these, I recommend the use of `DateTimeFormatter`, which I show you how to use in Recipe 6.2, or a `MessageFormat` (see Recipe 15.10) to control the order of arguments. I also urge you to read all of Chapter 15 to learn about internationalization. However, for "quick and dirty" work, as well as for writing log or data files that must be in a given format because some other program reads them, these are hard to beat.

Some date examples are shown in Example 10-3.

Example 10-3. src/main/java/io/FormatterDates.java

```java
public class FormatterDates {
    public static void main(String[] args) {

        // Format number as dates e.g., 2014-06-28
        System.out.printf("%4d-%02d-%2d%n", 2014, 6, 28);

        // Format fields directly from a Date object: multiple fields from "1$"
        // (hard-coded formatting for Date not advisable; see I18N chapter)
        Date today = Calendar.getInstance().getTime();
        // Might print e.g., July 4, 2015:
        System.out.printf("Today is %1$tB %1$td, %1$tY%n", today);
    }
}
```

Running this `FormatterDates` class produces the following output:

```
C:> java io.FormatterDates
2014-06-28
Today is April 07, 2014
```

The astute reader will notice that this mechanism requires that the Java language now contain a variable arguments mechanism. Variable argument lists have been the bane of developers on many platforms and, indeed, they have finally come to Java. Briefly: the variable argument, which must be the last declaration in the method's header, is declared as Type . . . name, and is treated as Type[] in the body of the method. The invocation must pass a comma-separated list of arguments of the same or compatible types. See *lang/VarArgsDemo.java* in the online source.

10.5. Scanning Input with StreamTokenizer

Problem

You need to scan a file with more fine-grained resolution than the readLine( ) method of the BufferedReader class and its subclasses (discussed in Recipe 10.16).

Solution

Use a StreamTokenizer, readLine(), and a StringTokenizer; the Scanner class (see Recipe 10.6); regular expressions (Chapter 4); or one of several third-party "parser generator" tools.

Discussion

Though you could, in theory, read a file one character at a time and analyze each character, that is a pretty low-level approach. The read( ) method in the Reader class is defined to return int so that it can use the time-honored value -1 (defined as EOF in Unix *<stdio.h>* for years) to indicate that you have read to the end of the file:

src/main/java/io/ReadCharsOneAtATime.java

```
public class ReadCharsOneAtATime {

    void doFile(Reader is) throws IOException {
        int c;
        while ((c=is.read( )) != -1) {
            System.out.print((char)c);
        }
    }
}
```

The cast to char is interesting. The program compiles fine without it, but does not print correctly because c is declared as int (which it must be, to be able to compare against the end-of-file value -1). For example, the integer value corresponding to capital A treated as an int prints as 65, whereas (char) prints the character A.

We discussed the StringTokenizer class extensively in Recipe 3.2. The combination of readLine() and StringTokenizer provides a simple means of scanning a file. Suppose you need to read a file in which each line consists of a name like *user@host.domain*, and you want to split the lines into users and host addresses. You could use this:

```java
public class ScanStringTok {
    protected LineNumberReader is;

    public static void main(String[] av) throws IOException {
        if (av.length == 0)
            new ScanStringTok(
                new InputStreamReader(System.in)).process();
        else
            for (int i=0; i<av.length; i++)
                new ScanStringTok(av[i]).process();
    }

    /** Construct a file scanner by name */
    public ScanStringTok(String fileName) throws IOException {
        is = new LineNumberReader(new FileReader(fileName));
    }

    /** Construct a file scanner by existing Reader */
    public ScanStringTok(Reader rdr) throws IOException {
        // no point adding another level of buffering, if already
        // being buffered...
        if (rdr instanceof LineNumberReader)
            is = (LineNumberReader)rdr;
        else
            is = new LineNumberReader(rdr);
    }

    protected void process() {
        String s = null;
        try {
            while ((s = is.readLine()) != null) {
                StringTokenizer st = new StringTokenizer(s, "@", true);
                String user = (String)st.nextElement();
                st.nextElement();
                String host = (String)st.nextElement();
                System.out.println("User name: " + user +
                    "; host part: " + host);

                // Presumably you would now do something
                // with the user and host parts...

            }
```

```
            } catch (NoSuchElementException ix) {
                System.err.println("Line " + is.getLineNumber() +
                    ": Invalid input " + s);
            } catch (IOException e) {
                System.err.println(e);
            }
        }
    }
}
```

The StreamTokenizer class in java.util provides slightly more capabilities for scanning a file. It reads characters and assembles them into words, or tokens. It returns these
tokens to you along with a type code describing the kind of token it found. This type
code is one of four predefined types (StringTokenizer.TT_WORD, TT_NUMBER, TT_EOF,
or TT_EOL for the end-of-line), or the char value of an ordinary character (such as 32
for the space character). Methods such as ordinaryCharacter() allow you to specify
how to categorize characters, while others such as slashSlashComment() allow you to
enable or disable features.

Example 10-4 shows a StreamTokenizer used to implement a simple immediate-mode
stack-based calculator:

```
2 2 + =
4
22 7 / =
3.141592857
```

I read tokens as they arrive from the StreamTokenizer. Numbers are put on the stack.
The four operators (+, -, *, and /) are immediately performed on the two elements at
the top of the stack, and the result is put back on the top of the stack. The = operator
causes the top element to be printed, but is left on the stack so that you can say:

```
4 5 * = 2 / =
20.0
10.0
```

Example 10-4. Simple calculator using StreamTokenizer

```java
public class SimpleCalcStreamTok {
    /** The StreamTokenizer Input */
    protected  StreamTokenizer tf;
    /** The Output File */
    protected PrintWriter out = new PrintWriter(System.out, true);
    /** The variable name (not used in this version) */
    protected String variable;
    /** The operand stack */
    protected Stack s;

    /* Driver - main program */
    public static void main(String[] av) throws IOException {
        if (av.length == 0)
            new SimpleCalcStreamTok(
```

```
            new InputStreamReader(System.in)).doCalc();
    else
        for (int i=0; i<av.length; i++)
            new SimpleCalcStreamTok(av[i]).doCalc();
}

/** Construct by filename */
public SimpleCalcStreamTok(String fileName) throws IOException {
    this(new FileReader(fileName));
}

/** Construct from an existing Reader */
public SimpleCalcStreamTok(Reader rdr) throws IOException {
    tf = new StreamTokenizer(rdr);
    // Control the input character set:
    tf.slashSlashComments(true);    // treat "//" as comments
    tf.ordinaryChar('-');            // used for subtraction
    tf.ordinaryChar('/');        // used for division

    s = new Stack();
}

/** Construct from a Reader and a PrintWriter
 */
public SimpleCalcStreamTok(Reader in, PrintWriter out) throws IOException {
    this(in);
    setOutput(out);
}

/**
 * Change the output destination.
 */
public void setOutput(PrintWriter out) {
    this.out = out;
}

protected void doCalc() throws IOException {
    int iType;
    double tmp;

    while ((iType = tf.nextToken()) != StreamTokenizer.TT_EOF) {
        switch(iType) {
        case StreamTokenizer.TT_NUMBER: // Found a number, push value to stack
            push(tf.nval);
            break;
        case StreamTokenizer.TT_WORD:
            // Found a variable, save its name. Not used here.
            variable = tf.sval;
            break;
        case '+':
            // + operator is commutative.
            push(pop() + pop());
```

```
                    break;
                case '-':
                    // - operator: order matters.
                    tmp = pop();
                    push(pop() - tmp);
                    break;
                case '*':
                    // Multiply is commutative
                    push(pop() * pop());
                    break;
                case '/':
                    // Handle division carefully: order matters!
                    tmp = pop();
                    push(pop() / tmp);
                    break;
                case '=':
                    out.println(peek());
                    break;
                default:
                    out.println("What's this? iType = " + iType);
                }
            }
        }
    void push(double val) {
        s.push(new Double(val));
    }
    double pop() {
        return ((Double)s.pop()).doubleValue();
    }
    double peek() {
        return ((Double)s.peek()).doubleValue();
    }
    void clearStack() {
        s.removeAllElements();
    }
}
```

10.6. Scanning Input with the Scanner Class

Problem

You want the ease of use that the java.util.Scanner class brings to *simple* reading tasks.

Solution

Use Scanner's next() methods for reading.

Discussion

The `Scanner` class lets you read an input source by tokens, somewhat analogous to the `StreamTokenizer` described in Recipe 10.5. The `Scanner` is more flexible in some ways (it lets you break tokens based on spaces or regular expressions) but less in others (you need to know the kind of token you are reading). This class bears some resemblance to the C-language `scanf()` function, but in the `Scanner` you specify the input token types by calling methods like `nextInt()`, `nextDouble()`, and so on. Here is a simple example of scanning:

```
String sampleDate = "25 Dec 1988";

try (Scanner sDate = new Scanner(sampleDate)) {
    int dayOfMonth = sDate.nextInt();
    String month = sDate.next();
    int year = sDate.nextInt();
    System.out.printf("%d-%s-%02d%n", year, month, dayOfMonth);
}
```

The `Scanner` recognizes Java's eight built-in types, in addition to `BigInteger` and `BigDecimal`. It can also return input tokens as `Strings` or by matching regular expressions (see Chapter 4). Table 10-3 lists the "next" methods and corresponding "has" methods; the "has" method returns true if the corresponding "next" method would succeed. There is no `nextString()` method; just use `next()` to get the next token as a `String`.

Table 10-3. Scanner methods

Returned type	"has" method	"next" method	Comment
String	hasNext()	next()	The next complete token from this scanner
String	hasNext(Pattern)	next(Pattern)	The next string that matches the given regular expression (regex)
String	hasNext(String)	next(String)	The next token that matches the regex pattern constructed from the specified string
BigDecimal	hasNextBigDecimal()	nextBigDecimal()	The next token of the input as a `BigDecimal`
BigInteger	hasNextBigInteger()	nextBigInteger()	The next token of the input as a `BigInteger`
boolean	hasNextBoolean()	nextBoolean()	The next token of the input as a `boolean`
byte	hasNextByte()	nextByte()	The next token of the input as a `byte`
double	hasNextDouble()	nextDouble()	The next token of the input as a `double`
float	hasNextFloat()	nextFloat()	The next token of the input as a `float`
int	hasNextInt()	nextInt()	The next token of the input as an `int`
String	N/A	nextLine()	Reads up to the end-of-line, including the line ending
long	hasNextLong()	nextLong()	The next token of the input as a `long`
short	hasNextShort()	nextShort()	The next token of the input as a `short`

The Scanner class is constructed with an input source, which can be a File object (Chapter 11), an InputStream, a String, or Readable (Readable is an interface that Reader and all its subclasses implement).

One way to use the Scanner is based on the Iterator pattern, using while (scanner.hasNext()) to control the iteration. Example 10-5 shows the simple calculator from Recipe 10.5 rewritten[3] to use the Scanner class.

Example 10-5. Simple calculator using java.util.Scanner

```
public class SimpleCalcScanner {
    /** The Scanner */
    protected  Scanner scan;

    /** The output */
    protected PrintWriter out = new PrintWriter(System.out);

    /** The variable name (not used in this version) */
    protected String variable;

    /** The operand stack; no operators are pushed, so it can be a stack of Double */
    protected Stack<Double> s = new Stack<>();

    /* Driver - main program */
    public static void main(String[] args) throws IOException {
        if (args.length == 0)
            new SimpleCalcScanner(
                new InputStreamReader(System.in)).doCalc();
        else
            for (String arg : args) {
                new SimpleCalcScanner(arg).doCalc();
            }
    }

    /** Construct a SimpleCalcScanner by name */
    public SimpleCalcScanner(String fileName) throws IOException {
        this(new FileReader(fileName));
    }

    /** Construct a SimpleCalcScanner from an open Reader */
    public SimpleCalcScanner(Reader rdr) throws IOException {
        scan = new Scanner(rdr);
    }

    /** Construct a SimpleCalcScanner from a Reader and a PrintWriter */
    public SimpleCalcScanner(Reader rdr, PrintWriter pw) throws IOException {
```

---

3. If this were code in a maintained project, I might factor out some of the common code among these two calculators, as well as the one in Recipe 5.18, and divide the code better using interfaces. However, this would detract from the simplicity of self-contained examples.

```
        this(rdr);
        setWriter(pw);
    }

    /** Change the output to go to a new PrintWriter */
    public void setWriter(PrintWriter pw) {
        out = pw;
    }

    protected void doCalc() throws IOException {
        double tmp;

        while (scan.hasNext()) {
            if (scan.hasNextDouble()) {
                push(scan.nextDouble());
            } else {
                String token = scan.next();
                if (token.equals("+")) {
                    // Found + operator, perform it immediately.
                    push(pop() + pop());
                } else if (token.equals("-")) {
                    // Found - operator, perform it (order matters).
                    tmp = pop();
                    push(pop() - tmp);
                } else if (token.equals("*")) {
                    // Multiply is commutative
                    push(pop() * pop());
                } else if (token.equals("/")) {
                    // Handle division carefully: order matters!
                    tmp = pop();
                    push(pop() / tmp);
                } else if (token.equals("=")) {
                    out.println(peek());
                } else {
                    out.println("What's this? " + token);
                }
            }
        }
    }

    void push(double val) {
        s.push(new Double(val));
    }

    double pop() {
        return ((Double)s.pop()).doubleValue();
    }

    double peek() {
        return ((Double)s.peek()).doubleValue();
    }
```

```
    void clearStack() {
        s.removeAllElements();
    }
}
```

10.7. Scanning Input with Grammatical Structure

Problem

You need to parse a file whose structure can be described as "grammatical" (in the sense of computer languages, not natural languages).

Solution

Use one of many parser generators.

Discussion

Although the `StreamTokenizer` class (see Recipe 10.5) and `Scanner` (see Recipe 10.6) are useful, they know only a limited number of tokens and have no way of specifying that the tokens must appear in a particular order. To do more advanced scanning, you need some special-purpose scanning tools. "Parser generators" have a long history in computer science. The best-known examples are the C-language `yacc` (Yet Another Compiler Compiler) and `lex`, released with Seventh Edition Unix in the 1970s and discussed in *lex & yacc* (O'Reilly), and their open source clones *bison* and *flex*. These tools let you specify the lexical structure of your input using some pattern language such as regular expressions (see Chapter 4). For example, you might say that an email address consists of a series of alphanumerics, followed by an at sign (@), followed by a series of alphanumerics with periods embedded, as:

```
name:   [A-Za-z0-9]+@[A-Za-z0-0.]
```

The tool then writes code that recognizes the characters you have described. These tools also have a grammatical specification, which says, for example, that the keyword `ADDRESS` must appear, followed by a colon, followed by a "name" token, as previously defined.

There are several good third-party parser generator tools for Java. They vary widely based on complexity, power, ease of use, and so on:

- One of the best known and most elaborate is ANTLR (*http://www.antlr.org*).
- JavaCC is an open source project on *java.net* (*https://javacc.java.net*).
- JParsec lets %%»%%you write the parser in straight Java, so it's all built at compile time (most of the others require a separate parse generation step, with the build and

debugging issues that that raises). JParsec is moving from Codehaus (*http://bit.ly/ 1qBe5Qr*) to GitHub (*http://bit.ly/SQYRLz*).

- JFlex (*http://jflex.de*) and CUP (*http://bit.ly/SQYUaq*) work together like the original *yacc* and *lex*.
- Parboiled uses *Parsing Expression Grammar* (PEG) to also build the parser at compile time. See GitHub (*http://bit.ly/1v5cAMW*) for more information.
- *Rats!* parser generator is part of the eXTensible Compiler Project (*http://bit.ly/ 1oTqQqd*) at New York University.
- There are others; a more complete list is maintained at Java Source (*http://bit.ly/ 1jmWHKi*).

These "compiler generators" can be used to write grammars for a wide variety of programs, from simple calculators—such as the one in Recipe 10.6—through HTML and CORBA/IDL, up to full Java and C/C++ compilers. Examples of these are included with the downloads. Unfortunately, the learning curve for parsers in general precludes providing a simple and comprehensive example here, let alone to compare them intelligently. Refer to the documentation and the numerous examples provided with each distribution.

As an alternative to using one of these, you could simply roll your own "recursive descent parser," and once you learn how to do so, you may find it's not really that difficult, quite possibly even less hassle than dealing with the extra parser generator software. (Depending on the complexity of the grammar involved, obviously.)

Java developers have a range of choices including simple line-at-a-time scanners using `StringTokenizer`, fancier token-based scanners using `StreamTokenizer`, a `Scanner` class to scan simple tokens (see Recipe 10.6), Regular Expressions (see Chapter 4), and third-party solutions include grammar-based scanners based on the parsing tools listed here.

10.8. Opening a File by Name

Problem

The Java documentation doesn't have methods for opening files. How do I connect a filename on disk with a `Reader`, `Writer`, or `Stream`?

Solution

Construct a `FileReader`, `FileWriter`, `FileInputStream`, or `FileOutputStream`.

Discussion

The action of constructing a `FileReader`, `FileWriter`, `FileInputStream`, or `FileOutputStream` corresponds to the "open" operation in most I/O packages. There is no explicit open operation, perhaps as a kind of rhetorical flourish of the Java API's object-oriented design. Therefore, to read a text file, you'd create, in order, a `FileReader` and a `BufferedReader`. To write a file a byte at a time, you'd create a `FileOutputStream` and probably a `BufferedOutputStream` for efficiency:

```
// OpenFileByName.java
BufferedReader is = new BufferedReader(new FileReader("myFile.txt"));
BufferedOutputStream bytesOut = new BufferedOutputStream(
    new FileOutputStream("bytes.dat"));
...
bytesOut.close( );
```

Remember that you need to handle `IOExceptions` around these calls.

10.9. Copying a File

Problem

You need to copy a file in its entirety.

Solution

Use a pair of `Streams` for binary data, or a `Reader` and a `Writer` for text, and a `while` loop to copy until end-of-file is reached on the input.

Discussion

This operation is fairly common, so I've packaged it as a set of methods in a class called `FileIO` in my utilities package `com.darwinsys.util`. Here's a simple test program that uses it to copy a source file to a backup file:

src/demo/java/io/FileIoDemo.java

```
package com.darwinsys.io;

import java.io.IOException;

public class FileIoDemo {
    public static void main(String[] av) {
        try {
            FileIO.copyFile("FileIO.java", "FileIO.bak");
            FileIO.copyFile("FileIO.class", "FileIO-class.bak");
        } catch (IOException e) {
            System.err.println(e);
```

```
            }
        }
    }
```

How does `FileIO` work? Its `copyFile` method takes several forms, depending on whether you have two filenames, a filename and a `PrintWriter`, and so on. The code for `FileIO` itself is shown in Example 10-6.

Example 10-6. src/main/java/com/darwinsys/io/FileIO.java

```java
package com.darwinsys.io;

import java.io.*;
import java.util.Enumeration;
import java.util.jar.JarEntry;
import java.util.jar.JarFile;

import com.darwinsys.lang.StringUtil;
import com.darwinsys.util.Debug;

/**
 * Some file I-O primitives reimplemented in Java.
 * All methods are static, since there is no state.
 */
public class FileIO {

    /** The size of blocking to use */
    protected static final int BLKSIZ = 16384;

    /** String for encoding UTF-8; copied by inclusion from StringUtil. */
    public static final String ENCODING_UTF_8 = StringUtil.ENCODING_UTF_8;

    /** Nobody should need to create an instance; all methods are static */
    private FileIO() {
        // Nothing to do
    }

    /** Copy a file from one filename to another */
    public static void copyFile(String inName, String outName)
    throws FileNotFoundException, IOException {
        BufferedInputStream is = null;
        BufferedOutputStream os = null;
        try {
            is = new BufferedInputStream(new FileInputStream(inName));
            os = new BufferedOutputStream(new FileOutputStream(outName));
            copyFile(is, os, false);
        } finally {
            if (is != null) {
                is.close();
            }
            if (os != null) {
                os.close();
```

```
        }
    }
}

/** Copy a file from an opened InputStream to opened OutputStream */
public static void copyFile(InputStream is, OutputStream os, boolean close)
throws IOException {
    byte[] b = new byte[BLKSIZ];              // the byte read from the file
    int i;
    while ((i = is.read(b)) != -1) {
        os.write(b, 0, i);
    }
    is.close();
    if (close)
        os.close();
}

/** Copy a file from an opened Reader to opened Writer */
public static void copyFile(Reader is, Writer os, boolean close)
throws IOException {
    int b;                    // the byte read from the file

    while ((b = is.read()) != -1) {
        os.write(b);
    }
    is.close();
    if (close)
        os.close();
}

/** Copy a file from a filename to a PrintWriter. */
public static void copyFile(String inName, PrintWriter pw, boolean close)
throws FileNotFoundException, IOException {
    BufferedReader ir = new BufferedReader(new FileReader(inName));
    copyFile(ir, pw, close);
}

/**
 * Copy a file to a directory, given File objects representing the files.
 * @param file File representing the source, must be a single file.
 * @param target File representing the location, may be file or directory.
 * @throws IOException
 */
public static void copyFile(File file, File target) throws IOException {
    if (!file.exists() || !file.isFile() || !(file.canRead())) {
        throw new IOException(file + " is not a readable file");
    }
    File dest = target;
    if (target.isDirectory()) {
        dest = new File(dest, file.getName());
    }
    InputStream is = null;
```

```
        OutputStream os  = null;
        try {
            is = new FileInputStream(file);
            os = new FileOutputStream(dest);
            int count = 0;            // the byte count
            byte[] b = new byte[BLKSIZ];    // the bytes read from the file
            while ((count = is.read(b)) != -1) {
                os.write(b, 0, count);
            }
        } finally {
            is.close();
            os.close();
        }
    }

    /** Copy a data file from one filename to another, alternative method.
     * As the name suggests, use my own buffer instead of letting
     * the BufferedReader allocate and use the buffer.
     */
    public void copyFileBuffered(String inName, String outName) throws
            FileNotFoundException, IOException {
        InputStream is = null;
        OutputStream os = null;
        try {
            is = new FileInputStream(inName);
            os = new FileOutputStream(outName);
            int count = 0;            // the byte count
            byte[] b = new byte[BLKSIZ];    // the bytes read from the file
            while ((count = is.read(b)) != -1) {
                os.write(b, 0, count);
            }
        } finally {
            if (is != null) {
                is.close();
            }
            if (os != null) {
                os.close();
            }
        }
    }

    /**
     * Copy all objects found in and under "fromdir", to their places in "todir".
     * @param fromDir
     * @param toDir
     * @throws IOException
     */
    public static void copyRecursively(File fromDir, File toDir, boolean create)
            throws IOException {

        Debug.printf("fileio", "copyRecursively(%s, %s%n", fromDir, toDir);
        if (!fromDir.exists()) {
```

```java
            throw new IOException(
                String.format("Source directory %s does not exist", fromDir));
        }
        if (create) {
            toDir.mkdirs();
        } else if (!toDir.exists()) {
            throw new IOException(
                String.format("Destination dir %s must exist", toDir));
        }
        for (File src : fromDir.listFiles()) {
            if (src.isDirectory()) {
                File destSubDir = new File(toDir, src.getName());
                copyRecursively(src, destSubDir, true);
            } else if (src.isFile()) {
                copyFile(src, toDir);
            } else {
                System.err.println(
                    String.format("Warning: %s is neither file nor directory", src));
            }
        }
    }

    public static void copyRecursively(File fromDir, File toDir) throws IOException {
        copyRecursively(fromDir, toDir, false);
    }

    public static void deleteRecursively(File startDir) throws IOException {

        String startDirPath = startDir.getCanonicalPath();

        // Pass one - delete recursively
        for (File f : startDir.listFiles()) {
            if (!f.getCanonicalPath().startsWith(startDirPath)) {
                throw new IOException("Attempted to go out of " + startDir);
            }
            if (f.isDirectory()) {
                deleteRecursively(f);
            }
        }
        // Pass two - delete whatever's left: files and (empty) directories
        for (File f : startDir.listFiles()) {
            f.delete();
            if (f.exists()) {
                System.err.println(f + " did not get deleted!");
            }
        }

        // Pass three - delete the (now empty) starting directory
        startDir.delete();
    }

    /**
```

```
 * Copy a tree of files to directory, given File objects representing the files.
 * @param base File representing the source, must be a single file.
 * @param startingDir
 * @param toDir File representing the location, may be file or directory.
 * @throws IOException
 */
public static void copyRecursively(JarFile base, JarEntry startingDir,
        File toDir) throws IOException {
    if (!startingDir.isDirectory()) {
        throw new IOException(String.format(
                "Starting point %s is not a directory", startingDir));
    }
    if (!toDir.exists()) {
        throw new IOException(String.format(
                "Destination dir %s must exist", toDir));
    }
    Enumeration<JarEntry> all = base.entries();
    while (all.hasMoreElements()) {
        JarEntry file = all.nextElement();
        // XXX ensure that it matches starting dir
        if (file.isDirectory()) {
            copyRecursively(base, file, new File(toDir, file.getName()));
        } else {
            InputStream is = null;
            OutputStream os = null;
            try {
                is = base.getInputStream(file);
                os = new FileOutputStream(new File(toDir, file
                        .getName()));
                copyFile(is, os, false);
            } finally {
                if (os != null)
                    os.close();
                if (is != null)
                    is.close();
            }
        }
    }
}

// Methods that do reading.
/** Open a file and read the first line from it. */
public static String readLine(String inName)
throws FileNotFoundException, IOException {
    BufferedReader is = null;
    try {
    is = new BufferedReader(new FileReader(inName));
    String line = null;
    line = is.readLine();
    is.close();
    return line;
    } finally {
```

```
        if (is != null)
            is.close();
    }
}

/** Read the entire content of a Reader into a String;
 * of course Readers should only be used for text files;
 * please do not use this to read a JPEG file, for example.
 */
public static String readerToString(Reader is) throws IOException {
    StringBuilder sb = new StringBuilder();
    char[] b = new char[BLKSIZ];
    int n;

    // Read a block. If it gets any chars, append them.
    while ((n = is.read(b)) > 0) {
        sb.append(b, 0, n);
    }

    // Only construct the String object once, here.
    return sb.toString();
}

/** Read the content of a Stream into a String */
public static String inputStreamToString(InputStream is)
throws IOException {
    return readerToString(new InputStreamReader(is));
}

public static String readAsString(String filename) throws IOException {
    return readerToString(new FileReader(filename));
}

/** Write a String as the entire content of a File */
public static void stringToFile(String text, String fileName)
throws IOException {
    BufferedWriter os = new BufferedWriter(new FileWriter(fileName));
    os.write(text);
    os.flush();
    os.close();
}

/** Open a BufferedReader from a named file. */
public static BufferedReader openFile(String fileName)
throws IOException {
    return new BufferedReader(new FileReader(fileName));
}
}
```

But wait: did you look closely at the body of copyFile(String inName, PrintWriter pw, boolean close)? If you didn't, have a look. You'll notice that I cheated and just delegated the work to `copyFile(Reader is,Writer os,boolean close)`. If I'm copying a file from one place on disk to another, why go through the overhead of converting it from external form to Unicode and back? Normally, you won't have to. But if you have something like a network filesystem mounted from Windows to Unix, or vice versa, it's better to do it a line at a time.

10.10. Reading a File into a String

Problem

You need to read the entire contents of a file into a string.

Solution

Use my `FileIO.readerToString()` method.

Discussion

This is not a common activity in Java, but sometimes you really want to do it. For example, you might want to load a file into a "text area" in a GUI, or process an entire file looking for multiline regular expressions (as in Recipe 4.11). Even though there's nothing in the standard API to do this, it's still easy to accomplish with the `readerTo-String()` method in `com.darwinsys.util.FileIO`, the source for which is included and discussed in Recipe 10.9. You just say something like the following:

```
Reader is = new FileReader(theFileName);
String input = FileIO.readerToString(is);
```

In Java 8, the standard API provides similar functionality in the `Files` class:

```
String input = new String(Files.readAllBytes(Paths.get(args[0])));
```

10.11. Reassigning the Standard Streams

Problem

You need to reassign one or more of the standard streams `System.in`, `System.out`, or `System.err`.

Solution

Construct an `InputStream` or `PrintStream` as appropriate, and pass it to the appropriate set method in the `System` class.

Discussion

The ability to reassign these streams corresponds to what Unix (or DOS command line) users think of as redirection, or piping. This mechanism is commonly used to make a program read from or write to a file without having to explicitly open it and go through every line of code changing the read, write, print, etc. calls to refer to a different stream object. The open operation is performed by the command-line interpreter in Unix or DOS, or by the calling class in Java.

Although you could just assign a new `PrintStream` to the variable `System.out`, you'd be considered antisocial because there is a defined method to replace it carefully:

```
String LOGFILENAME = "error.log";
System.setErr(new PrintStream(new FileOutputStream(LOGFILENAME)));
System.out.println("Please look for errors in " + LOGFILENAME);
// Now assume this is somebody else's code; you'll see it
//   writing to stderr...
int[] a = new int[5];
a[10] = 0;     // here comes an ArrayIndexOutOfBoundsException
```

The stream you use can be one that you've opened, as here, or one you inherited:

```
System.setErr(System.out);     // merge stderr and stdout to same output file.
```

It could also be a stream connected to or from another `Process` you've started (see Recipe 24.1), a network socket, or URL. Anything that gives you a stream can be used.

See Also

See Recipe 14.11, which shows how to reassign a file so that it gets "written" to a text window in a GUI application.

10.12. Duplicating a Stream as It Is Written

Problem

You want anything written to a stream, such as the standard output `System.out`, or the standard error `System.err`, to appear there but *also* be logged in to a file.

Solution

Subclass `PrintStream` and have its `write()` methods write to two streams. Then use `system.setErr()` or `setOut()`, as in "Discussion", to replace the existing standard stream with this "tee" `PrintStream` subclass.

Discussion

Classes are meant to be subclassed. Here we're just subclassing `PrintStream` and adding a bit of functionality: a second `PrintStream`! I wrote a class called `TeePrintStream`, named after the ancient Unix command *tee*. That command allowed you to duplicate, or "tee off," a copy of the data being written on a "pipeline" between two programs.

The original Unix *tee* command is used like this: the | character creates a pipeline in which the standard output of one program becomes the standard input to the next. This often-used example of pipes shows how many users are logged into a Unix server:

```
who | wc -l
```

This runs the *who* program (which lists who is logged in to the system, one name per line along with the terminal port and login time) and sends its output, not to the terminal, but rather into the standard input of the word count (*wc*) program. Here, *wc* is being asked to count lines, not words; hence the -l option. To *tee* a copy of the intermediate data into a file, you might say:

```
who | tee wholist | wc -l
```

which creates a file *wholist* containing the data. For the curious, the file *wholist* might look something like this:

```
ian      ttyC0    Mar 14 09:59
ben      ttyC3    Mar 14 10:23
ian      ttyp4    Mar 14 13:46   (laptop.darwinsys.com)
```

So both the previous command sequences would print 3 as their output.

`TeePrintStream` is an attempt to capture the spirit of the *tee* command. It can be used like this:

```
System.setErr(new TeePrintStream(System.err, "err.log"));
// ...lots of code that occasionally writes to System.err... Or might.
```

`System.setErr()` is a means of specifying the destination of text printed to `System.err` (there are also `System.setOut()` and `System.setIn()`). This code results in any messages that printed to `System.err` to print to wherever `System.err` was previously directed (normally the terminal, but possibly a text window in an IDE) and in to the file *err.log*.

This technique is not limited to the three standard streams. A `TeePrintStream` can be passed to any method that wants a `PrintStream`. Or, for that matter, an `OutputStream`. And you can adapt the technique for `BufferedInputStreams`, `PrintWriters`, `BufferedReaders`, and so on.

Example 10-7 shows the source code for `TeePrintStream`.

Example 10-7. TeePrintStream

```java
public class TeePrintStream extends PrintStream {
    /** The original/direct print stream */
    protected PrintStream parent;

    /** The filename we are tee-ing too, if known;
     * intended for use in future error reporting.
     */
    protected String fileName;

    /** The name for when the input filename is not known */
    private static final String UNKNOWN_NAME = "(opened Stream)";

    /** Construct a TeePrintStream given an existing PrintStream,
     * an opened OutputStream, and a boolean to control auto-flush.
     * This is the main constructor, to which others delegate via "this".
     */
    public TeePrintStream(PrintStream orig, OutputStream os, boolean flush)
    throws IOException {
        super(os, true);
        fileName = UNKNOWN_NAME;
        parent = orig;
    }

    /** Construct a TeePrintStream given an existing PrintStream and
     * an opened OutputStream.
     */
    public TeePrintStream(PrintStream orig, OutputStream os)
    throws IOException {
        this(orig, os, true);
    }

    /* Construct a TeePrintStream given an existing Stream and a filename.
     */
    public TeePrintStream(PrintStream os, String fn) throws IOException {
        this(os, fn, true);
    }

    /* Construct a TeePrintStream given an existing Stream, a filename,
     * and a boolean to control the flush operation.
     */
    public TeePrintStream(PrintStream orig, String fn, boolean flush)
    throws IOException {
        this(orig, new FileOutputStream(fn), flush);
        fileName = fn;
    }

    /** Return true if either stream has an error. */
    public boolean checkError() {
        return parent.checkError() || super.checkError();
    }
```

```
    /** override write(). This is the actual "tee" operation. */
    public void write(int x) {
        parent.write(x);     // "write once;
        super.write(x);       // write somewhere else."
    }

    /** override write(). This is the actual "tee" operation. */
    public void write(byte[] x, int o, int l) {
        parent.write(x, o, l);    // "write once;
        super.write(x, o, l);     // write somewhere else."
    }

    /** Close both streams. */
    public void close() {
        parent.close();
        super.close();
    }

    /** Flush both streams. */
    public void flush() {
        parent.flush();
        super.flush();
    }
}
```

It's worth mentioning that I do *not* need to override all the polymorphic forms of print() and println(). Because these all ultimately use one of the forms of write(), if you override the print and println methods to do the *tee*-ing as well, you can get several additional copies of the data written out.

10.13. Reading/Writing a Different Character Set

Problem

You need to read or write a text file using a particular encoding.

Solution

Convert the text to or from internal Unicode by specifying a converter when you construct an InputStreamReader or PrintWriter.

Discussion

Classes InputStreamReader and OutputStreamWriter are the bridge from byte-oriented Streams to character-based Readers. These classes read or write bytes and translate them to or from characters according to a specified character encoding. The UTF-16 character set used inside Java (char and String types) is a 16-bit character set.

But most character sets—such as ASCII, Swedish, Spanish, Greek, Turkish, and many others—use only a small subset of that. In fact, many European language character sets fit nicely into 8-bit characters. Even the larger character sets (script-based and pictographic languages) don't all use the same bit values for each particular character. The encoding, then, is a mapping between Java characters and an external storage format for characters drawn from a particular national or linguistic character set.

To simplify matters, the `InputStreamReader` and `OutputStreamWriter` constructors are the only places where you can specify the name of an encoding to be used in this translation. If you do not specify an encoding, the platform's (or user's) default encoding is used. `PrintWriters`, `BufferedReaders`, and the like all use whatever encoding the `InputStreamReader` or `OutputStreamWriter` class uses. Because these bridge classes only accept `Stream` arguments in their constructors, the implication is that if you want to specify a nondefault converter to read or write a file on disk, you must start by constructing not a `FileReader` or `FileWriter`, but a `FileInputStream` or `FileOutputStream`!

```
// UseConverters.java
BufferedReader fromKanji = new BufferedReader(
    new InputStreamReader(new FileInputStream("kanji.txt"), "EUC_JP"));
PrintWriter toSwedish = new PrinterWriter(
    new OutputStreamWriter(new FileOutputStream("sverige.txt"), "Cp278"));
```

Not that it would necessarily make sense to read a single file from Kanji and output it in a Swedish encoding; for one thing, most fonts would not have all the characters of both character sets, and, at any rate, the Swedish encoding certainly has far fewer characters in it than the Kanji encoding. Besides, if that were all you wanted, you could use a JDK tool with the ill-fitting name *native2ascii* (see its documentation for details). A list of the supported encodings is also in the JDK documentation, in the file *docs/guide/internat/encoding.doc.html*. A more detailed description is found in Appendix B of *Java I/O* (O'Reilly).

10.14. Those Pesky End-of-Line Characters

Problem

You really want to know about end-of-line characters.

Solution

Use \r and \n in whatever combination makes sense.

Discussion

If you are reading text (or bytes containing ASCII characters) in line mode using the readLine() method, you'll never see the end-of-line characters, and so you won't be cursed with having to figure out whether \n, \r, or \r\n appears at the end of each line. If you want that level of detail, you have to read the characters or bytes one at a time, using the read() methods. The only time I've found this necessary is in networking code, where some of the line-mode protocols assume that the line ending is \r\n. Even here, though, you can still work in line mode. When writing, pass \r\n into the print() (not println()!) method. When reading, use readLine() and you won't have to deal with the characters:

```
outputSocket.print("HELO " + myName + "\r\n");
String response = inputSocket.readLine( );
```

For the curious, the strange spelling of "hello" is used in SMTP, the mail sending protocol, where all commands must be four letters.

10.15. Beware Platform-Dependent File Code

Problem

Chastened by the previous recipe, you now wish to write only platform-independent code.

Solution

Use readLine() and println(). Never use \n by itself; use File.separator if you must.

Discussion

As mentioned in Recipe 10.14, if you just use readLine() and println(), you won't have to think about the line endings. But a particular problem, especially for former programmers of C and related languages, is using the \n character in text strings to mean a newline. What is particularly distressing about this code is that it works—sometimes—usually on the developer's own platform. But it will surely someday fail, on some other system:

```
String myName;
public static void main(String[] argv) {
    BadNewline jack = new BadNewline("Jack Adolphus Schmidt, III");
    System.out.println(jack);
}
/**
 * DON'T DO THIS. THIS IS BAD CODE.
 */
```

```
    public String toString() {
        return "BadNewlineDemo@" + hashCode() + "\n" + myName;
    }

    // The obvious Constructor is not shown for brevity; it's in the code
```

The real problem is not that it fails on some platforms, though. What's really wrong is that it mixes formatting and I/O, or tries to. Don't mix line-based display with `to-String()`; avoid "multiline strings"—output from `toString()` or any other string-returning method. If you need to write multiple strings, then say what you mean:

```
    String myName;
    public static void main(String[] argv) {
        GoodNewline jack = new GoodNewline("Jack Adolphus Schmidt, III");
        jack.print(System.out);
    }

    protected void print(PrintStream out) {
        out.println(toString());    // classname and hashcode
        out.println(myName);        // print name  on next line
    }
```

Alternatively, if you need multiple lines, you could return an array or `List` of strings.

10.16. Reading "Continued" Lines

Problem

You need to read lines that are continued with backslashes (\) or that are continued with leading spaces (such as email or news headers).

Solution

Use my `IndentContLineReader` or `EscContLineReader` classes.

Discussion

This functionality is likely to be reused, so it should be encapsulated in general-purpose classes. I offer the `IndentContLineReader` and `EscContLineReader` classes. `EscContLineReader` reads lines normally, but if a line ends with the escape character (by default, the backslash), the escape character is deleted and the following line is joined to the preceding line. So if you have lines like this in the input:

```
Here is something I wanted to say:\
Try and Buy in every way.
Go Team!
```

and you read them using `EscContLineReader`'s `readLine()` method, you get the following lines:

```
Here is something I wanted to say: Try and Buy in every way.
Go Team!
```

Note in particular that my reader *does* provide a space character between the abutted parts of the continued line because this is normally what you want when dealing with prose text. An `IOException` is thrown if a file ends with the escape character.

`IndentContLineReader` reads lines, but if a line begins with a space or tab, that line is joined to the preceding line. This is designed for reading email or news/message header lines. Here is an example input file:

```
From: ian Tuesday, January 1, 2000 8:45 AM EST
To: Book-reviewers List
Received: by darwinsys.com (OpenBSD 2.6)
    from localhost
    at Tuesday, January 1, 2000 8:45 AM EST
Subject: Hey, it's 2000 and MY computer is still up
```

When read using an `IndentContLineReader`, this text comes out with the continued lines joined together into longer single lines (we had to break this line to make it fit the margins of the print book):

```
From: ian Tuesday, January 1, 2000 8:45 AM EST
To: Book-reviewers List
Received: by darwinsys.com (OpenBSD 2.6) from localhost at Tuesday, January 1, ↵
2000 8:45 AM EST
Subject: Hey, it's 2000 and MY computer is still up
```

This class has a `setContinueMode(boolean)` method that lets you turn continuation mode off. This would normally be used to process the body of a message. Because the header and the body are separated by a null line in the text representation of messages, we can process the entire message correctly as follows:

src/test/java/io/IndentContLineReaderTest.java

```java
IndentContLineReader is = new IndentContLineReader(
    new StringReader(sampleTxt));
String aLine;
// Print Mail/News Header
System.out.println("----- Message Header -----");
while ((aLine = is.readLine()) != null && aLine.length() > 0) {
    System.out.println(is.getLineNumber() + ": " + aLine);
}
// Make "is" behave like normal BufferedReader
is.setContinuationMode(false);
System.out.println();
// Print Message Body
System.out.println("----- Message Body -----");
while ((aLine = is.readLine()) != null) {
```

```
            System.out.println(is.getLineNumber() + ": " + aLine);
        }
        is.close();
```

Each of the Reader classes is subclassed from LineNumberReader so that you can use getLineNumber(). This is a very useful feature when reporting errors back to the user who prepared an input file; it can save him considerable hunting around in the file if you tell him the line number on which the error occurred. The Reader classes are actually subclassed from an abstract ContLineReader subclass, which is first presented in Example 10-8. This class encapsulates the basic functionality for keeping track of lines that need to be joined together, and for enabling or disabling the continuation processing.

Example 10-8. ContLineReader.java

```java
/**
 * Subclass of LineNumberReader, parent of others, to allow reading of
 * continued lines using the readLine() method. The other Reader methods
 * (readInt()) etc.) must not be used. Must subclass to provide the actual
 * implementation of readLine().
 */
public abstract class ContLineReader extends LineNumberReader {
    /** Line number of first line in current (possibly continued) line */
    protected int firstLineNumber = 0;
    /** True if handling continuations, false if not; false == "PRE" mode */
    protected boolean doContinue = true;

    /** Set the continuation mode */
    public void setContinuationMode(boolean b) {
        doContinue = b;
    }

    /** Get the continuation mode */
    public boolean getContinuationMode() {
        return doContinue;
    }

    /** Read one (possibly continued) line, stripping out the \ that
     * marks the end of each line but the last in a sequence.
     */
    public abstract String readLine() throws IOException;

    /** Read one real line. Provided as a convenience for the
     * subclasses, so they don't embarrass themselves trying to
     * call "super.readLine()" which isn't very practical...
     */
    public String readPhysicalLine() throws IOException {
        return super.readLine();
    }

    // Can NOT override getLineNumber in this class to return the #
```

```
    // of the beginning of the continued line, since the subclasses
    // all call super.getLineNumber...

    /** Construct a ContLineReader with the default input-buffer size. */
    public ContLineReader(Reader in)  {
        super(in);
    }

    /** Construct a ContLineReader using the given input-buffer size. */
    public ContLineReader(Reader in, int sz)  {
        super(in, sz);
    }

    // Methods that do NOT work - redirect straight to parent

    /** Read a single character, returned as an int. */
    public int read() throws IOException {
        return super.read();
    }

    /** Read characters into a portion of an array. */
    public int read(char[] cbuf, int off, int len) throws IOException {
        return super.read(cbuf, off, len);
    }

    public boolean markSupported() {
        return false;
    }
}
```

The ContLineReader class ends with code for handling the read() calls so that the class
will work correctly. The IndentContLineReader class extends this to allow merging of
lines based on indentation. Example 10-9 shows the code for the IndentContLineR-
eader class.

Example 10-9. IndentContLineReader.java

```
public class IndentContLineReader extends ContLineReader {

    /** Line number of first line in current (possibly continued) line */
    public int getLineNumber() {
        return firstLineNumber;
    }

    protected String prevLine;

    /** Read one (possibly continued) line, stripping out the '\'s that
     * mark the end of all but the last.
     */
    public String readLine() throws IOException {
        String s;
```

```
        // If we saved a previous line, start with it. Else,
        // read the first line of possible continuation.
        // If non-null, put it into the StringBuffer and its line
        // number in firstLineNumber.
        if (prevLine != null) {
            s = prevLine;
            prevLine = null;
        }
        else {
            s = readPhysicalLine();
        }

        // save the line number of the first line.
        firstLineNumber = super.getLineNumber();

        // Now we have one line. If we are not in continuation
        // mode, or if a previous readPhysicalLine() returned null,
        // we are finished, so return it.
        if (!doContinue || s == null)
            return s;

        // Otherwise, start building a stringbuffer
        StringBuffer sb = new StringBuffer(s);

        // Read as many continued lines as there are, if any.
        while (true) {
            String nextPart = readPhysicalLine();
            if (nextPart == null) {
                // Egad! EOF within continued line.
                // Return what we have so far.
                return sb.toString();
            }
            // If the next line begins with space, it's continuation
            if (nextPart.length() > 0 &&
                Character.isWhitespace(nextPart.charAt(0))) {
                sb.append(nextPart);     // and add line.
            } else {
                // else we just read too far, so put in "pushback" holder
                prevLine = nextPart;
                break;
            }
        }

        return sb.toString();          // return what's left
    }
```

10.17. Reading/Writing Binary Data

Problem

You need to read or write binary data, as opposed to text.

Solution

Use a `DataInputStream` or `DataOutputStream`.

Discussion

The `Stream` classes have been in Java since the beginning of time and are optimal for reading and writing bytes rather than characters. The "data" layer over them, comprising `DataInputStream` and `DataOutputStream`, is configured for reading and writing binary values, including all of Java's built-in types. Suppose that you want to write a binary integer plus a binary floating-point value into a file and read it back later. This code shows the writing part:

```
public class WriteBinary {
    public static void main(String[] argv) throws IOException {
        int i = 42;
        double d = Math.PI;
        String FILENAME = "binary.dat";
        DataOutputStream os = new DataOutputStream(
            new FileOutputStream(FILENAME));
        os.writeInt(i);
        os.writeDouble(d);
        os.close();
        System.out.println("Wrote " + i + ", " + d + " to file " + FILENAME);
    }
}
```

The reading part is left as an exercise for the reader. Should you need to write all the fields from an object, you should probably use one of the methods described in Recipe 10.20.

10.18. Seeking to a Position within a File

Problem

You need to read from or write to a particular location in a file, such as an indexed file.

Solution

Use a `RandomAccessFile`.

Discussion

The class `java.io.RandomAccessFile` allows you to move the read or write position when writing to any location within a file or past the end. This allows you to create or access "files with holes" on some platforms and lets you read or write indexed or other database-like files in Java. The primary methods of interest are `void seek(long` where), which moves the position for the next read or write to where; int skip-Bytes(int howmany), which moves the position forward by howmany bytes; and long getFilePointer(), which returns the position.

The RandomAccessFile class also implements the DataInput and DataOutput interfaces, so everything I said about DataStreams in Recipe 10.17 also applies here. This example reads a binary integer from the beginning of the file, treats that as the position to read from, finds that position, and reads a string from that location within the file:

```java
public class ReadRandom {
    final static String FILENAME = "random.dat";
    protected String fileName;
    protected RandomAccessFile seeker;

    public static void main(String[] argv) throws IOException {
        ReadRandom r = new ReadRandom(FILENAME);

        System.out.println("Offset is " + r.readOffset());
        System.out.println("Message is \"" + r.readMessage() + "\".");
    }

    /** Constructor: save filename, construct RandomAccessFile */
    public ReadRandom(String fname) throws IOException {
        fileName = fname;
        seeker = new RandomAccessFile(fname, "r");
    }

    /** Read the Offset field, defined to be at location 0 in the file. */
    public int readOffset() throws IOException {
        seeker.seek(0);                  // move to very beginning
        return seeker.readInt();    // and read the offset
    }

    /** Read the message at the given offset */
    public String readMessage() throws IOException {
        seeker.seek(readOffset());   // move to the offset
        return seeker.readLine();    // and read the String
    }
}
```

10.19. Writing Data Streams from C

Problem

You need to exchange binary data between C and Java.

Solution

In your C code, use the network byte-ordering macros.

Discussion

The file *random.dat* read by the program in the previous recipe was not written by a Java program, but by a C program. Java is certainly capable of writing it, but I wanted to show that we can read binary data that was written in a language other than Java.

Since the earliest days of the TCP/IP protocol in the 1980s, and particularly on the 4.2 BSD version of Unix, there was an awareness that not all computer processors (CPUs) store the bytes within a word in the same order, and developers of the day came up with a means for dealing with it. The "big-endian" machines store the high-order bytes first, and "little-endian" machines store the bytes in the oppposite order (see Wikipedia (*http://en.wikipedia.org/wiki/Endianness*)). For this early heterogeneous network to function at all, it was necessary that a 32-bit word be interpreted correctly as a computer's network address, regardless of whether it originated on a PDP-11, a VAX, a Sun workstation, or any other kind of machine then prevalent. So "network byte order" was established, a standard for which bytes go in which order on the network. Network order is big-endian, whereas the Intel/AMD x86 architecture is little-endian.

For C programmers, the "network byte order macros" were written: ntohl for network-to-host order for a long (32 bits), htons for host-to-network order for a short (16 bits), and so on. In most Unix implementations, these C macros live in one of the Internet header files, although in some newer systems, they have been segregated out into a file like *<machine/endian.h>*, as on our OpenBSD system.

The designers of Java, working at Sun, were well aware of these issues and chose to use network byte order in the Java Virtual Machine. Thus, a Java program can read an IP address from a socket using a DataInputStream or write an integer to disk that will be read from C using read() and the network byte order macros.

The C program in Example 10-10 writes the file *random.dat* that we read in Recipe 10.18. It uses the network byte order macros to make sure that the long integer (32 bits on most C compilers) is in the correct order to be read as an int in Java:

Example 10-10. src/main/java/io/WriteRandom.c

```
/* C Program to create the random-access file for the RandomAccessFile example
 * Ian F. Darwin, http://www.darwinsys.com/
 */

#include <stdio.h>
#include <fcntl.h>
#include <stdlib.h>
#include <unistd.h>
#include <sys/types.h>
#include <machine/endian.h>

const off_t OFFSET = 1234;     // off_t is a C "typedef", usually == long integer
const char* FILENAME = "random.dat";
```

```c
const int MODE = 0644;
const char* MESSAGE = "Ye have sought, and ye have found!\r\n";

int
main(int argc, char **argv) {
    int fd;
    int java_offset;

    if ((fd = creat(FILENAME, MODE)) < 0) {
        perror(FILENAME);
        return 1;
    }

    /* Java's DataStreams etc. are defined to be in network byte order */
    java_offset = htonl(OFFSET);

    if (write(fd, &java_offset, sizeof java_offset) < 0) {
        perror("write");
        return 1;
    }

    if (lseek(fd, OFFSET, SEEK_SET) < 0) {
        perror("seek");
        return 1;
    }

    if (write(fd, MESSAGE, strlen(MESSAGE)) != strlen(MESSAGE)) {
        perror("write2");
        return 1;
    }

    if (close(fd) < 0) {
        perror("close!?");
        return 1;
    }

    return 0;
}
```

The same technique can be used in the other direction, of course, and when exchanging data over a network socket, and anyplace else you need to exchange binary data between Java and C.

10.20. Saving and Restoring Java Objects

Problem

You need to write and (later) read objects.

Solution

Use the object stream classes, `ObjectInputStream` and `ObjectOutputStream`.

Discussion

Object serialization is the ability to convert in-memory objects to an external form that can be sent serially (a byte at a time) and back again. The "and back again" may happen at a later time, or in another JVM on another computer (even one that has a different byte order)—Java handles differences between machines. `ObjectInputStream` and `ObjectOutputStream` are specialized stream classes designed to read and write objects. They can be used to save objects to disk, as I'll show here, and are also useful in passing objects across a network connection, as I'll show in Recipe 13.6.

As you might imagine, if we pass an object (e.g., a `MyData` object), to the `writeObject()` method, and `writeObject()` notices that one of the fields is itself a reference to an object such as a `String`, that data will get serialized properly. In other words, `writeObject` works *recursively*. And carefully: if an object is referenced multiple times, it will only be serializeed once. So, we can give it a `List` of `MyData` objects.

To be serializable, the data class must implement the empty `Serializable` interface. Also, the keyword `transient` can be used for any data that should *not* be serialized. You might need to do this for security or to prevent attempts to serialize a reference to an object of a nonserializable class.

That said, making a class `Serializable` is not a decision that should be taken lightly. Consideration should be given to enforcing class invariants during serialization, writing defensive `readObject` or `readResolve` methods, initializing transient variables, etc.

Here `transient` is used to prevent unencrypted passwords from being saved where they might be readable:

src/main/java/io/MyData.java

```java
/** Simple data class used in Serialization demos. */
public class MyData implements Serializable {

    private static final long serialVersionUID = -4965296908339881739L;
    String userName;
    String passwordCypher;
    transient String passwordClear;

    /** This constructor is required by most APIs */
    public MyData() {
        // Nothing to do
    }

    public MyData(String name, String clear) {
```

```
        setUserName(name);
        setPassword(clear);
    }

    public String getUserName() {
        return userName;
    }

    public void setUserName(String s) {
        this.userName = s;
    }

    public String getPasswordCypher() {
        return passwordCypher;
    }

    /** Save the clear text p/w in the object, it won't get serialized
     * So we must save the encryption! Encryption not shown here.
     */
    public void setPassword(String s) {
        this.passwordClear = s;
        passwordCypher = encrypt(passwordClear);
    }

    public String toString() {
        return "MyData[" + userName + ",------]";
    }
```

Because several methods are available for serializing, in Example 10-11, I define an abstract base class, called SerialDemoAbstractBase, which creates the data list and whose save() method calls the abstract write() method to actually save the data.

Example 10-11. src/main/java/io/SerialDemoAbstractBase.c

```c
/* C Program to create the random-access file for the RandomAccessFile example
 * Ian F. Darwin, http://www.darwinsys.com/
 */

#include <stdio.h>
#include <fcntl.h>
#include <stdlib.h>
#include <unistd.h>
#include <sys/types.h>
#include <machine/endian.h>

const off_t OFFSET = 1234;     // off_t is a C "typedef", usually == long integer
const char* FILENAME = "random.dat";
const int MODE = 0644;
const char* MESSAGE = "Ye have sought, and ye have found!\r\n";

int
main(int argc, char **argv) {
    int fd;
```

```
    int java_offset;

    if ((fd = creat(FILENAME, MODE)) < 0) {
        perror(FILENAME);
        return 1;
    }

    /* Java's DataStreams etc. are defined to be in network byte order */
    java_offset = htonl(OFFSET);

    if (write(fd, &java_offset, sizeof java_offset) < 0) {
        perror("write");
        return 1;
    }

    if (lseek(fd, OFFSET, SEEK_SET) < 0) {
        perror("seek");
        return 1;
    }

    if (write(fd, MESSAGE, strlen(MESSAGE)) != strlen(MESSAGE)) {
        perror("write2");
        return 1;
    }

    if (close(fd) < 0) {
        perror("close!?");
        return 1;
    }

    return 0;
}
```

The implementation for object stream serialization is shown here:

```
public class SerialDemoObjectStream extends SerialDemoAbstractBase {
    protected static final String FILENAME = "serial.dat";

    public static void main(String[] s) throws Exception {
        new SerialDemoObjectStream().save();    // in parent class; calls write
        new SerialDemoObjectStream().dump();    // here
    }

    /** Does the actual serialization */
    public void write(Object theGraph) throws IOException {
        // Save the data to disk.
        ObjectOutputStream os = new ObjectOutputStream(
            new BufferedOutputStream(
                new FileOutputStream(FILENAME)));
        os.writeObject(theGraph);
        os.close();
    }
```

```
public void dump() throws IOException, ClassNotFoundException {
    ObjectInputStream is = new ObjectInputStream(
        new FileInputStream(FILENAME));
    System.out.println(is.readObject());
    is.close();
    }
}
```

See Also

For more on the standard Serialization, see the chapter on this topic in *Effective Java* (*http://amzn.to/1iuJEVD*).

10.21. Preventing ClassCastExceptions with SerialVersionUID

Problem

Your classes were recompiled, and you're getting `ClassCastExceptions` that you shouldn't.

Solution

Run `serialver` to generate a "serial version UUID" and paste its output into your classes before you start. Or use your IDE's tools for this purpose.

Discussion

When a class is undergoing a period of evolution—particularly a class being used in a networking context such as RMI or servlets—it may be useful to provide a `serialVersionUID` value in this class. This is a `long` that is basically a hash of the methods and fields in the class. Both the object serialization API (see Recipe 10.20) and the JVM, when asked to cast one object to another (common when using collections, as in Chapter 7), either look up or, if not found, compute this value. If the value on the source and destination do not match, a `ClassCastException` is thrown. Most of the time, this is the correct thing for Java to do.

However, sometimes you may want to allow a class to evolve in a compatible way, but you can't immediately replace all instances in circulation. You must be willing to write code to account for the additional fields being discarded if restoring from the longer format to the shorter and having the default value (null for objects, 0 for numbers, and false for Boolean) if you're restoring from the shorter format to the longer. If you are only adding fields and methods in a reasonably compatible way, you can control the compatibility by providing a long int named `serialVersionUID`. The initial value should be obtained from a JDK tool called *serialver*, which takes just the class name. Consider a simple class called `SerializableUser`:

```
public class SerializableUser implements java.io.Serializable {
    public String name;
    public String address;
    public String country;
    public String phoneNum;

    // other fields, and methods, here...
    static final long serialVersionUID = -7978489268769667877L;
}
```

I first compiled it with two different compilers to ensure that the value is a product of the class structure, not of some minor differences in class file format that different compilers might emit:

```
$ javac SerializableUser.java
$ serialver SerializableUser
SerializableUser:    static final long serialVersionUID = -7978489268769667877L;
$ jikes +E SerializableUser.java
$ serialver SerializableUser
SerializableUser:    static final long serialVersionUID = -7978489268769667877L;
```

Sure enough, the class file from both compilers has the same hash. Now let's change the file. I go in with an editor and add a new field, phoneNum, right after `country`:

```
public String country;
public String phoneNum;        // Added this line.

$ javac SerializableUser.java
$ serialver SerializableUser
SerializableUser:    static final long serialVersionUID = -8339341455288589756L;
```

Notice how the addition of the field changed the `serialVersionUID`! Now, if I had wanted this class to evolve in a compatible fashion, here's what I should have done before I started expanding it. I copy and paste the original *serialver* output into the source file (again using an editor to insert a line before the last line):

```
// The following is the line I added to SerializableUser.java
private static final long serialVersionUID = -7978489268769667877L;
$ javac SerializableUser.java
$ serialver SerializableUser
SerializableUser:    static final long serialVersionUID = -7978489268769667877L;
$
```

Now all is well: I can interchange serialized versions of this file.

Note that `serialver` is part of the "object serialization" mechanism, and, therefore, it is meaningful only on classes that implement the `Serializable` interface described in Recipe 10.20.

Note also that some developers use serialVersionUID values that start at 1 (a choice offered by some IDEs when they note that a class that appears to be serializable lacks a serialVersionUID), and then simply increment it by one each time the class changes in an incompatible way.

10.22. Reading and Writing JAR or ZIP Archives

Problem

You need to create and/or extract from a JAR archive or a file in the well-known ZIP Archive format, as established by PkZip and used by Unix zip/unzip and WinZip.

Solution

You could use the *jar* program in the Java Development Kit because its file format is identical to the ZIP format with the addition of the *META-INF* directory to contain additional structural information. But because this is a book about programming, you are probably more interested in the ZipFile and ZipEntry classes and the stream classes to which they provide access.

Discussion

The class java.util.zip.ZipFile is not an I/O class *per se*, but a utility class that allows you to read or write the contents of a JAR or ZIP-format file.[4] When constructed, it creates a series of ZipEntry objects, one to represent each entry in the archive. In other words, the ZipFile represents the entire archive, and the ZipEntry represents one entry, or one file that has been stored (and compressed) in the archive. The ZipEntry has methods like getName( ), which returns the name that the file had before it was put into the archive, and getInputStream( ), which gives you an InputStream that will transparently uncompress the archive entry by filtering it as you read it. To create a Zip-File object, you need either the name of the archive file or a File object representing it:

```
ZipFile zippy = new ZipFile(fileName);
```

To see whether a given file is present in the archive, you can call the getEntry( ) method with a filename. More commonly, you'll want to process all the entries; for this, use the ZipFile object to get a list of the entries in the archive, in the form of an Enumeration (see Recipe 7.9):

---

4. There is no support for adding files to an existing archive, so make sure you put all the files in at once or be prepared to re-create the archive from scratch.

```
Enumeration all = zippy.entries( );
while (all.hasMoreElements( )) {
    ZipEntry entry = (ZipEntry)all.nextElement( );
    ...
}
```

We can then process each entry as we wish. A simple listing program could be:

```
if (entry.isDirectory( ))
    println("Directory: " + e.getName( ));
else
    println("File: " + e.getName( ));
```

A fancier version would extract the files. The program in Example 10-12 does both: it lists by default, but with the -x (extract) switch, it actually extracts the files from the archive.

Example 10-12. UnZip.java

```
public class UnZip {
    /** Constants for mode listing or mode extracting. */
    public static enum Mode {
        LIST,
        EXTRACT;
    };
    /** Whether we are extracting or just printing TOC */
    protected Mode mode = Mode.LIST;

    /** The ZipFile that is used to read an archive */
    protected ZipFile zippy;

    /** The buffer for reading/writing the ZipFile data */
    protected byte[] b = new byte[8092];;

    /** Simple main program, construct an UnZipper, process each
     * .ZIP file from argv[] through that object.
     */
    public static void main(String[] argv) {
        UnZip u = new UnZip();

        for (int i=0; i<argv.length; i++) {
            if ("-x".equals(argv[i])) {
                u.setMode(Mode.EXTRACT);
                continue;
            }
            String candidate = argv[i];
            // System.err.println("Trying path " + candidate);
            if (candidate.endsWith(".zip") ||
                candidate.endsWith(".jar"))
                    u.unZip(candidate);
            else System.err.println("Not a zip file? " + candidate);
        }
        System.err.println("All done!");
```

```
    }

    /** Set the Mode (list, extract). */
    protected void setMode(Mode m) {
        mode = m;
    }

    /** Cache of paths we've mkdir()ed. */
    protected SortedSet<String> dirsMade;

    /** For a given Zip file, process each entry. */
    public void unZip(String fileName) {
        dirsMade = new TreeSet<String>();
        try {
            zippy = new ZipFile(fileName);
            Enumeration all = zippy.entries();
            while (all.hasMoreElements()) {
                getFile((ZipEntry)all.nextElement());
            }
        } catch (IOException err) {
            System.err.println("IO Error: " + err);
            return;
        }
    }

    protected boolean warnedMkDir = false;

    /** Process one file from the zip, given its name.
     * Either print the name, or create the file on disk.
     */
    protected void getFile(ZipEntry e) throws IOException {
        String zipName = e.getName();
        switch (mode) {
        case EXTRACT:
            if (zipName.startsWith("/")) {
                if (!warnedMkDir)
                    System.out.println("Ignoring absolute paths");
                warnedMkDir = true;
                zipName = zipName.substring(1);
            }
            // if a directory, just return. We mkdir for every file,
            // since some widely used Zip creators don't put out
            // any directory entries, or put them in the wrong place.
            if (zipName.endsWith("/")) {
                return;
            }
            // Else must be a file; open the file for output
            // Get the directory part.
            int ix = zipName.lastIndexOf('/');
            if (ix > 0) {
                String dirName = zipName.substring(0, ix);
                if (!dirsMade.contains(dirName)) {
```

```
            File d = new File(dirName);
            // If it already exists as a dir, don't do anything
            if (!(d.exists() && d.isDirectory())) {
                // Try to create the directory, warn if it fails
                System.out.println("Creating Directory: " + dirName);
                if (!d.mkdirs()) {
                    System.err.println(
                    "Warning: unable to mkdir " + dirName);
                }
                dirsMade.add(dirName);
            }
        }
    }
    System.err.println("Creating " + zipName);
    FileOutputStream os = new FileOutputStream(zipName);
    InputStream  is = zippy.getInputStream(e);
    int n = 0;
    while ((n = is.read(b)) >0)
        os.write(b, 0, n);
    is.close();
    os.close();
    break;
case LIST:
    // Not extracting, just list
    if (e.isDirectory()) {
        System.out.println("Directory " + zipName);
    } else {
        System.out.println("File " + zipName);
    }
    break;
default:
    throw new IllegalStateException("mode value (" + mode + ") bad");
    }
    }
}
```

10.23. Finding Files in a Filesystem-Neutral Way with getResource() and getResourceAsStream()

Problem

You want to load objects or files without referring to their absolute location in the filesystem. This can be because you are in a server (Java EE) environment, or just because you want to be independent of file paths, or because you expect users to deploy the resource "somewhere" on the classpath (possibly even inside a JAR file).

Solution

Use getClass() or getClassLoader() and either getResource() or getResourceAs-Stream().

Discussion

There are three varieties of getResource() methods, some of which exist (with the exact same signature) both in the Class class (see Chapter 23) and in the ClassLoader class (see Recipe 23.5). The methods in Class delegate to the ClassLoader, so there is little difference between them. The methods are summarized in Table 10-4.

Table 10-4. The getResource* methods

Method signature	In Class	In ClassLoader
public InputStream getResourceAsStream(String);	Y	Y
public URL getResource(String);	Y	Y
public Enumeration<URL> getResources(String) throws IOException;	N	Y

The first is designed to quickly and easily locate a "resource" or file on your classpath. Using the Class version, or the other one with a standard classloader implementation, the resource can be a physical file, or a file inside a JAR file. If you define your own classloader, your imagination is the limit, as long as it can be represented as an Input-Stream. This is commonly used as:

```
InputStream is = getClass().getResourceAsStream("foo.properties");
// then do something with the InputStream...
```

The second form returns a URL, which again, can be interpreted in various ways (see the discussion of reading from a URL in Recipe 13.10).

The third form, only usable with a ClassLoader instance, returns an Enumeration of URL objects. This is intended to return all the resources that match a given string; remember that a CLASSPATH can consist of pretty much any number of directories and/or JAR files, so this will search all of them. Useful for finding a series of configuration files and merging them, perhaps. Or for finding out whether there is more than one resource/file of a given name on your classpath.

Note that the resource name can be given as either a relative path or as an absolute path. Assuming you are using Maven (see Recipe 1.7), then for the absolute path, place the file relative to *src/main/resources/* directory. For the absolute path, place the file in the same directory as your source code. The same rules apply in an IDE assuming you have made *src/main/java* and *src/main/resources* be treated as "source folders" in your IDE configuration. The idea is that "resource files" get copied to your classpath folder. For example, if you have two resource files, *src/main/resources/one.txt* and *src/main/java/*

MyPackage/two.txt, and your project is configured as described, these two lines would work, if accessed from a program in `MyPackage`:

```
Class<?> c = getClass();
InputStream isOne = getResourceAsStream("/one.txt");    // note leading slash
InputStream isTwo = getResourceAsStream("two.txt");     // without leading slash
```

 In either case, getResource() and getResourceAsStream() will return null if they don't find the resource; you should always check for null to guard against faulty deployment. However, if it doesn't find anything matching, getResources() will return an empty Enumeration.

If the file path has slashes between components (as in *package/subpackage*), the name you path into any of the `getResource` methods should have a "." in place of the "/".

10.24. Reading and Writing Compressed Files

Problem

You need to read or write files that have been compressed using GNU zip, or *gzip*. These files are usually saved with the extension *.gz*.

Solution

Use a `GZipInputStream` or `GZipOutputStream` as appropriate.

Discussion

The GNU *gzip/gunzip* utilities originated on Unix and are commonly used to compress files. Unlike the ZIP format discussed in Recipe 10.22, these programs do not combine the functionality of archiving and compressing, and, therefore, they are easier to work with. However, because they are not archives, people often use them in conjunction with an archiver. On Unix, *tar* and *cpio* are common, with *tar* and *gzip* being the *de facto* standard combination. Many websites and FTP sites make files available with the extension *.tar.gz* or *.tgz*; such files originally had to be first decompressed with *gunzip* and then extracted with *tar*. As this became a common operation, modern versions of *tar* have been extended to support a -z option, which means to *gunzip* before extracting, or to *gzip* before writing, as appropriate.

You may find archived files in *gzip* format on any platform. If you do, they're quite easy to read, again using classes from the `java.util.zip` package. This program assumes that the gzipped file originally contained text (Unicode characters). If not, you would treat it as a stream of bytes (i.e., use a BufferedInputStream instead of a Buffere-dReader):

```
public class ReadGZIP {
    public static void main(String[] argv) throws IOException {
        String FILENAME = "file.txt.gz";

        // Since there are 4 constructor calls here, I wrote them out in full.
        // In real life you would probably nest these constructor calls.
        FileInputStream fin = new FileInputStream(FILENAME);
        GZIPInputStream gzis = new GZIPInputStream(fin);
        InputStreamReader xover = new InputStreamReader(gzis);
        BufferedReader is = new BufferedReader(xover);

        String line;
        // Now read lines of text: the BufferedReader puts them in lines,
        // the InputStreamReader does Unicode conversion, and the
        // GZipInputStream "gunzip"s the data from the FileInputStream.
        while ((line = is.readLine()) != null)
            System.out.println("Read: " + line);
    }
}
```

If you need to write files in this format, everything works as you'd expect—you create a GZipOutputStream and write on it, usually using it through a DataOutputStream, BufferedWriter, or PrintWriter.

See Also

InflaterInputStream, InflaterOutputStream, DeflaterInputStream, and DeflaterOutputStream provide access to general-purpose compression and decompression; these stream classes provide an I/O-based implementation of Inflater and Deflater.

10.25. Learning about the Communications API for Serial and Parallel Ports

Problem

You have a computer with a serial or parallel port, and you want to read and write on such a port.

Solution

Find an implementation of the Java Communications API (javax.comm) and write code using it. Get a list of Communicaton Ports, and pick one port. You can use the CommPortIdentifier's open() method to get a SerialPort object.

Discussion

Peripheral devices are usually external to the computer.[5] Printers, mice, video cameras, scanners, data/fax modems, plotters, robots, telephones, light switches, weather gauges, smartphones, and many others exist "out there," beyond the confines of your desktop or server machine. We need a way to reach out to them.

The Java Communications API not only gave us that but cleverly unifies the programming model for dealing with a range of external devices. It supports both serial (RS232/434, COM, or tty) and parallel (printer, LPT) ports.

Before the USB (Universal Serial Bus) came along, it seemed that parallel ports would dominate for such peripherals because manufacturers were starting to make video cameras, scanners, and the like that worked over parallel ports. Now, however, USB has become the main attachment mode for such devices. A Java Standards Request (JSR-80) documents a standard API for accessing USB devices under Java, but it has not been widely used. You can download a reference implementation from Source Forge (*http://sourceforge.net/projects/javax-usb*). You can find a competing Java API for USB at jUSB (*http://jusb.sourceforge.net*).

Sadly, the Communications API has been languishing in recent years, and it is even hard to find copies of the official implementation. The download for this book includes "comm.jar," but does not have the native code libraries, so the examples will compile but not function. There is an alternative implementation called RxTx that may be usable for some of these examples.

Oracle has indicated that it plans to bring the "device access API" from Java ME into the Java SE world in 2014, and adapt it for Java SE conventions. This will replace the `javax.comm` API and hopefully do so as a full-fledged part of Java. Recipes will be added here when this API is fleshed out enough that it's possible to write about it.

The Communications API in a Nutshell

The Communications API is centered around the abstract class `CommPort` and its two subclasses, `SerialPort` and `ParallelPort`, which describe two types of ports found on desktop computers. The constructors for these classes are intentionally nonpublic; you use the static factory method `CommPortIdentifier.getPortIdentifiers()` to get a list of ports, choose (or let the user choose) a port from this list, and call this `CommPortIdentifier`'s `open()` method to receive a `CommPort` object. You cast the `CommPort` reference to a nonabstract subclass representing a particular type of communications device. At present, the subclass must be either `SerialPort` or `ParallelPort`.

---

5. Conveniently ignoring things like "internal modem cards" on desktop machines!

Each of these subclasses has some methods that apply only to that type. For example, the `SerialPort` class has a method to set baud rate, parity, and the like, while the `ParallelPort` class has methods for setting the "port mode" to original PC mode, bidirectional mode, etc.

Both subclasses also have methods that allow you to use the standard Java event model to receive notification of events such as data available for reading and output buffer empty. You can also receive notification of type-specific events such as ring indicator for a serial port and out-of-paper for a parallel port. (Parallel ports were originally for printers and still use their terminology in a few places.)

To summarize, the basic steps in using a communications port are as follows:

1. Get an `Enumeration` (see Recipe 7.9) of `CommPortIdentifiers` by calling the static `CommPortIdentifier` method `getPortIdentifiers()`, and choose the port you want.

2. Call the `CommPortIdentifier`'s `open()` method; cast the resulting `CommPort` object to a `SerialPort` object or `ParallelPort` as appropriate.

3. Set the communications parameters (i.e., baud rate, parity, stop bits, and the like), either individually or all at once, using the convenience routine `setSerialPort-Params()` for a serial port or "mode" for a parallel port.

4. Call the `getInputStream` and `getOutputStream` methods of the `CommPort` object, and construct any additional `Stream` or `Writer` objects (see Chapter 10).

You are then ready to read and write on the port. Example 10-13 is code that implements all these steps for a serial port. For parallel ports the API is similar; consult the online documentation.

Example 10-13. src/main/java/javacomm/CommPortSimple.java

```java
/**
 * Open a serial port using Java Communications.
 * @author    Ian F. Darwin, http://www.darwinsys.com/
 */
public class CommPortSimple {
    private static final String HELLO = "Hello?";
    /** How long to wait for the open to finish up. */
    public static final int TIMEOUTSECONDS = 30;
    /** The baud rate to use. */
    public static final int BAUD = 19200;
    /** The input stream */
    protected BufferedReader is;
    /** The output stream */
    protected PrintStream os;
    /** The chosen Port Identifier */
    CommPortIdentifier thePortID;
    /** The chosen Port itself */
```

```java
    CommPort thePort;

    public static void main(String[] argv) throws Exception {

        if (argv.length != 1) {
            System.err.println("Usage: CommPortSimple deviceName");
            System.exit(1);
        }

        new CommPortSimple(argv[0]).holdConversation();

        System.exit(0);
    }

    /* Constructor */
    public CommPortSimple(String devName) throws Exception {

        @SuppressWarnings("unchecked")
        Enumeration<CommPortIdentifier> pList =
                CommPortIdentifier.getPortIdentifiers();

        // Walk the list, looking for the given name
        CommPortIdentifier cpi = null;
        boolean atLeastOneSerialPresent = false;
        while (pList.hasMoreElements()) {
            CommPortIdentifier c = pList.nextElement();
            if (c.getPortType() !=CommPortIdentifier.PORT_SERIAL) {
                System.err.println("Not a serial port: " + c.getName());
                continue;
            }
            if (devName.equals(c.getName())) {
                cpi = c;
                break; // found!
            }
            atLeastOneSerialPresent = true;
            System.out.println("Not matched: " + c.getName());
        }
        if (cpi == null) {
            System.err.println("Did not find serial port '" + devName + "'");
            if (atLeastOneSerialPresent)
                System.err.println("Try again with one of the listed names");
            else
                System.err.println("In fact, I didn't see ANY serial ports!");
            System.exit(1);
        }

        thePort = cpi.open("JavaCook DataComm",
                TIMEOUTSECONDS * 1000);
        SerialPort myPort = (SerialPort) thePort;

        // set up the serial port
        myPort.setSerialPortParams(BAUD, SerialPort.DATABITS_8,
```

```
                    SerialPort.STOPBITS_1, SerialPort.PARITY_NONE);

        // Get the input and output streams
        is = new BufferedReader(new InputStreamReader(thePort.getInputStream()));
        os = new PrintStream(thePort.getOutputStream(), true);
    }

    /** Hold a conversation - in this case a *very* simple one.  */
    protected void holdConversation() throws IOException {

        System.out.println("Ready to read and write port.");

        os.println(HELLO);
        String response = is.readLine();

        System.out.printf("I said %s, and the other end replied %s%n",
                HELLO, response);

        // Finally, clean up.
        if (is != null)
            is.close();
        if (os != null)
            os.close();
    }
}
```

See Also

The online source includes `javacomm/CommPortOpen.java`, which provides a framework for using Java Communications API; it does pretty much all the work except for actually reading or writing. You subclass `CommPortOpen` and write a `converse()` method to read and write on the `InputStream` and `OutputStream`, which are exposed as the inherited fields `is` and `os`, respectively.

Table 10-5 lists additional programs in the online source package.

Table 10-5. Other Java Communications facilties, with examples

Program	Feature
ParallelPrint	Opens a printer and sends a file directly
CommPortModem	Talks to a Hayes-style "AT" command modem on a serial port
CommPortDial.java	As above but dials a number
TModem.java	Implements the 1980s era CP/M Modem Protocol to send/receive files
SerialLogger	Event-driven reading/writing, using `EventListener` model; reads from multiple serial ports
CommPortThreaded	Reading and writing using two `Threads` to allow "full duplex" style operation

Given the diminishing use of this API and its planned replacement, we don't discuss these examples in detail in the book.

10.26. Save User Data to Disk

Problem

You need to save user data to disk in a Java application. This may be in response to File→Save in a GUI application, saving the file in a text editor, or saving configuration data in a non-GUI application. You have heard (correctly) that a well-behaved application should never lose data.

Solution

Use this five-step plan, with appropriate variations:

1. Create a temporary file; arrange for it to be removed automatically with `deleteOnExit(true)`.

2. Write the user data to this file. Data format translation errors, if any, will be thrown during this process, leaving the previous version of the user's data file intact.

3. Delete the backup file if it exists.

4. Rename the user's previous file to *.bak*.

5. Rename the temporary file to the saved file.

Discussion

As developers, we have to deal with the fact that saving a file to disk is full of risk. There are many things that can go wrong in saving data, yet it is one of the most critical parts of most applications. If you lose data that a person has spent hours inputting, or even lost a setting that a user feels strongly about, she will despise your whole application. The disk might fill up while we're writing it, or be full before we start. This is a user's error, but we have to face it. So here's a more detailed discussion of the little five-step dance we should go through:

1. Create a temporary file that we will write to. Set this file to `deleteOnExit(true)`, so that if we fail in a later step we don't clutter the disk. Because we are later going to rename this file to become the user's real file, and we don't want to run out of disk space during the rename, it is important that we create the file on the same disk drive partition ("drive letter" or "mount point") as the user's real file, otherwise the rename will silently morph into a copy-and-delete, which could fail due to lack of disk space. The File API (see Chapter 11) makes this easy.

2. Write the user data to this new temporary file. If we are transforming data—say, getting it from a JDBC ResultSet (see Chapter 20) or writing objects using a XML

transformer (see Recipe 20.8)—an exception could be thrown. If we're not careful, these exceptions can cause the user's data to be lost.

3. Delete the backup file if it exists. First time we do this it won't exist; after that it probably will. Be prepared either way.

4. Rename the user's previous file to `*.bak`.

5. Rename the temporary file to the save file.

This may seem like overkill, but "It's not overkill, it prevents career kill." I've done pretty much this in numerous apps with various save file formats. This plan is the only really safe way around all the problems that can occur. For example, the final step has to be a rename not a copy, regardless of size considerations, to avoid the "disk fills up" problem. So, to be correct, you have to ensure that the temp file gets created on the same disk partition (drive letter or mount point) as the user's file:

src/main/java/com/darwinsys/io/FileSaver.java

```java
// package com.darwinsys.io;
public class FileSaver {

    private enum State {
        /** The state before and after use */
        AVAILABLE,
        /** The state while in use */
        INUSE
    }
    private State state;
    private final File inputFile;
    private final File tmpFile;
    private final File backupFile;

    public FileSaver(File input) throws IOException {

        // Step 1: Create temp file in right place
        this.inputFile = input;
        tmpFile = new File(inputFile.getAbsolutePath() + ".tmp");
        tmpFile.createNewFile();
        tmpFile.deleteOnExit();
        backupFile = new File(inputFile.getAbsolutePath() + ".bak");
        state = State.AVAILABLE;
    }

    /**
     * Return a reference to the contained File object, to
     * promote reuse (File objects are immutable so this
     * is at least moderately safe). Typical use would be:
     * <pre>
     * if (fileSaver == null ||
     *    !(fileSaver.getFile().equals(file))) {
     *         fileSaver = new FileSaver(file);
```

```
 * }
 * </pre>
 */
public File getFile() {
    return inputFile;
}

/** Return an output file that the client should use to
 * write the client's data to.
 * @return An OutputStream, which should be wrapped in a
 *      buffered OutputStream to ensure reasonable performance.
 * @throws IOException if the temporary file cannot be written
 */
public OutputStream getOutputStream() throws IOException {

    if (state != State.AVAILABLE) {
        throw new IllegalStateException("FileSaver not opened");
    }
    OutputStream out = new FileOutputStream(tmpFile);
    state = State.INUSE;
    return out;
}

/** Return an output file that the client should use to
 * write the client's data to.
 * @return A Writer, which should be wrapped in a
 *      buffered Writer to ensure reasonable performance.
 * @throws IOException if the temporary file cannot be written
 */
public Writer getWriter() throws IOException {

    if (state != State.AVAILABLE) {
        throw new IllegalStateException("FileSaver not opened");
    }
    Writer out = new FileWriter(tmpFile);
    state = State.INUSE;
    return out;
}

/** Close the output file and rename the temp file to the original name.
 * @throws IOException If anything goes wrong
 */
public void finish() throws IOException {

    if (state != State.INUSE) {
        throw new IllegalStateException("FileSaver not in use");
    }

    // Delete the previous backup file if it exists;
    backupFile.delete();

    // Rename the user's previous file to itsName.bak,
```

```
        // UNLESS this is a new file ;
        if (inputFile.exists() && !inputFile.renameTo(backupFile)) {
            throw new IOException("Could not rename file to backup file");
        }

        // Rename the temporary file to the save file.
        if (!tmpFile.renameTo(inputFile)) {
            throw new IOException("Could not rename temp file to save file");
        }
        state = State.AVAILABLE;
    }
}
```

See Also

The Preferences API (see Recipe 7.12) allows you to save small amounts of preference data, but is not convenient for saving program state. The Object Serialization API (see Recipe 10.20) will serialize objects to/from an external representation. To serialize using XML, consider using JAXB (see Recipe 20.1) or the XML Serializers (see Recipe 20.2). You could also save it in JSON (see Chapter 19). The XML and JSON forms have the benefit that they store text files (somewhat larger, but more portable).

Acknowledgements

The code in this program is my own, based on my experience in various applications. I was prompted to package it up this way, and write it up, by a posting made by Brendon McLean to the mailing list for the now-defunct Java Application Framework JSR-296 (*http://jcp.org/en/jsr/detail?id=296*).

10.27. Program: Text to PostScript

There are several approaches to printing in Java. In a GUI application, or if you want to use the graphical facilities that Java offers (fonts, colors, drawing primitives, and the like), you should refer to Recipe 12.12. However, sometimes you simply want to convert text into a form that prints nicely on a printer that isn't capable of handling raw text on its own (such as many of the PostScript devices on the market). The program in Example 10-14 shows code for reading one or more text files and outputting each of them in a plain font with PostScript around it. Because of the nature of PostScript, certain characters must be escaped; this is handled in toPsString(), which in turn is called from doLine(). There is also code for keeping track of the current position on the page. The output of this program can be sent directly to a PostScript printer.

Example 10-14. src/main/java/textproc/PSFormatter.java

```
public class PSFormatter {
    /** The current input source */
    protected BufferedReader br;
```

```java
/** The current page number */
protected int pageNum;
/** The current X and Y on the page */
protected int curX, curY;
/** The current line number on page */
protected int lineNum;
/** The current tab setting */
protected int tabPos = 0;
public static final int INCH = 72;     // PS constant: 72 pts/inch

// Page parameters
/** The left margin indent */
protected int leftMargin = 50;
/** The top of page indent */
protected int topMargin = 750;
/** The bottom of page indent */
protected int botMargin = 50;

// FORMATTING PARAMETERS
protected int points = 12;
protected int leading = 14;

public static void main(String[] av) throws IOException {
    if (av.length == 0)
        new PSFormatter(
            new InputStreamReader(System.in)).process();
    else for (int i = 0; i < av.length; i++) {
        new PSFormatter(av[i]).process();
    }
}

public PSFormatter(String fileName) throws IOException {
    br = new BufferedReader(new FileReader(fileName));
}

public PSFormatter(Reader in) throws IOException {
    if (in instanceof BufferedReader)
        br = (BufferedReader)in;
    else
        br = new BufferedReader(in);
}

/** Main processing of the current input source. */
protected void process() throws IOException {

    String line;

    prologue();                 // emit PostScript prologue, once.

    startPage();            // emit top-of-page (ending previous)

    while ((line = br.readLine()) != null) {
```

```java
            if (line.startsWith("\f") || line.trim().equals(".bp")) {
                startPage();
                continue;
            }
            doLine(line);
        }

        // finish last page, if not already done.
        if (lineNum != 0)
            System.out.println("showpage");
    }

    /** Handle start of page details. */
    protected void startPage() {
        if (pageNum++ > 0)
            System.out.println("showpage");
        lineNum = 0;
        moveTo(leftMargin, topMargin);
    }

    /** Process one line from the current input */
    protected void doLine(String line) {
        tabPos = 0;
        // count leading (not imbedded) tabs.
        for (int i=0; i<line.length(); i++) {
            if (line.charAt(i)=='\t')
                tabPos++;
            else
                break;
        }
        String l = line.trim(); // removes spaces AND tabs
        if (l.length() == 0) {
            ++lineNum;
            return;
        }
        moveTo(leftMargin + (tabPos * INCH),
            topMargin-(lineNum++ * leading));
        System.out.println('(' + toPSString(l)+ ") show");

        // If we just hit the bottom, start a new page
        if (curY <= botMargin)
            startPage();
    }

    /** Overly simplistic conversion to PS, e.g., breaks on "foo\)bar" */
    protected String toPSString(String o) {
        StringBuilder sb = new StringBuilder();
        for (int i=0; i<o.length(); i++) {
            char c = o.charAt(i);
            switch(c) {
                case '(':    sb.append("\\("); break;
                case ')':    sb.append("\\)"); break;
```

```
            default:    sb.append(c); break;
        }
    }
    return sb.toString();
}

protected void moveTo(int x, int y) {
    curX = x;
    curY = y;
    System.out.println(x + " " + y + " " + "moveto");
}

void prologue() {
    System.out.println("%!PS-Adobe");
    System.out.println("/Courier findfont " + points + " scalefont setfont ");
}
}
```

The program could certainly be generalized more, and certain features (such as wrapping long lines) could be handled. I could also wade into the debate among PostScript experts as to how much of the formatting should be done on the main computer and how much should be done by the PostScript program interpreter running in the printer. But perhaps I won't get into that discussion. At least, not today.

See Also

As mentioned, Recipe 12.12 contains "better" recipes for printing under Java.

For most topics in this chapter, Elliotte Rusty Harold's *Java I/O* should be considered the antepenultimate documentation. The penultimate reference is the javadoc documentation, while the ultimate reference is, if you really need it, the source code for the Java API, to which I have not needed to make a single reference in writing this chapter.

## CHAPTER 11

Directory and Filesystem Operations

11.0. Introduction

This chapter is largely devoted to one class: `java.io.File`. The `File` class gives you the ability to list directories, obtain file status, rename and delete files on disk, create directories, and perform other filesystem operations. Many of these would be considered "system programming" functions on some operating systems; Java makes them all as portable as possible.

Note that many of the methods of this class attempt to modify the permanent file store, or disk filesystem, of the computer you run them on. Naturally, you might not have permission to change certain files in certain ways. This can be detected by the Java Virtual Machine's (or the browser's, in an applet) `SecurityManager`, which will throw an instance of the unchecked exception `SecurityException`. But failure can also be detected by the underlying operating system: if the security manager approves it, but the user running your program lacks permissions on the directory, for example, you will either get back an indication (such as false) or an instance of the checked exception `IOException`. This must be caught (or declared in the `throws` clause) in any code that calls any method that tries to change the filesystem.

Java 7 introduced a potential replacement for `File`, called `Path`, which we will also investigate.

11.1. Getting File Information

Problem

You need to know all you can about a given file on disk.

Solution

Use a `java.io.File` object.

Discussion

The `File` class has a number of "informational" methods. To use any of these, you must construct a `File` object containing the name of the file it is to operate upon. It should be noted up front that creating a `File` object has no effect on the permanent filesystem; it is only an object in Java's memory. You must call methods on the `File` object in order to change the filesystem; as we'll see, there are numerous "change" methods, such as one for creating a new (but empty) file, one for renaming a file, etc., as well as many informational methods. Table 11-1 lists some of the informational methods.

Table 11-1. java.io.File methods

Return type	Method name	Meaning
boolean	exists()	True if something of that name exists
String	getCanonicalPath()	Full name
String	getName()	Relative filename
String	getParent()	Parent directory
boolean	canRead()	True if file is readable
boolean	canWrite()	True if file is writable
long	lastModified()	File modification time
long	length()	File size
boolean	isFile()	True if it's a file
		True if it's a directory (note: it might be neither)

You can't change the name stored in a `File` object; you simply create a new `File` object each time you need to refer to a different file:

```java
public class FileStatus {
    public static void main(String[] argv) throws IOException {

        // Ensure that a filename (or something) was given in argv[0]
        if (argv.length == 0) {
            System.err.println("Usage: FileStatus filename");
            System.exit(1);
        }
        for (String a : argv) {
            status(a);
        }
    }

    public static void status(String fileName) throws IOException {
        System.out.println("---" + fileName + "---");
```

```
        // Construct a File object for the given file.
        File f = new File(fileName);

        // See if it actually exists
        if (!f.exists()) {
            System.out.println("file not found");
            System.out.println();      // Blank line
            return;
        }
        // Print full name
        System.out.println("Canonical name " + f.getCanonicalPath());
        // Print parent directory if possible
        String p = f.getParent();
        if (p != null) {
            System.out.println("Parent directory: " + p);
        }
        // Check if the file is readable
        if (f.canRead()) {
            System.out.println("File is readable.");
        }
        // Check if the file is writable
        if (f.canWrite()) {
            System.out.println("File is writable.");
        }
        // Report on the modification time.
        Date d = new Date(f.lastModified());
        System.out.println("Last modified " + d);

        // See if file, directory, or other. If file, print size.
        if (f.isFile()) {
            // Report on the file's size
            System.out.println("File size is " + f.length() + " bytes.");
        } else if (f.isDirectory()) {
            System.out.println("It's a directory");
        } else {
            System.out.println("I dunno! Neither a file nor a directory!");
        }

        System.out.println();      // blank line between entries
    }
}
```

When run with the three arguments shown, it produces this output:

```
C:\javasrc\dir_file>java dir_file.FileStatus    / /tmp/id /autoexec.bat
---/---
Canonical name C:\
File is readable.
File is writable.
Last modified Thu Jan 01 00:00:00 GMT 1970
It's a directory
```

```
---/tmp/id---
file not found

---/autoexec.bat---
Canonical name C:\AUTOEXEC.BAT
Parent directory: \
File is readable.
File is writable.
Last modified Fri Sep 10 15:40:32 GMT 1999
File size is 308 bytes.
```

As you can see, the so-called "canonical name" not only includes a leading directory root of C:\, but also has had the name converted to uppercase. You can tell I ran that on Windows. On Unix, it behaves differently:

```
$ java dir_file.FileStatus / /tmp/id /autoexec.bat
---/---
Canonical name /
File is readable.
Last modified October 4, 1999 6:29:14 AM PDT
It's a directory

---/tmp/id---
Canonical name /tmp/id
Parent directory: /tmp
File is readable.
File is writable.
Last modified October 8, 1999 1:01:54 PM PDT
File size is 0 bytes.

---/autoexec.bat---
file not found

$
```

A typical Unix system has no *autoexec.bat* file. And Unix filenames (like those on a Mac) can consist of upper- and lowercase characters: what you type is what you get.

11.2. Creating a File

Problem

You need to create a new file on disk, but you don't want to write into it.

Solution

Use a java.io.File object's createNewFile() method.

Discussion

You could easily create a new file by constructing a `FileOutputStream` or `FileWriter` (see Recipe 10.8). But then you'd have to remember to close it as well. Sometimes you want a file to exist, but you don't want to bother putting anything into it. This might be used, for example, as a simple form of interprogram communication: one program could test for the presence of a file and interpret that to mean that the other program has reached a certain state. Here is code that simply creates an empty file for each name you give:

```
public class Creat {
    public static void main(String[] argv) throws IOException {

        // Ensure that a filename (or something) was given in argv[0]
        if (argv.length == 0) {
            System.err.println("Usage: Creat filename");
            System.exit(1);
        }

        for (String a : argv) {
            // Constructing a File object doesn't affect the disk, but
            // the createNewFile() method does.
            new File(a).createNewFile();
        }
    }
}
```

11.3. Renaming a File

Problem

You need to change a file's name on disk.

Solution

Use a `java.io.File` object's `renameTo()` method.

Discussion

For reasons best left to the gods of Java, the `renameTo()` method requires not the name you want the file renamed to, but another `File` object referring to the new name. So to rename a file you must create two `File` objects, one for the existing name and another for the new name. Then call the `renameTo` method of the existing name's `File` object, passing in the second `File` object. This is easier to see than to explain, so here goes:

```
public class Rename {
    public static void main(String[] argv) throws IOException {
```

```
        // Construct the file object. Does NOT create a file on disk!
        File f = new File("Rename.java~"); // backup of this source file.

        // Rename the backup file to "junk.dat"
        // Renaming requires a File object for the target.
        f.renameTo(new File("junk.dat"));
    }
}
```

11.4. Deleting a File

Problem

You need to delete one or more files from the disk.

Solution

Use a `java.io.File` object's `delete()` method; it deletes files (subject to permissions)
and directories (subject to permissions and to the directory being empty).

Discussion

This is not very complicated. Simply construct a `File` object for the file you wish to
delete, and call its `delete()` method:

```
public class Delete {
    public static void main(String[] argv) throws IOException {

        // Construct a File object for the backup created by editing
        // this source file. The file probably already exists.
        // Some text editors create backups by putting ~ at end of filename.
        File bkup = new File("Delete.java~");
        // Now, delete it:
        bkup.delete();
    }
}
```

Just recall the caveat about permissions in the Introduction to this chapter: if you don't
have permission, you can get a return value of false or, possibly, a `SecurityException`.
Note also that there are some differences between platforms. Some versions of Windows
allow Java to remove a read-only file, but Unix does not allow you to remove a file unless
you have write permission on the directory it's in, nor to remove a directory that isn't
empty. Here is a version of `Delete` with error checking (and reporting of success, too):

```
public class Delete2 {

    public static void main(String[] argv) {
        for (String a : argv) {
```

```
        delete(a);
    }
}

public static void delete(String fileName) {
    try {
        // Construct a File object for the file to be deleted.
        File target = new File(fileName);

        if (!target.exists()) {
            System.err.println("File " + fileName +
                " not present to begin with!");
            return;
        }

        // Now, delete it:
        if (target.delete())
            System.err.println("** Deleted " + fileName + " **");
        else
            System.err.println("Failed to delete " + fileName);
    } catch (SecurityException e) {
        System.err.println("Unable to delete " + fileName +
            "(" + e.getMessage() + ")");
    }
}
}
```

Running it looks something like this:

```
$ ls -ld ?
-rw-r--r--  1 ian  ian    0 Oct  8 16:50 a
drwxr-xr-x  2 ian  ian  512 Oct  8 16:50 b
drwxr-xr-x  3 ian  ian  512 Oct  8 16:50 c
$ java dir_file.Delete2 ?
**Deleted** a
**Deleted** b
Failed to delete c
$ ls -l  c
total 2
drwxr-xr-x  2 ian  ian  512 Oct  8 16:50 d
$ java dir_file.Delete2 c/d c
**Deleted** c/d
**Deleted** c
$
```

Note that on Unix, shell wildcard characters like "?" are converted to a list of filenames by the shell (command interpreter) before running the program; on Windows, this expansion may be done by the Java runtime.

11.5. Creating a Transient File

Problem

You need to create a file with a unique temporary filename, or arrange for a file to be deleted when your program is finished.

Solution

Use a `java.io.File` object's `createTempFile()` or `deleteOnExit()` method.

Discussion

The `File` object has a `createTempFile()` method and a `deleteOnExit()` method. The former creates a file with a unique name (in case several users run the same program at the same time on a server) and the latter arranges for any file (no matter how it was created) to be deleted when the program exits. Here we arrange for a backup copy of a program to be deleted on exit, and we also create a temporary file and arrange for it to be removed on exit. Both files are gone after the program runs:

```java
public class TempFiles {
    public static void main(String[] argv) throws IOException {

        // 1. Make an existing file temporary

        // Construct a File object for the backup created by editing
        // this source file. The file probably already exists.
        // My editor creates backups by putting ~ at the end of the name.
        File bkup = new File("Rename.java~");
        // Arrange to have it deleted when the program ends.
        bkup.deleteOnExit();

        // 2. Create a new temporary file.

        // Make a file object for foo.tmp, in the default temp directory
        File tmp = File.createTempFile("foo", "tmp");
        // Report on the filename that it made up for us.
        System.out.println("Your temp file is " + tmp.getCanonicalPath());
        // Arrange for it to be deleted at exit.
        tmp.deleteOnExit();
        // Now do something with the temporary file, without having to
        // worry about deleting it later.
        writeDataInTemp(tmp.getCanonicalPath());
    }

    public static void writeDataInTemp(String tempnam) {
        // This version is dummy. Use your imagination.
    }
}
```

Notice that the createTempFile() method is like createNewFile() (see Recipe 11.2) in that it does create the file. Also be aware that, should the Java Virtual Machine terminate abnormally, the deletion probably does not occur. There is no way to undo the setting of deleteOnExit() short of something drastic like powering off the computer before the program exits.

And, deleteOnExit() is probably not what you want to use in a long-running application, like most server-side apps. In these situations, the server could be running for weeks, months, or even years, and in the meantime all the temp files would accumulate, and the JVM would accumulate a large list of deferred work that it needs to perform upon shutdown. You'd probably run out of disk space or server memory or some other resource. For most long-running apps of this kind, it's better to use the explicit delete() operation, or else use a scheduler service to periodically trigger removal of old temporary files.

11.6. Changing File Attributes

Problem

You want to change attributes of a file other than its name.

Solution

Use setReadOnly() or setLastModified().

Discussion

As we saw in Recipe 11.1, many methods report on a file. By contrast, only a few change the file.

setReadOnly() turns on read-only for a given file or directory. This method returns true if it succeeds, otherwise false.

setLastModified() allows you to play games with the modification time of a file. This is normally not a good game to play, but it is useful in some types of backup/restore programs. This method takes an argument that is the number of milliseconds (not seconds) since the beginning of Unix time (January 1, 1970). You can get the original value for the file by calling getLastModified() (see Recipe 11.1), or you can get the value for a given date by calling the ZonedDateTime's toInstant().getEpochSecond() method (see Recipe 6.3) and multiplying by 1,000 to convert seconds to mSec. setLastModified() returns true if it succeeded and false otherwise.

The interesting thing is that the documentation reads, in part, that "Instances of the File class are immutable," which normally means that an object's fields don't change after the object is constructed. But does calling setReadOnly() affect the return value of canRead()? Let's find out:

```java
public class ReadOnly {
    public static void main(String[] a) throws IOException {

        File f = new File("f");

        if (!f.createNewFile()) {
            System.out.println("Can't create new file.");
            return;
        }

        if (!f.canWrite()) {
            System.out.println("Can't write new file!");
            return;
        }

        if (!f.setReadOnly()) {
            System.out.println("Grrr! Can't set file read-only.");
            return;
        }

        if (f.canWrite()) {
            System.out.println("Most immutable, captain!");
            System.out.println("But it still says canWrite() after setReadOnly");
            return;
        } else {
            System.out.println("Logical, captain!");
            System.out.println(
                "canWrite() correctly returns false after setReadOnly");
        }
    }
}
```

When I run it, this program reports what I (and I hope you) would expect:

```
$ javac -d . dir_file/ReadOnly.java
$ java dir_file.ReadOnly
Logical, captain!
canWrite( ) correctly returns false after setReadOnly
$
```

So the immutability of a File object refers only to *the pathname it contains, not to its read-only-ness*. Which of course makes perfect sense because another application could change a file's readability while the File object was in use in your application; this would have the same effect as my little demonstration.

11.7. Listing a Directory

Problem

You need to list the filesystem entries named in a directory.

Solution

Use a `java.io.File` object's `list()` or `listFiles()` method.

Discussion

The `java.io.File` class contains several methods for working with directories. For example, to list the filesystem entities named in the current directory, just write:

```
String[] list = new File(".").list( )
```

To get an array of already constructed `File` objects rather than `Strings`, use:

```
File[] list = new File(".").listFiles( );
```

This can become a complete program with as little as the following:

```
public class Ls {
    public static void main(String args[]) {
        String[] dirs = new java.io.File(".").list(); // Get list of names
        Arrays.sort(dirs);         // Sort it (see <<javacook-structure-SECT-8>>)
        for (String dir : dirs) {
            System.out.println(dir);       // Print the list
        }
    }
}
```

Of course, there's lots of room for elaboration. You could print the names in multiple columns across the page. Or even down the page because you know the number of items in the list before you print. You could omit filenames with leading periods, as does the Unix *ls* program. Or print the directory names first; I once used a directory lister called *lc* that did this, and I found it quite useful. By using `listFiles()`, which constructs a new `File` object for each name, you could print the size of each, as per the DOS *dir* command or the Unix *ls -l* command (see Recipe 11.1). Or you could figure out whether each is a file, a directory, or neither. Having done that, you could pass each directory to your top-level function, and you'd have directory recursion (the Unix *find* command, or *ls -R*, or the DOS *DIR /S* command).

A more flexible way to list filesystem entries is with `list(FilenameFilter ff)`. `FilenameFilter` is a little interface with only one method: `boolean accept(File inDir, String fileName)`. Suppose you want a listing of only Java-related files (*.java*, *.class*, *.jar*, etc.). Just write the `accept()` method so that it returns true for these files and false for any others. Here is the Ls class warmed over to use a FilenameFilter instance (my OnlyJava class implements this interface) to restrict the listing:

```java
public class FNFilter {
    public static void main(String argh_my_aching_fingers[]) {

        // Generate the selective list, with a one-use File object.
        String[] dirs = new java.io.File(".").list(new OnlyJava());
        Arrays.sort(dirs);           // Sort it (Data Structuring chapter))
        for (String d : dirs) {
            System.out.println(d);     // Print the list
        }
    }

    /** This class implements the FilenameFilter interface.
     * The Accept method returns true for .java, .class and .jar files.
     */
    private static class OnlyJava implements FilenameFilter {
        public boolean accept(File dir, String s) {
            if (s.endsWith(".java") ||
                s.endsWith(".class") ||
                s.endsWith(".jar")) {

                return true;
            }
            // others: projects, ... ?
            return false;
        }
    }
}
```

The FilenameFilter need not be a separate class; case in point, the online code example FNFilter2 implements the interface directly in the main class, resulting in a slightly shorter file. An anonymous inner class could be used. The example FNFilterL shows it as a lambda expression, which is shorter still:

dir_file/FNFilterL.java

```java
        // Generate the selective list, with a Lambda Expression
        String[] dirs = new java.io.File(dirName).list(
            (dir, s) -> {
                return s.endsWith(".java") ||
                    s.endsWith(".class") ||
                    s.endsWith(".jar");
            }
        );
        Arrays.sort(dirs);           // Sort it (see Data Structuring chapter))
        for (String d : dirs) {
            System.out.println(d);     // Print the list
        }
```

In a full-scale application, the list of files returned by the `FilenameFilter` would be chosen dynamically, possibly automatically, based on what you were working on. As we'll see in Recipe 14.13, the file chooser dialogs implement a superset of this functionality, allowing the user to select interactively from one of several sets of files to be listed. This is a great convenience in finding files, just as it is here in reducing the number of files that must be examined.

11.8. Getting the Directory Roots

Problem

You want to know about the top-level directories, such as C:\ and D:\ on Windows.

Solution

Use the static method `File.listRoots()`.

Discussion

Speaking of directory listings, you surely know that all modern desktop computing systems arrange files into hierarchies of directories. But you might not know that on Unix all filenames are somehow "under" the single root directory named /, whereas on Microsoft platforms, each disk drive has a root directory named \ (A:\ for the first floppy (if you still have one!), C:\ for the first hard drive, and other letters for CD-ROM and network drives). If you need to know about all the files on all the disks, you should find out what "directory root" names exist on the particular platform. The static method `listRoots()` returns (in an array of `File` objects) the available filesystem roots for whatever platform you are running on. Here is a short program to list these, along with its output:

dir_file/ListRoots.java

```java
public class ListRoots {
    public static void main(String argh_my_aching_fingers[]) {
        File[] drives = File.listRoots(); // Get list of names
        for (File dr : drives) {
            System.out.println(dr);        // Print the list
        }
    }
}

C:> java dir_file.DirRoots
A:\
C:\
D:\
C:>
```

As you can see, the program listed my floppy drive (even though the floppy drive was not only empty, but left at home while I wrote this recipe on my notebook computer in my car in a parking lot), the hard disk drive, and the CD-ROM drive.

On Unix there is only one:

```
$ java dir_file.DirRoots
/
$
```

One thing that is "left out" of the list of roots is the so-called UNC filename. UNC filenames are used on Microsoft platforms to refer to a network-available resource that hasn't been mounted locally on a particular drive letter. For example, my server (running Unix with the Samba SMB file server software) is named darian (made from my surname and first name), and my home directory on that machine is exported or shared with the name ian, so I could refer to a directory named *book* in my home directory under the UNC name *darian\ian\book*. Such a filename would be valid in any Java filename context (assuming you're running on Windows), but you would not learn about it from the File.listRoots() method.

11.9. Creating New Directories

Problem

You need to create a directory.

Solution

Use java.io.File's mkdir() or mkdirs() method.

Discussion

Of the two methods used for creating directories, mkdir() creates just one directory, whereas mkdirs() creates any parent directories that are needed. For example, if */home/ian* exists and is a directory, the calls:

```
new File("/home/ian/bin").mkdir( );
new File("/home/ian/src").mkdir( );
```

succeed, whereas:

```
new File("/home/ian/once/twice/again").mkdir( );
```

fails, assuming that the directory *once* does not exist. If you wish to create a whole path of directories, you would tell File to make all the directories at once by using mkdirs():

```
new File("/home/ian/once/twice/again").mkdirs( );
```

Both variants of this command return `true` if they succeed and `false` if they fail. Notice that it is possible (but not likely) for `mkdirs()` to create some of the directories and then fail; in this case, the newly created directories are left in the filesystem.

Notice that the spelling `mkdir()` is all lowercase. Although this might be said to violate the normal Java naming conventions (which would suggest `mkDir()` as the name), it is the name of the underlying operating system call and command on both Unix and DOS (though DOS allows *md* as an alias on the command line).

11.10. Using Path instead of File

Problem

You need more capability than the standard `File` class. You need to move, copy, delete, and otherwise work on files with a minimum of coding.

Solution

Consider using the `Path` class, an intended replacement for `File`, and the `Files` class.

Discussion

The `Path` object performs many of the same functions as the original `File` object. For simplest cases, its usage is similar, except you get an instance from the `Paths` factory class instead of by direct instantiation:

```
Path p = Paths.getPath("/home/ian/.profile");
if (!p.exists()) {
        // some warning here
} else {
        // use p.size() etc.
}
```

One way that `Path` goes beyond the original is in the ability (by calling its `register()` method) to set up a Watcher Service (see Recipe 11.11) to get notified of changes to a filesystem entry (such as new files created in a directory).

The `Files` class contains an array of methods for dealing with file paths, including:

- Copying
- Moving

- Deleting

The `PathsFilesDemo` program shown here illustrates some of these operations:

```
Path p = Paths.get("my_junk_file");                          ❶
boolean deleted = Files.deleteIfExists(p);                   ❷
InputStream is =                                             ❸
        PathsFilesDemo.class.getResourceAsStream("/demo.txt");
long newFileSize = Files.copy(is, p);                        ❹
System.out.println(newFileSize);                             ❺
final Path realPath = p.toRealPath();                        ❻
System.out.println(realPath);
realPath.forEach(pc-> System.out.println(pc));               ❼
Files.delete(p);                                             ❽
```

❶ Create an abstract `Path`

❷ Make sure the file doesn't exist

❸ Get an `InputStream` to copy from

❹ Copy the entire file contents

❺ Verify the file size

❻ Get the full path

❼ Iterate over the path elements (directories and file)

❽ Clean up

Legacy conversion

You can get a `Path` from a legacy `File` with the `File`'s `toPath()` method. You can go in the other direction using the `Path`'s `toFile()` method.

11.11. Using the FileWatcher Service to Get Notified about File Changes

Problem

You want to be notified when some other application updates one or more of the files in which you are interested.

Solution

Use the Java 7 FileWatchService to get notified of changes to files automatically, instead of having to examine the files periodically.

Discussion

It is fairly common for a large application to want to be notified of changes to files, without having to go and look at them periodically. For example, a Java Enterprise web server wants to know when Servlets and other components get updated. Many modern operating systems have had this capability for some time, and now it is available in Java.

The basic steps to using the FileWatchService are:

1. Create a Path object representing the directory you want to watch.
2. Get a WatchService by calling, for example, FileSystems.getDefault().new-WatchService().
3. Create an array of Kind enumerations for the things you want to watch (in our example we watch for files being created or modified).
4. Register the WatchService and the Kind array onto the Path object.
5. From then on, you wait for the watcher to notify you. A typical implementation is to enter a while (true) loop calling the WatchService's take() method to get an "event," and interpret these to figure out "what just happened."

Example 11-1 is a program that does just that. In addition, it starts another thread to actually do some filesystem operations, so that you can see the Watcher Service operating.

Example 11-1. src/main/java/nio/FileWatchServiceDemo.java

```java
public class FileWatchServiceDemo {

    final static String tempDirPath = "/tmp";
    static Thread mainRunner;
    static volatile boolean done = false;

    public static void main(String[] args) throws Throwable {
        String tempDirPath = "/tmp";
        System.out.println("Starting watcher for " + tempDirPath);
        Path p = Paths.get(tempDirPath);
        WatchService watcher =
            FileSystems.getDefault().newWatchService();
        Kind<?>[] watchKinds = { ENTRY_CREATE, ENTRY_MODIFY };
        p.register(watcher, watchKinds);
        mainRunner = Thread.currentThread();
        new Thread(new DemoService()).start();
        while (!done) {
```

```
            WatchKey key = watcher.take();
            for (WatchEvent<?> e : key.pollEvents()) {
                System.out.println(
                    "Saw event " + e.kind() + " on " +
                    e.context());
                if (e.context().toString().equals("MyFileSema.for")) {
                    System.out.println("Semaphore found, shutting down watcher");
                    done = true;
                }
            }
            if (!key.reset()) {
                System.err.println("Key failed to reset!");
            }
        }
    }
}

static class DemoService implements Runnable {
    public void run() {
        try {
            Thread.sleep(1000);
            System.out.println("Creating file");
            new File(tempDirPath + "/MyFileSema.for").createNewFile();
            Thread.sleep(1000);
            System.out.println("Stopping WatcherServiceDemo");
            done = true;
            Thread.sleep(1500);
            mainRunner.interrupt();
        } catch (Exception e) {
            System.out.println("Caught UNEXPECTED " + e);
        }
    }
}
}
```

11.12. Program: Find

The program shown in Example 11-2 implements a small subset of the Windows *Find Files* dialog or the Unix *find* command. However, it has much of the structure needed to build a more complete version of either of these. It uses a custom filename filter controlled by the -n command-line option, which is parsed using my GetOpt (see Recipe 2.6). It has a hook for filtering by file size, whose implementation is left as an exercise for the reader.

Example 11-2. src/main/java/dir_file/Find.java

```
/**
 * Find - find files by name, size, or other criteria. Non-GUI version.
 */
public class Find {
    /** Main program */
    public static void main(String[] args) {
```

```
        Find finder = new Find();
        GetOpt argHandler = new GetOpt("n:s:");
        int c;
        while ((c = argHandler.getopt(args)) != GetOpt.DONE) {
            switch(c) {
            case 'n': finder.filter.setNameFilter(argHandler.optarg()); break;
            case 's': finder.filter.setSizeFilter(argHandler.optarg()); break;
            default:
                System.out.println("Got: " + c);
                usage();
            }
        }
        if (args.length == 0 || argHandler.getOptInd()-1 == args.length) {
            finder.doName(".");
        } else {
            for (int i = argHandler.getOptInd()-1; i<args.length; i++)
                finder.doName(args[i]);
        }
    }

    protected FindFilter filter = new FindFilter();

    public static void usage() {
        System.err.println(
            "Usage: Find [-n namefilter][-s sizefilter][dir...]");
        System.exit(1);
    }

    /** doName - handle one filesystem object by name */
    private void doName(String s) {
        Debug.println("flow", "doName(" + s + ")");
        File f = new File(s);
        if (!f.exists()) {
            System.out.println(s + " does not exist");
            return;
        }
        if (f.isFile())
            doFile(f);
        else if (f.isDirectory()) {
            // System.out.println("d " + f.getPath());
            String objects[] = f.list(filter);

            for (String o : objects)
                doName(s + File.separator + o);
        } else
            System.err.println("Unknown type: " + s);
    }

    /** doFile - process one regular file. */
    private static void doFile(File f) {
        System.out.println("f " + f.getPath());
```

```
        }
}
```

Example 11-3 uses a class called `FindFilter`, my implementation of `FileNameFilter`, to implement matching.

Example 11-3. src/main/java/dir_file/FindFilter.java

```java
/** Class to encapsulate the filtration for Find.
 * For now just setTTTFilter() methods. Really needs to be a real
 * data structure to allow complex things like
 *    -n "*.html" -a \( -size < 0 -o mtime < 5 \).
 */
public class FindFilter implements FilenameFilter {
    boolean sizeSet;
    int size;
    String name;
    Pattern nameRE;
    boolean debug = false;

    void setSizeFilter(String sizeFilter) {
        size = Integer.parseInt(sizeFilter);
        sizeSet = true;
    }

    /** Convert the given shell wildcard pattern into internal form (an RE) */
    void setNameFilter(String nameFilter) {
        name = nameFilter;
        StringBuilder sb = new StringBuilder('^');
        for (char c : nameFilter.toCharArray()) {
            switch(c) {
                case '.':    sb.append("\\."); break;
                case '*':    sb.append(".*"); break;
                case '?':    sb.append('.'); break;
                // Some chars are special to RE and have to be escaped
                case '[':    sb.append("\\["); break;
                case ']':    sb.append("\\]"); break;
                case '(':    sb.append("\\("); break;
                case ')':    sb.append("\\)"); break;
                default:     sb.append(c); break;
            }
        }
        sb.append('$');
        if (debug)
            System.out.println("RE=\"" + sb + "\".");
        try {
            nameRE = Pattern.compile(sb.toString());
        } catch (PatternSyntaxException ex) {
            System.err.println("Error: RE " + sb.toString() +
                " didn't compile: " + ex);
        }
    }
```

```
/** Do the filtering. For now, only filter on name */
public boolean accept(File dir, String fileName) {
    File f = new File(dir, fileName);
    if (f.isDirectory()) {
        return true;     // allow recursion
    }

    if (nameRE != null) {
        return nameRE.matcher(fileName).matches();
    }

    // TODO size handling.

    // Catchall
    return false;
}

public String getName() {
    return name;
}
}
```

Exercise for the reader: in the online source directory, you'll find a class called Find-
NumFilter, which is meant to (someday) allow relational comparison of sizes, modification times, and the like, as most find services already offer. Make this work from the
command line, and write a GUI frontend to this program.

## CHAPTER 12

Media: Graphics, Audio, Video

12.0. Introduction

The `Graphics` class and the `Component` method `paint()` have survived virtually un-changed since the early days of Java. Together they provide a basic but quite functional graphics capability. The first printing API was put forward in 1.1, and it was promptly replaced in 1.2, and again in 1.4. These printing APIs, fortunately, are based on the `Graphics` object, so drawing code did not have to change; only the details of getting the right kind of `Graphics` object changed. The 2D (two-dimensional graphics) package is also based on `Graphics`; `Graphics2D` is a subclass of `Graphics`.

To put the 2D graphics in perspective, think about the tremendous boost that the Adobe PostScript language gave to desktop publishing and printing. PostScript is both a script-ing language and a *marking engine*: it has the capability to make a terrific variety of marks on paper. Because Java is already a comprehensive programming language, the 2D API needed only to add the marking engine. This it did very well, using several ideas imported from PostScript via Adobe's participation in the early design.

Also present from the beginning was the `AudioClip` class, which represents a playable sound file. This was soon extended to support additional formats (including MIDI) and to be usable from within an application as well. Meanwhile, the Java Media Framework (extension `javax.media`) and the newer JavaFX framework provide for playing audio, video, and possibly other media with much greater control over the presentation. You'll see examples in this chapter.

But first let's look at the `Graphics` class.

12.1. Painting with a Graphics Object

Problem

You want to draw something on the screen.

Solution

Write a Component subclass; in your paint() method, use the provided Graphics object's drawing methods:

```
public class PaintDemo extends Component {

    private static final long serialVersionUID = -5595189404659801913L;
    int rectX = 20, rectY = 30;
    int rectWidth = 50, rectHeight = 50;

    /**
     * Component subclasses can override paint(), but
     * JComponent subclasses should normally use paintComponent()
     * instead, to avoid clobbering border painting and the like.
     */
    @Override
    public void paint(Graphics g) {
        g.setColor(Color.red);
        g.fillRect(rectX, rectY, rectWidth, rectHeight);
    }

    @Override
    public Dimension getPreferredSize() {
        return new Dimension(100, 100);
    }
}
```

Discussion

The Graphics class has a large set of drawing primitives. Each shape—Rect(angle), Arc, Ellipse, and Polygon—has a draw method (draws just the outline) and a fill method (fills inside the outline). You don't need both, unless you want the outline and the interior (fill) of a shape to be different colors. The method drawString() and its relatives let you print text on the screen (see Recipe 12.3). There are also drawLine()—which draws straight line segments—setColor/getColor, setFont/getFont, and many other methods. Too many to list here, in fact; see the online documentation for java.awt.Graphics.

When to draw?

In the past, a common beginner's mistake was call getGraphics() and call the Graphics object's drawing methods from within a main program or the constructor of a

---

Component subclass. Fortunately, we now have any number of books to tell us that the correct way to draw anything is with your component's paint method. Why? Because you can't draw in a window until it's actually been created and (on most window systems) mapped to the screen, which takes much more time than your main program or constructor has. The drawing code needs to wait patiently until the window system notifies the Java runtime that it's time to paint the window.

Where do you put your drawing code? This is one situation where you need to think about AWT versus Swing. AWT, the basic windowing system, uses a method called paint(). This method is still available in Swing, but due to interaction with borders and the like, it is recommended that you override paintComponent() instead. Both are called with a single argument of type Graphics. Your paintComponent() should start by calling super.paintComponent() with the same argument to ensure that components are painted in proper back-to-front order, whereas paint() should not call its parent. Some examples in this chapter use paint() and others use paintComponent(); the latter also usually extend JPanel . This allows better interaction with Swing, and also allows you to place these as the main component in a JFrame by calling setContentPane(), which eliminates an extra layer of container. (JFrame's ContentPane is discussed in Recipe 14.1.)

12.2. Showing Graphical Components Without Writing Main

Problem

You don't want to have to write a little main program with a frame each time you write a subclass of Component.

Solution

Use my CompRunner class, which has a main method that builds a frame and installs your component into it.

Discussion

CompRunner is a small main program that takes a class name from the command line, instantiates it (see Recipe 23.4), and puts it in a JFrame. It also worries a bit over making sure the window comes out the right size. Many of these issues relate to the GUI rather than graphics and are discussed in Chapter 14.

The class to be tested must be a subclass of Component, or an error message is printed. This is very convenient for running small component classes, and I show a lot of these in this chapter and the next. Using it is simplicity itself; for example, to instantiate the DrawStringDemo2 class from Recipe 12.3, you just say:

```
java gui.CompRunner graphics.DrawStringDemo2
```

The result is shown on the left side of Figure 12-1. It's interesting to try running it on some of the predefined classes. A JTree (Java's tree view widget, used in Recipe 17.8) no-argument constructor creates a JTree that comes up with a demonstration set of data, as on the right side of Figure 12-1.

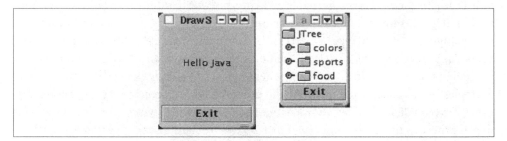

Figure 12-1. CompRunner showing DrawStringDemo2 (left) and javax.swing.JTree (right)

Because little of this relates to the material in this chapter, I don't show the source for CompRunner; however, it's included in the *gui* directory of the *javasrc* code examples for the book.

12.3. Drawing Text

Problem

You need to draw text in a component.

Solution

Simply call the drawString() method in the Graphics class:

```java
public class DrawStringDemo extends JComponent {

    private static final long serialVersionUID = -7199469682507443122L;

    int textX = 10, textY = 20;

    @Override
    public void paintComponent(Graphics g) {
        g.drawString("Hello Java", textX, textY);
    }
```

```
        public Dimension getPreferredSize() {
            return new Dimension(100, 100);
        }
    }
```

12.4. Drawing Centered Text in a Component

Problem

You want to draw text neatly centered in a component.

Solution

Measure the width and height of the string in the given font, and subtract it from the width and height of the component. Divide by two, and use this as your drawing location.

Discussion

The program `DrawStringDemo2` in Example 12-1 measures the width and height of a string (see Figure 12-2 for some attributes of the text). The program then subtracts the size of the text from the size of the component, divides this by two, and thereby centers the text in the given component.

Example 12-1. DrawStringDemo2.java

```
public class DrawStringDemo2 extends JComponent {

    private static final long serialVersionUID = -6593901790809089107L;
    //-
    String message = "Hello Java";

    /** Called by the window system to draw the text. */
    @Override
    public void paintComponent(Graphics g) {

        // Get the current Font, and ask it for its FontMetrics.
        FontMetrics fm = getFontMetrics(getFont());

        // Use the FontMetrics to get the width of the String.
        // Subtract this from width, divide by 2, that's our starting point.
        int textX = (getSize().width - fm.stringWidth(message))/2;
        if (textX<0)         // If string too long, start at 0
            textX = 0;

        // Same as above but for the height
        int textY = (getSize().height - fm.getAscent())/2 - fm.getDescent();
        if (textY < 0)
            textY = getSize().height - fm.getDescent() - 1;
```

```
        // Now draw the text at the computed spot.
        g.drawString(message, textX, textY);
    }
    //-

    public Dimension getPreferredSize() {
        return new Dimension(100, 100);
    }

    public static void main(final String[] args) {
        final JFrame jf = new JFrame();
        jf.add(new DrawStringDemo2());
        jf.setBounds(100, 100, 100, 100);
        jf.setVisible(true);
    }
}
```

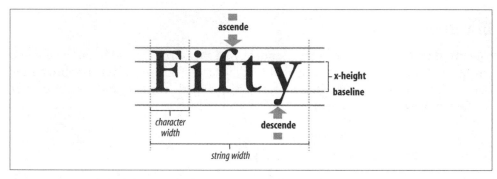

Figure 12-2. Font metrics

This is so common that you'd expect Java to have encapsulated the whole thing as a service, and in fact, Java does do this. What we have here is what most GUI component architectures call a *label*. As we'll see in Chapter 14, Java provides a `Label` component that allows for centered (or left- or right-aligned) text and supports the setting of fonts and colors. It also offers `JLabel`, which provides image icons in addition to or instead of text.

See Also

To draw formatted text—as in a word processor—requires considerably more complexity. You'll find an example in the online source under the `JabberPoint` program (see *ShowView.java*). This program also implements the Model-View-Controller pattern.

12.5. Drawing a Drop Shadow

Problem

You want to draw text or graphical objects with a "drop shadow" effect, as in Figure 12-3.

Figure 12-3. Drop shadow text

Solution

Draw the component twice, with the darker shadow behind and the "real" color, slightly offset, in front.

Discussion

Program `DropShadow` in Example 12-2 does just this. It also uses a `Font` object from `java.awt` to exercise some control over the typeface.

Example 12-2. DropShadow.java

```
public class DropShadow extends JComponent {
    /** The text to draw */
    protected String theLabel;
    /** The name of the font */
    protected String fontName;
    /** The font */
    protected Font theFont;
    /** The size of the font */
    protected int fontSize = 18;
    /** The offset for the drop shadow */
    protected int theOffset = 3;

    /**
     * Set up the GUI
     * limit ourselves to the ubiquitous IllegalArgumentException.
     */
    public DropShadow() {
        this("DropShadow");
    }

    public DropShadow(String theLabel) {
```

```
        this.theLabel = theLabel == null ? "DropShadow" : theLabel;
        // Now handle font stuff.
        fontName = "Sans";
        fontSize = 24;
        if (fontName != null || fontSize != 0) {
            theFont = new Font(fontName, Font.BOLD + Font.ITALIC, fontSize);
            System.out.println("Name " + fontName + ", font " + theFont);
        }
        setBackground(Color.green);
    }

    /** Paint method showing drop shadow effect */
    public void paint(Graphics g) {
        g.setFont(theFont);
        g.setColor(Color.black);
        g.drawString(theLabel, theOffset+30, theOffset+50);
        g.setColor(Color.white);
        g.drawString(theLabel, 30, 50);
    }
}
```

Standard AWT uses a very simple paint model for drawing. I guess that's why the method you have to write is called paint(). Let's go back to the paper age for a moment. If you paint something on a piece of paper and then paint over it with a different color, what happens? If you're old enough to remember paper, you'll know that the second color covers up the first color. Well, AWT works in pretty much the same way. No fair asking about water-based paints that run together; Java's painting is more like fast-drying oil paints. The fact that AWT retains all the bits (pixels, or picture elements) that you don't draw, plus the fact that methods like drawString() have extremely good aim, make it very easy to create a drop shadow and to combine graphics drawings in interesting ways.

Remember to draw from the back to the front, though. To see why, try interchanging the two calls to drawString() in the previous code.

A word of warning: don't mix drawing with added GUI components (see Chapter 14). For example, say you had a paint() method in an applet or other container and had add()ed a button to it. This works on some implementations of Java, but not on others: only the painting or the button appears, not both. It's not portable, so don't do it—you've been warned! Instead, you should probably use multiple components; see the JFrame's getContentPane() and getGlassPane(), discussed in Chapter 8 of *Java Swing*, for full details.

An alternative method of obtaining a drop shadow effect is covered in Recipe 12.6.

12.6. Drawing Text with 2D

Problem

You want fancier drawing abilities.

Solution

Use a `Graphics2D` object.

Discussion

The 2D graphics could be the subject of an entire book, and in fact, it is. *Java 2D Graphics* by Jonathan Knudsen (O'Reilly) covers every imaginable aspect of this comprehensive graphics package. Here I'll just show one example: drawing text with a textured background.

The `Graphics2D` class is a direct subclass of the original Java `Graphics` object. In fact, your `paint()` method is always called with an instance of `Graphics2D`. So begin your paint method by casting appropriately:

```
public void paint(Graphics g) {
    Graphics2D g2 = (Graphics2D) g;
```

You can then use any `Graphics2D` methods or any regular `Graphics` methods, getting to them with the object reference g2. One of the additional methods in `Graphics2D` is `setPaint()`, which can take the place of `setColor()` to draw with a solid color. However, it can also be called with several other types, and in this case we pass in an object called a `TexturePaint`, which refers to a pattern. Our pattern is a simple set of diagonal lines, but any pattern or even a bitmap from a file (see Recipe 12.8) can be used. Figure 12-4 shows the resulting screen (it looks even better in color); the program itself is shown in Example 12-3.

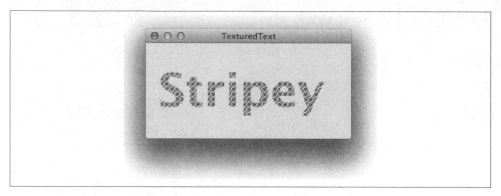

Figure 12-4. TexturedText in action

Example 12-3. TexturedText.java

```java
public class TexturedText extends JComponent {

    private static final long serialVersionUID = 8898234939386827451L;
    /** The image we draw in the texture */
    protected BufferedImage bim;
    /** The texture for painting. */
    TexturePaint tp;
    /** The string to draw. */
    String mesg = "Stripey";
    /** The font */
    Font myFont = new Font("Lucida Regular", Font.BOLD, 72);

    /** "main program" method - construct and show */
    public static void main(String[] av) {
        // create a TexturedText object, tell it to show up
        final Frame f = new Frame("TexturedText");
        TexturedText comp = new TexturedText();
        f.add(comp);
        f.addWindowListener(new WindowAdapter() {
            public void windowClosing(WindowEvent e) {
                f.setVisible(false);
                f.dispose();
                System.exit(0);
            }
        });
        f.pack();
        f.setLocation(200, 200);
        f.setVisible(true);
    }

    protected static Color[] colors = {
        Color.red, Color.blue, Color.yellow,
    };
```

```
    /** Construct the object */
    public TexturedText() {
        super();
        setBackground(Color.white);
        int width = 8, height = 8;
        bim = new BufferedImage(width, height, BufferedImage.TYPE_INT_ARGB);
        Graphics2D g2 = bim.createGraphics();
        for (int i=0; i<width; i++) {
            g2.setPaint(colors[(i/2)%colors.length]);
            g2.drawLine(0, i, i, 0);
            g2.drawLine(width-i, height, width, height-i);
        }
        Rectangle r = new Rectangle(0, 0, bim.getWidth(), bim.getHeight());
        tp = new TexturePaint(bim, r);
    }

    @Override
    public void paintComponent(Graphics g) {
        Graphics2D g2 = (Graphics2D)g;
        g2.setRenderingHint(RenderingHints.KEY_ANTIALIASING,
            RenderingHints.VALUE_ANTIALIAS_ON);
        g2.setPaint(tp);
        g2.setFont(myFont);
        g2.drawString(mesg, 20, 100);
    }

    @Override
    public Dimension getMinimumSize() {
        return new Dimension(250, 100);
    }

    @Override
    public Dimension getPreferredSize() {
        return new Dimension(320, 150);
    }
}
```

See Also

I have not discussed how to scale, rotate, or otherwise transmogrify an image using the AffineTransform class in Java 2D graphics because such topics are beyond the scope of this book. Consult the previously mentioned *Java 2D Graphics*.

12.7. Drawing Text with an Application Font

Problem

You want to provide a font with your application but do not want to require users to install it as a "system font" on all platforms.

Solution

Use `Font.createFont(…)`, which returns a scalable `Font` object, and scale it with `deriveFont(int nPoints)`.

Discussion

Java includes the static method `Font.createFont()`, which allows you to have a "private" font that can be used in your application without having it installed using the operating system's font mechanism. Users can then use your application and its custom font without having to have "root" or "administration" privileges on systems that require this in order to install fonts.

The `createFont()` method requires two arguments. The first is an `int`, which must be the public static field `Font.TRUETYPE_FONT`, and the second is an `InputStream` (see Recipe 10.17) that is open for reading the binary file. As you can infer from the requirement that the first argument be `Font.TRUETYPE_FONT`, only TrueType fonts are supported at present. The `Font` class documentation, ever the optimist, states that this field is to allow possible future addition of other font formats, though none is promised. Given the availability of free PostScript font renderers, such as the one in the X Window System XFree86, it should be possible to add PostScript font support in the future. Example 12-4 is a listing of a small standalone application that creates the window shown in Figure 12-5.

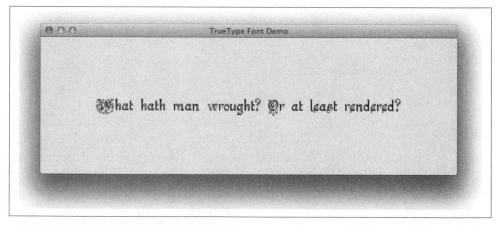

Figure 12-5. TTFontDemo in action

Example 12-4. Demo of an application font

```
public class TTFontDemo extends JLabel {

    private static final long serialVersionUID = -2774152065764538894L;
```

```
/** Construct a TTFontDemo -- Create a Font from TTF.
 */
public TTFontDemo(String fontFileName, String text)
throws IOException, FontFormatException {
    super(text, JLabel.CENTER);

    setBackground(Color.white);

    // First, see if we can load the font file.
    InputStream is = this.getClass().getResourceAsStream(fontFileName);
    if (is == null) {
        throw new IOException("Cannot open " + fontFileName);
    }

    // createFont makes a 1-point font, bit hard to read :-)
    Font ttfBase = Font.createFont(Font.TRUETYPE_FONT, is);

    // So scale it to 24 pt.
    Font ttfReal = ttfBase.deriveFont(Font.PLAIN, 24);

    setFont(ttfReal);
}

/** Simple main program for TTFontDemo */
public static void main(String[] args) throws Exception {

    String DEFAULT_MESSAGE =
        "What hath man wrought? Or at least rendered?";
    // Loaded as Resource so don't need graphics/ in front
    String DEFAULT_FONTFILE = "Kellyag_.ttf";
    String message = args.length == 1 ? args[0] : DEFAULT_MESSAGE;
    JFrame f = new JFrame("TrueType Font Demo");

    TTFontDemo ttfd = new TTFontDemo(DEFAULT_FONTFILE, message);
    f.getContentPane().add(ttfd);

    f.setBounds(100, 100, 700, 250);
    f.setVisible(true);
    f.setDefaultCloseOperation(JFrame.EXIT_ON_CLOSE);
}
}
```

This font technology has some restrictions. First, as noted in the comments, you can use this font only on a Swing JComponent, not on an AWT Component (see Chapter 14).

Also, this technique cannot easily be used in an applet due to security concerns (because it needs to create a local temporary file copy of the font). It should work in an application downloaded using Java WebStart (see Recipe 21.11).

12.8. Drawing an Image

Problem

You want to display an image, a preformatted bitmap, or raster file.

Solution

Use the `Graphics drawImage()` method in your paint routine. Image objects represent bitmaps. They are normally loaded from a file via `getImage()` but can also be synthesized using `createImage()`. You can't construct them yourself, however: the `Image` class is abstract. Once you have an image, displaying it is trivial:

```java
// File graphics/DrawImageDemo.java
public void paint(Graphics g) {
    g.drawImage(0, 0, myImage, this);
}
```

Discussion

You can get an image by using a routine named, naturally, `getImage()`. If your code is used only in an applet, you can use the `Applet` method `getImage()`, but if you want it to run in an application as well, you need to use the Toolkit version, which takes either a filename or a URL. The filename, of course, when it turns up in an applet, fails with a security exception unless the user installs a policy file. Program `GetImage` shows the code for doing this both ways:

```java
public class GetImage extends JApplet {

    private static final long serialVersionUID = 4288395022095915666L;
    private Image image;

    public void init() {
        loadImage();
    }

    public void loadImage() {

        // Portable version: getClass().getResource() works in either
        // applet or application, 1.1 or 1.3, returns URL for file name.
        URL url = getClass().getResource("Duke.gif");
        image = getToolkit().getImage(url);
        // Or just:
        // image = getToolkit().getImage(getClass().getResource("Duke.gif"));
    }

    @Override
    public void paint(Graphics g) {
        g.drawImage(image, 20, 20, this);
```

```
    }

    public static void main(String[] args) {
        JFrame f = new JFrame("GetImage");
        f.setDefaultCloseOperation(JFrame.EXIT_ON_CLOSE);
        GetImage myApplet = new GetImage();
        f.setContentPane(myApplet);
        myApplet.init();
        f.setSize(100, 100);
        f.setVisible(true);
        myApplet.start();
    }
}
```

You may sometimes want to display an image more than once in the same panel. Example 12-5 is a program that paints its background with the same image over and over. We use the image's getWidth() and getHeight() methods to find the image's size and the more regular getSize() method on the component itself. As usual, we don't hardcode the window size in the paint() method because the user has the option of resizing with the mouse.

Example 12-5. TiledImageComponent.java

```
public class TiledImageComponent extends JComponent {

    private static final long serialVersionUID = -8771306833824134974L;
    protected TextField nameTF, passTF, domainTF;
    protected Image im;
    public static final String DEFAULT_IMAGE_NAME =
        "graphics/background.gif";

    /** Set things up nicely. */
    public TiledImageComponent() {

        setLayout(new FlowLayout());
        add(new Label("Name:", Label.CENTER));
        add(nameTF=new TextField(10));

        add(new Label("Password:", Label.CENTER));
        add(passTF=new TextField(10));
        passTF.setEchoChar('*');

        add(new Label("Domain:", Label.CENTER));
        add(domainTF=new TextField(10));

        im = getToolkit().getImage(DEFAULT_IMAGE_NAME);
    }

    /** paint() - just tile the background.  */
    @Override
    public void paintComponent(Graphics g) {
        if (im == null)
```

```
            return;
        int iw = im.getWidth(this), ih=im.getHeight(this);
        if (iw < 0 || ih < 0)      // image not ready
            return;                // live to try again later.
        int w = getSize().width, h = getSize().height;

        for (int i = 0; i<=w; i+=iw) {
            for (int j = 0; j<=h; j+=ih) {
                Debug.println("draw", "drawImage(im,"+i+","+j+")");
                g.drawImage(im, i, j, this);
            }
        }
    }

    public static void main(String[] av) {
        JFrame f = new JFrame("TiledImageComponent Demo");
        f.getContentPane().add(new TiledImageComponent());
        f.setSize(200, 200);
        f.setVisible(true);
        f.setDefaultCloseOperation(JFrame.EXIT_ON_CLOSE);
    }
}
```

In the paint() method, we must check that the image is not null and has a nonnegative width and height—we are more careful than we were in the previous, somewhat cavalier, example. The image is null only if something went very wrong in the constructor, but it can have a negative size. How? In certain creation myths, time ran backward before the beginning of time; therefore, before an image is fully created, its size is backward (i.e., it has a width and height of –1). The getImage() method doesn't actually get the image, you see. It creates the Image object, true, but it doesn't necessarily load all the bits: it starts a background thread to do the reading and returns. This dates from the days when the Web was slower and took a long time to fully load an image. In particular, with some image file formats (some kinds of TIFF files, perhaps), you don't know the actual image size until you've read the entire file. Thus, when getImage() returns, the Image object is created, but its size is set to –1, –1. Because two threads are now running (see Chapter 22), two outcomes are possible. Either the image-reading thread reads enough to know the width and height before you need them, or you need them before the thread reads enough to know them. The curious-looking code in paint() is defensive about this. You should be, too.

But what if you really need the size of the image, for example to lay out a larger panel? If you read a bit of the Image documentation, you might think you can use the pre-pareImage() method to ensure that the object has been loaded. Unfortunately, this method can get you stuck in a loop if the image file is missing because prepare-Image() never returns true! If you need to be sure, you must construct a MediaTrack-er object to ensure that the image has been loaded successfully. That looks something like this:

```
/**
 * This CODE FRAGMENT shows using a MediaTracker to ensure
 * that an Image has been loaded successfully, then obtaining
 * its Width and Height. The MediaTracker can track an arbitrary
 * number of Images; the "0" is an arbitrary number used to track
 * this particular image.
 */
Image im;
int imWidth, imHeight;
public void setImage(Image i) {
    im = i;
    MediaTracker mt = new MediaTracker(this);
    // use of "this" assumes we're in a Component subclass.
    mt.addImage(im, 0);
    try {
        mt.waitForID(0);
    } catch(InterruptedException e) {
        throw new IllegalArgumentException(
            "InterruptedException while loading Image");
    }
    if (mt.isErrorID(0)) {
        throw new IllegalArgumentException(
                        "Couldn't load image");
    }
    imWidth  = im.getWidth(this);
    imHeight = im.getHeight(this);
}
```

You can ask the MediaTracker for its status at any time using the method status(int ID, boolean load), which returns an integer made by or-ing together the values shown in Table 12-1. The Boolean load flag, if true, tells the MediaTracker to start loading any images that haven't yet been started. A related method, statusAll(), returns the inclusive or of any flags applying to images that have started loading.

Table 12-1. MediaTracker status values

Flag	Meaning
ABORTED	Downloading of at least one item was aborted.
COMPLETE	Downloading of all items completed without error.
ERRORED	Something went wrong while downloading at least one item.
LOADING	Downloading is ongoing.

You can shorten the previous code by using the Swing ImageIcon class, which includes this functionality. The ImageIcon class has several constructor forms, one of which takes just a filename argument. ImageIcon uses a MediaTracker internally; you can ask for its status using the ImageIcon's getImageLoadStatus() method, which returns the same values as MediaTracker's statusAll()/statusID().

12.9. Reading and Writing Images with javax.imageio

Problem

You want to read a file, transform it, and write it back out.

Solution

Use the static ImageIO class from javax.imageio package; it provides static read() and write() methods.

Discussion

The imageio package provides java.awt.image.BufferedImage to represent an image in memory. It's a subclass of java.awt.Image, so normal graphics methods can be applied to it, starting with getGraphics(). The static ImageIO methods read() and write() can be used to load and store a BufferedImage.

The program shown here uses these methods to create the original versions of the circled 6/7/8 images that are used throughout this book to indicate the version of Java needed to run a particular code fragment, starting with a single coffee cup image created by artist *TikiGiki* and provided under the Creative Commons license from *http://OpenCli pArt.org.*

The Font method getStringBounds() is similar to the FontMetrics object used in Recipe 12.4 in that it measures the actual width of the characters being drawn. This plus a bit of simple arithmetic lets us put the large black version number (6 in this example) on top of the coffee cup, then we save the updated image to a file on disk; these are included in the book using the normal *AsciiDoc* image mechanism. Example 12-6 shows the complete code for generating the image.

Example 12-6. ReadWriteImage.java

```
int v = 6;
BufferedImage image = ImageIO.read(new File(dir + "coffeecup.png"));
Graphics2D g = image.createGraphics();
Font f = new Font("Serif", Font.BOLD, 160);
g.setFont(f);
g.setColor(Color.black);
String bigNumberLabel = Integer.toString(v);
Rectangle2D lineMetrics =
        f.getStringBounds(bigNumberLabel, g.getFontRenderContext() );
int x = (int) ((image.getWidth() - lineMetrics.getWidth() ) / 2);
x -= 10;                                      // ad-hoc fudge factor
int y = (int) ((image.getHeight() + lineMetrics.getHeight()) / 2);
g.drawString(bigNumberLabel, x, y);
ImageIO.write(image, "png", new File(String.format("%sjava%d.png",dir, v)));
```

The code needs to end with `System.exit(0);` because the graphics code starts a background thread.

See Also

The ImageIO tutorial (*http://docs.oracle.com/javase/tutorial/2d/images/index.html*) describes the ImageIO library in more detail.

12.10. Playing an Audio/Sound File

Problem

You want a quick and easy way to "make noise" or play an existing sound file.

Solution

Use the Audio API.

Discussion

This might seem out of place in the midst of all this Graphics code, but there's a pattern. We're moving from the simpler graphical forms to more dynamic multimedia. You can play audio file using an AudioClip to represent it:

```
public class AudioPlay {

    static String defSounds[] = {
        "/audio/test.wav",
        "/music/midi/Beet5th.mid",
    };

    public static void main(String[] av) {
        if (av.length == 0)
            main(defSounds);
        else for (String a : av) {
            System.out.println("Playing  " + a);
            try {
                URL snd = AudioPlay.class.getResource(a);
                if (snd == null) {
                    System.err.println("Cannot getResource "  + a);
                    continue;
                }
                AudioInputStream audioInputStream =
                    AudioSystem.getAudioInputStream(snd);
                final Clip clip = AudioSystem.getClip();
                clip.open(audioInputStream);
                clip.start();
            } catch (Exception e) {
```

```
                    System.err.println(e);
                }
            }
        }
    }
```

If you have *JavaFX* installed (see "The Evolution of Client-Side Java: Applets, Browser Wars, Swing, JavaFX" on page 843), you can also play using the JavaFX media APIs:

```
/** Simple Audio Playing with JavaFX */
public class AudioPlay {
    public static void main(String[] args) {
        String clipName = "demo.mp3";
        Media clip = new Media(clipName);
        MediaPlayer mediaPlayer = new MediaPlayer(clip);
        mediaPlayer.play();
    }
}
```

See Also

The JMFPlayer interface discussed in Recipe 12.11 plays sound files with a volume control panel.

12.11. Playing a Video File

Problem

You want to display a video file within a Java program.

Solution

Use the Java Media Framework (JMF), a standard extension, or some third-party tool like VLCJ, or use JavaFX.

Discussion

There are several media frameworks. Let's look first at the Java Media Framework (JMF).

JMF

JMF was released long ago by Sun and has not been well maintained over the years. It is an extension so it must be downloaded; there is a Maven dependency for it in the *javasrc* Maven *pom.xml* file. Example 12-7 shows code that displays a movie or other media file named on the command line. JMF is flexible; this program falls back to playing an audio file, supplying a volume control, if the media object that you name contains a sound clip instead of a movie. Figure 12-6 shows `JMFPlayer` displaying a sound file and a movie.

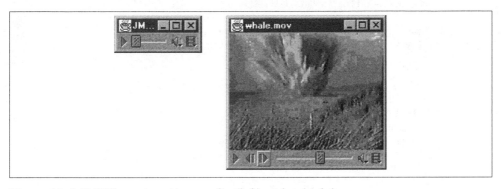

Figure 12-6. JMFPlayer in action: audio (left), video (right)

Example 12-7. JMFPlayer.java

```java
public class JMFPlayer extends JPanel implements ControllerListener {

    /** The player object */
    Player thePlayer = null;
    /** The parent Frame we are in. */
    JFrame parentFrame = null;
    /** Our contentpane */
    Container cp;
    /** The visual component (if any) */
    Component visualComponent = null;
    /** The default control component (if any) */
    Component controlComponent = null;
    /** The name of this instance's media file. */
    String mediaName;
    /** The URL representing this media file. */
    URL theURL;

    /** Construct the player object and the GUI. */
    public JMFPlayer(JFrame pf, String media) {
        parentFrame = pf;
        mediaName = media;
        // cp = getContentPane();
        cp = this;
        cp.setLayout(new BorderLayout());
        try {
            theURL = new URL(getClass().getResource("."), mediaName);
            thePlayer = Manager.createPlayer(theURL);
            thePlayer.addControllerListener(this);
        } catch (MalformedURLException e) {
            System.err.println("JMF URL creation error: " + e);
        } catch (Exception e) {
```

```java
            System.err.println("JMF Player creation error: " + e);
            return;
        }
        System.out.println("theURL = " + theURL);

        // Start the player: this will notify our ControllerListener.
        thePlayer.start();          // start playing
    }

    /** Called to stop the audio, as from a Stop button or menuitem */
    public void stop() {
        if (thePlayer == null)
            return;
        thePlayer.stop();           // stop playing!
        thePlayer.deallocate();     // free system resources
    }

    /** Called when we are really finished (as from an Exit button). */
    public void destroy() {
        if (thePlayer == null)
            return;
        thePlayer.close();
    }

    /** Called by JMF when the Player has something to tell us about. */
    public synchronized void controllerUpdate(ControllerEvent event) {
        // System.out.println("controllerUpdate(" + event + ")");
        if (event instanceof RealizeCompleteEvent) {
            if ((visualComponent = thePlayer.getVisualComponent()) != null)
                    cp.add(BorderLayout.CENTER, visualComponent);
            if ((controlComponent =
                thePlayer.getControlPanelComponent()) != null)
                    cp.add(BorderLayout.SOUTH, controlComponent);
            // resize the main window
            if (parentFrame != null) {
                parentFrame.pack();
                parentFrame.setTitle(mediaName);
            }
        }
    }

    public static void main(String[] argv) {
        JFrame f = new JFrame("JMF Player Demo");
        Container frameCP = f.getContentPane();
        final String musicURL = argv.length == 0 ?
                "file:/home/ian/Music/Classical/Rachmaninoff Prelude C_ min.mp3" :
                argv[0];
        JMFPlayer p = new JMFPlayer(f, musicURL);
        frameCP.add(BorderLayout.CENTER, p);
        f.setSize(200, 200);
        f.setDefaultCloseOperation(JFrame.EXIT_ON_CLOSE);
        f.setVisible(true);
```

```
        }
}
```

The optional Java Media Framework includes much more functionality than this example shows. However, the ability to display a QuickTime or MPEG movie with only a few lines of code is one of JMF's most endearing young charms. We load the media file from a URL and create a `Player` object to manage it. If it makes sense for the given player to have a controller, it will have one, and we add it to the bottom of the screen. Controllers may include volume controls, forward/backward buttons, position sliders, etc. However, we don't have to care: we get a component that contains all the appropriate controls for the kind of media clip for which we've created the player. If the given player represents a medium with a visual component (like a movie or a bitmap image), we add this to the center of the screen.

Of course, there is much more to the JMF API than this. You can, for example, coordinate playing of audio and video with each other or with other events.

VLCJ

A commonly used third-party solution uses the open source *VLC Media Player* program (*http://www.videolan.org*), connecting it to a Java `Canvas` to display video. Of course, in addition to downloading *vlcj*, you must download and install VLC itself. That is outside the scope of this book, and is quite platform-dependent.

This project depends on JNA, an unsupported *com.sun* package. You use this to tell VLCJ where VLC is installed; this is one of the first statements in the `MyVideoCanvas` constructor in Example 12-8. Next, you must create an `EmbeddedMediaPlayerComponent`, call its `getMediaPlayer()` method, and tell the resulting player object to `prepareMedia()`, `parseMedia()`, and `play()`. These steps are shown in the context of a full example in Example 12-8. The URL is supplied on the command line, and can be a local file, a remote streaming video, or anything else that the underlying VLC player can handle.

Example 12-8. VlcjVideo.java

```java
public class VlcjVideo extends JFrame {

    private static final long serialVersionUID = 1L;

    public static void main(String[] args) {
        new VlcjVideo(args[0]);
    }

    public VlcjVideo(String url) {
        setTitle("VLCJ Video");
        setDefaultCloseOperation(EXIT_ON_CLOSE);
        setSize(800, 600);
        JPanel player = new MyVideoPanel();
```

```
        add(player, BorderLayout.CENTER);
        pack();
        setVisible(true);
        ((MyVideoPanel)player).play(url);
    }

    class MyVideoPanel extends JPanel {
        private static final long serialVersionUID = 1L;
        private File vlcWhere = new File("/usr/local/lib");
        private EmbeddedMediaPlayer player;

        public MyVideoPanel() {
            NativeLibrary.addSearchPath("libvlc", vlcWhere.getAbsolutePath());
            EmbeddedMediaPlayerComponent videoCanvas =
                new EmbeddedMediaPlayerComponent();
            setLayout(new BorderLayout());
            add(videoCanvas, BorderLayout.CENTER);
            player = videoCanvas.getMediaPlayer();
        }

        public void play(String media) {
            player.prepareMedia(media);
            player.parseMedia();
            player.play();
        }
    }
}
```

JavaFX

JavaFX is integrated with most Java 7 JDKs and hopefully all Java 8 ones, or you can download it separately from Oracle. The code in Example 12-9 shows a simple JavaFX media player. We construct a Media clip with a test video (*http://www.mediacollege.com/ adobe/flash/video/tutorial/example-flv.html*) from *MediaCollege.com*, create a player, and call play(); we also have to set up the view window.

Example 12-9. JfxVideo.java

```
public class JfxVideo extends Application {

    public static void main(String[] args) {
        launch(args);
    }

    @Override
    public void start(Stage primaryStage) throws Exception {
        primaryStage.setTitle("JavaFX Video");
        final List<String> args = getParameters().getRaw();

        String url = args.size() > 0 ?
            args.get(args.size() - 1) :
                "http://www.mediacollege.com/" +
```

```
            "video-gallery/testclips/20051210-w50s.flv";
        Media media = new Media(url);

        MediaPlayer player = new MediaPlayer(media);
        player.play();

        MediaView view = new MediaView(player);
        Group root = new Group();
        root.getChildren().add(view);
        Scene scene = SceneBuilder.create().
                width(360).height(288).
                root(root).
                fill(Color.WHITE).
                build();
        primaryStage.setScene(scene);
        primaryStage.show();
    }
}
```

12.12. Printing in Java

Problem

You need to generate hardcopy or a print-formatted output stream.

Solution

Use the `javax.print` printing service.

Discussion

The Java Printing Service API allows you to communicate with operating system–defined print services. The basic steps are:

1. Obtain a `DocFlavor` for the kind of data you want to print.
2. Create an `AttributeSet` and fill in attributes such as paper size.
3. Look up a `PrintService` that can handle the job implied by the two objects just defined.
4. Create a `PrintJob` from the `PrintService`.
5. Call the `PrintJob`'s `print()` method.

The data you send will be paginated by the printer service, so it can be any input stream that would normally be acceptable for printing. In this case, I just send a small text file, and confirm that it shows up in my print queue and prints successfully.

The source code is shown in Example 12-10.

Example 12-10. PrintServiceDemo.java

```java
/**
 * Show the latest incarnation of printing, PrintService, from a GUI;
 * the GUI consists only of a "Print" button, and the filename is hardcoded,
 * but it's meant to be a minimal demo...
 */
public class PrintServiceDemo extends JFrame {

    private static final long serialVersionUID = 923572304627926023L;

    private static final String INPUT_FILE_NAME = "/demo.txt";

    /** main program: instantiate and show.
     * @throws IOException */
    public static void main(String[] av) throws Exception {
        SwingUtilities.invokeLater(new Runnable() {
            public void run() {
                try {
                    new PrintServiceDemo("Print Demo").setVisible(true);
                } catch (Exception e) {
                    e.printStackTrace();
                }
            }
        });
    }

    /** Constructor for GUI display with pushbutton to print */
    PrintServiceDemo(String title) {
        super(title);
        System.out.println("PrintServiceDemo.PrintServiceDemo()");
        setDefaultCloseOperation(EXIT_ON_CLOSE);
        setLayout(new FlowLayout());
        JButton b;
        add(b = new JButton("Print"));
        b.addActionListener(new ActionListener() {
            public void actionPerformed(ActionEvent e) {
                System.out.println(
                    "PrintServiceDemo.PrintServiceDemo...actionPerformed()");
                try {
                    print(INPUT_FILE_NAME);
                } catch (Exception e1) {
                    JOptionPane.showMessageDialog(
                        PrintServiceDemo.this, "Error: " + e1, "Error",
                        JOptionPane.ERROR_MESSAGE);
                    e1.printStackTrace();
                }
            }
        });
        pack();
        UtilGUI.center(this);
    }
```

```
/** Print a file by name
 * @throws IOException
 * @throws PrintException
 */
public void print(String fileName) throws IOException, PrintException {
    System.out.println("PrintServiceDemo.print(): Printing " + fileName);
    DocFlavor flavor = DocFlavor.INPUT_STREAM.TEXT_PLAIN_UTF_8;
    PrintRequestAttributeSet aset = new HashPrintRequestAttributeSet();
    //aset.add(MediaSize.NA.LETTER);
    aset.add(MediaSizeName.NA_LETTER);
    //aset.add(new JobName(INPUT_FILE_NAME, null));
    PrintService[] pservices =
        PrintServiceLookup.lookupPrintServices(flavor, aset);
    int i;
    switch(pservices.length) {
    case 0:
        System.err.println(0);
        JOptionPane.showMessageDialog(PrintServiceDemo.this,
            "Error: No PrintService Found", "Error",
            JOptionPane.ERROR_MESSAGE);
        return;
    case 1:
        i = 0;      // Only one printer, use it.
        break;
    default:
        i = JOptionPane.showOptionDialog(this,
            "Pick a printer", "Choice",
            JOptionPane.OK_OPTION, JOptionPane.QUESTION_MESSAGE,
            null, pservices, pservices[0]);
        break;
    }
    DocPrintJob pj = pservices[i].createPrintJob();
    InputStream is = getClass().getResourceAsStream(INPUT_FILE_NAME);
    if (is == null) {
        throw new NullPointerException("Input Stream is null: file not found?");
    }
    Doc doc = new SimpleDoc(is, flavor, null);

    pj.print(doc, aset);
    }
}
```

The command-line print queue verification, using `lpstat -t`:

```
MacKenzie$ lpstat -t
scheduler is running
system default destination: HP_Deskjet_F4200_series
device for HP_Deskjet_F4200_series: usb://HP/Deskjet%20F4200%20series
HP_Deskjet_F4200_series accepting requests since Wed Jan  1 15:04:16 2014
printer HP_Deskjet_F4200_series ...  enabled since Wed Jan  1 15:04:16 2014
HP_Deskjet_F4200_series-28 ian
```

```
1024    Wed Jan  1 15:03:22 2014
MacKenzie$
```

It is by no means required that the application be GUI-based (Swing or AWT). Example 12-11 shows a console-mode app that converts plain text to PostScript, without any GUI interaction.

Example 12-11. PrintPostScript, a command-line printing application

```java
/** Demonstrate finding a PrintService and printing to it */
public class PrintPostScript {

    private static final String INPUT_FILE_NAME = "/demo.txt";

    public static void main(String[] args) throws IOException, PrintException {
        new PrintPostScript().print();
    }

    public void print() throws IOException, PrintException {

        DocFlavor inputFlavor = DocFlavor.INPUT_STREAM.TEXT_PLAIN_UTF_8;

        // Lookup a print factory to convert from desired input to output.
        StreamPrintServiceFactory[] psfactories =
            StreamPrintServiceFactory.lookupStreamPrintServiceFactories(
                inputFlavor, DocFlavor.BYTE_ARRAY.POSTSCRIPT.getMimeType());
        if (psfactories.length == 0) {
            System.err.println("Ack! No StreamPrintFactory found for this job!");
        }
        StreamPrintService printService =
            psfactories[0].getPrintService(new FileOutputStream("demo.ps"));
        PrintRequestAttributeSet attrs = new HashPrintRequestAttributeSet();
        attrs.add(OrientationRequested.LANDSCAPE);
        attrs.add(MediaSizeName.NA_LETTER);
        attrs.add(new Copies(1));
        attrs.add(new JobName(INPUT_FILE_NAME, null));

        InputStream is = getClass().getResourceAsStream(INPUT_FILE_NAME);
        if (is == null) {
            throw new NullPointerException(
                "Input Stream is null: file not found?");
        }
        Doc doc = new SimpleDoc(is, inputFlavor, null);

        DocPrintJob printJob = printService.createPrintJob();
        printJob.print(doc, attrs);
    }
}
```

See Also

The Printing API has other useful methods described in the documentation, which you can also find at Oracle's website (*http://bit.ly/1gTPrEz*).

12.13. Program: PlotterAWT

In Recipe 8.12, we discussed a series of `Plotter` classes. The `PlotterAWT` class shown in Example 12-12 extends that recipe to provide a "plot preview" service: before being plotted on a (probably slow) plotter, the plot is displayed in an AWT window using the `Graphics` drawing primitives.

Example 12-12. PlotterAWT.java

```java
public class PlotterAWT extends Plotter {

    private JFrame f;
    private PCanvas p;
    private Graphics g;
    private Font font;
    private FontMetrics fontMetrics;

    PlotterAWT() {
        f = new JFrame("Plotter");
        Container cp = f.getContentPane();
        p = new PCanvas(MAXX, MAXY);
        cp.add(p, BorderLayout.CENTER);
        f.pack();
        f.setVisible(true);
        f.setDefaultCloseOperation(JFrame.EXIT_ON_CLOSE);
        g = p.getOsGraphics();
    }

    public void drawBox(int w, int h) {
        g.drawRect(curx, cury, w, h);
        p.repaint();
    }

    public void rmoveTo(int incrx, int incry){
        moveTo(curx += incrx, cury += incry);
    }

    public void moveTo(int absx, int absy){
        if (!penIsUp)
            g.drawLine(curx, cury, absx, absy);
        curx = absx;
        cury = absy;
    }

    public void setdir(float deg){}
    void penUp(){ penIsUp = true; }
```

```java
void penDown(){ penIsUp = false; }
void penColor(int c){
    switch(c) {
    case 0: g.setColor(Color.white); break;
    case 1: g.setColor(Color.black); break;
    case 2: g.setColor(Color.red); break;
    case 3: g.setColor(Color.green); break;
    case 4: g.setColor(Color.blue); break;
    default: g.setColor(new Color(c)); break;
    }
}
void setFont(String fName, int fSize) {
    font = new Font(fName, Font.BOLD, fSize);
    fontMetrics = p.getFontMetrics(font);
}
void drawString(String s) {
    g.drawString(s, curx, cury);
    curx += fontMetrics.stringWidth(s);
}

/** A Member Class that contains an off-screen Image that is
 * drawn into; this component's paint() copies from there to
 * the screen. This avoids having to keep a list of all the
 * things that have been drawn.
 */
class PCanvas extends Canvas {
    private static final long serialVersionUID = 6827371843858633606L;
    Image offScreenImage;
    int width;
    int height;
    Graphics pg;

    PCanvas(int w, int h) {
        width = w;
        height = h;
        setBackground(Color.white);
        setForeground(Color.red);
    }

    public Graphics getOsGraphics() {
        return pg;
    }

    /** This is called by AWT after the native window peer is created,
     * and before paint() is called for the first time, so
     * is a good time to create images and the like.
     */
    public void addNotify() {
        super.addNotify();
        offScreenImage = createImage(width, height);
        // assert (offScreenImage != null);
        pg = offScreenImage.getGraphics();
```

```
        }

        public void paint(Graphics pg) {
            pg.drawImage(offScreenImage, 0, 0, null);
        }
        public Dimension getPreferredSize() {
            return new Dimension(width, height);
        }
    }
}
```

12.14. Program: Grapher

Grapher is a simple program that reads a table of numbers and graphs them. The input format is two or more lines that each contain an X and a Y value. The output is an onscreen display that can also be printed. Figure 12-7 shows the results of running it with the following simple data; the first column is the X coordinate and the second is the Y coordinate of each point. The program scales the data to fit the window:

```
1.5  5
1.7  6
1.8  8
2.2  7
```

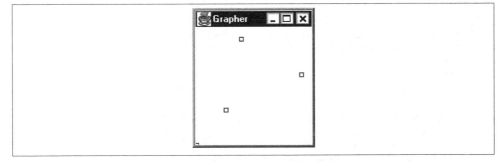

Figure 12-7. Grapher in action

Example 12-13 shows the code.

Example 12-13. Grapher.java

```
public class Grapher extends JPanel {

    private static final long serialVersionUID = -1813143391310613248L;

    /** Multiplier for range to allow room for a border */
    public final static double BORDERFACTOR = 1.1f;

    /** The list of Point points. */
```

```
    protected List<Point2D> data;

    /** The minimum and maximum X values */
    protected double minx = Integer.MAX_VALUE, maxx = Integer.MIN_VALUE;
    /** The minimum and maximum Y values */
    protected double miny = Integer.MAX_VALUE, maxy = Integer.MIN_VALUE;
    /** The range of X and Y values */
    protected double xrange, yrange;

    public Grapher() {
        data = new ArrayList<Point2D>();
        figure();
    }

    /** Set the list data from a list of Strings, where the
     * x coordinate is incremented automatically, and the y coordinate
     * is made from the String in the list.
     */
    public void setListDataFromYStrings(List<String> newData) {
        data.clear();
        for (int i=0; i < newData.size(); i++) {
            Point2D p = new Point2D.Double();
            p.setLocation(i, java.lang.Double.parseDouble(newData.get(i)));
            data.add(p);
        }
        figure();
    }

    /** Set the list from an existing List, as from GraphReader.read() */
    public void setListData(List<Point2D> newData) {
        data = newData;
        figure();
    }

    /** Compute new data when list changes */
    private void figure() {
        // find min & max
        for (int i=0 ; i < data.size(); i++) {
            Point2D d = (Point2D)data.get(i);
            if (d.getX() < minx) minx = d.getX();
            if (d.getX() > maxx) maxx = d.getX();
            if (d.getY() < miny) miny = d.getY();
            if (d.getY() > maxy) maxy = d.getY();
        }

        // Compute ranges
        xrange = (maxx - minx) * BORDERFACTOR;
        yrange = (maxy - miny) * BORDERFACTOR;
        Debug.println("range", "minx,x,r = " + minx +' '+ maxx +' '+ xrange);
        Debug.println("range", "miny,y,r = " + miny +' '+ maxy +' '+ yrange);
    }
```

```
/** Called when the window needs painting.
 * Computes X and Y range, scales.
 */
@Override
public void paintComponent(Graphics g) {
    super.paintComponent(g);
    Dimension s = getSize();
    if (data.size() < 2) {
        g.drawString("Insufficient data: " + data.size(), 10, 40);
        return;
    }

    // Compute scale factors
    double xfact =  s.width  / xrange;
    double yfact =  s.height / yrange;

    // Scale and plot the data
    for (int i=0 ; i < data.size(); i++) {
        Point2D d = (Point2D)data.get(i);
        double x = (d.getX() - minx) * xfact;
        double y = (d.getY() - miny) * yfact;
        Debug.println("point", "AT " + i + " " + d + "; " +
            "x = " + x + "; y = " + y);
        // Draw a 5-pixel rectangle centered, so -2 both x and y.
        // AWT numbers Y from 0 down, so invert:
        g.drawRect(((int)x)-2, s.height-2-(int)y, 5, 5);
    }
}


@Override
public Dimension getPreferredSize() {
    return new Dimension(150, 150);
}

public static void main(String[] args) throws IOException {
    final JFrame f = new JFrame("Grapher");
    f.setDefaultCloseOperation(JFrame.EXIT_ON_CLOSE);
    Grapher grapher = new Grapher();
    f.setContentPane(grapher);
    f.setLocation(100, 100);
    f.pack();
    List<Point2D> data = null;
    if (args.length == 0)
        data = GraphReader.read("Grapher.txt");
    else {
        String fileName = args[0];
        if ("-".equals(fileName)) {
            data = GraphReader.read(new InputStreamReader(System.in),
                "System.in");
        } else {
            data = GraphReader.read(fileName);
        }
```

```
        }
        grapher.setListData(data);
        f.setVisible(true);
    }
}
```

Most of the complexity of Grapher lies in determining the range and scaling. You could obviously extend this to draw fancier drawings such as bar charts and the like. If pie charts interest you, see ChartBean in the online source.

## CHAPTER 13

Network Clients

13.0. Introduction

Java can be used to write many types of networked programs. In traditional socket-based code, the programmer is responsible for structuring the interaction between the client and server; the TCP "socket" code simply ensures that whatever data you send gets to the other end. In higher-level types, such as RMI, CORBA, and EJB, the software takes over increasing degrees of control. Sockets are often used for connecting to "legacy" servers; if you were writing a new application from scratch, you'd be better off using a higher-level service.

It may be helpful to compare sockets with the telephone system. Telephones were originally used for analog voice traffic, which is pretty unstructured. Then it began to be used for some "layered" applications; the first widely popular one was facsimile transmission, or fax. Where would fax be without the widespread availability of voice telephony? The second wildly popular layered application historically was dial-up TCP/IP. This coexisted with the Web to become popular as a mass-market service. Where would dial-up IP be without widely deployed voice lines? And where would the Internet be without dial-up IP?

Sockets are layered like that too. The Web, RMI, JDBC, CORBA, and EJB are all layered on top of sockets. HTTP is now the most common protocol, and should generally be used for new applications when all you want is to get data from point b to point a.

Ever since the alpha release of Java (originally as a sideline to the HotJava browser) in May 1995, Java has been popular as a programming language for building network applications. It's easy to see why, particularly if you've ever built a networked application in C. First, C programmers have to worry about the platform they are on. Unix uses synchronous sockets, which work rather like normal disk files vis-a-vis reading and writing, whereas Microsoft OSes use asynchronous sockets, which use callbacks to notify when a read or write has completed. Java glosses over this distinction. Further, the amount of code needed to set up a socket in C is intimidating. Just for fun, Example 13-1 shows the "typical" C code for setting up a client socket. And remember, this is only the Unix part. And only the part that makes and closes the connection. To be portable to Windows, it would need some additional conditional code (using C's #ifdef mechanism). And C's #include mechanism requires that exactly the right files be included, and some files have to be listed in particular orders (Java's import mechanism is much more flexible).

Example 13-1. C client setup—src/main/java/network/Connect.c

```
#include <sys/types.h>
#include <sys/socket.h>
#include <netinet/in.h>
#include <netdb.h>
#include <stdio.h>
#include <string.h>
#include <fcntl.h>

int
main(int argc, char *argv[])
{
    char* server_name = "localhost";
    struct hostent *host_info;
    int sock;
    struct sockaddr_in server;

    /* Look up the remote host's IP address */
    host_info = gethostbyname(server_name);
    if (host_info == NULL) {
        fprintf(stderr, "%s: unknown host: %s\n", argv[0], server_name);
        exit(1);
    }

    /* Create the socket */
    if ((sock = socket(AF_INET, SOCK_STREAM, 0)) < 0) {
        perror("creating client socket");
        exit(2);
    }

    /* Set up the server's socket address */
    server.sin_family = AF_INET;
    memcpy((char *)&server.sin_addr, host_info->h_addr,
                    host_info->h_length);
    server.sin_port = htons(80);

    /* Connect to the server */
    if (connect(sock,(struct sockaddr *)&server,sizeof server) < 0) {
        perror("connecting to server");
        exit(4);
    }
```

```
/* Finally, we can read and write on the socket. */
/* ... */

(void) close(sock);
}
```

In the first recipe, we'll see how to do the connect in essentially one line of Java (plus a bit of error handling). We'll then cover error handling and transferring data over a socket. Next, we'll take a quick look at a `datagram` or UDP client that implements most of the TFTP (trivial file transfer protocol) that has been used for two decades to boot diskless workstations. We'll end with a program that connects interactively to a text-based server such as Telnet or email.

A common theme through most of these client examples is to use existing servers so that we don't have to generate both the client and the server at the same time. With one exception, all of these are services that exist on any standard Unix platform. If you can't find a Unix server near you to try them on, let me suggest that you take an old PC, maybe one that's underpowered for running the latest Microsoft software, and put up a free, open source Unix system on it. My personal favorite is OpenBSD, and the market's overall favorite is Linux. Both are readily available on CD-ROM or can be installed for free over the Internet, and offer all the standard services used in the client examples, including the time servers and TFTP. Both have free Java implementations available.

I also provide basic coverage of "web services" clients. The term "web services" has come to mean "program-to-program communication using HTTP." The two general categories are SOAP-based and REST-based. REST services are very simple—you send an HTTP request and get back a response in plain text, or JSON (Chapter 19) or XML (Chapter 20). SOAP requires a detailed XML specification for all aspects of the interaction, and requires that the entire interaction itself take place in fairly verbose XML. It does offer some services that REST does not, but these are rather advanced topics that we won't get into. There is more information on the client-side connections in *Java Network Programming* (O'Reilly). I don't cover the server-side APIs for building web services—JAX-RS and JAX-WS—because these are covered in several O'Reilly books (*http://bit.ly/orm-java*).

13.1. Contacting a Server

Problem

You need to contact a server using TCP/IP.

Solution

Just create a `java.net.Socket`, passing the hostname and port number into the constructor.

Discussion

There isn't much to this in Java. When creating a socket, you pass in the hostname and the port number. The `java.net.Socket` constructor does the `gethostbyname()` and the `socket()` system call, sets up the server's `sockaddr_in` structure, and executes the `connect()` call. All you have to do is catch the errors, which are subclassed from the familiar `IOException`. Example 13-2 sets up a Java network client, but doesn't actually do any I/O yet. It uses try-with-resources (see "Try With Resources" on page 840) to ensure that the socket is closed automatically when we are done with it.

Example 13-2. network/ConnectSimple.java (simple client connection)

```java
import java.net.Socket;

/* Client with NO error handling */
public class ConnectSimple {

    public static void main(String[] argv) throws Exception {

        try (Socket sock = new Socket("localhost", 8080)) {

            /* If we get here, we can read and write on the socket "sock" */
            System.out.println(" *** Connected OK ***");

            /* Do some I/O here... */

        }
    }
}
```

This version does no real error reporting, but a version called *ConnectFriendly* does; we'll see this version in Recipe 13.3.

See Also

Java supports other ways of using network applications. You can also open a URL and read from it (see Recipe 13.9). You can write code so that it will run from a URL, when opened in a web browser, or from an application.

13.2. Finding and Reporting Network Addresses

Problem

You want to look up a host's address name or number or get the address at the other end of a network connection.

Solution

Get an InetAddress object.

Discussion

The InetAddress object represents the Internet address of a given computer or host. It has no public constructors; you obtain an InetAddress by calling the static getBy-Name() method, passing in either a hostname like *www.darwinsys.com* or a network address as a string, like 1.23.45.67. All the "lookup" methods in this class can throw the checked UnknownHostException (a subclass of java.io.IOException), which must be caught or declared on the calling method's header. None of these methods actually contact the remote host, so they do not throw the other exceptions related to network connections.

The method getHostAddress() gives you the numeric IP address (as a string) corresponding to the InetAddress. The inverse is getHostName(), which reports the name of the InetAddress. This can be used to print the address of a host given its name, or vice versa:

```java
public class InetAddrDemo {
    public static void main(String[] args) throws IOException {
        String hostName = "www.darwinsys.com";
        String ipNumber = "8.8.8.8"; // currently a well-known Google DNS server

        // Show getting the InetAddress (looking up a host) by host name
        System.out.println(hostName + "'s address is " +
            InetAddress.getByName(hostName).getHostAddress());

        // Look up a host by address
        System.out.println(ipNumber + "'s name is " +
            InetAddress.getByName(ipNumber).getHostName());

        // Look up my localhost addresss
        final InetAddress localHost = InetAddress.getLocalHost();
        System.out.println("My localhost address is " + localHost);

        // Show getting the InetAddress from an open Socket
        String someServerName = "www.google.com";
        // assuming there's a web server on the named server:
        Socket theSocket = new Socket(someServerName, 80);
        InetAddress remote = theSocket.getInetAddress();
        System.out.printf("The InetAddress for %s is %s%n",
            someServerName, remote);
    }
}
```

You can also get an InetAddress from a Socket by calling its getInetAddress() method. You can construct a Socket using an InetAddress instead of a hostname string. So, to connect to port number myPortNumber on the same host as an existing socket, you'd use:

```
InetAddress remote = theSocket.getInetAddress( );
Socket anotherSocket = new Socket(remote, myPortNumber);
```

Finally, to look up all the addresses associated with a host—a server may be on more than one network—use the static method getAllByName(host), which returns an array of InetAddress objects, one for each IP address associated with the given name.

A static method getLocalHost() returns an InetAddress equivalent to "localhost" or 127.0.0.1. This can be used to connect to a server program running on the same machine as the client.

If you are using IPv6, you can use Inet6Address instead.

See Also

See NetworkInterface in Recipe 16.11, which lets you find out more about the networking of the machine you are running on.

There is not yet a way to look up services—i.e., to find out that the HTTP service is on port 80. Full implementations of TCP/IP have always included an additional set of resolvers; in C, the call getservbyname("http", "tcp"); would look up the given service[1] and return a servent (service entry) structure whose s_port member would contain the value 80. The numbers of established services do not change, but when services are new or installed in nonroutine ways, it is convenient to be able to change the service number for all programs on a machine or network (regardless of programming language) just by changing the services definitions. Java should provide this capability in a future release.

13.3. Handling Network Errors

Problem

You want more detailed reporting than just IOException if something goes wrong.

Solution

Catch a greater variety of exception classes. SocketException has several subclasses; the most notable are ConnectException and NoRouteToHostException. The names are

---

1. The location where it is looked up varies. It might be in a file named /etc/services on Unix; in the services file in a subdirectory of \windows or \winnt in Windows; in a centralized registry such as Sun's Network Information Services (NIS, formerly YP); or in some other platform- or network-dependent location.

---

self-explanatory: the first means that the connection was refused by the machine at the other end (the server machine), and the second completely explains the failure. Example 13-3 is an excerpt from the Connect program, enhanced to handle these conditions.

Example 13-3. ConnectFriendly.java

```java
public class ConnectFriendly {
    public static void main(String[] argv) {
        String server_name = argv.length == 1 ? argv[0] : "localhost";
        int tcp_port = 80;
        try (Socket sock = new Socket(server_name, tcp_port)) {

            /* If we get here, we can read and write on the socket. */
            System.out.println(" *** Connected to " + server_name  + " ***");

            /* Do some I/O here... */

        } catch (UnknownHostException e) {
            System.err.println(server_name + " Unknown host");
            return;
        } catch (NoRouteToHostException e) {
            System.err.println(server_name + " Unreachable" );
            return;
        } catch (ConnectException e) {
            System.err.println(server_name + " connect refused");
            return;
        } catch (java.io.IOException e) {
            System.err.println(server_name + ' ' + e.getMessage());
            return;
        }
    }
}
```

13.4. Reading and Writing Textual Data

Problem

Having connected, you wish to transfer textual data.

Solution

Construct a BufferedReader or PrintWriter from the socket's getInputStream() or getOutputStream().

Discussion

The Socket class has methods that allow you to get an InputStream or OutputStream to read from or write to the socket. It has no method to fetch a Reader or Writer, partly because some network services are limited to ASCII, but mainly because the Socket class was decided on before there were Reader and Writer classes. You can always create a Reader from an InputStream or a Writer from an OutputStream using the conversion classes. The paradigm for the two most common forms is:

```
BufferedReader is = new BufferedReader(
    new InputStreamReader(sock.getInputStream( )));
PrintWriter os = new PrintWriter(sock.getOutputStream( ), true);
```

Example 13-4 reads a line of text from the "daytime" service, which is offered by full-fledged TCP/IP suites (such as those included with most Unixes). You don't have to send anything to the Daytime server; you simply connect and read one line. The server writes one line containing the date and time and then closes the connection.

Running it looks like this. I started by getting the current date and time on the local host, then ran the DaytimeText program to see the date and time on the server (machine *darian* is one of my Unix servers):

```
C:\javasrc\network>date
Current date is Sun 01-23-2000
Enter new date (mm-dd-yy):
C:\javasrc\network>time
Current time is  1:13:18.70p
Enter new time:
C:\javasrc\network>java network.DaytimeText darian
Time on darian is Sun Jan 23 13:14:34 2000
```

The code is in class DaytimeText, shown in Example 13-4.

Example 13-4. DaytimeText.java

```java
public class DaytimeText {
    public static final short TIME_PORT = 13;

    public static void main(String[] argv) {
        String hostName;
        if (argv.length == 0)
            hostName = "localhost";
        else
            hostName = argv[0];

        try {
            Socket sock = new Socket(hostName, TIME_PORT);
            BufferedReader is = new BufferedReader(new
                InputStreamReader(sock.getInputStream()));
            String remoteTime = is.readLine();
            System.out.println("Time on " + hostName + " is " + remoteTime);
        } catch (IOException e) {
            System.err.println(e);
        }
    }
}
```

The second example, shown in Example 13-5, shows both reading and writing on the same socket. The Echo server simply echoes back whatever lines of text you send it. It's not a very clever server, but it is a useful one. It helps in network testing and also in testing clients of this type!

The converse() method holds a short conversation with the Echo server on the named host; if no host is named, it tries to contact localhost, a universal alias[2] for "the machine the program is running on."

Example 13-5. EchoClientOneLine.java

```java
public class EchoClientOneLine {
    /** What we send across the net */
    String mesg = "Hello across the net";

    public static void main(String[] argv) {
        if (argv.length == 0)
            new EchoClientOneLine().converse("localhost");
        else
            new EchoClientOneLine().converse(argv[0]);
    }

    /** Hold one conversation across the net */
    protected void converse(String hostName) {
        try {
            Socket sock = new Socket(hostName, 7); // echo server.
            BufferedReader is = new BufferedReader(new
                InputStreamReader(sock.getInputStream()));
            PrintWriter os = new PrintWriter(sock.getOutputStream(), true);
            // Do the CRLF ourself since println appends only a \r on
            // platforms where that is the native line ending.
            os.print(mesg + "\r\n"); os.flush();
            String reply = is.readLine();
            System.out.println("Sent \"" + mesg  + "\"");
            System.out.println("Got  \"" + reply + "\"");
        } catch (IOException e) {
            System.err.println(e);
        }
    }
}
```

It might be a good exercise to isolate the reading and writing code from this method into a NetWriter class, possibly subclassing PrintWriter and adding the \r\n and the flushing.

---

2. It used to be universal, when most networked systems were administered by full-time systems people who had been trained or served an apprenticeship. Today many machines on the Internet don't have localhost configured properly.

13.5. Reading and Writing Binary Data

Problem

Having connected, you wish to transfer binary data.

Solution

Construct a `DataInputStream` or `DataOutputStream` from the socket's `getInput-Stream()` or `getOutputStream()`.

Discussion

The simplest paradigm for reading/writing on a socket is:

```
DataInputStream is = new DataInputStream(sock.getInputStream());
DataOutputStream is = new DataOutputStream(sock.getOutputStream( ));
```

If the volume of data might be large, insert a buffered stream for efficiency. The paradigm is:

```
DataInputStream is = new DataInputStream(
    new BufferedInputStream(sock.getInputStream( )));
DataOutputStream is = new DataOutputStream(
    new BufferedOutputStream(sock.getOutputStream( )));
```

The program example in Example 13-6 uses another standard service that gives out the time as a binary integer representing the number of seconds since 1900. Because the Java `Date` class base is 1970, we convert the time base by subtracting the difference between 1970 and 1900. When I used this exercise in a course, most of the students wanted to *add* this time difference, reasoning that 1970 is later. But if you think clearly, you'll see that there are fewer seconds between 1999 and 1970 than there are between 1999 and 1900, so subtraction gives the correct number of seconds. And because the `Date` constructor needs milliseconds, we multiply the number of seconds by 1,000.

The time difference is the number of years multiplied by 365, plus the number of leap days between the two dates (in the years 1904, 1908, . . . , 1968)—i.e., 19 days.

The integer that we read from the server is a C-language `unsigned int`. But Java doesn't provide an unsigned integer type; normally when you need an unsigned number, you use the next-larger integer type, which would be `long`. But Java also doesn't give us a method to read an unsigned integer from a data stream. The `DataInputStream` method `readInt()` reads Java-style signed integers. There are `readUnsignedByte()` methods and `readUnsignedShort()` methods, but no `readUnsignedInt()` method. Accordingly, we synthesize the ability to read an unsigned `int` (which must be stored in a `long`, or else you'd lose the signed bit and be back where you started from) by reading unsigned bytes and reassembling them using Java's bit-shifting operators:

At the end of the code, we use the new date/time API (see Chapter 6) to construct and print a `LocalDateTime` object to show the current date and time on the local (client) machine:

```
$ java network.RDateClient dalai
Remote time is 3600895637
BASE_DIFF is 2208988800
Time diff == 1391906837
Time on dalai is Sat Feb 08 19:47:17 EST 2014
Local date/time = 2014-02-08T19:47:17.703
$
```

The name *dalai* is the hostname of one of my OpenBSD Unix computers. Looking at the output, you can see that the server agrees within a second. So the date calculation code in Example 13-6 is probably correct. This protocol is commonly known as rdate, so the client code is called `RDateClient`.

Example 13-6. RDateClient.java

```java
public class RDateClient {
    /** The TCP port for the binary time service. */
    public static final short TIME_PORT = 37;
    /** Seconds between 1970, the time base for Date(long) and Time.
     * Factors in leap years (up to 2100), hours, minutes, and seconds.
     * Subtract 1 day for 1900, add in 1/2 day for 1969/1970.
     */
    protected static final long BASE_DAYS =
        (long)((1970-1900)*365 + (1970-1900-1)/4);

    /* Seconds since 1970 */
    public static final long BASE_DIFF = (BASE_DAYS * 24 * 60 * 60);

    /** Convert from seconds to milliseconds */
    public static final int MSEC = 1000;

    public static void main(String[] argv) {
        String hostName;
        if (argv.length == 0)
            hostName = "localhost";
        else
            hostName = argv[0];

        try {
            Socket sock = new Socket(hostName, TIME_PORT);
            DataInputStream is = new DataInputStream(new
                BufferedInputStream(sock.getInputStream()));
            // Read 4 bytes from the network, unsigned.
            // Do it yourself; there is no readUnsignedInt().
            // Long is 8 bytes on Java, but we are using the
            // existing time protocol, which uses 4-byte ints.
            long remoteTime = (
                ((long)(is.readUnsignedByte()) << 24) |
```

```
                ((long)(is.readUnsignedByte()) << 16) |
                ((long)(is.readUnsignedByte()) <<  8) |
                ((long)(is.readUnsignedByte()) <<  0));
        System.out.println("Remote time is " + remoteTime);
        System.out.println("BASE_DIFF is " + BASE_DIFF);
        System.out.println("Time diff == " + (remoteTime - BASE_DIFF));
        Date d = new Date((remoteTime - BASE_DIFF) * MSEC);
        System.out.println("Time on " + hostName + " is " + d.toString());
        System.out.println("Local date/time = " + LocalDateTime.now());
    } catch (IOException e) {
        System.err.println(e);
    }
  }
}
```

13.6. Reading and Writing Serialized Data

Problem

Having connected, you wish to transfer serialized object data.

Solution

Construct an `ObjectInputStream` or `ObjectOutputStream` from the socket's `getInputStream()` or `getOutputStream()`.

Discussion

Object serialization is the ability to convert in-memory objects to an external form that can be sent serially (a byte at a time). This is discussed in Recipe 10.20.

This program (and its server) operate one service that isn't normally provided by TCP/IP, because it is Java-specific. It looks rather like the `DaytimeBinary` program in the previous recipe, but the server sends us a `Date` object already constructed. You can find the server for this program in Recipe 16.2; Example 13-7 shows the client code.

Example 13-7. DaytimeObject.java

```
public class DaytimeObject {
    /** The TCP port for the object time service. */
    public static final short TIME_PORT = 1951;

    public static void main(String[] argv) {
        String hostName;
        if (argv.length == 0)
            hostName = "localhost";
        else
            hostName = argv[0];
```

```
        try {
            Socket sock = new Socket(hostName, TIME_PORT);
            ObjectInputStream is = new ObjectInputStream(new
                BufferedInputStream(sock.getInputStream()));

            // Read and validate the Object
            Object o = is.readObject();
            if (o == null) {
                System.err.println("Read null from server!");
            } else if ((o instanceof Date)) {

                // Valid, so cast to Date, and print
                Date d = (Date) o;
                System.out.println("Server host is " + hostName);
                System.out.println("Time there is " + d.toString());

            } else {
                throw new IllegalArgumentException("Wanted Date, got " + o);
            }
        } catch (ClassNotFoundException e) {
            System.err.println("Wanted date, got INVALID CLASS (" + e + ")");
        } catch (IOException e) {
            System.err.println(e);
        }
    }
}
```

I ask the operating system for the date and time, and then run the program, which prints the date and time on a remote machine:

```
C:\javasrc\network>date /t
Current date is Sun 01-23-2000
C:\javasrc\network>time /t
Current time is  2:52:35.43p
C:\javasrc\network>java network.DaytimeObject aragorn
Time on aragorn is Sun Jan 23 14:52:25 GMT 2000
C:\javasrc\network>
```

13.7. UDP Datagrams

Problem

You need to use a datagram connection (UDP) instead of a stream connection (TCP).

Solution

Use DatagramSocket and DatagramPacket.

Discussion

Datagram network traffic is a kindred spirit to the underlying packet-based Ethernet and IP (Internet protocol) layers. Unlike a stream-based connection such as TCP, datagram transports like UDP transmit each "packet," or chunk of data, as a single "entity" with no necessary relation to any other.[3] A common analogy is that TCP is like talking on the telephone, whereas UDP is like sending postcards or maybe fax messages.

The differences show up most in error handling. Packets can, like postcards, go astray. When was the last time the postman rang your bell to tell you that the post office had lost one of several postcards it was supposed to deliver to you? That's not going to happen, because the post office doesn't keep track of postcards. On the other hand, when you're talking on the phone and there's a noise burst—like somebody yelling in the room, or even a bad connection—you notice the failure in real time, and you can ask the person at the other end to repeat what they just said.

With a stream-based connection like a TCP socket, the network transport layer handles errors for you: it asks the other end to retransmit. With a datagram transport such as UDP, you have to handle retransmission yourself. It's kind of like numbering the postcards you send so that you can go back and resend any that don't arrive—a good excuse to return to your vacation spot, perhaps.

Another difference is that datagram transmission preserves message boundaries. That is, if you write 20 bytes and then write 10 bytes when using TCP, the program reading from the other end will not know if you wrote one chunk of 30 bytes, two chunks of 15, or even 30 individual characters. With a `DatagramSocket`, you construct a `Datagram-Packet` object for each buffer, and its contents are sent as a *single* entity over the network; its contents will not be mixed together with the contents of any other buffer. The `Da-tagramPacket` object has methods like `getLength()`, `setPort()`, and so on.

Ian's Basic Steps: UDP Client

UDP is a bit more involved, so I'll list the basic steps for generating a UDP client:

1. Create a `DatagramSocket` with no arguments (the form that takes two arguments is used on the server).

2. Optionally `connect()` the socket to an `InetAddress` (see Recipe 13.2) and port number.

3. Create one or more `DatagramPacket` objects; these are wrappers around a byte array that contains data you want to send and is filled in with data you receive.

---

3. The UDP packet may need to be fragmented by some networks, but this is not germane to us at the UDP level, because it will re-assemble the network packets into our "single entity" UDP packet at the other end.

---

4. If you did not `connect()` the socket, provide the `InetAddress` and port when constructing the `DatagramPacket`.

5. Set the packet's length and use `sock.send(packet)` to send data to the server.

6. Use `sock.receive()` to retrieve data.

So why would we even use UDP? UDP has a lot less overhead than TCP, which can be particularly valuable when sending huge amounts of data over a reliable local network or a few hops on the Internet. Over long-haul networks, TCP is probably preferred because TCP handles retransmission of lost packets for you. And obviously, if preserving record boundaries makes your life easier, that may be a reason for considering UDP.

Example 13-8 is a short program that connects via UDP to the `Daytime` date and time server used in Recipe 13.4. Because UDP has no real notion of "connection," the client typically initiates the "conversation," which sometimes means sending an empty packet; the UDP server uses the address information it gets from that to return its response.

Example 13-8. DaytimeUDP.java

```java
public class DaytimeUDP {
    /** The UDP port number */
    public final static int DAYTIME_PORT = 13;

    /** A buffer plenty big enough for the date string */
    protected final static int PACKET_SIZE = 100;

    /** The main program that drives this network client.
     * @param argv[0] hostname, running daytime/udp server
     */
    public static void main(String[] argv) throws IOException {
        if (argv.length < 1) {
            System.err.println("usage: java DayTimeUDP host");
            System.exit(1);
        }
        String host = argv[0];
        InetAddress servAddr = InetAddress.getByName(host);
        DatagramSocket sock = new DatagramSocket();
        //sock.connect(servAddr, DAYTIME_PORT);
        byte[] buffer = new byte[PACKET_SIZE];

        // The udp packet we will send and receive
        DatagramPacket packet = new DatagramPacket(
            buffer, PACKET_SIZE, servAddr, DAYTIME_PORT);

        /* Send empty max-length (-1 for null byte) packet to server */
        packet.setLength(PACKET_SIZE-1);
        sock.send(packet);
        System.out.println("Sent request");
```

```
        // Receive a packet and print it.
        sock.receive(packet);
        System.out.println("Got packet of size " + packet.getLength());
        System.out.print("Date on " + host + " is " +
            new String(buffer, 0, packet.getLength()));

        sock.close();
    }
}
```

I'll run it to my Unix box just to be sure that it works:

```
$
$ java network.DaytimeUDP dalai
Sent request
Got packet of size 26
Date on dalai is Sat Feb  8 20:22:12 2014
$
```

13.8. Program: TFTP UDP Client

This program implements the client half of the TFTP application protocol, a once-well-known service that has been used in the Unix world for network booting of workstations since before Windows 3.1, now primarily used for network bootstrapping of computers. I chose this protocol because it's widely implemented on the server side, so it's easy to find a test server for it.

The TFTP protocol is a bit odd. The client contacts the server on the well-known UDP port number 69, from a generated port number,[4] and the server responds to the client from a generated port number. Further communication is on the two generated port numbers.

Getting into more detail, as shown in Figure 13-1, the client initially sends a read request with the filename and reads the first packet of data. The read request consists of two bytes (a short) with the read request code (short integer with a value of 1, defined as OP_RRQ), two bytes for the sequence number, then the ASCII filename, null termi- nated, and the mode string, also null terminated. The server reads the read request from the client, verifies that it can open the file and, if so, sends the first data packet (OP_DA- TA), and then reads again. The client reads from its end and, if the read is OK, turns the packet into an acknowledgement packet, and sends it. This read-acknowledge cycle is repeated until all the data is read. Note that each packet is 516 bytes (512 bytes of data,

---

4. When the application doesn't care, these port numbers are usually made up by the operating system. For example, when you call a company from a pay phone or cell phone, the company doesn't usually care what number you are calling from, and if it does, there are ways to find out. Generated port numbers generally range from 1024 (the first nonprivileged port; see Chapter 16) to 65535 (the largest value that can be held in a 16-bit port number).

---

plus 2 bytes for the packet type and 2 more for the packet number) except the last, which can be any length from 4 (zero bytes of data) to 515 (511 bytes of data). If a network I/O error occurs, the packet is resent. If a given packet goes astray, both client and server are supposed to perform a timeout cycle. This client does not, but the server does. You could add timeouts either using a thread (see Recipe 22.4) or by invoking `setSoTimeout()` on the socket and, if packets do get lost, catching the `SocketTimeoutException`, retransmitting the ACK (or RRQ), perhaps up to some max # of attempts. This is left as an exercise for the reader. The current version of the client code is shown in Example 13-9.

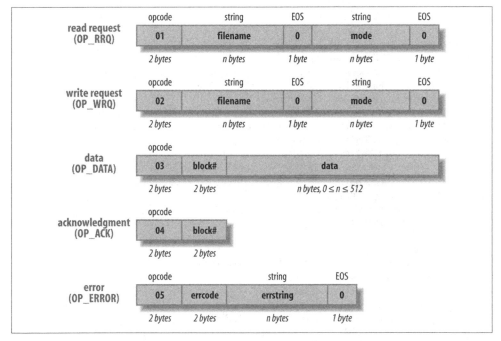

Figure 13-1. The TFTP protocol packet formats

Example 13-9. RemCat.java

```java
public class RemCat {
    /** The UDP port number */
    public final static int TFTP_PORT = 69;
    /** The mode we will use - octet for everything. */
    protected final String MODE = "octet";

    /** The offset for the code/response as a byte */
    protected final int OFFSET_REQUEST = 1;
    /** The offset for the packet number as a byte */
    protected final int OFFSET_PACKETNUM = 3;
```

```
/** Debugging flag */
protected static boolean debug = false;

/** TFTP op-code for a read request */
public final int OP_RRQ = 1;
/** TFTP op-code for a read request */
public final int OP_WRQ = 2;
/** TFTP op-code for a read request */
public final int OP_DATA = 3;
/** TFTP op-code for a read request */
public final int OP_ACK    = 4;
/** TFTP op-code for a read request */
public final int OP_ERROR = 5;

protected final static int PACKET_SIZE = 516;    // == 2 + 2 + 512
protected String host;
protected InetAddress servAddr;
protected DatagramSocket sock;
protected byte buffer[];
protected DatagramPacket inp, outp;

/** The main program that drives this network client.
 * @param argv[0] hostname, running TFTP server
 * @param argv[1..n] filename(s), must be at least one
 */
public static void main(String[] argv) throws IOException {
    if (argv.length < 2) {
        System.err.println("usage: rcat host filename[...]");
        System.exit(1);
    }
    if (debug)
        System.err.println("Java RemCat starting");
    RemCat rc = new RemCat(argv[0]);
    for (int i = 1; i<argv.length; i++) {
        if (debug)
            System.err.println("-- Starting file " +
                argv[0] + ":" + argv[i] + "---");
        rc.readFile(argv[i]);
    }
}

RemCat(String host) throws IOException {
    super();
    this.host = host;
    servAddr = InetAddress.getByName(host);
    sock = new DatagramSocket();
    buffer = new byte[PACKET_SIZE];
    outp = new DatagramPacket(buffer, PACKET_SIZE, servAddr, TFTP_PORT);
    inp = new DatagramPacket(buffer, PACKET_SIZE);
}

/* Build a TFTP Read Request packet. This is messy because the
```

```
 * fields have variable length. Numbers must be in
 * network order, too; fortunately Java just seems
 * naturally smart enough :-) to use network byte order.
 */
void readFile(String path) throws IOException {
    buffer[0] = 0;
    buffer[OFFSET_REQUEST] = OP_RRQ;          // read request
    int p = 2;                // number of chars into buffer

    // Convert filename String to bytes in buffer , using "p" as an
    // offset indicator to get all the bits of this request
    // in exactly the right spot.
    byte[] bTemp = path.getBytes();    // i.e., ASCII
    System.arraycopy(bTemp, 0, buffer, p, path.length());
    p += path.length();
    buffer[p++] = 0;          // null byte terminates string

    // Similarly, convert MODE ("stream" or "octet") to bytes in buffer
    bTemp = MODE.getBytes();    // i.e., ASCII
    System.arraycopy(bTemp, 0, buffer, p, MODE.length());
    p += MODE.length();
    buffer[p++] = 0;          // null terminate

    /* Send Read Request to tftp server */
    outp.setLength(p);
    sock.send(outp);

    /* Loop reading data packets from the server until a short
     * packet arrives; this indicates the end of the file.
     */
    int len = 0;
    do {
        sock.receive(inp);
        if (debug)
            System.err.println(
                "Packet # " + Byte.toString(buffer[OFFSET_PACKETNUM])+
                "RESPONSE CODE " + Byte.toString(buffer[OFFSET_REQUEST]));
        if (buffer[OFFSET_REQUEST] == OP_ERROR) {
            System.err.println("rcat ERROR: " +
                new String(buffer, 4, inp.getLength()-4));
            return;
        }
        if (debug)
            System.err.println("Got packet of size " +
                inp.getLength());

        /* Print the data from the packet */
        System.out.write(buffer, 4, inp.getLength()-4);

        /* Ack the packet. The block number we
         * want to ack is already in buffer so
         * we just change the opcode. The ACK is
```

```
      * sent to the port number which the server
      * just sent the data from, NOT to port
      * TFTP_PORT.
      */
     buffer[OFFSET_REQUEST] = OP_ACK;
     outp.setLength(4);
     outp.setPort(inp.getPort());
     sock.send(outp);
   } while (inp.getLength() == PACKET_SIZE);

   if (debug)
     System.err.println("** ALL DONE** Leaving loop, last size " +
       inp.getLength());
  }
}
```

To test this client, you need a TFTP server. If you are on a Unix system that you administer, you can enable the TFTP server to test this client just by editing the file */etc/inetd.conf* and restarting or reloading the *inetd* server. *inetd* is a program that listens for a wide range of connections and starts the servers only when a connection from a client comes along (a kind of lazy evaluation).[5] I set up the traditional */tftpboot* directory, put this line in my *inetd.conf*, and reloaded inetd:

```
tftp dgram udp wait root /usr/libexec/tftpd tftpd -s /tftpboot
```

Then I put a few test files, one named *foo*, into the */tftpboot* directory. Running:

```
$ java network.RemCat localhost foo
```

produced what looked like the file. But just to be safe, I tested the output of RemCat against the original file, using the Unix *diff* comparison program. No news is good news:

```
$ java network.RemCat localhost foo | diff - /tftpboot/foo
```

So far so good. Let's not slip this program on an unsuspecting network without exercising the error handling at least briefly:

```
$ java network.RemCat localhost nosuchfile
remcat ERROR: File not found
$
```

---

5. Beware of security holes; don't turn a TFTP server loose on the Internet without first reading a good security book, such as *Building Internet Firewalls*, (O'Reilly).

13.9. URI, URL, or URN?

Problem

Having heard these terms, you want to know the difference between a URI, URL, and URN.

Solution

Read on. Or see the javadoc for *java.net.uri*.

Discussion

A URL is the traditional name for a network address consisting of a scheme (like "http") and an address (site name) and resource or pathname. But there are three distinct terms in all:

- URI (Uniform Resource Identifier)
- URL (Uniform Resource Locator)
- URN (Uniform Resource Name)

A discussion near the end of the Java documentation for the new class explains the relationship among URI, URL, and URN. URIs form the set of all identifiers: URLs and URNs are subsets.

URIs are the most general; a URI is parsed for basic syntax without regard to the scheme, if any, that it specifies, and it need not refer to a particular server. A URL includes a hostname, scheme, and other components; the string is parsed according to rules for its scheme. When you construct a URL, an `InputStream` is created automatically. URNs name resources but do not explain how to locate them; typical examples of URNs that you will have seen include `mailto:` and `news:` references.

The main operations provided by the `URI` class are normalization (removing extraneous path segments including "..") and relativization (this should be called "making relative," but somebody wanted a single word to make a method name). A `URI` object does not have any methods for opening the URI; for that, you would normally use a string representation of the URI to construct a URL object, like so:

```
URL x = new URL(theURI.toString( ));
```

The program in Example 13-10 shows examples of normalizating, making relative, and constructing a URL from a URI.

Example 13-10. URIDemo.java

```java
public class URIDemo {
    public static void main(String[] args)
    throws URISyntaxException, MalformedURLException {

        URI u = new URI("http://www.darwinsys.com/java/../openbsd/../index.jsp");
        System.out.println("Raw: " + u);
        URI normalized = u.normalize();
        System.out.println("Normalized: " + normalized);
        final URI BASE = new URI("http://www.darwinsys.com");
        System.out.println("Relativized to " + BASE + ": " + BASE.relativize(u));

        // A URL is a type of URI
        URL url = new URL(normalized.toString());
        System.out.println("URL: " + url);

        // Junk
        URI uri = new URI("bean:WonderBean");
        System.out.println(uri);
    }
}
```

13.10. REST Web Service Client

Problem

You need to read from a URL (e.g., connect to a RESTful web service).

Solution

Use the standard URLConnection or the third-party Apache HttpClient library.

This technique applies anytime you need to read from a URL, not just a RESTful web service.

Discussion

Although the Apache HttpClient library gives you more flexibility, for most simple REST web services it is overkill. All we usually need is the ability to open and read from a URL. As our simple example, we'll use the free, open source freegeoip.net service. IP GeoLocation refers to finding the geographic location (geolocation) of a given IP connection, usually the address of a client or server (or its IP proxy, if it is behind a proxy).

The FreeGeoIP service supports three different output formats: CSV (see Recipe 3.13), JSON (see Chapter 19), and XML (see Chapter 20). As is typical of REST services that offer multiple formats, you choose your format simply by putting it as part of the URL. The service's documentation states that its URL usage is just:

```
http://freegeoip.net/{format}/{host}
```

The protocol can be either HTTP or HTTPS. The format can be csv, json, or xml (all lowercase). The "host" is optional: if not given, the IP address from which you are connecting will be looked up; if given, the host may be specified as a numeric IP or a resolvable hostname.

Here is the code:

```java
public class RestClientFreeGeoIp {
    public static void main(String[] args) throws Exception {
        URLConnection conn = new URL(
            "http://freegeoip.net/json/www.oreilly.com")
            .openConnection();
        try (BufferedReader is =
            new BufferedReader(new InputStreamReader(conn.getInputStream()))) {

            String line;
            while ((line = is.readLine()) != null) {
                System.out.println(line);
            }
        }
    }
}
```

The result comes back in the requested format. For a JSON request, we get a single long line with all the information, for the given (O'Reilly Media) web server. Here the line has been broken at commas to make it fit on the page:

```
{"ip":"207.152.124.48","country_code":"US","country_name":"United States",
"region_code":"CO","region_name":"Colorado","city":"Englewood",
"zipcode":"80111","latitude":39.6237,"longitude":-104.8738,
"metro_code":"751","areacode":"303"}
```

Like any commercially scaled organization, O'Reilly uses a distributed Content Distribution Network (CDN), so the answer you get will change over time; here is a different output obtained by running the same program a few minutes later:

```
{"ip":"69.31.106.26","country_code":"US","country_name":"United States",
"region_code":"MA","region_name":"Massachusetts","city":"Cambridge",
"zipcode":"02142","latitude":42.3626,"longitude":-71.0843,
"metro_code":"506","areacode":"617"}
```

You can find more information on REST services (including implementing the server-side components for them) in Bill Burke's *RESTful Java with JAX-RS 2.0, 2nd Edition* (O'Reilly).

13.11. SOAP Web Service Client

Problem

You need to communicate with a SOAP-based client, and have heard that it's more complex than REST services.

Solution

It is, but we'll get through it together, with help from JAX-WS. Get the WSDL. Process it with `wsimport`. Call the generated service factory to obtain the service stub, and call that to invoke the remote service.

Discussion

SOAP is the communications protocol used for XML Web Services. SOAP is not an acronym; it originally stood for "Simple Object Access Protocol" but by the time the standards committee got through with it it was certainly not "simple," and it was never really "object oriented," so they dropped the acronym but kept the name... Oh, and it's not *really* a "protocol" either—the protocol is usually HTTP or HTTPS. SOAP now is simply SOAP, although using "simple" and "SOAP" in the same breath tends to draw guffaws from the REST fans.

You need to get a copy of a "WSDL" (Web Services Description Language) document from the server. You run it through a JAX-WS program called `wsimport` (included with the JDK). You then invoke the generated service factory to get the service stub. Finally, call methods on the service stub to access the remote service.

WSDL defines the service in immense detail. Think of it somewhat like a Java interface on steroids. An interface tells you what methods can be called, their arguments, declared exceptions, and so on, but not where to find the service on the network, nor how to convert data into a format that the other end can accept. A WSDL does all that, in a standardized (albeit complex) way.

What's good about that is the client and the server do not have to be in the same programming language, or on the same OS, or even the same CPU type. You can have a Java EE server running the web service, and have clients on a mobile device (Android, iOS, BlackBerry, Windows, etc.) or a Perl, Python, or Ruby client on a Linux, Mac, or BSD desktop. The WSDL specifies all the formatting information so that word size issues and byte ordering issues are silently paved over for you. Even within the Java world, there are numerous toolkits for generating SOAP clients and services. We'll use JAX-WS (Java API for XML Web Services), because it's a standard part of the Java platform (both client-side, Java SE, and server-side, in Java EE).

Some people prefer generating WSDL files by hand. They call this "contract first" development. Not me. I'll start with an existing WSDL, or I'll generate a WSDL from a Java interface and then clean it up manually. A Java interface is a contract too, just not as complete (nor as full of legal mumbo jumbo, to stretch the analogy a bit).

Making a simple service

For this service, I have yet another variation of my Calc simple calculator. Note that all this code is in the *javasrcee* repository.

To get us to the client, I am going to digress very briefly to show how I made the service, because making the service makes the WSDL for us. In a real situation, you probably want to talk to an existing service so you will already have, or be given, "their" WSDL. In that case, you may want to skip ahead to "Generating the client artifacts, and writing the client" on page 446.

The Calc service starts off as an implementation class called Calc, in the service package jaxwsservice:

```
import javax.jws.WebService;

@WebService(targetNamespace="http://toy.service/")
public class Calc {

    public int add(int a, int b) {
        System.out.println("CalcImpl.add()");
        return a + b;
    }
    // The other three methods are pretty simple too
```

To make this into a service for testing, and for generating the WSDL file, the JDK includes an amazing tool called javax.xml.ws.Endpoint, which allows you to take any class (as long as it has an @WebService annotation) and publish it as a web service!

```
// Create the "service stub"
Calc impl = new Calc();
// Start the service running
Endpoint ep =
    Endpoint.publish("http://localhost:9090/calc", impl);
System.out.println("Endpoint running: " + ep);
```

Assuming you have done "mvn compile" at the top level of *javasrcee*, you can run the service as shown:

```
$ java -cp target/classes jaxwsservice.ServiceMain
Endpoint running:
 com.sun.xml.internal.ws.transport.http.server.EndpointImpl@f0f7074
```

What is impressive about this? If you haven't seen the complexity of "deployment" that some services require, you may not find it that interesting. Trust me, it is. Further, not only did it set up the server and "deploy" the plain old Java object (POJO) implementation as a web service, but it's also *generated the WSDL for us*, from scratch! Well, from the annotated implementation class, at least. So now I can show you the WSDL. While the service is running, point your web browser at the endpoint URL with the HTTP parameter wsdl appended (it doesn't need a value, so just ?wsdl will do). The full URL is thus *http://localhost:9090/calc?wsdl*.

Although you don't strictly need a copy of the WSDL for posterity, you can save it to disk. If you have a sensible FTP client like the BSD ftp or the third-party wget, you can save it directly to a file using something like this:

```
$ ftp -o calc.wsdl http://localhost:9090/calc?wsdl
Requesting http://localhost:9090/calc?wsdl
100% |*************************************************|  3745        00:00
3745 bytes received in 0.00 seconds (9.18 MB/s)
$ ls -l calc.wsdl
-rw-r--r--  1 ian  wheel  3745 Jan  3 09:53 calc.wsdl
$
```

You should probably look at the WSDL file, once, to see that it is as complex, or at least, as verbose, as I say. One argument for the "WSDL-first" people is that the handmade WSDL can be smaller and cleaner.

Generating the client artifacts, and writing the client

Well, now we can get back to generating the client code. wsimport reads the WSDL, either from the URL or from a file, and generates a whole pile of "artifacts":

```
$ mkdir jaxwsclient
$ wsimport -d jaxwsclient -keep 'http://localhost:9090/calc?wsdl'
parsing WSDL...

Generating code...

Compiling code...

$ ls jaxwsclient/service/toy/*.java
Add.java                Divide.java              ObjectFactory.java
AddResponse.java        DivideResponse.java      Subtract.java
Calc.java               Multiply.java            SubtractResponse.java
CalcService.java        MultiplyResponse.java    package-info.java
$
```

You need to examine the generated Calc and CalcService files (there are copies in the *javasrcee* repository in the *jaxwsclient* folder if you aren't building this as you go along; the copies in the repository were moved to a shorter-named package but should be otherwise identical). For a service with object arguments, you might have to examine the other generated artifacts, because there will be artifacts for the actual types the client has to pass into the stub. Examining CalcService will tell you the method name you need to create a connection to the service—in our case:

```
// First Half of jaxwsclient.TinyClientMain
Calc client = new CalcService().getCalcPort();
```

Examining Calc will tell you the arguments you need to the Calc interface—at this point you are supposed to pretend you've never seen the server-side version, and be particularly careful *not* to import anything from the server-side package! We can now write code like this:

```
// Second Half of jaxwsclient.TinyClientMain
System.out.println(client.add(2, 2));
```

And be very upset if the result is not 4! But yes, it really is possible to have a complete SOAP client in two lines of Java, given the fact that the arguments are primitives and given all the other work that wsimport and the toolkit have done for us:

```
// no imports!

/** Two-line client for Calc Service, complete code. */
public class TinyClientMain {
    public static void main(String[] args) {
        Calc client = new CalcService().getCalcPort();
        System.out.println(client.add(2, 2));
    }
}
$ java -cp target/classes jaxwsclient.TinyClientMain
4
$
```

The actual client in the jaxwsclient package provides an interactive calculator that lets you input lines like 2 + 2 and get the answer:

```
$ java -cp target/classes jaxwsclient.ClientMain
Interactive calculator. Put spaces around operators.
>> 2 + 2
2 + 2 = 4
>> 22 / 7
22 / 7 = 3
>> ^D
$
```

Brilliant, eh? Incidentally, there is both a unit test in the service package and an integration test (which just uses the static Endpoint.publish() to start and stop the service) in the client package.

To recap, we did the following:

1. Created the service (but usually that will already be done for you).

2. Got the WSDL from the service with endpoint via "the ?wsdl trick".

3. Ran the WSDL through wsimport to generate the client artifacts.

4. Examined the `Calc` and `CalcService` files (the pattern's the same for any service); the service name will be an interface and the factory for it will be the service name with the word `Service` appended.

5. Invoked the `getCalcService()` method on the factory, to get the client-side `Calc` "stub" object.

6. Invoked methods on the stub.

See Also

There is much more to SOAP Web Services than this. The issues surrounding larger, more complex web services are the same as for any type of network service: reliability, server uptime, and so on. The connection could fail at any time due to a server crash or network outage. There are higher-level protocols for reliability, security/encryption, and so on. But even with these, the network can still fail, so the client should be prepared for the possibility of a SOAP fault propagating back. It is somewhat common to structure the web service return value to be a tuple (sequence) of an integer indicating sucess or various error codes, implemented as an enumeration, a string error message (in case an old client meets a new server and doesn't understand some of the error codes), and the actual return data—the calculation result, in our example. *Java Web Services: Up and Running* (O'Reilly) has more details.

13.12. Program: Telnet Client

This program is a simple Telnet client. Telnet, as you probably know, is the oldest surviving remote login program in use on the Internet. It began on the original ARPAnet and was later translated for the Internet. A Unix command-line client lives on, and several windowed clients are in circulation. For security reasons, the use of Telnet as a means of logging in remotely over the Internet has largely been superseded by SSH (*http://www.openssh.com*). However, a Telnet client remains a necessity for such purposes as connecting locally, as well as debugging textual socket servers and understanding their protocols. For example, it is common to connect from a Telnet client to an SMTP (email) server; you can often intuit quite a bit about the SMTP server, even if you wouldn't normally type an entire mail session interactively.

When you need to have data copied in both directions at roughly the same time—from the keyboard to the remote program, and from the remote program to the screen—there are two approaches. Some I/O libraries in C have a function called `poll()` or `select()` that allows you to examine a number of files to see which ones are ready for reading or writing. Java does not support this model. The other model, which works on most platforms and is the norm in Java, is to use two threads,[6] one to handle the data transfer in each direction. That is our plan here; the class `Pipe` encapsulates one thread and the code for copying data in one direction; two instances are used, one to drive each direction of transfer independently of the other.

This program allows you to connect to any text-based network service. For example, you can talk to your system's SMTP (simple mail transport protocol) server, or the `Daytime` server (port 13) used in several earlier recipes in this chapter:

```
$ java network.Telnet darian 13
Host darian; port 13
Connected OK
Sat Apr 28 14:07:41 2001
^C
$
```

The source code is shown in Example 13-11.

Example 13-11. Telnet.java

```java
public class Telnet {
    String host;
    int portNum;
    public static void main(String[] argv) {
        new Telnet().talkTo(argv);
    }
    private void talkTo(String av[]) {
        if (av.length >= 1)
            host = av[0];
        else
            host = "localhost";
        if (av.length >= 2)
            portNum = Integer.parseInt(av[1]);
        else portNum = 23;
        System.out.println("Host " + host + "; port " + portNum);
        try {
            Socket s = new Socket(host, portNum);

            // Connect the remote to our stdout
            new Pipe(s.getInputStream(), System.out).start();

            // Connect our stdin to the remote
            new Pipe(System.in, s.getOutputStream()).start();

        } catch(IOException e) {
            System.out.println(e);
            return;
        }
        System.out.println("Connected OK");
```

---

6. A thread is one of (possibly) many separate flows of control within a single process; see Recipe 22.1.

```
        }

        /* This class handles one half of a full-duplex connection.
         * Line-at-a-time mode.
         */
        class Pipe extends Thread {
            BufferedReader is;
            PrintStream os;

            /** Construct a Pipe to read from is and write to os */
            Pipe(InputStream is, OutputStream os) {
                this.is = new BufferedReader(new InputStreamReader(is));
                this.os = new PrintStream(os);
            }

            /** Do the reading and writing. */
            public void run() {
                String line;
                try {
                    while ((line = is.readLine()) != null) {
                        os.print(line);
                        os.print("\r\n");
                        os.flush();
                    }
                } catch(IOException e) {
                    throw new RuntimeException(e.getMessage());
                }
            }
        }
    }
}
```

Of course this is far from a complete "real" Telnet client, but you should be using SSH instead of Telnet for real connectivity over the Internet; see *http://openssh.com*.

13.13. Program: Chat Client

This program is a simple chat program. You can't break in on ICQ or AIM with it, because they each use their own protocol;[7] this one simply writes to and reads from a server, locating the server with the applet method `getCodeBase()`. The server for this will be presented in Chapter 16. How does it look when you run it? Figure 13-2 shows me chatting all by myself one day.

---

7. For an open source program that "AIMs" to let you talk to both from the same program, check out Jabber at *http://www.jabber.org*.

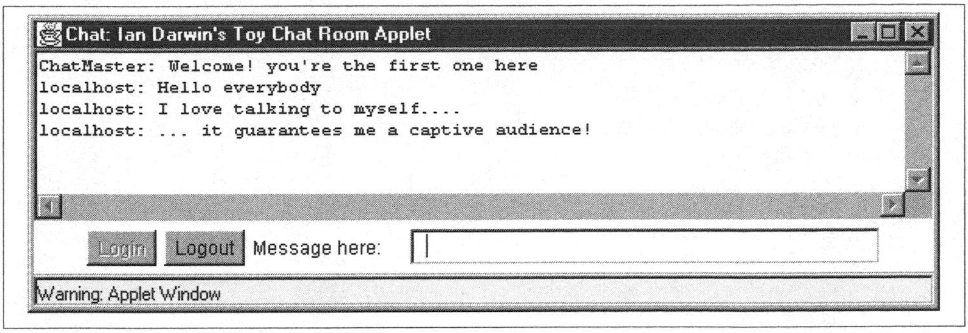

Figure 13-2. Chat client in action

The code is reasonably self-explanatory. We read from the remote server in a thread to make the input and the output run without blocking each other; this is discussed in Chapter 22. The reading and writing are discussed in this chapter. The program is shown in Example 13-12.

Example 13-12. ChatClient.java

```java
public class ChatClient extends JFrame {

    private static final long serialVersionUID = -3686334002367908392L;
    private static final String userName =
        System.getProperty("user.name", "User With No Name");
    /** The state of logged-in-ness */
    protected boolean loggedIn;
    /* The main Frame. */
    protected JFrame cp;
    /** The default port number */
    protected static final int PORTNUM = ChatProtocol.PORTNUM;
    /** The actual port number */
    protected int port;
    /** The network socket */
    protected Socket sock;
    /** BufferedReader for reading from socket */
    protected BufferedReader is;
    /** PrintWriter for sending lines on socket */
    protected PrintWriter pw;
    /** TextField for input */
    protected TextField tf;
    /** TextArea to display conversations */
    protected TextArea ta;
    /** The Login button */
    protected Button loginButton;
    /** The LogOUT button */
    protected Button logoutButton;
    /** The TitleBar title */
    final static String TITLE = "ChatClient: Ian Darwin's Toy Chat Room Client";
```

```java
/** set up the GUI */
public ChatClient() {
    cp = this;
    cp.setTitle(TITLE);
    cp.setLayout(new BorderLayout());
    port = PORTNUM;

    // The GUI
    ta = new TextArea(14, 80);
    ta.setEditable(false);          // readonly
    ta.setFont(new Font("Monospaced", Font.PLAIN, 11));
    cp.add(BorderLayout.NORTH, ta);

    Panel p = new Panel();

    // The login button
    p.add(loginButton = new Button("Login"));
    loginButton.setEnabled(true);
    loginButton.requestFocus();
    loginButton.addActionListener(new ActionListener() {
        public void actionPerformed(ActionEvent e) {
            login();
            loginButton.setEnabled(false);
            logoutButton.setEnabled(true);
            tf.requestFocus();    // set keyboard focus in right place!
        }
    });

    // The logout button
    p.add(logoutButton = new Button("Logout"));
    logoutButton.setEnabled(false);
    logoutButton.addActionListener(new ActionListener() {
        public void actionPerformed(ActionEvent e) {
            logout();
            loginButton.setEnabled(true);
            logoutButton.setEnabled(false);
            loginButton.requestFocus();
        }
    });

    p.add(new Label("Message here:"));
    tf = new TextField(40);
    tf.addActionListener(new ActionListener() {
        public void actionPerformed(ActionEvent e) {
            if (loggedIn) {
                pw.println(ChatProtocol.CMD_BCAST+tf.getText());
                tf.setText("");
            }
        }
    });
    p.add(tf);
```

```java
        cp.add(BorderLayout.SOUTH, p);

        cp.setDefaultCloseOperation(JFrame.EXIT_ON_CLOSE);
        cp.pack();
    }

    protected String serverHost = "localhost";

    /** LOG ME IN TO THE CHAT */
    public void login() {
        showStatus("In login!");
        if (loggedIn)
            return;
        try {
            sock = new Socket(serverHost, port);
            is = new BufferedReader(new InputStreamReader(sock.getInputStream()));
            pw = new PrintWriter(sock.getOutputStream(), true);
            showStatus("Got socket");

            // FAKE LOGIN FOR NOW - no password neede
            pw.println(ChatProtocol.CMD_LOGIN + userName);

            loggedIn = true;

        } catch(IOException e) {
            showStatus("Can't get socket to " +
                serverHost + "/" + port + ": " + e);
            cp.add(new Label("Can't get socket: " + e));
            return;
        }

        // Construct and start the reader: from server to textarea.
        // Make a Thread to avoid lockups.
        new Thread(new Runnable() {
            public void run() {
                String line;
                try {
                    while (loggedIn && ((line = is.readLine()) != null))
                        ta.append(line + "\n");
                } catch(IOException e) {
                    showStatus("Lost another client!\n" + e);
                    return;
                }
            }
        }).start();
    }

    /** Log me out, Scotty, there's no intelligent life here! */
    public void logout() {
        if (!loggedIn)
            return;
        loggedIn = false;
```

```
        try {
            if (sock != null)
                sock.close();
        } catch (IOException ign) {
            // so what?
        }
    }

    public void showStatus(String message) {
        System.out.println(message);
    }

    /** A main method to allow the client to be run as an Application */
    public static void main(String[] args) {
        ChatClient room101 = new ChatClient();
        room101.pack();
        room101.setVisible(true);
    }
}
```

See Also

There are many better structured ways to write a chat client, including WebSockets, RMI, and JMS. RMI is Java's RPC interface, and is included both in Java SE and in Java EE; it is not described in this edition of this book, but you can find the RMI chapter from previous editions on the author's website (*http://darwinsys.com/java/rmi*). The other technologies are part of the Java Enterprise so, again, we refer you to Arun Gupta's *Java EE 7 Essentials* (O'Reilly).

If you need to encrypt your socket connection, check out Sun's JSSE (Java Secure Socket Extension). (If you took our earlier advice and used the standard HTTP protocol, you can encrypt the conversation just by changing the URL to https).

For a good overview of network programming from the C programmer's point of view, see the late W. Richard Stevens' *Unix Network Programming* (*http://amzn.to/ 1hP3UkA*). Despite the book's name, it's really about socket and TCP/IP/UDP programming and covers all parts of the (Unix) networking API and protocols such as TFTP in amazing detail.

13.14. Program: Simple HTTP Link Checker

Checking links is an ongoing problem for website owners as well as those who write technical documentation that links to external sources (e.g., people like the author of the book you are now reading). *Link Checkers* are the tool they inevitably use to validate the links in their pages, be they web pages or book pages. Implementing a link checker is basically a matter of (a) extracting links and (b) opening them. Thus, this program. I call it KwikLinkChecker as it is a bit on the "quick and dirty" side—it doesn't validate the content of the link to be sure it still contains what it once did, so if, say, an open source project forgets to renew its domain registration, and it gets taken over by a porn site, well, KwikLinkChecker will never know. But that said, it does its job reasonably well, and reasonably quickly:

```
/**
 * Check one HTTP link; not recursive. Returns a LinkStatus with
 * boolean success, and the filename or an error message in the
 * message part of the LinkStatus.  The end of this method is one of
 * the few places where a whole raft of different "catch" clauses is
 * actually needed for the intent of the program.
 */
public LinkStatus check(String urlString) {
    URL url;
    HttpURLConnection conn = null;
    HttpURLConnection.setFollowRedirects(false);
    try {
        url = new URL(urlString);
        conn = (HttpURLConnection) url.openConnection();
        switch (conn.getResponseCode()) {
        case 200:
            return new LinkStatus(true, urlString);
        case 403:
            return new LinkStatus(false,"403: " + urlString );
        case 404:
            return new LinkStatus(false,"404: " + urlString );
        }
        conn.getInputStream();
        return new LinkStatus(true, urlString);
    } catch (IllegalArgumentException | MalformedURLException e) {
        // Oracle JDK throws IAE if host can't be determined from URL string
        return new LinkStatus(false, "Malformed URL: " + urlString);
    } catch (UnknownHostException e) {
        return new LinkStatus(false, "Host invalid/dead: " + urlString);
    } catch (FileNotFoundException e) {
        return new LinkStatus(false,"NOT FOUND (404) " + urlString);
    } catch (ConnectException e) {
        return new LinkStatus(false, "Server not listening: " + urlString);
    } catch (SocketException e) {
        return new LinkStatus(false, e + ": " + urlString);
    } catch (IOException e) {
        return new LinkStatus(false, e.toString()); // includes failing URL
    } catch (Exception e) {
        return new LinkStatus(false, "Unexpected exception! " + e);
    } finally {
        if (conn != null) {
            conn.disconnect();
        }
    }
}
```

Fancier link checkers are surely available, but this one works for me.

## CHAPTER 14

Graphical User Interfaces

14.0. Introduction

Java has had windowing capabilities since its earliest days. The first version made public was the Abstract Windowing Toolkit, or AWT. Because it used the native toolkit components, AWT was relatively small and simple. It suffered somewhat from being a "least common denominator"; a feature could not be added unless it could be implemented on all major platforms that Java supported. The second major implementation was the Swing classes, released in 1998 as part of the Java Foundation Classes. Swing is a full-function, professional-quality GUI toolkit designed to enable almost any kind of client-side GUI-based interaction. AWT lives inside, or rather underneath, Swing, and, for this reason, many programs begin by importing both `java.awt` and `javax.swing`. An alternative approach is exemplified by IBM's SWT (Standard Windowing Toolkit), which is a thin wrapper for direct access to the underlying toolkit. SWT is used in building the Eclipse IDE discussed in Recipe 1.3. It's possible to build new applications using SWT, but Swing is more portable and more widely used.

This chapter presents a few elements of Java windowing for the developer whose main exposure to Java has been on the server side. Most of the examples are shown using Swing, rather than the obsolescent AWT components; SWT is not covered at all. I assume that you have at least a basic understanding of what GUI components are, which ones should be used where, and so on. I will refer to `JButton`, `JList`, and `JFrame`, to name a few, without saying much more about their basics or functionality. This is not intended to be a complete tutorial; the reader needing more background should refer to *Java in a Nutshell* or *Head First Java*. For a very thorough presentation on all aspects of Swing, I recommend *Java Swing* by Marc Loy, Bob Eckstein, Dave Wood, Jim Elliott, and Brian Cole (O'Reilly). At around 1,250 pages, it's not an overnight read, but it *is* comprehensive.

Java's event model has evolved over time, too. In the earliest releases, the writer of a windowed application had to write a single large event-handling method to deal with button presses from all the GUI controls in the window. This was adequate for small programs, but it did not scale well. The early version of my `JabaDex` contacts application had one large event-handler method that tried to figure out which of 50 or 60 GUI controls had caused an event; this was tedious and error prone. Before long, a new delegation event model was introduced, which is still with us. In this model, events are given only to classes that request them, which is done by *registering a listener*. This is discussed in Recipe 14.5 and shown in Example 14-3. At the same time, the language was extended slightly to include the notion of inner classes. An inner class is simply a class whose definition is contained inside the body of another class. We use examples of two types of inner classes here; for details on the half-dozen different categories of inner classes, the reader is referred to *Java in a Nutshell*.

Most of the GUI construction techniques in this chapter can be done for you, in some cases more quickly, by an integrated development environment (IDE). I believe, however, that understanding what goes on inside the code should be a prerequisite for being allowed to use an IDE. Those who disagree may be inclined to skip this chapter, go press a few buttons, and have the computer do the work for them. But you should at least skim this chapter to see what's going on so that you'll know where to look when you need it later.

See Also

Before you unleash your GUI application upon the world, make sure to read the official *Java Look and Feel Design Guidelines* (*http://bit.ly/1poMpke*) (Addison-Wesley). This work presents the views of a large group of human factors and user-interface experts at Sun/Oracle who have worked with the Swing GUI package since its inception; they tell you how to make it work well.

14.1. Displaying GUI Components

Problem

You want to create some GUI components and have them appear in a window.

Solution

Create a `JFrame` and add the components to its `ContentPane`.

Discussion

The older AWT had a simple `Frame` component for making main windows; this allowed you to add components directly to it. "Good" programs usually created a panel to fit inside and populate the frame. But some less-educated folk, and those in a hurry, often added components directly to the frame. The Swing `JFrame` is more complex—it comes with not one but two containers already constructed inside it. The `ContentPane` is the main container; you should normally use it as your `JFrame`'s main container. The `GlassPane` has a clear background and sits over the top of the `ContentPane`; its primary use is in temporarily painting something over the top of the main `ContentPane`. Because of this, you need to use the `JFrame`'s `getContentPane()` method:

```
public class ContentPane extends JFrame {
    public ContentPane() {
        Container cp = getContentPane();
        // now add Components to "cp"...
        cp.add(new JLabel("A Really Simple Demo", JLabel.CENTER));
    }
}
```

You can add any number of components (including containers) into this existing container, using the `ContentPane` `add()` method:

```
public class JFrameDemo extends JFrame {

    private static final long serialVersionUID = -3089466980388235513L;
    JButton quitButton;

    /** Construct the object including its GUI */
    public JFrameDemo() {
        super("JFrameDemo");
        Container cp = getContentPane();
        cp.setLayout(new FlowLayout());
        cp.add(quitButton = new JButton("Exit"));

        // Set up so that "Close" will exit the program,
        // not just close the JFrame.
        setDefaultCloseOperation(JFrame.EXIT_ON_CLOSE);

        // This "action handler" will be explained later in the chapter.
        quitButton.addActionListener(new ActionListener() {
            public void actionPerformed(ActionEvent e) {
                setVisible(false);
                dispose();
                System.exit(0);
            }
        });

        pack();
        setLocation(500, 400);
```

```
    }
    public static void main(String[] args) {
        new JFrameDemo().setVisible(true);
    }
}
```

This code compiles fine. But when we try to run it, of course, there is no main method. We need to create one, either inside the JFrameDemo class or on its own:

```
public class JFrameDemoMain {
    // We need a main program to instantiate and show.
    public static void main(String[] args) {
        new JFrameDemo( ).setVisible(true);
    }
}
```

Now we can run it and have it display. But it has two obvious problems: it starts off tiny (on Windows) or huge (on X Windows). And, when we do resize it, only the buttons show, and it always takes up the full size of the window. To solve these problems, we need to discuss layout management, to which we will soon turn our attention.

A less obvious problem has to do with thread safety, which we discuss next, in Recipe 14.2.

14.2. Run Your GUI on the Event Dispatching Thread

Problem

Your application fails to start, with a message like Running on UI thread when not expected. Or, your application crashes very sporadically.

Solution

Run your UI on the UI thread, which Java names the "Event Dispatching Thread" or EDT.

Discussion

The UI objects in Java, as in most GUI systems, are not thread-safe (see Chapter 22), meaning you are only allowed to update GUI components from within a single thread, the system-provided UI thread or "event dispatcher thread" (EDT). The first GUI component that gets created in a given JVM instance starts this GUI Thread of control running, and both this thread and your main thread could be doing things to the GUI at the same time. A Java-language "main program" does not run on this thread, thus it should not run UI updates, even seemingly simple ones such as setVisible(true). In some versions of Java, this restriction is not enforced and, like jaywalking in a big city, can usually (but not always) be gotten away with. Apple's Java is particularly prone to enforcing this, yielding the message about `Cocoa AWT: Running on AppKit thread 0` `when not expected`.

There are two classes you can use to run your GUI startup on the event thread, with the same two static methods in each. In all cases, you pass a `Runnable` into the methods, which will get run on the correct thread. `EventQueue` and `SwingUtilities` are the classes; the methods are `invokeLater()` (shown in Example 14-1) and `invokeAnd-` `Wait()` (shown in Example 14-2). The former may be called on any thread; the latter may, of course, not be called on the EDT because it would result in the EDT thread waiting for itself, which never ends well. The code to start the GUI in a thread-safe way is only a few lines longer than calling it directly from main, but makes for a more reliable application.

Example 14-1. Run on EDT via EventQueue.invokeLater

```
public class JFrameDemoSafe {
    // We need a main program to instantiate and show.
    public static void main(String[] args) {

        // Create the GUI (variable is final because used by inner class).
        final JFrame demo = new JFrameDemo();

        // Create a Runnable to set the main visible, and get Swing to invoke.
        EventQueue.invokeLater(new Runnable() {
            public void run() {
                demo.setVisible(true);
            }
        });
    }
}
```

Example 14-2. Run on EDT via SwingUtilities.invoke

```
public class RunOnEdt {
    public static void main(String[] args) throws Exception {
        System.out.println("RunOnEdt.main()");
        SwingUtilities.invokeLater(new Runnable() {
            public void run() {
                try {
                    JOptionPane.showMessageDialog(null, "Hello Java");
                } catch (Exception e) {
                    e.printStackTrace();
                }
            }
        });
    }
}
```

Some books and articles on Swing GUIs do not mention Swing's thread-safety issues, but you can read about it on Oracle's Java website (*http://bit.ly/1fu2QTp*). *We will omit this code for brevity from most of the simple demos herein*, but production code should use it.

14.3. Designing a Window Layout

Problem

The default layout isn't good enough.

Solution

Learn to deal with a layout manager.

Discussion

The container classes such as `Panel` have the capability to contain a series of components, but you can arrange components in a window in many ways. Rather than clutter up each container with a variety of different layout computations, the designers of the Java API used a sensible design pattern to divide the labor. A layout manager is an object that performs the layout computations for a container.[1] The AWT package has five common layout manager classes (see Table 14-1), and Swing has a few more. Plus, as we'll see in Recipe 14.21, it's not that big a deal to write your own!

Table 14-1. Layout managers

Name	Notes	Default on
FlowLayout	Flows across the container	(J)Panel, (J)Applet
BorderLayout	Five "geographic" regions	(J)Frame, (J)Window
GridLayout	Regular grid (all items same size)	None
CardLayout	Display one of many components at a time; useful for wizard-style layouts	None
GridBagLayout	Very flexible but maximally complex	None
BoxLayout (Swing)	Single row or column of components	None

Because we've broached the subject of layout management, I should mention that each component has a method called `getPreferredSize()`, which the layout managers use in deciding how and where to place components. A well-behaved component overrides this method to return something meaningful. A button or label, for example, will indicate that it wishes to be large enough to contain its text and/or icon, plus a bit of space

---

1. The `LayoutManager` specification is actually a Java interface rather than a class. In fact, it's two interfaces: quoting the code, interface `LayoutManager2` extends `LayoutManager`. The differences between these two interfaces don't concern us here; we want to concentrate on using the layout managers.

for padding. And, if your JFrame is full of well-behaved components, you can set its size to be "just the size of all included components, plus a bit for padding," just by calling the pack() method, which takes no arguments. The pack() method goes around and asks each embedded component for its preferred size (and any nested container's get-PreferredSize() will ask each of its components, and so on). The JFrame is then set to the best size to give the components their preferred sizes as much as is possible. If not using pack(), you need to call the setSize() method, which requires either a width and a height, or a Dimension object containing this information.

A FlowLayout is the default in JPanel and Applet/JApplet. It simply lays the components out along the "normal" axis (left to right in European and English-speaking locales, right to left in Hebrew or Arabic locales, and so on, as set by the user's Locale settings). The overall collection of them is centered within the window.

The default for JFrame and JWindow is BorderLayout. This explains the problem of the single button appearing in the JFrameDemo class at the end of the previous recipe. BorderLayout divides the screen into the five areas shown in Figure 14-1. If you don't specify where to place a component, it goes into the center. And if you place multiple components in the same region (perhaps by adding several components without specifying where to place them!), only the last one appears.

Figure 14-1. BorderLayout's five regions

So we can fix the previous version of the JFrameDemo in one of two ways: either we can use a FlowLayout or specify BorderLayout regions for the label and the button. The former being simpler, we'll try it out:

```
public class JFrameFlowLayout extends JFrame {
    public JFrameFlowLayout() {
        Container cp = getContentPane();

        // Make sure it has a FlowLayout layoutmanager.
        cp.setLayout(new FlowLayout());

        // now add Components to "cp"...
        cp.add(new JLabel("Wonderful?"));
```

```
        cp.add(new JButton("Yes!"));
        pack();
    }

    // We need a main program to instantiate and show.
    public static void main(String[] args) {
        new JFrameFlowLayout().setVisible(true);
    }
}
```

See Also

I have not discussed the details of the advanced layouts. For an example of a dialog layout using nested panels, see the Font Chooser in Recipe 14.20. For an example of a GridBagLayout, see the file *graphics/GfxDemo2.java* in my *javasrc* collection. For more details, see the Layout Tutorial (*http://bit.ly/1lJqyPq*).

14.4. A Tabbed View of Life

Problem

These layouts don't include a tab layout, and you need one.

Solution

Use a JTabbedPane.

Discussion

The JTabbedPane class acts as a combined container and layout manager. It implements a conventional tab layout, which looks like Figure 14-2.

Figure 14-2. JTabbedPane: two views in Java Look and one in Windows Look

To add a tab to the layout, you do not use setLayout(). You simply create the JTabbedPane and call its addTab() method, passing in a String and a Component; you usually need to add JPanels or some similar Container to make a sophisticated layout. Example 14-3 is the code for our simple program.

Example 14-3. TabPaneDemo.java

```java
public class TabPaneDemo {
    protected JTabbedPane tabPane;
    public TabPaneDemo() {
        tabPane = new JTabbedPane();
        tabPane.add(new JLabel("One", JLabel.CENTER), "First");
        tabPane.add(new JLabel("Two", JLabel.CENTER), "Second");
    }

    public static void main(String[] a) {
        JFrame f = new JFrame("Tab Demo");
        f.getContentPane().add(new TabPaneDemo().tabPane);
        f.setSize(120, 100);
        f.setVisible(true);
    }
}
```

See Also

The third screenshot in Figure 14-2 shows the program with a Windows look and feel, instead of the default Java look and feel. See Recipe 14.17 for how to change the look and feel of a Swing-based GUI application.

14.5. Action Handling: Making Buttons Work

Problem

Your button doesn't do anything when the user presses it.

Solution

Add an ActionListener to do the work.

Discussion

Event listeners come in about half a dozen different types. The most common is the ActionListener, used by push buttons, text fields, and certain other components to indicate that the user has performed a high-level action, such as activating a push button or pressing Enter in a text field. The paradigm (shown in Figure 14-3) is that you create a Listener object, register it with the event source (such as the push button), and wait. Later, when and if the user pushes the button, the button will call your Listener.

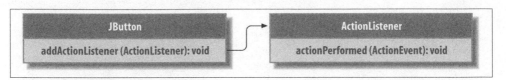

Figure 14-3. AWT listener relationships

Here's some simple code in which pushing a button causes the program to print a friendly message:

```
/** Demonstrate simple use of Button */
public class ButtonDemo extends JFrame implements ActionListener {
    JButton    b1;

    public ButtonDemo() {
        setLayout(new FlowLayout());
        add(b1 = new JButton("A button"));
        b1.addActionListener(this);
        setSize(300, 200);
    }

    public void actionPerformed(ActionEvent event) {
        System.out.println("Thanks for pushing my button!");
    }

    public static void main(String[] unuxed) {
        new ButtonDemo().setVisible(true);
    }
}
```

This version does not use an inner class to handle the events but does so itself by directly implementing the `ActionListener` interface. This works for small programs, but as an application grows, it quickly becomes unserviceable; how do you sort out which button was pressed? To solve this problem, we normally use an inner class as the action handler and have a different class for each button, or at least for each related set of actions. First, let's write the previous code with two buttons so that you can see what I mean:

```
public class ButtonDemo2a extends Applet implements ActionListener {
    Button b1, b2;

    public void init() {
        add(b1 = new Button("A button"));
        b1.addActionListener(this);

        add(b2 = new Button("Another button"));
        b2.addActionListener(this);
    }

    public void actionPerformed(ActionEvent e) {
        if (e.getSource() == b1)
```

```
        showStatus("Thanks for pushing my first button!");
    else
        showStatus("Thanks for pushing my second button!");
    }
}
```

Now here is the same program written using a *member inner class*—that is, a class that is a named part of its containing class:

```
public class ButtonDemo2b extends Applet {
    Button b1, b2;
    ActionListener handler = new ButtonHandler();

    public void init() {
        add(b1 = new Button("A button"));
        b1.addActionListener(handler);

        add(b2 = new Button("Another button"));
        b2.addActionListener(handler);
    }

    class ButtonHandler implements ActionListener {
        public void actionPerformed(ActionEvent e) {
            if (e.getSource() == b1)
                showStatus("Thanks for pushing my first button!");
            else
                showStatus("Thanks for pushing my second button!");
        }
    }
}
```

Note that merely breaking the action handling code into its own class doesn't really contribute much to readability. But there is a way to use inner classes that does promote readability and maintainability. We create an inner class (see Recipe 8.4) for each event source—each button, each menu item, and so on. Sounds like a lot of work, and it would be, if you used the previous method. But there is a shorter way, using anonymous inner classes, described next.

14.6. Action Handling Using Anonymous Inner Classes

Problem

You want action handling with less creation of special classes.

Solution

Use anonymous inner classes.

Discussion

Anonymous inner classes are declared and instantiated at the same time, using the new operator with the name of an existing class or interface. If you name a class, it will be subclassed; if you name an interface, the anonymous class will extend `java.lang.Object` and implement the named interface. The paradigm is:

```
b.addActionListener(new ActionListener( ) {
    public void actionPerformed(ActionEvent e) {
        showStatus("Thanks for pushing my second button!");
        }
});
```

Did you notice the `});` by itself on the last line? Good, because it's important. The `}` terminates the definition of the inner class, while the `)` ends the argument list to the `addActionListener` method; the single argument inside the parenthesis is an argument of type `ActionListener` that refers to the one and only instance created of your anonymous class. Example 14-4 contains a complete example.

Example 14-4. ButtonDemo2c.java

```
public class ButtonDemo2c extends Applet {
    Button     b;

    public void init() {
        add(b = new Button("A button"));
        b.addActionListener(new ActionListener() {
            public void actionPerformed(ActionEvent e) {
                showStatus("Thanks for pushing my first button!");
            }
        });
        add(b = new Button("Another button"));
        b.addActionListener(new ActionListener() {
            public void actionPerformed(ActionEvent e) {
                showStatus("Thanks for pushing my second button!");
            }
        });
    }
}
```

The real benefit of these anonymous inner classes, by the way, is that they keep the action handling code in the same place that the GUI control is being instantiated. This saves a lot of looking back and forth to see what a GUI control really does.

Those `ActionListener` objects have no instance name and appear to have no class name: is that possible? The former yes, but not the latter. In fact, class names are assigned to anonymous inner classes by the compiler. After compiling and testing `ButtonDemo2c`, I list the directory in which I ran the program:

```
C:\javasrc\gui>ls -1 ButtonDemo2c*
ButtonDemo2c$1.class
ButtonDemo2c$2.class
ButtonDemo2c.class
ButtonDemo2c.htm
ButtonDemo2c.java
C:\javasrc\gui>
```

Those first two are the anonymous inner classes. Note that a different compiler might assign different names to them; it doesn't matter to us. A word to the wise: don't depend on those names!

See Also

Most IDEs (see Recipe 1.1) have drag-and-drop GUI builder tools that make this task easier, at least for simpler projects.

14.7. Action Handling Using Lambdas

Problem

You want to use Java 8's lambda expressions to simplify GUI programming.

Solution

Write the lambda expression as the argument to, for example, `JComponent.addAction-Listener()`.

Discussion

The most common event method in Swing is JComponent's `addActionListener()` method. Because `ActionListener` is a functional method, as defined in Chapter 9, it can be used directly with lambda expressions:

```
/** Demonstrate a JButton with Lambda Action Listeners */
public class ButtonDemo2L extends JFrame {

    private static final long serialVersionUID = 1L;

    public ButtonDemo2L() {
        super("ButtonDemo Lambda");
        setDefaultCloseOperation(JFrame.EXIT_ON_CLOSE);
```

```
        setLayout(new FlowLayout());
        JButton    b;
        add(b = new JButton("A button"));
        // Minimalist style
        b.addActionListener(e -> JOptionPane.showMessageDialog(this,
            "Thanks for pushing my first button!"));

        add(b = new JButton("Another button"));
        // Longer style, with { } around body.
        b.addActionListener(e -> {
            JOptionPane.showMessageDialog(this,
                    "Thanks for pushing my second button!");
            }
        );

        pack();
    }

    public static void main(String[] args) {
        new ButtonDemo2L().setVisible(true);
    }
}
```

14.8. Terminating a Program with "Window Close"

Problem

Nothing happens when you click the close button on the title bar of an AWT `Frame`. When you do this on a Swing `JFrame`, the window disappears but the application does not exit.

Solution

Use `JFrame`'s `setDefaultCloseOperation()` method or add a `WindowListener` and have it exit the application.

Discussion

Main windows (subclasses of `java.awt.Window`, such as `(J)Frames` and `(J)Dialogs`) are treated specially. Unlike all other `Component` subclasses, `Window` and its subclasses are not initially visible. This is sensible because they have to be packed or resized, and you don't want the user to watch the components getting rearranged. Once you call a `Window`'s `setVisible(true)` method, all components inside it become visible. You can listen for `WindowEvents` on a `Window`.

The `WindowListener` interface contains a plenitude of methods to notify a listener when anything happens to the window. You can be told when the window is activated (gets keyboard and mouse events) or deactivated. Or you can find out when the window is iconified or deiconified: these are good times to suspend and resume processing, respectively. You can be notified the first time the window is opened. And, most importantly for us, you can be notified when the user requests that the window be closed. (Some sample close buttons are shown in Figure 14-4.) You can respond in two ways. With Swing's JFrame, you can set the "default close operation." Alternatively, with any Window subclass, you can provide a WindowListener to be notified of window events.

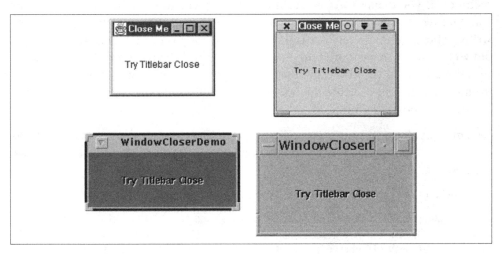

Figure 14-4. Some close buttons

In some cases, you may not need a window closer. The Swing JFrame has a setDefaultCloseOperation() method, which controls the default behavior. You can pass it one of the values defined in the Swing WindowConstants class:

WindowConstants.DO_NOTHING_ON_CLOSE
: Ignore the request. The window stays open. Useful for critical dialogs; probably antisocial for most "main application"–type windows.

WindowConstants.HIDE_ON_CLOSE
: Hide the window (default).

WindowConstants.DISPOSE_ON_CLOSE
: Hide and dispose the window.

WindowConstants.EXIT_ON_CLOSE
: Exit the application on close, obviating the need for a WindowListener! Does not give you a chance to save data; for that, you need a WindowListener.

The action set by setDefaultCloseOperation() will be performed after the last windowClosing() method on the Window (if you have one) returns.

The windowClosing() method of your WindowListener is called when the user clicks the close button (this depends on the window system and, on X Windows, on the window manager) or sends the close message from the keyboard (normally Alt-F4).

The method signature is:

```
public void windowClosing(WindowEvent);
```

But this method comes from the interface WindowListener, which has half a dozen other methods. If you define a WindowListener and implement only this one method, the compiler declares your class abstract and refuses to instantiate it. You might start by writing stub or dummy versions (methods whose body is just the two characters {}), but you'd then be doing more work than necessary; an "adapter" class already does this for all methods in the Listener interface. So you really need only to subclass from WindowAdapter and override the one method, windowClosing, that you care about. Figure 14-5 shows this model.

Let's put this all together in some code examples. Class WindowDemo2 puts up a JFrame and closes when you ask it to. The online source includes the older AWT Frame-based WindowDemo.

```
public class WindowDemo2 extends JFrame {

    public static void main(String[] argv) {
        JFrame f = new WindowDemo2();
        f.setVisible(true);
    }
    public WindowDemo2() {
        setSize(200, 100);
        setDefaultCloseOperation(WindowConstants.DO_NOTHING_ON_CLOSE);
        addWindowListener(new WindowDemoAdapter());
    }

    /** Named Inner class that closes a Window. */
    class WindowDemoAdapter extends WindowAdapter {
        public void windowClosing(WindowEvent e) {
            // whimsy - close randomly, ~ 1 times in 3
            if (Math.random() > 0.666) {
                System.out.println("Goodbye!");
                WindowDemo2.this.setVisible(false);    // window will close
                WindowDemo2.this.dispose();        // and be freed up.
                System.exit(0);
            }
            System.out.println("You asked me to close, but not to I chose.");
        }
    }
}
```

Because making a Window close—and optionally exit the program—is a common operation, I've encapsulated this into a small class called WindowCloser, which is in my

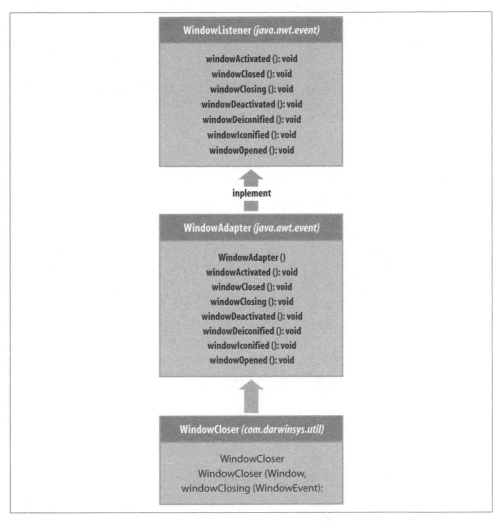

WindowListener *(java.awt.event)*

windowActivated (): void
windowClosed (): void
windowClosing (): void
windowDeactivated (): void
windowDeiconified (): void
windowIconified (): void
windowOpened (): void

inplement

WindowAdapter *(java.awt.event)*

WindowAdapter ()
windowActivated (): void
windowClosed (): void
windowClosing (): void
windowDeactivated (): void
windowDeiconified (): void
windowIconified (): void
windowOpened (): void

WindowCloser *(com.darwinsys.util)*

WindowCloser
WindowCloser (Window,
windowClosing (WindowEvent):

Figure 14-5. WindowListener, WindowAdapter, and my WindowCloser

public package `com.darwinsys.util`. Most AWT and Swing books have similar classes. Example 14-5 contains my `WindowCloser` class. Note that the class is marked deprecated; this serves as a reminder that, on Swing, you should just use `setDefaultCloseOperation()`. If you're writing an AWT-only application, you'll have to live with the deprecation warning.

Example 14-5. WindowCloser.java

```
package com.darwinsys.swingui;

import java.awt.Window;
```

```
import java.awt.event.WindowAdapter;
import java.awt.event.WindowEvent;

/** A WindowCloser - watch for Window Closing events, and
 * follow them up with setVisible(false), dispose(), and optionally
 * ends (it all) with a System.exit(0).
 * @deprecated For simple closing, just use JFrame.setDefaultCloseOperation().
 */
public class WindowCloser extends WindowAdapter {

    /** The window we are to close */
    Window win;

    /** True if we are to exit as well. */
    boolean doExit = false;

    /** Construct a WindowCloser that doesn't exit, just closes the window */
    public WindowCloser(Window w) {
        this(w, false);
    }

    /** Construct a WindowCloser with control over whether it exits */
    public WindowCloser(Window w, boolean exit) {
        win = w;
        doExit = exit;
    }

    /** Called by AWT when the user tries to close the window */
    public void windowClosing(WindowEvent e) {
        win.setVisible(false);
        win.dispose();
        if (doExit)
            System.exit(0);
    }
}
```

Using it is straightforward:

```
package com.darwinsys.swingui;

import java.awt.Frame;
import java.awt.Label;
import com.darwinsys.swingui.WindowCloser;

/* Example of closing a Window. */
public class WindowCloserDemo {

    /* Main method */
    public static void main(String[] argv) {
        Frame f = new Frame("Close Me");
        f.add(new Label("Try Titlebar Close", Label.CENTER));
        f.setSize(100, 100);
        f.setVisible(true);
```

```
        f.addWindowListener(new WindowCloser(f, true));
    }
}
```

Notice that some of this "quick and dirty" class extends Frame or JFrame directly. It is generally better to have a main program that creates a JFrame and installs the "main" GUI component into that. This scheme promotes greater reusability. For example, if your graphing program's main component extends JComponent, it can be added to a JPanel in another application; whereas if it extends JFrame, it cannot.

See Also

I've mentioned dispose() several times without saying much about it. Inherited from Window, the dispose() method causes the underlying (operating system–specific) window system resources to be released without totally destroying the Window. If you later call pack() or setVisible(true) on the Window, the native resources are re-created. It's a good idea to dispose() a window if you won't be using it for a while, but not if there's a good chance you'll need it again soon.

In addition to WindowListener, Swing has several other multimethod interfaces, including MouseListener and ComponentListener, and an Adapter class for each of these.

14.9. Dialogs: When Later Just Won't Do

Problem

You need a bit of feedback from the user *right now*.

Solution

Use a JOptionPane method to show a prebuilt dialog. Or subclass JDialog.

Discussion

It's fairly common to want to confirm an action with the user or to bring some problem to her attention right away, rather than waiting for her to read a logfile that she might or might not get around to. These pop-up windows are called dialogs. The JOption-Pane class has a number of show…Dialog() methods that let you display several commonly used dialogs, including those shown in Figure 14-6.

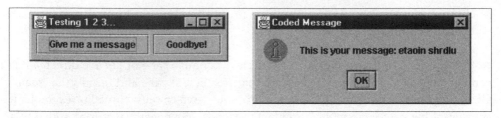

Figure 14-6. JOptionPane in action

The simplest form is showMessageDialog( ), and its first argument is the owning Frame or JFrame. If you don't know it, pass null, but Java doesn't guarantee to give input focus back to your main window when the dialog is dismissed. The second argument is the message text, and the third is the title bar title. Last but not least is code telling which of several prebuilt bitmaps should be displayed. This program produces the "Coded Message" dialog in the figure:

```java
public class JOptionDemo extends JFrame {

    private static final long serialVersionUID = 1L;

    private ResourceBundle rb;

    // Constructor
    JOptionDemo(String s) {
        super(s);

        Container cp = getContentPane();
        cp.setLayout(new FlowLayout());

        rb = ResourceBundle.getBundle("Widgets");

        JButton b = I18N.mkButton(rb, "getButton");
        b.addActionListener(new ActionListener() {
            public void actionPerformed(ActionEvent e) {
                JOptionPane.showMessageDialog(
                    JOptionDemo.this,
                    rb.getString("dialog1.text"),
                    rb.getString("dialog1.title"),
                    JOptionPane.INFORMATION_MESSAGE);
            }
        });
        cp.add(b);

        b = I18N.mkButton(rb, "goodbye");
        b.addActionListener(new ActionListener() {
            public void actionPerformed(ActionEvent e) {
                System.exit(0);
            }
        });
```

```
        cp.add(b);

        // the main window
        setSize(200, 150);
        pack();
    }

    public static void main(String[] arg) {
        JOptionDemo x = new JOptionDemo("Testing 1 2 3...");
        x.setVisible(true);
    }
}
```

You can use the JOptionPane class in several other ways. For example, you can call its showDialog() method with a list of strings; each is displayed on a push button in the dialog. This method blocks until the user selects one of the buttons; the return value of the method is an int telling which button the user clicked (it returns the array index of the string whose button was pressed). Another method, showInputDialog(), lets you prompt the user for a data value. Very, very convenient!

See Also

JDialog lets you write arbitrarily complicated dialogs. You subclass them in a manner similar to JFrame, specifying whether you want an application-modal or nonmodal dialog (a modal dialog locks out the rest of the application, which is less convenient for the user but much easier for the programmer). See *Java Swing* (O'Reilly) for information on JDialog.

14.10. Catching and Formatting GUI Exceptions

Problem

Your application code is throwing an exception, and you want to catch it, but the GUI runs in a different Thread (see Chapter 22), so you can't.

Solution

Use setDefaultUncaughtExceptionHandler().

Discussion

In days of yore, we had to use an unsupported feature for this! Now we use the Thread method setDefaultUncaughtExceptionHandler(), whose signature is:

```
public static void setDefaultUncaughtExceptionHandler(
    Thread.UncaughtExceptionHandler handler);
```

The code in Example 14-6 shows a tiny demonstration of this technique.

Example 14-6. ThreadBasedCatcher.java

```
[filename="src/main/java/gui/ThreadBasedCatcher.java", language="java", identifier="main"]
snippet~~~~
ERROR: Failed to load src/main/java/gui/ThreadBasedCatcher.java
snippet~~~~
```

Figure 14-7 shows the program running; pushing the button produced this output:

```
You crashed thread AWT-EventQueue-0
Exception was: java..lang.RuntimeException: You asked for it.
```

Figure 14-7. ThreadBasedCatcher running

To display the caught exceptions, you may want to show each one in a dialog. My API class `com.darwinsys.swingui.ErrorUtil` contains a method:

```
public static void showExceptions(Component parent, Throwable t)
```

The online version of ThreadBasedCatcher (Recipe 14.6) uses `showExceptions()`, but was omitted from the book to keep the code clearer. This method displays the `Throwable` (and, if applicable, any nested exceptions) in an error dialog:

```
/**
 * Show the given Exception (and any nested Exceptions) in JOptionPane(s).
 */
public static void showExceptions(Component parent, Throwable theExc) {

    Throwable next = null;

    do {
        String className = theExc.getClass().getName();
        String message = className;

        if (theExc instanceof SQLException) {
            SQLException sexc = (SQLException)theExc;
            message += "; code=" + sexc.getErrorCode();
            next = sexc.getNextException();
        } else {
            next = theExc.getCause();    // Comment out if < JDK 1.4
        }

        String[] choices = next != null ? choicesMore : choicesNoMore;

        /* Show the Dialog! */
```

```
            int response = JOptionPane.showOptionDialog(
                parent,
                message,
                className,                           // title
                JOptionPane.YES_NO_CANCEL_OPTION,    // icontType
                JOptionPane.ERROR_MESSAGE,           // messageType
                null,                                // icon
                choices,                             // options
                choices[0]                           // default
                );

        if (response == 0)          // "OK"
            return;
        if (response == 1) {        // "Details"
            // show ANOTHER JDialog with a JTextArea of printStackTrace();
            if (detailsDialog == null) // first time, lazy creation
                detailsDialog = new DetailsDialog((JFrame)parent);
            detailsDialog.showStackTrace(theExc);
        }
        // else resp = 2, "Next", let it fall through:

        theExc = next;

    } while (next != null);
}

/** JDialog class to display the details of an Exception */
protected static class DetailsDialog extends JDialog {

    private static final long serialVersionUID = -4779441441693785664L;
    JButton ok;
    JTextArea text;
    /** Construct a DetailsDialog given a parent (Frame/JFrame) */
    DetailsDialog(JFrame parent) {
        super(parent);
        Container cp = getContentPane();
        text = new JTextArea(40, 40);
        cp.add(text, BorderLayout.CENTER);
        ok = new JButton("Close");
        cp.add(ok, BorderLayout.SOUTH);
        ok.addActionListener(new ActionListener() {
            public void actionPerformed(ActionEvent evt) {
                dispose();
            }
        });
        pack();
    }

    /** Display the stackTrace from the given Throwable in this Dialog. */
    void showStackTrace(Throwable exc) {
        CharArrayWriter buff = new CharArrayWriter();
        PrintWriter pw = new PrintWriter(buff);
```

```
            exc.printStackTrace(pw);
            pw.close();
            text.setText(buff.toString());
            setVisible(true);
        }
    }
```

See the program ErrorUtilTest in the *darwinsys/src/test/java* directory for an example of running this program directly, and see ErrorUtilCatchTest in the same directory for an example of using it with uncaught exceptions from the GUI thread as described.

14.11. Getting Program Output into a Window

Problem

You want to capture an input/output stream and display it in a text field.

Solution

The easy way is to subclass OutputStream or Writer as appropriate, and override just the methods needed to get characters copied into the JTextArea. You may also want to redirect System.out and System.err to the stream; see "Discussion".

Discussion

This is such a common need that I've added it to the DarwinSys package (see Recipe 1.5). Here is the code for com.darwinsys.io.TextAreaWriter:

```
package com.darwinsys.io;

import java.io.IOException;
import java.io.Writer;

import javax.swing.JTextArea;

/**
 * Simple way to "print" to a JTextArea; just say
 * PrintWriter out = new PrintWriter(new TextAreaWriter(myTextArea));
 * Then out.println() et all will all appear in the TextArea.
 */
public final class TextAreaWriter extends Writer {

    private final JTextArea textArea;

    public TextAreaWriter(final JTextArea textArea) {
        this.textArea = textArea;
    }

    @Override
```

```
        public void flush(){ }

        @Override
        public void close(){ }

        @Override
        public void write(char[] cbuf, int off, int len) throws IOException {
            textArea.append(new String(cbuf, off, len));
        }
    }
```

As you can see, for the `Writer` case I only had to override one `write()` form; all the
other forms of `write()`, and the `print()`/`println()` methods in `PrintWriter`, call
down through this one method. The `flush()` and `close()` methods are also abstract in
`Writer`, but they don't have to do anything here (though `close()` could set the `tex-
tArea` field to `null`, and `write()` could check that, to guard against use of a closed
`Writer`).

As I may have said in Recipe 1.13, no code is complete until it has a working test. Here
is the JUnit test for `TextAreaWriter`:

```
public class TextAreaWriterTest extends TestCase {

    private static final String HELLO_WORLD = "Hello World";

    JTextArea ta = new JTextArea();

    public void testOne() {
        PrintWriter x = new PrintWriter(new TextAreaWriter(ta));
        x.print("Hello");
        x.print(' ');
        x.print("World");
        x.close();
        assertEquals(HELLO_WORLD, ta.getText());
    }
}
```

Note that my test creates a visual component but never uses it in a GUI. Because this is
the first time we've seen this technique, it's worth mentioning that it is acceptable (on
all platforms I've tried it) to have a JUnit test that creates a `Component` subclass without
setting it visible, if you only want to test methods that don't depend on actual graphics
being displayed, as we're doing here. On Mac OS X, this may cause a brief delay because
it creates a "running Java program" icon, but it seems otherwise harmless.

The `OutputStream` case is just a tiny bit more involved, but worth doing so we can reuse legacy code that writes to `System.out`. Here is `TextAreaOutputStream`:

```
package com.darwinsys.io;

import java.io.IOException;
```

```java
import java.io.OutputStream;

import javax.swing.JTextArea;

/**
 * Simple way to "print" to a JTextArea; just say
 * PrintStream out = new PrintStream(new TextAreaOutputStream(myTextArea));
 * Then out.println() et all will all appear in the TextArea.
 */
public final class TextAreaOutputStream extends OutputStream {

    private final JTextArea textArea;
    private final StringBuilder sb = new StringBuilder();

    public TextAreaOutputStream(final JTextArea textArea) {
        this.textArea = textArea;
    }

    @Override
    public void flush(){ }

    @Override
    public void close(){ }

    @Override
    public void write(int b) throws IOException {

        if (b == '\r')
            return;

        if (b == '\n') {
            textArea.append(sb.toString());
            sb.setLength(0);
        }

        sb.append((char)b);
    }
}
```

As with Writer, we only really need to override three methods; all the others (e.g.,
System.out.println()) ultimately call down to this write(int) method. The class
shown here uses a StringBuffer to build up a line of text and, when a line ending comes
along, appends the line to the JTextArea and resets the StringBuffer. A \r is ignored
because on UNIX a \n alone ends a line and on MS-DOS-based systems a \r\n ends a
line.

It's not reprinted here, but there is a JUnit test for this class as well. One of the tests is
similar to the one for TextAreaWriter, and the second uses System.setOut() followed
by System.out.println() to ensure that everything works as expected. It does.

Here's a longer example of using this. I have an existing console-based `CheckOpenMail-Relay` program (derived from the mail sender in Recipe 17.2), that I use to test whether remote servers are willing to accept mail from unknown third parties and forward it as their own. Figure 14-8 is the GUI for that program; both this and the main program are online in the email directory. Using the `JTextAreaWriter`, I was able to add a GUI wrapper to `CheckOpenMailRelay`, such that console output appears in a window, without having to change the code to know about `JTextArea`.

In the constructor of the GUI wrapper, I create a `JTextArea` and wrap it in a `TextAreaWriter` and then a `PrintWriter`. I pass this `PrintWriter` to the console program `CheckOpenMailRelay.process()` method. That method writes its output to the stream in addition to assigning standard output and standard error, so we should see anything it tries to print. Figure 14-8 shows three windows: the program output window (the goal of this whole exercise), a terminal window from which I copied the IP address (some parts of the text in this window have been deliberately obfuscated), and another command window in which I started the GUI program running. The code is shown in Example 14-7.

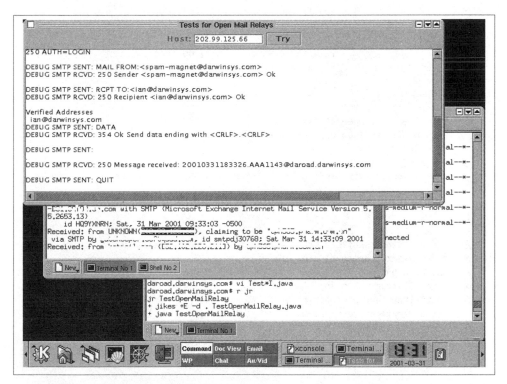

Figure 14-8. CheckOpenMailRelayGui in action

Example 14-7. CheckOpenMailRelayGui.java

```java
/**
 * GUI for TestOpenMailRelay, lets you run it multiple times in one JVM
 * Starts each invocation in its own Thread for faster return to ready state.
 * Uses TextAreaWriter to capture program into a window.
 */
public final class CheckOpenMailRelayGui extends JFrame {

    private static final long serialVersionUID = 1L;
    private static CheckOpenMailRelayGui gui;

    public static void main(String unused[]) throws Exception {
        Thread.setDefaultUncaughtExceptionHandler(
                new Thread.UncaughtExceptionHandler() {
                    public void uncaughtException(Thread t, final Throwable ex) {
                        try {
                            SwingUtilities.invokeAndWait(new Runnable() {
                                public void run() {
                                    ErrorUtil.showExceptions(gui, ex);
                                }
                            });
                        } catch (InvocationTargetException |
                            InterruptedException e) {

                            // Nothing we can really do here...
                            System.err.println("Sob! We failed: " + e);
                        }
                    }
                });
        gui = new CheckOpenMailRelayGui();
        SwingUtilities.invokeLater(new Runnable() {
            @Override
            public void run() {
                gui.setVisible(true);    // Can't do this on any non-EDT thread
            }
        });
    }


    /** The one-line textfield for the user to type Host name/IP */
    protected JTextField hostTextField;
    /** The push button to start a test; a field so can disable/enable it. */
    protected JButton goButton;
    /** Multi-line text area for results. */
    protected JTextArea results;
    /** The piped stream for the main class to write into "results" */
    protected PrintStream out;
    /** The piped stream to read from "ps" into "results" */
    protected BufferedReader iis;

    /** This inner class is the action handler both for pressing
     * the "Try" button and also for pressing <ENTER> in the text
     * field. It gets the IP name/address from the text field
```

```
 * and passes it to process() in the main class. Run in the
 * GUI Dispatch thread to avoid messing the GUI. -- tmurtagh.
 */
final ActionListener runner;
/** Construct a GUI and some I/O plumbing to get the output
 * of "TestOpenMailRelay" into the "results" textfield.
 */
public CheckOpenMailRelayGui() throws IOException {
    super("Tests for Open Mail Relays");

    runner = new ActionListener() {
        public void actionPerformed(ActionEvent evt) {
            goButton.setEnabled(false);
            SwingUtilities.invokeLater(new Runnable() {
                public void run() {
                    String host = hostTextField.getText().trim();
                    out.println("Trying " + host);
                    CheckOpenMailRelay.process(host, out);
                    goButton.setEnabled(true);
                }
            });
        }
    };

    JPanel p;
    Container cp = getContentPane();
    cp.add(BorderLayout.NORTH, p = new JPanel());

    // The entry label and text field.
    p.add(new JLabel("Host:"));
    p.add(hostTextField = new JTextField(10));
    hostTextField.addActionListener(runner);

    p.add(goButton = new JButton("Try"));
    goButton.addActionListener(runner);

    JButton cb;
    p.add(cb = new JButton("Clear Log"));
    cb.addActionListener(new ActionListener() {
        public void actionPerformed(ActionEvent evt) {
            results.setText("");
        }
    });
    JButton sb;
    p.add(sb = new JButton("Save Log"));
    sb.setEnabled(false);

    results = new JTextArea(20, 60);

    // Add the text area to the main part of the window (CENTER).
    // Wrap it in a JScrollPane to make it scroll automatically.
    cp.add(BorderLayout.CENTER, new JScrollPane(results));
```

```
        setDefaultCloseOperation(JFrame.EXIT_ON_CLOSE);

        pack();            // end of GUI portion

        out = new PrintStream(new TextAreaOutputStream(results));
    }
}
```

14.12. Choosing a Value with JSpinner

Problem

You want to let the user choose from a fixed set of values, but do not want to use a JList
or JComboBox because they take up too much "screen real estate."

Solution

Use a JSpinner.

Discussion

The JSpinner class lets the user click up or down to cycle through a set of values. The
values can be of any type because they are managed by a helper of type SpinnerModel
and displayed by another helper of type SpinnerEditor. A series of predefined Spin-
nerModels handle Numbers, Dates, and Lists (which can be arrays or Collections). A
demonstration program is listed in Example 14-8; its output is shown in Figure 14-9.

Example 14-8. SpinnerDemo.java

```java
public class SpinnerDemo {

    public static void main(String[] args) {
        JFrame jf = new JFrame("It Spins");
        Container cp = jf.getContentPane();
        cp.setLayout(new GridLayout(0,1));

        // Create a JSpinner using one of the pre-defined SpinnerModels
        JSpinner dates = new JSpinner(new SpinnerDateModel());
        cp.add(dates);

        // Create a JSpinner using a SpinnerListModel.
        String[] data = { "One", "Two", "Three" };
        JSpinner js = new JSpinner(new SpinnerListModel(data));
        cp.add(js);

        jf.setSize(100, 80);
        jf.setVisible(true);
```

```
    }
}
```

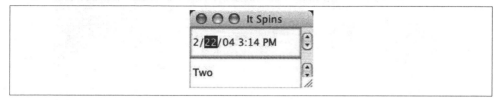

Figure 14-9. SpinnerDemo output

JSpinner's editors are reasonably clever. For example, if you select the leading zero of a number (such as the 04 in 2004), and try to increment it, the editor updates the entire number (04 to 05) rather than producing something silly like 15.

See Also

The earlier Swing classes JList and JComboBox also let you choose among values.

14.13. Choosing a File with JFileChooser

Problem

You want to allow the user to select a file by name using a traditional windowed file dialog.

Solution

Use a JFileChooser.

Discussion

The JFileChooser dialog provides a fairly standard file chooser. It has elements of both a Windows chooser and a Mac chooser, with more resemblance to the former than the latter. If you want to have control over which files appear, you need to provide one or more FileFilter subclasses. Each FileFilter subclass instance passed into the JFileChooser's addChoosableFileFilter() method becomes a selection in the chooser's Files of Type: choice. The default is All Files (.). Figure 14-10 shows my demo program in action.

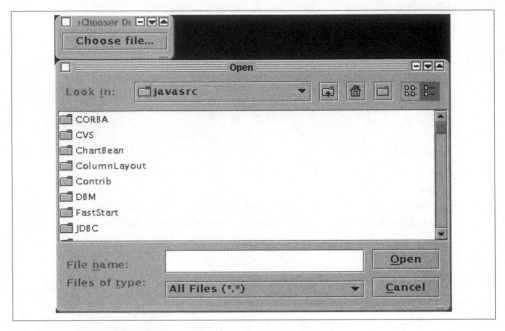

Figure 14-10. JFileChooserDemo in action

Let's look at the code for using `JFileChooser`:

```
public class JFileChooserDemo extends JPanel {

    private static final long serialVersionUID = 2615629432967419176L;

    /** Constructor */
    public JFileChooserDemo(JFrame f) {
        final JFrame frame = f;
        final JFileChooser chooser = new JFileChooser();

        // If you want the user to select only directories, use this.
        // Default is to allow selection of files only.
        // Note if you set the selection mode to DIRECTORIES_ONLY,
        // it no longer displays any files, even with the file view.

        // chooser.setFileSelectionMode(JFileChooser.DIRECTORIES_ONLY);

        // If want it to only show certain file types, use a FileFilter.
        // N.B. JFileFilter is not in javax.swing; it is my implementation
        // of interface javax.swing.filechooser.FileFilter, and is similar
        // to the ExtentionFilter in demo/jfc accompanying the J2SE SDK.
        JFileFilter filter = new JFileFilter();
        filter.addType("java");
        filter.addType("class");
        filter.addType("jar");
        filter.setDescription("Java-related files");
```

```
        chooser.addChoosableFileFilter(filter);
        JButton b = new JButton("Choose file...");
        add(b);
        b.addActionListener(new ActionListener() {
            public void actionPerformed(ActionEvent e) {
            int returnVal = chooser.showOpenDialog(frame);
            if (returnVal == JFileChooser.APPROVE_OPTION) {
                File file = chooser.getSelectedFile();
                System.out.println("You chose a " +
                    (file.isFile() ? "file" : "directory") +
                    " named: " + file.getPath());
            } else {
                System.out.println("You did not choose a filesystem object.");
            }
            }
        });
    }


    public static void main(String[] args) {
        JFrame f = new JFrame("JFileChooser Demo");
        f.getContentPane().add(new JFileChooserDemo(f));
        f.pack();
        f.setDefaultCloseOperation(JFrame.EXIT_ON_CLOSE);
        f.setVisible(true);
    }
}
```

In this example, I set up a FileFilter for Java files. Note that FileFilter exists both in javax.swing.filechooser and java.io (an older version, not for use here; see Recipe 11.7). The javax.swing.filechooser.FileFilter interface has only two methods: boolean accept(File) and String getDescription( ). This is enough for a totally fixed-function file filter: you could hardcode the list of extensions that should be accepted, for example. The following class is similar in spirit to the ExampleFileFilter included in the JDK demo directory:

```
[filename="src/main/java/gui/JFileFilter.java", language="java", identifier="main"]
snippet~~~~
ERROR: Failed to load src/main/java/gui/JFileFilter.java
snippet~~~~
```

14.14. Choosing a Color

Problem

You want to allow the user to select a color from all the colors available on your computer.

Solution

Use Swing's `JColorChooser`.

Discussion

OK, so it may be just glitz or a passing fad, but with today's displays, the 13 original AWT colors are too limiting. Swing's `JColorChooser` lets you choose from zillions of colors. From a program's view, it can be used in three ways:

- Construct it and place it in a panel
- Call its `createDialog()` and get a `JDialog` back
- Call its `showDialog()` and get back the chosen color

We use the last method because it's the simplest and the most likely to be used in a real application. The user has several methods of operating the chooser, too:

Swatches mode
> The user can pick from one of a few hundred color variants.

HSB mode
> This one's my favorite. The user picks one of Hue, Saturation, or Brightness, a standard way of representing color value. The user can adjust each value by slider. There is a huge range of different pixel values to choose from, by clicking (or, more fun, *dragging*) in the central area. See Figure 14-11.

RGB mode
> The user picks Red, Green, and Blue components by sliders.

Example 14-9 contains a short program that makes it happen.

Example 14-9. JColorDemo.java

```java
public class JColorChooserDemo extends JFrame {
    /** A canvas to display the color in. */
    protected JLabel demo;

    /** Constructor - set up the entire GUI for this program */
    public JColorChooserDemo() {
        super("Swing Color Demo");
        Container cp = getContentPane();
        JButton jButton;
        cp.add(jButton = new JButton("Change Color..."), BorderLayout.NORTH);
        jButton.setToolTipText("Click here to see the Color Chooser");
        jButton.addActionListener(new ActionListener() {
            public void actionPerformed(ActionEvent actionEvent)
            {
                Color ch = JColorChooser.showDialog(
                    JColorChooserDemo.this,                  // parent
```

```
                    "Swing Demo Color Popup",     // title
                    demo.getForeground());            // default
                System.out.println("Your selected color is " + ch);
                if (ch != null) {
                    demo.setForeground(ch);
                    demo.repaint();
                }
            }
        });
        cp.add(BorderLayout.CENTER, demo =
            new JLabel("Your One True Color", JLabel.CENTER));
        demo.setToolTipText("This is the last color you chose");
        pack();
        setDefaultCloseOperation(JFrame.EXIT_ON_CLOSE);
    }

    /** good old main */
    public static void main(String[] argv) {
        new JColorChooserDemo().setVisible(true);
    }
}
```

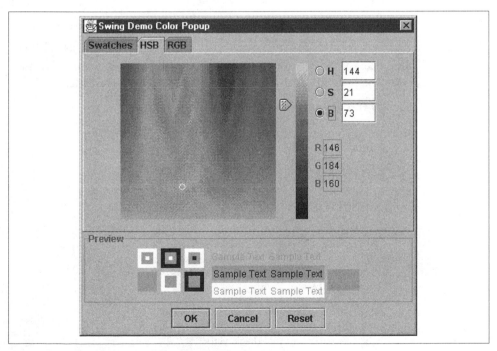

Figure 14-11. JColorChooser: HSB view in action

See Also

This program introduces `setToolTipText()`, a method to set the text for pop-up "tool-tips" that appear when you position the mouse pointer over a component and don't do anything for a given time (initially half a second). Tooltips originated with Macintosh Balloon Help and were refined into ToolTips under Microsoft Windows.[2] Tooltips are easy to use; the simplest form is shown here. For more documentation, see Chapter 3 of *Java Swing*.

14.15. Formatting JComponents with HTML

Problem

You want more control over the formatting of text in `JLabel` and friends.

Solution

Use HTML in the text of the component.

Discussion

The Swing components that display text, such as `JLabel`, format the text as HTML—instead of as plain text—if the first six characters are the obvious tag `<html>`. The program `JLabelHTMLDemo` just puts up a `JLabel` formatted using this Java code:

```
public class JLabelHTMLDemo extends JFrame {

    /** Construct the object including its GUI */
    public JLabelHTMLDemo() {
        super("JLabelHTMLDemo");
        Container cp = getContentPane();

        JButton component = new JButton(
            "<html>" +
            "<body bgcolor='white'>" +
            "<h1><font color='red'>Welcome</font></h1>" +
            "<p>This button will be formatted according to the usual " +
            "HTML rules for formatting of paragraphs.</p>" +
            "</body></html>");

        component.addActionListener(new ActionListener() {
            public void actionPerformed(ActionEvent evt) {
                System.out.println("Thank you!");
            }
        });
```

2. See? I even said something nice about Microsoft. I do believe in credit where credit's due.

```
        cp.add(BorderLayout.CENTER, component);

        setSize(200, 400);

        setDefaultCloseOperation(JFrame.EXIT_ON_CLOSE);
    }
    public static void main(String[] args) {
        new JLabelHTMLDemo().setVisible(true);
    }
}
```

Figure 14-12 shows the program in operation.

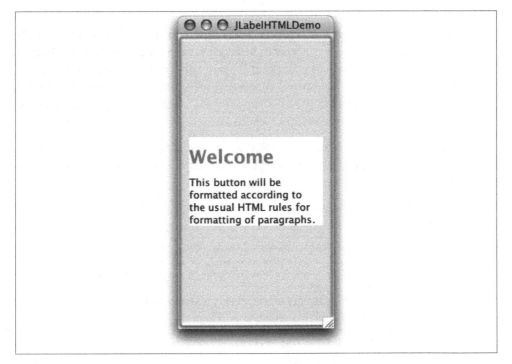

Figure 14-12. JLabel with HTML text

14.16. Centering a Main Window

Problem

You want your main window to be centered on the screen.

Solution

First, be aware that some users on some platforms would rather that you didn't do this because they have existing "placement" schemes. However, at least on Windows, this technique is useful.

Subtract the width and height of the window from the width and height of the screen, divide by two, and go there. Be aware that some platforms (Mac, Unix) make it pretty easy for the power user to have multiple monitors active, so you don't always want to do this.

Discussion

The code for this is pretty simple. The part that might take a while to figure out is the Dimension of the screen. Two methods can help: getScreenSize() in the Toolkit class and the static method getDefaultToolkit(). The Toolkit class relates to the under-lying windowing toolkit; it has several subclasses, including two different ones for X Windows on Unix (Motif and non-Motif), another for Macintosh, and so on. Put these together and you have the Dimension you need.

Centering a Window is such a common need that I have packaged it in its own little class: UtilGUI. Here is the complete source for UtilGUI, which I'll use without comment from now on:

```
// package com.darwinsys.swingui;
public class UtilGUI {

    /** Centre a Window, Frame, JFrame, Dialog, etc. */
    public static void centre(final Window w) {
        // After packing a Frame or Dialog, centre it on the screen.
        Dimension us = w.getSize(),
            them = Toolkit.getDefaultToolkit().getScreenSize();
        int newX = (them.width - us.width) / 2;
        int newY = (them.height- us.height)/ 2;
        w.setLocation(newX, newY);
    }

    /** Center a Window, Frame, JFrame, Dialog, etc.,
     * but do it the American Spelling Way :-)
     */
    public static void center(final Window w) {
        UtilGUI.centre(w);
    }

    /** Maximize a window, the hard way. */
    public static void maximize(final Window w) {
        Dimension them =
            Toolkit.getDefaultToolkit().getScreenSize();
        w.setBounds(0,0, them.width, them.height);
```

```
}

/**
 * Copy a string value to the system copy buffer
 */
public static void setSystemClipboardContents(Component c, String srcData) {
    if (srcData != null) {
        Clipboard clipboard = c.getToolkit().getSystemClipboard();
        StringSelection contents = new StringSelection(srcData);
        clipboard.setContents(contents, new ClipboardOwner() {
            public void lostOwnership(Clipboard clipboard,
                Transferable contents) {

                // don't care
            }
        });
    }
}

/** Print a yes/no prompt; return true if the user presses yes
 */
public static boolean confirm(JFrame parent, String message) {
    int confirm = JOptionPane.showConfirmDialog(parent, message, "Confirm",
            JOptionPane.YES_NO_OPTION,
            JOptionPane.QUESTION_MESSAGE);
    // Only selecting Yes choice will result in true
    return confirm == 0;
}

/**    Save the X and Y locations in Preferences node provided.
 */
public static void setSavedLocation(
    final Preferences pNode, final Window w) {

    Point where = w.getLocation();
    int x = (int)where.getX();
    pNode.putInt("mainwindow.x", Math.max(0, x));
    int y = (int)where.getY();
    pNode.putInt("mainwindow.y", Math.max(0, y));
}

/** Retrieve the saved X and Y from Preferences
 */
public static Point getSavedLocation(final Preferences pNode) {
    int savedX = pNode.getInt("mainwindow.x", -1);
    int savedY = pNode.getInt("mainwindow.y", -1);
    return new Point(savedX, savedY);
}

/**
 * Track a Window's position across application restarts; location is saved
 * in a Preferences node that you pass in; we attach a ComponentListener to
```

```
     * the Window.
     */
    public static void monitorWindowPosition(
        final Window w, final Preferences pNode) {

        // Get the current saved position, if any
        Point p = getSavedLocation(pNode);
        int savedX = (int)p.getX();
        int savedY = (int)p.getY();
        if (savedX != -1) {
            // Move window to is previous location
            w.setLocation(savedX, savedY);
        } else {
            // Not saved yet, at least make it look nice
            centre(w);
        }
        // Now make sure that if the user moves the window,
        // we will save the new position.
        w.addComponentListener(new ComponentAdapter() {
            @Override
            public void componentMoved(ComponentEvent e) {
                setSavedLocation(pNode, w);
            }
        });
    }
}
```

To use it after the relevant import, you can simply say, for example:

```
myFrame.pack( );
UtilGUI.centre(myFrame);
myFrame.setVisible(true);
```

14.17. Changing a Swing Program's Look and Feel

Problem

You want to change the look and feel of an application.

Solution

Use the static UIManager.setLookAndFeel() method. Maybe.

Discussion

If you wish to specify the entire look and feel for a program, set it with the static UIManager.setLookAndFeel() method; the name you pass in must be the full name (as a string) of a class that implements a Java look and feel. The details of writing a look and feel class are beyond the scope of this book; refer to *Java Swing* or the Sun documentation. But using these classes is easy. For example:

```
UIManager.setLookAndFeel("javax.swing.plaf.metal.MetalLookAndFeel");
```

This must appear before you create the GUI of the program, and it can throw an exception if the class name is invalid.

People sometimes like to show off the fact that you can change the look and feel on the fly. As earlier, you call `setLookAndFeel()`, and then call the static `SwingUtilities.updateComponentTree()` for your `JFrame` and all detached trees, such as dialog classes. But before you rush out to do it, be advised that the official Sun position is that you shouldn't! The first edition of the official *Java Look and Feel Design Guideline* book says, on page 23 (Oracle):

> Because there is far more to the design of an application than the look and feel of components, it is unwise to give end users the ability to swap look and feel while [running] your application. Switching look and feel designs in this way only swaps the look and feel designs from one platform to another. The layout and vocabulary used are platform-specific and do not change. For instance, swapping look and feel designs does not change the titles of the menus.

The book does recommend that you let users specify an alternative look and feel, presumably in your properties file, at program startup time. Even so, the capability to switch while an application is running is too tempting to ignore; even Sun's own Swing Demonstration (included with the JDK) offers a menu item to change its look and feel. Figure 14-13 is my nice little program in the Java style; see Example 14-10 for the source code.

Figure 14-13. Java, Windows, and Motif look and feel under Windows

Of course, not all looks work on all platforms. If I try the Mac OS look and feel under Windows, I get the error dialog shown in Figure 14-14, which shows what happens when you request any look and feel that is unavailable on the current platform.

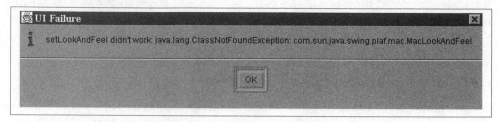

Figure 14-14. Look and feel request refused on Windows

The OPEN LOOK design alluded to in the code is, well, not written yet. Vaporware. That's why it's grayed out.

Under Mac OS X, the default look and feel is, of course, the Mac OS look and feel. You can also select the Java or Motif look, but not the Windows look. See Figure 14-15.

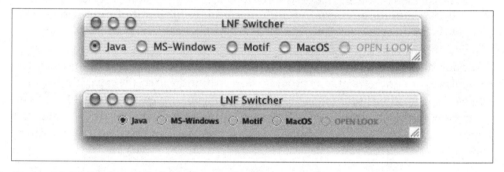

Figure 14-15. Look and feel switcher under Mac OS X

Example 14-10 shows the code that implements the look and feel switcher. It's pretty straightforward based on what we've seen already. The only neat trick is that I've set the selected button back to what it was if the look and feel that the user selects is not available.

Example 14-10. LNFSwitcher.java

```java
public class LNFSwitcher {
    /** The frame. */
    protected JFrame theFrame;
    /** Its content pane */
    protected Container cp;

    /** Start with the Java look-and-feel, if possible */
    final static String PREFERREDLOOKANDFEELNAME =
        "javax.swing.plaf.metal.MetalLookAndFeel";
    protected String curLF = PREFERREDLOOKANDFEELNAME;
    protected JRadioButton previousButton;

    /** Construct a program... */
```

```
public LNFSwitcher() {
    super();
    theFrame = new JFrame("LNF Switcher");
    theFrame.setDefaultCloseOperation(JFrame.EXIT_ON_CLOSE);
    cp = theFrame.getContentPane();
    cp.setLayout(new FlowLayout());

    ButtonGroup bg = new ButtonGroup();

    JRadioButton bJava = new JRadioButton("Java");
    bJava.addActionListener(new LNFSetter(
        "javax.swing.plaf.metal.MetalLookAndFeel", bJava));
    bg.add(bJava);
    cp.add(bJava);

    JRadioButton bMSW  = new JRadioButton("MS-Windows");
    bMSW.addActionListener(new LNFSetter(
        "com.sun.java.swing.plaf.windows.WindowsLookAndFeel", bMSW));
    bg.add(bMSW);
    cp.add(bMSW);

    JRadioButton bMotif = new JRadioButton("Motif");
    bMotif.addActionListener(new LNFSetter(
        "com.sun.java.swing.plaf.motif.MotifLookAndFeel", bMotif));
    bg.add(bMotif);
    cp.add(bMotif);

    JRadioButton bMac = new JRadioButton("Sun-MacOS");
    bMac.addActionListener(new LNFSetter(
        "com.sun.java.swing.plaf.mac.MacLookAndFeel", bMac));
    bg.add(bMac);
    cp.add(bMac);

    String defaultLookAndFeel = UIManager.getSystemLookAndFeelClassName();
    // System.out.println(defaultLookAndFeel);
    JRadioButton bDefault = new JRadioButton("Default");
    bDefault.addActionListener(new LNFSetter(
        defaultLookAndFeel, bDefault));
    bg.add(bDefault);
    cp.add(bDefault);

    (previousButton = bDefault).setSelected(true);

    theFrame.pack();
}

/* Class to set the Look and Feel on a frame */
class LNFSetter implements ActionListener {
    String theLNFName;
    JRadioButton thisButton;

    /** Called to setup for button handling */
```

```
            LNFSetter(String lnfName, JRadioButton me) {
                theLNFName = lnfName;
                thisButton = me;
            }

            /** Called when the button actually gets pressed. */
            public void actionPerformed(ActionEvent e) {
                try {
                    UIManager.setLookAndFeel(theLNFName);
                    SwingUtilities.updateComponentTreeUI(theFrame);
                    theFrame.pack();
                } catch (Exception evt) {
                    JOptionPane.showMessageDialog(null,
                        "setLookAndFeel didn't work: " + evt,
                        "UI Failure", JOptionPane.INFORMATION_MESSAGE);
                    previousButton.setSelected(true);          // reset the GUI to agree
                }
                previousButton = thisButton;
            }
        }

        public static void main(String[] argv) {
            LNFSwitcher o = new LNFSwitcher();
            o.theFrame.setVisible(true);
        }
    }
```

See Also

You can find some alternative look-and-feel implementations on the Web. If you'd like to build your own look and feel, perhaps for corporate identity reasons, some of these, in conjunction with O'Reilly's *Java Swing*, would be a good starting point.

14.18. Enhancing Your Swing GUI for Mac OS X

Problem

You tried running your Swing GUI application on Mac OS X, and it didn't look right.

Solution

There are a variety of small steps you can take to improve your GUI's appearance and behavior under Mac OS X.

Discussion

Although Swing aims to be a portable GUI, Apple's implementation for Mac OS X does not automatically do "the right thing" for everyone. For example, a JMenuBar menu container appears by default at the top of the application window. This is the norm on Windows and on most Unix platforms, but Mac users expect the menu bar for the active application to appear at the top of the screen. To enable "normal" behavior, you have to set the System property apple.laf.useScreenMenuBar to the value true, as in **java - Dapple.laf.useScreenMenuBar=true SomeClassName**. You might want to set some other properties too, such as a short name for your application to appear in the menu bar (the default is the full class name of your main application class).

But there is no point in setting these properties unless you are, in fact, running on Mac OS X. How do you tell? Apple's recommended way is to check for the system property mrj.runtime and, if so, assume you are on Mac OS X:

```
boolean isMacOS = System.getProperty("mrj.version") != null;
if (isMacOS) {
  System.setProperty("apple.laf.useScreenMenuBar", "true");
  System.setProperty("com.apple.mrj.application.apple.menu.about.name",
  "JabaDex");
}
```

Or, because these properties are likely harmless on non-Mac systems, you could just skip the test, and set the two properties unconditionally, as is done in Example 14-11.

Example 14-11. MacOsUiHints.java

```java
/**
 * Interactive test for "macosui" package.
 * Class cannot extend JFrame; must set properties before first
 * call to any Swing constructor.
 */
public class MacOsUiHints {

    public static void main(String[] args) throws Exception {
        // OS X Tester:
        // check that the File Edit View menu appears atop the desktop not the window
        System.setProperty("apple.laf.useScreenMenuBar", "true");
        // OS X Tester: check that this string appears in the Application Menu.
        System.setProperty("com.apple.mrj.application.apple.menu.about.name",
            "MacOsUiHints");
        final MacOsUiHints gui = new MacOsUiHints( );
        SwingUtilities.invokeAndWait(new Runnable() {
            @Override
            public void run() {
                gui.getFrame().setVisible(true);
            }
        });
    }

    JFrame jf;

    protected JFrame getFrame() {
        return jf;
```

```
        }

    public MacOsUiHints( ) {
        jf = new JFrame("MacOsUiHints");
        JButton button = new JButton("Exit");
        button.addActionListener(new ActionListener( ) {
            public void actionPerformed(ActionEvent arg0) {
                System.exit(0);
            }
        });
        jf.getContentPane( ).add(button);

        JMenuBar mb = new JMenuBar();
        jf.setJMenuBar(mb);

        JMenu fileMenu = new JMenu("File");
        mb.add(fileMenu);
        fileMenu.add(new JMenuItem("Quit"));

        mb.add(new JMenu("Edit"));

        // Tester: see that Application->About produces our popup
        // Ditto for Preferences and Shutdown.
        // MacOSAppAdapter adapter =
        //    new MacOSAppAdapter(jf, abouter, prefser, printer, shutter);
        //adapter.register( );
        jf.setSize(300, 200);

    }
}
```

But there's more! You still don't get to handle "normal" (to Mac users) Mac-style Quit, Preferences, Print, or About requests (Cmd-Q, Cmd-comma, Cmd-P, or Application→About, respectively). For these options, you need to use some classes in the com.apple.eawt package, which are not included in current JDKs.

See Also

For older releases, you can read about this in the Apple Developer Documentation that comes with Mac OS X.

See *Mac OS X for Java Geeks* by Will Iverson (O'Reilly) for more information on Mac OS X. Apple has been slowly moving away from Java, so it no longer maintains very much documentation on it. However, Apple's list of System Properties was still available at Apple's developer site (*http://bit.ly/1fat0j9*) as of January 2014. As of that same time, Oracle has some ancient Sun articles on Mac Java: "Bringing your Java Application to Mac OS X" (*http://bit.ly/1nJ37qN*) and "Bringing your Java Application to Mac OS X Part Two" (*http://bit.ly/1fatndE*). Unfortunately, these refer to classes in com.apple.eawt, which in Java 7 fail to compile with the following error message:

```
Access restriction: The method addApplicationListener(ApplicationListener)
from the type Application is not accessible due to restriction on required
library
/Library/Java/JavaVirtualMachines/1.7.0.jdk/Contents/Home/jre/lib/rt.jar
```

I used to provide an adapter class, com.darwinsys.macosui.MacOSAppAdapter, which made the now-restricted classes easier to use, but discontinued it when the corresponding classes disappeared from the JDK. The code is still available on my GitHub repo (*http://bit.ly/TNQIs2*). You may be able to find some additional articles on Apple's developer site (*http://bit.ly/1fHRMVr*).

It seems you may be best off living with the use of System properties to adapt to the OS X environmnent.

14.19. Building Your GUI Application with JavaFX

Problem

You want to build GUI applications with less work than writing Swing code.

Solution

JavaFX provides one alternative.

Discussion

JavaFX is a GUI package that ships with some releases of Java SE 7 and probably all releases of Java SE 8. It is simpler to use, and also provides its own "standard" drag-and-drop GUI builder (which is a separate download). Here is a "Hello, world" program in JavaFX that simply prints to the standard output when a button is pressed:

```
import javafx.application.Application;          ❶
import javafx.event.ActionEvent;
import javafx.event.EventHandler;
import javafx.scene.Scene;
import javafx.scene.control.Button;
import javafx.scene.layout.StackPane;
import javafx.stage.Stage;

public class HelloFx extends Application {       ❷

    @Override
    public void start(Stage stage) {             ❸
        stage.setTitle("JavaFX Hello!");
        Button btn = new Button();
        btn.setText("Run Greeting");
        btn.setOnAction(new EventHandler<ActionEvent>() {  ❹
            @Override
```

```
            public void handle(ActionEvent e) {
                System.out.println("Hello from JavaFX");
            }
        });

        StackPane rootPane = new StackPane();        ❺
        rootPane.getChildren().add(btn);
        stage.setScene(new Scene(rootPane, 300, 200));
        stage.show();
    }

    public static void main(String[] args) {        ❻
        launch(args);
    }
}
```

❶   Note that no Swing imports are used; Button is from JavaFX, not from Swing.

❷   The main program has to extend the JavaFX Application class.

❸   Like an applet, no constructor is provided; instead, the override of start() is
      called, passing in a Stage (which is analogous to a JFrame).

❹   Different action handling method, but exactly the same concepts as in
      Recipe 14.5.

❺   A Pane (StackPane), analogous to a JPanel, is created, and the button added
      into it; the Pane is then wrapped in a Scene, which is added to the Stage. Now
      the whole thing is ready to show.

❻   The main program doesn't need to instantiate anything, but just calls the
      inherited launch() method, passing in the command-line arguments.

Figure 14-16 shows this program on display.

To learn about using the drag-and-drop GUI builder for JavaFX, consult the Oracle
article, "Installing JavaFX Scene Builder" (*http://bit.ly/1hrOAKL*). There is tutorial information on full development of applications using JavaFX (*http://bit.ly/1mNrGjU*).
Although the IDE notes there are mainly or only for NetBeans, you can adapt them (I
ran Figure 14-16 under Eclipse).

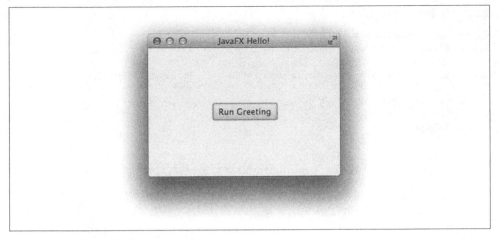

Figure 14-16. Hello JavaFX In Action

14.20. Program: Custom Font Chooser

Problem

You want to allow the user to select a font, but standard Java doesn't yet include a Font Chooser dialog.

Solution

Use my `FontChooser` dialog class.

Discussion

As we saw in Recipe 12.3, you can manually select a font by calling the `java.awt.Font` class constructor, passing in the name of the font, the type you want (plain, bold, italic, or bold+italic), and the point size:

```
Font f = new Font("Helvetica", Font.BOLD, 14);
setfont(f);
```

This is not very flexible for interactive applications. You normally want the user to be able to choose fonts with the same ease as using a File Chooser dialog. Until the Java API catches up with this, you are more than welcome to use the Font Chooser that I wrote when faced with a similar need.

The source code is shown in Example 14-12; it ends, as many of my classes do, with a short main method that is both a test case and an example of using the class in action. The display is shown in Figure 14-17.

Example 14-12. FontChooser.java

```java
// package com.darwinsys.swingui;
public class FontChooser extends JDialog {

    private static final long serialVersionUID = 5363471384675038069L;

    public static final String DEFAULT_TEXT = "Lorem ipsem dolor";

    // Results:

    /** The font the user has chosen */
    protected Font resultFont = new Font("Serif", Font.PLAIN, 12);
    /** The resulting font name */
    protected String resultName;
    /** The resulting font size */
    protected int resultSize;
    /** The resulting boldness */
    protected boolean isBold;
    /** The resulting italicness */
    protected boolean isItalic;

    // Working fields

    /** Display text */
    protected String displayText = DEFAULT_TEXT;
    /** The font name chooser */
    protected JList fontNameChoice;
    /** The font size chooser */
    protected JList fontSizeChoice;
    /** The bold and italic choosers */
    JCheckBox bold, italic;

    /** The list of font sizes */
    protected Integer fontSizes[] = {
            8, 9, 10, 11, 12, 14, 16, 18, 20, 24, 30, 36, 40, 48, 60, 72
    };
    /** The index of the default size (e.g., 14 point == 4) */
    protected static final int DEFAULT_SIZE = 4;
    /** The font display area.
     */
    protected JLabel previewArea;

    /** Construct a FontChooser -- Sets title and gets
     * array of fonts on the system. Builds a GUI to let
     * the user choose one font at one size.
     */
    public FontChooser(JFrame f) {
        super(f, "Font Chooser", true);

        Container cp = getContentPane();

        JPanel top = new JPanel();
```

```
top.setBorder(new TitledBorder(new EtchedBorder(), "Font"));
top.setLayout(new FlowLayout());

// This gives a longish list; most of the names that come
// with your OS (e.g., Helvetica, Times), plus the Sun/Java ones (Lucida,
// Lucida Bright, Lucida Sans...)
String[] fontList = GraphicsEnvironment.getLocalGraphicsEnvironment().
    getAvailableFontFamilyNames();

fontNameChoice = new JList(fontList);
top.add(new JScrollPane(fontNameChoice));

fontNameChoice.setVisibleRowCount(fontSizes.length);
fontNameChoice.setSelectedValue("Serif", true);

fontSizeChoice = new JList(fontSizes);
top.add(fontSizeChoice);

fontSizeChoice.setSelectedIndex(fontSizes.length * 3 / 4);

cp.add(top, BorderLayout.NORTH);

JPanel attrs = new JPanel();
top.add(attrs);
attrs.setLayout(new GridLayout(0,1));
attrs.add(bold  =new JCheckBox("Bold", false));
attrs.add(italic=new JCheckBox("Italic", false));

// Make sure that any change to the GUI will trigger a font preview.
ListSelectionListener waker = new ListSelectionListener() {
    public void valueChanged(ListSelectionEvent e) {
        previewFont();
    }
};
fontSizeChoice.addListSelectionListener(waker);
fontNameChoice.addListSelectionListener(waker);
ItemListener waker2 = new ItemListener() {
    public void itemStateChanged(ItemEvent e) {
        previewFont();
    }
};
bold.addItemListener(waker2);
italic.addItemListener(waker2);

previewArea = new JLabel(displayText, JLabel.CENTER);
previewArea.setSize(200, 50);
cp.add(previewArea, BorderLayout.CENTER);

JPanel bot = new JPanel();

JButton okButton = new JButton("Apply");
bot.add(okButton);
```

```
        okButton.addActionListener(new ActionListener() {
            public void actionPerformed(ActionEvent e) {
                previewFont();
                dispose();
                setVisible(false);
            }
        });

        JButton canButton = new JButton("Cancel");
        bot.add(canButton);
        canButton.addActionListener(new ActionListener() {
            public void actionPerformed(ActionEvent e) {
                // Set all values to null. Better: restore previous.
                resultFont = null;
                resultName = null;
                resultSize = 0;
                isBold = false;
                isItalic = false;

                dispose();
                setVisible(false);
            }
        });

        cp.add(bot, BorderLayout.SOUTH);

        previewFont(); // ensure view is up to date!

        pack();
        setLocation(100, 100);
    }

    /** Called from the action handlers to get the font info,
     * build a font, and set it.
     */
    protected void previewFont() {
        resultName = (String)fontNameChoice.getSelectedValue();
        String resultSizeName = fontSizeChoice.getSelectedValue().toString();
        int resultSize = Integer.parseInt(resultSizeName);
        isBold = bold.isSelected();
        isItalic = italic.isSelected();
        int attrs = Font.PLAIN;
        if (isBold) attrs = Font.BOLD;
        if (isItalic) attrs |= Font.ITALIC;
        resultFont = new Font(resultName, attrs, resultSize);
        // System.out.println("resultName = " + resultName + "; " +
        //         "resultFont = " + resultFont);
        previewArea.setFont(resultFont);
        pack();                      // ensure Dialog is big enough.
    }

    /** Retrieve the selected font name. */
```

```
    public String getSelectedName() {
        return resultName;
    }
/** Retrieve the selected size */
    public int getSelectedSize() {
        return resultSize;
    }

/** Retrieve the selected font, or null */
    public Font getSelectedFont() {
        return resultFont;
    }

    public String getDisplayText() {
        return displayText;
    }

    public void setDisplayText(String displayText) {
        this.displayText = displayText;
        previewArea.setText(displayText);
        previewFont();
    }

    public JList getFontNameChoice() {
        return fontNameChoice;
    }

    public JList getFontSizeChoice() {
        return fontSizeChoice;
    }

    public boolean isBold() {
        return isBold;
    }

    public boolean isItalic() {
        return isItalic;
    }
}
```

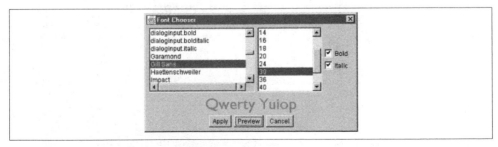

Figure 14-17. Font Chooser in action

14.21. Program: Custom AWT/Swing Layout Manager

Problem

None of the standard layout managers does quite what you need.

Solution

Roll your own. All you need to do is implement the methods of the java.awt.Layout-Manager interface.

Discussion

Although many people are intimidated by the thought of writing their own layout manager, it beats the alternative of using only "the big five" layouts (BorderLayout, CondLayout, FlowLayout, GridBagLayout, and GridLayout). BorderLayout isn't quite flexible enough, and GridBaglayout is too complex for many applications. Suppose, for instance, that you wanted to lay out an arbitrary number of components in a circle. In a typical X Windows or Windows application, you would write the geometry calculations within the code for creating the components to be drawn. This would work, but the code for the geometry calculations would be unavailable to anybody who needed it later. The LayoutManager interface is another great example of how the Java API's design promotes code reuse: if you write the geometry calculations as a layout manager, then anybody needing this type of layout could simply instantiate your CircleLayout class to get circular layouts.

As another example, consider the layout shown in Figure 14-18, where the labels column and the textfield column have different widths. Using the big five layouts, there's no good way to ensure that the columns line up and that you have control over their relative widths. Suppose you wanted the label field to take up 40% of the panel and the entry field to take up 60%. I'll implement a simple layout manager here, both to show you how easy it is and to give you a useful class for making panels like the one shown.

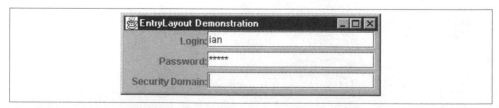

Figure 14-18. EntryLayout in action

The methods for the LayoutManager interface are shown in Table 14-2.

Table 14-2. LayoutManager methods

Method name	Description
preferredLayoutSize(Container)	Like getPreferredSize() for a component: the "best" size for the container
minimumLayoutSize(Container)	Same, but for the minimum workable size
layoutContainer(Container)	Perform the layout calculations, and resize and reposition all the components at the current size of the container
addLayoutComponent(String, Compo-nent)	Associate a constraint with a given component (you normally store these mappings in a java.util.Map)
removeLayoutComponent(Component)	Remove a component from the HashMap

If you don't need Constraint objects (such as BorderLayout.NORTH or a GridBagCon-straint object), you can ignore the last two methods. Well, you can't ignore them com-pletely. Because this is an interface, you must implement them. But they can be as simple as {} (i.e., a null-bodied method).

That leaves only three serious methods. The first, preferredLayoutSize(), normally loops through all the components—either in the HashMap if using constraints, or in an array returned by the container's getComponents() method—asking each for its pre-ferred size and adding them up, while partly doing the layout calculations. And mini-mumLayoutSize() is the same for the smallest possible layout that will work. It may be possible for these methods to delegate either to a common submethod or to invoke layoutContainer(), depending on how the given layout policy works.

The most important method is layoutContainer(). This method needs to examine all the components and decide where to put them and how big to make each one. Having made the decision, it can use setBounds() to set each one's position and size.

Other than a bit of error checking, that's all that's involved. Here's an example, Entry-Layout, that implements the multicolumn layout shown in Figure 14-18. Quoting its javadoc documentation:

> A simple layout manager, for Entry areas like:
>
> Login: __
>
> Password: __
>
> Basically two (or more) columns of different, but constant, widths.
>
> Construct instances by passing an array of the column width percentages (as doubles, fractions from 0.1 to 0.9, so 40%, 60% would be {0.4, 0.6}). The length of this array uniquely determines the number of columns. Columns are forced to be the relevant widths. As with GridLayout, the number of items added must be an even multiple of the number of columns. If not, exceptions may be thrown!

First, let's look at the program that uses this layout to produce Figure 14-18. This program simply creates a JFrame, gets the contentPane container, and sets its layout to an instance of EntryLayout, passing an array of two doubles representing the relative widths (decimal fractions, not percentages) into the EntryLayout constructor. Then we add an even number of components, and call pack( )—which in turn calls our preferredLayoutSize( )—and setVisible(true):

```java
public class EntryLayoutTest {

    /** "main program" method - construct and show */
    public static void main(String[] av) {
        testTwoCols();
        testFiveCols();
    }

    static void testTwoCols() {
        final JFrame f = new JFrame("EntryLayout Demonstration");
        Container cp = f.getContentPane();
        double widths[] = { .33, .66 };
        cp.setLayout(new EntryLayout(widths));
        cp.add(new JLabel("Login:", SwingConstants.RIGHT));
        cp.add(new JTextField(10));
        cp.add(new JLabel("Password:", SwingConstants.RIGHT));
        cp.add(new JPasswordField(20));
        cp.add(new JLabel("Security Domain:", SwingConstants.RIGHT));
        cp.add(new JTextField(20));
        // cp.add(new JLabel("Monkey wrench in works"));
        f.pack();
        f.setDefaultCloseOperation(JFrame.EXIT_ON_CLOSE);
        f.setLocation(200, 200);
        f.setVisible(true);
    }

    static void testFiveCols() {
        final JFrame f = new JFrame("EntryLayout Five Columns");
        Container cp = f.getContentPane();
        double widths[] = { .25, .33, .10, .10, .20 };
        cp.setLayout(new EntryLayout(widths));
        cp.add(new JLabel("Login:", SwingConstants.RIGHT));
        cp.add(new JTextField(10));
        cp.add(new JCheckBox());
        cp.add(new JCheckBox());
        cp.add(new JCheckBox());
        cp.add(new JLabel("Password:", SwingConstants.RIGHT));
        cp.add(new JPasswordField(20));
        cp.add(new JCheckBox());
        cp.add(new JCheckBox());
        cp.add(new JCheckBox());
        cp.add(new JLabel("Security Domain:", SwingConstants.RIGHT));
        cp.add(new JTextField(20));
        cp.add(new JCheckBox());
```

```
        cp.add(new JCheckBox());
        cp.add(new JCheckBox());
        f.pack();
        f.setDefaultCloseOperation(JFrame.EXIT_ON_CLOSE);
        f.setLocation(200, 200);
        f.setVisible(true);
    }

    @Test
    public void trivialTest() {
        try {
            main(null);
        } catch (HeadlessException he) {
            System.out.println("EntryLayoutTest.test(): cannot test Headless");
        }
    }
}
```

Nothing complicated about it. The last JLabel ("Monkey wrench in works") is commented out because, as noted, the LayoutManager throws an exception if the number of components is not evenly divisible by the number of columns. It was put in during testing and then commented out, but was left in place for further consideration. Note that this layout operates correctly with more than two columns, but it does assume that all columns are approximately the same height (relaxing this requirement has been left as an exercise for the reader).

Finally, let's look at the code for the layout manager itself, shown in Example 14-13. After some constants and fields and two constructors, the methods are listed in about the same order as the discussion earlier in this recipe: the dummy add/remove component methods; then the preferredSize() and minimumLayoutSize() methods (which delegate to computeLayoutSize); and, finally, layoutContainer, which does the actual laying out of the components within the container. As you can see, the entire EntryLayout layout manager class is only about 140 lines, including a lot of comments.

Example 14-13. EntryLayout.java

```
// package com.darwinsys.swingui.layout;
public class EntryLayout implements LayoutManager {
    /** The array of widths, as decimal fractions (0.4 == 40%, etc.). */
    protected final double[] widthPercentages;

    /** The number of columns. */
    protected final int COLUMNS;

    /** The default padding */
    protected final static int HPAD = 5, VPAD = 5;
    /** The actual padding */
    protected final int hpad, vpad;

    /** True if the list of widths was valid. */
```

```java
    protected boolean validWidths = false;

    /** Construct an EntryLayout with widths and padding specified.
     * @param relWidths    Array of doubles specifying relative column widths.
     * @param h            Horizontal padding between items
     * @param v            Vertical padding between items
     */
    public EntryLayout(double[] relWidths, int h, int v) {
        COLUMNS = relWidths.length;
        widthPercentages = new double[COLUMNS];
        for (int i=0; i<relWidths.length; i++) {
            if (relWidths[i] >= 1.0)
                throw new IllegalArgumentException(
                    "EntryLayout: widths must be fractions < 1");
            widthPercentages[i] = relWidths[i];
        }
        validWidths = true;
        hpad = h;
        vpad = v;
    }

    /** Construct an EntryLayout with widths and with default padding amounts.
     * @param relWidths    Array of doubles specifying column widths.
     */
    public EntryLayout(double[] relWidths) {
        this(relWidths, HPAD, VPAD);
    }

    /** Adds the specified component with the specified constraint
     * to the layout; required by LayoutManager but not used.
     */
    public void addLayoutComponent(String name, Component comp) {
        // nothing to do
    }

    /** Removes the specified component from the layout;
     * required by LayoutManager, but does nothing.
     */
    public void removeLayoutComponent(Component comp)  {
        // nothing to do
    }

    /** Calculates the preferred size dimensions for the specified panel
     * given the components in the specified parent container. */
    public Dimension preferredLayoutSize(Container parent)  {
        // System.out.println("preferredLayoutSize");
        return computeLayoutSize(parent, hpad, vpad);
    }

    /** Find the minimum Dimension for the
     * specified container given the components therein.
     */
```

```java
    public Dimension minimumLayoutSize(Container parent)  {
        // System.out.println("minimumLayoutSize");
        return computeLayoutSize(parent, 0, 0);
    }

    /** The width of each column, as found by computLayoutSize(). */
    int[] widths;
    /** The height of each row, as found by computLayoutSize(). */
    int[] heights;

    /** Compute the size of the whole mess. Serves as the guts of
     * preferredLayoutSize() and minimumLayoutSize().
     * @param parent The container in which to do the layout.
     * @param hp The horizontal padding (may be zero)
     * @param vp The Vertical Padding (may be zero).
     */
    protected Dimension computeLayoutSize(Container parent, int hp, int vp) {
        if (!validWidths)
            return null;
        Component[] components = parent.getComponents();
        int preferredWidth = 0, preferredHeight = 0;
        widths = new int[COLUMNS];
        heights = new int[components.length / COLUMNS];
        // System.out.println("Grid: " + widths.length + ", " + heights.length);

        int i;
        // Pass One: Compute largest widths and heights.
        for (i=0; i<components.length; i++) {
            int row = i / widthPercentages.length;
            int col = i % widthPercentages.length;
            Component c = components[i];
            Dimension d = c.getPreferredSize();
            widths[col] = Math.max(widths[col], d.width);
            heights[row] = Math.max(heights[row], d.height);
        }

        // Pass two: agregate them.
        for (i=0; i<widths.length; i++)
            preferredWidth += widths[i] + hp;
        for (i=0; i<heights.length; i++)
            preferredHeight += heights[i] + vp;

        // Finally, pass the sums back as the actual size.
        return new Dimension(preferredWidth, preferredHeight);
    }

    /** Lays out the container in the specified panel. This is a row-column
     * type layout; find x, y, width and height of each Component.
     * @param parent The Container whose children we are laying out.
     */
    public void layoutContainer(Container parent) {
        Debug.println("layout","layoutContainer:");
```

```
    if (!validWidths)
        return;
    Component[] components = parent.getComponents();
    Dimension contSize = parent.getSize();
    int x = 0;
    for (int i=0; i<components.length; i++) {
        int row = i / COLUMNS;
        int col = i % COLUMNS;
        Component c = components[i];
        Dimension d = c.getPreferredSize();
        int colWidth = (int)(contSize.width * widthPercentages[col]);

        if (col == 0) {
            x = hpad;
        } else {
            x += hpad * (col-1) +
                (int)(contSize.width * widthPercentages[col-1]);
        }
        int y = vpad * (row) + (row * heights[row]) + (heights[row]-d.height);
        Rectangle r = new Rectangle(x, y, colWidth, d.height);
        c.setBounds(r);
    }
  }
}
```

See Also

For more on layouts, see Jim Elliott's RelativeLayout, described at On Java (*http://bit.ly/1kml7q0*). This is not to be confused with the like-named but much simpler Relative-Layout in the source distribution accompanying the *Java Cookbook*; Jim's is more complete.

The JGoodies Forms package (*http://bit.ly/1lcHuev*) provides a number of useful additions to help build complex layouts.

MetaWidget (*http://bit.ly/1q8mIVe*) provides a facility for mapping Javabean properties to Swing UI, but can also build Android, HTML, and several other layout types.

As mentioned in the Introduction, there are many good books on windowed application programming with Java. O'Reilly's *Java Swing* discusses the many Swing components not covered here, such as JTable, JScrollPane, JList, and JTree, and many more. Some Swing components not covered in this chapter are nonetheless used in later recipes in this book (for example, JTree is discussed in Recipe 17.8).

## CHAPTER 15

Internationalization and Localization

15.0. Introduction

"All the world's a stage," wrote William Shakespeare. But not all the players upon that great and turbulent stage speak the great Bard's native tongue. To be usable on a global scale, your software needs to communicate in many different languages. The menu labels, button strings, dialog messages, title bar titles, and even command-line error messages must be settable to the user's choice of language. This is the topic of *internationalization* and *localization*. Because these words take a long time to say and write, they are often abbreviated by their first and last letters and the count of omitted letters, that is, I18N and L10N.

Java provides a `Locale` class to discover/control the internationalization settings. A default `Locale` is inherited from operating system runtime settings when Java starts up and can be used most of the time!

Ian's Basic Steps: Internationalization

Internationalization and localization consist of:

Sensitivity training (Internationalization or I18N)
   Making your software sensitive to these issues

Language lessons (Localization or L10N)
   Writing configuration files for each language

Culture lessons (optional)
   Customizing the presentation of numbers, fractions, dates, and message formatting

---

For more information, see *Java Internationalization* by Andy Deitsch and David Czarnecki.

15.1. Creating a Button with I18N Resources

Problem

You want your program to take "sensitivity lessons" so that it can communicate well internationally.

Solution

Your program must obtain all control and message strings via the internationalization software. Here's how:

1. Get a ResourceBundle.

   ```
   ResourceBundle rb = ResourceBundle.getBundle("Menus");
   ```

   I'll talk about ResourceBundle in Recipe 15.6, but briefly, a ResourceBundle represents a collection of name-value pairs (resources). The names are names you assign to each GUI control or other user interface text, and the values are the text to assign to each control in a given language.

2. Use this ResourceBundle to fetch the localized version of each control name.

   Old way:

   ```
   somePanel.add(new JButton("Exit"));
   ```

   New way:

   ```
   try { label = rb.getString("exit.label"); }
   catch (MissingResourceException e) { label="Exit"; } // fallback
   somePanel.add(new JButton(label));
   ```

This is quite a bit of code for one button, but distributed over all the widgets (buttons, menus, etc.) in a program, it can be as little as one line with the use of *convenience routines*, which I'll show in Recipe 15.4.

What happens at runtime?

The default locale is used, because we didn't specify one. The default locale is platform-dependent:

Unix/POSIX
: LANG environment variable (per user)

Windows
: Control Panel→Regional Settings

Mac OS X
: System Preferences→Language & Text

Others

See platform documentation

`ResourceBundle.getBundle()` locates a file with the named resource bundle name (`Menus`, in the previous example), plus an underscore and the locale name (if any locale is set), plus another underscore and the locale variation (if any variation is set), plus the extension *.properties*. If a variation is set but the file can't be found, it falls back to just the country code. If that can't be found, it falls back to the original default. Table 15-1 shows some examples for various locales.

Note that Android apps—usually written in Java—use exactly the same mechanism, except for some small changes in the name of the file in which the properties files are found.

Table 15-1. Property filenames for different locales

Locale	Filename
Default locale	*Menus.Properties*
Swedish	*Menus_sv.properties*
Spanish	*Menus_es.properties*
French	*Menus_fr.properties*
French-Canadian	*Menus_fr_CA.properties*

Locale names are two-letter ISO-639 language codes (lowercase), and normally abbreviate the country's *endonym* (the name its language speakers refer to it by), thus Sweden is *sv* for *Sverige*, etc.; locale variations are two-letter ISO country codes (uppercase).

Setting the locale

On Windows, go into Regional Settings in the Control Panel. Changing this setting may entail a reboot, so exit any editor windows.

On Unix, set your LANG environment variable. For example, a Korn shell user in Mexico might have this line in her *.profile*:

```
export LANG=es_MX
```

On either system, for testing a different locale, you need only define the locale in the System Properties at runtime using the command-line option `-D`, as in:

```
java -Duser.language=es i18n.Browser
```

to run the Java program named `Browser` in package `i18n` in the Spanish locale.

15.2. Listing Available Locales

Problem

You want to see what locales are available.

Solution

Call `Locale.getAvailableLocales()`.

Discussion

A typical runtime may have dozens of locales available. The program `ListLocales` uses the method `getAvailableLocales()` and prints the list:

```
// File ListLocales.java
Locale[] list = Locale.getAvailableLocales( );
for (Locale loc : list) {
    System.out.println(loc);
}
```

The list is far too long to show here, as you can judge by the first few entries:

```
> java i18n.ListLocales
en
en_US
ar
ar_AE
ar_BH
ar_DZ
ar_EG
ar_IQ
ar_JO
ar_KW
ar_LB
ar_LY
ar_MA
ar_OM
ar_QA
ar_SA
ar_SD
ar_SY
ar_TN
ar_YE
be
be_BY
```

On my laptop, the complete list has more than a dozen dozen locales:

```
$ java i18n.ListLocales | wc -l
    160
$
```

15.3. Creating a Menu with I18N Resources

Problem

You want to internationalize an entire Menu.

Solution

Get the Menu's label, and each MenuItem's label, from a ResourceBundle.

Discussion

Fetching a single menu item is the same as fetching a button:

```
rb = getResourceBundle("Widgets");
try { label = rb.getString("exitMenu.label"); }
catch (MissingResourceException e) { label="Exit"; } // fallback
someMenu.add(new JMenuItem(label));
```

This is a lot of code, so we typically consolidate it in convenience routines (see Recipe 15.4). Here is sample code, using our convenience routines:

```
JMenu fm = mkMenu(rb, "file");
fm.add(mkMenuItem(rb, "file", "open"));
fm.add(mkMenuItem(rb, "file", "new"));
fm.add(mkMenuItem(rb, "file", "save"));
fm.add(mkMenuItem(rb, "file", "exit"));
mb.add(fm);
Menu um = mkMenu(rb, "edit");
um.add(mkMenuItem(rb, "edit", "copy"));
um.add(mkMenuItem(rb, "edit", "paste"));
mb.add(um);
```

15.4. Writing Internationalization Convenience Routines

Problem

You want convenience.

Solution

I've got it.

Discussion

Convenience routines are mini-implementations that can be more convenient and effective than the general-purpose routines. Here I present the convenience routines to create buttons, menus, etc. First, a simple one, mkMenu():

```
/** Convenience routine to make up a Menu with its name L10N'd */
Menu mkMenu(ResourceBundle b, String menuName) {
    String label;
    try { label = b.getString(menuName+".label"); }
    catch (MissingResourceException e) { label=menuName; }
    return new Menu(label);
}
```

There are many such routines that you might need; I have consolidated several of them into my class *I18N.java*, which is part of the com.darwinsys.swingui package. All methods are static, and can be used without having to instantiate an I18N object because they do not maintain any state across calls. The method mkButton() creates and returns a localized Button, and so on. The method mkDialog is slightly misnamed because the JOptionPane method showMessageDialog() doesn't create and return a Dialog object, but it seemed more consistent to write it as shown here:

```
package com.darwinsys.swingui;

import java.util.MissingResourceException;
import java.util.ResourceBundle;

import javax.swing.*;

/** Convenience routines for internationalized code.
 * All methods are static, for ease of use.
 */
public class I18N {

    /** Convenience routine to make a JButton */
    public static JButton mkButton(ResourceBundle b, String name) {
        String label;
        try { label = b.getString(name+".label"); }
        catch (MissingResourceException e) { label=name; }
        return new JButton(label);
    }

    /** Convenience routine to make a JMenu */
    public static JMenu mkMenu(ResourceBundle b, String name) {
        String menuLabel;
        try { menuLabel = b.getString(name+".label"); }
        catch (MissingResourceException e) { menuLabel=name; }
        return new JMenu(menuLabel);
    }

    /** Convenience routine to make a JMenuItem */
```

```
public static JMenuItem mkMenuItem(ResourceBundle b,
        String menu, String name) {

    String miLabel;
    try { miLabel = b.getString(menu + "." + name + ".label"); }
    catch (MissingResourceException e) { miLabel=name; }
    String key = null;
    try { key = b.getString(menu + "." + name + ".key"); }
    catch (MissingResourceException e) { key=null; }

    if (key == null)
        return new JMenuItem(miLabel);
    else
        return new JMenuItem(miLabel, key.charAt(0));
}

/** Show a JOptionPane message dialog */
public static void mkDialog(ResourceBundle b,JFrame parent,
    String dialogTag, String titleTag, int messageType) {
        JOptionPane.showMessageDialog(
            parent,
            getString(b, dialogTag, "DIALOG TEXT MISSING: " + dialogTag),
            getString(b, titleTag, "DIALOG TITLE MISSING: "  + titleTag),
            messageType);
}

/** Just get a String (for dialogs, labels, etc.) */
public static String getString(ResourceBundle b, String name, String dflt) {
    String result;
    try {
        result = b.getString(name);
    } catch (MissingResourceException e) {
        result = dflt;
    }
    return result;
}
}
```

15.5. Creating a Dialog with I18N Resources

Problem

You want to internationalize a dialog.

Solution

Use a ResourceBundle.

Discussion

This is similar to the use of ResourceBundle in the previous recipes and shows the code for an internationalized version of the JOptionDemo program from Recipe 14.9:

```java
public class JOptionDemo extends JFrame {

    private static final long serialVersionUID = 1L;

    private ResourceBundle rb;

    // Constructor
    JOptionDemo(String s) {
        super(s);

        Container cp = getContentPane();
        cp.setLayout(new FlowLayout());

        rb = ResourceBundle.getBundle("Widgets");

        JButton b = I18N.mkButton(rb, "getButton");
        b.addActionListener(new ActionListener() {
            public void actionPerformed(ActionEvent e) {
                JOptionPane.showMessageDialog(
                    JOptionDemo.this,
                    rb.getString("dialog1.text"),
                    rb.getString("dialog1.title"),
                    JOptionPane.INFORMATION_MESSAGE);
            }
        });
        cp.add(b);

        b = I18N.mkButton(rb, "goodbye");
        b.addActionListener(new ActionListener() {
            public void actionPerformed(ActionEvent e) {
                System.exit(0);
            }
        });
        cp.add(b);

        // the main window
        setSize(200, 150);
        pack();
    }

    public static void main(String[] arg) {
        JOptionDemo x = new JOptionDemo("Testing 1 2 3...");
        x.setVisible(true);
    }
}
```

15.6. Creating a Resource Bundle

Problem

You need to create a resource bundle for use by I18N.

Solution

A resource bundle is simply a collection of names and values. You can write a `java.util.ResourceBundle` subclass, but it is easier to create textual Properties files (see Recipe 7.12) that you then load with `ResourceBundle.getBundle( )`. The files can be created using any text editor. Leaving it in a text file format also allows user customization; a user whose language is not provided for, or who wishes to change the wording somewhat due to local variations in dialect, will have no trouble editing the file.

Note that the resource bundle text file should not have the same name as any of your Java classes. The reason is that the `ResourceBundle` constructs a class dynamically with the same name as the resource files. You can confirm this by running **java -verbose** on any of the programs that use the I18N class from this chapter.

Discussion

Here is a sample properties file for a simple browser (see the `MenuIntl` program in Recipe 15.11):

```
# Default Menu properties
# The File Menu
file.label=File Menu
file.new.label=New File
file.new.key=N
```

Creating the default properties file is usually not a problem, but creating properties files for other languages might be. Unless you are a large multinational corporation, you will probably not have the resources (pardon the pun) to create resource files in-house. If you are shipping commercial software, you need to identify your target markets and understand which of these are most sensitive to wanting menus and the like in their own languages. Then, hire a professional translation service that has expertise in the required languages to prepare the files. Test them well before you ship, as you would any other part of your software.

If you need special characters, multiline text, or other complex entry, remember that a `ResourceBundle` is also a `Properties` file.

As an alternative approach, the next recipe describes a program that automates some of the work of isolating strings, creating resource files, and translating them to other languages.

15.7. Extracting Strings from Your Code

Problem

You have existing code that contains hardcoded strings.

Solution

Localize as you go along. For existing code, use JILT, Eclipse, or your favorite IDE.

Discussion

Of course it's best if you internationalize your code as you write it. But this often doesn't happen for one reason or another. Hence the need to retroactively internationalize your code.

Many tools extract Strings into resource bundles. This process is also known as externalization. Nothing to do with jilting your lover, JILT is Sun's Java Internationalization and Localization Toolkit, Version 2.0.[1] JILTing your code means processing it with JILT, which facilitates I18N and L10N'ing the Java classes. JILT has four GUI-based tools, which can be used independently, started from a GUI frontend called JILKIT. Figure 15-1 shows JILT in action.

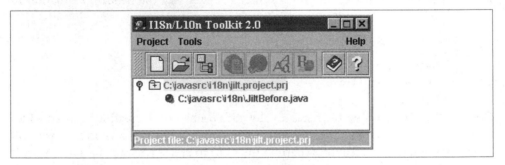

Figure 15-1. JILT in action

The tools are listed in Table 15-2.

---

1. Ironically, though, Sun appears to be jilting JILT; it's nearing the end of its lifecycle, so you may want to look at the externalization support offered by your IDE instead.

Table 15-2. JILT programs

Tool	Function
I18N Verifier	Tests program for international use and suggests improvements.
Message Tool	Finds and allows you to edit hardcoded or inconsistent messages.
Translator	Translates messages in a resource bundle file into a given locale/language.
Resource Tool	Merges multiple resource files into a new resource bundle. Can also find differences between resource files

It's worth noting that the time it takes to learn these tools may overshadow their benefits on small projects, but on large projects they will likely prove worthwhile.

Version 2 of the Translator ships with a Chinese dictionary, but you can provide your own dictionaries as well.

The Java Internationalization and Localization Toolkit has reached end-of-life in terms of support but can, as of this writing, still be downloaded for free from the Java Archived software page (*http://bit.ly/java-dwnlds*).

Almost all IDEs now provide an externalization mechanism. Under Eclipse, for example, select a Java source file, then select Externalize Strings from the Source menu. Eclipse generates a Properties file and a class with static methods to retrieve the values of the Strings and replace the strings in your code with calls to those methods. Other IDEs provide similar mechanisms.

15.8. Using a Particular Locale

Problem

You want to use a locale other than the default in a particular operation.

Solution

Use Locale.getInstance(Locale).

Discussion

Classes that provide formatting services, such as DateFormat and NumberFormat, provide an overloaded getInstance() method that can be called either with no arguments or with a Locale argument.

To use these, you can employ one of the predefined locale variables provided by the Locale class, or you can construct your own Locale object giving a language code and a country code:

```
Locale locale1 = Locale.FRANCE;     // predefined
Locale locale2 = new Locale("en", "UK");    // English, UK version
```

Either of these can be used to format a date or a number, as shown in class `UseLocales`:

```java
public class UseLocales {
    public static void main(String[] args) {

        Locale frLocale = Locale.FRANCE;     // predefined
        Locale ukLocale = new Locale("en", "UK");    // English, UK version

        DateFormat defaultDateFormatter = DateFormat.getDateInstance(
            DateFormat.MEDIUM);
        DateFormat frDateFormatter = DateFormat.getDateInstance(
            DateFormat.MEDIUM, frLocale);
        DateFormat ukDateFormatter = DateFormat.getDateInstance(
            DateFormat.MEDIUM, ukLocale);

        Date now = new Date();
        System.out.println("Default: " + ' ' +
            defaultDateFormatter.format(now));
        System.out.println(frLocale.getDisplayName() + ' ' +
            frDateFormatter.format(now));
        System.out.println(ukLocale.getDisplayName() + ' ' +
            ukDateFormatter.format(now));
    }
}
```

The program prints the locale name and formats the date in each of the locales:

```
$ java i18n.UseLocales
Default:  Nov 30, 2000
French (France) 30 nov. 00
English (UK) Nov 30, 2000
$
```

15.9. Setting the Default Locale

Problem

You want to change the default `Locale` for all operations within a given Java runtime.

Solution

Set the system property `user.language` or call `Locale.setDefault()`.

Discussion

Here is a program called `SetLocale`, which takes the language and country codes from the command line, constructs a `Locale` object, and passes it to `Locale.setDefault()`. When run with different arguments, it prints the date and a number in the appropriate locale:

```
C:\javasrc\i18n>java i18n.SetLocale en US
6/30/00 1:45 AM
123.457

C:\javasrc\i18n>java i18n.SetLocale fr FR
30/06/00 01:45
123,457
```

The code is similar to the previous recipe in how it constructs the locale:

```java
public class SetLocale {
    public static void main(String[] args) {

        switch (args.length) {
        case 0:
            Locale.setDefault(Locale.FRANCE);
            break;
        case 1:
            throw new IllegalArgumentException();
        case 2:
            Locale.setDefault(new Locale(args[0], args[1]));
            break;
        default:
            System.out.println("Usage: SetLocale [language [country]]");
            // FALLTHROUGH
        }

        DateFormat df = DateFormat.getInstance();
        NumberFormat nf = NumberFormat.getInstance();

        System.out.println(df.format(new Date()));
        System.out.println(nf.format(123.4567));
    }
}
```

Note that it is only appropriate to do this in a standalone application, not one that will be used by multiple users at the same time, such as a Chat server or a web application; there you should use a specific locale (Recipe 15.8) for each user.

15.10. Formatting Messages with MessageFormat

Problem

Messages may need to be formatted differently in different languages.

Solution

Use a MessageFormat object.

Discussion

In English, for example, we say "file not found." But in other languages the word order is different: the words for "not found" might need to precede the word for "file." Java accounts for this using the MessageFormat class. Suppose we want to format a message as follows:

```
$ java i18n.MessageFormatDemoIntl
At 3:33:02 PM on 01-Jul-00, myfile.txt could not be opened.
$ java -Duser.language=es i18n.MessageFormatDemoIntl
A 3:34:49 PM sobre 01-Jul-00, no se puede abrir la fila myfile.txt.
$
```

The MessageFormat in its simplest form takes a format string with a series of numeric indexes and an array of objects to be formatted. The objects are inserted into the resulting string, where the given array index appears. Here is a simple example of a MessageFormat in action:

```
public class MessageFormatDemo {

    static Object[] data = {
            new java.util.Date(),
            "myfile.txt",
            "could not be opened"
    };

    public static void main(String[] args) {
        String result = MessageFormat.format(
            "At {0,time} on {0,date}, {1} {2}.", data);
        System.out.println(result);
    }
}
```

But we still need to internationalize this, so we'll add some lines to our widget's properties files. In the default (English) version:

```
# These are for MessageFormatDemo
#
filedialogs.cantopen.format=At {0,time} on {0,date}, {1} could not be opened.
```

In the Spanish version, we'll add the format as follows:

```
# These are for MessageFormatDemo
#
filedialogs.cantopen.formta=A {0,time} sobre {0,date}, no pude abrir la fila {1}.
```

Then MessageFormatDemo still needs to have a ResourceBundle and get the format string from the bundle. Here is MessageFormatDemoIntl:

```
public class MessageFormatDemoIntl {

    private static Date date = new Date();
    private static String fileName = "myfile.txt";
```

```
    public static void main(String[] args) {
        ResourceBundle rb = ResourceBundle.getBundle("Widgets");
        String format = rb.getString("filedialogs.cantopen.format");
        String result = MessageFormat.format(format, date, fileName);
        System.out.println(result);
    }
}
```

Running it might produce the following output in the default locale:

```
$ java i18n.MessageFormatDemoIntl
At 9:10:13 PM on 23-Feb-2014, myfile.txt could not be opened.
$
```

MessageFormat is more complex than this; see the javadoc page for more details and examples.

15.11. Program: MenuIntl

MenuIntl (shown in Example 15-1) is a complete version of the menu code presented in Recipe 15.3.

Example 15-1. MenuIntl.java

```java
public class MenuIntl extends JFrame {

    /** "main program" method - construct and show */
    public static void main(String[] av) {
        // create an MenuIntl object, tell it to show up
        new MenuIntl().setVisible(true);
    }

    /** Construct the object including its GUI */
    public MenuIntl() {
        super("MenuIntlTest");
        JMenuItem mi;          // used in various spots

        Container cp = getContentPane();
        cp.setLayout(new FlowLayout());
        JLabel lab;
        cp.add(lab = new JLabel());

        setDefaultCloseOperation(EXIT_ON_CLOSE);
        JMenuBar mb = new JMenuBar();
        setJMenuBar(mb);

        ResourceBundle b = ResourceBundle.getBundle("i18n.Widgets");

        String titlebar;
        try { titlebar = b.getString("program"+".title"); }
        catch (MissingResourceException e) { titlebar="MenuIntl Demo"; }
```

```
        setTitle(titlebar);

        String message;
        try { message = b.getString("program"+".message"); }
        catch (MissingResourceException e) {
            message="Welcome to the world of Java";
        }
        lab.setText(message);

        JMenu fm = mkMenu(b, "file");
        // In finished code there would be a call to
        // mi.addActionListener(...) after *each* of
        // these mkMenuItem calls!
        fm.add(mi = mkMenuItem(b, "file", "open"));
        fm.add(mi = mkMenuItem(b, "file", "new"));
        fm.add(mi = mkMenuItem(b, "file", "save"));
        fm.add(mi = mkMenuItem(b, "file", "exit"));
        mi.addActionListener(new ActionListener() {
            public void actionPerformed(ActionEvent e) {
                MenuIntl.this.setVisible(false);
                MenuIntl.this.dispose();
                System.exit(0);
            }
        });
        mb.add(fm);

        JMenu vm = mkMenu(b,  "view");
        vm.add(mi = mkMenuItem(b, "view", "tree"));
        vm.add(mi = mkMenuItem(b, "view", "list"));
        vm.add(mi = mkMenuItem(b, "view", "longlist"));
        mb.add(vm);

        JMenu hm = mkMenu(b,  "help");
        hm.add(mi = mkMenuItem(b, "help", "about"));
        // mb.setHelpMenu(hm);    // needed for portability (Motif, etc.).

        // the main window
        JLabel jl = new JLabel("Menu Demo Window");
        jl.setSize(200, 150);
        cp.add(jl);
        pack();
    }

    // Copies of routines that are in darwinsys.jar,
    // just here for compilation convenience

    /** Convenience routine to make a JMenu */
    public JMenu mkMenu(ResourceBundle b, String name) {
        String menuLabel;
        try { menuLabel = b.getString(name+".label"); }
        catch (MissingResourceException e) { menuLabel=name; }
        return new JMenu(menuLabel);
```

```
    }

    /** Convenience routine to make a JMenuItem */
    public JMenuItem mkMenuItem(ResourceBundle b, String menu, String name) {
        String miLabel;
        try { miLabel = b.getString(menu + "." + name + ".label"); }
        catch (MissingResourceException e) { miLabel=name; }
        String key = null;
        try { key = b.getString(menu + "." + name + ".key"); }
        catch (MissingResourceException e) { key=null; }

        if (key == null)
            return new JMenuItem(miLabel);
        else
            return new JMenuItem(miLabel, key.charAt(0));
    }

    private String lookupWithDefault(ResourceBundle rb, String key, String dflt)
    {
        try {
            return rb.getString(key);
        } catch (MissingResourceException e) {
            return dflt;
        }
    }
}
```

15.12. Program: BusCard

This program may seem a bit silly, but it's a good example of configuring a variety of user interface controls from a resource bundle. The BusCard program allows you to create a digital business card ("interactive business card") onscreen (see Figure 15-2). The labels for all the GUI controls, and even the pull-down menu options, are loaded from a ResourceBundle.

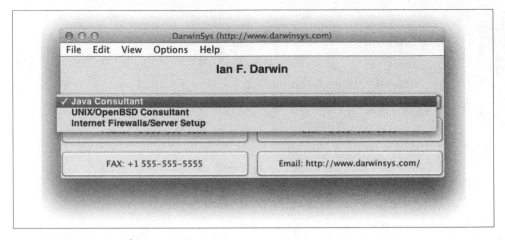

Figure 15-2. BusCard program in action

Example 15-2 shows the code for the `BusCard` program.

Example 15-2. BusCard.java

```java
public class BusCard extends JFrame {

    private static final long serialVersionUID = 1L;
    private JLabel nameTF;
    private JComboBox<String> jobChoice;
    private JButton B1, B2, B3, B4;

    /** "main program" method - construct and show */
    public static void main(String[] av) {
        // create a BusCard object, tell it to show up
        new BusCard().setVisible(true);
    }

    /** Construct the object including its GUI */
    public BusCard() {

        Container cp = getContentPane();

        cp.setLayout(new GridLayout(0, 1));

        addWindowListener(new WindowAdapter() {
            public void windowClosing(WindowEvent e) {
                setVisible(false);
                dispose();
                System.exit(0);
            }
        });

        JMenuBar mb = new JMenuBar();
```

```java
setJMenuBar(mb);

ResourceBundle b = ResourceBundle.getBundle("i18n.BusCard");

JMenu aMenu;
aMenu = I18N.mkMenu(b, "filemenu");
mb.add(aMenu);
JMenuItem mi = I18N.mkMenuItem(b, "filemenu", "exit");
aMenu.add(mi);
mi.addActionListener(new ActionListener() {
    public void actionPerformed(ActionEvent e) {
        System.exit(0);
    }
});
aMenu = I18N.mkMenu(b, "editmenu");
mb.add(aMenu);
aMenu = I18N.mkMenu(b, "viewmenu");
mb.add(aMenu);
aMenu = I18N.mkMenu(b, "optionsmenu");
mb.add(aMenu);
aMenu = I18N.mkMenu(b, "helpmenu");
mb.add(aMenu);
//mb.setHelpMenu(aMenu);        // needed for portability (Motif, etc.).

setTitle(I18N.getString(b, "card"+".company", "TITLE"));

JPanel p1 = new JPanel();
p1.setLayout(new GridLayout(0, 1, 50, 10));

nameTF = new JLabel("My Name", JLabel.CENTER);
nameTF.setFont(new Font("helvetica", Font.BOLD, 18));
nameTF.setText(I18N.getString(b, "card"+".myname", "MYNAME"));
p1.add(nameTF);

jobChoice = new JComboBox<>();
jobChoice.setFont(new Font("helvetica", Font.BOLD, 14));

// Get Job Titles from the Properties file loaded into "b"!
String next;
int i=1;
do {
    next = I18N.getString(b, "job_title" + i++, null);
    if (next != null)
        jobChoice.addItem(next);
} while (next != null);
p1.add(jobChoice);

cp.add(p1);

JPanel p2 = new JPanel();
p2.setLayout(new GridLayout(2, 2, 10, 10));
```

```
        B1 = new JButton();
        B1.setText(I18N.getString(b, "button1.label", "BUTTON LABEL"));
        p2.add(B1);

        B2 = new JButton();
        B2.setText(I18N.getString(b, "button2.label", "BUTTON LABEL"));
        p2.add(B2);

        B3 = new JButton();
        B3.setText(I18N.getString(b, "button3.label", "BUTTON LABEL"));
        p2.add(B3);

        B4 = new JButton();
        B4.setText(I18N.getString(b, "button4.label", "BUTTON LABEL"));
        p2.add(B4);
        cp.add(p2);

        pack();
    }
}
```

See Also

Other things may need to be internationalized as well:

Character comparisons
> These are set separately on Unix/POSIX; on other operating systems, they depend on the default `Locale`.

Date and time formats
> See the Introduction to Chapter 6.

Number formats
> See `java.util.NumberFormat` in Recipe 5.8.

Message insertions
> These appear in different orders in different languages (something the C-language `printf()` could never handle). See `java.util.MessageFormat` in Recipe 15.10.

Internationalization Caveats

Internationalizing your menus and buttons is only one step. You also need to internationalize message text in dialogs as well as help files (see the JavaHelp API (see "Javadoc Versus JavaHelp" on page 693).

Some items, such as AWT `FileDialog`, use native components—their appearance depends on the native operating system (your application can change its own default locale, but not the system's; if your customer has a differently internationalized copy of the same OS, the file dialogs will appear differently).

Documentation

A short, readable, non-Java-specific introduction to the overall topic of internationalization is *The Guide to Translation and Localization*, written by the staff of Lingo Systems and published by the IEEE Computer Society. For more on Java I18N, see the online documentation that ships with the JDK; start at *docs/guide/intl/index.html*. See also the O'Reilly book *Java Internationalization*.

The Oracle Java tutorials feature an I18N section ("Trail") (*http://bit.ly/1mNs8ie*).

The Last Word

Good luck. Bonne chance. Buena suerte…

## CHAPTER 16

Server-Side Java

16.0. Introduction

Sockets form the underpinnings of almost all networking protocols. JDBC, RMI, COR-BA, EJB, and the non-Java RPC (Remote Procedure Call) and NFS (Network File System) are all implemented by connecting various types of sockets together. Socket connections can be implemented in most any language, not just Java: C, C++, Perl, and Python are also popular, and many others are possible. A client or server written in any one of these languages can communicate with its opposite written in any of the other languages. Therefore, it's worth taking a quick look at how the ServerSocket behaves, even if you wind up utilizing the higher-level services such as RMI, JDBC, CORBA, or EJB.

The discussion looks first at the ServerSocket itself, then at writing data over a socket in various ways. Finally, I show a complete implementation of a usable network server written in Java: the chat server from the client in the previous chapter.

 Most production work in server-side Java uses the Java Enterprise Edition (Java EE). Java EE provides scalability and support for building well-structured, multi-tiered distributed applications. EE provides the "servlet" framework; a servlet is a strategy object that can be installed into any standard Java EE web server. EE also provides two web "view" technologies: the original JSP (JavaServer Pages) and the newer, component-based JSF (JavaServer Faces). Finally, EE provides a number of other network-based services, including EJB3 remote access and Java Messaging Service (JMS). These are unfortunately outside the scope of this book, and are covered in several other books such as Arun Gupta's *Java EE 7 Essentials: Enterprise Developer Handbook. This chapter is only for those who need or want to build their own server from the ground up.*

16.1. Opening a Server Socket for Business

Problem

You need to write a socket-based server.

Solution

Create a ServerSocket for the given port number.

Discussion

The ServerSocket represents the "other end" of a connection, the server that waits patiently for clients to come along and connect to it. You construct a ServerSocket with just the port number.[1] Because it doesn't need to connect to another host, it doesn't need a particular host's address as the client socket constructor does.

Assuming the ServerSocket constructor doesn't throw an exception, you're in business. Your next step is to await client activity, which you do by calling accept(). This call blocks until a client connects to your server; at that point, the accept() returns to you a Socket object (not a ServerSocket) that is connected in both directions to the Socket object on the client (or its equivalent, if written in another language). Example 16-1 shows the code for a socket-based server.

Example 16-1. Listen.java

```java
public class Listen {
    /** The TCP port for the service. */
    public static final short PORT = 9999;

    public static void main(String[] argv) throws IOException {
        ServerSocket sock;
        Socket  clientSock;
        try {
            sock = new ServerSocket(PORT);
            while ((clientSock = sock.accept()) != null) {

                // Process it.
                process(clientSock);
            }
```

---

1. You may not be able to pick just any port number for your own service, of course. Certain well-known port numbers are reserved for specific services and listed in your *services* file, such as 22 for Secure Shell, 25 for SMTP, and hundreds more. Also, on server-based operating systems, ports below 1024 are considered "privileged" ports and require root or administrator privilege to create. This was an early security mechanism; today, with zillions of single-user desktops connected to the Internet, it provides little real security, but the restriction remains.

```
        } catch (IOException e) {
            System.err.println(e);
        }
    }

    /** This would do something with one client. */
    static void process(Socket s) throws IOException {
        System.out.println("Accept from client " + s.getInetAddress());
        // The conversation would be here.
        s.close();
    }
}
```

You would normally use the same socket for both reading and writing, as shown in the next few recipes.

You may want to listen only on a particular network interface. Though we tend to think of network addresses as computer addresses, the two are not the same. A network address is actually the address of a particular network card, or network interface connection, on a given computing device. A desktop computer, laptop, Palm handheld, or cellular phone might have only a single interface, hence a single network address. But a large server machine might have two or more interfaces, usually when it is connected to several networks. A network router is a box, either special purpose (e.g., a Cisco router), or general purpose (e.g., a Unix host), that has interfaces on multiple networks *and* has both the capability and the administrative permission to forward packets from one network to another. A program running on such a server machine might want to provide services only to its inside network or its outside network. One way to accomplish this is by specifying the network interface to be listened on. Suppose you want to provide a different view of web pages for your intranet than you provide to outside customers. For security reasons, you probably wouldn't run both these services on the same machine. But if you wanted to, you could do this by providing the network interface addresses as arguments to the ServerSocket constructor.

However, to use this form of the constructor, you don't have the option of using a string for the network address's name, as you did with the client socket; you must convert it to an InetAddress object. You also have to provide a backlog argument, which is the number of connections that can queue up to be accepted before clients are told that your server is too busy. The complete setup is shown in Example 16-2.

Example 16-2. ListenInside.java

```
public class ListenInside {
    /** The TCP port for the service. */
    public static final short PORT = 9999;
    /** The name of the network interface. */
    public static final String INSIDE_HOST = "acmewidgets-inside";
    /** The number of clients allowed to queue */
```

```
    public static final int BACKLOG = 10;

    public static void main(String[] argv) throws IOException {
        ServerSocket sock;
        Socket   clientSock;
        try {
            sock = new ServerSocket(PORT, BACKLOG,
                InetAddress.getByName(INSIDE_HOST));
            while ((clientSock = sock.accept()) != null) {

                // Process it.
                process(clientSock);
            }

        } catch (IOException e) {
            System.err.println(e);
        }
    }

    /** Hold server's conversation with one client. */
    static void process(Socket s) throws IOException {
        System.out.println("Connected from  " + INSIDE_HOST +
            ": " + s.getInetAddress(  ));
        // The conversation would be here.
        s.close();
    }
}
```

The InetAddress.getByName( ) looks up the given hostname in a system-dependent way, referring to a configuration file in the */etc* or *\windows* directory, or to some kind of resolver such as the Domain Name System. Consult a good book on networking and system administration if you need to modify this data.

16.2. Returning a Response (String or Binary)

Problem

You need to write a string or binary data to the client.

Solution

The socket gives you an InputStream and an OutputStream. Use them.

Discussion

The client socket examples in the previous chapter called the getInputStream( ) and getOutputStream( ) methods. These examples do the same. The main difference is that these ones get the socket from a ServerSocket's accept( ) method. Another distinction is, by definition, that normally the server creates or modifies the data and sends it to the client. Example 16-3 is a simple Echo server, which the Echo client of Recipe 13.4 can connect to. This server handles one complete connection with a client, then goes back and does the accept() to wait for the next client.

Example 16-3. EchoServer.java

```java
public class EchoServer {
    /** Our server-side rendezvous socket */
    protected ServerSocket sock;
    /** The port number to use by default */
    public final static int ECHOPORT = 7;
    /** Flag to control debugging */
    protected boolean debug = true;

    /** main: construct and run */
    public static void main(String[] args) {
        int p = ECHOPORT;
        if (args.length == 1) {
            try {
                p = Integer.parseInt(args[0]);
            } catch (NumberFormatException e) {
                System.err.println("Usage: EchoServer [port#]");
                System.exit(1);
            }
        }
        new EchoServer(p).handle();
    }

    /** Construct an EchoServer on the given port number */
    public EchoServer(int port) {
        try {
            sock = new ServerSocket(port);
        } catch (IOException e) {
            System.err.println("I/O error in setup");
            System.err.println(e);
            System.exit(1);
        }
    }

    /** This handles the connections */
    protected void handle() {
        Socket ios = null;
        BufferedReader is = null;
        PrintWriter os = null;
        while (true) {
            try {
                System.out.println("Waiting for client...");
                ios = sock.accept();
                System.err.println("Accepted from " +
                    ios.getInetAddress().getHostName());
                is = new BufferedReader(
```

```
            new InputStreamReader(ios.getInputStream(), "8859_1"));
        os = new PrintWriter(
                new OutputStreamWriter(
                    ios.getOutputStream(), "8859_1"), true);
        String echoLine;
        while ((echoLine = is.readLine()) != null) {
            System.err.println("Read " + echoLine);
            os.print(echoLine + "\r\n");
            os.flush();
            System.err.println("Wrote " + echoLine);
        }
        System.err.println("All done!");
    } catch (IOException e) {
        System.err.println(e);
    } finally {
        try {
            if (is != null)
                is.close();
            if (os != null)
                os.close();
            if (ios != null)
                ios.close();
        } catch (IOException e) {
            // These are unlikely, but might indicate that
            // the other end shut down early, a disk filled up
            // but wasn't detected until close, etc.
            System.err.println("IO Error in close");
        }
    }
  }
 }
 /*NOTREACHED*/
    }
}
```

To send a string across an arbitrary network connection, some authorities recommend sending both the carriage return and the newline character; many protocol specifications require that you do so. This explains the \r\n in the code. If the other end is a DOS program or a Telnet-like program, it may be expecting both characters. On the other hand, if you are writing both ends, you can simply use println()—followed always by an explicit flush() before you read--to prevent the deadlock of having both ends trying to read with one end's data still in the PrintWriter's buffer!

If you need to process binary data, use the data streams from java.io instead of the readers/writers. I need a server for the DaytimeBinary program of Recipe 13.5. In operation, it should look like the following:

```
C:\javasrc\network>java network.DaytimeBinary
Remote time is 3161316799
BASE_DIFF is 2208988800
Time diff == 952284799
```

```
Time on localhost is Sun Mar 08 19:33:19 GMT 2014

C:\javasrc\network>time/t
Current time is  7:33:23.84p

C:\javasrc\network>date/t
Current date is Sun 03-08-2014

C:\javasrc\network>
```

Well, it happens that I have such a program in my arsenal, so I present it in
Example 16-4. Note that it directly uses certain public constants defined in the client
class. Normally these are defined in the server class and used by the client, but I wanted
to present the client code first.

Example 16-4. DaytimeServer.java

```java
public class DaytimeServer {
    /** Our server-side rendezvous socket */
    ServerSocket sock;
    /** The port number to use by default */
    public final static int PORT = 37;

    /** main: construct and run */
    public static void main(String[] argv) {
        new DaytimeServer(PORT).runService();
    }

    /** Construct a DaytimeServer on the given port number */
    public DaytimeServer(int port) {
        try {
            sock = new ServerSocket(port);
        } catch (IOException e) {
            System.err.println("I/O error in setup\n" + e);
            System.exit(1);
        }
    }

    /** This handles the connections */
    protected void runService() {
        Socket ios = null;
        DataOutputStream os = null;
        while (true) {
            try {
                System.out.println("Waiting for connection on port " + PORT);
                ios = sock.accept();
                System.err.println("Accepted from " +
                    ios.getInetAddress().getHostName());
                os = new DataOutputStream(ios.getOutputStream());
                long time = System.currentTimeMillis();

                time /= RDateClient.MSEC;    // Daytime Protocol is in seconds
```

```
                // Convert to Java time base.
                time += RDateClient.BASE_DIFF;

                // Write it, truncating cast to int since it is using
                // the Internet Daytime protocol which uses 4 bytes.
                // This will fail in the year 2038, along with all
                // 32-bit timekeeping systems based from 1970.
                // Remember, you read about the Y2038 crisis here first!
                os.writeInt((int)time);
                os.close();
            } catch (IOException e) {
                System.err.println(e);
            }
        }
    }
}
```

16.3. Returning Object Information Across a Network Connection

Problem

You need to return an object across a network connection.

Solution

Create the object you need, and write it using an `ObjectOutputStream` created on top of the socket's output stream.

Discussion

The program in Example 13-7 in the previous chapter reads a `Date` object over an `ObjectInputStream`. Example 16-5, the `DaytimeObjectServer` (the other end of that process), is a program that constructs a `Date` object each time it's connected to and returns it to the client.

Example 16-5. DaytimeObjectServer.java

```
public class DaytimeObjectServer {
    /** The TCP port for the object time service. */
    public static final short TIME_PORT = 1951;

    public static void main(String[] argv) {
        ServerSocket sock;
        Socket    clientSock;
        try {
            sock = new ServerSocket(TIME_PORT);
```

```
        while ((clientSock = sock.accept()) != null) {
            System.out.println("Accept from " +
                clientSock.getInetAddress());
            ObjectOutputStream os = new ObjectOutputStream(
                clientSock.getOutputStream());

            // Construct and write the Object
            os.writeObject(new Date());

            os.close();
        }

    } catch (IOException e) {
        System.err.println(e);
    }
  }
}
```

16.4. Handling Multiple Clients

Problem

Your server needs to handle multiple clients.

Solution

Use a thread for each.

Discussion

In the C world, several mechanisms allow a server to handle multiple clients. One is to use a special "system call" select() or poll(), which notifies the server when any of a set of file/socket descriptors is ready to read, ready to write, or has an error. By including its rendezvous socket (equivalent to our ServerSocket) in this list, the C-based server can read from any of a number of clients in any order. Java does not provide this call, because it is not readily implementable on some Java platforms. Instead, Java uses the general-purpose Thread mechanism, as described in Recipe 22.11. Threads are, in fact, one of the other mechanisms available to the C programmer on most platforms. Each time the code accepts a new connection from the ServerSocket, it immediately constructs and starts a new thread object to process that client.[2]

---

2. There are some limits to how many threads you can have, which affect only very large, enterprise-scale servers. You can't expect to have thousands of threads running in the standard Java runtime. For large, high-performance servers, you may wish to resort to native code (see Recipe 24.6) using select() or poll().

The Java code to implement accepting on a socket is pretty simple, apart from having to catch IOExceptions:

```
/** Run the main loop of the Server. */
void runServer( ) {
    while (true) {
        try {
            Socket clntSock = sock.accept( );
            new Handler(clntSock).start( );
        } catch(IOException e) {
            System.err.println(e);
        }
    }
}
```

To use a thread, you must either subclass Thread or implement Runnable. The Handler class must be a subclass of Thread for this code to work as written; if Handler instead implemented the Runnable interface, the code would pass an instance of the Runnable into the constructor for Thread, as in:

```
Thread t = new Thread(new Handler(clntSock));
t.start( );
```

But as written, Handler is constructed using the normal socket returned by accept( ), and normally calls the socket's getInputStream( ) and getOutputStream( ) methods and holds its conversation in the usual way. I'll present a full implementation, a threaded echo client. First, a session showing it in use:

```
$ java network.EchoServerThreaded
EchoServerThreaded ready for connections.
Socket starting: Socket[addr=localhost/127.0.0.1,port=2117,localport=7]
Socket starting: Socket[addr=darian/192.168.1.50,port=13386,localport=7]
Socket starting: Socket[addr=darian/192.168.1.50,port=22162,localport=7]
Socket ENDED: Socket[addr=darian/192.168.1.50,port=22162,localport=7]
Socket ENDED: Socket[addr=darian/192.168.1.50,port=13386,localport=7]
Socket ENDED: Socket[addr=localhost/127.0.0.1,port=2117,localport=7]
```

Here, I connected to the server once with my EchoClient program and, while still connected, called it up again (and again) with an operating system–provided Telnet client. The server communicated with all the clients concurrently, sending the answers from the first client back to the first client, and the data from the second client back to the second client. In short, it works. I ended the sessions with the end-of-file character in the program and used the normal disconnect mechanism from the Telnet client. Example 16-6 is the code for the server.

Example 16-6. EchoServerThreaded.java

```
public class EchoServerThreaded {

    public static final int ECHOPORT = 7;
```

```java
public static void main(String[] av)
{
    new EchoServerThreaded().runServer();
}

public void runServer()
{
    ServerSocket sock;
    Socket clientSocket;

    try {
        sock = new ServerSocket(ECHOPORT);

        System.out.println("EchoServerThreaded ready for connections.");

        /* Wait for a connection */
        while(true){
            clientSocket = sock.accept();
            /* Create a thread to do the communication, and start it */
            new Handler(clientSocket).start();
        }
    } catch(IOException e) {
        /* Crash the server if IO fails. Something bad has happened */
        System.err.println("Could not accept " + e);
        System.exit(1);
    }
}

/** A Thread subclass to handle one client conversation. */
class Handler extends Thread {
    Socket sock;

    Handler(Socket s) {
        sock = s;
    }

    public void run() {
        System.out.println("Socket starting: " + sock);
        try {
            BufferedReader is =
                new BufferedReader(
                    new InputStreamReader(sock.getInputStream()));
            PrintStream os = new PrintStream(sock.getOutputStream(), true);
            String line;
            while ((line = is.readLine()) != null) {
                os.print(line + "\r\n");
                os.flush();
            }
            sock.close();
        } catch (IOException e) {
            System.out.println("IO Error on socket " + e);
            return;
```

```
        }
        System.out.println("Socket ENDED: " + sock);
    }
}
}
```

A lot of short transactions can degrade performance, because each client causes the creation of a new threaded object. If you know or can reliably predict the degree of concurrency that is needed, an alternative paradigm involves the precreation of a fixed number of threads. But then how do you control their access to the ServerSocket? A look at the ServerSocket class documentation reveals that the accept() method is not synchronized, meaning that any number of threads can call the method concurrently. This could cause bad things to happen. So I use the synchronized keyword around this call to ensure that only one client runs in it at a time, because it updates global data. When no clients are connected, you will have one (randomly selected) thread running in the ServerSocket object's accept() method, waiting for a connection, plus *n-1* threads waiting for the first thread to return from the method. As soon as the first thread manages to accept a connection, it goes off and holds its conversation, releasing its lock in the process so that another randomly chosen thread is allowed into the accept() method. Each thread's run() method has an infinite loop beginning with an ac-cept() and then holding the conversation. The result is that client connections can get started more quickly, at a cost of slightly greater server startup time. Doing it this way also avoids the overhead of constructing a new Handler or Thread object each time a request comes along. This general approach is similar to what the popular Apache web server does, although it normally creates a number or pool of identical processes (instead of threads) to handle client connections. Accordingly, I have modified the EchoSer-verThreaded class shown in Example 16-6 to work this way, as you can see in Example 16-7.

Example 16-7. EchoServerThreaded2.java

```
public class EchoServerThreaded2 {

    public static final int ECHOPORT = 7;

    public static final int NUM_THREADS = 4;

    /** Main method, to start the servers. */
    public static void main(String[] av) {
        new EchoServerThreaded2(ECHOPORT, NUM_THREADS);
    }

    /** Constructor */
    public EchoServerThreaded2(int port, int numThreads) {
        ServerSocket servSock;

        try {
```

```
            servSock = new ServerSocket(port);

        } catch(IOException e) {
            /* Crash the server if IO fails. Something bad has happened */
            throw new RuntimeException("Could not create ServerSocket ", e);
        }

        // Create a series of threads and start them.
        for (int i=0; i<numThreads; i++) {
            new Handler(servSock, i).start();
        }
    }
}

/** A Thread subclass to handle one client conversation. */
class Handler extends Thread {
    ServerSocket servSock;
    int threadNumber;

    /** Construct a Handler. */
    Handler(ServerSocket s, int i) {
        servSock = s;
        threadNumber = i;
        setName("Thread " + threadNumber);
    }

    public void run() {
        /* Wait for a connection. Synchronized on the ServerSocket
         * while calling its accept() method.
         */
        while (true) {
            try {
                System.out.println( getName() + " waiting");

                Socket clientSocket;
                // Wait here for the next connection.
                synchronized(servSock) {
                    clientSocket = servSock.accept();
                }
                System.out.println(getName() + " starting, IP=" +
                    clientSocket.getInetAddress());
                BufferedReader is = new BufferedReader(
                    new InputStreamReader(clientSocket.getInputStream()));
                PrintStream os = new PrintStream(
                    clientSocket.getOutputStream(), true);
                String line;
                while ((line = is.readLine()) != null) {
                    os.print(line + "\r\n");
                    os.flush();
                }
                System.out.println(getName() + " ENDED ");
                clientSocket.close();
            } catch (IOException ex) {
```

```
                System.out.println(getName() + ": IO Error on socket " + ex);
                return;
            }
        }
    }
}
```

It is quite possible to implement a server of this sort with NIO, the "new" (back in J2SE 1.4) IO package. However, the code to do so outweighs anything in this chapter, and it is fraught with "issues." There are several good tutorials on the Internet for the person who truly needs the performance gain of using NIO to manage server connections.

16.5. Serving the HTTP Protocol

Problem

You want to serve up a protocol such as HTTP.

Solution

Create a ServerSocket and write some code that "speaks" the particular protocol. Or, better, use a Java-powered web server such as Apache Tomcat or a Java Enterprise Edition (Java EE) server such as JBoss WildFly.

Discussion

You can implement your own HTTP protocol server for very simple applications, which we'll do here. For any serious development, you want to use the Java Enterprise Edition; see the note at the beginning of this chapter.

This example just constructs a ServerSocket and listens on it. When connections come in, they are replied to using the HTTP protocol. So it is somewhat more involved than the simple Echo server presented in Recipe 16.2. However, it's not a complete web server; the filename in the request is ignored, and a standard message is always returned. This is thus a *very* simple web server; it follows only the bare minimum of the HTTP protocol needed to send its response back. A somewhat more complete example is presented in Recipe 22.11, after the issues of multithreading have been covered. For a real web server written in Java, get Tomcat from the Apache Tomcat website (*http://tomcat.apache.org*). The code shown in Example 16-8, however, is enough to understand how to structure a simple server that communicates using a protocol.

Example 16-8. WebServer0.java

```
public class WebServer0 {
    public static final int HTTP = 80;
```

```java
public static final String CRLF = "\r\n";
ServerSocket s;
static final String VIEW_SOURCE_URL =
  "https://github.com/IanDarwin/javasrc/tree/master/src/main/java/network";

/**
 * Main method, just creates a server and call its runServer().
 */
public static void main(String[] argv) throws Exception {
    System.out.println("DarwinSys JavaWeb Server 0.0 starting...");
    WebServer0 w = new WebServer0();
    w.runServer(HTTP);          // never returns!!
}

/** Get the actual ServerSocket; deferred until after Constructor
 * so subclass can mess with ServerSocketFactory (e.g., to do SSL).
 * @param port The port number to listen on
 */
protected ServerSocket getServerSocket(int port) throws Exception {
    return new ServerSocket(port);
}

/** RunServer accepts connections and passes each one to handler. */
public void runServer(int port) throws Exception {
    s = getServerSocket(port);
    while (true) {
        try {
            Socket us = s.accept();
            Handler(us);
        } catch(IOException e) {
            System.err.println(e);
            return;
        }

    }
}

/** Handler() handles one conversation with a Web client.
 * This is the only part of the program that "knows" HTTP.
 */
public void Handler(Socket s) {
    BufferedReader is;      // inputStream, from Viewer
    PrintWriter os;         // outputStream, to Viewer
    String request;         // what Viewer sends us.
    try {
        String from = s.getInetAddress().toString();
        System.out.println("Accepted connection from " + from);
        is = new BufferedReader(new InputStreamReader(s.getInputStream()));
        request = is.readLine();
        System.out.println("Request: " + request);

        os = new PrintWriter(s.getOutputStream(), true);
```

```
            os.print("HTTP/1.0 200 Here is your data" + CRLF);
            os.print("Content-type: text/html" + CRLF);
            os.print("Server-name: DarwinSys NULL Java WebServer 0" + CRLF);
            String reply1 = "<html><head>" +
                "<title>Wrong System Reached</title></head>\n" +
                "<h1>Welcome, ";
            String reply2 = ", but...</h1>\n" +
                "<p>You have reached a desktop machine " +
                "that does not run a real Web service.\n" +
                "<p>Please pick another system!</p>\n" +
                "<p>Or view <a href=\"" + VIEW_SOURCE_URL + "\">" +
                "the WebServer0 source on github</a>.</p>\n" +
                "<hr/><em>Java-based WebServer0</em><hr/>\n" +
                "</html>\n";
            os.print("Content-length: " +
                (reply1.length() + from.length() + reply2.length()) + CRLF);
            os.print(CRLF);
            os.print(reply1 + from + reply2 + CRLF);
            os.flush();
            s.close();
        } catch (IOException e) {
            System.out.println("IOException " + e);
        }
        return;
    }
}
```

16.6. Securing a Web Server with SSL and JSSE

Problem

You want to protect your network traffic from prying eyes or malicious modification, while the data is in transit.

Solution

Use the Java Secure Socket Extension, JSSE, to encrypt your traffic.

Discussion

JSSE provides services at a number of levels, but the simplest way to use it is simply to get your ServerSocket from an SSLServerSocketFactory instead of using the ServerSocket constructor directly. SSL is the Secure Sockets Layer; a revised version is known as TLS. It is specifically for use on the Web. To secure other protocols, you'd have to use a different form of the SocketFactory.

The SSLServerSocketFactory returns a ServerSocket that is set up to do SSL encryption. Example 16-9 uses this technique to override the getServerSocket() method in Recipe 16.5. If you're thinking this is too easy, you're wrong!

Example 16-9. JSSEWebServer0

```
/**
 * JSSEWebServer - subclass trivial WebServer0 to make it use SSL.
 * N.B. You MUST have set up a server certificate (see the
 * accompanying book text), or you will get the dreaded
 * javax.net.ssl.SSLHandshakeException: no cipher suites in common
 * (because without it JSSE can't use any of its built-in ciphers!).
 */
public class JSSEWebServer0 extends WebServer0 {

    public static final int HTTPS = 8443;

    public static void main(String[] args) throws Exception {
        if (System.getProperty("javax.net.ssl.keyStore") == null) {
            System.err.println(
                "You must pass in a keystore via -D; see the documentation!");
            System.exit(1);
        }
        System.out.println("DarwinSys JSSE Server 0.0 starting...");
        JSSEWebServer0 w = new JSSEWebServer0();
        w.runServer(HTTPS);        // never returns!!
    }

    /** Get an HTTPS ServerSocket using JSSE.
     * @see WebServer0#getServerSocket(int)
     * @throws ClassNotFoundException if the SecurityProvider cannot be instantiated.
     */
    protected ServerSocket getServerSocket(int port) throws Exception {

        SSLServerSocketFactory ssf =
            (SSLServerSocketFactory)SSLServerSocketFactory.getDefault();

        return ssf.createServerSocket(port);
    }

}
```

That is, indeed, all the Java code one needs to write. You do have to set up an SSL Certificate. For demonstration purposes, this can be a self-signed certificate; the steps in Recipe 21.12 (Steps 1–4) will suffice. You have to tell the JSSE layer where to find your keystore:

```
java -Djavax.net.ssl.keyStore=/home/ian/.keystore -Djavax.net.ssl.
keyStorePassword=secrit JSSEWebServer0
```

The typical client browser raises its eyebrows at a self-signed certificate (see Figure 16-1), but, if the user OKs it, will accept the certificate.

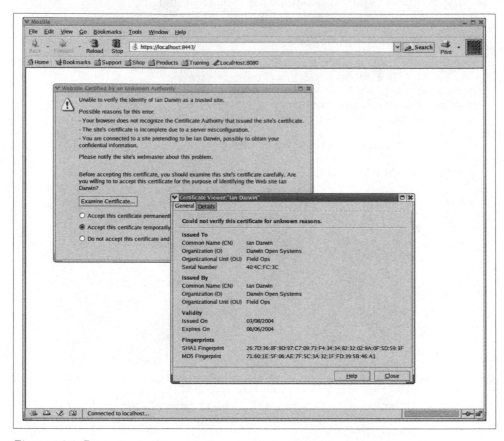

Figure 16-1. Browser caution

Figure 16-2 shows the output of the simple WebServer0 being displayed over the HTTPS protocol (notice the padlock in the lower-right corner).

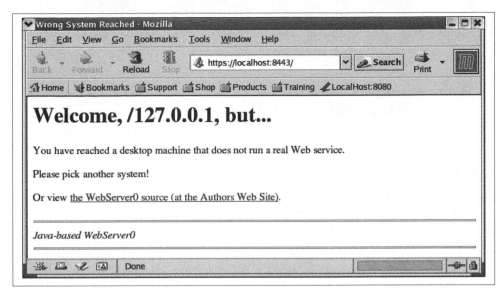

Figure 16-2. With encryption

See Also

JSSE can do much more than encrypt web server traffic; this is, however, sometimes seen as its most exciting application. For more information on JSSE, see the Sun website (*http://java.sun.com/products/jsse*) or *Java Security* by Scott Oaks (O'Reilly).

16.7. Network Logging

Problem

Your class is running inside a server container, and its debugging output is hard to obtain.

Solution

Use a network-based logger like the Java Logging API, Apache Logging Services Project's log4j, or the simple one shown here.

Discussion

Getting the debug output from a desktop client is fairly easy on most operating systems. But if the program you want to debug is running in a "container" like a servlet engine or an EJB server, it can be difficult to obtain debugging output, particularly if the container is running on a remote computer. It would be convenient if you could have your program send messages back to a program on your desktop machine for immediate display. Needless to say, it's not that hard to do this with Java's socket mechanism.

Many logging APIs can handle this:

- Java has had for years a standard logging API (discussed in Recipe 16.10) that talks to various logging mechanisms including Unix `syslog`.
- The Apache Logging Services Project produces `log4j`, which is used in many open source projects that require logging (see Recipe 16.9).
- The Apache Jakart Commons Logging (JCL) (*http://bit.ly/1pNZl0T*). Not discussed here; similar to the others.
- SLF4J (Simple Logging Facade For Java, see Recipe 16.8) is the newest and, as the name implies, a facade that can use the others.
- And, before these became widely used, I wrote a small, simple API to handle this type of logging function. My `netlog` is not discussed here because it is preferable to use one of the standard logging mechanisms; its code is in the *logging* subdirectory of the *javasrc* repo if you want to exhume it.

The JDK logging API, `log4j`, and `SFL4J` are more fully fleshed out and can write to such destinations as a file, an `OutputStream` or `Writer`, or a remote `log4j`, Unix `syslog`, or Windows Event Log server.

The program being debugged is the "client" from the logging API's point of view—even though it may be running in a server-side container such as a web server or application server—because the "network client" is the program that initiates the connection. The program that runs on your desktop machine is the "server" program for sockets because it waits for a connection to come along.

If you want to run any network-based logger reachable from any public network, you need to be more aware of security issues. One common form of attack is a simple denial-of-service (DoS), during which the attacker makes a lot of connections to your server in order to slow it down. If you are writing the logto disk, for example, the attacker could fill up your disk by sending lots of garbage. In common use, your log listener would be behind a firewall and not reachable from outside, but if this is not the case, beware of the DoS attack.

16.8. Network Logging with SLF4J

Problem

You want to use a logging API that lets you use any of the other logging APIs, for example, so your code can be used in other projects without requiring them to switch logging APIs.

Solution

Use SLF4J: get a `Logger` from the `LoggerFactory`, and use its various methods for logging.

Discussion

Using SLF4j requires only one JAR file to compile, *slf4j-api-1.x.y.jar* (where x and y will change over time). To actually get logging output, you need to add one of several implementation JARs to your runtime classpath, the simplest of which is *slf4j-simple-1.x.y.jar* (where x and y should match between the two files).

Get a `Logger` by calling `LoggerFactory.getLogger()`, passing either the string name of a class or package, or just the current `Class` reference. Then call the logger's logging methods. A simple example is in Example 16-10.

Example 16-10. logging/Slf4jDemo.java

```
public class Slf4jDemo {

    final static Logger theLogger = LoggerFactory.getLogger(Slf4jDemo.class);

    public static void main(String[] args) {

        Object o = new Object();
        theLogger.info("I created an object: " + o);

    }
}
```

There are various methods used to log information at different levels of severity, which are shown in Table 16-1.

Table 16-1. SLF4j logging methods

Name	Meaning
trace	Verbose debugging (disabled by default)
debug	Verbose debugging
info	low-level informational message
warn	Possible error
error	Serious error

One of the advantages of SLF4j over most of the other logging APIs is the avoidance of the "dead string" anti-pattern. In many other logger APIs you may find code like:

```
logger.log("The value is " + object + "; this is not good");
```

This can lead to a performance problem, in that the object's `toString()` is implicitly called, and two string concatenations performed, before we even know if the logger is going to use them! If this is in code that is called repeatedly, a lot of overhead can be wasted.

This led the other logging packages to offer "code guards," based on logger methods that can find out very quickly if a logger is enabled, leading to code like the following:

```
if (logger.isEnabled()) {
        logger.log("The value is " + object + "; this is not good");
}
```

This solves the performance problem, but clutters the code! SLF4J's solution is to use a mechanism similar to (but not quite compatible with) Java's `MessageFormat` mechanism (see Recipe 15.10), as shown in Example 16-11.

Example 16-11. logging/Slf4jDemo2.java

```
public class Slf4jDemo2 {

    final static Logger theLogger = LoggerFactory.getLogger(Slf4jDemo2.class);

    public static void main(String[] args) {

        try {
            Person p = new Person();
            // populate person's fields here...
            theLogger.info("I created an object {}", p);

            if (p != null) {     // bogus, just to show logging
                throw new IllegalArgumentException("Just testing");
            }
        } catch (Exception ex) {
            theLogger.error("Caught Exception: " + ex, ex);
        }
    }
}
```

Although this doesn't demonstrate network logging, it is easy to accomplish this in conjunction with a logging implementation like Log4J or JUL which allow you to provide configurable logging. Log4J is described in the next recipe.

See Also

The SLF4J website contains a Getting Started manual (*http://bit.ly/1oTvlkK*) that discusses the various classpath options. There is also the Maven artifacts (*http://bit.ly/1l5xIRm*) for the various options.

16.9. Network Logging with log4j

Problem

You wish to write log file messages using log4j.

Solution

Get a Logger and use its log() method or the convenience methods. Control logging by changing a properties file. Use the org.apache.log4j.net package to make it network based.

Discussion

Logging using log4j is simple, convenient, and flexible. You need to get a Logger object from the static method Logger.getLogger(), pass in a configuration identifier that can either be a hierarchical name (e.g., com.darwinsys) or a Class object (e.g., MyApp.class) that generates the full package and class name. This name can be used in the configuration file to specify the level of detail that you want to see from the logger. The Logger has public void methods (debug(), info(), warn(), error(), and fatal()), each of which takes one Object to be logged (and an optional Throwable). As with System.out.println(), if you pass in anything that is not a String, its toString() method is called. A generic logging method is also included:

```
public void log(Level level, Object message);
```

The Level class is defined in the log4j package. The standard levels are in this order: DEBUG < INFO < WARN < ERROR < FATAL. So debug messages are least important, and fatal are most important. Each Logger has a level associated with it; messages whose level is less than the Logger's level are silently discarded.

A simple application can log messages using these few statements:

```
public class Log4JDemo {
    public static void main(String[] args) {

        Logger myLogger = Logger.getLogger("com.darwinsys");

        // PropertyConfigurator.configure("log4j.properties");

        Object o = new Object();
        myLogger.info("I created an object: " + o);

    }
}
```

If you compile and run this program with no *log4j.properties* file, it complains and does not produce any logging output:

```
ant run.log4jdemo
Buildfile: build.xml
run.log4jdemo:
    [java] log4j:WARN No appenders could be found for logger (com.darwinsys).
    [java] log4j:WARN Please initialize the log4j system properly.
```

So we need to create a configuration file, whose default name is *log4j.properties*. You can also provide the logfile name via System Properties: -Dlog4j.configuration=URL.

Every Logger has a Level to specify what level of messages to write, and an Appender, which is the code that writes the messages out. A ConsoleAppender writes to System.out, of course; other loggers write to files, operating system–level loggers, and so on. A simple configuration file looks something like this:

```
# Set root logger level to DEBUG and its only appender to APP1.
log4j.rootLogger=DEBUG, APP1

# APP1 is set to be a ConsoleAppender.
log4j.appender.APP1=org.apache.log4j.ConsoleAppender

# APP1 uses PatternLayout.
log4j.appender.APP1.layout=org.apache.log4j.PatternLayout
log4j.appender.APP1.layout.ConversionPattern=%-4r [%t] %-5p %c %x - %m%n
```

This file gives the root logger a level of DEBUG—write all messages—and an appender of APP1, which is configured on the next few lines. Note that I didn't have to refer to the com.darwinsys Logger; because every Logger inherits from the root logger, a simple application needs to configure only the root logger. The properties file can also be an XML document or you can write your own configuration parser (almost nobody does this). With the preceding file in place, the demonstration works better:

```
$ ant run.log4jdemo
Buildfile: build.xml

init:

build:

run.log4jdemo:
    [java] 1    [main] INFO  com.darwinsys  - I created an object: java.lang.
Object@bb6086

BUILD SUCCESSFUL
Total time: 1 second
```

A more typical use of logging might be to catch an Exception and log it, as shown in Example 16-12.

Example 16-12. Log4j—catching and logging

```java
public class Log4JDemo2 {
    public static void main(String[] args) {

        Logger theLogger = Logger.getLogger("com.darwinsys");

        try {
            Object o = new Object();
            theLogger.info("I created an object: " + o);
            if (o != null) {    // bogus, just to show logging
                throw new IllegalArgumentException("Just testing");
            }
        } catch (Exception ex) {
            theLogger.error("Caught Exception: " + ex, ex);
        }
    }
}
```

Much of the flexibility of the log4j package stems from its use of external configuration files; you can enable or disable logging without recompiling the application. A properties file that eliminates all logging might have this entry:

```
log4j.rootLogger=FATAL, APP1
```

Only fatal error messages print; all levels less than that are ignored.

To log from a client to a server on a remote machine, the org.apache.log4j.net package includes several Appenders and servers to connect them to.

For more information on log4j, visit its website (*http://logging.apache.org/log4j*). log4j is free software, distributed under the Apache Software Foundation license.

16.10. Network Logging with java.util.logging

Problem

You wish to write logging messages using the Java logging mechanism.

Solution

Get a Logger, and use it to log your messages and/or exceptions.

Discussion

The Java Logging API (package java.util.logging) is similar to, and obviously inspired by, the log4j package. You acquire a Logger object by calling the static Logger.getLogger() with a descriptive String. You then use instance methods to write to the log; these methods include:

```
public void log(java.util.logging.LogRecord);
public void log(java.util.logging.Level,String);
// and a variety of overloaded log( ) methods
public void logp(java.util.logging.Level,String,String,String);
public void logrb(java.util.logging.Level,String,String,String,String);

// Convenience routines for tracing program flow
public void entering(String,String);
public void entering(String,String,Object);
public void entering(String,String,Object[]);
public void exiting(String,String);
public void exiting(String,String,Object);
public void throwing(String,String,Throwable);

// Convenience routines for log( ) with a given level
public void severe(String);
public void warning(String);
public void info(String);
public void config(String);
public void fine(String);
public void finer(String);
public void finest(String);
```

As with log4j, every Logger object has a given logging level, and messages below that level are silently discarded:

```
public void setLevel(java.util.logging.Level);
public java.util.logging.Level getLevel( );
public boolean isLoggable(java.util.logging.Level);
```

As with log4j, objects handle the writing of the log. Each logger has a Handler:

```
public synchronized void addHandler(java.util.logging.Handler);
public synchronized void removeHandler(java.util.logging.Handler);
public synchronized java.util.logging.Handler[] getHandlers( );
```

and each Handler has a Formatter, which formats a LogRecord for display. By providing your own Formatter, you have more control over how the information being passed into the log gets formatted.

Unlike log4j, the Java SE logging mechanism has a default configuration, so Example 16-13 is a minimal logging example program.

Example 16-13. Log14Demo.java

```
public class Log14Demo {
    public static void main(String[] args) {

        Logger myLogger = Logger.getLogger("com.darwinsys");

        Object o = new Object();
        myLogger.info("I created an object: " + o);
```

```
        }
}
```

Running it prints the following:

```
C:> java logging.Log14Demo
Mar 8, 2014 7:48:26 PM Log14Demo main
INFO: I created an object: java.lang.Object@57f0dc
C:>
```

As with log4j, the typical use is in logging caught exceptions; the code for this is in Example 16-14.

Example 16-14. Log14Demo2—catching and logging

```java
public class Log14Demo2 {
    public static void main(String[] args) {

        System.setProperty("java.util.logging.config.file",
            "logging/logging.properties");

        Logger logger = Logger.getLogger("com.darwinsys");

        try {
            Object o = new Object();
            logger.info("I created an object: " + o);
            if (o != null) {    // bogus, just to show logging
                throw new IllegalArgumentException("Just testing");
            }
        } catch (Exception t) {
            // All-in-one call:
            logger.log(Level.SEVERE, "Caught Exception", t);
            // Alternate: Long form, more control.
            // LogRecord msg = new LogRecord(Level.SEVERE, "Caught exception");
            // msg.setThrown(t);
            // logger.log(msg);
        }
    }
}
```

16.11. Finding Network Interfaces

Problem

You wish to find out about the computer's networking arrangements.

Solution

Use the NetworkInterface class.

Discussion

Every computer on a network has one or more "network interfaces." On typical desktop machines, a network interface represents a network card or network port or some software network interface, such as the loopback interface. Each interface has an operating system–defined name. On most versions of Unix, these devices have a two- or three-character device driver name plus a digit (starting from 0); for example, `eth0` or `en0` for the first Ethernet on systems that hide the details of the card manufacturer, or `de0` and `de1` for the first and second Digital Equipment[3] DC21x4x-based Ethernet card, `xl0` for a 3Com EtherLink XL, and so on. The loopback interface is almost invariably `lo0` on all Unix-like platforms.

So what? Most of the time this is of no consequence to you. If you have only one network connection, like a cable link to your ISP, you really don't care. Where this matters is on a server, where you might need to find the address for a given network, for example. The `NetworkInterface` class lets you find out. It has static methods for listing the interfaces and other methods for finding the addresses associated with a given interface. The program in Example 16-15 shows some examples of using this class. Running it prints the names of all the local interfaces. If you happen to be on a computer named *laptop*, it prints the machine's network address; if not, you probably want to change it to accept the local computer's name from the command line; this is left as an exercise for the reader.

Example 16-15. NetworkInterfaceDemo.java

```
public class NetworkInterfaceDemo {
    public static void main(String[] a) throws IOException {
        Enumeration list = NetworkInterface.getNetworkInterfaces();
        while (list.hasMoreElements()) {
            // Get one NetworkInterface
            NetworkInterface iface = (NetworkInterface) list.nextElement();
            // Print its name
            System.out.println(iface.getDisplayName());
            Enumeration addrs = iface.getInetAddresses();
            // And its address(es)
            while (addrs.hasMoreElements()) {
                InetAddress addr = (InetAddress) addrs.nextElement();
                System.out.println(addr);
            }

        }
        // Try to get the Interface for a given local (this machine's) address
        InetAddress destAddr = InetAddress.getByName("laptop");
        try {
```

3. Digital Equipment was absorbed by Compaq, which was then absorbed by HP, but the name remains de because the engineers who name such things don't care for corporate mergers anyway.

```
        NetworkInterface dest = NetworkInterface.getByInetAddress(destAddr);
        System.out.println("Address for " + destAddr + " is " + dest);
    } catch (SocketException ex) {
        System.err.println("Couldn't get address for " + destAddr);
    }
}
}
```

16.12. Program: A Java Chat Server

This program implements a simple chat server (see Example 16-16) that works with the chat client program from Recipe 13.13. It accepts connections from an arbitrary number of clients; any message sent from one client is broadcast to all clients. In addition to ServerSockets, it demonstrates the use of threads (see Chapter 22). Because there are interactions among clients, this server needs to keep track of all the clients it has at any one time. I use an ArrayList (see Recipe 7.4) to serve as an expandable list and am careful to use the synchronized keyword around all accesses to this list to prevent one thread from accessing it while another is modifying it (this is discussed in Chapter 22).

Example 16-16. ChatServer.java

```
public class ChatServer {
    /** What I call myself in system messages */
    protected final static String CHATMASTER_ID = "ChatMaster";
    /** What goes between any handle and the message */
    protected final static String SEP = ": ";
    /** The Server Socket */
    protected ServerSocket servSock;
    /** The list of my current clients */
    protected List<ChatHandler> clients;
    /** Debugging state */
    private static boolean DEBUG = false;

    /** Main just constructs a ChatServer, which should never return */
    public static void main(String[] argv) throws IOException {
        System.out.println("DarwinSys ChatServer 0.1 starting...");
        if (argv.length == 1 && argv[0].equals("-debug"))
            DEBUG = true;
        ChatServer w = new ChatServer();
        w.runServer();              // should never return.
        System.out.println("**ERROR* ChatServer 0.1 quitting");
    }

    /** Construct (and run!) a Chat Service
     * @throws IOException
     */
    ChatServer() throws IOException {
        clients = new ArrayList<>();

        servSock = new ServerSocket(ChatProtocol.PORTNUM);
```

```
            System.out.println("DarwinSys Chat Server Listening on port " +
                ChatProtocol.PORTNUM);
    }

    public void runServer() {
        try {
            while (true) {
                Socket userSocket = servSock.accept();
                String hostName = userSocket.getInetAddress().getHostName();
                System.out.println("Accepted from " + hostName);
                ChatHandler cl = new ChatHandler(userSocket, hostName);
                String welcomeMessage;
                synchronized (clients) {
                    clients.add(cl);
                    if (clients.size() == 1) {
                        welcomeMessage = "Welcome! you're the first one here";
                    } else {
                        welcomeMessage = "Welcome! you're the latest of " +
                                    clients.size() + " users.";
                    }
                }
                cl.start();
                cl.send(CHATMASTER_ID, welcomeMessage);
            }
        } catch(IOException e) {
            log("IO Exception in runServer: " + e);
        }
    }

    protected void log(String s) {
        System.out.println(s);
    }

    /**
     * The remainder of this file is an inner class that is
     * instantiated once to handle each conversation.
     */
    protected class ChatHandler extends Thread {
        /** The client socket */
        protected Socket clientSock;
        /** BufferedReader for reading from socket */
        protected BufferedReader is;
        /** PrintWriter for sending lines on socket */
        protected PrintWriter pw;
        /** The client's host */
        protected String clientIP;
        /** String form of user's handle (name) */
        protected String login;

        /* Construct a Chat Handler */
        public ChatHandler(Socket sock, String clnt) throws IOException {
            clientSock = sock;
```

```
            clientIP = clnt;
            is = new BufferedReader(
                new InputStreamReader(sock.getInputStream()));
            pw = new PrintWriter(sock.getOutputStream(), true);
    }

    /** Each ChatHandler is a Thread, so here's the run() method,
     * which handles this conversation.
     */
    public void run() {
        String line;
        try {
            /*
             * We should stay in this loop as long as the Client remains
             * connected, so when this loop ends, we disconnect the client.
             */
            while ((line = is.readLine()) != null) {
                char c = line.charAt(0);
                line = line.substring(1);
                switch (c) {
                case ChatProtocol.CMD_LOGIN:
                    if (!ChatProtocol.isValidLoginName(line)) {
                        send(CHATMASTER_ID, "LOGIN " + line + " invalid");
                        log("LOGIN INVALID from " + clientIP);
                        continue;
                    }
                    login = line;
                    broadcast(CHATMASTER_ID, login +
                        " joins us, for a total of " +
                        clients.size() + " users");
                    break;
                case ChatProtocol.CMD_MESG:
                    if (login == null) {
                        send(CHATMASTER_ID, "please login first");
                        continue;
                    }
                    int where = line.indexOf(ChatProtocol.SEPARATOR);
                    String recip = line.substring(0, where);
                    String mesg = line.substring(where+1);
                    log("MESG: " + login + "-->" + recip + ": "+ mesg);
                    ChatHandler cl = lookup(recip);
                    if (cl == null)
                        psend(CHATMASTER_ID, recip + " not logged in.");
                    else
                        cl.psend(login, mesg);
                    break;
                case ChatProtocol.CMD_QUIT:
                    broadcast(CHATMASTER_ID,
                        "Goodbye to " + login + "@" + clientIP);
                    close();
                    return;            // The end of this ChatHandler
```

```
            case ChatProtocol.CMD_BCAST:
                if (login != null)
                    broadcast(login, line);
                else
                    log("B<L FROM " + clientIP);
                break;
            default:
                log("Unknown cmd " + c + " from " + login + "@" + clientIP);
            }
        }
    } catch (IOException e) {
        log("IO Exception: " + e);
    } finally {
        // the sock ended (darn it), so we're done, bye now
        System.out.println(login + SEP + "All Done");
        String message = "This should never appear.";
        synchronized(clients) {
            clients.remove(this);
            if (clients.size() == 0) {
                System.out.println(CHATMASTER_ID + SEP +
                    "I'm so lonely I could cry...");
            } else if (clients.size() == 1) {
                message =
                    "Hey, you're talking to yourself again";
            } else {
                message =
                    "There are now " + clients.size() + " users";
            }
        }
        broadcast(CHATMASTER_ID, message);
    }
}

protected void close() {
    if (clientSock == null) {
        log("close when not open");
        return;
    }
    try {
        clientSock.close();
        clientSock = null;
    } catch (IOException e) {
        log("Failure during close to " + clientIP);
    }
}

/** Send one message to this user */
public void send(String sender, String mesg) {
    pw.println(sender + SEP + mesg);
}

/** Send a private message */
```

```java
        protected void psend(String sender, String msg) {
            send("<*" + sender + "*>", msg);
        }

        /** Send one message to all users */
        public void broadcast(String sender, String mesg) {
            System.out.println("Broadcasting " + sender + SEP + mesg);
            clients.forEach(sib -> {
                if (DEBUG)
                    System.out.println("Sending to " + sib);
                sib.send(sender, mesg);
            });
            if (DEBUG) System.out.println("Done broadcast");
        }

        protected ChatHandler lookup(String nick) {
            synchronized (clients) {
                for (ChatHandler cl : clients) {
                    if (cl.login.equals(nick))
                        return cl;
                }
            }
            return null;
        }

        /** Present this ChatHandler as a String */
        public String toString() {
            return "ChatHandler[" + login + "]";
        }
    }
}
```

This code can be used with any reasonable number of clients connected concurrently.

See Also

A good general reference on this chapter's topic is *Java Network Programming* (O'Reilly).

The server side of any network mechanism is extremely sensitive to security issues. It is easy for one misconfigured or poorly written server program to compromise the security of an entire network! Of the many books on network security, two stand out: *Firewalls and Internet Security* by William R. Cheswick, Steven M. Bellovin, and Aviel D. Rubin (Addison-Wesley) and a series of books with *Hacking Exposed* in the title, the first in the series by Stuart McClure, Joel Scambray, and George Kurtz (McGraw-Hill).

This completes my discussion of server-side Java using sockets. A chat server could be implemented using several other technologies, such as RMI (Remote Methods Invocation), an HTTP web service, JMS (Java Message Service), and a Java Enterprise API that handles store-and-forward message processing. This is beyond the scope of this book, but there's an example of a JMS chat server in *Java Message Service* by Mark Richards, Richard Monson-Haefel, and David Chappell.

## CHAPTER 17

Java and Electronic Mail

17.0. Introduction

Sending and receiving email from a program is easy with Java. If you are writing an applet, you can simply get the browser to compose and send it for you. Otherwise, you can use the JavaMail Extension (package `javax.mail`) to both send and read mail. Java-Mail provides three general categories of classes: `Messages`, `Transports`, and `Stores`. A `Message`, of course, represents one email message. A `Transport` is a way of sending a `Message` from your application into the network or Internet. A `Store` represents stored email messages and can be used to retrieve them as `Message` objects. Thus, a `Transport` is for sending email and a `Store` is for reading it. One other class, `Session`, is used to obtain references to the appropriate `Store` and/or `Transport` objects that you need to use.

The JavaMail package is included in JavaEE and can be downloaded for JavaSE use. It's worth it: for the cost of a few minutes' downloading time, you get the ability to send and receive electronic mail over a variety of network protocols. The JavaMail project is hosted on `java.net` (*http://bit.ly/1mNtFEY*). You can download a JAR file containing all the standard protocol providers (SMTP, IMAP, POP3), or an API JAR just to compile against, or download the basic API and download the protocols individually. There are Maven artifacts in [Maven Central (*http://bit.ly/1v5iHAR*) as well. There is a JavaMail home page (*http://bit.ly/SDw1xT*) at Oracle. Finally, there is at least one alternative implementation, GNU JavaMail.

As you might have guessed from Chapter 13, it's also not that big a stretch to write code yourself that contacts an SMTP server and pretends to be a mail program. Hey, why pretend? You really have a mail program at that point! This is not shown in the book, but is available in the *javasrc* repo under *src/main/java/email/SmtpTalk.java*, for use as an aid to understanding the SMTP protocol.

17.1. Sending Email: Browser Version

Problem

You want an applet to permit the user to compose and send email, but hide your email address.

Solution

One approach is to use a `mailto:` URL hidden in some Java code. This is a somewhat heavyweight approach—you could do this with a shorter piece of JavaScript code—but this is the *Java Cookbook*, and this is one of the places where Java applets remain useful.

Discussion

Because most web browsers are now configured with either built-in or connected email clients, you can use the `mailto:` URL as a poor-person's email composer to have users contact you. Many people prefer this to a fill-in-the-blank "mail" form connected to a script or servlet because they can use a specialized tool and save their own copy of the mail either in their log file or by CC'ing their own account. Although you could use a `mailto:` URL directly in HTML, experience suggests that a species of parasite called a spam perpetrator will attach itself permanently to your mailbox if you do:

```
<h1>Test</h1> <p>Here is how to <a
href="mailto:spam-magnet@somedomainnamehere.com?subject=Testing Mailto URL
&amp;cc=dilbert@office.comics">contact us</a>
```

(The `href` line should be written as one long line in a real HTML file; the *&cc* is intentionally expanded as an HTML entity inside the `href` attribute).

My approach is to hide the `mailto:` URL inside a Java applet, where spam perps are less likely to notice it. The applet uses `showDocument()` to activate the `mailto:` URL:

```
String theURL = "mailto:" + username;
URL targetURL = new URL(theURL);
getAppletContext.showDocument(targetURL);
```

Further, I break the email address into two parts and provide the @ separately, so it won't be seen as an email address even if the spam-spider is clever enough to look into the `param` parts of the `applet` tag. Because I know you won't actually deploy this code without changing `Target1` and `Target2`—the `param` tags for the mail receiver's email name and host domain—you're fairly safe from spam with this. Example 17-1 is the Java applet class.

Example 17-1. MailtoButton.java

```java
public class MailtoButton extends Applet {

    private static final long serialVersionUID = -3186706180199804315L;
    /** The label that is to appear in the button */
    protected String label = null;
    /** The width and height */
    protected int width, height;
    /** The string form of the URL to jump to */
    protected String targetName, targetHost;
    /** The URL to jump to when the button is pushed. */
    protected URL targetURL;
    /** The name of the font */
    protected String fontName;
    protected String DEFAULTFONTNAME = "helvetica";
    /** The font */
    protected Font theFont;
    /** The size of the font */
    protected int fontSize = 18;
    /** The HTML PARAM for the user account -- keep it short */
    private String TARGET1 = "U";      // for User
    /** The HTML PARAM for the hostname -- keep it short */
    private String TARGET2 = "H";      // for Host
    // Dummy
    //private String BOGON1 = "username";    // happy strings-ing, SPAM perps
    //private String BOGON2 = "hostname";    // ditto.
    /** The string for the Subject line, if any */
    private String subject;

    /** Called from the browser to set up. We want to throw various
     * kinds of exceptions but the API predefines that we don't, so we
     * limit ourselves to the ubiquitous IllegalArgumentException.
     */
    public void init() {
        // System.out.println("In LinkButton::init");
        try {
            if ((targetName = getParameter(TARGET1)) == null)
                throw new IllegalArgumentException(
                    "TARGET parameter REQUIRED");
            if ((targetHost = getParameter(TARGET2)) == null)
                throw new IllegalArgumentException(
                    "TARGET parameter REQUIRED");

            String theURL = "mailto:" + targetName + "@" + targetHost;

            subject = getParameter("subject");
            if (subject != null)
                theURL += "?subject=" + subject;

            targetURL = new URL(theURL);

        } catch (MalformedURLException rsi) {
```

```
            throw new IllegalArgumentException("MalformedURLException " +
                rsi.getMessage());
        }


        label = getParameter("label");       // i.e., "Send feedback"
        if (label == null)
                throw new IllegalArgumentException("LABEL is REQUIRED");

        // Now handle font stuff.
        fontName = getParameter("font");
        if (fontName == null)
            fontName = DEFAULTFONTNAME;
        String s;
        if ((s = getParameter("fontsize")) != null)
            fontSize = Integer.parseInt(s);
        if (fontName != null || fontSize != 0) {
            // System.out.println("Name " + fontName + ", size " + fontSize);
            theFont = new Font(fontName, Font.BOLD, fontSize);
        }

        Button b = new Button(label);
        b.addActionListener(new ActionListener() {
            public void actionPerformed(ActionEvent e) {
                if (targetURL != null) {
                    // showStatus("Going to " + target);
                    getAppletContext().showDocument(targetURL);
                }
            }
        });
        if (theFont != null)
            b.setFont(theFont);
        add(b);
    }

    /** Give Parameter info to the AppletViewer, just for those
     * writing HTML without hardcopy documentation :-)
     */
    public String[][] getParameterInfo() {
        String info[][] = {
            { "label",       "string",    "Text to display" },
            { "fontname",    "name",        "Font to display it in" },
            { "fontsize",    "10-30?",    "Size to display it at" },

            // WARNING - these intentionally lie, to mislead spammers who
            // are incautious enough to download and run (or strings) the
            // .class file for this Applet.

            { "username",    "email-account",
                "Where do you want your mail to go today? Part 1" },
            { "hostname",    "host.domain",
                "Where do you want your mail to go today? Part 2" },
```

```
            { "subject",    "subject line",
                "What your Subject: field will be." },
        };
        return info;
    }
}
```

Example 17-2 shows the program in a simple HTML page to show you the syntax of using it.

Example 17-2. MailtoButton.htm

```
<html><head>
<title>Some Domain Name Systems: Feedback Page</title></head>
<body bgcolor="White">
<h1>Some Domain Name Systems: Feedback Page</H1>
<p>So, please, send us your feedback!</P>
<applet code=MailtoButton width=200 height=40>
    <param name="H" value="www.somedomainnamehere.com"/>
    <param name="U" value="wile_e_coyote"/>
    <param name="subject" value="Acme Widgets Feedback"/>
    <param name="label" value="Send Feedback by Mail"/>
    <param name="font" value="Helvetica"/>
    <param name="fontsize" value="16"/>
    <p>Your browser doesn't recognize Java Applets.
    Please use the HTML-based feedback form.</P>
</applet>
<p>You should get an acknowledgement by email shortly. Thank you
for your comments!</p>
<hr/>
<p>Here is a traditional form to let you to send feedback
if you aren't running Java or if your browser doesn't support
email composition.</P>
<form method="post" action="/java/feedback.cgi">
    <textarea name="message" rows="5" cols="60"/>
    <br/>
    <input type="submit" value="Send Feedback"/>
</form>
<p>Thank you for your comments.</p>
```

The page features a traditional CGI-based form for the benefit of those poor souls in need of a Java-based browser. Figure 17-1 is a screenshot showing the Compose window resulting from clicking the Feedback button.

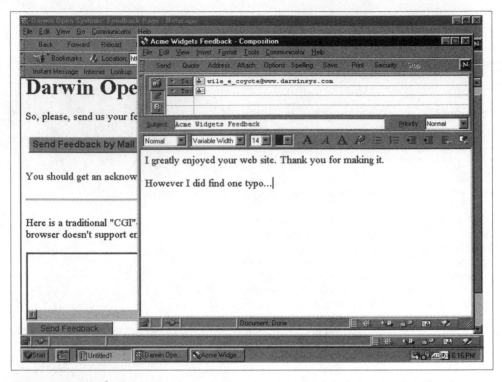

Figure 17-1. MailtoButton

The form is a workaround, so it's better to provide a full-blown mail composer.

17.2. Sending Email: For Real

Problem

You need to send email, and the browser trick in Recipe 17.1 won't cut it.

Solution

Provide a real email client.

Discussion

A real email client allows the user considerably more control. Of course, it also requires more work. In this recipe, I'll build a simple version of a mail sender, relying upon the JavaMail API. This first example shows the steps of sending mail over SMTP, the standard Internet mail protocol. The steps are listed in the sidebar.

Ian's Basic Steps: Sending Email over SMTP

Here are the steps for sending email over SMTP:

1. Create a `java.util.Properties` object (see Recipe 7.4) to pass information about the mail server, because the JavaMail API allows room for many settings.

2. Load the `Properties` with at least the hostname of the SMTP mail server.

3. Create a `Session` object.

4. Create a `Message` from the `Session` object.

5. Set the From, To, CC addresses, and Subject in the `Message`.

6. Set the message text into the message body.

7. Finally, use the static method `Transport.send()` to send the message!

This API requires that you catch the `MessagingException`, which indicates some failure of the transmission. Class `Sender` is shown in Example 17-3.

Example 17-3. Sender.java

```java
public class Sender {

    /** The message recipient. */
    protected String message_recip = "spam-magnet@darwinsys.com";
    /* What's it all about, Alfie? */
    protected String message_subject = "Re: your mail";
    /** The message CC recipient. */
    protected String message_cc = "nobody@erewhon.com";
    /** The message body */
    protected String message_body =
        "I am unable to attend to your message, as I am busy sunning " +
        "myself on the beach in Maui, where it is warm and peaceful." +
        "Perhaps when I return I'll get around to reading your mail. " +
        "Or not.";

    /** The JavaMail session object */
    protected Session session;
    /** The JavaMail message object */
    protected Message mesg;

    /** Do the work: send the mail to the SMTP server.  */
    public void doSend() {

        // We need to pass info to the mail server as a Properties, since
        // JavaMail (wisely) allows room for LOTS of properties...
        Properties props = new Properties();
```

```
    // Your LAN must define the local SMTP server as "mailhost"
    // for this simple-minded version to be able to send mail...
    props.put("mail.smtp.host", "mailhost");

    // Create the Session object
    session = Session.getDefaultInstance(props, null);
    session.setDebug(true);          // Verbose!

    try {
        // create a message
        mesg = new MimeMessage(session);

        // From Address - this should come from a Properties...
        mesg.setFrom(new InternetAddress("nobody@host.domain"));

        // TO Address
        InternetAddress toAddress = new InternetAddress(message_recip);
        mesg.addRecipient(Message.RecipientType.TO, toAddress);

        // CC Address
        InternetAddress ccAddress = new InternetAddress(message_cc);
        mesg.addRecipient(Message.RecipientType.CC, ccAddress);

        // The Subject
        mesg.setSubject(message_subject);

        // Now the message body.
        mesg.setText(message_body);
        // XXX I18N: use setText(msgText.getText(), charset)

        // Finally, send the message!
        Transport.send(mesg);

    } catch (MessagingException ex) {
        while ((ex = (MessagingException)ex.getNextException()) != null) {
            ex.printStackTrace();
        }
    }
}

/** Simple test case driver */
public static void main(String[] av) {
    Sender sm = new Sender();
    sm.doSend();
}
}
```

Of course, a program that can only send one message to one address is not useful in the long run. The second version (not shown here, but in the source tree accompanying this book) allows the To, From, Mailhost, and Subject to come from the command line and reads the mail text either from a file or from the standard input.

17.3. Mail-Enabling a Server Program

Problem

You want to send mail notification from within a program.

Solution

Use the `javax.mail` API directly, or use this `Mailer` wrapper.

Discussion

It is not uncommon to want to send email from deep within a non-GUI program such as a server. Here, I package all the standard code into a class called `Mailer`, which has a series of "set" methods to set the sender, recipient, mail server, etc. You simply call the `Mailer` method `doSend()` after setting the recipient, sender, subject, and the message text, and `Mailer` does the rest. Very convenient! So convenient, in fact, that `Mailer` is part of the `com.darwinsys.util` package.

For extra generality, the lists of To, CC, and BCC recipients can be set in one of three ways:

- By passing a string containing one or more recipients, such as "ian, robin"
- By passing a `List` containing all the recipients as strings
- By adding each recipient as a string

A "full" version allows the user to type the recipients, the subject, the text, and so on into a GUI and have some control over the header fields. The `MailComposeBean` (in Recipe 17.8) does all of these, using a Swing-based GUI. `MailComposeBean` uses this `Mailer` class to interface with the JavaMail API. Example 17-4 contains the code for the `Mailer` class.

Example 17-4. Mailer.java

```java
package com.darwinsys.mail;

public class Mailer {
    /** The javamail session object. */
    protected Session session;
    /** The sender's email address */
    protected String from;
    /** The subject of the message. */
    protected String subject;
    /** The recipient ("To:"), as Strings. */
    protected List<String> toList = new ArrayList<>();
    /** The CC list, as Strings. */
    protected List<String> ccList = new ArrayList<String>();
```

```java
/** The BCC list, as Strings. */
protected List<String> bccList = new ArrayList<String>();
/** The text of the message. */
protected String body;
/** The SMTP relay host */
protected String mailHost;
/** The verbosity setting */
protected boolean verbose;

/** Get from */
public String getFrom() {
    return from;
}

/** Set from */
public void setFrom(String fm) {
    from = fm;
}

/** Get subject */
public String getSubject() {
    return subject;
}

/** Set subject */
public void setSubject(String subj) {
    subject = subj;
}

// SETTERS/GETTERS FOR TO: LIST

/** Get tolist, as an array of Strings */
public List<String> getToList() {
    return toList;
}

/** Set to list to an ArrayList of Strings */
public void setToList(ArrayList<String> to) {
    toList = to;
}

/** Set to as a string like "tom, mary, robin@host". Loses any
 * previously set values. */
public void setToList(String s) {
    toList = Arrays.asList(s.split(",\\s+"));
}

/** Add one "to" recipient */
public void addTo(String to) {
    toList.add(to);
}
```

```java
// SETTERS/GETTERS FOR CC: LIST

/** Get cclist, as an array of Strings */
public List<String> getCcList() {
    return ccList;
}

/** Set cc list to an ArrayList of Strings */
public void setCcList(ArrayList<String> cc) {
    ccList = cc;
}

/** Set cc as a string like "tom, mary, robin@host". Loses any
 * previously set values. */
public void setCcList(String s) {
    ccList = Arrays.asList(s.split(",\\s+"));
}

/** Add one "cc" recipient */
public void addCc(String cc) {
    ccList.add(cc);
}

// SETTERS/GETTERS FOR BCC: LIST

/** Get bcclist, as an array of Strings */
public List<String> getBccList() {
    return bccList;
}

/** Set bcc list to an ArrayList of Strings */
public void setBccList(List<String> bcc) {
    bccList = bcc;
}

/** Set bcc as a string like "tom, mary, robin@host". Loses any
 * previously set values. */
public void setBccList(String s) {
    bccList = Arrays.asList(s.split(",\\s+"));
}

/** Add one "bcc" recipient */
public void addBcc(String bcc) {
    bccList.add(bcc);
}

// SETTER/GETTER FOR MESSAGE BODY

/** Get message */
public String getBody() {
    return body;
}
```

```java
/** Set message */
public void setBody(String text) {
    body = text;
}


// SETTER/GETTER FOR VERBOSITY

/** Get verbose */
public boolean isVerbose() {
    return verbose;
}

/** Set verbose */
public void setVerbose(boolean v) {
    verbose = v;
}

/** Check if all required fields have been set before sending.
 * Normally called before doSend; called by doSend for verification.
 */
public boolean isComplete() {
    if (from == null     || from.length()==0) {
        System.err.println("doSend: no FROM");
        return false;
    }
    if (subject == null || subject.length()==0) {
        System.err.println("doSend: no SUBJECT");
        return false;
    }
    if (toList.size()==0) {
        System.err.println("doSend: no recipients");
        return false;
    }
    if (body == null || body.length()==0) {
        System.err.println("doSend: no body");
        return false;
    }
    if (mailHost == null || mailHost.length()==0) {
        System.err.println("doSend: no server host");
        return false;
    }
    return true;
}

public void setServer(String s) {
    mailHost = s;
}

/** Send the message.
 */
public synchronized void doSend() throws MessagingException {
```

```
        if (!isComplete())
            throw new IllegalArgumentException(
                "doSend called before message was complete");

        /** Properties object used to pass props into the MAIL API */
        Properties props = new Properties();
        props.put("mail.smtp.host", mailHost);

        // Create the Session object
        if (session == null) {
            session = Session.getDefaultInstance(props, null);
            if (verbose)
                session.setDebug(true);          // Verbose!
        }

        // create a message
        final Message mesg = new MimeMessage(session);

        InternetAddress[] addresses;

        // TO Address list
        addresses = new InternetAddress[toList.size()];
        for (int i=0; i<addresses.length; i++)
            addresses[i] = new InternetAddress((String)toList.get(i));
        mesg.setRecipients(Message.RecipientType.TO, addresses);

        // From Address
        mesg.setFrom(new InternetAddress(from));

        // CC Address list
        addresses = new InternetAddress[ccList.size()];
        for (int i=0; i<addresses.length; i++)
            addresses[i] = new InternetAddress((String)ccList.get(i));
        mesg.setRecipients(Message.RecipientType.CC, addresses);

        // BCC Address list
        addresses = new InternetAddress[bccList.size()];
        for (int i=0; i<addresses.length; i++)
            addresses[i] = new InternetAddress((String)bccList.get(i));
        mesg.setRecipients(Message.RecipientType.BCC, addresses);

        // The Subject
        mesg.setSubject(subject);

        // Now the message body.
        mesg.setText(body);

        Transport.send(mesg);
    }

    /** Convenience method that does it all with one call.
```

```
 * @param mailhost - SMTP server host
 * @param recipient - domain address of email (user@host.domain)
 * @param sender - your email address
 * @param subject - the subject line
 * @param message - the entire message body as a String with embedded \n's
 */
public static void send(String mailhost,
    String recipient, String sender,
    String subject, String message)
    throws MessagingException {

    Mailer m = new Mailer();
    m.setServer(mailhost);
    m.addTo(recipient);
    m.setFrom(sender);
    m.setSubject(subject);
    m.setBody(message);
    m.doSend();
    }
}
```

17.4. Sending MIME Mail

Problem

You need to send a multipart, MIME-encoded message.

Solution

Use the Part, which is "part" of the JavaMail API.

Discussion

Way back in the old days when the Internet was being invented, most email was composed using the seven-bit ASCII character set. You couldn't send messages containing characters from international character sets. Then some enterprising soul got the idea to convert non-ASCII files into ASCII using a form of encoding known as UUENCODE (the UU is a reference to UUCP, one of the main transport protocols used for email and file transfer at a time when Internet access was prohibitively expensive for the masses). But this was pretty cumbersome, so eventually the Multimedia Internet Mail Extensions, or MIME, was born. MIME has grown over the years to support, as its name implies, a variety of multimedia types in addition to supporting odd characters. MIME typing has become very pervasive due to its use on the Web. As you probably know, every file that your web browser downloads—and a typical web page may contain from dozens to hundreds of individual files—is classified by the web server; this "MIME type" tells the browser how to display the contents of the file. Normal HTML pages are given a type of text/html. Plain text is, as you might guess, text/plain. Images have types such as image/gif, image/jpeg, image/png, and so on. Other types include application/ms-word, application/pdf, audio/au, etc.

Mail *attachments* are files attached to a mail message. MIME is used to classify attachments so that they can be deciphered by a mail reader the same way that a browser decodes files it downloads. Plain text and HTML text are the two most popular, but something called Visual Basic Script, or VBS, was popularized (along with major weaknesses in the design of a certain desktop operating system) by several famous viruses.

The point of all this? The JavaMail extension is designed to make it easy for you to send and receive all normal types of mail, including mail containing MIME-typed data. For example, if you wish to encode a stream containing audio data, you can do so. And, as importantly for Java, if you wish to encode a Reader containing characters in an 8- or 16-bit character encoding, you can do that, too.

The API makes you specify each separate MIME-encoded portion of your message as a Part. A Part represents a chunk of data that may need special handling by MIME encoders when being sent, and MIME decoders (in your email client) when being read. Example 17-5 is an example of sending a text/html attachment along with plain text.

Example 17-5. SendMime.java (partial listing)

```java
public class SendMime {

    /** The message recipient. */
    protected String message_recip = "spam-magnet@somedomainnamehere.com";
    /* What's it all about, Alfie? */
    protected String message_subject = "Re: your mail";
    /** The message CC recipient. */
    protected String message_cc = "nobody@erewhon.com";
    /** The text/plain message body */
    protected String message_body =
        "I am unable to attend to your message, as I am busy sunning " +
        "myself on the beach in Maui, where it is warm and peaceful. " +
        "Perhaps when I return I'll get around to reading your mail. " +
        "Or not.";
    /* The text/html data. */
    protected String html_data =
        "<html><head><title>My Goodness</title></head>" +
        "<body><p>You <em>do</em> look a little " +
        "<font color='green'>GREEN</font> " +
        "around the edges..." +
        "</body></html>";

    /** The JavaMail session object */
    protected Session session;
    /** The JavaMail message object */
    protected Message mesg;
```

```java
/** Do the work: send the mail to the SMTP server.  */
public void doSend() throws IOException, MessagingException {

    // We need to pass info to the mail server as a Properties, since
    // JavaMail (wisely) allows room for LOTS of properties...
    FileProperties props =
        new FileProperties(MailConstants.PROPS_FILE_NAME);

    // Copy the value of Mail.send.host into mail.smtp.host
    props.setProperty("mail.smtp.host",
        props.getProperty(MailConstants.SEND_HOST));

    // Create the Session object
    session = Session.getDefaultInstance(props, null);
    session.setDebug(true);          // Verbose!

    try {
        // create a message
        mesg = new MimeMessage(session);

        // From Address - this should come from a Properties...
        mesg.setFrom(new InternetAddress("nobody@host.domain"));

        // TO Address
        InternetAddress toAddress = new InternetAddress(message_recip);
        mesg.addRecipient(Message.RecipientType.TO, toAddress);

        // CC Address
        InternetAddress ccAddress = new InternetAddress(message_cc);
        mesg.addRecipient(Message.RecipientType.CC, ccAddress);

        // The Subject
        mesg.setSubject(message_subject);

        // Now the message body.
        Multipart mp = new MimeMultipart();

        BodyPart textPart = new MimeBodyPart();
        textPart.setText(message_body);     // sets type to "text/plain"

        BodyPart pixPart = new MimeBodyPart();
        pixPart.setContent(html_data, "text/html");

        // Collect the Parts into the MultiPart
        mp.addBodyPart(textPart);
        mp.addBodyPart(pixPart);

        // Put the MultiPart into the Message
        mesg.setContent(mp);

        // Finally, send the message!
        Transport.send(mesg);
```

```
        } catch (MessagingException ex) {
            System.err.println(ex);
            ex.printStackTrace(System.err);
        }
    }
}
```

17.5. Providing Mail Settings

Problem

You want a way to automatically provide server host, protocol, user, and password.

Solution

Use a `Properties` object.

Discussion

You may remember from Recipe 7.12 that `java.util.Properties` is a list of name/value pairs, and that my `FileProperties` extends `Properties` to provide loading and saving. In several places in this chapter, I use a `FileProperties` object to preload a large variety of settings, instead of hardcoding them or having to type them all on the command line. When dealing with JavaMail, you must specify the mail hostname, username and password, protocol to use (IMAP, POP, or mailbox for reading), and so on. I store this information in a properties file, and most of the programs in this chapter will use it. Here is my default file, *MailClient.properties*:

```
# This file contains my default Mail properties.
#
# Values for sending
Mail.address=ian@darwinsys.com
Mail.send.proto=smtp
Mail.send.host=localhost
Mail.send.debug=true
#
# Values for receiving
Mail.receive.host=localhost
Mail.receive.protocol=mbox
Mail.receive.user=*
Mail.receive.pass=*
Mail.receive.root=/var/mail/ian
```

The last two, `pass` and `root`, can have certain predefined values. Because nobody concerned with security would store unencrypted passwords in a file on disk, I allow you to set `pass=*` (in uppercase), which causes some of my programs to prompt for a password. The JavaMail API allows use of `root=INBOX` to mean the default storage location for your mail.

The keys in this list of properties intentionally begin with a capital letter because the property names used by the JavaMail API begin with a lowercase letter. The names are rather long, so they, too, are coded. It would be circular to encode them in a `Proper-ties` object, though; instead, they are embedded in a Java class called `MailConstants`, shown in Example 17-6.

Example 17-6. email/MailConstants.java

```java
/** Simple list of Properties keys for the Mail System. */
public class MailConstants {
    public static final String PROPS_FILE_NAME = "MailClient.properties";

    public static final String SEND_PROTO = "Mail.send.protocol";
    public static final String SEND_USER  = "Mail.send.user";
    public static final String SEND_PASS  = "Mail.send.password";
    public static final String SEND_ROOT  = "Mail.send.root";
    public static final String SEND_HOST  = "Mail.send.host";
    public static final String SEND_DEBUG = "Mail.send.debug";

    public static final String RECV_PROTO = "Mail.receive.protocol";
    public static final String RECV_PORT  = "Mail.receive.port";
    public static final String RECV_USER  = "Mail.receive.user";
    public static final String RECV_PASS  = "Mail.receive.password";
    public static final String RECV_ROOT  = "Mail.receive.root";
    public static final String RECV_HOST  = "Mail.receive.host";
    public static final String RECV_DEBUG = "Mail.receive.debug";
}
```

The fields in this class can be referred to by their full names—for example, `MailConst-ants.RECV_PROTO`. However, that is almost as much typing as the original long string (`Mail.receive.protocol`). As a shortcut, programs that use more than a few of the fields will want to use the `static import` mechanism, and then can refer to the fields as part of their class (e.g., `RECV_PROTO`). This is used to good effect in Example 17-10.

17.6. Reading Email

Problem

You need to read electronic mail in a program.

Solution

Use a JavaMail `Store`.

Discussion

The JavaMail API is designed to be easy to use. `Store` encapsulates the information and access methods for a particular type of mail storage; the steps for using it are listed in the sidebar.

Ian's Basic Steps: Reading Email Using Store

Here is how you read email using `Store`:

1. Get a `Session` object using `Session.getDefaultInstance()`. You can pass `System.getProperties()` as the `Properties` argument.

2. Get a `Store` from the `Session` object.

3. Get the root `Folder`.

4. If the root `Folder` can contain subfolders, list them.

5. For each `Folder` that can contain messages, call `getMessages()`, which returns an array of `Message` objects.

6. Do what you will with the messages (usually, display the headers and let the user select which message to view).

Java provides a `Store` class for the IMAP and POP3 transport mechanisms. The programs in this chapter will work more-or-less the same whether you use either of these, or a third-party store. I've tested some of the programs using the Unix mbox protocol,[1] which reads the mailbox "spool file" typically found on Unix mail servers. I've tested others using the POP and IMAP stores. The programs can be made to use any of these (assuming it's on your classpath, of ourse) just by passing the appropriate protocol name where "pop3" appears in the following examples. I've tested several of the programs using Sun's POP store and several POP servers (CUCIpop and PMDF).

I (try to) delete most of the email I get on one of my systems, so there were only two messages to be read when I ran my first "mailbox lister" program:

```
$ java email.MailLister pop3 dalai ian '*' /var/mail/ian
Password: (not shown)
Getting folder /var/mail/ian.
Name: ian(/var/mail/ian)
No New Messages
irate_client@nosuchd  Contract in Hawaii
mailer-daemon@kingcr  Returned mail: Data format error
$
```

---

1. This is free (GPL) software, originally downloaded from the Giant Java Tree, formerly at *http://www.gjt.org*.

The main program shown in Example 17-7 takes all five arguments from its command line.

Example 17-7. MailLister.java

```java
public class MailLister {
    static StringFormat fromFmt =
        new StringFormat(20, StringFormat.JUST_LEFT);
    static StringFormat subjFmt =
        new StringFormat(40, StringFormat.JUST_LEFT);

    public static void main(String[] argv) throws Exception {
        String fileName = MailConstants.PROPS_FILE_NAME;
        String protocol = null;
        String host = null;
        String user = null;
        String password = null;
        String root = null;

        // If argc == 1, assume it's a Properties file.
        if (argv.length == 1) {
            fileName = argv[0];
            FileProperties fp = new FileProperties(fileName);
            fp.load();
            protocol = fp.getProperty(MailConstants.RECV_PROTO);
            host = fp.getProperty(MailConstants.RECV_HOST);
            user = fp.getProperty(MailConstants.RECV_USER);
            password = fp.getProperty(MailConstants.RECV_PASS);
            root = fp.getProperty(MailConstants.RECV_ROOT);
        }
        // If not, assume listing all args in long form.
        else if (argv.length == 5) {
            protocol = argv[0];
            host = argv[1];
            user = argv[2];
            password = argv[3];
            root = argv[4];
        }
        // Otherwise give up.
        else {
            System.err.println(
                "Usage: MailLister protocol host user pw root");
            System.exit(0);
        }

        boolean recursive = false;

        // Start with a JavaMail Session object
        Session session = Session.getDefaultInstance(
            System.getProperties(), null);
        session.setDebug(false);
```

```
        // Get a Store object for the given protocol
        Store store = session.getStore(protocol);
        if (password.equals("*")) {
            final char[] passBytes =
                System.console().readPassword("Password:", (Object[])null);
            password = new String(passBytes);
        }
        store.connect(host, user, password);

        // Get Folder object for root, and list it
        // If root name = "", getDefaultFolder(), else getFolder(root)
        Folder rf;
        if (root.length() != 0) {
            System.out.println("Getting folder " + root + ".");
            rf = store.getFolder(root);
        } else {
            System.out.println("Getting default folder.");
            rf = store.getDefaultFolder();
        }
        rf.open(Folder.READ_WRITE);

        if (rf.getType() == Folder.HOLDS_FOLDERS) {
            Folder[] fs = rf.list();
            for (Folder f : fs) {
                listFolder(f, "", recursive);
            }
        } else {
            listFolder(rf, "", false);
        }
    }

    static void listFolder(Folder folder, String tab, boolean recurse)
    throws Exception {
        folder.open(Folder.READ_WRITE);
        System.out.println(tab + "Name: " + folder.getName() + '(' +
            folder.getFullName() + ')');
        if (!folder.isSubscribed())
            System.out.println(tab + "Not Subscribed");
        if ((folder.getType() & Folder.HOLDS_MESSAGES) != 0) {
            if (folder.hasNewMessages())
                System.out.println(tab + "Has New Messages");
            else
                System.out.println(tab + "No New Messages");
            Message[] msgs = folder.getMessages();
            for (Message m : msgs) {
                Address from = m.getFrom()[0];
                String fromAddress;
                if (from instanceof InternetAddress)
                    fromAddress = ((InternetAddress)from).getAddress();
                else
                    fromAddress = from.toString();
                StringBuffer sb = new StringBuffer();
```

```
                    fromFmt.format(fromAddress, sb, null);
                    sb.      append("  ");
                    subjFmt.format(m.getSubject(), sb, null);
                    System.out.println(sb.toString());
                }
            }
            if ((folder.getType() & Folder.HOLDS_FOLDERS) != 0) {
                System.out.println(tab + "Is Directory");
            }
            if (recurse) {
                Folder[] fs = folder.list();
                for (Folder f : fs) {
                    listFolder(f, tab + "", recurse);
                }
            }
        }
    }
}
```

This program has the core of a full mail reader but doesn't actually fetch the articles. To display a message, you have to get it (by number) from the folder, then call methods like getSubject(), getFrom(), and others. The listFolder() method does this to obtain identifying information on each message, and formats them using the StringAlign class from Recipe 3.5.

If we add a GUI and a bit of code to get all the relevant header fields, we can have a working mail reader. We'll show the messages in a tree view, because some protocols let you have more than one folder containing messages. For this we'll use a JTree widget, the Swing GUI component for displaying text or icons in a tree-like view. The objects stored in a JTree must be Node objects, but we also want them to be Folders and Messages. I handled this by subclassing DefaultMutableNode and adding a field for the folder or message, although you could also subclass Folder and implement the Node interface. Arguably, the way I did it is less "pure OO," but also less work. Example 17-8 is my MessageNode; FolderNode is similar, but simpler in that its toString() method calls only the Folder's getName() method.

Example 17-8. MessageNode.java

```
public class MessageNode extends DefaultMutableTreeNode {
    Message m;

    StringFormat fromFmt = new StringFormat(20, StringFormat.JUST_LEFT);
    StringFormat subjFmt = new StringFormat(30, StringFormat.JUST_LEFT);

    MessageNode(Message m) {
        this.m = m;
    }

    public String toString() {
        try {
```

```
            Address from = m.getFrom()[0];

            String fromAddress;
            if (from instanceof InternetAddress)
                fromAddress = ((InternetAddress)from).getAddress();
            else
                fromAddress = from.toString();

            StringBuffer sb = new StringBuffer();
            fromFmt.format(fromAddress, sb, null);
            sb.    append(" ");
            subjFmt.format(m.getSubject(), sb, null);
            return sb.toString();
        } catch (Exception e) {
            return e.toString();
        }
    }
}
```

These are all put together into a mail reader component in Recipe 17.7.

17.7. Program: MailReaderBean

Example 17-9 shows the complete MailReaderBean program. As the name implies, it can be used as a bean in larger programs but also has a main method for standalone use. Clicking a message displays it in the message view part of the window; this is handled by the TreeSelectionListener called tsl.

Example 17-9. MailReaderBean.java

```
import javax.mail.Address;
import javax.mail.Folder;
import javax.mail.Message;
import javax.mail.Session;
import javax.mail.Store;
import javax.mail.internet.InternetAddress;
import javax.swing.JFrame;
import javax.swing.JScrollPane;
import javax.swing.JSplitPane;
import javax.swing.JTextArea;
import javax.swing.JTree;
import javax.swing.event.TreeSelectionEvent;
import javax.swing.event.TreeSelectionListener;

/**
 * Display a mailbox or mailboxes.
 * This is a generic GUI component for displaying email.
 */
public class MailReaderBean extends JSplitPane {

    private static final long serialVersionUID = 1L;
```

```java
private JTextArea bodyText;

/* Construct a mail reader bean with all defaults.
 */
public MailReaderBean() throws Exception {
    this("imap", "mailhost", "user", "*", "/");
}

/* Construct a mail reader bean with all values. */
public MailReaderBean(
    String protocol,
    String host,
    String user,
    String password,
    String rootName)
throws Exception {

    super(VERTICAL_SPLIT);

    boolean recursive = false;

    // Start with a Mail Session object
    Session session = Session.getDefaultInstance(
        System.getProperties(), null);
    session.setDebug(false);

    // Get a Store object for the given protocol
    Store store = session.getStore(protocol);
    store.connect(host, user, password);

    // Get Folder object for root, and list it
    // If root name = "", getDefaultFolder(), else getFolder(root)
    FolderNode top;
    if (rootName.length() != 0) {
        // System.out.println("Getting folder " + rootName + ".");
        top = new FolderNode(store.getFolder(rootName));
    } else {
        // System.out.println("Getting default folder.");
        top = new FolderNode(store.getDefaultFolder());
    }
    if (top == null || !top.f.exists()) {
        System.out.println("Invalid folder " + rootName);
        return;
    }

    if (top.f.getType() == Folder.HOLDS_FOLDERS) {
        Folder[] fs = top.f.list();
        for (Folder f : fs)
            listFolder(top, new FolderNode(f), recursive);
    } else
            listFolder(top, top, false);
```

```
// Now that (all) the foldernodes and treenodes are in,
// construct a JTree object from the top of the list down,
// make the JTree scrollable (put in JScrollPane),
// and add it as the MailComposeBean's Northern child.
JTree tree = new JTree(top);
JScrollPane treeScroller = new JScrollPane(tree);
treeScroller.setBackground(tree.getBackground());
this.setTopComponent(treeScroller);

// The Southern (Bottom) child is a textarea to display the msg.
bodyText = new JTextArea(15, 80);
this.setBottomComponent(new JScrollPane(bodyText));

// Add a notification listener for the tree; this will
// display the clicked-upon message
TreeSelectionListener tsl = new TreeSelectionListener() {
    public void valueChanged(TreeSelectionEvent evt) {
        Object[] po = evt.getPath().getPath();     // yes, repeat it.
        Object o = po[po.length - 1];     // last node in path
        if (o instanceof FolderNode) {
            // System.out.println("Select folder " + o.toString());
            return;
        }
        if (o instanceof MessageNode) {
            bodyText.setText("");
            try {
                Message m = ((MessageNode)o).m;

                bodyText.append("To: ");
                Object[] tos = m.getAllRecipients();
                for (Object to : tos) {
                    bodyText.append(to.toString());
                    bodyText.append(" ");
                }
                bodyText.append("\n");

                bodyText.append("Subject: " + m.getSubject() + "\n");
                bodyText.append("From: ");
                Object[] froms = m.getFrom();
                for (Object from : froms) {
                    bodyText.append(from.toString());
                    bodyText.append(" ");
                }
                bodyText.append("\n");

                bodyText.append("Date: " + m.getSentDate() + "\n");
                bodyText.append("\n");

                bodyText.append(m.getContent().toString());

                // Start reading at top of message(!)
```

```
                        bodyText.setCaretPosition(0);
                    } catch (Exception e) {
                        bodyText.append(e.toString());
                    }
                } else
                    System.err.println("UNEXPECTED SELECTION: " + o.getClass());
            }
        };
        tree.addTreeSelectionListener(tsl);
    }


    /** Process one folder. */
    static void listFolder(FolderNode top, FolderNode folder, boolean recurse)
        throws Exception {

        if ((folder.f.getType() & Folder.HOLDS_MESSAGES) != 0) {
            Message[] msgs = folder.f.getMessages();
            for (Message ms : msgs) {
                MessageNode m = new MessageNode(ms);
                Address from = m.m.getFrom()[0];
                String fromAddress;
                if (from instanceof InternetAddress)
                    fromAddress = ((InternetAddress)from).getAddress();
                else
                    fromAddress = from.toString();
                top.add(new MessageNode(ms));
            }
        }
        if ((folder.f.getType() & Folder.HOLDS_FOLDERS) != 0) {
            if (recurse) {
                Folder[] fs = folder.f.list();
                for (Folder f : fs) {
                    listFolder(new FolderNode(f), top, recurse);
                }
            }
        }
    }


    /* Demo unit - main program */
    public static void main(String[] args) throws Exception {
        final JFrame jf = new JFrame("MailReaderBean");
        jf.setDefaultCloseOperation(JFrame.EXIT_ON_CLOSE);
        String mbox = "INBOX";
        if (args.length > 0)
            mbox = args[0];
        MailReaderBean mb = new MailReaderBean("imap", "localhost",
            System.getProperty("user.name"), "*", mbox);
        jf.getContentPane().add(mb);
        jf.setSize(640,480);
        jf.setVisible(true);
    }
}
```

It's a minimal, but working, mail reader. We'll merge it with a mail sender in Recipe 17.8 to make a complete mail client program.

17.8. Program: MailClient

This program is a simplistic GUI-based mail client. It uses the Swing GUI components (see Chapter 14) along with JavaMail. The program loads a Properties file (see Recipe 7.12) to decide which mail server to use for outgoing mail (see Recipe 17.2), as well as the name of a mail server for incoming mail and a Store class (see this chapter's Introduction and Recipe 17.6). The main class, MailClient, is simply a JComponent with a JTabbedPane to let you switch between reading mail and sending mail.

When first started, the program behaves as a mail reader, as shown in Figure 17-2.

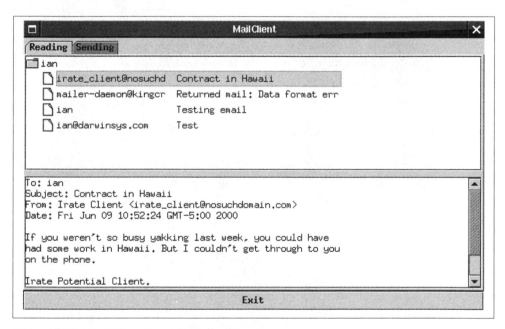

Figure 17-2. MailClient in reading mode

You can click the Sending tab to make it show the Mail Compose window, shown in Figure 17-3. I am typing a message to an ISP about some spam I received.

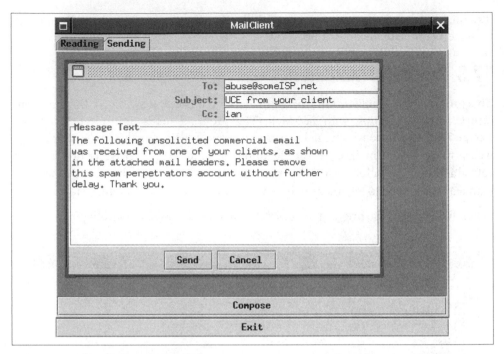

Figure 17-3. MailClient in compose mode

The code reuses the `MailReaderBean` presented earlier and a similar `MailCompose-Bean` for sending mail. Example 17-10 is the main program.

Example 17-10. MailClient.java

```java
public class MailClient extends JComponent {

    private static final long serialVersionUID = 1L;
    /** The quit button */
    JButton quitButton;
    /** The read mode */
    MailReaderBean mrb;
    /** The send mode */
    MailComposeFrame mcb;
    /** The Aliases panel */
    AliasBean alb;

    /** Construct the MailClient JComponent a default Properties filename */
    public MailClient() throws Exception {
        this(PROPS_FILE_NAME);
    }

    /** Construct the MailClient JComponent with a Properties filename */
    public MailClient(String propsFileName) throws Exception {
        super();
```

```
        // Construct and load the Properties for the mail reader and sender.
        Properties mailProps = new FileProperties(propsFileName);

        // Gather some key values
        String proto = mailProps.getProperty(RECV_PROTO);
        String user  = mailProps.getProperty(RECV_USER);
        String pass  = mailProps.getProperty(RECV_PASS);
        String host  = mailProps.getProperty(RECV_HOST);

        if (proto==null)
            throw new IllegalArgumentException(RECV_PROTO + "==null");

        // Protocols other than "mbox" need a password.
        if (!proto.equals("mbox") && (pass == null || pass.equals("ASK"))) {
            String np;
            do {
                // Make JOptionPane prompt for password in no-echo.
                // Create "message" using JPanel, JLabel, & JPasswordField
                // Courtesy of Marc Loy.
                JPanel p = new JPanel();
                p.add(new JLabel("Password for " + proto + " user " +
                        user + " on " + host));
                JPasswordField jpf = new JPasswordField(20);
                p.add(jpf);
                JOptionPane.showMessageDialog(null, p,
                    "Password request", JOptionPane.QUESTION_MESSAGE);
                np = new String(jpf.getPassword());
            } while (np == null || (np != null && np.length() == 0));
            mailProps.setProperty(RECV_PASS, np);
        }

        // Dump them all into System.properties so other code can find.
        System.getProperties().putAll(mailProps);

        // Construct the GUI
        // System.out.println("Constructing GUI");
        setLayout(new BorderLayout());
        JTabbedPane tbp = new JTabbedPane();
        add(BorderLayout.CENTER, tbp);
        tbp.addTab("Reading", mrb = new MailReaderBean());
        tbp.addTab("Sending", mcb = new MailComposeFrame());
        tbp.addTab("Aliases", alb = new AliasBean());
        tbp.addTab("List sending", new JLabel("Under construction",
            JLabel.CENTER));
        add(BorderLayout.SOUTH, quitButton = new JButton("Exit"));
        // System.out.println("Leaving Constructor");
    }

    /** "main program" method - run the program */
    public static void main(String[] av) throws Exception {
```

```
final JFrame f = new JFrame("MailClient");

// Start by checking that the javax.mail package is installed!
try {
    Class.forName("javax.mail.Session");
} catch (ClassNotFoundException cnfe) {
    JOptionPane.showMessageDialog(f,
        "Sorry, the javax.mail package was not found\n(" + cnfe + ")",
        "Error", JOptionPane.ERROR_MESSAGE);
    return;
}

// create a MailClient object
MailClient comp;
if (av.length == 0)
    comp = new MailClient();
else
    comp = new MailClient(av[0]);
f.getContentPane().add(comp);

// Set up action handling for GUI
comp.quitButton.addActionListener(new ActionListener() {
    public void actionPerformed(ActionEvent e) {
        f.setVisible(false);
        f.dispose();
        System.exit(0);
    }
});
f.addWindowListener(new WindowAdapter() {
    public void windowClosing(WindowEvent e) {
        f.setVisible(false);
        f.dispose();
        System.exit(0);
    }
});

f.pack();

f.setVisible(true);
    }
}
```

The `MailReaderBean` used in the Reading tab is exactly the same as the one shown in Recipe 17.7.

The `MailComposeBean` used for the Sending tab is a GUI component for composing a mail message. It uses the `Mailer` class from Recipe 17.3 to do the actual sending. Example 17-11 shows the `MailComposeBean` program.

Example 17-11. MailComposeBean.java

```java
public class MailComposeBean extends JPanel {

    /** The parent frame to be hidden/disposed; may be JFrame, JInternalFrame
     * or JPanel, as necessary */
    private Container parent;

    private JButton sendButton, cancelButton;
    private JTextArea msgText;          // The message!

    // The To, Subject, and CC lines are treated a bit specially,
    // any user-defined headers are just put in the tfs array.
    private JTextField tfs[], toTF, ccTF, subjectTF;
    // tfsMax MUST == how many are current, for focus handling to work
    private int tfsMax = 3;
    private final int TO = 0, SUBJ = 1, CC = 2, BCC = 3, MAXTF = 8;

    /** The JavaMail session object */
    private Session session = null;
    /** The JavaMail message object */
    private Message mesg = null;

    private int mywidth;
    private int myheight;

    /** Construct a MailComposeBean with no default recipient */
    MailComposeBean(Container parent, String title, int height, int width) {
        this(parent, title, null, height, width);
    }

    /** Construct a MailComposeBean with no arguments (needed for Beans) */
    MailComposeBean() {
        this(null, "Compose", null, 300, 200);
    }

    /** Constructor for MailComposeBean object.
     *
     * @param parent    Container parent. If JFrame or JInternalFrame,
     *                      will setvisible(false) and dispose() when
     *                      message has been sent. Not done if "null" or JPanel.
     * @param title       Title to display in the titlebar
     * @param recipient   Email address of recipient
     * @param height    Height of mail compose window
     * @param width        Width of mail compose window
     */
    MailComposeBean(Container parent, String title, String recipient,
            int width, int height) {
        super();

        this.parent = parent;

        mywidth = width;
```

```
        myheight = height;

        // THE GUI
        Container cp = this;
        cp.setLayout(new BorderLayout());


        // Top is a JPanel for name, address, etc.
        // Center is the TextArea.
        // Bottom is a panel with Send and Cancel buttons.
        JPanel tp = new JPanel();
        tp.setLayout(new GridLayout(3,2));
        cp.add(BorderLayout.NORTH, tp);

        tfs = new JTextField[MAXTF];

        tp.add(new JLabel("To: ", JLabel.RIGHT));
        tp.add(tfs[TO] = toTF = new JTextField(35));
        if (recipient != null)
            toTF.setText(recipient);
        toTF.requestFocus();

        tp.add(new JLabel("Subject: ", JLabel.RIGHT));
        tp.add(tfs[SUBJ] = subjectTF = new JTextField(35));
        subjectTF.requestFocus();

        tp.add(new JLabel("Cc: ", JLabel.RIGHT));
        tp.add(tfs[CC] = ccTF = new JTextField(35));

        // Center is the TextArea
        cp.add(BorderLayout.CENTER, msgText = new JTextArea(70, 10));
        msgText.setBorder(BorderFactory.createTitledBorder("Message Text"));

        // Bottom is the apply/cancel button
        JPanel bp = new JPanel();
        bp.setLayout(new FlowLayout());
        bp.add(sendButton = new JButton("Send"));
        sendButton.addActionListener(new ActionListener() {
            public void actionPerformed(ActionEvent e) {
                try {
                    doSend();
                } catch(Exception err) {
                    System.err.println("Error: " + err);
                    JOptionPane.showMessageDialog(null,
                        "Sending error:\n" + err.toString(),
                        "Send failed", JOptionPane.ERROR_MESSAGE);
                }
            }
        });
        bp.add(cancelButton = new JButton("Cancel"));
        cancelButton.addActionListener(new ActionListener() {
            public void actionPerformed(ActionEvent e) {
```

```
                maybeKillParent();
            }
        });
        cp.add(BorderLayout.SOUTH, bp);
    }

    public Dimension getPreferredSize() {
        return new Dimension(mywidth, myheight);
    }
    public Dimension getMinimumSize() {
        return getPreferredSize();
    }

    /** Do the work: send the mail to the SMTP server.
     *
     * ASSERT: must have set at least one recipient.
     */
    public void doSend() {

        try {
            Mailer m = new Mailer();

            FileProperties props =
                new FileProperties(MailConstants.PROPS_FILE_NAME);
            String serverHost = props.getProperty(MailConstants.SEND_HOST);
            if (serverHost == null) {
                JOptionPane.showMessageDialog(parent,
                    "\"" + MailConstants.SEND_HOST +
                        "\" must be set in properties",
                    "No server!",
                    JOptionPane.ERROR_MESSAGE);
                return;
            }
            m.setServer(serverHost);

            String tmp = props.getProperty(MailConstants.SEND_DEBUG);
            m.setVerbose(tmp != null && tmp.equals("true"));

            String myAddress = props.getProperty("Mail.address");
            if (myAddress == null) {
                JOptionPane.showMessageDialog(parent,
                    "\"Mail.address\" must be set in properties",
                    "No From: address!",
                    JOptionPane.ERROR_MESSAGE);
                return;
            }
            m.setFrom(myAddress);

            m.setToList(toTF.getText());
            m.setCcList(ccTF.getText());
            // m.setBccList(bccTF.getText());
```

```
                if (subjectTF.getText().length() != 0) {
                    m.setSubject(subjectTF.getText());
                }

                // Now copy the text from the Compose TextArea.
                m.setBody(msgText.getText());
                // XXX I18N: use setBody(msgText.getText(), charset)

                // Finally, send the sucker!
                m.doSend();

                // Now hide the main window
                maybeKillParent();

            } catch (MessagingException me) {
                me.printStackTrace();
                while ((me = (MessagingException)me.getNextException()) != null) {
                    me.printStackTrace();
                }
                JOptionPane.showMessageDialog(null,
                    "Mail Sending Error:\n" + me.toString(),
                    "Error", JOptionPane.ERROR_MESSAGE);
            } catch (Exception e) {
                JOptionPane.showMessageDialog(null,
                    "Mail Sending Error:\n" + e.toString(),
                    "Error", JOptionPane.ERROR_MESSAGE);
            }
        }

        private void maybeKillParent() {
            if (parent == null)
                return;
            if (parent instanceof Frame) {
                ((Frame)parent).setVisible(true);
                ((Frame)parent).dispose();
            }
            if (parent instanceof JInternalFrame) {
                ((JInternalFrame)parent).setVisible(true);
                ((JInternalFrame)parent).dispose();
            }
        }


        /** Simple test case driver */
        public static void main(String[] av) {
            final JFrame jf = new JFrame("DarwinSys Compose Mail Tester");
            System.getProperties().setProperty("Mail.server", "mailhost");
            System.getProperties().setProperty("Mail.address", "nobody@home");
            MailComposeBean sm =
                new MailComposeBean(jf,
                "Test Mailer", "spam-magnet@darwinsys.com", 500, 400);
            sm.setSize(500, 400);
```

```
        jf.getContentPane().add(sm);
        jf.setLocation(100, 100);
        jf.setVisible(true);
        jf.addWindowListener(new WindowAdapter() {
            public void windowClosing(WindowEvent e) {
            jf.setVisible(false);
            jf.dispose();
            System.exit(0);
            }
        });
        jf.pack();
    }
}
```

Further, the MailComposeBean program is a JavaBean, so it can be used in GUI builders and even have its fields set within a JSP. It has a main method, which allows it to be used standalone (primarily for testing).

To let you compose one or more email messages concurrently, messages being composed are placed in a JDesktopPane, Java's implementation of Multiple-Document Interface (MDI). Example 17-12 shows how to construct a multiwindow email implementation. Each MailComposeBean must be wrapped in a JInternalFrame, which is what you need to place components in the JDesktopPane. This wrapping is handled inside the Mail-ReaderFrame method, one instance of which is created in the MailClient constructor. The MailReaderFrame method newSend() creates an instance of MailComposeBean and shows it in the JDesktopFrame, returning a reference to the MailComposeBean so that the caller can use methods such as addRecipient() and send(). It also creates a Compose button and places it below the desktop pane so that you can create a new composition window by clicking the button.

Example 17-12. MailComposeFrame.java

```
public class MailComposeFrame extends JPanel {
    JDesktopPane dtPane;
    JButton newButton;
    protected int nx, ny;

    /** To be useful here, a MailComposeBean has to be inside
     * its own little JInternalFrame.
     */
    public MailComposeBean newSend() {

        // Make the JInternalFrame wrapper
        JInternalFrame jf = new JInternalFrame();

        // Bake the actual Bean
        MailComposeBean newBean =
            new MailComposeBean(this, "Compose", 400, 250);

        // Arrange them on the diagonal.
```

```
        jf.setLocation(nx+=10, ny+=10);

        // Make the new Bean be the contents of the JInternalFrame
        jf.setContentPane(newBean);
        jf.pack();
        jf.toFront();

        // Add the JInternalFrame to the JDesktopPane
        dtPane.add(jf);
        return newBean;
    }

    /* Construct a MailComposeFrame, with a Compose button. */
    public MailComposeFrame() {

        setLayout(new BorderLayout());

        dtPane = new JDesktopPane();
        add(dtPane, BorderLayout.CENTER);

        newButton = new JButton("Compose");
        newButton.addActionListener(new ActionListener() {
            public void actionPerformed(ActionEvent e) {
                newSend();
            }
        });
        add(newButton, BorderLayout.SOUTH);
    }
}
```

The file *TODO.txt* in the email source directory lists a number of improvements that would have to be added to the `MailClient` program to make it functional enough for daily use (delete and reply functionality, menus, templates, aliases, and much more). But it is a start and provides a structure to build on.

See Also

There are several books that discuss Internet mail. Start with Elliotte Rusty Harold's *JavaMail API* (O'Reilly). Kevin Johnson's *Internet Email Protocols: A Developer's Guide* (Addison-Wesley) covers the protocols and has appendixes on various programming languages, including Java. *The Programmer's Guide to Internet Mail: SMTP, POP, IMAP, and LDAP*, by John Rhoton (Digital Press) and *Essential E-Mail Standards: RFCs and Protocols Made Practical* by Pete Loshin (Wiley) cover the protocols without much detail on Java implementation. Finally, the books *Stopping Spam: Stamping Out Unwanted Email and News Postings* by Alan Schwartz and Simson Garfinkel (O'Reilly) and *Removing the Spam: Email Processing and Filtering* by Geoff Mulligan (Addison-Wesley) aren't about JavaMail, but they discuss what is now perhaps the biggest problem facing many Internet mail users.

## CHAPTER 18

Database Access

18.0. Introduction

Java can be used to access many kinds of databases. A database can be something as simple as a text file or a fast key/value pairing on disk (DBM format), as sophisticated as a SQL-based relational database management system (DBMS), as scalable as a cloud-based "NoSQL" database, or as exotic as an object database. That said, this chapter focuses on relational databases.

Regardless of how your data is actually stored, in many applications you'll want to write a class called an *accessor*[1] to mediate between the database and the rest of the application. For example, if you are using JDBC, the answers to your query come back packaged in an object called a ResultSet, but it would not make sense to structure the rest of your application around the ResultSet because it's JDBC-specific. In a Personal Information Manager application, the primary classes might be Person, Address, and Meeting. You would probably write a PersonAccessor class to request the names and addresses from the database and generate Person and Address objects from them. The DataAccessor objects would also take updates from the main program and store them into the database.

If this reminds you of Enterprise JavaBeans, you're right. If you're familiar with EJB 2 Entity Beans or JPA Entities (incorrectly but frequently called "EJ3 Entities"), you can think of simple entity beans as a specialized kind of data accessor. In fact, JPA provides a high-level mechanism for easily building accessors, and is discussed in Recipe 18.1.

Java DataBase Connectivity (JDBC) consists of classes in package java.sql and some extensions in package javax.sql. (SQL is the ANSI-standardized Structured Query Language, used by relational database software for ages to provide a reasonably standard

---

1. The Design Pattern for this is called Data Accessor Object, or DAO for short.

command language for creating, modifying, updating, and querying relational databases.)

Why was JDBC invented? Java is highly portable, but many databases previously lacked a portable interface and were tied to one particular language or platform. JDBC is designed to fill that gap. JDBC is patterned very loosely on Microsoft's Open DataBase Connectivity (ODBC). Sun's Java group borrowed several general ideas from Microsoft, which in turn borrowed some of it from prior art in relational databases. Whereas ODBC is C- and pointer-based (and void * at that), JDBC is based on Java and is therefore portable as well as being network-aware and having better type checking.

JDBC comes in two parts: the portable JDBC API provided with Java and the database-specific driver usually provided by the DBMS vendor or sometimes by a third party. These drivers have to conform to the Driver interface, and map from the generic calls into something the existing database code can understand.

JDBC is designed for *relational databases* only. But JDBC can provide access to any relational database, be it local or remote (remote databases are accessed just by using a JDBC URL containing a hostname, in drivers that support this; they are, of course, implemented under the hood using client sockets, as discussed in Chapter 16). In addition to the drivers from database vendors, versions of the JDK/JRE running on Microsoft Windows provide a JDBC-ODBC that allows you to use JDBC with an existing Windows database. Its performance is slightly less than some other drivers because it adds an extra layer, but it does work.

One formerly common form of database that I do not cover is the so-called Xbase format, which is implemented by several commercial databases (dBase, FoxBase, etc.) common in the MS-DOS and Windows world. If you wanted to decode such a database in Java, you'd probably start with the Xbase file format, documented by Erik Bachmann (*http://bit.ly/1lq4Stw*). Alternatively, you might find a useful driver in the Microsoft ODBC-32 software and use the JDBC-to-ODBC bridge to convert your data to a newer format such as a relational database.

Another special-purpose database is the DB/DBM file format. This is a key/value store, something like a java.util.Map but stored on disk, and with a special API to access it. DBM originated with Bell Labs Unix, was extended to "ndbm" at UC Berkeley, and was cloned as "gdbm" by the Free Software Foundation. A company called SleepyCat software was formed to continue development of Berkeley DB, and produced a Java implementation, but was eventually absorbed by Oracle. This product is not covered here, but you can download it manually from the Oracle website (*http://bit.ly/oracle-berk-db*).

This chapter provides an overview of several database techniques, starting with JPA and its kin Hibernate, and emphasizing JDBC, so that you know what this technology looks and feels like.

The code examples use parts of the API used that are required in client apps; when you run your code in a Java EE server, a lot of details—things like security, transactions, configuration, dependency injection (see Recipe 8.11) of needed resources)—are taken care of for you by the EE server.

18.1. Easy Database Access with JPA and/or Hibernate

Problem

You want an easy, high-level way to access your relational database.

Solution

Use the Java Persistence API (JPA) Entity annotations, and either the JPA or Hibernate APIs.

Ian's Basic Steps: JPA

To set up a JPA application:

1. Write, annotate, and compile the POJO data classes.

2. Create an XML file *persistence.xml* (this name is mandatory), containing the database access informtion, and listing the entity classes.

3. Obtain an `EntityManagerFactory` from the `Persistence` factory class.

4. Obtain an `EntityManager` from the `EntityManagerFactory`.

5. To save data, get the transaction, make the objects persistent by calling, e.g., `your-EntityManager.save(yourObject)`, and commit.

6. To load data objects, load them by primary key or use a query.

Discussion

As mentioned, JPA and Hibernate provide easy, high-level access to databases, and they are similar enough that they can be treated together for simple cases. Hibernate is an open source project, originated by Gavin King and now maintained by JBoss. JPA is an official Java specification, and a "hollow API"; you need one of the many implementations or "providers" (just as you need a Driver implementation to use JDBC, see Recipe 18.3). Indeed, one of the more common JPA implementations *is* Hibernate.

Hibernate originally required an XML configuration file specifying the "mappings" between, for example, Java classes and database tables, between fields or properties on the Java entities and columns in the database. This XML format is considered obsolete, and I do not cover it here, although many online examples still use it. After Hibernate had been around for some years, Sun (before Oracle consumed it) began a committee charged with defining what became JPA, a new high-level API to replace its JDO and EJB·specs, taking the best of Hibernate and other persistence APIs. JPA settled both on using good defaults throughout, and on using Java annotations on the source code to specify these mappings. Although the Hibernate people had started building their own annotations, they wisely decided to adopt the JPA annotations, knowing that they'd have to recognize these in order for Hibernate to be usable as a JPA provider. So, at present, Hibernate recognizes both its own annotations and the JPA ones; you should use the JPA ones so you can use a different provider if you need to.

The two bare-minimum annotations you need on every data class to be used with JPA (or Hibernate in annotations mode) are @Entity, which goes on the class itself, and @Id, which goes on the primary key field. A minimally annotated class might look like this:

```
import javax.persistence.*;

@Entity
public class Address {

    private int id;

    private String streetAddress;
    private String city;
    private String country;

    @Id @GeneratedValue(strategy=GenerationType.AUTO)
    public int getId() {
        return id;
    }
}
// Other accessors and methods omitted for brevity
```

Java annotations always appear directly before their target. The @Id (and many other property annotations) can appear either on the field (e.g., private int id) or on the get method (getId()), never on the set method. Within a given project, JPA *requires* you to be consistent: either use field annotations or method annotations, but not both.

There are many annotations, and a full treatment of them is book-length, so consult any good book on JPA or Hibernate for details.

Once you have annotated your entity classes, and created a bit of XML configuration, you need to write code using either the JPA or Hibernate APIs to actually load or save data (see "Ian's Basic Steps: JPA" on page 611).

Example 18-1 uses JPA to persist a simple entity object.

Example 18-1. JPASimple

```java
public class JPASimple {

    @SuppressWarnings("unchecked")
    public static void main(String[] args) {

        System.out.println("JPASimple.main()");

        EntityManagerFactory entityMgrFactory = null;
        EntityManager entityManager = null;
        try {
            entityMgrFactory = Persistence.createEntityManagerFactory("jpademo");
            entityManager = entityMgrFactory.createEntityManager();

            EntityTransaction transaction = entityManager.getTransaction();
            transaction.begin();

            // Create an entity in the database.
            Person np = new Person("Tom", "Boots");
            System.out.println(np);
            entityManager.persist(np);
            transaction.commit();

            int id = np.getId();
            System.out.println("Created Person with Id " + id);

            transaction = entityManager.getTransaction();
            transaction.begin();

            Query query = entityManager.createQuery(
                "select p from Person p order by p.lastName");

            List<Person> list = query.getResultList();
            System.out.println("There are " + list.size() + " persons:");
            list.forEach(p ->
                System.out.println(
                    p.getFirstName() + ' ' + p.getLastName())
            );
        } finally {
            if (entityManager != null)
                entityManager.close();
            if (entityMgrFactory != null)
                entityMgrFactory.close();
        }
    }
}
```

Besides the annotations, only a bit of configuration is needed. To tell JPA how to access the database, a configuration file named *persistence.xml* is loaded. This specifies one or more *persistence units*—think of each of these as one set of classes and a relational database to keep them in—and some other parameters: the JPA Provider to use, and either a JNDI resource or the database driver, URL, and username and password (details of JDBC parameters are discussed in Recipe 18.3). Here's the code you'll need:

```
<persistence xmlns="http://java.sun.com/xml/ns/persistence"
    xmlns:xsi="http://www.w3.org/2001/XMLSchema-instance"
    xsi:schemaLocation="http://java.sun.com/xml/ns/persistence
    http://java.sun.com/xml/ns/persistence/persistence_1_0.xsd"
    version="1.0">

<persistence-unit name="jpademo">
    <provider>org.hibernate.ejb.HibernatePersistence</provider>

    <exclude-unlisted-classes>false</exclude-unlisted-classes>

    <properties>

<!-- Properties for Hibernate -->
    <property name="hibernate.hbm2ddl.auto" value="create-drop"/>
    <property name="hibernate.show_sql" value="true"/>
    <property name="hibernate.format_sql" value="false"/>
    <property name="hibernate.archive.autodetection" value="class"/>
    <property name="hibernate.connection.driver_class"
        value="org.hsqldb.jdbcDriver"/>
    <property name="hibernate.connection.url"
        value="jdbc:hsqldb:mem:jpademo.db"/>
    <property name="hibernate.connection.username" value="sa"/>
    <property name="hibernate.connection.password" value=""/>
    <property name="hibernate.transaction.factory.class"
        value="org.hibernate.transaction.JTATransactionFactory"/>
    <property name="hibernate.dialect"
        value="org.hibernate.dialect.HSQLDialect"/>

    <!-- Properties for other providers -->

    </properties>
</persistence-unit>
```

Once all these pieces are in place, the program in Example 18-1 can be run. The data objects are saved to disk and displayed by the program.

Example 18-2 shows the exact same example, using the exact same annotated entity classes, using the Hibernate API.

Example 18-2. HibernateSimple

```
public class HibernateSimple {
    @SuppressWarnings("unchecked")
    public static void main(String[] args) {

        System.out.println("HibernateSimple.main()");
```

```java
Configuration cf = new AnnotationConfiguration();
cf.configure();
SessionFactory sf = null;
Session session = null;
try {
    sf = cf.buildSessionFactory();
    session = sf.openSession();

    Transaction tx = session.beginTransaction();

    // Create an entity in the database.
    Person np = new Person("Tom", "Boots");
    System.out.println(np);
    session.save(np);
    tx.commit();

    int id = np.getId();
    System.out.println("Created Person with Id " + id);

    tx = session.beginTransaction();

    Query query = session.createQuery(
        "select p from Person p order by p.lastName");

    List<Person> list = query.list();
    System.out.println("There are " + list.size() + " persons:");
    list.forEach(p ->
        System.out.println(
                p.getFirstName() + ' ' + p.getLastName())
    );
    System.out.println();
} finally {
    if (session != null) {
        session.close();
    }
}
}
}
```

For Hibernate, the configuration file is named *hibernate.cfg.xml*, and might look like this:

```xml
<hibernate-configuration>
    <session-factory>
        <!-- Using HSQLDB -->
        <property name="connection.url">jdbc:hsqldb:tmp/hibdemo.db
                    </property>
        <property name="connection.username">sa</property>
        <property name="connection.password"></property>
        <property name="connection.driver_class">org.hsqldb.jdbcDriver
                        </property>
```

```
                    <property name="dialect">org.hibernate.dialect.HSQLDialect
                                    </property>

                    <property name="hibernate.connection.isolation">2</property>
                    <property name="hibernate.jdbc.batch_size">0</property>

                    <!-- Make hibernate manage session contexts -->
                    <property name="hibernate.current_session_context_class">
                        org.hibernate.context.ThreadLocalSessionContext</property>

                    <!-- Nice setting for dev; do not use in production! :-) -->
                    <property name="hibernate.hbm2ddl.auto">create-drop</property>

                    <property name="show_sql">true</property>

                    <!-- Hibernate wants to be told about each class,
                                 like a strict JPA implementation -->
                    <mapping class="domain.Address"/>
                    <mapping class="domain.Country"/>
                    <mapping class="domain.Person"/>
                    <mapping class="domain.Preference"/>

                    <mapping class="domain.model.Recording"/>
                    <mapping class="domain.model.MusicRecording"/>
                    <mapping class="domain.model.Track"/>
                    <mapping class="domain.model.VideoRecording"/>
                    <mapping class="domain.model.Actor"/>

                    <mapping class="domain.sales.Customer"/>
                    <mapping class="domain.sales.SalesPerson"/>

            </session-factory>
        </hibernate-configuration>
```

See Also

This example gives a quick look at JPA and Hibernate for storing and retrieving objects.
There is much more to JPA and Hibernate than I've covered here. There are several
good books on each. This website (*http://bit.ly/1kqOX9L*) contains JPA information,
articles, and links to many implementations. You'll also want to take a look at the official
Hibernate website (*http://www.hibernate.org*). Finally, I maintain a separate GitHub
repo (*https://github.com/IanDarwin/jpademo*) with JPA and Hibernate demos.

The next few recipes concentrate on using the lower-level JDBC.

18.2. JDBC Setup and Connection

Problem

You want to access a database via JDBC.

Solution

Use `Class.forName()` and `DriverManager.getConnection()`.

Discussion

Though DB and friends have their place, most of the modern database action is in relational databases, and accordingly, Java database action is in JDBC. So the bulk of this chapter is devoted to JDBC.

I assume that you know a little bit about SQL, the universal language used to control relational databases. SQL has queries like "SELECT * from userdb," which means to select all columns (the *) from all rows (entries) in a database table named `userdb` (all rows are selected because the SELECT statement has no "where" clause). SQL also has updates like INSERT, DELETE, CREATE, and DROP. If you need more information on SQL or relational databases, many good books can introduce you to the topic in more detail.

JDBC has two Levels, JDBC 1 and JDBC 2. Level 1 is included in all JDBC implementation and drivers; Level 2 is optional and requires a Level 2 driver. This chapter concentrates on common features, primarily Level 1.

Ian's Basic Steps: Using a JDBC Query

To create a JDBC query:

1. Load the appropriate `Driver` class, which has the side effect of registering with the `DriverManager`.

2. Get a `Connection` object, using `DriverManager.getConnection()`:

        Connection con = DriverManager.getConnection (dbURL, name, pass);

3. Get a `Statement` object, using the `Connection` object's `prepareStatement` or `createStatement()`:

        Statement stmt = con.prepareStatement("select * from MyTable");

4. Get a `ResultSet` object, using the `Statement` object's `executeQuery()`:

        ResultSet rs = stmt.executeQuery();

5. Iterate over the `ResultSet`:

```
while (rs.next( )) {
    int x = rs.getInt("CustNO");
```

6. Close the `Statement`.

7. Close the `ResultSet`.

8. If you are all done with it, close the `Connection`.

The first step in using JDBC is to load your database's driver. This is performed using some Java JVM magic. The class `java.lang.Class` has a method called `forName( )` that takes a string containing the full Java name for a class and loads the class, returning a `Class` object describing it. This is part of the introspection or reflection API (see Chapter 23), but can be used any time to ensure that a class has been correctly configured into your CLASSPATH. This is the use that we'll see here. And, in fact, part of the challenge of installing JDBC drivers is ensuring that they are in your CLASSPATH at deployment time. The advantage of my slightly convoluted approach is that the drivers do not have to be on your CLASSPATH at compile time. In some cases, this can allow customers to use your software with database drivers that didn't even exist when your software was written; how's that for flexibility?

But wait, there's more! In addition to checking your CLASSPATH, this method also registers the driver with another class called the `DriverManager`. How does it work? Each valid JDBC driver has a bit of method-like code called a static initializer. This is used whenever the class is loaded—just what the doctor ordered! So the static block registers the class with the `DriverManager` when you call `Class.forName()` on the driver class.

For the curious, the static code block in a `Driver` called `BarFileDriver` looks something like this:

```
/** Static code block, to initialize with the DriverManager. */
static {
    try {
        DriverManager.registerDriver(new BarFileDriver());
    } catch (SQLException e) {
        DriverManager.println("Can't load driver" +
            BarFileDriver.getClass().getName());
    }
}
```

Example 18-3 shows a bit of code that tries to load two drivers. The first is the JDBC-to-ODBC bridge described in the Introduction. The second is one of the commercial drivers from Oracle.

Example 18-3. LoadDriver.java

```
public class LoadDriver {
    public static void main(String[] av) {
```

```
    try {
        // Try to load the jdbc-odbc bridge driver
        // Should be present on Sun JDK implementations.
        Class<?> c = Class.forName("sun.jdbc.odbc.JdbcOdbcDriver");
        System.out.println("Loaded " + c.getName());
        // Try to load an Oracle driver.
        Class<?> d = Class.forName("oracle.jdbc.driver.OracleDriver");
        System.out.println("Loaded " + d.getName());
    } catch (ClassNotFoundException ex) {
        System.err.println(ex);
    }
  }
}
```

The first load succeeded; the second failed because I didn't have the Oracle driver installed at the time:

```
$ java LoadDriver
Loaded class sun.jdbc.odbc.JdbcOdbcDriver
java.lang.ClassNotFoundException: oracle/jdbc/driver/OracleDriver
$
```

It is also possible to preregister a driver using the -D option to load it into the System Properties; in this case, you can skip the Class.forName() step:

```
$ java -Djdbc.drivers=com.acmewidgets.AcmeDriver:foo.bar.OhMyDriver MyClass
```

Once you have registered the driver, you are ready to connect to the database.

18.3. Connecting to a JDBC Database

Problem

You need to get a Connection to the relational database.

Solution

Use DriverManager.getConnection().

Discussion

The static method DriverManager.getConnection() lets you connect to the database using a URL-like syntax for the database name (for example, *jdbc:dbmsnetproto://server:4567/mydatabase*) and a login name and password. The "dbURL" that you give must begin with jdbc:. The rest of it can be in whatever form the driver vendor's documentation requires and is checked by the driver. The DriverManager asks each driver you have loaded (if you've loaded any) to see if it can handle a URL of the form you provided.

The first one that responds in the affirmative gets to handle the connection, and its connect() method is called for you (by DriverManager.getConnection()).

Four types of drivers are defined (not in the JDBC specification but in the less formal documentation); these are shown in Table 18-1.

Table 18-1. JDBC driver types

Type	Name	Notes
1	JDBC-ODBC bridge	Provides JDBC API access.
2	Java and Native driver	Java code calls Native DB driver.
3	Java and Middleware	Java contacts Middleware server.
4	Pure Java	Java contacts (possibly remote) DB directly.

Table 18-2 shows some interesting drivers. I'll use the ODBC bridge driver and InstantDB in examples for this chapter. Some drivers work only locally (like the JDBC-ODBC bridge), whereas others work across a network. For details on different types of drivers, refer to the books referenced at the end of this chapter. Most of these drivers are commercial products. InstantDB is a clever freeware[2] product; the driver and the entire database management system reside inside the same Java Virtual Machine as the client (the database is stored on disk like any other, of course). This eliminates the interprocess communication overhead of some databases. However, you can't have multiple JVM processes updating the same database at the same time.

Table 18-2. Some JDBC drivers

Driver class	Start of dbURL	Database
sun.jdbc.odbc.JdbcOdbcDriver	jdbc:odbc:	Bridge to Microsoft ODBC (included with JDK on Windows platforms)
jdbc.idbDriver	jdbc:idb:	Instant Database (IDB)
oracle.jdbc.Driver.OracleDriver	jdbc:oracle:thin:@server:port#:dbname	Oracle
postgresql.Driver	jdbc:postgres://host/database	PostgreSQL (*http://www.postgresql.org*) (freeware database)
org.gjt.mm.mysql.Driver	jdbc:mysql://host/database	MySql (*http://www.mysql.com*) (freeware database)

Example 18-4 is a sample application that connects to a database. Note that we now have to catch the checked exception SQLException because we're using the JDBC API. (The Class.forName() method is in java.lang, and so it is part of the standard Java API, not part of JDBC.)

---

2. At this writing, it is also a freeware product in flux; use Google to see if you can find it.

Example 18-4. Connect.java

```java
public class Connect {

    public static void main(String[] av) {
        String dbURL = "jdbc:odbc:Companies";
        try {
            // Load the jdbc-odbc bridge driver
            Class.forName("sun.jdbc.odbc.JdbcOdbcDriver");

            // Enable logging
            DriverManager.setLogWriter(new PrintWriter((System.err)));

            System.out.println("Getting Connection");
            Connection conn =
                DriverManager.getConnection(dbURL, "ian", "");     // user, passwd

            // If a SQLWarning object is available, print its
            // warning(s).  There may be multiple warnings chained.

            SQLWarning warn = conn.getWarnings();
            while (warn != null) {
                System.out.println("SQLState: " + warn.getSQLState());
                System.out.println("Message:  " + warn.getMessage());
                System.out.println("Vendor:   " + warn.getErrorCode());
                System.out.println("");
                warn = warn.getNextWarning();
            }

            // Do something with the connection here...

            conn.close();     // All done with that DB connection

        } catch (ClassNotFoundException e) {
            System.out.println("Can't load driver " + e);
        } catch (SQLException e) {
            System.out.println("Database access failed " + e);
        }
    }
}
```

I've enabled two verbosity options in this example. The use of `DriverManager.set-LogStream()` causes any logging to be done to the standard error, and the `Connection` object's `getWarnings()` prints any additional warnings that come up.

When I run it on a system that doesn't have ODBC installed, I get the following outputs. They are all from the `setLogStream()` except for the last one, which is a fatal error:

```
Getting Connection
JDBC to ODBC Bridge: Checking security
*Driver.connect (jdbc:odbc:Companies)
JDBC to ODBC Bridge: Checking security
```

```
JDBC to ODBC Bridge 1.2001
Current Date/Time: Fri Jun 16 16:18:45 GMT-5:00 2000
Loading JdbcOdbc library
Unable to load JdbcOdbc library
Unable to load JdbcOdbc library
Unable to allocate environment
Database access failed java.sql.SQLException: driver not found:
jdbc:odbc:Companies
```

On a system with JDBC installed, the connection goes further and verifies that the named database exists and can be opened.

See Also

Performance will suffer if a program repeatedly opens and closes JDBC connections, because getting a Connection object involves "logging in" to the database. One solution is to use a *connection pool*: the pool preallocates a certain number of Connection objects, hands them out on demand, and the application code returns its connection to the pool when done. Writing a simple connection pool is easy, but writing a connection pool reliable enough to be used in production is very hard. For this reason, JDBC 2 introduced the notion of having the driver provide connection pooling. However, this feature is optional—check your driver's documentation. Also, if you are running in a Java EE application server, the server will provide connection pooling; for example, if a servlet is using EJBs and the servlet engine runs in the same "application server" process, this can be a very efficient solution. See *Enterprise JavaBeans* (O'Reilly).

18.4. Sending a JDBC Query and Getting Results

Problem

You want to query a database using JDBC and get results back.

Solution

Having done the setup steps in Recipe 18.4, you can get a Statement and use it to execute a query. You'll get a set of results, a ResultSet object.

Discussion

The Connection object can generate various kinds of statements. The simplest is a Statement created by createStatement( ), which is used to send your SQL query as an arbitrary string:

```
Statement stmt = conn.createStatement( );
stmt.executeQuery("select * from myTable");
```

The result of the query is returned as a ResultSet object. The ResultSet works like an iterator in that it lets you access all the rows of the result that match the query. This process is shown in Figure 18-1.

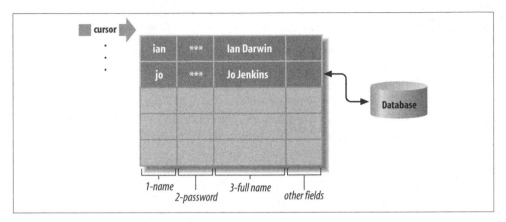

Figure 18-1. ResultSet illustrated

Typically, you use it like this:

```
while (rs.next( )) {
    int i = rs.getInt(1);          // or getInt("UserID");
```

As the comment suggests, you can retrieve elements from the ResultSet either by their column index (which starts at one, unlike most Java things, which typically start at zero) or column name. In JDBC 1, you must retrieve the values in increasing order by the order of the SELECT (or by their column order in the database if the query is SELECT *). In JDBC 2, you can retrieve them in any order (and, in fact, many JDBC 1 drivers don't enforce the retrieving of values in certain orders). If you want to learn the column names (a sort of introspection), you can use a ResultSet 's getResultSetMetaData() method, described in Recipe 18.10. SQL handles many types of data, and JDBC offers corresponding methods to get them from a ResultSet. The common ones are shown in Table 18-3.

Table 18-3. Data type mappings between SQL and JDBC

JDBC method	SQL type	Java type
getBit( )	BIT	boolean
getByte( )	TINYINT	byte
getShort( )	SMALLINT	short
getInt( )	INTEGER	int
getLong( )	BIGINT	long
getFloat( )	REAL	float

JDBC method	SQL type	Java type
getDouble( )	DOUBLE	double
getString( )	CHAR	String
getString( )	VARCHAR	String
getString( )	LONGVARCHAR	String
getDate( )	DATE	java.sql.Date
getTimeStamp()	TIME	java.sql.Date
getObject( )	BLOB	Object

Assuming that we have a relational database containing the User data, we can retrieve it as demonstrated in Example 18-5. This program retrieves any or all entries that have a username of ian and prints the ResultSets in a loop. It prints lines like:

```
User ian is named Ian Darwin
```

The source code is shown in Example 18-5.

Example 18-5. UserQuery.java

```java
public class UserQuery {

    public static void main(String[] fn)
    throws ClassNotFoundException, SQLException, IOException {

        // Load the database driver
        Class.forName(JDConstants.getProperty("jabadot.jabadb.driver"));

        System.out.println("Getting Connection");
        Connection conn = DriverManager.getConnection(
            JDConstants.getProperty("jabadot.dburl"));

        Statement stmt = conn.createStatement();

        ResultSet rs = stmt.executeQuery(
            "SELECT * from jabadb where name='ian'");

        // Now retrieve (all) the rows that matched the query
        while (rs.next()) {

            // Field 1 is login name
            String name = rs.getString(1);

            // Password is field 2 - do not display.

            // Column 3 is fullname
            String fullName = rs.getString(3);

            System.out.println("User " + name + " is named " + fullName);
        }
```

```
        rs.close();         // All done with that resultset
        stmt.close();       // All done with that statement
        conn.close();       // All done with that DB connection
        System.exit(0);     // All done with this program.
    }
}
```

Note that a ResultSet is tied to its Connection object; if the Connection is closed, the ResultSet becomes invalid. You should either extract the data from the ResultSet before closing it or cache it in a CachedRowSet (for more on RowSets, see Recipe 18.8).

18.5. Using JDBC Prepared Statements

Problem

You want to save the overhead of parsing, compiling, and otherwise setting up a statement that will be called multiple times.

Solution

Use a PreparedStatement.

Discussion

An SQL query consists of textual characters. The database must first parse a query and then compile it into something that can be run in the database. This can add up to a lot of overhead if you are sending a lot of queries. In some types of applications, you'll use a number of queries that are the same syntactically but have different values:

```
select * from payroll where personnelNo = 12345;
select * from payroll where personnelNo = 23740;
select * from payroll where personnelNo = 97120;
```

In this case, the statement needs to be parsed and compiled only once. But if you keep making up select statements and sending them, the database mindlessly keeps parsing and compiling them. Better to use a prepared statement, in which the variable part is replaced by a parameter marker (a question mark). Then the statement need only be parsed (or organized, optimized, compiled, or whatever) once:

```
PreparedStatement ps = conn.prepareStatement(
    "select * from payroll where personnelNo = ?;")
```

Before you can use this prepared statement, you must fill in the blanks with the appropriate set methods. These take a parameter number (starting at one, not zero like most things in Java) and the value to be plugged in. Then use executeQuery() with no arguments because the query is already stored in the statement:

```
ps.setInt(1, 12345);
rs = ps.executeQuery( );
```

If there are multiple parameters, you address them by number; for example, if there were a second parameter of type double, its value would be set by:

```
ps.setDouble(2, 12345);
```

Example 18-6 is the JDBC version of the User accessor, UserDBJDBC. It uses prepared statements for inserting new users, changing passwords, and setting the last login date.

Example 18-6. UserDBJDBC.java

```
public class UserDBJDBC extends UserDB {

    protected PreparedStatement setPasswordStatement;
    protected PreparedStatement addUserStmt;
    protected PreparedStatement setLastLoginStmt;
    protected PreparedStatement deleteUserStmt;

    /** insert the dozen or so fields into the user database */
    final static String SQL_INSERT_USER =
        "insert into users " +
        " values (?,?,?,?,?,?,?,?,?,?,?,?,?)";

    /** Default constructor */
    protected UserDBJDBC() throws NamingException, SQLException, IOException {
        super();

        System.out.println("UserDBJDBC.<init> starting...");

        System.out.println("Loading Driver Class");
        try {
            Class.forName("org.hsqldb.jdbcDriver");
        } catch (ClassNotFoundException ex) {
            System.out.println("FAILED: " + ex.toString());
            throw new IllegalStateException(ex.toString());
        }
        Connection conn = DriverManager.getConnection(
            "jdbc:hsqldb:/home/ian/src/jabadot/WEB-INF/jabadot",
            "jabadmin", "fredonia");

        Statement stmt = conn.createStatement();

        ResultSet rs = stmt.executeQuery("select * from users");

        while (rs.next()) {
            //name:password:fullname:City:Prov:Country:privs

            // Get the fields from the query.
            // Could be an Entity EJB with CMP: this is unnecessarily
            // chummy with the SQL. See CreateUserDatabase.java for field#'s!
            int i = 1;
```

```
                String nick = rs.getString(i++).trim();
                String pass = rs.getString(i++).trim();
                // System.err.println(nick + " (" + pass + ")");
                String first = rs.getString(i++);
                String last = rs.getString(i++);
                String email = rs.getString(i++);
                String city = rs.getString(i++);
                String prov = rs.getString(i++);
                String ctry = rs.getString(i++);
                java.sql.Date credt = rs.getDate(i++);
                java.sql.Date lastlog = rs.getDate(i++);
                String skin = rs.getString(i++);
                boolean editPrivs = rs.getBoolean(i++);
                boolean adminPrivs = rs.getBoolean(i++);

                // Construct a user object from the fields
                // System.out.println("Constructing User object");
                User u = new User(nick, pass, first, last, email,
                    prov, ctry, credt, lastlog,
                    skin, editPrivs, adminPrivs);
                // System.out.println("Adding User object " + u + " to " + users);
                // Add it to the in-memory copy.
                users.add(u);
                // System.err.println("User " + nick + "; pass " + pass.charAt(0));
        }
        rs.close();          // All done with that resultset
        stmt.close();

        // Set up the PreparedStatements now so we don't have to
        // re-create them each time needed.
        addUserStmt = conn.prepareStatement(SQL_INSERT_USER);
        setPasswordStatement = conn.prepareStatement(
            "update users SET password = ? where name = ?");
        setLastLoginStmt = conn.prepareStatement(
            "update users SET lastLogin = ? where name = ?");
        deleteUserStmt = conn.prepareStatement(
            "delete from users where name = ?");

        conn.close();
    }

    /** Add one user to the list, both in-memory and on disk. */
    public synchronized void addUser(User nu)
    throws IOException, SQLException {
        // Add it to the in-memory list
        super.addUser(nu);

        // Copy fields from user to DB
        // XXX WAY INCOMPLETE NOW
        int i = 1;
        addUserStmt.setString(i++, nu.getName());
        addUserStmt.setString(i++, nu.getPassword());
```

```java
        addUserStmt.setString(i++, nu.getFirstName());
        addUserStmt.setString(i++, nu.getLastName());
        addUserStmt.setString(i++, nu.getEmail());
        addUserStmt.setString(i++, nu.getCity());
        addUserStmt.setString(i++, nu.getProvince());
        addUserStmt.setString(i++, nu.getCountry());
        java.sql.Date now = new java.sql.Date(System.currentTimeMillis());
        addUserStmt.setDate(i++, now);
        addUserStmt.setDate(i++, now);
        addUserStmt.setString(i++, nu.getSkin());
        addUserStmt.setBoolean(i++, false);
        addUserStmt.setBoolean(i++, false);
        --i;

        if (i != 13) {
            System.out.println("Warning: not enough fields set! i = " + i);
        }

        // Store in persistent DB
        addUserStmt.executeUpdate();
    }

    public void deleteUser(String nick) throws SQLException {
        // Find the user object
        User u = getUser(nick);
        if (u == null) {
            throw new SQLException("User " + nick + " not in in-memory DB");
        }
        deleteUserStmt.setString(1, nick);
        int n = deleteUserStmt.executeUpdate();
        if (n != 1) {     // not just one row??
            /*CANTHAPPEN */
            throw new SQLException("ERROR: deleted " + n + " rows!!");
        }

        // IFF we deleted it from the DB, also remove from the in-memory list
        users.remove(u);
    }

    public synchronized void setPassword(String nick, String newPass)
    throws SQLException {

        // Find the user object
        User u = getUser(nick);

        // Change it in DB first; if this fails, the info in
        // the in-memory copy won't be changed either.
        setPasswordStatement.setString(1, newPass);
        setPasswordStatement.setString(2, nick);
        setPasswordStatement.executeUpdate();

        // Change it in-memory
```

```
        u.setPassword(newPass);
    }

    /** Update the Last Login Date field. */
    public synchronized void setLoginDate(String nick, java.util.Date date)
    throws SQLException {

        // Find the user object
        User u = getUser(nick);

        // Change it in DB first; if this fails, the date in
        // the in-memory copy won't be changed either.
        // Have to convert from java.util.Date to java.sql.Date here.
        // Would be more efficient to use java.sql.Date everywhere.
        setLastLoginStmt.setDate(1, new java.sql.Date(date.getTime()));
        setLastLoginStmt.setString(2, nick);
        setLastLoginStmt.executeUpdate();

        // Change it in-memory
        u.setLastLoginDate(date);
    }
}
```

Another example of prepared statements is given in Recipe 18.9.

18.6. Using Stored Procedures with JDBC

Problem

You want to use a procedure stored in the database (a stored procedure).

Solution

Use a `CallableStatement`.

Discussion

A *stored procedure* is a series of SQL statements[3] stored as part of the database for use by any SQL user or programmer, including JDBC developers. Stored procedures are used for the same reasons as prepared statements: efficiency and convenience. Typically, the database administrator (DBA) at a large database shop sets up stored procedures and tells you what they are called, what parameters they require, and what they return. Putting the stored procedure itself into the database is totally database-dependent and not discussed here.

---

3. And possibly some database-dependent utility statements.

Suppose that I wish to see a list of user accounts that have not been used for a certain length of time. Instead of coding this logic into a JDBC program, I might define it using database-specific statements to write and store a procedure in the database and then use the following code. Centralizing this logic in the database has some advantages for maintenance and also, in most databases, for speed:

```
CallableStatment cs = conn.prepareCall("{ call ListDefunctUsers }");
ResultSet rs = cs.executeQuery( );
```

I then process the `ResultSet` in the normal way.

18.7. Changing Data Using a ResultSet

Problem

You want to change the data using a `ResultSet`.

Solution

If you have JDBC 2 and a conforming driver, you can request an updatable `Result-Set` when you create the statement object. When you're on the row you want to change, use the `update( )` methods and end with `updateRow( )`.

Discussion

You need to create the statement with the attribute `ResultSet.CONCUR_UPDATABLE` as shown in Example 18-7. Do an SQL SELECT with this statement. When you are on the row (only one row matches this particular query because it is selecting on the primary key), use the appropriate update method for the type of data in the column you want to change, passing in the column name or number and the new value. You can change more than one column in the current row this way. When you're done, call `updateRow( )` on the `ResultSet`. Assuming that you didn't change the autocommit state, the data is committed to the database.

Example 18-7. ResultSetUpdate.java (partial listing)

```
try {
   con = DriverManager.getConnection(url, user, pass);
   stmt = con.createStatement(
       ResultSet.TYPE_SCROLL_SENSITIVE, ResultSet.CONCUR_UPDATABLE);
   rs = stmt.executeQuery("SELECT * FROM Users where nick=\"ian\"");

   // Get the resultset ready, update the passwd field, commit
   rs.first( );
   rs.updateString("password", "unguessable");
   rs.updateRow( );
```

```
    rs.close( );
    stmt.close( );
    con.close( );
} catch(SQLException ex) {
    System.err.println("SQLException: " + ex.getMessage( ));
}
```

18.8. Storing Results in a RowSet

Problem

You need to save some results in a JDBC form without maintaining a database connection. Or you want some JDBC results to have JavaBean semantics.

Solution

Use a RowSet—in particular, a CachedRowSet.

Discussion

The RowSet interface, a subinterface of ResultSet, was introduced with JDBC 2 and updated in JDBC 4.1 (with JavaSE 7). Because a RowSet is a ResultSet, you can use any of the ResultSet processing methods previously discussed. But RowSets tend to be more self-contained; you typically do not need to specify a driver, and performing queries is done in a new way. You call setCommand( ) to specify the query and execute( ) to perform the query (this takes the place of creating a Statement and calling its execute-Query( ) method).

The five subinterfaces are listed in Table 18-4. For each of these, a reference implementation is provided in the com.sun.rowset package.

Table 18-4. RowSet subinterfaces

Interface name	RowSetFactory Method	Purpose
CachedRowSet	createCachedRowSet	Caches results in memory; disconnected Rowset
FilteredRowSet	createFilteredRowSet	Implements lightweight querying, using javax.sql.rowset.Predicate
JdbcRowSet	createJdbcRowSet	Makes results available as a JavaBean component
JoinRowSet	createJoinRowSet	Combine multiple RowSets into one, like an SQL join
WebRowSet	createWebRowSet	Convert between XML data and RowSet

The Java 7 RowSetFactory has the static methods shown in Table 18-4 to create RowSet instances. Prior to Java 7, you had to instantiate the corresponding "Impl" classes from the unsupported com.sun.rowset package.

The CachedRowSet looks the most interesting and useful. In Example 18-8, a CachedRowSet is created and populated with setCommand() and execute(). Then (hypothetically some time later) the user changes some data. After that is completed, we call updateRow(), which tells the CachedRowSet to put the changes back into the JDBC database.

Example 18-8. CachedRowSetDemo

```
public class CachedRowSetDemo {
    public static void main(String[] args) throws Exception {
        RowSet rs;

        RowSetFactory rsFactory = RowSetProvider.newFactory();
        rs = rsFactory.createCachedRowSet();

        rs.setUrl("jdbc:postgresql:tmclub");
        rs.setUsername("ian");
        rs.setPassword("secret");

        rs.setCommand("select * from members where name like ?");
        rs.setString(1, "I%");

        // This will cause the RowSet to connect, fetch its data, and
        // disconnect
        rs.execute();

        // Some time later, the client tries to do something.

        // Suppose we want to update data:
        while (rs.next()) {
            if (rs.getInt("id") == 42) {
                rs.setString(1, "Marvin");
                rs.updateRow();    // Normal JDBC

                // This additional call tells the CachedRowSet to connect
                // to its database and send the updated data back.
                rs.updateRow();
            }
        }

        // If we're all done...
        rs.close();
    }
}
```

The WebRowSet has several uses that involve converting database results to or from XML. I have used a WebRowSet in conjunction with JUnit (see Recipe 1.13) to preload a ResultSet (because a RowSet is a ResultSet) to a known populated state before testing the SQL formatting code in Recipe 18.11. Because it writes data in a known format (public DTD), it could also be used with web services to exchange data across different vendors' systems.

See Also

The documentation for JDBC that accompanies the JDK provides more details on the various RowSet implementations and their usages. The changes for JDBC 4.1 are documented by Oracle (*http://bit.ly/1jknB5J*).

18.9. Changing Data Using SQL

Problem

You wish to insert or update data, create a new table, delete a table, or otherwise change the database.

Solution

Instead of using the Statement method executeQuery(), use executeUpdate() with SQL commands to make the change.

Discussion

The executeUpdate() method is used when you want to make a change to the database as opposed to getting a list of rows with a query. You can implement either data changes like insert or update, data structure changes like create table, or almost anything that you can do by sending SQL directly to the database through its own update command interface or GUI.

The program listed in Example 18-9 loads a text file format into a relational database. Note that I *optionally* drop the table before creating it, just in case an older version was in place (this is *not* the default behavior!). Then the program creates the table and its index. Finally, it goes into a loop reading the lines from the text file; for each, a prepared statement is used to insert the user's information into the database.

Example 18-9. TextToJDBC.java

```
/** Load the database from text file into JDBC relational database.
 * Text format is: name:password:fullname:city:prov:country:privs
 */
public class TextToJDBC {

    protected final static String TEXT_NAME = "users.txt";
    protected final static String DB_URL = "jdbc:idb:userdb.prp";
    protected static boolean dropAndReCreate = false;
```

```java
public static void main(String[] fn) throws Exception {

    BufferedReader is = new BufferedReader(new FileReader(TEXT_NAME));

    // Load the database driver
    Class.forName("jdbc.idbDriver");

    System.out.println("Getting Connection");
    Connection conn = DriverManager.getConnection(
        DB_URL, "admin", "");    // user, password

    System.out.println("Creating Statement");
    Statement stmt = conn.createStatement();

    System.out.println("Re-creating table and index");
    if (dropAndReCreate)
        stmt.executeUpdate("DROP TABLE IF EXISTS users");
    stmt.executeUpdate("CREATE TABLE users (\n" +
        "name     char(12) PRIMARY KEY,\n" +
        "password char(20),\n" +
        "fullName char(30),\n" +
        "email    char(60),\n" +
        "city     char(20),\n" +
        "prov     char(20),\n" +
        "country  char(20),\n" +
        "privs    int\n" +
        ")");
    stmt.executeUpdate("CREATE INDEX nickIndex ON users (name)");
    stmt.close();

    // put the data in the table
    PreparedStatement ps = conn.prepareStatement(
        "INSERT INTO users VALUES (?,?,?,?,?,?,?,?)");

    String line;
    while ((line = is.readLine()) != null) {

        if (line.startsWith("#")) {        // comment
            continue;
        }

        StringTokenizer st =
            new StringTokenizer(line, ":");
        String nick = st.nextToken();
        String pass = st.nextToken();
        String full = st.nextToken();
        String email = st.nextToken();
        String city = st.nextToken();
        String prov = st.nextToken();
        String ctry = st.nextToken();
        // User u = new User(nick, pass, full, email,
        //     city, prov, ctry);
```

```
            String privs = st.nextToken();
            int iprivs = 0;
            if (privs.indexOf("A") != -1) {
                iprivs |= User.P_ADMIN;
            }
            if (privs.indexOf("E") != -1) {
                iprivs |= User.P_EDIT;
            }
            ps.setString(1, nick);
            ps.setString(2, pass);
            ps.setString(3, full);
            ps.setString(4, email);
            ps.setString(5, city);
            ps.setString(6, prov);
            ps.setString(7, ctry);
            ps.setInt(8, iprivs);
            ps.executeUpdate();
        }
        ps.close();      // All done with that statement
        conn.close();    // All done with that DB connection
        return;          // All done with this program.
    }
}
```

Once the program has run, the database is populated and ready for use by the UserDBJDBC data accessor shown in Recipe 18.5.

18.10. Finding JDBC Metadata

Problem

You want to learn about a database or table.

Solution

Read the documentation provided by your vendor or database administrator. Or ask the software for a MetaData object.

Discussion

There are two classes relating to *metadata* (data about data) that you can ask for in the JDBC API: DatabaseMetaData and ResultSetMetaData. Each of these has methods that let you interrogate particular aspects. The former class is obtained from a get method in a Connection object; the latter from a get method in the given ResultSet.

ResultSetMetaData

First, let's look at the class `ResultsDecoratorHTML`, a "generic query" formatter shown in Example 18-10. This is one of several "ResultSet Formatters" used in the SQLRunner program of Recipe 18.11 (the parent class `ResultsDecorator`, discussed with SQLRunner, simply defines a `Constructor` that saves the given `PrintWriter` as a field, as well as providing two abstract methods that `ResultsDecoratorHTML` implements). When a program using `ResultsDecoratorHTML` calls the `write()` method, the `ResultSet` is interrogated and formatted into a neat little HTML table, using the column names from the `ResultSetMetaData` as the headings for the HTML table. The nice part about this program is that it responds to whatever columns are in the `ResultSet`, which need not be in the same order as they are in the database. Consider the two queries:

```
select name, address from userdb
select address, name from userdb
```

Any code that depends upon knowing the order in the database would look very strange indeed if the user query requested fields in a different order than they were stored in the database.

Example 18-10. ResultsDecoratorHTML.java

```java
import java.io.*;
import java.sql.*;

import com.darwinsys.util.Verbosity;

/** Print ResultSet in HTML
 */
public class ResultsDecoratorHTML extends ResultsDecorator {

    public ResultsDecoratorHTML(PrintWriter out, Verbosity v) {
        super(out, v);
    }

    public int write(ResultSet rs) throws IOException, SQLException {

        ResultSetMetaData md = rs.getMetaData();
        int colCount = md.getColumnCount();
        println("<table border=1>");
        print("<tr>");
        for (int i=1; i<=colCount; i++) {
            print("<th>");
            print(md.getColumnLabel(i));
        }
        println("</tr>");
        int rowCount = 0;
        while (rs.next()) {
            ++rowCount;
            print("<tr>");
            for (int i=1; i<=colCount; i++) {
```

```
                print("<td>");
                print(rs.getString(i));
            }
            println("</tr>");
        }
        println("</table>");
        return rowCount;
    }

    @Override
    public void displayTable(String table, ResultSet rs) throws IOException, SQLException {
        write(rs);
    }

    /** Return a printable name for this decorator
     * @see ResultsDecorator#getName()
     */
    public String getName() {
        return "HTML";
    }
}
```

DatabaseMetaData

Example 18-11 uses `DatabaseMetaData` to print out the name and version number of the database product and uses a helper method in my `ConnectionUtil` class to format the default transaction isolation (basically, the extent to which users of a database can interfere with each other; see any good book on databases for information on transactions and why it's often really important to know your database's default transaction isolation).

Example 18-11. DatabaseMetaDemo.java

```java
/** A database MetaData query */
public class DatabaseMetaDemo {

    public static void main(String[] args) {
        try {
                // Get the connection
            Connection conn =
                ConnectionUtil.getConnection(args[0]);

            // Get a Database MetaData as a way of interrogating
            // the names of the tables in this database.
            DatabaseMetaData meta = conn.getMetaData();

            System.out.println("We are using " + meta.getDatabaseProductName());
            System.out.println("Version is " + meta.getDatabaseProductVersion() );

            int txisolation = meta.getDefaultTransactionIsolation();
            System.out.println("Database default transaction isolation is " +
                txisolation + " (" +
```

```
            transactionIsolationToString(txisolation) + ").");

        conn.close();

        System.out.println("All done!");

    } catch (SQLException ex) {
        System.out.println("Database access failed:");
        System.out.println(ex);
    }
}

/** Convert a TransactionIsolation int (defined in java.sql.Connection)
 * to the corresponding printable string.
 *
 * XXX Remove from here once darwinsys.jar gets committed.
 */
public static String transactionIsolationToString(int txisolation) {
    switch(txisolation) {
        case Connection.TRANSACTION_NONE:
            // transactions not supported.
            return "TRANSACTION_NONE";
        case Connection.TRANSACTION_READ_UNCOMMITTED:
            // All three phenomena can occur
            return "TRANSACTION_NONE";
        case Connection.TRANSACTION_READ_COMMITTED:
        // Dirty reads are prevented; non-repeatable reads and
        // phantom reads can occur.
            return "TRANSACTION_READ_COMMITTED";
        case Connection.TRANSACTION_REPEATABLE_READ:
            // Dirty reads and non-repeatable reads are prevented;
            // phantom reads can occur.
            return "TRANSACTION_REPEATABLE_READ";
        case Connection.TRANSACTION_SERIALIZABLE:
            // All three phenomena prvented; slowest!
            return "TRANSACTION_SERIALIZABLE";
        default:
            throw new IllegalArgumentException(
                txisolation + " not a valid TX_ISOLATION");
    }
}
}
}
```

When you run it, in addition to some debugging information, you'll see something like
this. The details, of course, depend on your database:

```
C:> java database.DatabaseMetaDemo
Enhydra InstantDB - Version 3.13
The Initial Developer of the Original Code is Lutris Technologies Inc.
Portions created by Lutris are Copyright (C) 1997-2000 Lutris Technologies, Inc.
We are using InstantDB
Version is Version 3.13
```

```
Database default transaction isolation is 0 (TRANSACTION_NONE).
All done!
C:>
```

18.11. Program: SQLRunner

The SQLRunner program is a simple interface to any SQL database for which you have a JDBC driver and a login name and password. Most databases provide such a program, and most of them are more powerful. However, this program has the advantage that it works with any database. The program reads SQL commands from a console window (up to a semicolon), passes them to the driver, and prints the results. If the result is a ResultSet, it is printed using a ResultsDecorator; otherwise, it is printed as a Row-Count.

The abstract ResultsDecorator class (ResultsFormatter might have been a better name) is shown in Example 18-12. A text-mode decorator is used by default; an HTML decorator (discussed earlier in Example 18-10) and an SQL generator (potentially useful in dumping the data for insertion into another database) is also available. You can specify the decorator using command-line options or switch using the escape mechanism; for example, a line with \mh; sets the mode to HTML for the results of all following output.

To avoid hardcoding database parameters, they are fetched from a properties file, which defaults to *${user.home}/.db.properties*. For example, my *.db.properties* file contains entries like the following:

```
# Connection for the "lhbooks" database
lhbooks.DBDriver=org.postgresql.Driver
lhbooks.DBURL=jdbc:postgresql:ecom
lhbooks.DBUser=thisoneistopsecrettoo
lhbooks.DBPassword=fjkdjsj

# Connection for the "tmclub " database
tmclub.DBDriver=org.postgresql.Driver
tmclub.DBURL=jdbc:postgresql:tmclub_alliston
tmclub.DBUser=dontshowthereaderstherealpassword
tmclub.DBPassword=dlkjklzj
```

I wish I could connect to one of these databases just by saying:

```
java com.darwinsys.sql.SQLRunner -c tmclub
```

But that won't work because I have to provide the driver JAR files in the CLASSPATH. So a Unix shell script *sqlrunner* runs this java command and sets the classpath to include my drivers. So I can say:

```
sqlrunner -c tmclub
```

This connects me to my Toastmasters Club[4] database. In this example, I select all the meetings that are scheduled for the year 2014; just to show the use of different ResultsDecorators, I then switch to HTML and print the resultset as HTML, which I paste into an HTML page (in a web application, a servlet would get the results and call the ResultsDecorator directly):

```
SQLRunner: Loading driver org.postgresql.Driver
SQLRunner: Connecting to DB jdbc:postgresql:tmclub_alliston
SQLRunner: Connected to PostgreSQL
SQLRunner: ready.
select * from meetings where date > '2014-01-01';
Executing : select * from meetings where date > '2014-01-01'

id      date      theme      maxspeakers      roles_order
21      2014-01-07      Everything Old is New Again      7      null
22      2014-01-14      T.B.A.  7      null
23      2014-01-21      T.B.A.  7      null
24      2014-01-28      T.B.A.  7      null
25      2014-02-04      T.B.A.  7      null
26      2014-02-11      T.B.A.  7      null
27      2014-02-18      T.B.A.  7      null
28      2014-02-25      g Somehing New  7      null
29      2014-03-03      Spring is in the air?  null      null
2       2014-03-05      Peak Performance      null      null
30      2014-03-10      Peak Performance      5      null
31      2014-03-17      Spring Break    null      null

\mh;
select * from meetings where date > '2014-01-01';
Executing : select * from meetings where date > '2014-01-01'
<table border=1>
<tr><th>id<th>date<th>theme<th>maxspeakers<th>roles_order</tr>
<tr><td>21<td>2014-01-07<td>Everything Old is New Again<td>7<td>null</tr>
<tr><td>22<td>2014-01-14<td>T.B.A.<td>7<td>null</tr>
<tr><td>23<td>2014-01-21<td>T.B.A.<td>7<td>null</tr>
<tr><td>24<td>2014-01-28<td>T.B.A.<td>7<td>null</tr>
<tr><td>25<td>2014-02-04<td>T.B.A.<td>7<td>null</tr>
<tr><td>26<td>2014-02-11<td>T.B.A.<td>7<td>null</tr>
<tr><td>27<td>2014-02-18<td>T.B.A.<td>7<td>null</tr>
<tr><td>28<td>2014-02-25<td>g Somehing New<td>7<td>null</tr>
<tr><td>29<td>2014-03-03<td>Spring is in the air?<td>null<td>null</tr>
<tr><td>2<td>2014-03-05<td>Peak Performance<td>null<td>null</tr>
<tr><td>30<td>2014-03-10<td>Peak Performance<td>5<td>null</tr>
<tr><td>31<td>2014-03-17<td>Spring Break<td>null<td>null</tr>
</table>
```

---

4. Toastmasters is an international nonprofit organization dedicated to public speaking and leadership; see *http://www.toastmasters.org/* for information on clubs and programs.

The code for ResultsDecorator and ResultsDecoratorText is shown in Examples 18-12 and 18-13, respectively. These programs are quite general and have no dependency on SQLRunner.

Example 18-12. ResultsDecorator.java

```java
package com.darwinsys.sql;

import java.io.IOException;
import java.io.PrintWriter;
import java.sql.ResultSet;
import java.sql.SQLException;

import com.darwinsys.util.Verbosity;

/** Base class for a series of ResultSet printers. */
public abstract class ResultsDecorator {
    PrintWriter out;
    Verbosity verbosity;

    ResultsDecorator(PrintWriter wr, Verbosity v) {
        this.out = wr;
        this.verbosity = v;
    }

    /** Print the name of this Decorator's output format */
    public abstract String getName();

    /** Print the contents of a ResultSet */
    public abstract int write(ResultSet rs) throws IOException, SQLException;

    /** Print the resultset as a table info */
    public abstract void displayTable(String table, ResultSet rs)
        throws IOException, SQLException;

    public void printRowCount(int n) throws IOException {
        out.println("Row Count = " + n);
    }
    public void println(String line) throws IOException {
        out.println(line);
    }
    public void println() throws IOException {
        out.println();
    }
    public void print(String lineSeg) throws IOException {
        out.print(lineSeg);
    }

    public void flush() {
        out.flush();
    }
```

```
        public void setWriter(PrintWriter out) {
            this.out = out;
        }
    }
```

Example 18-13. ResultsDecoratorText.java

```java
package com.darwinsys.sql;

import java.io.IOException;
import java.io.PrintWriter;
import java.sql.ResultSet;
import java.sql.ResultSetMetaData;
import java.sql.SQLException;

import com.darwinsys.util.Verbosity;

/**
 * Print a ResultSet in plain text.
 */
public class ResultsDecoratorText extends ResultsDecorator {

    public ResultsDecoratorText(PrintWriter out, Verbosity v) {
        super(out, v);
    }

    @Override
    public int write(ResultSet rs) throws IOException,SQLException {
        ResultSetMetaData md = rs.getMetaData();
        int colCount = md.getColumnCount();
        for (int i = 1; i <= colCount; i++) {
            print(md.getColumnName(i) + "\t");
        }
        println();
        int rowCount = 0;
        while (rs.next()) {
            ++rowCount;
            for (int i = 1; i <= colCount; i++) {
                print(rs.getString(i) + "\t");
            }
            println();
        }
        return rowCount;
    }

    @Override
    public void displayTable(String table, ResultSet rs)
        throws IOException, SQLException {

        write(rs);
    }

    @Override
```

```java
    public void printRowCount(int rowCount) throws IOException {
        println("Rows: " + rowCount);
    }

    /* (non-Javadoc)
     * @see ResultsDecorator#getName()
     */
    @Override
    public String getName() {
        return "Plain text";
    }
}
```

Finally, the main program, SQLRunner, is shown in Example 18-14.

Example 18-14. SQLRunner.java

```java
// package com.darwinsys.sql;
public class SQLRunner {

    OutputMode outputMode = OutputMode.t;

    private static boolean okToExit = false;

    public static void setOkToExit(final boolean setting) {
        okToExit = setting;
    }

    public static boolean isOkToExit() {
        return okToExit;
    }

    public static void exit(final int exitStatus) {
        if (okToExit) {
            System.exit(exitStatus);
        } else {
            // do nothing
        }
    }

    /** Database connection */
    private Connection conn;

    private DatabaseMetaData dbMeta;

    /** SQL Statement */
    private Statement statement;

    /** Where the output is going */
    private PrintWriter out;

    private ResultsDecorator currentDecorator;
```

```java
/** Must be set at beginning */
private ResultsDecorator textDecorator =
    new ResultsDecoratorText(out, verbosity);

private ResultsDecorator sqlDecorator;

private ResultsDecorator htmlDecorator;

private ResultsDecorator xmlDecorator;

private ResultsDecorator jtableDecorator;

private boolean debug;

private boolean escape;

/** DB2 is the only one I know of today that requires table names
 * be given in uppercase when getting table metadata
 */
private boolean upperCaseTableNames;

private SQLRunnerGUI gui;

private static Verbosity verbosity = Verbosity.QUIET;

/** Construct a SQLRunner object
 * @param driver String for the JDBC driver
 * @param dbUrl String for the JDBC URL
 * @param user String for the username
 * @param password String for the password, normally in cleartext
 * @param outputMode One of the MODE_XXX constants.
 * @throws ClassNotFoundException
 * @throws SQLException
 */
public SQLRunner(String driver, String dbUrl, String user, String password,
        String outputFile, String outputMode)
        throws IOException, ClassNotFoundException, SQLException {
    conn = ConnectionUtil.getConnection(driver, dbUrl, user, password);
    commonSetup(outputFile, outputMode);
}

public SQLRunner(Connection c, String outputFile, String outputModeName)
    throws IOException, SQLException {

    // set up the SQL input
    conn = c;
    commonSetup(outputFile, outputModeName);
}

private void commonSetup(String outputFileName, String outputModeName)
    throws IOException, SQLException {
```

```
        dbMeta = conn.getMetaData();
        upperCaseTableNames =
            dbMeta.getDatabaseProductName().indexOf("DB2") >= 0;
        String dbName = dbMeta.getDatabaseProductName();
        System.out.println("SQLRunner: Connected to " + dbName);
        statement = conn.createStatement();

        if (outputFileName == null) {
            out = new PrintWriter(System.out);
        } else {
            out = new PrintWriter(new FileWriter(outputFileName));
        }

        setOutputMode(outputModeName);
    }

    /** Set the output mode.
     * @param outputMode Must be a value equal to one of the MODE_XXX values.
     * @throws IllegalArgumentException if the mode is not valid.
     */
    void setOutputMode(String outputModeName) {
        if (outputModeName == null ||
            outputModeName.length() == 0) {
            System.err.println(
            "invalid mode: " + outputMode + "; must be t, h or s"); }

        outputMode = OutputMode.valueOf(outputModeName);
        setOutputMode(outputMode);
    }

    /** Assign the correct ResultsDecorator, creating them on the fly
     * using lazy evaluation.
     */
    void setOutputMode(OutputMode outputMode) {
        ResultsDecorator newDecorator = null;
        switch (outputMode) {
            case t:
                newDecorator = textDecorator;
                break;
            case h:
                if (htmlDecorator == null) {
                    htmlDecorator = new ResultsDecoratorHTML(out, verbosity);
                }
                newDecorator = htmlDecorator;
                break;
            case s:
                if (sqlDecorator == null) {
                    sqlDecorator = new ResultsDecoratorSQL(out, verbosity);
                }
                newDecorator = sqlDecorator;
                break;
            case x:
```

```
            if (xmlDecorator == null) {
                xmlDecorator = new ResultsDecoratorXML(out, verbosity);
            }
            newDecorator = xmlDecorator;
            break;
        case j:
            if (jtableDecorator == null) {
                if (gui == null) {
                    throw new IllegalArgumentException(
                    "Can't set mode to JTable before calling setGUI()");
                }
                jtableDecorator =
                    new ResultsDecoratorJTable(gui.getJTable(), out, verbosity);
            }
            newDecorator = jtableDecorator;
            break;
        default:
            System.err.println("invalid mode: "
                            + outputMode + "; must be one of: ");
            for (OutputMode t : OutputMode.values()) {
                out.print(t); out.print(' ');
            }
            out.println();
    }
    if (currentDecorator != newDecorator) {
        currentDecorator = newDecorator;
        if (debug)
            System.out.println("Mode set to  " + outputMode);
    }
    currentDecorator.setWriter(out);
}

/** Run one script file, by name. Called from cmd line main
 * or from user code. Deprecated because of the poor capability
 * for error handling; it would be better for the user interface
 * code to create a Reader and then say:
 * <pre>while ((stmt = SQLRunner.getStatement(is)) != null) {
        stmt = stmt.trim();
        try {
            myRunner.runStatement(stmt);
        } catch (Exception e) {
            // Display the message to the user ...
        }
    }
 * </pre>
 * @throws SyntaxException
 */
@Deprecated
public void runScript(String scriptFile)
throws IOException, SQLException, SyntaxException {

    BufferedReader is;
```

```
        // Load the script file first, it's the most likely error
        is = new BufferedReader(new FileReader(scriptFile));

        runScript(is, scriptFile);
    }

    /** Run one script, by name, given a BufferedReader.
     * Deprecated because of the poor capability
     * for error handling; it would be better for the
     * user interface code to do:
     * <pre>while ((stmt = SQLRunner.getStatement(is)) != null) {
     *      stmt = stmt.trim();
     *      try {
     *          myRunner.runStatement(stmt);
     *      } catch (Exception e) {
     *          // Display the message to the user ...
     *      }
     *  }
     * </pre>
     * @throws SyntaxException
     */
    @Deprecated
    public void runScript(BufferedReader is, String name)
    throws IOException, SQLException, SyntaxException {
        String stmt;

        while ((stmt = getStatement(is)) != null) {
            stmt = stmt.trim();
            runStatement(stmt);
        }
    }

    /**
     * Process an escape, like "\ms;" for mode=sql.
     * @throws SyntaxException
     */
    private void doEscape(String str)
        throws IOException, SQLException, SyntaxException  {

        String rest = null;
        if (str.length() > 2) {
            rest = str.substring(2);
        }

        if (str.startsWith("\\d")) {     // Display
            if (rest == null){
                throw new SyntaxException("\\d needs display arg");
            }
            display(rest);
        } else if (str.startsWith("\\m")) {     // MODE
            if (rest == null){
```

```
                throw new SyntaxException("\\m needs output mode arg");
            }
            setOutputMode(rest);
        } else if (str.startsWith("\\o")){
            if (rest == null){
                throw new SyntaxException("\\o needs output file arg");
            }
            setOutputFile(rest);
        } else if (str.startsWith("\\q")){
            exit(0);
        } else {
            throw new SyntaxException("Unknown escape: " + str);
        }
    }

    /**
     * Display - generate output for \dt and similar escapes
     * @param rest - what to display - the argument with the \d stripped off
     * XXX: Move more formatting to ResultsDecorator: listTables(rs), listColumns(rs)
     */
    private void display(String rest)
        throws IOException, SQLException, SyntaxException {

        // setOutputMode(OutputMode.t);
        if (rest.equals("t")) {
            // Display list of tables
            DatabaseMetaData md = conn.getMetaData();
            ResultSet rs =
                md.getTables(null, null, "%", new String[]{"TABLE","VIEW"});
            textDecorator.setWriter(out);
            textDecorator.write(rs);
            textDecorator.flush();
        } else if (rest.startsWith("t")) {
            // Display one table. Some DatabaseMetaData implementations
            // don't do ignorecase so, for now, convert to UPPERCASE.
            String tableName = rest.substring(1).trim();
            if (upperCaseTableNames) {
                tableName = tableName.toUpperCase();
            }
            System.out.println("-- Display table " + tableName);
            DatabaseMetaData md = conn.getMetaData();
            ResultSet rs = md.getColumns(null, null, tableName, "%");
            currentDecorator.displayTable(tableName, rs);
            textDecorator.flush();
        } else
            throw new SyntaxException("\\d"  + rest + " invalid");
    }

    /**
     * @param rs
     * @return
     * @throws SQLException
     */
```

```java
    */
    private static CachedRowSet cacheResultSet(ResultSet rs) throws SQLException {
        CachedRowSet rows = null;//new com.sun.rowset.WebRowSetImpl();
        rows.populate(rs);
        return rows;
    }

    /** Set the output to the given filename.
     * @param fileName
     */
    public void setOutputFile(String fileName) throws IOException {
        if (fileName == null) {
            /* Set the output file back to System.out */
            setOutputFile(new PrintWriter(System.out, true));
        } else {
            File file = new File(fileName);
            setOutputFile(new PrintWriter(new FileWriter(file), true));
            System.out.println("Output set to " + file.getCanonicalPath());
        }
    }

    /** Set the output to the given Writer; immediately
     * update the textDecorator so \dt works...
     * @param writer
     */
    public void setOutputFile(PrintWriter writer) {
        out = writer;
        currentDecorator.setWriter(out);
    }

    /** Run one Statement, and format results as per Update or Query.
     * Called from runScript or from user code.
     * @throws SyntaxException
     */
    public void runStatement(final String rawString)
        throws IOException, SQLException, SyntaxException {

        final String inString = rawString.trim();

        if (verbosity != Verbosity.QUIET) {
            out.println("Executing : <<" + inString + ">>");
            out.flush();
        }
        currentDecorator.println(
            String.format("-- output from command -- \"%s\"%n", inString));

        escape = false;
        if (inString.startsWith("\\")) {
            escape = true;
            doEscape(inString);
            return;
        }
```

```
        boolean hasResultSet =
            statement.execute(inString);        // DO IT - call the database.

        if (!hasResultSet) {
            currentDecorator.printRowCount(statement.getUpdateCount());
        } else {
            int n = currentDecorator.write(cacheResultSet(statement.getResultSet()));
            if (verbosity == Verbosity.VERBOSE || verbosity == Verbosity.DEBUG) {
                currentDecorator.printRowCount(n);
            }
        }
        currentDecorator.flush();
    }

    /** Extract one statement from the given Reader.
     * Ignore comments and null lines.
     * @return The SQL statement, up to but not including the ';' character.
     * May be null if no statement found.
     */
    public static String getStatement(BufferedReader is)
    throws IOException {
        StringBuilder sb = new StringBuilder();
        String line;
        while ((line = is.readLine()) != null) {
            if (verbosity == Verbosity.DEBUG) {
                System.out.println("SQLRunner.getStatement(): LINE " + line);
            }
            if (line == null || line.length() == 0) {
                continue;
            }
            line = line.trim();
            if (line.startsWith("#") || line.startsWith("--")) {
                continue;
            }
            if (line.startsWith("\\")) {
                if (sb.length() != 0) {
                    throw new IllegalArgumentException(
                        "Escape command found inside statement");
                }
            }
            sb.append(line);
            int nb = sb.length();

            // If the buffer currently ends with ';', return it.
            if (nb > 0 && sb.charAt(nb-1) == ';') {
                if (nb == 1) {
                    return null;
                }
                sb.setLength(nb-1);
                return sb.toString();
            }
```

```
            // Add a space in case the SQL is generated by a tool
            // that doesn't remember to add spaces (hopefully this won't
            // break tools that output newlines inside quoted strings!).
            sb.append(' ');
        }
        return null;
    }

    public void close() throws SQLException {
        if (statement != null) {
            statement.close();
        }
        if (conn != null) {
            conn.close();
        }
        out.flush();
        out.close();
    }

    public static Verbosity getVerbosity() {
        return verbosity;
    }

    public static void setVerbosity(Verbosity verbosity) {
        SQLRunner.verbosity = verbosity;
    }

    public void setErrorHandler(SQLRunnerErrorHandler eHandler) {
        gui.setErrorHandler(eHandler);
    }

    public void setGUI(SQLRunnerGUI gui) {
        this.gui = gui;
    }

    public String toString() {
        return "sqlrunner";
    }

    public boolean isEscape() {
        return escape;
    }
}

}
```

I used to use this program fairly regularly, so it evolved quite a lot. Now that most of my projects use the excellent open source PostgresQL database, I tend to use "psql," a tool which heavily influenced SqlRunner.

See Also

There are many good books on JDBC from O'Reilly and other major publishers. The same is true of relational databases, relational theory, and so on. The list changes too frequently to be kept up to date here.

## CHAPTER 19

Processing JSON Data

19.0. Introduction

JSON, or JavaScript Object Notation, is:

- A simple, lightweight data interchange format.

- A simpler, lighter alternative to XML (see Chapter 20).

- Easy to generate with `println`s or with one of several APIs.

- Recognized directly by the JavaScript parser in all web browsers.

- Supported with add-on frameworks for all common languages (Java, C/C++, Perl, Ruby, Python, Lua, Erlang, Haskell, to name a few); a ridiculously long list of supported languages (including two dozen parsers for Java alone) is right on the homepage (*http://json.org*).

A simple JSON message might look like this:

softwareinfo.json

```
{
  "name": "robinparse",
  "version": "1.2.3",
  "description": "Another Parser for JSON",
  "className": "RobinParse",
  "contributors": [
      "Robin Smythe",
      "Jon Jenz",
      "Jan Ardann"
  ]
}
```

As you can see, the syntax is simple, nestable, and amenable to human inspection.

The JSON home page (*http://json.org*) provides a concise summary of JSON syntax. There are two kinds of structure: JSON Objects (maps) and JSON Arrays (lists). JSON Objects are sets of name and value pairs, which can be represented either as a `java.util.Map` *or* as the properties of a Java object. For example, the fields of a `Local-Date` (see Recipe 6.1) object for April 1, 2014, might be represented as:

```
{
        "year": 2014,
        "month": 4,
        "day" : 1
}
```

JSON Arrays are ordered lists, represented in Java either as arrays or as `java.util.Lists`. A list of two dates might look like this:

```
{
        [{
                "year": 2014,
                "month": 4,
                "day" : 1
        },{
                "year": 2014,
                "month": 5,
                "day" : 15
        }]
}
```

JSON is free-format, so the preceding could also be written, with some loss of human-readability but no loss of information or functionality, as:

```
{[{"year":2014,"month":4,"day":1},{"year":2014,"month":5,"day":15}]}
```

Hundreds of parsers have, I'm sure, been written for JSON. A few that come to mind in the Java world include the following:

`stringtree.org`
    Very small and light weight

`json.org parser`
    Widely used because it's free and has a good domain name

`jackson.org parser`
    Widely used because it's very powerful, and used with Spring Framework

`javax.json`
    Oracle's new official but currently EE-only standard

This chapter shows several ways of processing JSON data using some of the various APIs just listed. Disturbingly, the "official" `javax.json` API is only included in the Java EE, not the Java SE, so it is unlikely to see very much use on the client side. This API uses some names in common with the `org.json` API, but not enough to be consdered "compatible."

Because this is a book for client-side Java developers, nothing will be made of the ability to process JSON directly in server-generated browser-based JavaScript, though this can be very useful in building enterprise applications.

19.1. Generating JSON Directly

Problem

You want to generate JSON without bothering to use an API.

Solution

Get the data you want, and use `println()` or `String.format()` as appropriate.

Discussion

There is nothing the APIs do that you can't do yourself. For the utterly trivial cases, you can just use the `PrintWriter.println()` or `String.format()`.

This code prints the year, month, and date from a `LocalTime` object (see Recipe 6.1). Some of the JSON formatting is delegated to the `toJson()` object:

```java
public class LocalDateToJsonManually {

    private static final String OPEN = "{";
    private static final String CLOSE = "}";

    public static void main(String[] args) {
        LocalDate dNow = LocalDate.now();
        System.out.println(toJson(dNow));
    }

    public static String toJson(LocalDate dNow) {
        StringBuilder sb = new StringBuilder();
        sb.append(OPEN).append("\n");
        sb.append(jsonize("year", dNow.getYear()));
        sb.append(jsonize("month", dNow.getMonth()));
        sb.append(jsonize("day", dNow.getDayOfMonth()));
        sb.append(CLOSE).append("\n");
        return sb.toString();
    }

    public static String jsonize(String key, Object value) {
        return String.format("\"%s\": \"%s\",\n", key, value);
    }
}
```

Of course, this is an extremely trivial example. For anything more involved, or for the common case of having to parse JSON objects, using one of the frameworks will be easier on your nerves.

19.2. Parsing and Writing JSON with Jackson

Problem

You want to read and/or write JSON using a full-function JSON API.

Solution

Use Jackson, the full-blown JSON API.

Discussion

Jackson provides many ways of working. For simple cases, you can have POJO (plain old Java objects) converted to/from JSON more-or-less automatically, as is illustrated in Example 19-1.

Example 19-1. Reading and Writing POJOs with Jackson

```
public class ReadWriteJackson {

    public static void main(String[] args) throws IOException {
        ObjectMapper mapper = new ObjectMapper();                       ❶

        String jsonInput =                                             ❷
                "{\"id\":0,\"firstName\":\"Robin\",\"lastName\":\"Wilson\"}";
        Person q = mapper.readValue(jsonInput, Person.class);
        System.out.println("Read and parsed Person from JSON: " + q);

        Person p = new Person("Roger", "Rabbit");                      ❸
        System.out.print("Person object " + p +" as JSON = ");
        mapper.writeValue(System.out, p);
    }
}
```

❶   Create a Jackson `ObjectMapper` which can map POJOs to/from JSON.

❷   Map the string `jsonInput` into a `Person` object with one call to `readValue()`.

❸   Convert the `Person` object p into JSON with one call to `writeValue()`.

Running this example produces the following output:

```
Read and parsed Person from JSON: Robin Wilson
Person object Roger Rabbit as JSON = {"id":0,"firstName":"Roger",
        "lastName":"Rabbit","name":"Roger Rabbit"}
```

As another example, this code reads the "parser description" example file that opened this chapter; notice the declaration List<String> for the array of contributors:

```
public class SoftwareParseJackson {
    final static String FILE_NAME = "/json/softwareinfo.json";

    public static void main(String[] args) throws Exception {
        ObjectMapper mapper = new ObjectMapper();   ❶

        InputStream jsonInput =
            SoftwareParseJackson.class.getResourceAsStream(FILE_NAME);
        if (jsonInput == null) {
            throw new NullPointerException("can't find" + FILE_NAME);
        }
        SoftwareInfo sware = mapper.readValue(jsonInput, SoftwareInfo.class);
        System.out.println(sware);
    }

}
```

❶　The ObjectMapper does the actual parsing of the JSON input.

Running this example produces the following output:

```
Software: robinparse (1.2.3) by [Robin Smythe, Jon Jenz, Jan Ardann]
```

Of course there are cases where the mapping gets more involved; for this purpose, Jackson provides a set of annotations to control the mapping. But the default mapping is pretty good!

19.3. Parsing and Writing JSON with org.json

Problem

You want to read/write JSON using a mid-sized, widely used JSON API.

Solution

Consider using the org.json API; it's widely used and is also used in Android.

Discussion

The *org.json* package is not as advanced as Jackson, nor as high-level; it makes you think and work in terms of the underlying JSON abstractions instead of at the Java code level. For example, here is the *org.json* version of reading the software description from the opening of this chapter:

```
public class SoftwareParseOrgJson {
    final static String FILE_NAME = "/json/softwareinfo.json";
```

```
    public static void main(String[] args) throws Exception {

        InputStream jsonInput =
            SoftwareParseOrgJson.class.getResourceAsStream(FILE_NAME);
        if (jsonInput == null) {
            throw new NullPointerException("can't find" + FILE_NAME);
        }
        JSONObject obj = new JSONObject(new JSONTokener(jsonInput));        ❶
        System.out.println("Software Name: " + obj.getString("name"));      ❷
        System.out.println("Version: " + obj.getString("version"));
        System.out.println("Description: " + obj.getString("description"));
        System.out.println("Class: " + obj.getString("className"));
        JSONArray contribs = obj.getJSONArray("contributors");             ❸
        for (int i = 0; i < contribs.length(); i++) {                      ❹
            System.out.println("Contributor Name: " + contribs.get(i));
        }
    }

}
```

❶   Create the JSONObject from the input.

❷   Retrieve individual String fields.

❸   Retrieve the JSONArray of contributor names.

❹   org.json.JSONArray doesn't implement *Iterable* so you can't use a foreach loop.

Running it does produce the expected output:

```
Software Name: robinparse
Version: 1.2.3
Description: Another Parser for JSON
Class: RobinParse
Contributor Name: Robin Smythe
Contributor Name: Jon Jenz
Contributor Name: Jan Ardann
```

JSONObject and JSONArray use their toString() method to produce (correctly for-matted) JSON strings. For example:

```
public class WriteOrgJson {
    public static void main(String[] args) {
        JSONObject jsonObject = new JSONObject();
        jsonObject.put("Name", "robinParse").          ❶
            put("Version", "1.2.3").
            put("Class", "RobinParse");
        String printable = jsonObject.toString();       ❷
        System.out.println(printable);
    }
}
```

❶ Nice that it offers a "fluent API" to allow chaining of method calls

❷ `toString()` converts to textual JSON representation.

Running this produces the following:

```
{"Name":"robinParse","Class":"RobinParse","Version":"1.2.3"}
```

See Also

The *org.json* API javadoc is online at *http://www.json.org/java/index.html*.

Summary

Many APIs exist for Java. Jackson is the biggest and most powerful; org.json and javax.json are in the middle; StringTree (which I didn't give an example of because it doesn't have a Maven Artifact available) is the smallest. For a list of these and other JSON APIs, consult *http://www.json.org/java/* and scroll past the syntax summary.

## CHAPTER 20

Processing XML

20.0. Introduction

The Extensible Markup Language, or XML, is a portable, human-readable format for exchanging text or data between programs. XML is derived from the parent standard SGML, as is the HTML language used on web pages worldwide. XML, then, is HTML's younger but more capable sibling. And because most developers know at least a bit of HTML, parts of this discussion compare XML with HTML. XML's lesser-known grandparent is IBM's GML (General Markup Language), and one of its cousins is Adobe FrameMaker's Maker Interchange Format (MIF). Figure 20-1 depicts the family tree.

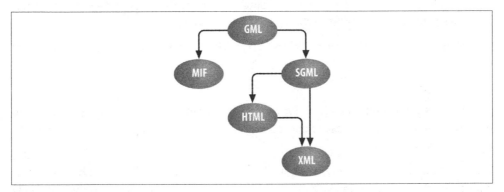

Figure 20-1. XML's ancestry

One way of thinking about XML is that it's like HTML cleaned up, consolidated, and—most importantly—with the ability for you to define your own tags. It's HTML with tags that can and should identify the informational content as opposed to the formatting. Another way of perceiving XML is as a general interchange format for such things as business-to-business communications over the Internet or as a human-editable[1] description of things as diverse as word-processing files and Java documents. XML is all these things, depending on where you're coming from as a developer and where you want to go today—and tomorrow.

Because it is text, XML can be generated from Java in a number of ways. For very simple cases, you can just use good old `out.println()`, but this is not recommended. The Java Architecture for XML Binding (JAXB, see Recipe 20.1), and the XML Serializers (Recipe 20.2) provide mechanisms for moving information in both directions between Java objects and XML documents. Some other third-party packages provide this as well, but we'll keep the coverage to these two.

Because of the wide acceptance of XML, it is used as the basis for many other formats, including the Open Office (*http://www.openoffice.org*) save file format, the SVG graphics file format, and many more.

From SGML, both HTML and XML inherit the syntax of using angle brackets (< and >) around *tags*, each pair of which delimits one part of an XML document, called an *element*. An element may contain content (like a <P> tag in HTML) or may not (like an <hr> in HTML). Whereas HTML documents can begin with either an <html> tag or a <DOCTYPE...> tag (or, informally, with neither), an XML file may begin with an XML declaration. Indeed, it must begin with an XML processing instruction (<? ... ?>) if the file's character encoding is other than UTF-8 or UTF-16:

```
<?xml version="1.0" encoding="iso-8859-1"?>
```

The question mark is a special character used to identify the XML "processing instruction" (it's syntactically similar to the % used in ASP and JSP).

HTML has a number of elements that accept attributes, such as those in this (very old) web page:

```
<BODY bgcolor=white> ... </body>
```

In XML, attribute values (such as the 1.0 for the version in the processing instruction or the `white` of `BGCOLOR`) must be quoted. In other words, quoting is optional in HTML, but required in XML.

The `BODY` example shown here, though allowed in traditional HTML, would draw complaints from any XML parser. XML is case sensitive; in XML, `BODY`, `Body`, and `body` represent three different element names. In addition, each XML start tag must have a

---

1. Although you can edit XML using *vi*, Emacs, Notepad, or simpletext, it is often considered preferable to use an XML-aware editor. XML's structure is more complex, and parsing programs are far less tolerant of picayune error, than was ever the case in the HTML world. XML files are kept as plain text for debugging purposes, for ease of transmission across wildly incompatible operating systems, and (as a last resort) for manual editing to repair software disasters.

matching end tag. This is one of a small list of basic constraints detailed in the XML specification. Any XML file that satisfies all of these constraints is said to be well-formed and is accepted by an XML parser. A document that is not well-formed will be rejected by an XML parser.

Speaking of XML parsing, quite a few XML parsers are available. A parser is simply a program or class that reads an XML file, looks at it at least syntactically, and lets you access some or all of the elements. Most of these parsers in the Java world conform to the Java bindings for one of the two well-known XML APIs, SAX and DOM. SAX, the Simple API for XML, reads the file and calls your code when it encounters certain events, such as start-of-element, end-of-element, start-of-document, and the like. DOM, the Document Object Model, reads the file and constructs an in-memory tree or graph corresponding to the elements and their attributes and contents in the file. This tree can be traversed, searched, modified (even constructed from scratch, using DOM), or written to a file.

An alternative API called JDOM (*http://www.jdom.org*) has also been released into the open source field. JDOM, originally by Brett McLaughlin and Jason Hunter and now shepherded by Rolf Lear, has the advantage of being aimed primarily at Java (DOM itself is designed to work with many different programming languages).

But how does the parser know if an XML file contains the correct elements? Well, the simpler, "nonvalidating" parsers don't—their only concern is the well-formedness (see the following list) of the document. Validating parsers check that the XML file conforms to a given Document Type Definition (DTD) or an XML Schema. DTDs are inherited from SGML; their syntax is discussed in Recipe 20.7. Schemas are newer than DTDs and, though slightly more complex, provide more flexibility, including such object-based features as inheritance. DTDs are written in a special syntax derived from SGML's document type definition specification, whereas XML Schemas are expressed using ordinary XML elements and attributes.

These definitions give more precise meaning to terms used with XML:

Well Formed
> An XML document that conforms to the syntax of all XML documents (i.e., one root element, correct tag/element syntax, correct nesting, etc.).

Valid
> An XML document that in addition to being well-formed has been tested to conform to the requirements of an XML schema (or DocType).

In addition to parsing XML, you can use an XML processor to transform XML into some other format, such as HTML. This is a natural for use in a web servlet: if a given web browser client can support XML, just write the data as-is, but if not, transform the data into HTML. We'll look at two approaches to XML transformation: transformation using a generic XSLT processor and then later some parsing APIs suitable for customized operations on XML.

If you need to control how an XML document is formatted, for screen or print, you can use XSL (Extensible Style Language). XSL is a more sophisticated variation on the HTML stylesheet concept that allows you to specify formatting for particular elements. XSL has two parts: tree transformation (for which XSLT was designed, though it can also be used independently, as we'll see) and formatting (the non-XSLT part is informally known as XSL-FO or XSL Formatting Objects).

XSL stylesheets can be complex; you are basically specifying a batch formatting language to describe how your textual data is formatted for the printed page. A comprehensive reference implementation is FOP (Formatting Objects Processor), which produces Acrobat PDF output and is available from *http://xml.apache.org*. Indeed, the third edition of this book is being produced using a complex toolchain that converts from AsciiDoc to XML and then XML to various output formats using XSLT.

When Java first appeared, writing portable XML-based Java programs was difficult because there was no single standard API. However, for a long time we have had JAXP, the Java API for XML Processing, which provides standard means for processing XML.

20.1. Converting Between Objects and XML with JAXB

Problem

You want to generate XML directly from Java objects, or vice versa.

Solution

One way is to use the Java Architecture for XML Bindings, JAXB.

Discussion

JAXB requires a Schema (see Recipe 20.7) document to work; this document is a standard schema that describes how to write the fields of your object into XML or how to recognize them in an incoming XML document.

In Example 20-1, we'll serialize a `Configuration` document, a subset of the information a multiuser app needs to keep track of about each user. We've already annotated this class with some JAXB annotations, which we'll discuss after the code.

Example 20-1. Configuration.java

```
/**
 * Demo of XML via JAXB; meant to represent some of the (many!)
 * fields in a typical GUI for user<-->application configuration
 * (it is not configuring JAXB; it is used to configure a larger app).
```

```
    */
@XmlAccessorType(XmlAccessType.FIELD)
@XmlType(name = "configuration",
    propOrder={"screenName", "webProxy", "verbose", "colorName"})
@XmlRootElement(name = "config")
public class Configuration {

    private String webProxy;
    private boolean verbose;
    private String colorName;
    private String screenName;

    public String getColorName() {
        return colorName;
    }
    public void setColorName(String colorName) {
        this.colorName = colorName;
    }

    // Remaining accessors, hashCode/equals(), are uninteresting.
```

The `Configuration` class has four fields, and we want them written in a particular order.
Normally JAXB would find the fields in Reflection (see Chapter 23) order, which isn't
well defined. So we list them in the first annotation (these are all from
`javax.xml.bind.annotation`):

```
@XmlType(name = "configuration",
propOrder={"screenName", "webProxy", "verbose", "colorName"})
@XmlAccessorType(XmlAccessType.FIELD)
@XmlRootElement(name = "config")
```

We could write the XML schema by hand, using `vi` or `notepad`, but regular readers such
as yourself undoubtedly expect that I will refuse to do so whenever possible. Instead,
I'll use a JAXB-provided utility, `schemagen`, to generate the XML:

```
$ schemagen -cp $js/target -d /tmp Configuration.java
```

This generates a schema file with the hardcoded filename *schema1.xsd* (*.xsd* is the normal filename extension for XML Schema Definition):

```
<xs:schema version="1.0" xmlns:xs="http://www.w3.org/2001/XMLSchema">

  <xs:element name="config" type="configuration"/>

  <xs:complexType name="configuration">
    <xs:sequence>
      <xs:element name="screenName" type="xs:string" minOccurs="0"/>
      <xs:element name="webProxy" type="xs:string" minOccurs="0"/>
      <xs:element name="verbose" type="xs:boolean"/>
      <xs:element name="colorName" type="xs:string" minOccurs="0"/>
    </xs:sequence>
```

```
        </xs:complexType>
    </xs:schema>
```

The online source has a commented-up version of this file, renamed to *xml.jaxb.xsd*.

Now we are ready to serialize or deserialize objects. Example 20-2 shows writing a `Configuration` object out to an XML file and then, some time later in the same program (maybe a subsequent invocation of the program) reading it back in. This code is written as a JUnit test (see Recipe 1.13) to make it easy to prove that it actually saves the fields and rereads them.

Example 20-2. JAXB Demonstration Main

```
// We set up JAXB: the context arg is the package name!
JAXBContext jc = JAXBContext.newInstance("xml.jaxb");
Marshaller saver = jc.createMarshaller();
final File f = new File("config.save");

// We save their preferences
// Configuration c = ... - set above
Writer saveFile = new FileWriter(f);
saver.marshal(c, saveFile);
saveFile.close();

// Confirm that the XML file got written
assertTrue(f.exists());
System.out.println("JAXB output saved in " + f.getAbsolutePath());

// Sometime later, we read it back in.
Unmarshaller loader = jc.createUnmarshaller();
Configuration c2 = (Configuration) loader.unmarshal(f);

// Outside of the simulation, we test that what we
// read back is the same as what we started with.
assertEquals("saved and loaded back the object", c, c2);
```

After the test runs, the *config.save* file is left in the testing directory; I grabbed a copy of this, reformatted it, and saved it in the source directory with *.xml* appended to the filename. The content looks as you'd expect:

```
<config>
        <screenName>idarwin</screenName>
        <verbose>true</verbose>
        <colorName>inky green</colorName>
</config>
```

20.2. Converting Between Objects and XML with Serializers

Problem

You want to generate XML directly from Java objects, or vice versa.

Solution

Another way is to use the XML Object Serializers.

Discussion

The Serialization demonstration in Recipe 10.20 showed an abstract base class that called upon abstract methods to write the file out in some format. Example 20-3 is the XML subclass for it. If you haven't read that section, all that matters is that write() is called with one argument, the tree of objects to be saved.

Example 20-3. SerialDemoXML.java

```java
public class SerialDemoXML extends SerialDemoAbstractBase {

    public static final String FILENAME = "serial.xml";

    public static void main(String[] args) throws IOException {
        new SerialDemoXML().save();
        new SerialDemoXML().dump();
    }

    /** Save the data to disk. */
    public void write(Object theGraph) throws IOException {
        XMLEncoder os = new XMLEncoder(
                new FileOutputStream(FILENAME));
        os.writeObject(theGraph);
        os.close();
    }

    /** Display the data */
    public void dump() throws IOException {
        XMLDecoder inp = new XMLDecoder(
                new FileInputStream(FILENAME));
        System.out.println(inp.readObject());
        inp.close();
    }
}
```

20.3. Transforming XML with XSLT

Problem

You need to make significant changes to the output format.

Solution

Use XSLT; it is fairly easy to use and does not require writing much Java.

Discussion

XSLT, the Extensible Stylesheet Language for Transformations, allows you a great deal of control over the output format. It can be used to change an XML file from one vocabulary into another, as might be needed in a business-to-business (B2B) application where information is passed from one industry-standard vocabulary to a site that uses another. It can also be used to render XML into another format such as HTML. Some open source projects even use XSLT as a tool to generate Java source files from an XML description of the required methods and fields. Think of XSLT as a scripting language for transforming XML.

This example uses XSLT to transform a document containing people's names, addresses, and so on—such as the file *people.xml*, shown in Example 20-4—into printable HTML.

Example 20-4. people.xml

```
<people>
<person>
    <name>Ian Darwin</name>
    <email>http://www.darwinsys.com/contact.html</email>
    <country>Canada</country>
</person>
<person>
    <name>Another Darwin</name>
    <email type="intranet">afd@node1</email>
    <country>Canada</country>
</person>
</people>
```

You can transform the *people.xml* file into HTML by using the following command:

```
$ java xml.JAXPTransform people.xml people.xsl  people.html
```

The output is something like the following:

```
<html>
<head>
<META http-equiv="Content-Type" content="text/html; charset=UTF-8">
<title>Our People</title>
</head>
```

```
<body>
<table border="1">
<tr>
<th>Name</th><th>EMail</th>
</tr>
<tr>
<td>Ian Darwin</td><td>http://www.darwinsys.com/</td>
</tr>
<tr>
<td>Another Darwin</td><td>afd@node1</td>
</tr>
</table>
</body>
</html>
```

Figure 20-2 shows the resulting HTML file opened in a browser.

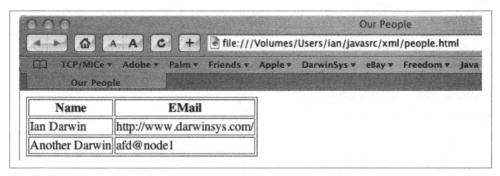

Figure 20-2. XML to HTML final result

Let's look at the file *people.xsl* (shown in Example 20-5). Because an XSL file is an XML file, it must be well-formed according to the syntax of XML. As you can see, it contains some XML elements but is mostly (well-formed) HTML.

Example 20-5. people.xsl

```
<xsl:stylesheet xmlns:xsl="http://www.w3.org/1999/XSL/Transform" version="1.0">
<xsl:template match="/">

<html>
<head><title>Our People</title></head>
<body>

    <table border="1">
    <tr>
        <th>Name</th>
        <th>EMail</th>
    </tr>

    <xsl:for-each select="people/person">
```

```
        <tr>
            <td><xsl:value-of select="name"/></td>
            <td><xsl:value-of select="email"/></td>
        </tr>
    </xsl:for-each>

    </table>

</body></html>
</xsl:template>
</xsl:stylesheet>
```

I haven't shown my XSLT-based JAXPTransform program yet. To transform XML using XSL, you use a set of classes called an *XSLT processor*, which Java includes as part of JAXP. Another freely available XSLT processor is the Apache XML Project's Xalan. To use JAXP's XSL transformation, you create an XSL processor by calling the factory method TransformerFactory.newInstance().newTransformer(), passing in a Streamsource for the stylesheet. You then call its transform() method, passing in a StreamSource for the XML document and a StreamResult for the output file. The code for JAXPTransform appears in Example 20-6.

Example 20-6. JAXPTransform.java

```
public class JAXPTransform {

    /**
     * @param args three filenames: XML, XSL, and Output (this order is historical).
     * @throws Exception
     */
    public static void main(String[] args) throws Exception {

        // Require three input args
        if (args.length != 3) {
            System.out.println(
            "Usage: java JAXPTransform inputFile.xml inputFile.xsl outputFile");
            System.exit(1);
        }

        // Create a transformer object
        Transformer tx = TransformerFactory.newInstance().newTransformer(
                new StreamSource(new File(args[1]))); // not 0

        // Use its transform() method to perform the transformation
        tx.transform(new StreamSource(new File(args[0])), // not 1
                new StreamResult(new File(args[2])));
    }
}
```

See also the JAXP "XML Transformer," which does not necessarily use stylesheets, in Recipe 20.8.

See Also

An optimization fort XSLT is the use of *translets*. The *translet* framework reads a stylesheet and generates a Translet class, which is a compiled Java program that transforms XML according to that particular stylesheet. This eliminates the overhead of reading the stylesheet each time a document is translated. Translets have been incorporated under the name XSLTC into the Apache XML Xerces-Java project (*http://xml.apache.org/xalan-j/xsltc_usage.html*).

20.4. Parsing XML with SAX

Problem

You want to make one quick pass over an XML file, extracting certain tags or other information as you go.

Solution

Simply use SAX to create a document handler and pass it to the SAX parser.

Discussion

The XML DocumentHandler interface specifies a number of "callbacks" that your code must provide. In one sense, this is similar to the Listener interfaces in AWT and Swing, as briefly described in Recipe 14.5. The most commonly used methods are startElement(), endElement(), and characters(). The first two, obviously, are called at the start and end of an element, and characters() is called when there is character data. The characters are stored in a large array, and you are passed the base of the array and the offset and length of the characters that make up your text. Conveniently, there is a string constructor that takes exactly these arguments. Hmmm, I wonder if they thought of that . . .

To demonstrate this, I wrote a simple program using SAX to extract names and email addresses from an XML file. The program itself is reasonably simple and is shown in Example 20-7.

Example 20-7. SAXLister.java

```java
public class SAXLister {
    final boolean DEBUG = false;
    public static void main(String[] args) throws Exception {
        new SAXLister(args);
    }

    public SAXLister(String[] args) throws SAXException, IOException {
        XMLReader parser = XMLReaderFactory.createXMLReader();
```

```
            parser.setContentHandler(new PeopleHandler());
            parser.parse(args.length == 1 ? args[0] : "xml/people.xml");
    }

    /** Inner class provides DocumentHandler
     */
    class PeopleHandler extends DefaultHandler {
        boolean person = false;
        boolean email = false;
        public void startElement(String nsURI, String localName,
                String rawName, Attributes attributes) throws SAXException {
            if (DEBUG) {
                System.out.println("startElement: " + localName + ","
                    + rawName);
            }
            // Consult rawName since we aren't using xmlns prefixes here.
            if (rawName.equalsIgnoreCase("name"))
                person = true;
            if (rawName.equalsIgnoreCase("email"))
                email = true;
        }
        public void characters(char[] ch, int start, int length) {
            if (person) {
                System.out.println("Person:  " +
                    new String(ch, start, length));
                person = false;
            } else if (email) {
                System.out.println("Email: " +
                    new String(ch, start, length));
                email = false;
            }
        }
    }
}
```

When run against the *people.xml* file shown in Example 20-4, it prints the listing:

```
$ $ java -cp $js/target/classes xml.SAXLister
Person:  Ian Darwin
Email: http://www.darwinsys.com/
Person:  Another Darwin
Email: afd@node1.com
$
```

In version 2 of the XML DOM API, you can use the new XMLReaderFactory.crea-teXMLReader(). Incidentally, the SAX specification and code are maintained by the SAX Project (*http://www.saxproject.org*), not by Oracle. The no-argument form of createXMLReader() is expected first to try loading the class defined in the system property org.xml.sax.driver, and if that fails, to load an implementation-defined SAX parser. On extremely old versions, the Sun implementation would simply throw an exception to the effect of System property org.xml.sax.driver not specified. An overloaded form of `createXMLReader()` takes the name of the parser as a string argument (e.g., `"org.apache.xerces.parsers.SAXParser"` or `"org.apache.crimson.parser.XMLReaderImpl"`). This class name would normally be loaded from a properties file (see Recipe 7.12) to avoid having the parser class name compiled into your application.

One problem with SAX is that it is, well, simple, and therefore doesn't scale well, as you can see by thinking about this program. Imagine trying to handle 12 different tags and doing something different with each one. For more involved analysis of an XML file, the Document Object Model (DOM) or the JDOM API may be better suited. (On the other hand, DOM requires keeping the entire tree in memory, so there are scalability issues with very large XML documents.) And with SAX, you can't really "navigate" a document because you have only a stream of events, not a real structure. For that, you want DOM or JDOM.

20.5. Parsing XML with DOM

Problem

You want to examine an XML file in detail.

Solution

Use DOM to parse the document and process the resulting in-memory tree.

Discussion

The Document Object Model (DOM) is a tree-structured representation of the information in an XML document. It consists of several interfaces, the most important of which is the *node*. All are in the package `org.w3c.dom`, reflecting the influence of the World Wide Web Consortium (*http://www.w3.org*) in creating and promulgating the DOM. The major DOM interfaces are shown in Table 20-1.

Table 20-1. Major DOM interfaces

Interface	Function
Document	Top-level representation of an XML document
Node	Representation of any node in the XML tree
Element	An XML element
Text	A textual string

You don't have to implement these interfaces; the parser generates them. When you start creating or modifying XML documents in Recipe 20.8, you can create nodes. But even then there are implementing classes. Parsing an XML document with DOM is syntactically similar to processing a file with XSL; that is, you get a reference to a parser and call its methods with objects representing the input files. The difference is that the parser returns an XML DOM, a tree of objects in memory. XParse in Example 20-8 simply parses an XML document. Despite the simplicity, I use it a lot; whenever I have an XML file whose validity is in question, I just pass it to XParse.

Example 20-8. XParse.java

```java
public static void main(String[] av) throws SAXException {
    if (av.length == 0) {
        System.err.println("Usage: XParse file");
        return;
    }
    boolean validate = false;
    Schema schema = null;
    try {
        for (int i=0; i<av.length; i++) {
            if (av[i].equals("-v"))
                validate = true;
            else if (av[i].equals("-a")) {
                // "create a SchemaFactory capable of understanding W3C schemas"
                //    -- from the Javadoc page
                SchemaFactory schemaFactory =
                SchemaFactory.newInstance(XMLConstants.W3C_XML_SCHEMA_NS_URI);

                // load the W3c XML schema, represented by a Schema instance
                String schemaLocation = av[++i];
                File schemaFile = new File(schemaLocation);
                if (!schemaFile.exists()) {
                    throw new IOException(
                    "Schema location = " + schemaLocation + " does not exist");
                }
                schema = schemaFactory.newSchema(schemaFile);

            } else {
                File xmlFile = new File(av[i]);
                System.err.println(
                    "Parsing " + xmlFile.getAbsolutePath() + "...");

                DocumentBuilderFactory dbFactory =
                    DocumentBuilderFactory.newInstance();
                if (validate) {
                    if (schema != null) {
                        dbFactory.setSchema(schema);
                    } else {
                        dbFactory.setValidating(true);
                        dbFactory.setNamespaceAware(true);
                        dbFactory.setAttribute(
                        "http://java.sun.com/xml/jaxp/properties/schemaLanguage",
                                XMLConstants.W3C_XML_SCHEMA_NS_URI);
                    }
                }
```

```
            DocumentBuilder parser = dbFactory.newDocumentBuilder();
            // If not using schema, Get local copies of DTDs...
            if (schema == null) {
                parser.setEntityResolver(new MyDTDResolver());
            }
            parser.parse(xmlFile);
            System.out.println("Parsed/Validated OK");
        }
    }
    // Just +catch+ statements below here...
```

To enable validation for Schema, DTD, RelaxNG, etc., you need to set validation true on the `DocumentBuilderFactory` before creating the `DocumentBuilderParser`. The XParse program has code for doing this; it's done differently for DTD (`-v`) and Schema (`-v` and `-a` *schemalocation*).

DOM also provides tools to traverse the document. You can use the defined `TreeWalker` interface, or you can just use the algorithm shown in Example 20-9.

Example 20-9. XTW.java

```
public class XTW {

    public static void main(String[] av) {
        if (av.length == 0) {
            System.err.println("Usage: XTW file [...]");
            return;
        }
        for (int i=0; i<av.length; i++) {
            String name = av[i];
            new XTW().convert(name, true);
        }
    }

    /** Convert the file */
    protected void convert(String fileName, boolean verbose) {

        try {
            if (verbose)
                System.err.println(">>>Parsing " + fileName + "...");
            // Make the document a URL so relative DTD works.
            String uri = "file:" + new File(fileName).getAbsolutePath();

            DocumentBuilderFactory factory =
                DocumentBuilderFactory.newInstance();
            DocumentBuilder builder = factory.newDocumentBuilder();
            Document doc = builder.parse( uri );

            if (verbose)
                System.err.println(">>>Walking " + fileName + "...");
            doRecursive(doc);
```

```
        } catch (Exception ex) {
            System.err.println("+============================+");
            System.err.println("|          XTW Error         |");
            System.err.println("+============================+");
            System.err.println(ex.getClass());
            System.err.println(ex.getMessage());
            System.err.println("+============================+");
        }
        if (verbose) {
            System.err.println(">>>Done " + fileName + "...");
        }
    }
}

/* Process all the nodes, recursively. */
protected void doRecursive(Node p) {
    if (p == null) {
        return;
    }
    NodeList nodes = p.getChildNodes();
    Debug.println("xml-tree", "Element has " +
        nodes.getLength() + " children");
    for (int i = 0; i < nodes.getLength(); i++) {
        Node n = nodes.item(i);
        if (n == null) {
            continue;
        }

        doNode(n);

    }
}

protected void doNode(Node n) {

    switch(n.getNodeType()) {
        case Node.ELEMENT_NODE:
            System.out.println("ELEMENT<" + n.getNodeName() + ">");
            doRecursive(n);
            break;
        case Node.TEXT_NODE:
            String text = n.getNodeValue();
            if (text.length() == 0 ||
                text.equals("\n") || text.equals("\\r")) {
                break;
            }
            System.out.println("TEXT: " + text);
            break;
        default:
            System.err.println( "OTHER NODE " +
                n.getNodeType() + ": " + n.getClass());
            break;
    }
```

```
        }
}
```

20.6. Finding XML Elements with XPath

Problem

You want to extract elements from an XML document, without writing code to find
them.

Solution

Create a `Document` instance and use the XPath API to search it.

Discussion

XPath is a World Wide Web Consortium (W3C)–defined API for searching XML documents and performing certain operations on them. It includes a searching language that
looks somewhat like a filesystem directory hierarchy (with forward slashes), so that "/
people/person/name" in our *people* example would match the person's name.
Example 20-10 shows a simple demonstration of using XPath to retrieve a nested element containing a number rather than a `String`.

Example 20-10. XPathDemo.java

```java
/**
 * Simple demo of XPath, supported in JAXP (in JavaSE package javax.xml.xpath)
 */
public class XPathDemo {

    public static void main(String[] args) throws Exception {

        DocumentBuilder parser =
            DocumentBuilderFactory.newInstance().newDocumentBuilder();   ❶

        String doc = "<?xml version='1.0'?>" +                           ❷
        "<section><sectiontitle>A Discourse of Numbers</sectiontitle>" +
        "<sectionnumber>1.2</sectionnumber>" +
        "<SC>Introduction</SC><p></p></section>";

        Document document =
            parser.parse(new ByteArrayInputStream(doc.getBytes()));      ❸

        // Evaluate the XPath expression against the Document
        XPath xpath = XPathFactory.newInstance().newXPath();             ❹
        String expression = "/section/sectionnumber";                    ❺
        Number secNum = (Number) xpath.evaluate(                         ❻
            expression, document, XPathConstants.NUMBER);
        System.out.printf("Section number = %s (a %s)",
```

```
            secNum, secNum.getClass().getName());        ❼
    }
}
```

❶   Create a Document parser.

❷   Here the input XML document is a hardcoded String.

❸   Create a Document from the XML document created in ❷.

❹   Create an XPath execution wrapper.

❺   Specify the string to match; this says to find the `sectionnumber` element inside a `section` element.

❻   Finally, evaluate the XPath expression.

❼   Print the result.

There is more to XPath's query language, such as the ability to request attribute matching, using "@", for example, and "." and ".." meaning current and parent nodes (as in a filesystem). Consult one of the general XML books listed at the end of this chapter for more guidance on XPath. See also the Wikipedia article (*http://en.wikipedia.org/wiki/Xpath*) for more on the levels of path search syntax.

20.7. Verifying Structure with Schema or DTD

Problem

Up to now, I have simply provided XML and asserted that it is valid. Now you want to verify the structure using an XML Schema or, rarely, the older Document Type Definition (DTD).

Solution

Write or locate the Schema or DTD and refer to it in one or more XML documents.

Discussion

XML Schema

Due to some limitations of Document Type Definitions, the XML community has been moving to use of Schema. Although it takes a few seconds longer to write a Schema, there are tools that will help generate them in most IDEs, and there are tools that can generate a Schema from existing Java objects (we saw `schemagen` in Recipe 20.1). A schema describes the type system for an open-ended series of valid XML document instances. Example 20-11 is one possible schema for the *people.xml* file. This was generated by XMLSpy (*http://www.altova.com*).

Example 20-11. people.xsd

```
<xs:schema xmlns:xs="http://www.w3.org/2001/XMLSchema"
    targetNamespace="urn:darwinsys:people"
    xmlns:tns="urn:darwinsys:people"                        ❶
    elementFormDefault="qualified">

    <xs:element name="country">                             ❷
        <xs:simpleType>
            <xs:restriction base="xs:string">               ❸
                <xs:enumeration value="Canada"/>
                <xs:enumeration value="USA"/>
            </xs:restriction>
        </xs:simpleType>
    </xs:element>
    <xs:element name="email">
        <xs:complexType mixed="true">
            <xs:attribute name="type">
                <xs:simpleType>
                    <xs:restriction base="xs:string">
                        <xs:enumeration value="intranet"/>
                    </xs:restriction>
                </xs:simpleType>
            </xs:attribute>
        </xs:complexType>
    </xs:element>
    <xs:element name="name" type="xs:string">
    </xs:element>
    <xs:element name="people">                              ❹
        <xs:complexType>
            <xs:sequence>
                <xs:element ref="tns:person" maxOccurs="unbounded"/>
            </xs:sequence>
        </xs:complexType>
    </xs:element>
    <xs:element name="person">
        <xs:complexType>
            <xs:sequence>
                <xs:element ref="tns:name"/>
                <xs:element ref="tns:email"/>
                <xs:element ref="tns:country"/>
            </xs:sequence>
        </xs:complexType>
    </xs:element>
</xs:schema>
```

❶ Define my namespace as a URN (see Recipe 16.9).

❷ Define one of the person components, the country (others done similary).

❸ Define country as an enumeration (could become a Java enum).

❹   Finally, define the root element, a sequence of `person` elements.

Example 20-12 shows how we assert our claim to the schema in a document.

Example 20-12. people-schema.xml

```
<people xmlns:xsi="http://www.w3.org/2001/XMLSchema-instance" ❶
    xmlns="urn:darwinsys:people"                               ❷
    xsi:schemaLocation="urn:darwinsys:people ./people.xsd" >   ❸
    // <person> elements here...
</people>
```

❶   Define on the root element the `xmlns` (namespace) with `xsi` prefix to map to the XML Schema Instance namespace.

❷   The default `xmlns` maps to my namespace (❶ in the schema file in Example 20-12).

❸   Define the schema location for my namespace to be the file *people.xsd*; it is more common to use an `http:` URL, but a physical file is acceptable if not scaleable.

Then you need to enable the parser for validation; this is discussed in Recipe 20.5. Any elements in the document not valid according to the schema will result in an exception being thrown.

XML Document Type Definition

This is not the place for a full dissertation on Document Type Definition syntax. Briefly, a DTD is a means of restricting the structure of an XML document by listing all the elements allowed, where they are permitted, and what attributes they have, if any. The DTD uses a special syntax inherited from SGML. Example 20-13 is *people.dtd*, a DTD for the *people.xml* file shown earlier in this chapter.

Example 20-13. people.dtd

```
<!ELEMENT people (person)*>
<!ELEMENT person (name, email, country)>

<!ELEMENT name (#PCDATA)>
<!ATTLIST email type CDATA #IMPLIED>
<!ELEMENT email (#PCDATA)>
<!ELEMENT country (#PCDATA)>
```

To assert that a file conforms to a DTD—that is, to validate the file—you need to refer to the DTD from within the XML file, as is sometimes seen in HTML documents. The `<!DOCTYPE>` line should follow the XML PI line if present but precede any actual data:

```
<!DOCTYPE people SYSTEM "people.dtd">
<people>
<person>
```

```
        <name>Ian Darwin</name>
        <email>someone@someplace.dom</email>
        <country>Canada</country>
    </person>
```

Then you need to enable the parser for validation; this is discussed in Recipe 20.5. Any elements in the document not valid according to the DTD will result in an exception being thrown.

See Also

Document Type Definitions are simpler to write than XML Schemas. In some parts of the industry, people seem to be going on the assumption that XML Schemas will completely replace DTDs, and they probably will, eventually. But other developers continue to use DTDs. There are also other options for constraining structure and data types, including RelaxNG (an ISO standard).

20.8. Generating Your Own XML with DOM and the XML Transformer

Problem

You want to generate your own XML files or modify existing documents.

Solution

Generate a DOM tree; pass the `Document` and an output stream to a `Transformer`'s `transform()` method.

Discussion

JAXP supports the notion of XML `Transformer` objects (in `javax.xml.transform`), which have wide-ranging applicability for modifying XML content. Their simplest use, however, is as a "null transformer"—one that doesn't actually transform the XML—used to transport it from an in-memory tree to an output stream or writer.

Create a `Document` consisting of nodes (either directly as in this example, or by reading it). Create the `Transformer`, setting any properties (in the example we set the "indent" property, which doesn't actually indent but at least causes line breaks). Wrap the document in a `DomSource` object, and the output stream in a `StreamResult` object. Pass the wrapped input and output into the `Transformer`'s `transform()` method, and it will convert the in-memory tree to text and write it to the given `StreamResult`.

For example, suppose you want to generate a poem in XML. Example 20-14 shows what running the program and letting the XML appear on the standard output might look like.

Example 20-14. DocWrite.java

```
$ java xml.DocWriteDOM
Writing the tree now...
<?xml version="1.0" encoding="UTF-8"?>
<Poem>
<Stanza>
<Line>Once, upon a midnight dreary</Line>
<Line>While I pondered, weak and weary</Line>
</Stanza>
</Poem>
$
```

The code for this is fairly short; see Example 20-15 for the code using DOM. Code for using JDOM is similar but used JDOM's own classes; see *DocWriteJDOM.java* in the *javasrc* project.

Example 20-15. DocWriteDOM.java

```java
public class DocWriteDOM {

    public static void main(String[] av) throws Exception {
        DocWriteDOM dw = new DocWriteDOM();
        Document doc = dw.makeDoc();

        System.out.println("Writing the tree now...");
        Transformer tx = TransformerFactory.newInstance().newTransformer();
        tx.setOutputProperty(OutputKeys.INDENT, "yes");
        tx.transform(new DOMSource(doc), new StreamResult(System.out));
    }

    /** Generate the XML document */
    protected Document makeDoc() {
        try {
            DocumentBuilderFactory fact = DocumentBuilderFactory.newInstance();
            DocumentBuilder parser = fact.newDocumentBuilder();
            Document doc = parser.newDocument();

            Node root = doc.createElement("Poem");
            doc.appendChild(root);

            Node stanza = doc.createElement("Stanza");
            root.appendChild(stanza);

            Node line = doc.createElement("Line");
            stanza.appendChild(line);
            line.appendChild(doc.createTextNode("Once, upon a midnight dreary"));
            line = doc.createElement("Line");
```

```
                stanza.appendChild(line);
                line.appendChild(doc.createTextNode("While I pondered, weak and weary"));

                return doc;

        } catch (Exception ex) {
            System.err.println("+==============================+");
            System.err.println("|          XML Error           |");
            System.err.println("+==============================+");
            System.err.println(ex.getClass());
            System.err.println(ex.getMessage());
            System.err.println("+==============================+");
            return null;
        }
    }
}
```

A more complete program would create an output file and have better error reporting. It would also have more lines of the poem than I can remember.

20.9. Program: xml2mif

Adobe FrameMaker[2] uses an interchange language called MIF (Maker Interchange Format), which is vaguely related to XML but is not well-formed. Let's look at a program that uses DOM to read an entire document and generate code in MIF for each node. This program was in fact used to create some chapters of the first edition.

The main program, shown in Example 20-16, is called XmlForm; it parses the XML and calls one of several output generator classes. This could be used as a basis for generating other formats.

Example 20-16. XmlForm.java

```
public class XmlForm {
    protected Reader is;
    protected String fileName;

    protected static PrintStream msg = System.out;

    /** Construct a converter given an input filename */
    public XmlForm(String fn) {
        fileName = fn;
    }

    /** Convert the file */
    public void convert(boolean verbose) {
        try {
```

---

2. Previously from Frame Technologies, a company that Adobe ingested. See note in Preface.

```
            if (verbose)
                System.err.println(">>>Parsing " + fileName + "...");
            // Make the document a URL so relative DTD works.
            //String uri = "file:" + new File(fileName).getAbsolutePath();
            InputStream uri = getClass().getResourceAsStream(fileName);
            DocumentBuilderFactory factory =
                DocumentBuilderFactory.newInstance();
            DocumentBuilder builder = factory.newDocumentBuilder();
            Document doc = builder.parse( uri );
            if (verbose)
                System.err.println(">>>Walking " + fileName + "...");
            XmlFormWalker c = new GenMIF(doc, msg);
            c.convertAll();

        } catch (Exception ex) {
            System.err.println("+=================================+");
            System.err.println("|           *Parse Error*         |");
            System.err.println("+=================================+");
            System.err.println(ex.getClass());
            System.err.println(ex.getMessage());
            System.err.println("+=================================+");
        }
        if (verbose)
            System.err.println(">>>Done " + fileName + "...");
    }

    public static void main(String[] av) {
        if (av.length == 0) {
            System.err.println("Usage: XmlForm file");
            return;
        }
        for (int i=0; i<av.length; i++) {
            String name = av[i];
            new XmlForm(name).convert(true);
        }
        msg.close();
    }
}
```

The actual MIF generator *GenMIF* is not shown here—it's not really XML-related—but is included in the *javasrc* code package.

See Also

XML-related technology continues to evolve. New APIs (and acronyms!) continue to appear. XML-RPC, REST services, and SOAP let you build distributed applications known as web services using XML and HTTP as the program interchange. JAX-WS is a Java EE API for SOAP-based web services; JAX-RS for REST services (we covered the client side of these in Chapter 13). The W3C has additional XML standards coming out.

Several websites track the changing XML landscape, including the official W3C site (*http://www.w3.org/xml*) and O'Reilly's XML site (*http://www.xml.com*).

For an interesting historical perspective on HTML and XML by the person who primarily invented the Web and HTML, see Tim Berners-Lee's book, *Weaving the Web* (Harper).

Many books cover XML. These range from the simple *XML: A Primer* by Simon St.Laurent to the comprehensive *XML Bible* by the prolific Elliotte Rusty Harold. In between is *Learning XML* by Erik T. Ray (O'Reilly). *Java and XML* by Brett McLaughlin and Justin Edelson (O'Reilly) covers these topics in more detail and also covers XML publishing frameworks such as Apache's Cocoon, and developing XML information channels using RSS, often used for blogging.

## CHAPTER 21

Packages and Packaging

21.0. Introduction

One of the better aspects of the Java language is that it has defined a very clear packaging mechanism for categorizing and managing its large API. Contrast this with most other languages, where symbols may be found in the C library itself or in any of dozens of other libraries, with no clearly defined naming conventions.[1] APIs consist of one or more packages; packages consist of classes; classes consist of methods and fields. Anybody can create a package, with one important restriction: you or I cannot create a package whose name begins with the four letters java. Packages named java. or javax. are reserved for use by Oracle's Java developers, under the management of the Java Community Process (JCP). When Java was new, there were about a dozen packages in a structure that is very much still with us, though it has quadrupled in size; some of these are shown in Table 21-1.

Table 21-1. Java packages basic structure

Name	Function
java.applet	Applets for browser use
java.awt	Graphical User Interface
java.io	Reading and writing
java.lang	Intrinsic classes (String, etc.)
java.lang.annotation	Library support for annotation processing
java.math	Math library

---

1. This is not strictly true. On Unix in C, at least, there is a distinction between normal include files and those in the *sys* subdirectory, and many structures have names beginning with one or two letters and an underscore, like pw_name, pw_passwd, pw_home, and so on in the password structure. But this is nowhere near as consistent as Java's java.* naming conventions.

Name	Function
java.net	Networking (sockets)
java.nio	"New" I/O (not new anymore): Channel-based I/O
java.sql	Java database connectivity
java.text	Handling and formatting/parsing dates, numbers, messages
java.time	Java 8: Modern date/time API (JSR-311)
java.util	Utilities (collections, date)
java.util.regex	Regular Expressions
javax.naming	JNDI
javax.print	Support for printing
javax.script	Java 6: Scripting engines support
javax.swing	Modern Graphical User Interface

Many packages have been added over the years, but the initial structure has stood the test of time fairly well. In this chapter, I show you how to create and document your own packages, and then discuss a number of issues related to deploying your package in various ways on various platforms.

21.1. Creating a Package

Problem

You want to be able to import classes and/or organize your classes, so you want to create your own package.

Solution

Put a package statement at the front of each file, and recompile with -d or a build tool or IDE.

Discussion

The package statement must be the very first noncomment statement in your Java source file—preceding even import statements—and it must give the full name of the package. Package names are expected to start with your domain name backward; for example, my Internet domain is *darwinsys.com*, so most of my packages begin with com.darwinsys and a project name. The utility classes used in this book and meant for reuse are in one of the com.darwinsys packages listed in Recipe 1.5, and each source file begins with a statement, such as:

```
package com.darwinsys.util;
```

The demonstration classes in the *JavaSrc* repository do not follow this pattern; they are in packages with names related to the chapter they are in or the java.* package they relate to; for example, lang for basic Java stuff, structure for examples from the data structuring chapter (Chapter 7), threads for the threading chapter (Chapter 22), and so on. It is hoped that you will put them in a "real" package if you reuse them in your application!

Once you have package statements in place, be aware that the Java runtime, and even the compiler, will expect the compiled *.class* files to be found in their rightful place (i.e., in the subdirectory corresponding to the full name somewhere in your CLASSPATH settings). For example, the class file for com.darwinsys.util.FileIO must *not* be in the file *FileIO.class* in my CLASSPATH but must be in *com/darwinsys/util/FileIO.class* relative to one of the directories or archives in my CLASSPATH. Accordingly, if you are compiling with the command-line compiler, it is customary (almost mandatory) to use the -d command-line argument when compiling. This argument must be followed by the name of an existing directory (often . is used to signify the current directory) to specify where to build the directory tree. For example, to compile all the *.java* files in the current directory, and create the directory path under it (e.g., create *./com/darwinsys/util* in the example):

```
javac -d . *.java
```

This creates the path (e.g., *com/darwinsys/util/*) relative to the current directory, and puts the class files into that subdirectory. This makes life easy for subsequent compilations, and also for creating archives, which I will do in Recipe 21.4.

Of course, if you use a build tool such as Ant (see Recipe 1.6) or Maven (see Recipe 1.7), this will be done once in your configuration file (Ant) or done correctly by default (Maven), so you won't have to remember to keep doing it!

Note that in all modern Java environments, classes that do not belong to a package (the "anonymous package") cannot be listed in an import statement, although they can be referred to by other classes in that package.

21.2. Documenting Classes with Javadoc

Problem

You have heard about this thing called "code reuse" and would like to promote it by allowing other developers to use your classes.

Solution

Use Javadoc. Write the comments when you write the code.

Discussion

Javadoc is one of the great inventions of the early Java years. Like so many good things, it was not wholly invented by the Java folks; earlier projects such as Knuth's Literate Programming had combined source code and documentation in a single source file. But the Java folks did a good job on it and came along at the right time. Javadoc is to Java classes what "man pages" are to Unix, or what Windows Help is to Windows applications: it is a standard format that everybody expects to find and knows how to use. Learn it. Use it. Write it. Live long and prosper (well, perhaps that's not guaranteed). But all that HTML documentation that you learned from writing Java code, the complete reference for the JDK—did you think they hired dozens of tech writers to produce it? Nay, that's not the Java way. Java's developers wrote the documentation comments as they went along, and when the release was made, they ran javadoc on all the zillions of public classes and generated the documentation bundle at the same time as the JDK. You can, should, and really must do the same when you are preparing classes for other developers to use.

All you have to do to use javadoc is to put special "javadoc comments" into your Java source files. These are similar to multiline Java comments, but begin with a slash and *two* stars, and end with the normal star-slash. Javadoc comments must appear immediately before the definition of the class, method, or field that they document; if placed elsewhere, they are ignored.

A series of keywords, prefixed by the at sign (@), can appear inside doc comments in certain contexts. Some are contained in braces ("{…}"). The keywords as of Java 8 are listed in Table 21-2.

Table 21-2. Javadoc keywords

Keyword	Use
@author	Author name(s)
{@code *text*}	Displays text in code font without HTML interpretation
@deprecated	Causes deprecation warning
{@docroot}	Refers to the root of the generated documentation tree
@exception	Alias for @throws
{@inheritDoc}	Inherits documentation from nearest superclass/superinterface
@link	Generates inline link to another class or member
@linkplain	As @link but displays in plain text
{@literal *text*}	Displays text without interpretation
@param *name description*	Argument name and meaning (methods only)
@return	Return value
@see	Generate Cross-reference link to another class or member
@serial	Describes serializable field

Keyword	Use
@serialData	Describes order and types of data in serialized form
@serialField	Describes serializable field
@since	JDK version in which introduced (primarily for Sun use)
@throws	Exception class and conditions under which thrown
{@value [ref]}	Displays values of this or another constant field
@version	Version identifier

Example 21-1 is a somewhat contrived example that shows some common *javadoc* keywords in use. The output of running this through javadoc is shown in a browser in Figure 21-1.

Example 21-1. JavadocDemo.java

```java
public class JavadocDemo extends JPanel {

    /**
     * Construct the GUI
     * @throws java.lang.IllegalArgumentException if constructed on a Sunday.
     */
    public void JavadocDemo() {
        // We create and add a pushbutton here,
        // but it doesn't do anything yet.
        Button b = new Button("Hello");
        add(b);                         // connect Button into component
        // Totally capricious example of what you should not do
        if (Calendar.getInstance().get(Calendar.DAY_OF_WEEK) == Calendar.SUNDAY) {
            throw new IllegalArgumentException("Never On A Sunday");
        }
    }

    /** paint() is an AWT Component method, called when the
     *  component needs to be painted. This one just draws colored
     * boxes in the window.
     *
     * @param g A java.awt.Graphics that we use for all our
     * drawing methods.
     */
    public void paint(Graphics g) {
        int w = getSize().width, h = getSize().height;
        g.setColor(Color.YELLOW);
        g.fillRect(0, 0, w/2, h);
        g.setColor(Color.GREEN);
        g.fillRect(w/2, 0, w, h);
        g.setColor(Color.BLACK);
        g.drawString("Welcome to Java", 50, 50);
    }
}
```

The javadoc tool works fine for one class but really comes into its own when dealing with a package or collection of packages. You can provide a package summary file for each package, which will be incorporated into the generated files. Javadoc generates thoroughly interlinked and crosslinked documentation, just like that which accompanies the standard JDK. There are several command-line options; I normally use -author and -version to get it to include these items, and often -link to tell it where to find the standard JDK to link to.

Run javadoc -help for a complete list of options, or see the full documentation online at Oracle's website (*http://bit.ly/SQsaOy*). Figure 21-1 shows one view of the documentation that the class shown in Example 21-1 generates when run as:

```
$ javadoc -author -version JavadocDemo.java
```

Figure 21-1. Javadoc in action

Be aware that one of the (many) generated files have the same name as the class, with the extension *.html*. If you are still using applets and have a sample HTML file to invoke it, and generate javadoc in the source directory, the *.html* file is silently overwritten with the javadoc output. For this reason, I recommend applet writers use the -d *directory* option to tell javadoc where to put the generated files so you don't have them in the source directory; it works the same as the same option on `javac`. Alternatively, you could use the filename extension *.htm* for the HTML page that invokes the applet.

See Also

Javadoc has numerous other command-line arguments. If documentation is for your own use only and will not be distributed, you can use the -link option to tell it where your standard JDK documentation is installed so that links can be generated to standard Java classes (like `String`, `Object`, and so on). If documentation is to be distributed, you can omit -link or use -link with a URL to the appropriate Java API page on Oracle's website. See the online tools documentation for all the command-line options.

The output that javadoc generates is fine for most purposes. It is possible to write your own `Doclet` class to make the javadoc program into a class documentation verifier, a Java-to-MIF or Java-to-RTF documentation generator, or whatever you like. Those are actual examples; see the javadoc tools documentation that comes with the JDK for documents and examples, or go to Oracle's website (*http://bit.ly/SQsaOy*). Visit Doclet (*http://www.doclet.com*) for a somewhat dated but useful collection of Doclets and other javadoc-based tools.

Javadoc Versus JavaHelp

Javadoc is for programmers using your classes; for a GUI application, end users will probably appreciate standard online help. This is the role of the Java Help API, which is not covered in this book but is fully explained in *Creating Effective JavaHelp* (O'Reilly), which every GUI application developer should read. JavaHelp is another useful specification that was somewhat left to coast during the Sun sellout to Oracle; it is now hosted on *java.net* at JavaHelp (*http://javahelp.java.net*).

21.3. Beyond Javadoc: Annotations/Metadata

Problem

You want to generate not just documentation, but also other code artifacts, from your source code. You want to mark code for additional compiler verification.

Solution

Use the Java Annotations or "Metadata" facility.

Discussion

The continuing success of the open source tool XDoclet (*http://xdoclet.sourceforge.net*) —originally used to generate the tedious auxiliary classes and deployment descriptor files for the widely criticized EJB2 framework—led to a demand for a similar mechanism in standard Java. Java *Annotations* were the result. The *annotation* mechanism uses an interface-like syntax, in which both declaration and use of Annotations use the name preceded by an at character (@). This was chosen, according to the designers, to be reminiscent of "Javadoc tags, a preexisting ad hoc annotation facility in the Java programming language." Javadoc is ad hoc only in the sense that its @ tags were never fully integrated into the language; most were ignored by the compiler, but @deprecated was always understood by the compiler (see Recipe 1.9).

Annotations can be read at runtime by use of the Reflection API; this is discussed in Recipe 23.9, where I also show you how to define your own annotations. Annotations can also be read post–compile time by tools such as the RMI and EJB stub generators (and others to be invented, perhaps by you, gentle reader!).

Annotations are also read by `javac` at compile time to provide extra information to the compiler.

For example, a common coding error is overloading a method when you mean to override it, by mistakenly using the wrong argument type. Consider overriding the equals method in `Object`. If you mistakenly write:

```
public boolean equals(MyClass obj) {
    ...
}
```

then you have created a new overload that will likely never be called, and the default version in `Object` will be called. To prevent this, an annotation included in `java.lang` is the `Override` annotation. This has no parameters but simply is placed before the method call. For example:

```
/**
 * AnnotationOverrideDemo - Simple demonstation of Metadata being used to
 * verify that a method does in fact override (not overload) a method
 * from the parent class. This class provides the method.
 */
abstract class Top {
    public abstract void myMethod(Object o);
}

/** Simple demonstation of Metadata being used to verify
 * that a method does in fact override (not overload) a method
 * from the parent class. This class is supposed to do the overriding,
 * but deliberately introduces an error to show how the modern compiler
 * behaves
 */
```

```
class Bottom {

    @Override
    public void myMethod(String s) {     // EXPECT COMPILE ERROR
        // Do something here...
    }
}
```

Attempting to compile this results in a compiler error that the method in question does not override a method, even though the annotation says it does; this is a fatal compile-time error:

```
C:> javac AnnotationOverrideDemo.java
AnnotationOverrideDemo.java:16: method does not override a method
        from its superclass
        @Override public void myMethod(String s) {     // EXPECT COMPILE ERROR
          ^
1 error
C:>
```

21.4. Archiving with jar

Problem

You want to create a Java archive (JAR) file from your package (or any other collection of files).

Solution

Use *jar*.

Discussion

The *jar* archiver is Java's standard tool for building archives. Archives serve the same purpose as the program libraries that some other programming languages use. Java normally loads its standard classes from archives, a fact you can verify by running a simple Hello World program with the -verbose option:

```
java -verbose HelloWorld
```

Creating an archive is a simple process. The *jar* tool takes several command-line arguments: the most common are c for create, t for table of contents, and x for extract. The archive name is specified with -f and a filename. The options are followed by the files and directories to be archived. For example:

```
jar cvf /tmp/MyClasses.jar .
```

The dot at the end is important; it means "the current directory." This command creates an archive of all files in the current directory and its subdirectories into the file */tmp/ MyClasses.jar*.

Most applications of JAR files depend on an extra file that is always present in a true JAR file, called a *manifest*. This file always lists the contents of the JAR and their attributes; you can add extra information into it. The attributes are in the form `name:` `value`, as used in email headers, properties files (see Recipe 7.12), and elsewhere. Some attributes are required by the application, whereas others are optional. For example, Recipe 21.5 discusses running a main program directly from a JAR; this requires a `Main-` `Program` header. You can even invent your own attributes, such as:

```
MySillyAttribute: true
MySillynessLevel: high (5'11")
```

You store this in a file called, say, *manifest.stub*,[2] and pass it to *jar* with the `-m` switch. *jar* includes your attributes in the manifest file it creates:

```
jar -cv -m manifest.stub -f /tmp/com.darwinsys.util.jar .
```

The *jar* program and related tools add additional information to the manifest, including a listing of all the other files included in the archive.

> If youuse a tool like Maven (see Recipe 1.7), it will automatically create a JAR file from your source project just by saying `mvn package`.

21.5. Running a Program from a JAR

Problem

You want to distribute a single large file containing all the classes of your application and run the main program from within the JAR.

Solution

Create a JAR file with a `Main-Class:` line in the manifest; run the program with the `java` `-jar` option.

---

2. Some people like to use names like *MyPackage.mf* so that it's clear which package it is for; the extension *.mf* is arbitrary, but it's a good convention for identifying manifest files.

Discussion

The java command has a -jar option that tells it to run the main program found within a JAR file. In this case, it will also find classes it needs to load from within the same JAR file. How does it know which class to run? You must tell it. Create a one-line entry like this, noting that *the attribute fields are case-sensitive and that the colon must be followed by a space*:

```
Main-Class: com.somedomainhere.HelloWorld
```

Place that in a file called, say, *manifest.stub*, and assuming that you want to run the program HelloWorld from the given package. You can then use the following commands to package your app and run it from the JAR file:

```
C:> javac HelloWorld.java
C:> jar cvmf manifest.stub hello.jar HelloWorld.class
C:> java -jar hello.jar
Hello, World of Java
C:>
```

You can now copy the JAR file anywhere and run it the same way. You do not need to add it to your CLASSPATH or list the name of the main class.

On GUI platforms that support it, you can also launch this application by double-clicking the JAR file. This works at least on Mac OS X and on Windows with the Sun Java runtime installed.

Mac OS X Specifics

On Mac OS X, you can use the Jar Bundler (available under */usr/share/java/Tools/Jar Bundler.app*). This provides a windowed tool to specify the options set by my MacO-SUI package (see Recipe 14.18) as well as CLASSPATH and other attributes. See Figure 21-2.

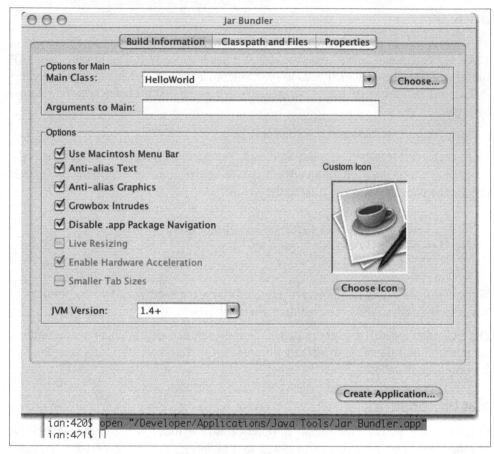

Figure 21-2. Mac OS Jar Bundler (OS X 10.3.2 version)

Applet Specifics

jar up the applet and supporting files into a single JAR file. Deploy the JAR file in place of the class file on the web server. Use `<applet code="MyClass" archive="MyApplet-Jar.jar" …>`.

Once you've deployed the JAR file on the web server in place of the class file, you need to refer to it in the applet tag in the HTML. The syntax for doing this is to use an `archive="`*name of jar file*`"` attribute on the applet tag.

You can also store other resources such as GIF images for use by the applet. You can then use `getResource()` instead of trying to open the file directly; see Step 5 in the sidebar in Recipe 21.11.

21.6. Preparing a Class as a JavaBean

Problem

You have a class that you would like to install as a JavaBean.

Solution

Make sure the class meets the JavaBeans requirements; create a JAR file containing the class, a manifest, and any ancillary entries.

Discussion

Several kinds of Java components are called either Beans or JavaBeans:

- Visual components for use in GUI builders, as discussed in this chapter.
- Plain Old Java Objects (POJOs), or components meant for reuse.
- Java Enterprise has "Enterprise JavaBeans" (EJBs), "JSP JavaBeans," "JSF managed Beans," and "CDI Beans," containing features for building enterprise-scale applications. Creating and using Java EE components is more involved than regular JavaBeans and would take us very far afield, so they are not covered in this book. When you need to learn about enterprise functionality, turn to *Java EE 7 Essentials* by Arun Gupta (O'Reilly).
- The Spring Framework (*http://springframework.org*) also uses the term "Beans" for the objects it manages.

What all these types of beans have in common are certain naming paradigms. All public properties should be accessible by get/set accessor methods. For a given property `Prop` of type `Type`, the following two methods should exist (note the capitalization):

```
public Type getProp( );
public void setProp(Type)
```

The one commonly permitted variance to this pattern is that, for `boolean` or `Boolean` arguments, the "get" method is usually called `isProp( )` rather than `getProp( )`.

For example, the various AWT and Swing components that have textual labels all have the following pair of methods:

```
public String getText( );
public void setText(String newText);
```

You should use this set/get design pattern (set/get methods) for methods that control a bean. Indeed, this technique is useful even in nonbean classes for regularity. The "bean containers" for the APIs listed at the start of this section, generally use Java introspection (see Chapter 23) to find the set/get method pairs, and some use these to construct properties editors for your bean. Bean-aware IDEs, for example, provide editors for all standard types (colors, fonts, labels, etc.). You can supplement this with a `BeanInfo` class to provide or override information.

The bare minimum a class requires to be usable as a JavaBean in a GUI builder is the following:

- The class must implement `java.io.Serializable`.
- The class must have a no-argument constructor.
- The class should use the set/get paradigm.
- The class file should be packaged into a JAR file with the *jar* archiver program (see Recipe 21.7).

Note that a JavaBean with no *required* inheritance or `implements` is also called a POJO, or "Plain Old Java Object." Most new Java frameworks accept POJO components, instead of (as in days of yore) requiring inheritance (e.g., Struts 1 `org.struts.Action` class) or implementation of interfaces (e.g., EJB2 `javax.ejb.SessionBean` interface).

Here is a sample bean that may be a useful addition to your Java GUI toolbox, the `LabelText` widget. It combines a label and a one-line text field into a single unit, making it easier to compose GUI applications. A test program in the online source directory sets up three `LabelText` widgets, as shown in Figure 21-3.

Figure 21-3. LabelText bean

The code for `LabelText` is shown in Example 21-2. Notice that it is serializable and uses the set/get paradigm for most of its public methods. Most of the public set/get methods simply delegate to the corresponding methods in the label or the text field. There isn't really a lot to this bean, but it's a good example of aggregation, in addition to being a good example of a bean.

Example 21-2. LabelText.java

```
// package com.darwinsys.swingui;
public class LabelText extends JPanel implements java.io.Serializable {

    private static final long serialVersionUID = -83430407071105763298L;
    /** The label component */
    protected JLabel theLabel;
    /** The text field component */
```

```
    protected JTextField theTextField;
    /** The font to use */
    protected Font myFont;

    /** Construct the object with no initial values.
     * To be usable as a JavaBean there must be a no-argument constructor.
     */
    public LabelText() {
        this("(LabelText)",  12);
    }

    /** Construct the object with the label and a default textfield size */
    public LabelText(String label) {
        this(label, 12);
    }

    /** Construct the object with given label and textfield size */
    public LabelText(String label, int numChars) {
        this(label, numChars, null);
    }

    /** Construct the object with given label, textfield size,
     * and "Extra" component
     * @param label The text to display
     * @param numChars The size of the text area
     * @param extra A third component such as a cancel button;
     * may be null, in which case only the label and textfield exist.
     */
    public LabelText(String label, int numChars, JComponent extra) {
        super();
        setLayout(new BoxLayout(this, BoxLayout.X_AXIS));
        theLabel = new JLabel(label);
        add(theLabel);
        theTextField = new JTextField(numChars);
        add(theTextField);
        if (extra != null) {
            add(extra);
        }
    }

    /** Get the label's horizontal alignment */
    public int getLabelAlignment() {
        return theLabel.getHorizontalAlignment();
    }

    /** Set the label's horizontal alignment */
    public void setLabelAlignment(int align) {
        theLabel.setHorizontalAlignment(align);
    }

    /** Get the text displayed in the text field */
    public String getText() {
```

```
        return theTextField.getText();
    }

    /** Set the text displayed in the text field */
    public void setText(String text) {
        theTextField.setText(text);
    }

    /** Get the text displayed in the label */
    public String getLabel() {
        return theLabel.getText();
    }

    /** Set the text displayed in the label */
    public void setLabel(String text) {
        theLabel.setText(text);
    }

    /** Set the font used in both subcomponents. */
    public void setFont(Font f) {
        // This class' constructors call to super() can trigger
        // calls to setFont() (from Swing.LookAndFeel.installColorsAndFont),
        // before we create our components, so work around this.
        if (theLabel != null)
            theLabel.setFont(f);
        if (theTextField != null)
            theTextField.setFont(f);
    }

    /** Adds the ActionListener to receive action events from the textfield */
    public void addActionListener(ActionListener l) {
        theTextField.addActionListener(l);
    }

    /** Remove an ActionListener from the textfield. */
    public void removeActionListener(ActionListener l) {
        theTextField.removeActionListener(l);
    }
}
```

Once it's compiled, it's ready to be pickled into a JAR. JavaBeans people really talk like that!

21.7. Pickling Your Bean into a JAR

Problem

You need to package your bean for deployment.

Solution

"Pickle your bean into a JAR" (i.e., create a JAR archive containing it and a manifest file).

Discussion

Although most containers now use reflection to access POJO bean properties, you may wish to package your Java bean into a self-contained JAR file for separate distribution. In addition to the compiled file, you need a manifest prototype, which needs the following entries as a minimum; you can also put such information as your vendor URL or a copyright notice:

```
Name: LabelText.class
Java-Bean: true
```

If these lines are stored in a file called *LabelText.stub*, we can prepare the whole mess for use as a bean by running the *jar* command (see Recipe 21.4). Because the JAR file must contain the class files in their correct package location (see Recipe 21.1), and because LabelText is part of my com.darwinsys package (see Recipe 1.5), I start off in the source directory and refer to the class file by its full path (the Stub file can be anywhere, but I keep it with the source file so I can find it easily, thus I have to refer to it by its full path, too):

```
$ cd $js/darwinsys/src
$ jar cvfm labeltext.jar com/darwinsys/swingui/LabelText.stub \
com/darwinsys/swingui/LabelText.class
added manifest
adding: com/darwinsys/swingui/LabelText.class(in=1607) (out=776)(deflated 51%)
$
```

Of course, in production you would want to automate this with a build tool such as Ant (see Recipe 1.6) or Maven (see Recipe 1.7).

Now we're ready to install *labeltext.jar* as a JavaBean. However, the curious may wish to examine the JAR file in detail. The x option to *jar* asks it to extract files:

```
$ jar xvf labeltext.jar
  created: META-INF/
extracted: META-INF/MANIFEST.MF
extracted: com/darwinsys/swingui/LabelText.class
$
```

The *MANIFEST.MF* file is based on the manifest file (*LabelText.stub*); let's examine it:

```
$ more META-INF/MANIFEST.MF
Manifest-Version: 1.0
Created-By: 1.4.2_03 (Apple Computer, Inc.)
Java-Bean: true
Name: LabelText.class
```

Not much exciting has happened besides the addition of a few lines. But the class is now ready for use as a JavaBean. For a GUI builder, either copy it into the *beans* directory or use the bean installation wizard, as appropriate.

21.8. Packaging a Servlet into a WAR File

Problem

You have a servlet and other web resources and want to package them into a single file for deploying to the server.

Solution

Use *jar* to make a web archive (WAR) file. Or, as mentioned earlier, use Maven with `packaging=war`.

Discussion

Servlets are server-side components for use in web servers. They can be packaged for easy installation into a web server. A *web application* in the Servlet API specification is a collection of HTML and/or JSP pages, servlets, and other resources. A typical directory structure might include the following:

index.html, foo.jsp
> Web pages

WEB-INF
> Server directory

WEB-INF/web.xml
> Descriptor

WEB-INF/classes
> Directory for servlets and any classes used by them or by JSPs

WEB-INF/lib
> Directory for any JAR files of classes needed by classes in the *WEB-INF/classes* directory

Once you have prepared the files in this way, you just package them up with *jar*:

```
jar cvf MyWebApp.war .
```

You then deploy the resulting WAR file into your web server. For details on this, consult the web server documentation.

21.9. "Write Once, Install Anywhere"

Problem

You want your application program to be installable on a variety of platforms by users who have not yet earned a Ph.D. in software installation.

Solution

Use an installer.

Discussion

The process of installing desktop software is nontrivial. Unix command-line geeks are quite happy to extract a gzipped TAR file and set their PATH manually, but if you want your software to be used by the larger masses, you need something simpler—in other words, point and click. Several tools try to automate this process. The better ones will create startup icons on Mac OS, Windows, and even some of the Unix desktops (CDE, KDE, GNOME).

I had good results some years back with ZeroG Software's commercial InstallAnywhere. It ensures that a JVM is installed and has both web-based and application installation modes (i.e., you can install the application from a web page or you can run the installer explicitly). This software has changed hands several times and appears to be currently available from Flexera (*http://bit.ly/1n5vDRa*).

InstallShield (*http://www.installshield.com*) has long been the leader in the Windows installation world, but it has had more competition in the Java world.

Recipe 21.11 discusses Java Web Start, Sun's new web-based application installer.

You can find my early attempts at building a standalone installer for Java in the *yajinstaller* (Yet Another unfinished Java Installer) project at GitHub (*http://github.com/IanDarwin/yajinstaller*)). If you make it better, send me diffs or a pull request!

21.10. "Write Once, Install on Mac OS X"

Problem

You want to install your Java program as a first-class application under Mac OS X.

Solution

Structure your build directory as shown here. Or use a tool such as a commercial installer (see Recipe 21.9) or the Eclipse IDE Export Mac OS Application wizard.

Discussion

To be a first-class, fully supported participant in OS X, Mac applications require a specific installation format, which is fairly easy to understand. Each Mac OS X application, regardless of programming language, is installed in a separate directory called an "Application Bundle," whose name should end in *.app*. This is the preferred way of installing applications under Mac OS X. Unlike simple JAR files, Application Bundles will be shown as icons in Finder ("explorer") windows and elsewhere, can be saved in the Dock for single-click startup, and can have file types associated with them (so that double-clicking or opening a file will launch your application and have it open the file).

Figure 21-4 shows a listing of the files in a simple Java application's directory.

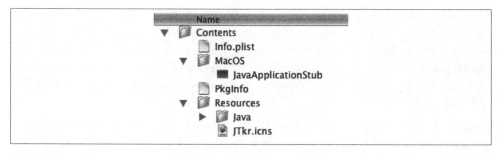

Figure 21-4. Files in the Java application directory on Mac OS X

As you can see, there is one directory *Contents* with two subdirectories: *MacOS* and *Resources*. *Contents/MacOS* contains the executable program, in the Java case *JavaApplicationStub*, a native-language Java launcher for Mac OS (provided with the Developer Tools package). *Contents/Resources/*.icns* contains icons in various resolutions for display by the Finder; this file can be created using the IconComposer program (found in */Developer/Applications/Utilities/Icon Composer.app*). The directory *Contents/Resources/Java* contains your Java classes and/or JAR files. *Contents/Info.plist* ties the whole thing together, specifying the names of the various files, the file types your application can open, and other information.

The better commercial installer tools (discussed in Recipe 21.9) generate this structure for you. You can create this structure using Ant. Eclipse 3.0 (since "Milestone 7") can generate a Mac OS X application. Just select your Project in the Eclipse navigator, select Export Mac OS X application from the Export menu, and fill in two screens specifying the output destination and some other information, as shown in Figure 21-5. In the case of Ant or Eclipse, you probably want to use Disk Copy to build a *dmg* (disk image) file of your directory; *dmg* files can be downloaded by Mac OS X users and are normally expanded automatically upon download to re-create the Application Bundle.

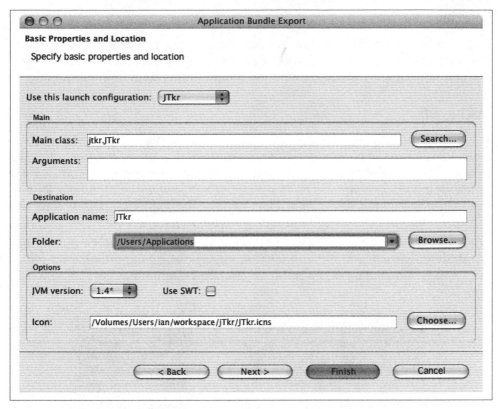

Figure 21-5. Eclipse Application Bundle Export screen

See Also

Chapter 7 of *Mac OS X for Java Geeks*, by Will Iverson (O'Reilly), covers Application Bundles. This book is recommended for any Java developer concerned with making good use of Java on OS X, and especially for anyone shipping applications who is concerned with making a good impression on OS X users.

21.11. Java Web Start

Problem

You have an application (not an applet) and need to distribute it electronically.

Solution

Sun's Java Web Start combines browser-based ease of use with applet-like "sandbox" security (which can be overridden on a per-application basis) and "instant update" downloading but also lets you run a full-blown application on the user's desktop.

Discussion

Java Web Start (JWS) provides application downloads over the Web. It is distinct from the old Java applet mechanism, which required special methods and ran inside the browser framework. JWS lets you run ordinary GUI-based applications. It is aimed at people who want the convenience of browser access combined with full application capabilities. The user experience is as follows. You see a link to an application you'd like to launch. If you've previously installed JWS (explained toward the end of this recipe), you can just click its Launch link and be running the application in a few seconds to a few minutes, depending on your download speed. Figure 21-6 shows the startup screen that appears after clicking a Launch link for my JabaDex application.

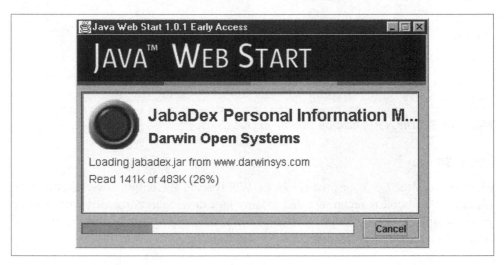

Figure 21-6. Starting JabaDex as a JWS application

After the application is downloaded successfully, it starts running. This is shown in slightly compressed form in Figure 21-7.

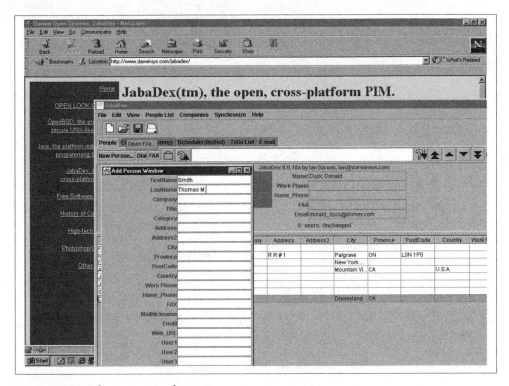

Figure 21-7. JabaDex up and running

For your convenience, JWS caches the JAR files and other pieces needed to run the application. You can later restart the application (even when not connected to the Web) using the JWS application launcher. In Figure 21-8, I have JabaDex in my JWS launcher. JWS also allows you to create desktop shortcuts and start menu entries on systems that support these.

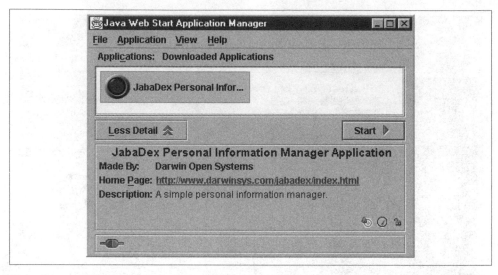

Figure 21-8. JWS application control screen

The basic steps in setting up your application for JWS are shown in the following sidebar.

Ian's Basic Steps: Java Web Start

To set up Java Web Start:

1. Package your application in one or more JAR files.

2. Optionally, provide icons to represent your application in JWS format.

3. Describe your application in a JNLP (Java Net Launch Protocol) description file.

4. If necessary, set your web server's MIME types list to return JNLP files as type `application/x-java-jnlp-file`.

5. If necessary, modify your application to use `ClassLoader`'s `getResource()` method instead of opening files.

6. If necessary, sign the application's JAR files.

7. Make links to your application's JNLP file and a download link for JWS itself.

8. Enjoy using your application locally with easy web downloading!

Let's go over these instructions in detail. The first step is to package your application in one or more JAR files. The *jar* program was described earlier in this chapter. The main JAR file should include the application classes and any resources such as properties files, images, and the like.

You should also include on the website any JAR files containing extra APIs, such as JavaMail, `com.darwinsys.util`, or any other APIs. You can even include native code files, but they are platform-dependent.

Optionally, you can provide icons to represent your application in JWS format. The application icons should be in GIF or JPEG format and should be 64x64 pixels.

The next step is to describe your application in a JNLP (Java Net Launch Protocol) description file. The JNLP file is an XML file; see the official documentation (*http://docs.oracle.com/javase/7/docs/technotes/guides/javaws/index.html*). The file I used for enabling JabaDex to run with JWS is a subset of the allowable XML elements but should be moderately self-explanatory. See Example 21-3.

Example 21-3. JabaDex.jnlp

```
<!-- JNLP File for JabaDex Application -->
<jnlp spec="1.0+"
    codebase="http://www.darwinsys.com/"
    href="/jabadex/">
    <information>
      <title>JabaDex Personal Information Manager Application</title>
      <vendor>Darwin Open Systems</vendor>
      <homepage href="/"/>
      <description>JabaDex Personal Information Manager Application</description>
      <description kind="short">A simple personal information manager.</description>
      <icon href="images/jabadex.jpg"/>
      <offline-allowed/>
    </information>
    <security>
        <all-permissions/>
    </security>
    <resources>
      <j2se version="1.5"/>
      <jar href="jabadex.jar"/>
      <jar href="com-darwinsys-util.jar"/>
    </resources>
    <application-desc main-class="JDMain"/>
  </jnlp>
```

If necessary, set your web server's MIME types list to return JNLP files as of type `application/x-java-jnlp-file`. How you do this depends entirely on what web server you are running; it should be just a matter of adding an entry for the filename extension *.jnlp* to map to this type.

Also if necessary, modify your application to get its `ClassLoader` and use one of its `getResource()` methods, instead of opening files. Any images or other resources that you need should be opened this way. For example, to explicitly load a properties file, you could use `getClassLoader()` and `getResource()`, as shown in Example 21-4.

Example 21-4. packaging/GetResourceDemo (partial listing)

```
// Find the ClassLoader that loaded us.
// Regard it as the One True ClassLoader for this app.
ClassLoader loader = this.getClass().getClassLoader();

// Use the loader's getResource() method to open the file.
InputStream is = loader.getResourceAsStream("widgets.properties");
if (is == null) {
    System.err.println("Can't load properties file");
    return;
}

// Create a Properties object
Properties p = new Properties();

// Load the properties file into the Properties object
try {
    p.load(is);
} catch (IOException ex) {
    System.err.println("Load failed: " + ex);
    return;
}

// List it to confirm that we loaded it.
p.list(System.out);
```

Notice that getResource() returns a java.net.URL object here whereas getResour-ceAsStream() returns an InputStream.

If you want the application to have "nonsandbox" (i.e., full application) permissions, you must sign the application's JAR files. The procedure to sign a JAR file digitally is described in Recipe 21.12. If you request full permissions and don't sign all your application JAR files, the sad note shown in Figure 21-9 displays.

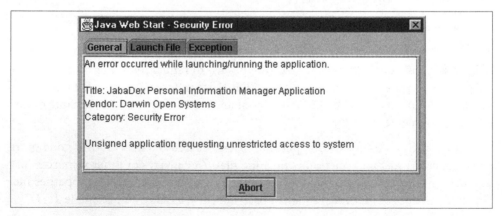

Figure 21-9. Unsigned application failure

If you self-sign (i.e., use a test certificate), the user sees a warning dialog like the one in Figure 21-10.

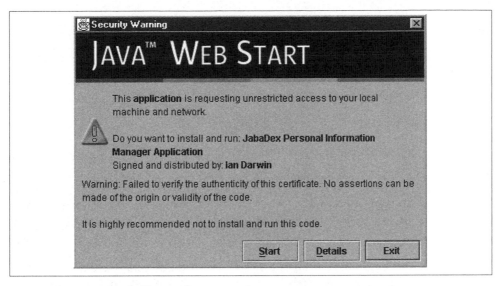

Figure 21-10. Unverifiable certificate warning

Finally, make links to your application's JNLP file in the web page and, optionally, a download link for JWS itself. JWS is a compiled program that must be loaded before the user can download any JWS-enabled applications; it runs as a "helper application" for the browsers. You can download it as a binary program from the JWS home page. In theory, you could write your own implementation of this helper from the JNLP Specification, if you needed to.

Actually, if the user has JWS installed, you don't need the download link; if he doesn't, the Launch link does not function correctly. The Developer's Guide shows how you can use client-side HTML scripting (JavaScript or VBScript) to make only one of these links appear. The Launch link must refer to the JNLP file:

```
If you have JWS installed, you can <a href="jabadex.jnlp">launch JabaDex<</a>
If not, you should
<a href="http://www.oracle.com/technetwork/java/javase/javawebstart/">
read about Java Web Start</a>.
```

You should now be ready to use your application in a downloadable fashion!

See Also

See the JWS home page (*http://bit.ly/1oFWie2*).

21.12. Signing Your JAR File

Problem

You want to digitally sign your JAR file.

Solution

Get or forge a digital certificate, and use the `jarsigner` program.

Discussion

A JAR file can be digitally signed to verify the identity of its creator. This is very similar to digital signing of websites: consumers are trained not to enter sensitive information such as credit card numbers into a web form unless the "padlock" icon shows that it is digitally signed. Signing JAR files uses the Security API in the core Java 2 platform. You can sign JAR files for use with Java applets (see Chapter 16) or JWS (see Recipe 21.11). In either case, the `jarsigner` tool included in the JDK is used.

You can purchase a certificate from one of the commercial signing agencies when you are ready to go live. Meanwhile, for testing, you can "self-sign" a certificate. Here are the steps needed to sign a JAR file with a test certificate:

1. Create a new key in a new "keystore" as follows:

   ```
   keytool -genkey -keystore myKeystore -alias myself
   ```

   The alias `myself` is arbitrary; its intent is to remind you that it is a self-signed key so you don't put it into production by accident.

2. The program prompts you in the terminal window for information about the new key. It asks for a password for protecting the keystore. Then it asks for your name, department, organization, city, state, country, and so on. This information goes into the new keystore file on disk.

3. Create a self-signed test certificate:

   ```
   keytool -selfcert -alias myself -keystore myKeystore
   ```

   You enter the keystore password and `keytool` generates the certificate.

4. You may want to verify that the steps up to here worked correctly. You can list the contents of the keystore:

   ```
   keytool -list -keystore myKeystore
   ```

   The output should look something like the following:

   ```
   Keystore type: jks
   Keystore provider: SUN
   Your keystore contains 1 entry:
   ```

```
    myself, Mon Dec 18 11:05:27 EST 2000, keyEntry,
    Certificate fingerprint (MD5): 56:9E:31:81:42:07:BF:FF:42:01:CB:42:51:42:96:B6
```

5. You can now sign the JAR file with your test certificate:

   ```
   jarsigner -keystore myKeystore test.jar myself
   ```

   The `jarsigner` tool updates the *META-INF* directory of your JAR file to contain certificate information and digital signatures for each entry in the archive. This can take a while, depending on the speed of your CPU, the number of entries in the archive, and so on. The end result is a signed JAR file that is acceptable to applet-enabled browsers, Java Web Start, and any other mechanisms that require a signed JAR file.

See Also

For more information on signing and permissions, see *Java Security* by Scott Oaks (O'Reilly). For more information on the JDK tools mentioned here, see the documentation that accompanies the JDK you are using.

## CHAPTER 22

Threaded Java

22.0. Introduction

We live in a world of multiple activities. A person may be talking on the phone while doodling or reading a memo. A multifunction office machine may scan one fax while receiving another and printing a document from somebody's computer. We expect the GUI programs we use to be able to respond to a menu while updating the screen. But ordinary computer programs can do only one thing at a time. The conventional computer programming model—that of writing one statement after another, punctuated by repetitive loops and binary decision making—is sequential at heart.

Sequential processing is straightforward but not as efficient as it could be. To enhance performance, Java offers threading, the capability to handle multiple flows of control within a single application or process. Java provides thread support and, in fact, requires threads: the Java runtime itself is inherently multithreaded. For example, window system action handling and Java's garbage collection—that miracle that lets us avoid having to free everything we allocate, as others must do when working in languages at or below C level—run in separate threads.

Just as multitasking allows a single operating system to give the appearance of running more than one program at the same time on a single-processor computer, so multithreading can allow a single program or process to give the appearance of working on more than one thing at the same time. With multithreading, applications can handle more than one activity at the same time, leading to more interactive graphics and more responsive GUI applications (the program can draw in a window while responding to a menu, with both activities occurring more or less independently), more reliable network servers (if one client does something wrong, the server continues communicating with the others), and so on.

Note that I did not say "multiprocessing" in the previous paragraph. The term multitasking is sometimes erroneously called multiprocessing, but that term in fact refers to different issue: it's the case of two or more CPUs running under a single operating system. Multiprocessing per se is nothing new: IBM mainframes did it in the 1970s, Sun SPARCstations did it in the late 1980s, and Intel PCs did it in the 1990s. Since the mid-2010s, it has become increasingly hard to buy a single-processor computer packaged inside anything larger than a wristwatch. True multiprocessing allows you to have more than one process running concurrently on more than one CPU. Java's support for threading includes multiprocessing, as long as the operating system supports it. Consult your system documentation for details.

Though most modern operating systems provide threads, Java was the first mainstream programming language to have intrinsic support for threaded operations built right into the language. The semantics of `java.lang.Object`, of which all objects are instances, includes the notion of "monitor locking" of objects, and some methods (`notify`, `notifyAll`, `wait`) that are meaningful only in the context of a multithreaded application. Java also has language keywords such as `synchronized` to control the behavior of threaded applications.

Now that the world has had years of experience with threaded Java, experts have started building better ways of writing threaded applications. The Concurrency Utilities, specified in JSR 166[1] and included in all modern Java releases, are heavily based on the `util.concurrent` package by Professor Doug Lea of the Computer Science Department at the State University of New York at Oswego. This package aims to do for the difficulties of threading what the Collections classes (see Chapter 7) did for structuring data. This is no small undertaking, but they pulled it off.

The `java.util.concurrent` package includes several main sections:

- Executors, thread pools, and `Futures`
- Queues and `BlockingQueues`
- Locks and conditions, with JVM support for faster locking and unlocking
- Synchronizers, including `Semaphores` and `Barriers`
- Atomic variables

An implementation of the `Executor` interface is, of course, a class that can execute code for you. The code to be executed can be the familiar `Runnable` or a new interface `Callable`. One common kind of `Executor` is a "thread pool." A `Future` represents the future state of something that has been started; it has methods to wait until the result is ready.

---

1. JSR stands for Java Specification Request. The Java Community Process calls standards, both proposed and adopted, JSRs. See *http://www.jcp.org* for details.

These brief definitions are certainly oversimplifications. Addressing all the issues is beyond the scope of this book, but I do provide several examples.

22.1. Running Code in a Different Thread

Problem

You need to write a threaded application.

Solution

Write code that implements Runnable; instantiate and start it.

Discussion

There are several ways to implement threading, and they all require you to implement the Runnable interface. Runnable has only one method, whose signature is:

```
public void run( );
```

You must provide an implementation of the run() method. When this method returns, the thread is used up and can never be restarted or reused. Note that there is nothing special in the compiled class file about this method; it's an ordinary method and you could call it yourself. But then what? There wouldn't be the special magic that launches it as an independent flow of control, so it wouldn't run concurrently with your main program or flow of control. For this, you need to invoke the magic of thread creation.

One way to do this is simply to subclass from java.lang.Thread (which also implements this interface; you do not need to declare redundantly that you implement it). This approach is shown in Example 22-1. Class ThreadsDemo1 simply prints a series of "Hello from X" and "Hello from Y" messages; the order in which they appear is indeterminate because there is nothing in either Java or the program to determine the order of things.

Example 22-1. ThreadsDemo1.java

```java
public class ThreadsDemo1 extends Thread {
    private String mesg;
    private int count;

    /** Run does the work: print a message, "count" number of times */
    public void run() {
        while (count-- > 0) {
            System.out.println(mesg);
            try {
                Thread.sleep(100);    // in mSec
            } catch (InterruptedException e) {
                return;
```

```
            }
        }
        System.out.println(mesg + " all done.");
    }

    /**
     * Construct a ThreadsDemo1 object.
     * @param m Message to display
     * @param n How many times to display it
     */
    public ThreadsDemo1(final String mesg, int n) {
        this.mesg = mesg;
        count = n;
        setName(mesg + " runner Thread");
    }

    /**
     * Main program, test driver for ThreadsDemo1 class.
     */
    public static void main(String[] argv) {
        // could say: new ThreadsDemo1("Hello from X", 10).run();
        // could say: new ThreadsDemo1("Hello from Y", 15).run();
        // But then it wouldn't be multi-threaded!
        new ThreadsDemo1("Hello from X", 10).start();
        new ThreadsDemo1("Hello from Y", 15).start();
    }
}
```

What if you can't subclass Thread because you're already subclassing another class?
There are two other ways to do it: have a class implement the Runnable interface, or use
an inner class to provide the Runnable implementation. Example 22-2 is code that implements Runnable.

Example 22-2. ThreadsDemo2.java

```
public class ThreadsDemo2 implements Runnable {
    private String mesg;
    private Thread t;
    private int count;

    /**
     * Main program, test driver for ThreadsDemo2 class.
     */
    public static void main(String[] argv) {
        new ThreadsDemo2("Hello from X", 10);
        new ThreadsDemo2("Hello from Y", 15);
    }

    /**
     * Construct a ThreadsDemo2 object
     * @param m Message to display
     * @param n How many times to display it
```

```
        */
    public ThreadsDemo2(String m, int n) {
        count = n;
        mesg  = m;
        t = new Thread(this);
        t.setName(m + " runner Thread");
        t.start();
    }

    /** Run does the work. We override the run() method in Runnable. */
    public void run() {
        while (count-- > 0) {
            System.out.println(mesg);
            try {
                Thread.sleep(100);      // 100 msec
            } catch (InterruptedException e) {
                return;
            }
        }
        System.out.println(mesg + " thread all done.");
    }
}
```

The run() method itself does not change, so I've omitted it from this listing. Example 22-3 is a version of this class that uses an inner class to provide the run() method.

Example 22-3. ThreadsDemo3.java

```
public class ThreadsDemo3 {
    private Thread t;
    private int count;

    /**
     * Main program, test driver for ThreadsDemo3 class.
     */
    public static void main(String[] argv) {
        new ThreadsDemo3("Hello from X", 10);
        new ThreadsDemo3("Hello from Y", 15);
    }

    /**
     * Construct a ThreadDemo object
     * @param m Message to display
     * @param n How many times to display it
     */
    public ThreadsDemo3(final String mesg, int n) {
        count = n;
        t = new Thread(new Runnable() {
            public void run() {
                while (count-- > 0) {
                    System.out.println(mesg);
```

```
                    try {
                        Thread.sleep(100);    // 100 msec
                    } catch (InterruptedException e) {
                        return;
                    }
                }
                System.out.println(mesg + " thread all done.");
            }
        });
        t.setName(mesg + " runner Thread");
        t.start();
    }
}
```

Here the `run()` method is part of the anonymous inner class declared in the statement beginning `t = new Thread(…)`. This runs with no interaction with other classes, so it's a good use of an inner class.

Finally, with Java 8, as shown in Recipe 9.0, you can in most cases simplify this code by using a lambda expression in place of the anonymous inner class, as shown in Example 22-4.

Example 22-4. ThreadsDemo4.java

```
public class ThreadsDemo4 {
    private String mesg;
    private Thread t;
    private int count;

    /**
     * Main program, test driver for ThreadsDemo4 class.
     */
    public static void main(String[] argv) {
        new ThreadsDemo4("Hello from X", 10);
        new ThreadsDemo4("Hello from Y", 15);
    }

    /**
     * Construct a ThreadDemo object
     * @param m Message to display
     * @param n How many times to display it
     */
    public ThreadsDemo4(final String mesg, int n) {
        count = n;
        t = new Thread(() -> {
                while (count-- > 0) {
                    System.out.println(mesg);
                    try {
                        Thread.sleep(100);    // 100 msec
                    } catch (InterruptedException e) {
                        return;
                    }
                }
```

```
        }
        System.out.println(mesg + " thread all done.");

    });
    t.setName(mesg + " runner Thread");
    t.start();
    }
}
```

To summarize, you can create a Runnable in one of several ways:

- Extend Thread as ThreadsDemo1 did. This works best for standalone applications that don't need to extend another class.

- Implement the Runnable interface. This works for classes that extend another class and thus cannot extend Thread due to single inheritance.

- Construct a Thread passing an inner class that is a Runnable. This is best for tiny run() methods with little outside interaction.

- In Java 8, construct a Thread passing a lambda expression that is compatible with Runnable, which is a functional interface.

Thread lifecycle methods

I should mention a few other methods briefly, starting with the Thread constructors: Thread(), Thread("Thread Name"), and Thread(Runnable). The no-argument and name-argument constructors are used only when subclassing. But what's in a name? Well, by default, a thread's name is composed of the class name and a number such as a sequence number or the object's hashcode; on the standard JDK it uses sequence numbers, such as Thread-0, Thread-1, and so on. These names are not very descriptive when you need to look at them in a debugger, so assigning names like "Clock Ticker Thread" or "Background Save Thread" will make your life easier when (not if) you wind up having to debug your threaded application. Because of this, getName()/set-Name(String) methods return or change the thread's name, respectively.

We've seen already that the start() method begins the process of assigning CPU time to a thread, resulting in its run() method being called. The corresponding stop( ) method is deprecated; see Recipe 22.3, where I also discuss interrupt(), which interrupts whatever the thread is doing. The method boolean isAlive() returns true if the thread has neither finished nor been terminated by a call to its stop() method. Also deprecated are suspend()/resume(), which pause and continue a thread; they are prone to corruption and deadlocking, so they should not be used. If you've created multiple threads, you can join() a thread to wait for it to finish; see Recipe 22.4.

The methods int getPriority()/void setPriority(int) show and set the priority of a thread; higher priority threads get first chance at the CPU. Finally, wait()/notify()/notifyAll() allow you to implement classical semaphore handling for such paradigms as producer/consumer relationships. See the javadoc page for the Thread class for information on a few other methods.

Each of these techniques will get you started, but they tend not to scale well. For any volume work, use of a thread pool is considered essential. Thread pools are provided by the Executors class, as described in Recipe 22.6.

22.2. Displaying a Moving Image with Animation

Problem

You need to update a graphical display while other parts of the program are running.

Solution

Use a background thread to drive the animation.

Discussion

One common use of threads is an animator, a class that displays a moving image. This "animator" program does just that. It draws a graphical image (see Recipe 12.8) at locations around the screen; the location is updated and redrawn from a Thread for each such image. This version is an applet, so we see it here in the AppletViewer (Figure 22-1).

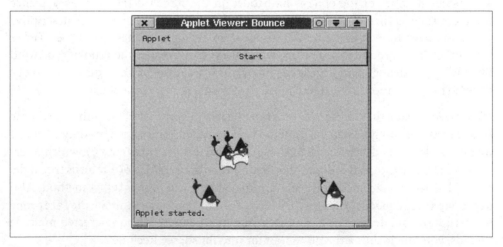

Figure 22-1. Animator

The code for the animator program consists of two classes, Sprite (see Example 22-5) and Bounce[2] (see Example 22-6). A Sprite is one image that moves around; Bounce is the main program.

Example 22-5. threads/Sprite.java (part of animator program)

```java
/** A Sprite is one Image that moves around the screen on its own */
public class Sprite extends Component implements Runnable {
    protected static int spriteNumber = 0;
    protected Thread t;
    protected int x, y;
    protected Component parent;
    protected Image img;
    protected volatile boolean done = false;
    /** The time in mSec to pause between each move. */
    protected volatile int sleepTime = 250;
    /** The direction for this particular sprite. */
    protected int direction;
    /** The direction for going across the page */
    public static final int HORIZONTAL = 1;
    /** The direction for going up and down */
    public static final int VERTICAL = 2;
    /** The direction for moving diagonally */
    public static final int DIAGONAL = 3;

    /** Construct a Sprite with a Component parent, image and direction.
     * Construct and start a Thread to drive this Sprite.
     */
    public Sprite(Component parent, Image img, int dir) {
        this.parent = parent;
        this.img = img;
        switch(dir) {
            case VERTICAL: case HORIZONTAL: case DIAGONAL:
                direction = dir;
                break;
            default:
                throw new IllegalArgumentException(
                    "Direction " + dir + " invalid");
        }
        setSize(img.getWidth(this), img.getHeight(this));
    }

    /** Construct a sprite with the default direction */
    public Sprite(Component parent, Image img) {
        this(parent, img, DIAGONAL);
    }

    /** Start this Sprite's thread. */
```

2. The title belies some unfulfilled ambitions to make the animations follow the bouncing curves seen in some flashier animation demonstrations.

```java
public void start() {
    t = new Thread(this);
    t.setName("Sprite #" + ++spriteNumber);
    t.start();
}

/** Stop this Sprite's thread. */
public void stop() {
    if (t == null)
        return;
    System.out.println("Stopping " + t.getName());
    done = true;
}

/** Adjust the motion rate */
protected void setSleepTime(int n) {
    sleepTime = n;
}

/**
 * Run one Sprite around the screen.
 * This version just moves them around either across, down, or
 * at some 45-degree angle.
 */
public void run() {
    int width = parent.getSize().width;
    int height = parent.getSize().height;
    // Set initial location
    x = (int)(Math.random() * width);
    y = (int)(Math.random() * height);
    // Flip coin for x & y directions
    int xincr = Math.random()>0.5?1:-1;
    int yincr = Math.random()>0.5?1:-1;
    while (!done) {
        width = parent.getSize().width;
        height = parent.getSize().height;
        if ((x+=xincr) >= width)
            x=0;
        if ((y+=yincr) >= height)
            y=0;
        if (x<0)
            x = width;
        if (y<0)
            y = height;
        switch(direction) {
            case VERTICAL:
                x = 0;
                break;
            case HORIZONTAL:
                y = 0;
                break;
            case DIAGONAL: break;
```

```
        }
        //System.out.println("from " + getLocation() + "->" + x + "," + y);
        setLocation(x, y);
        repaint();
        try {
            Thread.sleep(sleepTime);
        } catch (InterruptedException e) {
            return;
        }
        }
    }
}

    /** paint -- just draw our image at its current location */
    public void paint(Graphics g) {
        g.drawImage(img, 0, 0, this);
    }
}
```

Example 22-6. Bounce.java (part of animator program)

```
public class Bounce extends Applet implements ActionListener {

    private static final long serialVersionUID = -53591626217195202213L;
    /** The main Panel */
    protected Panel p;
    /** The image, shared by all the Sprite objects */
    protected Image img;
    /** A Vector of Sprite objects. */
    protected List<Sprite> v;

    public void init() {
        Button b = new Button("Start");
        b.addActionListener(this);
        setLayout(new BorderLayout());
        add(b, BorderLayout.NORTH);
        add(p = new Panel(), BorderLayout.CENTER);
        p.setLayout(null);
        String imgName = getParameter("imagefile");
        if (imgName == null) imgName = "duke.gif";
        img = getImage(getCodeBase(), imgName);
        MediaTracker mt = new MediaTracker(this);
        mt.addImage(img, 0);
        try {
            mt.waitForID(0);
        } catch(InterruptedException e) {
            throw new IllegalArgumentException(
                "InterruptedException while loading image " + imgName);
        }
        if (mt.isErrorID(0)) {
            throw new IllegalArgumentException(
                "Couldn't load image " + imgName);
        }
        v = new Vector<Sprite>(); // multithreaded, use Vector
```

```
    }

    public void actionPerformed(ActionEvent e) {
        System.out.println("Creat-ing another one!");
        Sprite s = new Sprite(this, img);
        s.start();
        p.add(s);
        v.add(s);
    }

    public void stop() {
        for (int i=0; i<v.size(); i++) {
            v.get(i).stop();
        }
        v.clear();
    }
}
```

22.3. Stopping a Thread

Problem

You need to stop a thread.

Solution

Don't use the `Thread.stop()` method; instead, use a `boolean` tested at the top of the main loop in the `run()` method.

Discussion

Though you can use the thread's `stop()` method, Sun recommends against it. That's because the method is so drastic that it can never be made to behave reliably in a program with multiple active threads. That is why, when you try to use it, the compiler will generate deprecation warnings. The recommended method is to use a `boolean` variable in the main loop of the `run()` method. The program in Example 22-7 prints a message endlessly until its `shutDown()` method is called; it then sets the controlling variable `done` to false, which terminates the loop. This causes the `run()` method to return, ending the thread. The `ThreadStoppers` program in the source directory for this chapter has a main program that instantiates and starts this class and then calls the `shutDown()` method.

Example 22-7. StopBoolean.java

```
public class StopBoolean extends Thread {

    // MUST be volatile to ensure changes visible to other threads.
    protected volatile boolean done = false;
```

```
    public void run() {
        while (!done) {
            System.out.println("StopBoolean running");
            try {
                sleep(720);
            } catch (InterruptedException ex) {
                // nothing to do
            }
        }
        System.out.println("StopBoolean finished.");
    }
    public void shutDown() {
        done = true;
    }

    public static void main(String[] args)
    throws InterruptedException {
        StopBoolean t1 = new StopBoolean();
        t1.start();
        Thread.sleep(1000*5);
        t1.shutDown();
    }
}
```

Running it looks like this:

```
StopBoolean running
StopBoolean running
StopBoolean running
StopBoolean running
StopBoolean running
StopBoolean running
StopBoolean running
StopBoolean finished.
```

But what if your thread is blocked reading from a network connection? You then cannot check a Boolean, because the thread that is reading is asleep. This is what the `stop` method was designed for, but, as we've seen, it is now deprecated. Instead, you can simply close the socket. The program shown in Example 22-8 intentionally deadlocks itself by reading from a socket that you are supposed to write to, simply to demonstrate that closing the socket does in fact terminate the loop.

Example 22-8. StopClose.java

```
public class StopClose extends Thread {
    protected Socket io;

    public void run() {
        try {
            io = new Socket("java.sun.com", 80);      // HTTP
            BufferedReader is = new BufferedReader(
                new InputStreamReader(io.getInputStream()));
```

```
        System.out.println("StopClose reading");

        // The following line will deadlock (intentionally), since HTTP
        // enjoins the client to send a request (like "GET / HTTP/1.0")
        // and a null line, before reading the response.

        String line = is.readLine();      // DEADLOCK

        // Should only get out of the readLine if an interrupt
        // is thrown, as a result of closing the socket.

        // So we shouldn't get here, ever:
        System.out.printf("StopClose FINISHED after reading %s!?", line);
    } catch (IOException ex) {
        System.out.println("StopClose terminating: " + ex);
    }
}

public void shutDown() throws IOException {
    if (io != null) {
        // This is supposed to interrupt the waiting read.
        synchronized(io) {
            io.close();
        }
    }
    System.out.println("StopClose.shutDown() completed");
}

public static void main(String[] args)
throws InterruptedException, IOException {
    StopClose t = new StopClose();
    t.start();
    Thread.sleep(1000*5);
    t.shutDown();
}
}
```

When run, it prints a message that the close is happening:

```
StopClose reading
StopClose terminating: java.net.SocketException: Resource temporarily unavailable
```

"But wait," you say. "What if I want to break the wait, but not really terminate the socket?"
A good question, indeed, and there is no perfect answer. But you can *interrupt* the thread
that is reading; the read is interrupted by a java.io.InterruptedIOException, and you
can retry the read. The file *Intr.java* in this chapter's source code shows this.

22.4. Rendezvous and Timeouts

Problem

You need to know whether something finished or whether it finished in a certain length of time.

Solution

Start that "something" in its own thread and call its `join()` method with or without a timeout value.

Discussion

The `join()` method of the target thread is used to suspend the current thread until the target thread is finished (returns from its `run()` method). This method is overloaded; a version with no arguments waits forever for the thread to terminate, whereas a version with arguments waits up to the specified time. For a simple example, I create (and start!) a simple thread that just reads from the console terminal, and the main thread simply waits for it. When I run the program, it looks like this:

```
darwinsys.com$ java threads.Join
Starting
Joining
Reading
hello from standard input # waits indefinitely for me to type this line
Thread Finished.
Main Finished.
darwinsys.com$
```

Example 22-9 lists the code for the join( ) demo.

Example 22-9. Join.java

```java
public class Join {
    public static void main(String[] args) {
        Thread t = new Thread() {
            public void run() {
                System.out.println("Reading");
                try {
                    System.in.read();
                } catch (java.io.IOException ex) {
                    System.err.println(ex);
                }
                System.out.println("Thread Finished.");
            }
        };
        System.out.println("Starting");
        t.start();
```

```
        System.out.println("Joining");
        try {
            t.join();
        } catch (InterruptedException ex) {
            // should not happen:
            System.out.println("Who dares interrupt my sleep?");
        }
        System.out.println("Main Finished.");
    }
}
```

As you can see, it uses an inner class Runnable (see Recipe 22.1) in Thread t to be runnable.

22.5. Synchronizing Threads with the synchronized Keyword

Problem

You need to protect certain data from access by multiple threads.

Solution

Use the synchronized keyword on the method or code you wish to protect.

Discussion

I discussed the synchronized keyword briefly in Recipe 16.4. This keyword specifies that only one thread at a time is allowed to run the given method (or any other synchronized method in the same class) in a given object instance (for static methods, only one thread is allowed to run the method at a time). You can synchronize methods or smaller blocks of code. It is easier and safer to synchronize entire methods, but this can be more costly in terms of blocking threads that could run. You can simply add the synchronized keyword on the method. For example, many of the methods of Vector (see Recipe 7.4) are synchronized, to ensure that the vector does not become corrupted or give incorrect results when two threads update or retrieve from it at the same time.

Bear in mind that threads can be interrupted at almost any time, in which case control is given to another thread. Consider the case of two threads appending to a data structure at the same time. Let's suppose we have the same methods as Vector, but we're operating on a simple array. The add() method simply uses the current number of objects as an array index, then increments it:

```
public void add(Object obj) {
    data[max] = obj; // ❶
```

```
    max = max + 1;   // ❷
}
```

Threads A and B both wish to call this method. Suppose that Thread A gets interrupted after ❶ but before ❷, and then Thread B gets to run.

❶   Thread B does ❶, overwriting the contents of data[max]; we've now lost all reference to the object that Thread A passed in!

❷   Thread B then increments max at ❷ and returns. Later, Thread A gets to run again; it resumes at ❷ and increments max past the last valid object. So not only have we lost an object, but we have an uninitialized reference in the array. This state of affairs is shown in Figure 22-2.

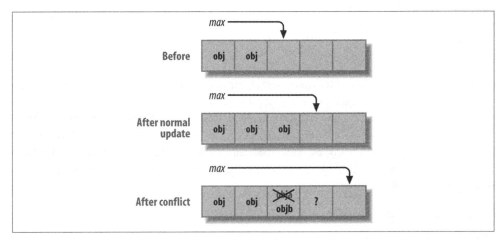

Figure 22-2. Nonthreadsafe add method in operation: normal and failed updates

Now you might think, "No problem, I'll just combine the two lines of code!":

```
data[max++] = obj;
```

As the game show host sometimes says, "Bzzzzt! Thanks for playing!" This change makes the code a bit shorter but has absolutely no effect on reliability. Interrupts don't happen conveniently on Java statement boundaries; they can happen between any of the many JVM machine instructions that correspond to your program. The code can still be interrupted after the store and before the increment. The only good solution is to use proper synchronization.

Making the method synchronized means that any invocations of it will wait if one thread has already started running the method:

```
public synchronized void add(Object obj) {
    ...
}
```

Anytime you wish to synchronize some code, but not an entire method, use the synchronized keyword on an unnamed code block within a method, as in:

```
public void add(Object obj) {
    synchronized (someObject) {
        // this code will execute in one thread at a time
    }
}
```

The choice of object to synchronize on is up to you. Sometimes it makes sense to synchronize on the object containing the code, as in Example 22-10. For synchronizing access to an ArrayList, it would make sense to use the ArrayList instance, as in:

```
synchronized(myArrayList) {
    if (myArrayList.indexOf(someObject) != -1) {
        // do something with it.
    } else {
        create an object and add it...
    }
}
```

Example 22-10 is a web servlet that I wrote for use in the classroom, following a suggestion from Scott Weingust (*scottw@sysoft.ca*).[3] It lets you play a quiz show game of the style where the host asks a question and the first person to press her buzzer (buzz in) gets to try to answer the question correctly. To ensure against having two people buzz in simultaneously, the code uses a synchronized block around the code that updates the Boolean buzzed variable. And for reliability, any code that accesses this Boolean is also synchronized.

Example 22-10. BuzzInServlet.java

```
public class BuzzInServlet extends HttpServlet {

    /** The attribute name used throughout. */
    protected final static String WINNER = "buzzin.winner";

    /** doGet is called from the contestants web page.
     * Uses a synchronized code block to ensure that
     * only one contestant can change the state of "buzzed".
     */
    public void doGet(HttpServletRequest request, HttpServletResponse response)
    throws ServletException, IOException
    {
        ServletContext application = getServletContext();

        boolean iWon = false;
        String user = request.getRemoteHost() + '@' + request.getRemoteAddr();
```

---

3. A *servlet* is a low-level server-side API for interacting with remote clients; today it would probably be written in the form of a JavaServer Faces (JSF) handler.

```
        // Do the synchronized stuff first, and all in one place.
        synchronized(application) {
            if (application.getAttribute(WINNER) == null) {
                application.setAttribute(WINNER, user);
                application.log("BuzzInServlet: WINNER " + user);
                iWon = true;
            }
        }

        response.setContentType("text/html");
        PrintWriter out = response.getWriter();

        out.println("<html><head><title>Thanks for playing</title></head>");
        out.println("<body bgcolor=\"white\">");

        if (iWon) {
            out.println("<b>YOU GOT IT</b>");
            // TODO - output HTML to play a sound file :-)
        } else {
                out.println("Thanks for playing, " + request.getRemoteAddr());
                out.println(", but " + application.getAttribute(WINNER) +
                    " buzzed in first");
        }
        out.println("</body></html>");
}

/** The Post method is used from an Administrator page (which should
 * only be installed in the instructor/host's localweb directory).
 * Post is used for administrative functions:
 * 1) to display the winner;
 * 2) to reset the buzzer for the next question.
 */
public void doPost(HttpServletRequest request, HttpServletResponse response)
throws ServletException, IOException
{
    ServletContext application = getServletContext();

    response.setContentType("text/html");
    HttpSession session = request.getSession();

    PrintWriter out = response.getWriter();

    if (request.isUserInRole("host")) {
        out.println("<html><head><title>Welcome back, " +
            request.getUserPrincipal().getName() + "</title><head>");
        out.println("<body bgcolor=\"white\">");
        String command = request.getParameter("command");
        if (command.equals("reset")) {

            // Synchronize what you need, no more, no less.
            synchronized(application) {
```

```
            application.setAttribute(WINNER, null);
        }
        session.setAttribute("buzzin.message", "RESET");
    } else if (command.equals("show")) {
        String winner = null;
        synchronized(application) {
            winner = (String)application.getAttribute(WINNER);
        }
        if (winner == null) {
            session.setAttribute("buzzin.message",
                "<b>No winner yet!</b>");
        } else {
            session.setAttribute("buzzin.message",
                "<b>Winner is: </b>" + winner);
        }
    }
    else {
        session.setAttribute("buzzin.message",
            "ERROR: Command " + command + " invalid.");
    }
    RequestDispatcher rd = application.getRequestDispatcher(
        "/hosts/index.jsp");
    rd.forward(request, response);
} else {
    out.println("<html><head><title>Nice try, but... </title><head>");
    out.println("<body bgcolor=\"white\">");
    out.println(
        "I'm sorry, Dave, but you know I can't allow you to do that.");
    out.println("Even if you are " + request.getUserPrincipal());
}
    out.println("</body></html>");
    }
}
```

Two HTML pages lead to the servlet. The contestant's page simply has a large link (<a href=/servlet/BuzzInServlet>). Anchor links generate an HTML GET, so the servlet engine calls doGet():

```
<html><head><title>Buzz In!</title></head>
<body>
<h1>Buzz In!</h1>
<p>
<font size=+6>
<a href="servlet/BuzzInServlet">
Press here to buzz in!
</a>
</font>
```

The HTML is pretty plain, but it does the job. Figure 22-3 shows the look and feel.

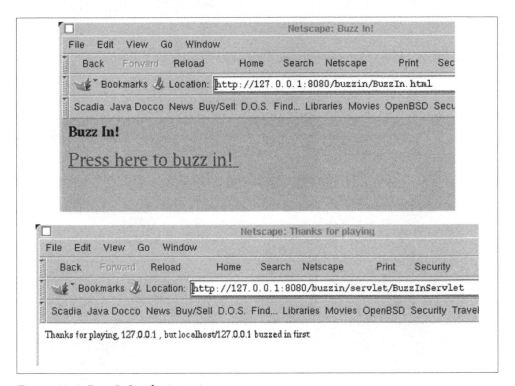

Figure 22-3. BuzzInServlet in action

The game show host has access to an HTML form with a POST method, which calls the doPost() method. This displays the winner to the game show host and resets the "buzzer" for the next question. A password is provided; it's hardcoded here, but in reality the password would come from a properties file (Recipe 7.12) or a servlet initialization parameter (as described in *Java Servlet Programming* [O'Reilly]):

```
<html><head><title>Reset Buzzer</title></head>
<body>
<h1>Display Winner</h1>
<p>
<b>The winner is:</b>
<form method="post" action="servlet/BuzzInServlet">
    <input type="hidden" name="command" value="show">
    <input type="hidden" name="password" value="syzzy">
    <input type="submit" name="Show" value="Show">
</form>
<h1>Reset Buzzer</h1>
<p>
<b>Remember to RESET before you ask the contestants each question!</b>
<form method="post" action="servlet/BuzzInServlet">
    <input type="hidden" name="command" value="reset">
    <input type="hidden" name="password" value="syzzy">
```

```
        <input type="submit" name="Reset" value="RESET!">
    </form>
```

The game show host functionality is shown in Figure 22-4.

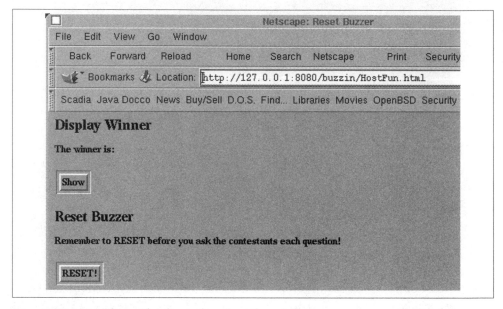

Figure 22-4. BuzzInServlet game show host function

For a more complete game, of course, the servlet would keep a `Stack` (see Recipe 7.18) of people in the order they buzzed in, in case the first person doesn't answer the question correctly. Access to this would have to be synchronized, too.

22.6. Simplifying Synchronization with Locks

Problem

You want an easier means of synchronizing threads.

Solution

Use the `Lock` mechanism in `java.util.concurrent.locks`.

Discussion

Use the `java.util.concurrent.locks` package; its major interface is `Lock`. This interface has several methods for locking and one for unlocking. The general pattern for using it is:

```
Lock thelock = ....
try {
        lock.lock( );
        // do the work that is protected by the lock
} finally {
        lock.unlock( );
}
```

The point of putting the unlock( ) call in the finally block is, of course, to ensure that it is not bypassed if an exception occurs (the code may also include one or more catch blocks, as required by the work being performed).

The improvement here, compared with the traditional synchronized methods and blocks, is that using a Lock actually looks like a locking operation! And, as I mentioned, several means of locking are available, shown in Table 22-1.

Table 22-1. Locking methods of the Lock class

Return type	Method	Meaning
void	lock( )	Get the lock, even if you have to wait until another thread frees it first.
boolean	tryLock( )	Get the lock only if it is free right now.
boolean	tryLock(long time, TimeUnit units) throws InterruptedException	Try to get the lock, but only wait for the length of time indicated.
void	lockInterruptibly( ) throws InterruptedException	Get the lock, waiting unless interrupted.
void	unlock( )	Release the lock.

The TimeUnit class lets you specify the units for the amount of time specified, including TimeUnit.SECONDS, TimeUnit.MILLISECONDS, TimeUnit.MICROSECONDS, and TimeUnit.NANOSECONDS.

In all cases, the lock must be released with unlock( ) before it can be locked again.

The standard Lock is useful in many applications, but depending on the application's requirements, other types of locks may be more appropriate. Applications with asymmetric load patterns may benefit from a common pattern called the "reader-writer lock"; I call this one a Readers-Writer lock to emphasize that there can be many readers but only one writer. It's actually a pair of interconnected locks; any number of readers can hold the read lock and read the data, as long as it's not being written (shared read access). A thread trying to lock the write lock, however, waits until all the readers are finished, then locks them out until the writer is finished (exclusive write access). To support this pattern, both the ReadWriteLock interface and the implementing class ReentrantReadWriteLock are available. The interface has only two methods, readLock( ) and writeLock( ), which provide a reference to the appropriate Lock implementation. *These methods do not, in themselves, lock or unlock the locks*; they only provide access to them, so it is common to see code like:

```
rwlock.readLock( ).lock( );
...
rwlock.readLock( ).unlock( );
```

To demonstrate ReadWriteLock in action, I wrote the business logic portion of a web-based voting application. It could be used in voting for candidates or for the more common web poll. Presuming that you display the results on the home page and change the data only when somebody takes the time to click a response to vote, this application fits one of the intended criteria for ReadWriteLock—i.e., that you have more readers than writers. The main class, ReadersWritersDemo, is shown in Example 22-11. The helper class BallotBox is online; it simply keeps track of the votes and returns a read-only Iterator upon request. Note that in the run( ) method of the reading threads, you could obtain the iterator while holding the lock but release the lock before printing it; this allows greater concurrency and better performance, but could (depending on your application) require additional locking against concurrent update.

Example 22-11. ReadersWriterDemo.java

```
public class ReadersWriterDemo {
    private static final int NUM_READER_THREADS = 3;

    public static void main(String[] args) {
        new ReadersWriterDemo().demo();
    }

    /** Set this to true to end the program */
    private volatile boolean done = false;

    /** The data being protected. */
    private BallotBox theData;

    /** The read lock / write lock combination */
    private ReadWriteLock lock = new ReentrantReadWriteLock();

    /**
     * Constructor: set up some quasi-random initial data
     */
    public ReadersWriterDemo() {
        List<String> questionsList = new ArrayList<>();
        questionsList.add("Agree");
        questionsList.add("Disagree");
        questionsList.add("No opinion");
        theData = new BallotBox(questionsList);
    }

    /**
     * Run a demo with more readers than writers
```

```
 */
private void demo() {

    // Start two reader threads
    for (int i = 0; i < NUM_READER_THREADS; i++) {
        new Thread() {
            public void run() {
                while (!done) {
                    lock.readLock().lock();
                    try {
                        theData.forEach(p ->
                            System.out.printf("%s: votes %d%n",
                                p.getName(),
                                p.getVotes())));
                    } finally {
                        // Unlock in "finally" to be sure it gets done.
                        lock.readLock().unlock();
                    }

                    try {
                        Thread.sleep(((long)(Math.random()* 1000)));
                    } catch (InterruptedException ex) {
                        // nothing to do
                    }
                }
            }
        }.start();
    }

    // Start one writer thread to simulate occasional voting
    new Thread() {
        public void run() {
            while (!done) {
                lock.writeLock().lock();
                try {
                    theData.voteFor(
                        // Vote for random candidate :-)
                        // Performance: should have one PRNG per thread.
                        (((int)(Math.random()*
                        theData.getCandidateCount())))));
                } finally {
                    lock.writeLock().unlock();
                }
                try {
                    Thread.sleep(((long)(Math.random()*1000)));
                } catch (InterruptedException ex) {
                    // nothing to do
                }
            }
        }
    }.start();
```

```
        // In the main thread, wait a while then terminate the run.
        try {
            Thread.sleep(10 * 1000);
        } catch (InterruptedException ex) {
            // nothing to do
        } finally {
            done = true;
        }
    }
}
```

Because this is a simulation and the voting is random, it does not always come out 50/50. In two consecutive runs, the following were the last line of each run:

```
Agree(6), Disagree(6)
Agree(9), Disagree(4)
```

See Also

The Lock interface also makes available Condition objects, which provide even more flexibility. Consult the online documentation for more information.

22.7. Synchronizing Threads the Hard Way with wait( ) and notifyAll( )

Problem

The synchronized keyword lets you lock out multiple threads but doesn't give you much communication between them.

Solution

Use wait() and notifyAll(). Very carefully.

Discussion

Three methods appear in java.lang.Object that allow you to use any object as a synchronization target: wait(), notify(), and notifyAll():

wait()
:   This causes the current thread to block on the given object until awakened by a notify() or notifyAll().

notify()
:   This causes a randomly selected thread waiting on this object to be awakened. It will then try to regain the monitor lock.

notifyAll()

> This causes all threads waiting on the object to be awakened; each will then try to regain the monitor lock. Hopefully one will succeed.

Most programs will use `notifyAll()` instead of `notify()`, because, in waking all the threads, the one that needs to run next will eventually get to run.

This sounds complicated, but most of the work happens inside the thread mechanism.

Do note that both `wait()` and the notification methods can be used only if you are already synchronized on the object; that is, you must be in a synchronized method within—or a code block synchronized on—the object that you wish your current thread to `wait()` or `notify()` upon.

For a simple introduction to `wait()` and `notify()`, I'll use a simple producer/consumer model. This pattern can be used to simulate a variety of real-world situations in which one object is creating or allocating objects (producing them), usually with a random delay, while another is grabbing the objects and doing something with them (consuming them). A single-threaded producer/consumer model is shown in Example 22-12. As you can see, no threads are created, so the entire program—the `read()` in main as well as `produce()` and `consume()`—runs in the same thread. You control the production and consumption by entering a line consisting of letters. Each p causes one unit to be produced, while each c causes one unit to be consumed. So if I run it and type pcpcpcpc, the program alternates between producing and consuming. If I type pppccc, the program will produce three units and then consume them.

Example 22-12. ProdCons1.java

```
public class ProdCons1 {

    protected LinkedList<Object> list = new LinkedList<>();

    protected void produce() {
        int len = 0;
        synchronized(list) {
            Object justProduced = new Object();
            list.addFirst(justProduced);
            len = list.size();
            list.notifyAll();
        }
        System.out.println("List size now " + len);
    }

    protected void consume() {
        Object obj = null;
        int len = 0;
        synchronized(list) {
            while (list.size() == 0) {
                try {
```

```
            list.wait();
        } catch (InterruptedException ex) {
            return;
        }
    }
    obj = list.removeLast();
    len = list.size();
}
System.out.println("Consuming object " + obj);
System.out.println("List size now " + len);
}

public static void main(String[] args) throws IOException {
    ProdCons1 pc = new ProdCons1();
    System.out.println("Ready (p to produce, c to consume):");
    int i;
    while ((i = System.in.read()) != -1) {
        char ch = (char)i;
        switch(ch) {
            case 'p':    pc.produce(); break;
            case 'c':    pc.consume(); break;
        }
    }
}
}
```

The part that may seem strange is using `list` instead of the main class as the synchronization target. Each object has its own wait queue, so it does matter which object you use. In theory, any object can be used as long as your `synchronized` target and the object in which you run `wait()` and `notify()` are one and the same. Of course, it is good to refer to the object that you are protecting from concurrent updates, so I used `list` here.

Hopefully, you're now wondering what this has to do with thread synchronization. There is only one thread, but the program *seems* to work:

```
> javac +E -d . threads.ProdCons1.java
> java ProdCons1
pppccc
List size now 1
List size now 2
List size now 3
Consuming object java.lang.Object@d9e6a356
List size now 2
Consuming object java.lang.Object@d9bea356
List size now 1
Consuming object java.lang.Object@d882a356
List size now 0
```

But this program is not quite right. If I enter even one more c than there are p's, think about what happens. The `consume()` method does a `wait()`, but it is no longer possible for the `read()` to proceed. The program, we say, is *deadlocked*: it is waiting on something that can never happen. Fortunately, this simple case is detected by some versions of the Java runtime:

```
ppccc
List size now 1
List size now 2
Consuming object java.lang.Object@18faf0
List size now 1
Consuming object java.lang.Object@15bc20
List size now 0
Dumping live threads:
 'gc' tid 0x1a0010, status SUSPENDED flags DONTSTOP
  blocked@0x19c510 (0x1a0010-&gt;|)
 'finaliser' tid 0x1ab010, status SUSPENDED flags DONTSTOP
  blocked@0x10e480 (0x1ab010-&gt;|)
 'main' tid 0xe4050, status SUSPENDED flags NOSTACKALLOC
  blocked@0x13ba20 (0xe4050-&gt;|)
Deadlock: all threads blocked on internal events
Abort (core dumped)
```

Indeed, the read() is never executed because there's no way for produce() to get called and so the notifyAll() can't happen. To fix this, I want to run the producer and the consumer in separate threads. There are several ways to accomplish this. I'll just make consume() and produce() into inner classes Consume and Produce that extend Thread, and their run() method will do the work of the previous methods. In the process, I'll replace the code that reads from the console with code that causes both threads to loop for a certain number of seconds, and change it to be a bit more of a simulation of a distributed producer/consumer mechanism. The result of all this is the second version, ProdCons2, shown in Example 22-13.

Example 22-13. ProdCons2.java

```java
public class ProdCons2 {

    /** Throughout the code, this is the object we synchronize on so this
     * is also the object we wait() and notifyAll() on.
     */
    protected LinkedList<Object> list = new LinkedList<>();
    protected int MAX = 10;
    protected boolean done = false; // Also protected by lock on list.

    /** Inner class representing the Producer side */
    class Producer extends Thread {

        public void run() {
            while (true) {
                Object justProduced = getRequestFromNetwork();
                // Get request from the network - outside the synch section.
                // We're simulating this actually reading from a client, and it
                // might have to wait for hours if the client is having coffee.
                synchronized(list) {
```

```
                        while (list.size() == MAX) { // queue "full"
                            try {
                                System.out.println("Producer WAITING");
                                list.wait();      // Limit the size
                            } catch (InterruptedException ex) {
                                System.out.println("Producer INTERRUPTED");
                            }
                        }
                        list.addFirst(justProduced);
                        list.notifyAll();    // must own the lock
                        System.out.println("Produced 1; List size now " + list.size());
                        if (done)
                            break;
                        // yield();     // Useful for green threads & demo programs.
                    }
                }
            }

            Object getRequestFromNetwork() {    // Simulation of reading from client
                // try {
                //      Thread.sleep(10); // simulate time passing during read
                // } catch (InterruptedException ex) {
                //      System.out.println("Producer Read INTERRUPTED");
                // }
                return(new Object());
            }
        }

        /** Inner class representing the Consumer side */
        class Consumer extends Thread {
            public void run() {
                while (true) {
                    Object obj = null;
                    synchronized(list) {
                        while (list.size() == 0) {
                            try {
                                System.out.println("CONSUMER WAITING");
                                list.wait();     // must own the lock
                            } catch (InterruptedException ex) {
                                System.out.println("CONSUMER INTERRUPTED");
                            }
                        }
                        obj = list.removeLast();
                        list.notifyAll();
                        int len = list.size();
                        System.out.println("List size now " + len);
                        if (done)
                            break;
                    }
                    process(obj);     // Outside synch section (could take time)
                    //yield(); DITTO
                }
```

```
        }

        void process(Object obj) {
            // Thread.sleep(1234) // Simulate time passing
            System.out.println("Consuming object " + obj);
        }
    }

    ProdCons2(int nP, int nC) {
        for (int i=0; i<nP; i++)
            new Producer().start();
        for (int i=0; i<nC; i++)
            new Consumer().start();
    }

    public static void main(String[] args)
    throws IOException, InterruptedException {

        // Start producers and consumers
        int numProducers = 4;
        int numConsumers = 3;
        ProdCons2 pc = new ProdCons2(numProducers, numConsumers);

        // Let it run for, say, 10 seconds
        Thread.sleep(10*1000);

        // End of simulation - shut down gracefully
        synchronized(pc.list) {
            pc.done = true;
            pc.list.notifyAll();
        }
    }
}
```

I'm happy to report that all is well with this. It runs for long periods of time, neither crashing nor deadlocking. After running for some time, I captured this tiny bit of the log:

```
Produced 1; List size now 118
Consuming object java.lang.Object@2119d0
List size now 117
Consuming object java.lang.Object@2119e0
List size now 116
```

By varying the number of producers and consumers started in the constructor method, you can observe different queue sizes that all seem to work correctly.

One caveat is that, in real life, you generally would not want to perform I/O while holding the monitor lock, because doing so is bad for performance.

22.8. Simplifying Producer/Consumer with the Queue Interface

Problem

You need to control producer/consumer implementations involving multiple threads.

Solution

Use the Queue interface or the BlockingQueue subinterface.

Discussion

As an example of the simplifications possible with java.util.Concurrent package, consider the producer/consumer program in Recipe 22.7. Example 22-14, Prod-Cons15.java, uses the java.util.BlockingQueue (itself a subinterface of the java.util.Queue interface) to reimplement the program ProdCons2 from Example 22-13 in about two-thirds the number of lines of code. With these new features, the application need not be concerned with wait() or the vagaries of notify() and the use of notifyAll() in its place.

The application simply puts items into a queue and takes them from it. In the example, I have (as before) four producers and only three consumers, so the producers eventually wait. Running the application on one of my older notebooks, the producers' lead over the consumers increases to about 350 over the 10 seconds or so of running it.

Example 22-14. ProdCons15.java

```java
public class ProdCons15 {

    protected volatile boolean done = false;

    /** Inner class representing the Producer side */
    class Producer implements Runnable {

        protected BlockingQueue<Object> queue;

        Producer(BlockingQueue<Object> theQueue) { this.queue = theQueue; }

        public void run() {
            try {
                while (true) {
                    Object justProduced = getRequestFromNetwork();
                    queue.put(justProduced);
                    System.out.println(
                        "Produced 1 object; List size now " + queue.size());
                    if (done) {
                        return;
```

```
                }
            }
        } catch (InterruptedException ex) {
            System.out.println("Producer INTERRUPTED");
        }
    }

    Object getRequestFromNetwork() {    // Simulation of reading from client
        try {
                Thread.sleep(10); // simulate time passing during read
        } catch (InterruptedException ex) {
            System.out.println("Producer Read INTERRUPTED");
        }
        return new Object();
    }
}

/** Inner class representing the Consumer side */
class Consumer implements Runnable {
    protected BlockingQueue<Object> queue;

    Consumer(BlockingQueue<Object> theQueue) { this.queue = theQueue; }

    public void run() {
        try {
            while (true) {
                Object obj = queue.take();
                int len = queue.size();
                System.out.println("List size now " + len);
                process(obj);
                if (done) {
                    return;
                }
            }
        } catch (InterruptedException ex) {
                System.out.println("CONSUMER INTERRUPTED");
        }
    }

    void process(Object obj) {
        // Thread.sleep(123) // Simulate time passing
        System.out.println("Consuming object " + obj);
    }
}

ProdCons15(int nP, int nC) {
    BlockingQueue<Object> myQueue = new LinkedBlockingQueue<>();
    for (int i=0; i<nP; i++)
        new Thread(new Producer(myQueue)).start();
    for (int i=0; i<nC; i++)
        new Thread(new Consumer(myQueue)).start();
}
```

```
    public static void main(String[] args)
    throws IOException, InterruptedException {

        // Start producers and consumers
        int numProducers = 4;
        int numConsumers = 3;
        ProdCons15 pc = new ProdCons15(numProducers, numConsumers);

        // Let the simulation run for, say, 10 seconds
        Thread.sleep(10*1000);

        // End of simulation - shut down gracefully
        pc.done = true;
    }
}
```

ProdCons15 is superior to the implementation in the previous recipe in almost all aspects. However, the queue sizes that are output no longer necessarily exactly reflect the size of the queue after the object is inserted or removed. Because there's no longer any locking ensuring atomicity here, any number of queue operations could occur on other threads between thread A's queue insert or removal, and thread A's queue size query.

22.9. Optimizing Parallel Processing with Fork/Join

Problem

You want to optimize use of multiple processors and/or large problem spaces.

Solution

Use the Fork/Join framework.

Discussion

Fork/Join is an ExecutorService intended mainly for reasonably large tasks that can naturally be divided recursively, where you don't have to ensure equal timing for each division. It uses work-stealing to keep threads busy.

The basic means of using Fork/Join is to extend RecursiveTask or RecursiveAction and override its compute() method along these lines:

```
if (assigned portion of work is "small enough") {
        perform the work myself
} else {
        split my work into two pieces
        invoke the two pieces and await the results
}
```

There are two classes: RecursiveTask and RecursiveAction. The main difference is that RecursiveTask has each step of the work returning a value, whereas RecursiveAction does not. In other words, the RecursiveAction method compute() has a return type of void, whereas the RecursiveAction method of the same name has a return type of T, some Type Parameter. You might use RecursiveTask when each call returns a value that represents the computation for its subset of the overall task, in other words, to divide a problem like summarizing data—each task would summarize one part and return that. You might use RecursiveAction to operate over a large data structure performing some transform of the data in place.

There are two demos of the Fork/Join framework here, named after the ForkJoinTask that each subclasses:

- RecursiveTaskDemo uses fork() and join() directly.

- RecursiveActionDemo uses invokeAll() to invoke the two subtasks. invoke() is just a fork() and a join(); and invokeAll() just does this repeatedly until done. Compare the versions of compute() in Examples 22-15 and 22-16 and this will make sense.

Example 22-15. RecursiveActionDemo.java

```
/** A trivial demonstration of the "Fork-Join" framework:
 * square a bunch of numbers using RecursiveAction.
 * We use RecursiveAction here b/c we don't need each
 * compute() call to return its result; the work is
 * accumulated in the "dest" array.
 * @author Ian Darwin
 */
public class RecursiveActionDemo extends RecursiveAction {

    private static final long serialVersionUID = 37427743740013520116L;

    static int[] raw = {
        19, 3, 0, -1, 57, 24, 65, Integer.MAX_VALUE, 42, 0, 3, 5
    };
    static int[] sorted = null;

    int[] source;
    int[] dest;
    int length;
    int start;
```

```java
    final static int THRESHOLD = 4;

    public static void main(String[] args) {
        sorted = new int[raw.length];
        RecursiveActionDemo fb =
            new RecursiveActionDemo(raw, 0, raw.length, sorted);
        ForkJoinPool pool = new ForkJoinPool();
        pool.invoke(fb);
        System.out.print('[');
        for (int i : sorted) {
            System.out.print(i + ",");
        }
        System.out.println(']');
    }

    public RecursiveActionDemo(int[] src, int start, int length, int[] dest) {
        this.source = src;
        this.start = start;
        this.length = length;
        this.dest = dest;
    }

    @Override
    protected void compute() {
        System.out.println("ForkJoinDemo.compute()");
        if (length <= THRESHOLD) { // Compute Directly
            for (int i = start; i < start + length; i++) {
                dest[i] = source[i] * source[i];
            }
        } else {                        // Divide and Conquer
            int split = length / 2;
            invokeAll(
              new RecursiveActionDemo(source, start,         split,         dest),
              new RecursiveActionDemo(source, start + split, length - split, dest));
        }
    }
}
```

Example 22-16. RecursiveTaskDemo.java

```java
/**
 * Demonstrate the Fork-Join Framework to average a large array.
 * Running this on a multi-core machine as e.g.,
 * $ time java threads.RecursiveTaskDemo
 * shows that the CPU time is always greater than the elapsed time,
 * indicating that we are making use of multiple cores.
 * That said, it is a somewhat contrived demo.
 *
 * Use RecursiveTask<T> where, as in this example, each call returns
 * a value that represents the computation for its subset of the overall task.
 * @author Ian Darwin
 */
public class RecursiveTaskDemo extends RecursiveTask<Long> {
```

```java
private static final long serialVersionUID = 37427743740013520116L;

static final int N = 10000000;
final static int THRESHOLD = 500;

int[] data;
int start, length;

public static void main(String[] args) {
    int[] source = new int[N];
    loadData(source);
    RecursiveTaskDemo fb = new RecursiveTaskDemo(source, 0, source.length);
    ForkJoinPool pool = new ForkJoinPool();
    long before = System.currentTimeMillis();
    pool.invoke(fb);
    long after = System.currentTimeMillis();
    long total = fb.getRawResult();
    long avg = total / N;
    System.out.println("Average: " + avg);
    System.out.println("Time :" + (after - before) + " mSec");
}

static void loadData(int[] data) {
    Random r = new Random();
    for (int i = 0; i < data.length; i++) {
        data[i] = r.nextInt();
    }
}

public RecursiveTaskDemo(int[] data, int start, int length) {
    this.data = data;
    this.start = start;
    this.length = length;
}

@Override
protected Long compute() {
    if (length <= THRESHOLD) { // Compute Directly
        long total = 0;
        for (int i = start; i < start + length; i++) {
            total += data[i];
        }
        return total;
    } else {                        // Divide and Conquer
        int split = length / 2;
        RecursiveTaskDemo t1 =
            new RecursiveTaskDemo(data, start,          split);
        t1.fork();
        RecursiveTaskDemo t2 =
            new RecursiveTaskDemo(data, start + split, length - split);
        return t2.compute() + t1.join();
```

```
        }
    }
}
```

The biggest undefined part there is "small enough"; you may have to do some experimentation to see what works well as a "chunk size." Or, better yet, write more code using a feedback control system, measuring the system throughput as the parameter is dynamically tweaked up and down, and have the system automatically arrive at the optimal value for that particular computer system and runtime. This is left as an extended exercise for the reader.

22.10. Background Saving in an Editor

Problem

You need to save the user's work periodically in an interactive program.

Solution

Use a background thread.

Discussion

This code fragment creates a new thread to handle background saves, as in most word processors:

```java
public class AutoSave extends Thread {
    /** The FileSave interface is implemented by the main class. */
    protected FileSaver model;
    /** How long to sleep between tries */
    public static final int MINUTES = 5;
    private static final int SECONDS = MINUTES * 60;

    public AutoSave(FileSaver m) {
        super("AutoSave Thread");
        setDaemon(true);          // so we don't keep the main app alive
        model = m;
    }

    public void run() {
        while (true) {            // entire run method runs forever.
            try {
                sleep(SECONDS*1000);
            } catch (InterruptedException e) {
                // do nothing with it
            }
            if (model.wantAutoSave() && model.hasUnsavedChanges())
                model.saveFile(null);
```

```
            }
        }

        // Not shown:
        // 1) saveFile() must now be synchronized.
        // 2) method that shuts down main program be synchronized on *SAME* object
    }

    /** Local copy of FileSaver interface, for compiling AutoSave demo. */
    interface FileSaver {
        /** Load new model from fn; if null, prompt for new fname */
        public void loadFile(String fn);

        /** Ask the model if it wants AutoSave done for it */
        public boolean wantAutoSave();

        /** Ask the model if it has any unsaved changes, don't save otherwise */
        public boolean hasUnsavedChanges();

        /** Save the current model's data in fn.
         * If fn == null, use current fname or prompt for a filename if null.
         */
        public void saveFile(String fn);
    }
```

As you can see in the run() method, this code sleeps for five minutes (300 seconds), then checks whether it should do anything. If the user has turned autosave off, or hasn't made any changes since the last save, nothing needs to be done. Otherwise, we call the saveFile() method in the main program, which saves the data to the current file. It would be smarter to save it to a recovery file of some name, as the better word processors do.

What's not shown is that now all the methods must be synchronized. It's easy to see why if you think about how the save method would work if the user clicked the Save button at the same time that the autosave method called it, or if the user clicked Exit while the file save method had just opened the file for writing. The "save to recovery file" strategy gets around some of this, but it still needs a great deal of care.

22.11. Program: Threaded Network Server

Problem

You want a network server to be multithreaded.

Solution

Either create a thread when you accept a connection or create a pool of threads in advance and have each wait on the accept() call.

Discussion

Networking (see Chapters 13 and 16) and threads are two very powerful APIs that are a standard part of the Java platform. Used alone, each can increase the reach of your Java programming skills. A common paradigm is a threaded network server, which can either preallocate a certain number of threads or can start a new thread each time a client connects. The big advantage is that each thread can block on read without causing other client threads to delay.

One example of a threaded socket server was discussed in Recipe 16.4; another is shown here. It seems to be some kind of rite (or wrong) of passage for Java folks to write a web server entirely in Java. This one is fairly small and simple; if you want a full-bodied flavor, check out the Apache Foundation's Apache (written in C) and Tomcat (pure Java) servers (I may be biased because I coauthored *Tomcat: The Definitive Guide* [O'Reilly], recommended for administering Tomcat). The main program of my simple server here constructs one instance of class `Httpd`. This creates a socket and waits for incoming clients in the `accept( )` method. Each time there is a return from `accept()`, we have another client, so we create a new thread to process that client. This happens in the `main()` and `runserver()` methods, which are near the beginning of Example 22-17.

Example 22-17. Httpd.java

```
/**
 * A very very simple Web server.
 * <p>
 * NO SECURITY. ALMOST NO CONFIGURATION. NO CGI. NO SERVLETS.
 *<p>
 * This version is threaded. I/O is done in Handler.
 */
public class Httpd {
    /** The default port number */
    public static final int HTTP = 80;
    /** The server socket used to connect from clients */
    protected ServerSocket sock;
    /** A Properties, for loading configuration info */
    private Properties wsp;
    /** A Properties, for loading mime types into */
    private Properties mimeTypes;
    /** The root directory */
    private String rootDir;

    public static void main(String argv[]) throws Exception {
        System.out.println("DarwinSys JavaWeb Server 0.1 starting...");
        Httpd w = new Httpd();
        if (argv.length == 2 && argv[0].equals("-p")) {
            w.startServer(Integer.parseInt(argv[1]));
        } else {
            w.startServer(HTTP);
        }
}
```

```
        w.runServer();
        // NOTREACHED
}

/** Run the main loop of the Server. Each time a client connects,
 * the ServerSocket accept() returns a new Socket for I/O, and
 * we pass that to the Handler constructor, which creates a Thread,
 * which we start.
 */
void runServer() throws Exception  {
    while (true) {
            final Socket clntSock = sock.accept();
            Thread t = new Thread(){
                public void run() {
                    new Handler(Httpd.this).process(clntSock);
                }
            };
            t.start();
    }
}

/** Construct a server object for a given port number */
Httpd() throws Exception {
    wsp=new FileProperties("httpd.properties");
    rootDir = wsp.getProperty("rootDir", ".");
    mimeTypes =
        new FileProperties(
            wsp.getProperty("mimeProperties",
                "mime.properties"));
}

public void startServer(int portNum) throws Exception {
    String portNumString = null;
    if (portNum == HTTP) {
        portNumString = wsp.getProperty("portNum");
        if (portNumString != null) {
            portNum = Integer.parseInt(portNumString);
        }
    }
    sock = new ServerSocket(portNum);
    System.out.println("Listening on port " + portNum);

}

public String getMimeType(String type) {
    return mimeTypes.getProperty(type);
}
public String getMimeType(String type, String dflt) {
    return mimeTypes.getProperty(type, dflt);
}
public String getServerProperty(String name) {
    return wsp.getProperty(name);
```

```
    }

    public String getRootDir() {
        return rootDir;
    }
}
```

The Handler class—shown in Example 22-18—is the part that knows the HTTP protocol, or at least a small subset of it. You may notice near the middle that it parses the incoming HTTP headers into a HashMap but does nothing with them. Here is a log of one connection with debugging enabled:

```
Connection accepted from localhost/127.0.0.1
Request: Command GET, file /, version HTTP/1.0
hdr(Connection,Keep-Alive)
hdr(User-Agent,Mozilla/4.6 [en] (X11; U; OpenBSD 2.8 i386; Nav))
hdr(Pragma,no-cache)
hdr(Host,127.0.0.1)
hdr(Accept,image/gif, image/jpeg, image/pjpeg, image/png, */*)
hdr(Accept-Encoding,gzip)
hdr(Accept-Language,en)
hdr(Accept-Charset,iso-8859-1,*,utf-8)
Loading file //index.html
END OF REQUEST
```

At this stage, the server is getting ready to create an HttpServletRequest object, but it is not sufficiently evolved to do so. This file is a snapshot of work in progress. More interesting is the Hashtable used as a cache; to save disk I/O overhead, once a file has been read from disk, the program does not reread it. This means you have to restart the server if you change files; comparing the timestamps (see Recipe 11.1) and reloading files if they have changed is left as an exercise for the reader.

Example 22-18. Handler.java

```
public class Handler {

    /** inputStream, from Viewer */
    protected BufferedReader is;
    /** outputStream, to Viewer */
    protected PrintStream os;
    /** Main program */
    protected WebProxy parent;
    /** The default filename in a directory. */
    protected final static String DEF_NAME = "/index.html";

    /** The Hashtable used to cache all URLs we've read.
     * Static, shared by all instances of Handler (one Handler per request;
     * this is probably quite inefficient, but simple. Need ThreadPool).
     * Note that Hashtable methods *are* synchronized.
     */
    private static Map<String,Object> cache  = new HashMap<String,Object>();
```

```
static {
    cache.put("", "<html><body><b>Unknown server error</b>".getBytes());
}

/** Construct a Handler */
Handler(WebProxy parent) {
    this.parent = parent;
}

protected enum RequestType {
    RQ_INVALID, RQ_GET, RQ_HEAD, RQ_POST
};

String requestURL;

public void process(Socket clntSock) {
    String request;           // what Viewer sends us.
    RequestType methodType = RequestType.RQ_INVALID;
    try {
        System.out.println("Connection accepted from " +
            clntSock.getInetAddress());
        is = new BufferedReader(new InputStreamReader(
            clntSock.getInputStream()));
        // Must do before any chance of errorResponse being called!
        os = new PrintStream(clntSock.getOutputStream());

        request = is.readLine();
        if (request == null || request.length() == 0) {
            // No point nattering: the sock died, nobody will hear
            // us if we scream into cyberspace...
            System.err.println("The sock has died...");
            return;
        }

        // Use a StringTokenizer to break the request into its three parts:
        // HTTP method, resource name, and HTTP version
        StringTokenizer st = new StringTokenizer(request);
        if (st.countTokens() != 3) {
            errorResponse(444, "Unparseable input " + request);
            clntSock.close();
            return;
        }
        String requestCommand = st.nextToken();
        requestURL = st.nextToken();
        String requestHTTPVersion = st.nextToken();
        System.out.println("Request: Command " + requestCommand +
                ", file " + requestURL + ", version " + requestHTTPVersion);

        // First, check that rqCode is either GET or HEAD or ...
        if ("get".equalsIgnoreCase(requestCommand))
            methodType = RequestType.RQ_GET;
```

```java
        else if ("head".equalsIgnoreCase(requestCommand))
            methodType = RequestType.RQ_HEAD;
        else if ("post".equalsIgnoreCase(requestCommand))
            methodType = RequestType.RQ_POST;
        else {
            errorResponse(400, "invalid method: " + requestCommand);
            clntSock.close();
            return;
        }

        // Read headers, up to the null line before the body,
        // so the body can be read directly if it's a POST.
        Map<String,String> headersMap = new HashMap<String,String>();
        String hdrLine;
        while ((hdrLine = is.readLine()) != null &&
                hdrLine.length() != 0) {
            int ix;
            if ((ix=hdrLine.indexOf(':')) != -1) {
                String hdrName = hdrLine.substring(0, ix);
                String hdrValue = hdrLine.substring(ix+1).trim();
                Debug.println("hdr", hdrName+","+hdrValue);
                headersMap.put(hdrName, hdrValue);
            } else {
                System.err.println("INVALID HEADER: " + hdrLine);
            }
        }

        if (methodType == RequestType.RQ_POST) {
            errorResponse(501, "Protocol not written yet");
            clntSock.close();
            return;
        }

        // Make a URL from the request
        URL url = new URL(requestURL);
        String protocol = url.getProtocol();
        if (!"http".equals(protocol)) {
            errorResponse(401, "protocol not supported: " + requestURL);
            clntSock.close();
            return;
        }

        returnURL(url, os);
        os.flush();
        clntSock.close();

        System.out.println("END OF REQUEST");
    } catch (FileNotFoundException e) {
        errorResponse(404, "Server can't find " + requestURL);
    } catch (IOException e) {
        errorResponse(500, "IO Error on proxy");
        System.out.println("IOException " + e);
```

```java
                e.printStackTrace();
            }
        }

    private void returnURL(URL url, PrintStream os) throws IOException {
        InputStream is = url.openStream();
        int c;
        while ((c = is.read()) != -1) {
            os.write(c);
        }
    }

    /** Sends an error response, by number, hopefully localized. */
    protected void errorResponse(final int errNum, final String errMsg) {

        // Check for localized messages
        ResourceBundle messages = null;
        try {
            messages = ResourceBundle.getBundle("errors");
        } catch (MissingResourceException e) {
            System.err.println(e);
        }

        String response = errMsg;

        if (messages != null) {
            try {
                response = messages.getString(Integer.toString(errNum));
            } catch (MissingResourceException e) {
                response = errMsg;
            }
        }

        // Generate and send the response
        os.println("HTTP/1.0 " + errNum + " " + response);
        os.println("Content-type: text/html");
        os.println();
        os.println("<html>");
        os.println("<head><title>Error " + errNum + "--" + response +
            "</title></head>");
        os.println("<h1>" + errNum + " " + response + "</h1>");
        os.println("<hr>");
        os.println("<address>Java Web Proxy,");
        String myAddr = "http://www.darwinsys.com/freeware/";
        os.println("<a href=\"" + myAddr + "\">" +
            myAddr + "</a>");
        os.println("</address>");
        os.println("</html>");
        os.println();
        os.close();
    }
}
```

From a performance and security point of view, it will be better to precreate a pool of threads and cause each one to run the Handler when a connection comes along. This is how servlet engines drive ordinary servlets to high levels of performance; it avoids the overhead of creating a Thread object for each request. This can be done easily, using the Concurrency Utilities.

22.12. Simplifying Servers Using the Concurrency Utilities

Problem

You need to implement a multithreaded server.

Solution

Use a Thread Pool implementation of the Executor interface.

Discussion

The java.util.concurrent package includes Executors; an Executor is, as its name implies, a class that can execute code for you. The code to be executed can be the familiar Runnable or a new interface Callable. One common kind of Executor is a "thread pool." The code in Example 22-19 subclasses the main class of the Threaded Web Server from Recipe 22.11 to use a pool of Threads to schedule multiple clients concurrently.

Example 22-19. HttpdConcurrent.java

```java
/**
 * HttpConcurrent - Httpd Subclass using java.lang.concurrent
 */
public class HttpdConcurrent extends Httpd {

    private final Executor myThreadPool;

    public HttpdConcurrent() throws Exception {
        super();
        myThreadPool = Executors.newFixedThreadPool(5);
    }

    public static void main(String[] argv) throws Exception {
        System.out.println("DarwinSys JavaWeb Server 0.1 starting...");
        HttpdConcurrent w = new HttpdConcurrent();
        if (argv.length == 2 && argv[0].equals("-p")) {
            w.startServer(Integer.parseInt(argv[1]));
        } else {
            w.startServer(HTTP);
        }
        w.runServer();
    }
```

```
public void runServer() throws Exception {
    while (true) {
        final Socket clientSocket = sock.accept();
        myThreadPool.execute(new Runnable() {
            public void run() {
                new Handler(HttpdConcurrent.this).process(clientSocket);
            }
        });
    }
}
```

You can see this program in action in Figure 22-5.

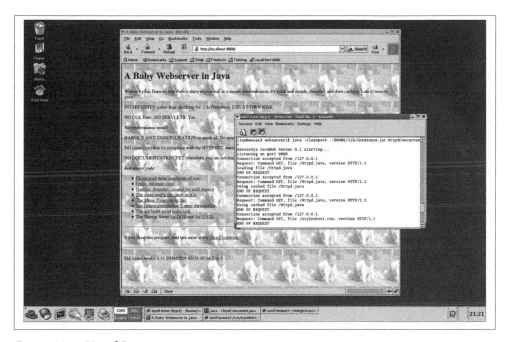

Figure 22-5. HttpdConcurrent in action

See Also

For details on `java.util.concurrent`, see the online documentation accompanying the JDK. For background on JSR 166, see Doug Lea's home page (*http://gee.cs.oswe go.edu*) and his JSR 166 page (*http://bit.ly/1jMds0W*).

An alternative to Java threads has been proposed (and implemented and released) by an organization called Parallel Universe, a good pun. Its Quasar library is described as:

> "Quasar is a library that adds true lightweight threads to the JVM. Lightweight threads, or fibers, are like regular threads, except they consume far less resources, and are able to

task-switch much faster than plain Java (OS) threads. You can easily have hundreds of thousands, or even millions of running fibers on one JVM instance.

"What are fibers good for? They allow you to enjoy the performance and scalability (across cores) of asynchronous, callback based, code, while keeping the natural, simple and intuitive blocking style of threaded code. Quasar includes various constructs for inter-fiber communication, including channels for CSP-style programming (just like those in the Go language). On top of this core, Quasar provides a full Erlang-like actor system, complete with behaviors, supervisors and selective receive, as well as distribution across a cluster.

"Quasar also has a Clojure API, called Pulsar, that closely mimics Erlang functionality."

— Parallel Universe Blog
http://blog.paralleluniverse.co/2014/01/22/introducing-comsat/

## CHAPTER 23

Reflection, or "A Class Named Class"

23.0. Introduction

The class `java.lang.Class`, and the reflection package `java.lang.reflect`, provide a number of mechanisms for gathering information from the Java Virtual Machine. Known collectively as *reflection*, these facilities allow you to load classes on the fly, to find methods and fields in classes, to generate listings of them, and to invoke methods on dynamically loaded classes. There is even a mechanism to let you construct a class from scratch (well, actually, from an array of bytes) while your program is running. This is about as close as Java lets you get to the magic, secret internals of the Java machine.

The JVM itself is a large program, normally written in C and/or C++, that implements the Java Virtual Machine abstraction. You can get the source for OpenJDK and other JVMs via the Internet, which you could study for months. Here we concentrate on just a few aspects, and only from the point of view of a programmer using the JVM's facilities, not how it works internally; that is an implementation detail that could vary from one vendor's JVM to another.

I'll start with loading an existing class dynamically, move on to listing the fields and methods of a class and invoking methods, and end by creating a class on the fly using a `ClassLoader`. One of the more interesting aspects of Java, and one that accounts for both its flexibility (applets, servlets) and part of its perceived speed problem, is the notion of *dynamic loading*. For example, even the simplest "Hello Java" program has to load the class file for your `HelloJava` class, the class file for its parent (usually `java.lang.Object`), the class for `PrintStream` (because you used `System.out`), the class for `PrintStream`'s parent, and `IOException`, and its parent, and so on. To see this in action, try something like:

```
java -verbose HelloJava | more
```

To take another example, a browser can download an applet's bytecode file over the Internet and run it on your desktop. How does it load the class file into the running JVM? We discuss this little bit of Java magic in Recipe 23.4. The chapter ends with replacement versions of the JDK tools *javap* and AppletViewer—the latter doing what a browser does, loading applets at runtime—and a cross-reference tool that you can use to become a famous Java author by publishing your very own reference to the complete Java API.

23.1. Getting a Class Descriptor

Problem

You want to get a Class object from a class name or instance.

Solution

If the type name is known at compile time, you can get the class instance using the compiler keyword `.class`, which works on any type that is known at compile time, even the eight primitive types.

Otherwise, if you have an object (an instance of a class), you can call the `java.lang.Object` method `getClass()`, which returns the Class object for the object's class (now that was a mouthful!):

```
System.out.println("Trying the ClassName.class keyword:");
System.out.println("Object class: " + Object.class);
System.out.println("String class: " + String.class);
System.out.println("String[] class: " + String[].class);
System.out.println("Calendar class: " + Calendar.class);
System.out.println("Current class: " + ClassKeyword.class);
System.out.println("Class for int: " + int.class);
System.out.println();

System.out.println("Trying the instance.getClass() method:");
System.out.println("Sir Robin the Brave".getClass());
System.out.println(Calendar.getInstance().getClass());
```

When we run it, we see:

```
C:\javasrc\reflect>java ClassKeyword
Trying the ClassName.class keyword:
Object class: class java.lang.Object
String class: class java.lang.String
String[] class: class [Ljava.lang.String;
Calendar class: class java.util.Calendar
Current class: class ClassKeyword
Class for int: int

Trying the instance.getClass( ) method:
```

```
class java.lang.String
class java.util.GregorianCalendar
```

```
C:\javasrc\reflect>
```

Nothing fancy, but as you can see, you can get the `Class` object for almost anything known at compile time, whether it's part of a package or not.

23.2. Finding and Using Methods and Fields

Problem

You need to find arbitrary method or field names in arbitrary classes.

Solution

Use the reflection package `java.lang.reflect`.

Discussion

If you just wanted to find fields and methods in one particular class, you wouldn't need this recipe; you could simply create an instance of the class using `new` and refer to its fields and methods directly. But this allows you to find methods and fields in any class, even classes that have not yet been written! Given a class object created as in Recipe 23.1, you can obtain a list of constructors, a list of methods, or a list of fields. The method `getMethods()` lists the methods available for a given class as an array of `Method` objects. Similarly, `getFields()` returns a list of `Field` objects. Because constructor methods are treated specially by Java, there is also a `getConstructors()` method, which returns an array of `Constructor` objects. Even though `Class` is in the package `java.lang`, the `Constructor`, `Method`, and `Field` objects it returns are in `java.lang.reflect`, so you need an import of this package. The `ListMethods` class (see Example 23-1) shows how get a list of methods in a class whose name is known at runtime.

Example 23-1. ListMethods.java

```java
public class ListMethods {
    public static void main(String[] argv) throws ClassNotFoundException {
        if (argv.length == 0) {
            System.err.println("Usage: ListMethods className");
            return;
        }
        Class<?> c = Class.forName(argv[0]);
        Constructor<?>[] cons = c.getConstructors();
        printList("Constructors", cons);
        Method[] meths = c.getMethods();
        printList("Methods", meths);
```

```
    }
    static void printList(String s, Object[] o) {
        System.out.println("*** " + s + " ***");
        for (int i=0; i<o.length; i++)
            System.out.println(o[i].toString());
    }
}
```

For example, you could run Example 23-1 on a class like `java.lang.String` and get a fairly lengthy list of methods; I'll only show part of the output so you can see what it looks like:

```
> java reflection.ListMethods java.lang.String
*** Constructors ***
public java.lang.String( )
public java.lang.String(java.lang.String)
public java.lang.String(java.lang.StringBuffer)
public java.lang.String(byte[])
// and many more...
*** Methods ***
public static java.lang.String java.lang.String.copyValueOf(char[])
public static java.lang.String java.lang.String.copyValueOf(char[],int,int)
public static java.lang.String java.lang.String.valueOf(char)
// and more valueOf( ) forms...
public boolean java.lang.String.equals(java.lang.Object)
public final native java.lang.Class java.lang.Object.getClass( )
// and more java.lang.Object methods...
public char java.lang.String.charAt(int)
public int java.lang.String.compareTo(java.lang.Object)
public int java.lang.String.compareTo(java.lang.String)
```

You can see that this could be extended (almost literally) to write a `BeanMethods` class that would list only the set/get methods defined in a JavaBean (see Recipe 21.6).

Alternatively, you can find a particular method and invoke it, or find a particular field and refer to its value. Let's start by finding a given field, because that's the easiest. Example 23-2 is code that, given an `Object` and the name of a field, finds the field (gets a `Field` object) and then retrieves and prints the value of that `Field` as an `int`.

Example 23-2. FindField.java

```
public class FindField {

    public static void main(String[] unused)
    throws NoSuchFieldException, IllegalAccessException {

        // Create instance of FindField
        FindField gf = new FindField();

        // Create instance of target class (YearHolder defined below).
        Object o = new YearHolder();
```

```
        // Use gf to extract a field from o.
        System.out.println("The value of 'currentYear' is: " +
            gf.intFieldValue(o, "currentYear"));
    }

    int intFieldValue(Object o, String name)
    throws NoSuchFieldException, IllegalAccessException {
        Class<?> c = o.getClass();
        Field fld = c.getField(name);
        int value = fld.getInt(o);
        return value;
    }
}

/** This is just a class that we want to get a field from */
class YearHolder {
    /** Just a field that is used to show getting a field's value. */
    public int currentYear = Calendar.getInstance().get(Calendar.YEAR);
}
```

What if we need to find a method? The simplest way is to use the methods getMethod()
and invoke(). But this is not altogether trivial. Suppose that somebody gives us a reference to an object. We don't know its class but have been told that it should have this
method:

```
public void work(String s) { }
```

We wish to invoke work(). To find the method, we must make an array of Class objects,
one per item in the parameter list. So, in this case, we make an array containing only a
reference to the class object for String. Because we know the name of the class at compile
time, we'll use the shorter invocation String.class instead of Class.forName(). This,
plus the name of the method as a string, gets us entry into the getMethod() method of
the Class object. If this succeeds, we have a Method object. But guess what? In order to
invoke the method, we have to construct yet another array, this time an array of Object
references actually containing the data to be passed to the invocation. We also, of course,
need an instance of the class in whose context the method is to be run. For this demonstration class, we need to pass only a single string, because our array consists only of
the string. Example 23-3 is the code that finds the method and invokes it.

Example 23-3. GetAndInvokeMethod.java

```
/**
 * Get a given method, and invoke it.
 * @author Ian F. Darwin, http://www.darwinsys.com/
 */
public class GetAndInvokeMethod {

    /** This class is just here to give us something to work on,
     * with a println() call that will prove we got into it.
     */
```

```
    static class X {
        public void work(int i, String s) {
            System.out.printf("Called: i=%d, s=%s%n", i, s);
        }
        // The main code does not use this overload.
        public void work(int i) {
            System.out.println("Unexpected call!");
        }
    }
    public static void main(String[] argv) {
        try {
            Class<?> clX = X.class; // or Class.forName("X");

            // To find a method we need the array of matching Class types.
            Class<?>[] argTypes = {
                int.class,
                String.class
            };

            // Now find a Method object for the given method.
            Method worker = clX.getMethod("work", argTypes);

            // To INVOKE the method, we need the invocation
            // arguments, as an Object array.
            Object[] theData = {
                42,
                "Chocolate Chips"
            };

            // The obvious last step: invoke the method.
            // First arg is an instance, null if static method
            worker.invoke(new X(), theData);

        } catch (Exception e) {
            System.err.println("Invoke() failed: " + e);
        }
    }
}
```

Not tiny, but it's still not bad. In most programming languages, you couldn't do that in the 40 lines it took us here.

A word of caution: when the arguments to a method are of a primitive type, such as int, you do not pass Integer.class into getMethod(). Instead, you must use the class object representing the primitive type int. The easiest way to find this class is in the Integer class, as a public constant named TYPE, so you'd pass Integer.TYPE. The same is true for all the primitive types; for each, the corresponding wrapper class has the primitive class referred to as TYPE.

23.3. Accessing Private Methods and Fields via Reflection

Problem

You want to access private fields and have heard you can do so using the Reflection API.

Solution

You bad kid, you! You're not supposed to go after other classes' private parts. But if you have to, and the SecurityManager allows you to use Reflection, you can.

Discussion

There is occasionally a need to access private fields in other classes. For example, I did so recently in writing a JUnit test case that needed to see all the fields of a target class. The secret is to call the `Field` or `Method` descriptor's `setAccessible()` method passing the value `true` before trying to get the value or invoke the method. It really is that easy, as shown in Example 23-4.

Example 23-4. DefeatPrivacy.java

```
class X {
    @SuppressWarnings("unused") // Used surreptitiously below.
    private int p = 42;
    int q = 3;
}

/**
 * Demonstrate that it is, in fact, all too easy to access private members
 * of an object using Reflection, using the default SecurityManager (so this
 * will probably not work in an Applet, for example...).
 */
public class DefeatPrivacy {

    public static void main(String[] args) throws Exception {
        new DefeatPrivacy().process();
    }

    private void process() throws Exception {
        X x = new X();
        System.out.println(x);
        // System.out.println(x.p); // Won't compile
        System.out.println(x.q);
        Class<? extends X> class1 = x.getClass();
        Field[] flds = class1.getDeclaredFields();
        for (Field f : flds) {
            f.setAccessible(true);      // bye-bye "private"
            System.out.println(f + "==" + f.get(x));
            f.setAccessible(false);     // reset to "correct" state
```

```
        }
    }
}
```

 Use this with *extreme care*, because it can defeat some of the most cherished principles of Java programming.

23.4. Loading and Instantiating a Class Dynamically

Problem

You want to load classes dynamically, just like browsers load your applets and web servers load your servlets.

Solution

Use `class.forName("ClassName");` and the class's `newInstance( )` method.

Discussion

Suppose you are writing a Java application and want other developers to be able to extend your application by writing Java classes that run in the context of your application. In other words, these developers are, in essence, using Java as an extension language, in the same way that applets are an extension of a web browser. You would probably want to define a small set of methods that these extension programs would have and that you could call for such purposes as initialization, operation, and termination. The best way to do this is, of course, to publish a given, possibly abstract, class that provides those methods and get the developers to subclass from it. Sound familiar? It should. This is just how web browsers such as Netscape allow the deployment of applets.

We'll leave the thornier issues of security and of loading a class file over a network socket for now, and assume that the user can install the classes into the application directory or into a directory that appears in CLASSPATH at the time the program is run. First, let's define our class. We'll call it `Cooklet` (see Example 23-5) to avoid infringing on the overused word *applet*. And we'll initially take the easiest path from ingredients to cookies before we complicate it.

Example 23-5. Cooklet.java

```
/** A simple class, just to provide the list of methods that
 * users need to provide to be usable in our application.
 * Note that the class is abstract so you must subclass it,
 * but the methods are non-abstract so you don't have to provide
```

```
 * dummy versions if you don't need a particular functionality.
 */
public abstract class Cooklet {

    /** The initialization method. The Cookie application will
     * call you here (AFTER calling your no-argument constructor)
     * to allow you to initialize your code
     */
    public void initialize( ) {
    }

    /** The work method. The cookie application will call you
     * here when it is time for you to start cooking.
     */
    public void work( ) {
    }

    /** The termination method. The cookie application will call you
     * here when it is time for you to stop cooking and shut down
     * in an orderly fashion.
     */
    public void terminate( ) {
    }
}
```

Now, because we'll be baking, err, making this available to other people, we'll probably want to cook up a demonstration version too; see Example 23-6.

Example 23-6. DemoCooklet.java

```
public class DemoCooklet extends Cooklet {
    public void work() {
        System.out.println("I am busy baking cookies.");
    }
    public void terminate() {
        System.out.println("I am shutting down my ovens now.");
    }
}
```

But how does our application use it? Once we have the name of the user's class, we need to create a Class object for that class. This can be done easily using the static method Class.forName() . Then we can create an instance of it using the Class object's newInstance() method; this calls the class's no-argument constructor. Then we simply cast the newly constructed object to our Cooklet class, and we can call its methods! It actually takes longer to describe this code than to look at the code, so let's do that now; see Example 23-7.

Example 23-7. Cookies.java

```
public class Cookies {
    public static void main(String[] argv) {
```

```
        System.out.println("Cookies Application Version 0.0");
        Cooklet cooklet = null;
        String cookletClassName = argv[0];
        try {
            Class<Cooklet> cookletClass =
                (Class<Cooklet>) Class.forName(cookletClassName);
            cooklet = cookletClass.newInstance();
        } catch (Exception e) {
            System.err.println("Error " + cookletClassName + e);
        }
        cooklet.initialize();
        cooklet.work();
        cooklet.terminate();
    }
}
```

And if we run it?

```
$ java  Cookies DemoCooklet
Cookies Application Version 0.0
I am busy baking cookies.
I am shutting down my ovens now.
$
```

Of course, this version has rather limited error handling. But you already know how to fix that. Your ClassLoader can also place classes into a package by constructing a Package object; you should do this if loading any medium-sized set of application classes.

23.5. Constructing a Class from Scratch with a ClassLoader

Problem

You need to load a class from a nonstandard location and run its methods.

Solution

Examine the existing loaders such as java.net.URLClassLoader. If none is suitable, write and use your own ClassLoader.

Discussion

A ClassLoader, of course, is a program that loads classes. One class loader is built into the Java Virtual Machine, but your application can create others as needed. Learning to write and run a working class loader and using it to load a class and run its methods is a nontrivial exercise. In fact, you rarely need to write a class loader, but knowing how is helpful in understanding how the JVM finds classes, creates objects, and calls methods.

ClassLoader itself is abstract; you must subclass it, presumably providing a load-Class() method that loads classes as you wish. It can load the bytes from a network connection, a local disk, RAM, a serial port, or anywhere else. Or you can construct the class file in memory yourself, if you have access to a compiler.

There is a general-purpose loader called java.net.URLClassLoader that can be used if all you need is to load classes via the Web protocol (or, more generally, from one or more URLs).

You must call the class loader's loadClass() method for any classes you wish to explicitly load from it. Note that this method is called to load all classes required for classes you load (superclasses that aren't already loaded, for example). However, the JVM still loads classes that you instantiate with the new operator "normally" via CLASSPATH.

When writing a class loader, your loadClass() method needs to get the class file into a byte array (typically by reading it), convert the array into a Class object, and return the result.

What? That sounds a bit like "And Then a Miracle Occurs…" And it is. The miracle of class creation, however, happens down inside the JVM, where you don't have access to it. Instead, your ClassLoader has to call the protected defineClass() method in your superclass (which is java.lang.ClassLoader). This is illustrated in Figure 23-1, where a stream of bytes containing a hypothetical Chicken class is converted into a ready-to-run Chicken class in the JVM by calling the defineClass() method.

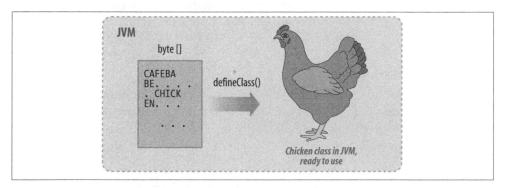

Figure 23-1. ClassLoader in action

What next?

To use your ClassLoader subclass, you need to instantiate it and call its loadClass() method with the name of the class you want to load. This gives you a Class object for the named class; the Class object in turn lets you construct instances, find and call methods, etc. Refer back to Recipe 23.2.

23.6. Performance Timing

Problem

Slow performance?

Solution

Use a *profiler*, or, time individual methods using `System.currentTimeMillis()` before and after invoking the target method; the difference is the time that method took.

Discussion

Profilers

Profiling tools—profilers—have a long history as one of the important tools in a programmer's toolkit. A commercial profiling tool will help find bottlenecks in your program by showing both the number of times each method was called, and the amount of time in each.

Quite a bit of useful information can be obtained from a Java application by use of the `JVisualVM` tool, a standard part of the Oracle JDK. See Oracle's documentation on JavaVisual VM (*http://bit.ly/1mMFNWL*). A newer tool that is part of the JDK as of JDK 7 Update 40 is *Java Flight Recorder* profiler, a component of *Java Mission Control* (*http://bit.ly/1lj3OYG*). There are also third-party profilers that will give more detailed information. NewRelic (*http://newrelic.com*) claims to have a powerful commercial performance analyzer.

Measuring one method

The simplest technique is to save the JVM's accumulated time before and after dynamically loading a main program, and calculate the difference between those times. Code to do just this is presented in Example 23-10; for now, just remember that we have a way of timing a given Java class.

One way of measuring the efficiency of a particular operation is to run it many times in isolation. The overall time the program takes to run thus approximates the total time of many invocations of the same operation. Gross numbers like this can be compared if you want to know which of two ways of doing something is more efficient. Consider the case of string concatenation versus `println()`. The code:

```
println("Time is " + n.toString( ) + " seconds");
```

will probably work by creating a `StringBuilder`, appending the string `"Time is "`, the value of n as a string, and `" seconds"`, and finally converting the finished `StringBuilder` to a `String` and passing that to `println()`. Suppose you have a program that does a lot of this, such as a Java servlet that creates a lot of HTML this way, and you expect (or at least hope) your web site to be sufficiently busy so that doing this efficiently will make a difference. There are two ways of thinking about this:

- Theory A: This string concatenation is inefficient.

- Theory B: String concatenation doesn't matter; `println()` is inefficient, too.

A proponent of Theory A might say that because `println()` just puts stuff into a buffer, it is very fast and that string concatenation is the expensive part.

How to decide between Theory A and Theory B? Assume you are willing to write a simple test program that tests both theories. Let's just write a simple program both ways and time it. Example 23-8 is the timing program for Theory A.

Example 23-8. StringPrintA.java

```
public class StringPrintA {
    public static void main(String[] argv) {
        Object o = "Hello World";
        for (int i=0; i<100000; i++) {
            System.out.println("<p><b>" + o.toString() + "</b></p>");
        }
    }
}
```

`StringPrintAA` (in the *javasrc* repo but not printed here) is the same but explicitly uses a `StringBuilder` for the string concatenation. Example 23-9 is the tester for Theory B.

Example 23-9. StringPrintB.java

```
public class StringPrintB {
    public static void main(String[] argv) {
        Object o = "Hello World";
        for (int i=0; i<100000; i++) {
            System.out.print("<p><b>");
            System.out.print(o.toString());
            System.out.print("</b></p>");
            System.out.println();
        }
    }
}
```

Timing results

I ran `StringPrintA`, `StringPrintAA`, and `StringPrintB` twice each on the same computer. To eliminate JVM startup times, I ran them from a program called `TimeNoArgs`, which takes a class name and invokes its `main()` method, using the Reflection API. `TimeNoArgs` and a shell script to run it, *stringprinttimer.sh*, are in the *performance* folder of the *javasrc* source repository. Here are the results:

2004 Results	
StringPrintA	17.23, 17.20 seconds
StringPrintAA	17.23, 17.23 seconds
StringPrintB	27.59, 27.60 seconds
2014 Results	
StringPrintA	0.714, 0.525 seconds
StringPrintAA	0.616, 0.561 seconds
StringPrintB	1.091, 1.039 seconds

Although the times went down by a factor of roughly 20 over a decade, the ratios remain remarkably consistent: `StringPrintB`, which calls `print()` and `println()` multiple times, takes roughly twice as long.

Moral: Don't guess. If it matters, time it.

Another moral: Multiple calls to `System.out.print()` cost more than the same number of calls to a `StringBuilder`'s `append()` method, by a factor of roughly 1.5 (or 150%). Theory B wins; the extra `println` calls appear to save a string concatenation but make the program take substantially longer.

Other aspects of performance: GC

There are many other aspects of software performance. One that is fundamental to Java is garbage collection behavior. Sun/Oracle usually talk about this at JavaOne. See, for example, the JavaOne 2003 paper "Garbage Collection in the Java HotSpot Virtual Machine" (*http://bit.ly/1krch7x*). You should also see the JavaOne 2007 talk by the same GC Development team, "Garbage-Collection-Friendly Programming", TS-2906. Unfortunately it seems to have gotten lost from Oracle's website, but is still available online (*http://bit.ly/1l4VJYN*). JavaOne 2010 featured an updated presentation entitled "The Garbage Collection MythBusters." (*http://bit.ly/1iqTKbF*)

A timing program

It's pretty easy to build a simplified `time` command in Java, given that you have `System.currentTimeMillis()` to start with. Run my `Time` program, and, on the command line, specify the name of the class to be timed, followed by the arguments (if any) that class needs for running. The program is shown in Example 23-10. The time that the class took is displayed. But remember that `System.currentTimeMillis()` returns clock time, not necessarily CPU time. So you must run it on a machine that isn't running a lot of background processes. And note also that I use dynamic loading (see Recipe 23.4) to let you put the Java class name on the command line.

Example 23-10. Time.java

```java
public class Time {
    public static void main(String[] argv) throws Exception {
        // Instantiate target class, from argv[0]
        Class<?> c = Class.forName(argv[0]);

        // Find its static main method (use our own argv as the signature).
        Class<?>[] classes = { argv.getClass() };
        Method main = c.getMethod("main", classes);

        // Make new argv array, dropping class name from front.
        // (Normally Java doesn't get the class name, but in
        // this case the user puts the name of the class to time
        // as well as all its arguments...
        String nargv[] = new String[argv.length - 1];
        System.arraycopy(argv, 1, nargv, 0, nargv.length);

        Object[] nargs = { nargv };

        System.err.println("Starting class " + c);

        // About to start timing run. Important to not do anything
        // (even a println) that would be attributed to the program
        // being timed, from here until we've gotten ending time.

        // Get current (i.e., starting) time
        long t0 = System.currentTimeMillis();

        // Run the main program
        main.invoke(null, nargs);

        // Get ending time, and compute usage
        long t1 = System.currentTimeMillis();

        long runTime = t1 - t0;

        System.err.println(
            "runTime=" + Double.toString(runTime/1000D));
    }
}
```

Of course, you can't directly compare the results from the operating system `time` command with results from running this program. There is a rather large, but fairly constant, initialization overhead—the JVM startup and the initialization of `Object` and `System.out`, for example—that is included in the former and excluded from the latter. One could even argue that my `Time` program is more accurate because it excludes this constant overhead. But, as noted, it must be run on a single-user machine to yield repeatable results. And no fair running an editor in another window while waiting for your timed program to complete!

See Also

Java Performance: The Definitive Guide by Scott Oaks (O'Reilly) provides information on tuning Java performance.

23.7. Printing Class Information

Problem

You want to print all the information about a class, similar to the way *javap* does.

Solution

Get a `Class` object, call its `getFields()` and `getMethods()`, and print the results.

Discussion

The JDK includes a program called *javap*, the Java Printer. Sun's JDK version normally prints the outline of a class file—a list of its methods and fields—but can also print out the Java bytecodes or machine instructions. The Kaffe package did not include a version of *javap*, so I wrote one and contributed it (see Example 23-11). The Kaffe folks have expanded it somewhat, but it still works basically the same. My version doesn't print the bytecodes; it behaves rather like Sun's behaves when you don't give theirs any command-line options.

The `getFields()` and `getMethods()` methods return arrays of `Field` and `Method`, respectively; these are both in package `java.lang.reflect`. I use a `Modifiers` object to get details on the permissions and storage attributes of the fields and methods. In many Java implementations, you can bypass this and simply call `toString()` in each `Field` and `Method` object (as I do here for `Constructors`). Doing it this way gives me a bit more control over the formatting.

Example 23-11. MyJavaP.java

```
public class MyJavaP {

    /** Simple main program, construct self, process each class name
     * found in argv.
     */
    public static void main(String[] argv) {
        MyJavaP pp = new MyJavaP();

        if (argv.length == 0) {
            System.err.println("Usage: MyJavaP className [...]");
            System.exit(1);
        } else for (int i=0; i<argv.length; i++)
            pp.doClass(argv[i]);
```

```
        }

    /** Format the fields and methods of one class, given its name.
     */
    protected void doClass(String className) {
        try {
            Class<? extends Object> c = Class.forName(className);

            final Annotation[] annotations = c.getAnnotations();
            for (Annotation a : annotations) {
                System.out.println(a);
            }

            System.out.println(c + " {");

            Field fields[] = c.getDeclaredFields();
            for (Field f : fields) {
                final Annotation[] fldAnnotations = f.getAnnotations();
                for (Annotation a : fldAnnotations) {
                    System.out.println(a);
                }
                if (!Modifier.isPrivate(f.getModifiers()))
                    System.out.println("\t" + f + ";");
            }

            Constructor<? extends Object>[] constructors = c.getConstructors();
            for (Constructor<? extends Object> con : constructors) {
                System.out.println("\t" + con + ";");
            }

            Method methods[] = c.getDeclaredMethods();
            for (Method m : methods) {
                final Annotation[] methodAnnotations = m.getAnnotations();
                for (Annotation a : methodAnnotations) {
                    System.out.println(a);
                }
                if (!Modifier.isPrivate(m.getModifiers())) {
                    System.out.println("\t" + m + ";");
                }
            }
            System.out.println("}");
        } catch (ClassNotFoundException e) {
            System.err.println("Error: Class " +
                className + " not found!");
        } catch (Exception e) {
            System.err.println("JavaP Error: " + e);
        }
    }
}
```

23.8. Listing Classes in a Package

Problem

You want to get a list of all the classes in a package.

Solution

You can't, in the general case. There are some limited approaches, most involving "classpath scanning."

Discussion

There is no way to find out all the classes in a package, in part because, as we just saw in Recipe 23.5, you can add classes to a package at any time! And, for better or for worse, the JVM and standard classes such as `java.lang.Package` do not even allow you to enumerate the classes currently in a given package.

The nearest you can come is to look through the classpath. And this will surely work only for local directories and JAR files; if you have locally defined or network-loaded classes, this is not going to help. In other words, it will find compiled classes, but not dynamically loaded ones. There are several libraries that can automate this for you, and you're welcome to use them. The code to scan the classpath is fairly simple at heart, though, so classy developers with heart will want to examine it. Example 23-12 shows my `ClassesInPackage` class with its one static method. The code works but is rather short on error handling, and will crash on non-existent packages and other failures.

The code goes through a few gyrations to get the classpath as an enumeration of URLs, then looks at each element. "file:" URLs will contain the pathname of the file containing the *.class* file, so we can just list it. "jar:" URLs contain the filename as "file:/path_to_jar_file!package/name," so we have to pull this apart; the "package name" suffix is slightly redundant in this case because it's the package we asked the `ClassLoader` to give us.

Example 23-12. ClassesInPackage.java

```
public class ClassesInPackage {

    /** This approach began as a contribution by Paul Kuit at
     * http://stackoverflow.com/questions/1456930/, but his only
     * handled single files in a directory in classpath, not in Jar files.
     * N.B. Does NOT handle system classes!
     * @param packageName
     * @return
     * @throws IOException
     */
    public static String[] getPackageContent(String packageName)
```

```
        throws IOException {

        final String packageAsDirName = packageName.replace(".", "/");
        final List<String> list = new ArrayList<>();
        final Enumeration<URL> urls =
                Thread.currentThread().
                getContextClassLoader().
                getResources(packageAsDirName);
        while (urls.hasMoreElements()) {
            URL url = urls.nextElement();
            // System.out.println("URL = " + url);
            String file = url.getFile();
            switch (url.getProtocol()) {
            case "file":
                // This is the easy case: "file" is
                // the full path to the classpath directory
                File dir = new File(file);
                for (File f : dir.listFiles()) {
                    list.add(packageAsDirName + "/" + f.getName());
                }
                break;
            case "jar":
                // This is the harder case; "file" is of the form
                // "jar:/home/ian/bleah/darwinsys.jar!com/darwinsys/io"
                // for some jar file that contains at least one class from
                // the given package.
                int colon = file.indexOf(':');
                int bang = file.indexOf('!');
                String jarFileName = file.substring(colon + 1, bang);
                JarFile jarFile = new JarFile(jarFileName);
                Enumeration<JarEntry> entries = jarFile.entries();
                while (entries.hasMoreElements()) {
                    JarEntry e = entries.nextElement();
                    String jarEntryName = e.getName();
                    if (!jarEntryName.endsWith("/") &&
                        jarEntryName.startsWith(packageAsDirName)) {
                        list.add(jarEntryName);
                    }
                }
                break;
            default:
                throw new IllegalStateException(
                "Dunno what to do with URL " + url);
            }
        }
        return list.toArray(new String[] {});
    }

    public static void main(String[] args) throws IOException {
        String[] names = getPackageContent("com.darwinsys.io");
        for (String name : names) {
            System.out.println(name);
```

```
        }
        System.out.println("Done");
    }
}
```

Note that if you run this application in the "javasrc" project, it will list the members of the demonstration package (com.darwinsys.io) twice, because it will find them both in the build directory and in the JAR file. If this is an issue, change the List to a Set (see Recipe 7.3).

23.9. Using and Defining Annotations

Problem

You need to know how to use annotations in code or to define your own annotations.

Solution

Apply annotations in your code using @*AnnotationName* before a class, method, field, etc. Define annotations with @interface at the same level as class, interface, etc.

Discussion

Annotations are a way of adding additional information beyond what the source code conveys. Annotations may be directed at the compiler or at runtime examination. Their syntax was somewhat patterned after javadoc annotations (such as @author, @version inside "doc comments"). Annotations are what I call *class-like things* (so they have initial-cap names), but are prefixed by @ sign where used (e.g., @Override). You can place them on classes, methods, fields, and a few other places; they must appear immediately before what they annotate (ignoring space and comments). A given annotation may only appear once in a given position (this is relaxed in Java 8 or 9).

As an example of the benefits of a compile-time annotation, consider the common error made when overriding: as shown in Example 23-13, a small error in the method signature can result it an overload when an override was intended.

Example 23-13. MyClass.java: Why annotations?

```
public class MyClass {

public boolean equals(MyClass object2) {
// compare, return boolean
}
```

The code will compile just fine on any release of Java, but it is incorrect. The standard contract of the equals() method (see Recipe 8.2) requires an equals method whose solitary argument is of type `java.lang.Object`. The preceding version creates an accidental overload. Because the main use of `equals()` (and its buddy method `hashCode()`, see Recipe 8.2) is in the Collections classes (see Chapter 7), this overloaded method will never get called, resulting both in dead code and in incorrect operation of your class within Sets and Maps.

The solution is very simple: using the annotation `java.lang.Override`, as in Example 23-14, informs the compiler that the annotated method is required to be overriding a method inherited from a supertype (either a superclass or an interface). If not, the code will not compile.

Example 23-14. MyClass.java: @Override Annotation

```
public class MyClass {

@Override
public boolean equals(MyClass object2) {
// compare, return boolean
}
```

This version of `equals()`, while still incorrect, will be flagged as erroneous at compile time, potentially avoiding a lot of debugging time. This annotation, on your own classes, will help both at the time you write new code and as you maintain your codebase; if a method is removed from a superclass, all the subclasses that still attempt to override it *and* have the `@Override` annotation, will cause an error message, allowing you to remove a bunch of dead code.

The second major use of annotations is to provide metatdata at runtime. For example, the Java Persistence API (JPA, see Recipe 18.1) uses its own set of annotations defined in the package `javax.persistence` to "mark up" entity classes to be loaded and/or persisted. A JPA Entity Class might look like Example 23-15:

Example 23-15. Person.java: JPA annotations

```
@Entity
public class Person {

    int id;
    protected String firstName;
    protected String lastName;

    public Person() {
        // required by JPA; must code it since we need 2-arg form.
    }

    public Person(String firstName, String lastName) {
        this.firstName = firstName;
        this.lastName = lastName;
    }
```

```
@Id @GeneratedValue(strategy=GenerationType.AUTO, generator="my_poid_gen")
public int getId() {
    return id;
}

public void setId(int id) {
    this.id = id;
}

public String getFirstName() {
    return firstName;
}

public void setFirstName(String firstName) {
    this.firstName = firstName;
}

@Column(name="surname")
public String getLastName() {
    return lastName;
}

public void setLastName(String lastName) {
    this.lastName = lastName;
}

@Override
public String toString() {
    return getFullName();
}

@Transient /* synthetic: cannot be used in JPA queries. */
public String getFullName() {
    StringBuilder sb = new StringBuilder();
    if (firstName != null)
        sb.append(firstName).append(' ');
    if (lastName != null)
        sb.append(lastName);
    if (sb.length() == 0)
        sb.append("NO NAME");
    return sb.toString();
}
}
```

The @Entity annotation at class level directs JPA to treat this as a data object to be mapped into the database. The @Id informs JPA that this id is the primary key property, and the @GeneratedValue tells it how to assign the primary key values for newly created objects. The @Column annotation is only needed when the column name in the relational database differs from the expected name based on the property; in this case, the SQL database designer has used surname, whereas the Java developer wants to use lastName.

I said that annotations are class-like things, and so, you can define your own. The syntax here is a bit funky; you use @interface. It is rumored that the team developing this feature was either told not to, or was afraid to, introduce a new keyword into the language, due to the trouble that doing so had caused when the enum keyword was introduced in Java SE 1.4. Or, maybe they just wanted to use a syntax that was more reminiscent of the annotation's usage. At any rate, Example 23-16 is a trivial example of a custom annotation.

Example 23-16. Trivial annotation defined

```
package lang;

public @interface MyToyAnnotation {
}
```

Annotations are "class-like things" so they should be named the same way—that is, names that begin with a capital letter and, if public, stored in a source file of the same name (e.g, *MyToyAnnotation.java*).

Compile the Example 23-16 with javac and you'll see there's a new *MyToyAnnotation.class* file. In Example 23-17, we examine this with javap, the standard JDK class inspection tool.

Example 23-17. Running javap on trivial annotation

```
$ javap lang.MyToyAnnotation
Compiled from "MyToyAnnotation.java"
public interface lang.MyToyAnnotation extends java.lang.annotation.Annotation {
}
$
```

As it says, an Annotation is represented in the class file format as just an interface that extends Annotation (to answer the obvious question, you could write simple interfaces this way, but it would be a truly terrible idea). Let's have a quick look at Annotation itself:

```
$ javap java.lang.annotation.Annotation
Compiled from "Annotation.java"
public interface java.lang.annotation.Annotation {
  public abstract boolean equals(java.lang.Object);
  public abstract int hashCode();
  public abstract java.lang.String toString();
  public abstract java.lang.Class<? extends java.lang.annotation.Annotation>
    annotationType();
}
$
```

Annotations can be made such that the compiler will only allow them in certain points in your code. Here is one that can only go on classes or interfaces:

```
@Target(ElementType.TYPE)
@Retention(RetentionPolicy.RUNTIME)
public @interface MyAnnotation {
}
```

The @Target specifies where the annotation can be used: ElementType.TYPE makes it usable on classes, interfaces, class-like things such as enums, even annotations! To restrict it to use just on annotations, there is ElementType.ANNOTATION_TYPE. Other types include METHOD, FIELD, CONSTRUCTOR, LOCAL_VARIABLE, PACKAGE, and PARAMETER. So, this annotation is itself annotated with two @ANNOTATION_TYPE-targeted annotations.

Usage of annotations with an existing framework requires consulting their documentation. Using annotations for your own purpose at runtime requires use of the Reflection API, as shown in Example 23-18.

One more thing to note about annotations is that they may have attributes. These are defined as methods in the annotation source code, but used as attributes where the annotation is used. Example 23-18 is an annotated annotation with one such attribute:

Example 23-18. Annotation demo

```
/**
 * A sample annotation for types (classes, interfaces);
 * it will be available at run time.
 */
@Target(ElementType.TYPE)
@Retention(RetentionPolicy.RUNTIME)
public @interface AnnotationDemo {
    public boolean fancy() default false;
    public int order() default 42;
}

/** A simple example of using the annotation */
@AnnotationDemo(fancy=true)
@Resource(name="Dumbledore")
class FancyClassJustToShowAnnotation {

    /** Print out the annotations attached to this class */
    public static void main(String[] args) {
        Class<?> c = FancyClassJustToShowAnnotation.class;
        System.out.println("Class " + c.getName() + " has these annotations:");
        for (Annotation a : c.getAnnotations()) {
            if (a instanceof AnnotationDemo) {
                AnnotationDemo ad = (AnnotationDemo)a;
                System.out.println("\t" +a +
                    " with fancy=" + ad.fancy() +
                    " and order " + ad.order());
            } else {
                System.out.println("\tSomebody else's annotation: " + a);
            }
        }
    }
```

```
        }
}
```

`AnnotationDemo` has the meta-annotation `@Target(ElementType.TYPE)` to indicate that it can annotate user-defined types (such as classes). Other `ElementType` choices include `METHOD`, `FIELD`, `PARAMETER` and a few more. If more than one is needed, use array initializer syntax.

`AnnotationDemo` also has the `@Retention(RetentionPolicy.RUNTIME)` annotation to request that it be preserved until runtime. This is obviously required for any annotation that will be examined by a framework at runtime.

These two meta-annotations are common on user-defined annotations that will be examined at runtime.

The class `FancyClassJustToShowAnnotation` shows using the `AnnotationDemo` annotation, along with a standard Java one (the `@Resource` annotation).

Refer to Recipe 23.10 for a full example of using this mechanism.

23.10. Finding Plug-in-like Classes via Annotations

Problem

You want to do plug-in-like things without using an explicit plug-in API.

Solution

Define an annotation for the purpose, and use it to mark the plug-in classes.

Discussion

Suppose we want to model how the Java EE standard `javax.annotations.Named` or `javax.faces.ManagedBean` annotations work; for each class that is so annotated, convert the class name to an instance-like name (e.g, lowercase the first letter), and do something special with it. You'd want to do something like the following:

1. Get the list of classes in the given package(s) (see Recipe 23.8).
2. Check if the class is annotated.
3. If so, save the name and `Class` descriptor for later use.

This is implemented in Example 23-19.

Example 23-19. PluginsViaAnnotations::findAnnotatedClasses

```
/** Discover "plugins" or other add-in classes via Reflection using Annotations */
public class PluginsViaAnnotations {

    /**
     * Find all classes in the given package which have the given
     * class-level annotation class.
     */
    public static List<Class<?>> findAnnotatedClasses(String packageName,
        Class<? extends Annotation> annotationClass) throws Exception {

        List<Class<?>> ret = new ArrayList<>();
        String[] classes = ClassesInPackage.getPackageContent(packageName);
        for (String clazz : classes) {
            Class<?> c = Class.forName(clazz);
            if (c.isAnnotationPresent(annotationClass))
                ret.add(c);
        }
        return ret;
    }
}
```

We can take this one step further, and support particular method annotations, similar to `javax.annotations.PostCreate`, which is meant to decorate a method that is to be called after an instance of the bean has been instantiated by the framework. Our flow is now something like this, and the code is shown in Example 23-20:

1. Get the list of classes in the given package(s) (again, see Recipe 23.8).

2. If you are using a class-level annotation, check if the class is annotated.

3. If this class is still of interest, get a list of its methods.

4. For each method, see if it contains a given method-specific annotation.

5. If so, add the class and method to a list of invocable methods.

Example 23-20. PluginsViaAnnotations::findAnnotatedMethods

```
    /**
     * Find all classes in the given package which have the given
     * method-level annotation class on at least one method.
     */
    public static List<Class<?>> findClassesWithAnnotatedMethods(String packageName,
            Class<? extends Annotation> methodAnnotationClass) throws Exception {
        List<Class<?>> ret = new ArrayList<>();
        String[] classes = ClassesInPackage.getPackageContent(packageName);
        for (String clazz : classes) {
            Class<?> c = Class.forName(clazz);
            for (Method m : c.getMethods()) {
                if (m.isAnnotationPresent(methodAnnotationClass)) {
                    ret.add(c);
                }
```

```
            }
        }
        return ret;
    }
```

See Also

Recipe 23.9, and the rest of this chapter.

23.11. Program: CrossRef

You've probably seen those other Java books that consist entirely of listings of the Java API for version thus-and-such of the JDK. I don't suppose you thought the authors of these works sat down and typed the entire contents from scratch. As a programmer, you would have realized, I hope, that there must be a way to obtain that information from Java. But you might not have realized how easy it is! If you've read this chapter faithfully, you now know that there is one true way: make the computer do the walking. Example 23-21 is a program that puts most of the techniques together. This version generates a cross-reference listing, but by overriding the last few methods, you could easily convert it to print the information in any format you like, including an API Reference book. You'd need to deal with the details of this or that publishing software—FrameMaker, troff, T$_E$X, or whatever—but that's the easy part.

This program makes fuller use of the Reflection API than did MyJavaP in Recipe 23.7. It also uses the java.util.zip classes (see Recipe 10.22) to crack the JAR archive containing the class files of the API. Each class file found in the archive is loaded and listed; the listing part is similar to MyJavaP.

Example 23-21. CrossRef.java

```java
public class CrossRef extends APIFormatter {

    /** Simple main program, construct self, process each .ZIP file
     * found in CLASSPATH or in argv.
     */
    public static void main(String[] argv) throws IOException {
        CrossRef xref = new CrossRef();
        xref.doArgs(argv);
    }

    /**
     * Print the fields and methods of one class.
     */
    protected void doClass(Class<?> c) {
        startClass(c);
        try {
            Field[] fields = c.getDeclaredFields();
            Arrays.sort(fields, new Comparator<Field>() {
```

```
            public int compare(Field o1, Field o2) {
                return o1.getName().compareTo(o2.getName());
            }
        });
        for (int i = 0; i < fields.length; i++) {
            Field field = (Field)fields[i];
            if (!Modifier.isPrivate(field.getModifiers()))
                putField(field, c);
            // else System.err.println("private field ignored: " + field);
        }

        Method methods[] = c.getDeclaredMethods();
        Arrays.sort(methods, new Comparator<Method>() {
            public int compare(Method o1, Method o2) {
                return o1.getName().compareTo(o2.getName());
            }
        });
        for (int i = 0; i < methods.length; i++) {
            if (!Modifier.isPrivate(methods[i].getModifiers()))
                putMethod(methods[i], c);
            // else System.err.println("pvt: " + methods[i]);
        }
    } catch (Exception e) {
        e.printStackTrace();
    }
    endClass();
}

/** put a Field's information to the standard output.  */
protected void putField(Field fld, Class<?> c) {
    println(fld.getName() + " field " + c.getName() + " ");
}

/** put a Method's information to the standard output.  */
protected void putMethod(Method method, Class<?> c) {
    String methName = method.getName();
    println(methName + " method " + c.getName() + " ");
}

/** Print the start of a class. Unused in this version,
 * designed to be overridden */
protected void startClass(Class<?> c) {
}

/** Print the end of a class. Unused in this version,
 * designed to be overridden */
protected void endClass() {
}

/** Convenience routine, short for System.out.println */
protected final void println(String s) {
    System.out.println(s);
```

```
        }
}
```

You probably noticed the methods startClass() and endClass(), which are null. These methods are placeholders designed to make subclassing easy for when you need to write something at the start and end of each class. One example might be a fancy text formatting application in which you need to output a bold header at the beginning of each class. Another would be XML (see Chapter 20), where you'd want to write a tag like <class> at the front of each class, and </class> at the end. Example 23-22 is, in fact, a working XML-specific subclass that generates (limited) XML for each field and method.

Example 23-22. CrossRefXML.java

```java
public class CrossRefXML extends CrossRef {

    public static void main(String[] argv) throws IOException {
        CrossRef xref = new CrossRefXML();
        xref.doArgs(argv);
    }

    /** Print the start of a class.
     */
    protected void startClass(Class<?> c) {
        println("<class><classname>" + c.getName() + "</classname>");
    }

    protected void putField(Field fld, Class<?> c) {
        println("<field>" + fld + "</field>");
    }

    /** put a Method's information to the standard output.
     * Marked protected so you can override it (hint, hint).
     */
    protected void putMethod(Method method, Class<?> c) {
        println("<method>" + method + "</method>");
    }

    /** Print the end of a class.
     */
    protected void endClass() {
        println("</class>");
    }
}
```

By the way, if you publish a book using either of these and get rich, "Remember, remember me!"

23.12. Program: AppletViewer

Though I don't say much about applets in this edition of this book, another JDK tool that can be replicated is the *AppletViewer*. This uses the reflection package to load a class that is subclassed from `Applet`, instantiate an instance of it, and `add()` this to a frame at a given size. Writing a replacement version of such a tool is a good example of reflection in action: you can use these techniques to dynamically load any subclass of a given class. Suppose we have a simple applet like `HelloApplet` in Example 23-23.

Example 23-23. HelloApplet.java

```java
public class HelloApplet extends JApplet {

    /** The flag which controls drawing the message. */
    protected boolean requested;

    /** init() is an Applet method called by the browser to initialize */
    public void init() {
        JButton b;
        requested = false;
        Container cp = (Container)getContentPane();
        cp.setLayout(new FlowLayout());
        String buttonLabel = getParameter("buttonlabel");
        if (buttonLabel == null) {
            buttonLabel = "Draw/Don't Draw";
        }
        cp.add(b = new JButton(buttonLabel));
        b.addActionListener(new ActionListener() {
            /*  Button - toggle the state of the "requested" flag, to draw or
             *  not to draw.
             */
            public void actionPerformed(ActionEvent e) {
                String arg = e.getActionCommand();
                // Invert the state of the draw request.
                requested = !requested;
                do_the_work();
            }
        });
    }

    /** paint() is an AWT Component method, called when the
     * component needs to be painted.
     */
    public void do_the_work() {
        /* If the Draw button is selected, draw something */
        if (requested) {
            showStatus("Welcome to Java!");
        } else {
            showStatus("");     // retract welcome? :-)
        }
```

```
        }
}
```

If we run it in my `AppletViewer`,[1] it shows up as a window with just the Draw button showing; if you click the button an odd number of times, the screen shows the welcome label (Figure 23-2).

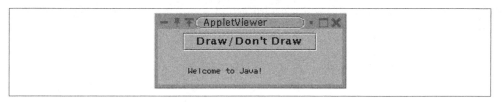

Figure 23-2. My AppletViewer showing simple applet

Example 23-24 is the code for the main part of the `AppletViewer`, which creates a `JFrame` and then loads the `Applet` class dynamically and adds it to the `JFrame`.

Example 23-24. AppletViewer.java main program

```
public class AppletViewer {
    /** The main Frame of this program */
    JFrame f;
    /** The AppletAdapter (gives AppletStub, AppletContext, showStatus) */
    static AppletAdapter aa = null;
    /** The name of the Applet subclass */
    String appName = null;
    /** The Class for the actual applet type */
    Class<?> ac = null;
    /** The Applet instance we are running, or null. Can not be a JApplet
     * until all the entire world is converted to JApplet. */
    Applet ai = null;
    /** The width of the Applet */
    final int WIDTH = 250;
    /** The height of the Applet */
    final int HEIGHT = 200;

    /** Main is where it all starts.
     * Construct the GUI. Load the Applet. Start it running.
     */
    public static void main(String[] av) {
        new AppletViewer(av.length==0?"HelloApplet":av[0]);
    }
```

---

1. My `AppletViewer` doesn't parse HTML like the real one does, so you invoke it with just the name of the `Applet` subclass on its command line. The size is therefore hardcoded, at least until somebody gets around to writing code to extract the `class`, `width`, and `height` attributes from the `applet` tag in the HTML page like the real McCoy does.

```
/** Construct the GUI for an Applet Viewer */
AppletViewer(String appName) {
    super();

    this.appName = appName;

    f = new JFrame("AppletViewer");
    f.addWindowListener(new WindowAdapter() {
        public void windowClosing(WindowEvent e) {
            f.setVisible(false);
            f.dispose();
            System.exit(0);
        }
    });
    Container cp = f.getContentPane();
    cp.setLayout(new BorderLayout());

    // Instantiate the AppletAdapter which gives us
    // AppletStub and AppletContext.
    if (aa == null)
        aa = new AppletAdapter();

    // The AppletAdapter also gives us showStatus.
    // Therefore, must add() it very early on, since the Applet's
    // Constructor or its init() may use showStatus()
    cp.add(BorderLayout.SOUTH, aa);

    showStatus("Loading Applet " + appName);

    loadApplet(appName , WIDTH, HEIGHT);    // sets ac and ai
    if (ai == null)
        return;

    // Now right away, tell the Applet how to find showStatus et al.
    ai.setStub(aa);

    // Connect the Applet to the Frame.
    cp.add(BorderLayout.CENTER, ai);

    Dimension d = ai.getSize();
    d.height += aa.getSize().height;
    f.setSize(d);
    f.setVisible(true);             // make the Frame and all in it appear

    showStatus("Applet " + appName + " loaded");

    // Here we pretend to be a browser!
    ai.init();
    ai.start();
}
```

```
/*
 * Load the Applet into memory. Should do caching.
 */
void loadApplet(String appletName, int w, int h) {
    // appletName = ... extract from the HTML CODE= somehow ...;
    // width =          ditto
    // height =         ditto
    try {
        // get a Class object for the Applet subclass
        ac = Class.forName(appletName);
        // Construct an instance (as if using no-argument constructor)
        ai = (Applet) ac.newInstance();
    } catch(ClassNotFoundException e) {
        showStatus("Applet subclass " + appletName + " did not load");
        return;
    } catch (Exception e ){
        showStatus("Applet " + appletName + " did not instantiate");
        return;
    }
    ai.setSize(w, h);
}

public void showStatus(String s) {
    aa.getAppletContext().showStatus(s);
}
}
```

For `Applet` methods to work, two additional classes must be defined: `AppletStub` and `AppletContext`. The `AppletStub` is the tie-in between the applet and the browser, and the `AppletContext` is a set of methods used by the applet. In a real browser, they are probably implemented separately, but I have combined them into one class (see Example 23-25). Note that the scope of applets that will work without throwing exceptions is rather limited, because so many of the methods here are, at present, dummied out. This `AppletViewer` is not a full replacement for the standard `AppletViewer`; it has been tested only with a basic Hello World applet, and it is simply provided as a starting point for those who want to fill in the gaps and make a full-blown applet viewer program or some other reflection-based tool that works in a similar fashion.

Example 23-25. AppletAdapter.java, partial AppletStub, and AppletContext

```
public class AppletAdapter extends Panel implements AppletStub, AppletContext {

    private static final long serialVersionUID = 1L;
    /** The status window at the bottom */
    Label status = null;

    /** Construct the GUI for an Applet Status window */
    AppletAdapter() {
        super();
```

```java
        // Must do this very early on, since the Applet's
        // Constructor or its init() may use showStatus()
        add(status = new Label());

        // Give "status" the full width
        status.setSize(getSize().width, status.getSize().height);

        showStatus("AppletAdapter constructed");    // now it can be said
    }

    /***************** AppletStub *********************/
    /** Called when the applet wants to be resized.  */
    public void appletResize(int w, int h) {
        // applet.setSize(w, h);
    }

    /** Gets a reference to the applet's context.  */
    public AppletContext getAppletContext() {
        return this;
    }

    /** Gets the base URL.  */
    public URL getCodeBase() {
        return getClass().getResource(".");
    }

    /** Gets the document URL.  */
    public URL getDocumentBase() {
        return getClass().getResource(".");
    }

    /** Returns the value of the named parameter in the HTML tag.  */
    public String getParameter(String name) {
        String value = null;
        return value;
    }
    /** Determines if the applet is active.  */
    public boolean isActive() {
        return true;
    }


    /********************** AppletContext **********************/

    /** Finds and returns the applet with the given name. */
    public Applet getApplet(String an) {
        return null;
    }

    /** Finds all the applets in the document
     * XXX NOT REALLY IMPLEMENTED
     */
    public Enumeration<Applet> getApplets()  {
```

```
        class AppletLister implements Enumeration<Applet> {
            public boolean hasMoreElements() {
                return false;
            }
            public Applet nextElement() {
                return null;
            }
        }
        return new AppletLister();
    }

    /** Create an audio clip for the given URL of a .au file */
    public AudioClip getAudioClip(URL u) {
        return null;
    }

    /** Look up and create an Image object that can be paint()ed */
    public Image getImage(URL u)  {
        return null;
    }

    /** Request to overlay the current page with a new one - ignored */
    public void showDocument(URL u) {
    }

    /** as above but with a Frame target */
    public void showDocument(URL u, String frame)  {
    }

    /** Called by the Applet to display a message in the bottom line */
    public void showStatus(String msg) {
        if (msg == null)
            msg = "";
        status.setText(msg);
    }

    /* StreamKey stuff - new in JDK1.4 */
    Map<String,InputStream> streamMap = new HashMap<>();

    /** Associate the stream with the key. */
    public void setStream(String key, InputStream stream) throws IOException {
        streamMap.put(key, stream);
    }

    public InputStream getStream(String key) {
        return (InputStream)streamMap.get(key);
    }

    public Iterator<String> getStreamKeys() {
        return streamMap.keySet().iterator();
    }
}
```

It is left as an exercise for the reader to implement `getImage()` and other methods in terms of other recipes used in this book.

See Also

We have not investigated all the ins and outs of reflection or the `ClassLoader` mechanism, but by now you should have a basic idea of how it works.

Perhaps the most important omissions are `SecurityManager` and `ProtectionDomain`. Only one `SecurityManager` can be installed in a given instance of the JVM (e.g., to prevent a malicious applet from providing its own!). A browser, for example, provides a `SecurityManager` that is far more restrictive than the standard one. Writing such a `SecurityManager` is left as an exercise for the reader—an important exercise for anyone planning to load classes over the Internet! (For more information about security managers and the Java Security APIs, see *Java Security* by Scott Oaks (O'Reilly). A `ProtectionDomain` can be provided with a `ClassLoader` to specify all the permissions needed for the class to run.

I've also left unexplored many topics in the JVM; see the (somewhat dated) O'Reilly books *Java Virtual Machine* and *Java Language*, or Sun/Oracle's *Java Language Specification* and *JVM Specification* documents (both updated with new releases, and available online (*http://docs.oracle.com/javase/specs*)) for a lifetime of reading enjoyment and edification!

The Apache Software Foundation maintains a vast array of useful software packages that are free to get and use. Source code is always available without charge from its website. Two packages you might want to investigate include the Commons BeanUtils and the Byte Code Engineering Library (BCEL). The Commons BeanUtils (*http://bit.ly/1q7MvNs*) claims to provide easier-to-use wrappers around some of the Reflection API. BCEL is a third-party toolkit for building and manipulating "bytecode" class files. Written by Markus Dahm, BCEL has become part of the Apache Commons Project (*http://bit.ly/1lqln94*).

## CHAPTER 24

Using Java with Other Languages

24.0. Introduction

Java has several methods of running programs written in other languages. You can invoke a compiled program or executable script using `Runtime.exec()`, as I'll describe in Recipe 24.1. There is an element of system dependency here, because you can only run external applications under the operating system they are compiled for. Alternatively, you can invoke one of a number of scripting languages (or "dynamic languages") —running the gamut: awk, bsh, Clojure, Ruby, Perl, Python, Scala—using `javax.script`, as illustrated in Recipe 24.3. Or you can drop down to C level with Java's "native code" mechanism and call compiled functions written in C/C++; see Recipe 24.6. From native code, you can call to functions written in just about any language. Not to mention that you can contact programs written in any language over a socket (see Chapter 16), with HTTP services (see Chapter 16), or with Java clients in RMI or CORBA clients in a variety of languages.

There is a wide range of other JVM languages, including:

- BeanShell, a general scripting language for Java.
- Groovy (*http://groovy.codehaus.org*) is a Java-based scripting language that pioneered the use of closures in the Java language ecosystem. It also has a rapid-development web package called Grails (*http://grails.org*) and a build tool called Gradle (see Recipe 1.8).
- Jython (*http://jython.org*), a full Java implementation of Python.
- JRuby (*http://jruby.org*), a full Java implementation of the Ruby language.
- Scala (*http://scala-lang.org*), a "best of functional and OO" language for the JVM.
- Clojure (*http://clojure.org*), a predominantly functional Lisp-1 dialect for the JVM.

- Renjin (pronounced "R Engine") (*http://renjin.org*), a fairly complete open source clone of the R statistics package with the ability to scale to the cloud.

These are JVM-centric and some can be called directly from Java to script or vice versa, without using `javax.script`. A list of these can be found at Wikipedia (*http://bit.ly/1phtZAo*).

24.1. Running an External Program from Java

Problem

You want to run an external program from within a Java program.

Solution

Use one of the `exec()` methods in the `java.lang.Runtime` class. Or set up a `Process-Builder` and call its `start()` method.

Discussion

The `exec()` method in the `Runtime` class lets you run an external program. The command line you give is broken into strings by a simple `StringTokenizer` (see Recipe 3.2) and passed on to the operating system's "execute a program" system call. As an example, here is a simple program that uses `exec()` to run *kwrite*, a windowed text editor program.[1] On Windows, you'd have to change the name to `notepad` or `wordpad`, possibly including the full pathname; for example, *c:/windows/notepad.exe* (you can also use backslashes, but be careful to double them because the backslash is special in Java strings):

```
public class ExecDemoSimple {
    public static void main(String av[]) throws Exception {

        // Run the "notepad" program or a similar editor
        Process p = Runtime.getRuntime().exec("kwrite");

        p.waitFor();
    }
}
```

When you compile and run it, the appropriate editor window appears:

```
$ javac -d . ExecDemoSimple.java
$ java otherlang.ExecDemoSimple # causes a KWrite window to appear.
$
```

---

1. *kwrite* is Unix-specific; it's a part of the K Desktop Environment (KDE) (*http://www.kde.org*).

This version of exec() assumes that the pathname contains no blanks because these break proper operation of the StringTokenizer. To overcome this potential problem, use an overloaded form of exec(), taking an array of strings as arguments. Example 24-1 runs the Windows or Unix version of Netscape, assuming Netscape was installed in the default directory. It passes the name of a help file as an argument, offering a kind of primitive help mechanism, as displayed in Figure 24-1.

Example 24-1. ExecDemoNS.java

```java
public class ExecDemoNS extends JFrame {
    private static final String NETSCAPE = "netscape";

    /** The name of the help file. */
    protected final static String HELPFILE = "./help/index.html";

    /** A stack of process objects; each entry tracks one external running process */
    Stack<Process> pStack = new Stack<>();

    /** main - instantiate and run */
    public static void main(String av[]) throws Exception {
        String program = av.length == 0 ? NETSCAPE : av[0];
        new ExecDemoNS(program).setVisible(true);
    }

    /** The path to the binary executable that we will run */
    protected static String program;

    /** Constructor - set up strings and things. */
    public ExecDemoNS(String prog) {
        super("ExecDemo: " + prog);
        String osname = System.getProperty("os.name");
        if (osname == null)
            throw new IllegalArgumentException("no os.name");
        if (prog.equals(NETSCAPE))
            program = // Windows or UNIX only for now, sorry Mac fans
                (osname.toLowerCase().indexOf("windows")!=-1) ?
                "c:/program files/netscape/communicator/program/netscape.exe" :
                "/usr/local/netscape/netscape";
        else
            program = prog;

        Container cp = getContentPane();
        cp.setLayout(new FlowLayout());
        JButton b;
        cp.add(b=new JButton("Exec"));
        b.addActionListener(new ActionListener() {
            public void actionPerformed(ActionEvent evt) {
                runProg();
            }
        });
        cp.add(b=new JButton("Wait"));
```

```
        b.addActionListener(new ActionListener() {
            public void actionPerformed(ActionEvent evt) {
                doWait();
            }
        });
        cp.add(b=new JButton("Exit"));
        b.addActionListener(new ActionListener() {
            public void actionPerformed(ActionEvent evt) {
                System.exit(0);
            }
        });
        pack();
    }

    /** Start the help, in its own Thread. */
    public void runProg() {

        new Thread() {
            public void run() {

                try {
                    // Get the URL for the Help File
                    URL helpURL = this.getClass().getClassLoader().
                        getResource(HELPFILE);

                    // Start Netscape from the Java Application.

                    pStack.push(Runtime.getRuntime().exec(program + " " + helpURL));

                    Debug.println("trace", "In main after exec " + pStack.size());

                } catch (Exception ex) {
                    JOptionPane.showMessageDialog(ExecDemoNS.this,
                        "Error" + ex, "Error",
                        JOptionPane.ERROR_MESSAGE);
                }
            }
        }.start();

    }

    public void doWait() {
        if (pStack.size() == 0) return;
        Debug.println("trace", "Waiting for process " + pStack.size());
        try {
            pStack.peek().waitFor();
            // wait for process to complete
            // (may not work as expected for some old Windows programs)
            Debug.println("trace", "Process " + pStack.size() + " is done");
        } catch (Exception ex) {
            JOptionPane.showMessageDialog(this,
                "Error" + ex, "Error",
```

```
                JOptionPane.ERROR_MESSAGE);
        }
        pStack.pop();
    }

}
```

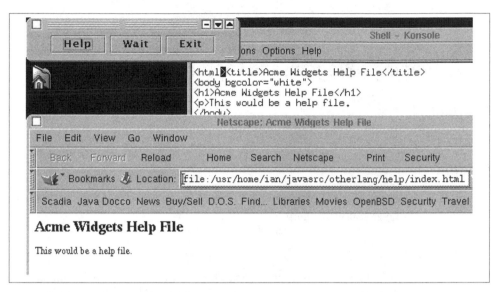

Figure 24-1. ExecDemoNS in action

A newer class, `ProcessBuilder`, replaces most nontrivial uses of `Runtime.exec()`. This `ProcessBuilder` uses Generic Collections to let you modify or replace the environment, as shown in Example 24-2.

Example 24-2. ProcessBuilderDemo.java

```
        List<String> command = new ArrayList<>();          ❶
        command.add("notepad");
        command.add("foo.txt");
        ProcessBuilder builder = new ProcessBuilder(command); ❷
        builder.environment().put("PATH",
                "/windows;/windows/system32;/winnt");       ❸
        final Process godot = builder.directory(
            new File(System.getProperty("user.home"))).      ❹
            start();
        System.err.println("Waiting for Godot");            ❺
        godot.waitFor();                                    ❻
```

❶   Set up the command-line argument list: editor program name and filename.

❷   Use that to start configuring the `ProcessBuilder`.

❸ Configure the builder's environment to a list of common MS Windows directories.

❹ Set the initial directory to the user's home, and start the process!

❺ I always wanted to be able to use this line in code.

❻ Wait for the end of our little play.

For more on `ProcessBuilder`, see the javadoc for `java.lang.ProcessBuilder`.

24.2. Running a Program and Capturing Its Output

Problem

You want to run a program but also capture its output.

Solution

Use the `Process` object's `getInputStream()`; read and copy the contents to `System.out` or wherever you want them.

Discussion

The original notion of standard output and standard error was that they would always be connected to "the terminal"; this notion dates from an earlier time when almost all computer users worked at the command line. Today, a program's standard and error output does not always automatically appear anywhere. Arguably, there should be an automatic way to make this happen. But for now, you need to add a few lines of code to grab the program's output and print it:

```
public class ExecDemoLs {
    /** The program to run */
    public static final String PROGRAM = "ls"; // "dir" for Windows
    /** Set to true to end the loop */
    static volatile boolean done = false;

    public static void main(String argv[]) throws IOException {

        final Process p;        // Process tracks one external native process
        BufferedReader is;      // reader for output of process
        String line;

        p = Runtime.getRuntime().exec(PROGRAM);

        Debug.println("exec", "In Main after exec");

        // Optional: start a thread to wait for the process to terminate.
        // Don't just wait in main line, but here set a "done" flag and
```

```
            // use that to control the main reading loop below.
            Thread waiter = new Thread() {
                public void run() {
                    try {
                        p.waitFor();
                    } catch (InterruptedException ex) {
                        // OK, just quit.
                        return;
                    }
                    System.out.println("Program terminated!");
                    done = true;
                }
            };
            waiter.start();

            // getInputStream gives an Input stream connected to
            // the process p's standard output (and vice versa). We use
            // that to construct a BufferedReader so we can readLine() it.
            is = new BufferedReader(new InputStreamReader(p.getInputStream()));

            while (!done && ((line = is.readLine()) != null))
                System.out.println(line);

            Debug.println("exec", "In Main after EOF");

            return;
        }
    }
```

This is such a common occurrence that I've packaged it up into a class called ExecAnd-
Print, which is part of my com.darwinsys.lang package. ExecAndPrint has several
overloaded forms of its run() method (see the documentation for details), but they all
take at least a command and optionally an output file to which the command's output
is written. Example 24-3 shows the code for some of these methods.

Example 24-3. ExecAndPrint.java (partial listing)

```
/** Need a Runtime object for any of these methods */
protected final static Runtime r = Runtime.getRuntime();

/** Run the command given as a String, printing its output to System.out */
public static int run(String cmd) throws IOException {
    return run(cmd, new OutputStreamWriter(System.out));
}

/** Run the command given as a String, print its output to "out" */
public static int run(String cmd, Writer out) throws IOException {

    Process p = r.exec(cmd);

    FileIO.copyFile(new InputStreamReader(p.getInputStream()), out, true);
    try {
```

```
        p.waitFor();     // wait for process to complete
    } catch (InterruptedException e) {
        return -1;
    }
    return p.exitValue();
}
```

As a simple example of using exec() directly along with ExecAndPrint, I'll create three temporary files, list them (directory listing), and then delete them. When I run the ExecDemoFiles program, it lists the three files it has created:

```
-rw-------  1 ian   wheel   0 Jan 29 14:29 file1
-rw-------  1 ian   wheel   0 Jan 29 14:29 file2
-rw-------  1 ian   wheel   0 Jan 29 14:29 file3
```

Its source code is in Example 24-4.

Example 24-4. ExecDemoFiles.java

```
// Get and save the Runtime object.
Runtime rt = Runtime.getRuntime();

// Create three temporary files (the slow way!)
rt.exec("mktemp file1");
rt.exec("mktemp file2");
rt.exec("mktemp file3");

// Run the "ls" (directory lister) program
// with its output sent into a file
String[] args = { "ls", "-l", "file1", "file2", "file3" };
ExecAndPrint.run(args);

rt.exec("rm file1 file2 file3");
```

A process isn't necessarily destroyed when the Java program that created it exits or bombs out. Simple text-based programs will be, but window-based programs like *kwrite*, Netscape, or even a Java-based JFrame application will not. For example, our ExecDemoNS program started Netscape, and when ExecDemoNS's Exit button is clicked, ExecDemoNS exits but Netscape stays running. What if you want to be sure a process has completed? The Process object has a waitFor() method that lets you do so, and an exitValue() method that tells you the "return code" from the process. Finally, should you wish to forcibly terminate the other process, you can do so with the Process object's destroy() method, which takes no argument and returns no value. Example 24-5 is ExecDemoWait, a program that runs whatever program you name on the command line (along with arguments), captures the program's standard output, and waits for the program to terminate.

Example 24-5. ExecDemoWait.java

```java
// A Runtime object has methods for dealing with the OS
Runtime r = Runtime.getRuntime();
Process p;          // Process tracks one external native process
BufferedReader is;    // reader for output of process
String line;

// Our argv[0] contains the program to run; remaining elements
// of argv contain args for the target program. This is just
// what is needed for the String[] form of exec.
p = r.exec(argv);

System.out.println("In Main after exec");

// getInputStream gives an Input stream connected to
// the process p's standard output. Just use it to make
// a BufferedReader to readLine() what the program writes out.
is = new BufferedReader(new InputStreamReader(p.getInputStream()));

while ((line = is.readLine()) != null)
    System.out.println(line);

System.out.println("In Main after EOF");
System.out.flush();
try {
    p.waitFor();     // wait for process to complete
} catch (InterruptedException e) {
    System.err.println(e);     // "Can'tHappen"
    return;
}
System.err.println("Process done, exit status was " + p.exitValue());
```

See Also

You wouldn't normally use any form of exec() to run one Java program from another in this way; instead, you'd probably create it as a thread within the same process, because this is generally quite a bit faster (the Java interpreter is already up and running, so why wait for another copy of it to start up?). See Chapter 22.

When building industrial-strength applications, note the cautionary remarks in the Java API docs for the Process class concerning the danger of losing some of the I/O due to insufficient buffering by the operating system.

24.3. Calling Other Languages via javax.script

Problem

You want to invoke a script written in some other language from within your Java program, running in the JVM, with the ability to pass variables directly to/from the other language.

Solution

If the script you want is written in any of the two-dozen-plus supported languages, just use `javax.script`. Languages include awk, perl, python, Ruby, BeanShell, PNuts, Ksh/Bash, R ("Renjin"), several implementations of JavaScript, and more.

Discussion

Example 24-6 is a very simple demo where we know the name of the scripting engine we want to use. R (*http://www.r-project.org*) is a well-known statistical computing/scripting language, itself cloned from Bell Labs' "S" language. Renjin (*http://www.renjin.org*) is a pure-Java reimplementation of R.

Example 24-6. RenjinScripting.java

```
/**
 * Demonstrate interacting with the "R" implementation called "Renjin"
 */
public static void main(String[] args) throws ScriptException {
    ScriptEngineManager manager = new ScriptEngineManager();
    ScriptEngine engine = manager.getEngineByName("Renjin");
    engine.put("a", 42);
    Object ret = engine.eval("b <- 2; a*b");
    System.out.println(ret);
}
```

Because R treats all numbers as floating point, like many interpreters, the value printed is `84.0`.

You can also find out the installed scripting engines and pick one that is on your classpath. The `ScriptEnginesDemo` program in Example 24-7 lists the installed engines, and runs a simple script in the default language, ECMAScript (aka JavaScript).

Example 24-7. ScriptEnginesDemo.java

```
public class ScriptEnginesDemo {

    public static void main(String[] args) throws ScriptException {
        ScriptEngineManager scriptEngineManager = new ScriptEngineManager();

        // Print list of supported languages
```

```
    scriptEngineManager.getEngineFactories().forEach(factory ->
        System.out.println(factory.getLanguageName()));

    // Run a script in the JavaScript language
    String lang = "ECMAScript";
    ScriptEngine engine =
        scriptEngineManager.getEngineByName(lang);
    if (engine == null) {
        System.err.println("Could not find engine");
        return;
    }
    engine.eval("print(\"Hello from " + lang + "\");");
    }
}
```

See Also

To see the full list of languages, and download the "script engines"—the interfaces from Java to each of the languages—visit the Oracle page (*http://bit.ly/UwuoUx*) or the *java.net* page (*http://bit.ly/1xOyZAt*).

At present, the website is borked; to view the list of engines at *Java.net* (*http://bit.ly/ UwutHU*) you have to save the file and open it manually; the web server dishes it with the wrong content type.

The list maintained as part of the scripting project per se can be found at the source code repository, by viewing *Java.net* (*http://bit.ly/1ubXIKI*). A dozen or so other engines are maintained by others outside this project; for example, there is a Perl5 script engine from Google (*http://bit.ly/1xOA2jQ*).

24.4. Roll Your Own Scripting Engine

Problem

You like javax.script but there isn't yet a script engine for your favorite language.

Solution

Roll your own: implement ScriptEngine and ScriptEngineFactory and add one trivial configuration file.

Discussion

Hooking into an existing Scripting language sounds easy. It may or may not be, depending on the language. Before you do implement one, check the set of languages available at Java's website (*https://java.net/projects/scripting*).

ScriptEngine is a fairly simple interface, with just over a dozen methods, of which six are overloads of the popular eval method. There is an AbstractScriptEngine that handles all these overloads and some other bookkeeping, leaving only four abstract methods. When you extend AbstractScriptEngine, you only are required to implement four methods:

```java
public class CalcScriptEngine extends AbstractScriptEngine {

    private ScriptEngineFactory factory;

    CalcScriptEngine(ScriptEngineFactory factory) {
        super();
        this.factory = factory;
    }

    @Override
    public Object eval(String script, ScriptContext context)
            throws ScriptException {
        System.out.println("CalcScriptEngine.eval(): Running: " + script);
        Stack<Integer> stack = new Stack<>();
        StringTokenizer st = new StringTokenizer(script);
        while (st.hasMoreElements()) {
            String tok = st.nextToken();
            if (tok.equals("+")) {
                return stack.pop() + stack.pop();
            }
            if (tok.equals("-")) {
                final Integer tos = stack.pop();
                return stack.pop() - tos;
            }
            if (tok.equals("*")) {
                return stack.pop() * stack.pop();
            }
            if (tok.equals("/")) {
                final Integer tos = stack.pop();
                return stack.pop() / tos;
            }
            // else ... check for other operators
            // If nothing else, must be a name. get and stack its value
            stack.push((Integer) context.getAttribute(tok));
        }
        return 0;
    }

    @Override
    public Object eval(Reader reader, ScriptContext context)
            throws ScriptException {
        System.out.println("CalcScriptEngine.eval()");
        // should read the file into a String, then
        // return eval(scriptString, context);
        throw new IllegalStateException("eval(Reader) not written yet");
```

```
        }

        @Override
        public Bindings createBindings() {
            Bindings ret = new SimpleBindings();
            return ret;
        }

        @Override
        public ScriptEngineFactory getFactory() {
            return factory;
        }
    }
```

A slightly longer file is the required `ScriptEngineFactory` implementation:

```
public class CalcScriptEngineFactory implements ScriptEngineFactory {

    private static final String THY_NAME = "SimpleCalc";

    @Override
    public String getEngineName() {
        return THY_NAME;
    }

    @Override
    public String getEngineVersion() {
        return "0.1";
    }

    @Override
    public String getLanguageName() {
        return THY_NAME;
    }


    @Override
    public List<String> getExtensions() {
        ArrayList<String> ret = new ArrayList<>(1);
        ret.add("calc");
        return ret;
    }

    @Override
    public List<String> getMimeTypes() {
        ArrayList<String> ret = new ArrayList<String>(0);
        return ret;
    }

    @Override
    public List<String> getNames() {
        ArrayList<String> ret = new ArrayList<String>(1);
        ret.add(THY_NAME);
```

```
        return ret;
    }

    @Override
    public String getLanguageVersion() {
        return "0.1";
    }

    @Override
    public Object getParameter(String key) {
        switch(key) {
        case ScriptEngine.ENGINE:
            return getEngineName();
        case ScriptEngine.ENGINE_VERSION:
            return getEngineVersion();
        case ScriptEngine.LANGUAGE:
            return getLanguageName();
        case ScriptEngine.LANGUAGE_VERSION:
            return getLanguageVersion();
        default:
            throw new IllegalArgumentException("Unknown parameter " + key);
        }
    }

    @Override
    public String getMethodCallSyntax(String obj, String m, String... args) {
        // TODO Auto-generated method stub
        return null;
    }

    @Override
    public String getOutputStatement(String toDisplay) {
        return toDisplay;
    }

    @Override
    public String getProgram(String... statements) {
        return statements.toString();
    }

    @Override
    public ScriptEngine getScriptEngine() {
        return new CalcScriptEngine(this);
    }

}
```

Finally, a configuration file is required. This file must be named exactly *jav-ax.script.ScriptEngineFactory* and must be located precisely in the *META-INF/services* directory of the same classpath element as your JAR files. This file must contain exactly one line with just the full name of your factory class. For example:

```
otherlang.calcscriptengine.CalcScriptEngineFactory
```

Of course, most scripts need parameters or "variables" passed in. The scripting demo implements the most trivial calculator, a four-function stack-based ("reverse Polish notation") integer calculator. Just enough to show that values are getting in and the value back out. For example, if the script input is

```
+i j *+
```

that is an instruction to get the values i and j and multiply them together. Then these variables' values have to be passed in before the script can execute successfully; that is the function of the

```
engine.put("i", 99);
engine.put("j", 1);
```

in the demo program. The one eval() overload that's implemented puts numbers into a stack and, when an operator is found, pops two values off the stack and performs one of the four basic operators that are implemented, and stacks and returns the value. Obviously it's not usable for anything at this stage, but it shows the mechanism for getting values in and out. Oh, and it gets the correct answer:

```
CalcScriptEngine.eval(): Running: i j +
Script returned 100
```

As an advanced feature, if you are writing an engine for a scripting language that supports compiling scripts into some kind of saveable file format (as javac produces *.class* files, python produces *.pyc*, etc.) you should investigate the Compilable and Invocable interfaces.

This example can be run as part of the *javasrc* repository (see Recipe 1.5). It is typical, but not required, to bundle up the two classes and the configuration file into a separate JAR file for distribution (and ease of installation).

You now have the ability to include arbitrary languages into your Java application. Before you do so, make sure there isn't already an implementation available, at the URL shown in the introduction to this recipe!

24.5. Marrying Java and Perl

Problem

You want to call Java from Perl.

Solution

To call Java from Perl, use the Perl Inline::Java module. To go the other way—calling Perl from Java—use javax.script, as in Recipe 24.3.

Discussion

Perl is often called a "glue language" that can be used to bring together diverse parts of the software world. But, in addition, it is a full-blown language in its own right for creating software. A wealth of extension modules provide ready-to-run solutions for quite diverse problems, and most of these modules are available free from CPAN, the Comprehensive Perl Archive Network (*http://www.cpan.org*). Also, as a scripting language, it is ideally suited for rapid prototyping. On the other hand, although building graphical user interfaces is definitely possible in Perl, it is not exactly one of the language's strengths. So you might want to construct your GUI using Java Swing, and, at the same time, reuse business logic implemented in Perl.

Fortunately, among the many CPAN modules, `Inline::Java` makes the integration of Perl and Java a breeze. Let's assume first that you want to call into Java from Perl. For business logic, I have picked a CPAN module that measures the similarity of two strings (the so-called *Levenshtein edit distance*). Example 24-8 shows the complete source. You need at least version 0.44 of the module `Inline::Java`; previous versions did not support threaded applications properly, so use of Swing wasn't possible.

Using the module this way requires that the Java source be included in the Perl script with special delimiters, as shown in Example 24-8.

Example 24-8. Swinging.pl

```
#! /usr/bin/perl
# Calling Java from Perl

use strict;
use warnings;

use Text::Levenshtein qw( );
  # Perl module from CPAN to measure string similarity

use Inline 0.44 "JAVA" => "DATA";  # pointer to the Inline java source
use Inline::Java qw(caught);  # helper function to determine exception type

my $show = new Showit;      # construct Java object using Perl syntax
$show->show("Just another Perl hacker");                # call method on that object

eval {
  # Call a method that will call back to Perl;
  # catch exceptions, if any.
  print "matcher: ", $show->match("Japh", shift||"Java"),
  " (displayed from Perl)\n";
};
if ($@) {
  print STDERR "Caught:", caught($@), "\n";
  die $@ unless caught("java.lang.Exception");
  print STDERR $@->getMessage( ), "\n";
}
```

```
__END__

__JAVA__
// Java starts here
import javax.swing.*;
import org.perl.inline.java.*;

class Showit extends InlineJavaPerlCaller {
  // extension only neeeded if calling back into Perl

  /** Simple Java class to be called from Perl, and to call back to Perl
   */
  public Showit( ) throws InlineJavaException { }

  /** Simple method */
  public void show(String str) {
    System.out.println(str + " inside Java");
  }

  /** Method calling back into Perl */
  public int match(String target, String pattern)
      throws InlineJavaException, InlineJavaPerlException {

    // Calling a function residing in a Perl Module
    String str = (String)CallPerl("Text::Levenshtein", "distance",
        new Object [] {target, pattern});

    // Show result
    JOptionPane.showMessageDialog(null, "Edit distance between '" + target +
        "' and '" + pattern + "' is " + str,
        "Swinging Perl", JOptionPane.INFORMATION_MESSAGE);
    return Integer.parseInt(str);
  }

}
```

In simple cases like this, you don't even need to write a separate Java source file: you combine all the code, Perl and Java alike, in one single file. You do not need to compile anything, either; just execute it by typing:

```
perl Swinging.pl
```

(You can also add a string argument.) After a little churning, a Java message box pops up, telling you that the distance between "Japh" and "Java" is 2. At the same time, your console shows the string "Just another Perl hacker inside Java." When you close the message box, you get the final result "matcher: 2 (displayed from Perl)."

In between, your Perl program has created an instance of the Java class Showit by calling its constructor. It then called that object's show( ) method to display a string from within Java. It then proceeded to call the match( ) method, but this time, something more complicated happens: the Java code calls back into Perl, accessing method distance of module Text::Levenshtein and passing it two strings as arguments. It receives the result, displays it in a message box, and finally, for good measure, returns it to the Perl main program that it had been called from.

Incidentally, the eval { } block around the method call is the Perlish way of catching exceptions. In this case, the exception is thrown from within Java.

If you restart the program, you will notice that startup time is much shorter, which is always good news. Why is that so? On the first call, Inline::Java took the input apart, precompiled the Java part, and saved it to disk (usually, in a subdirectory called _Inline_). On subsequent calls, it just makes sure that the Java source has not changed and then calls the class file that is already on disk. (Of course, if you surreptitiously changed the Java code, it is recompiled just as automagically.) Behind the scenes, even stranger things are going on, however. When the Perl script is executed, a Java server is constructed and started unbeknownst to the user, and the Perl part and the Java bits communicate through a TCP socket (see Chapter 16).

Marrying two platform-independent languages, like Perl and Java, in a portable way skirts many portability problems. When distributing inlined applications, be sure to supply not just the source files but also the contents of the _Inline_ directory. (It is advisable to purge that directory and to rebuild everything just before distribution time; otherwise, old compiled versions left lying around might make it into the distribution.) Each target machine needs to repeat the magic steps of Inline::Java, which requires a Java compiler. In any case, the Inline::Java module must be installed.

Because Perl has Inline modules for a number of other languages (ordinary languages like C, but others as exotic as Befunge), one might even consider using Perl as glue for interoperation between those other languages, jointly or separately, and Java. I am sure many happy hours can be spent working out the intricacies of such interactions.

See Also

You can find full information on Inline::Java on CPAN (*http://search.cpan.org*) or in the POD (plain old documentation) that is installed along with the module itself.

24.6. Calling Other Languages via Native Code

Problem

You wish to call native C/C++ functions from Java, either for efficiency or to access hardware- or system-specific features.

Solution

Use JNI, the Java Native Interface.

Discussion

Java lets you load native or compiled code into your Java program. Why would you want to do such a thing? The best reason would probably be to access OS-dependent functionality, or existing code written in another language. A less good reason would be speed: native code can sometimes run faster than Java, though this is becoming less important. Like everything else in Java, the "native code" mechanism is subject to security restrictions; for example, applets are not allowed to access native code.

The native code language bindings are defined for code written in C or C++. If you need to access a language other than C/C++, write a bit of C/C++ and have it pass control to other functions or applications, using any mechanism defined by your operating system.

Due to such system-dependent features as the interpretation of header files and the allocation of the processor's general-purpose registers, your native code may need to be compiled by the same C compiler used to compile the Java runtime for your platform. For example, on Solaris you can use SunPro C or maybe gcc. On Win32 platforms, use Microsoft visual C++ Version 4.x or higher (32 bit). For Linux and Mac OS X, you should be able to use the provided gcc-based compiler. For other platforms, see your Java vendor's documentation.

Also note that the details in this section are for the Java Native Interface (JNI) of Java 1.1 and later, which differs in some details from 1.0 and from Microsoft's native interface.

Ian's Basic Steps: Java Calling Native Code

To call native code from Java:

1. Write Java code that calls a native method.
2. Compile this Java code.
3. Create an *.h* file using *javah*.
4. Write a C function that does the work.
5. Compile the C code into a loadable object.
6. Try it!

The first step is to write Java code that calls a native method. To do this, use the keyword `native` to indicate that the method is native, and provide a static code block that loads your native method using `System.loadLibrary()`. (The dynamically loadable module is created in Step 5.) Static blocks are executed when the class containing them is loaded; loading the native code here ensures it is in memory when needed!

Object variables that your native code may modify should carry the `volatile` modifier. The file *HelloJni.java*, shown in Example 24-9, is a good starting point.

Example 24-9. HelloJni.java

```java
/**
 * A trivial class to show Java Native Interface 1.1 usage from Java.
 */
public class HelloJni {
  int myNumber = 42; // used to show argument passing

  // declare native class
  public native void displayHelloJni();

  // Application main, call its display method
  public static void main(String[] args) {
    System.out.println("HelloJni starting; args.length="+
                        args.length+"...");
    for (int i=0; i<args.length; i++)
                        System.out.println("args["+i+"]="+args[i]);
    HelloJni hw = new HelloJni();
    hw.displayHelloJni();// call the native function
    System.out.println("Back in Java, \"myNumber\" now " + hw.myNumber);
  }

  // Static code blocks are executed once, when class file is loaded
  static {
    System.loadLibrary("hello");
  }
}
```

The second step is simple; just use *javac HelloJni.java* as you normally would. You probably won't get any compilation errors on a simple program like this; if you do, correct them and try the compilation again.

Next, you need to create an *.h* file. Use *javah* to produce this file:

```
javah jni.HelloJni          // produces HelloJni.h
```

The *.h* file produced is a "glue" file, not really meant for human consumption and particularly not for editing. But by inspecting the resulting *.h* file, you'll see that the C method's name is composed of the name Java, the package name (if any), the class name, and the method name:

```
JNIEXPORT void JNICALL Java_HelloJni_displayHelloWorld(JNIEnv *env,
    jobject this);
```

Then create a C function that does the work. You must use the same function signature as is used in the *.h* file.

This function can do whatever it wants. Note that it is passed two arguments: a JVM environment variable and a handle for the this object. Table 24-1 shows the correspondence between Java types and the C types (JNI types) used in the C code.

Table 24-1. Java and JNI types

Java type	JNI	Java array type	JNI
byte	jbyte	byte[]	jbyteArray
short	jshort	short[]	jshortArray
int	jint	int[]	jintArray
long	jlong	long[]	jlongArray
float	jfloat	float[]	jfloatArray
double	jdouble	double[]	jdoubleArray
char	jchar	char[]	jcharArray
boolean	jboolean	boolean[]	jbooleanArray
void	jvoid		
Object	jobject	Object[]	jobjectArray
Class	jclass		
String	jstring		
array	jarray		
Throwable	jthrowable		

Example 24-10 is a complete C native implementation. Passed an object of type Hel-loJni, it increments the integer myNumber contained in the object.

Example 24-10. HelloJni.c

```c
#include <jni.h>
#include "HelloJni.h"
#include <stdio.h>
/*
 * This is the Java Native implementation of displayHelloJni.
 */
JNIEXPORT void JNICALL Java_HelloJni_displayHelloJni(JNIEnv *env, jobject this) {
  jfieldID fldid;
  jint n, nn;

  (void)printf("Hello from a Native Method\n");

  if (this == NULL) {
    fprintf(stderr, "'this.' pointer is null!\n");
    return;
  }
  if ((fldid = (*env)->GetFieldID(env,
        (*env)->GetObjectClass(env, this), "myNumber", "I")) == NULL) {
    fprintf(stderr, "GetFieldID failed");
```

```
      return;
  }

  n = (*env)->GetIntField(env, this, fldid);/* retrieve myNumber */
  printf("\"myNumber\" value is %d\n", n);

  (*env)->SetIntField(env, this, fldid, ++n);/* increment it! */
  nn = (*env)->GetIntField(env, this, fldid);

  printf("\"myNumber\" value now %d\n", nn); /* make sure */
  return;
}
```

Finally, you compile the C code into a loadable object. Naturally, the details depend on platform, compiler, etc. For example, on Windows:

```
> set JAVA_HOME=C:\java                # or wherever
> set INCLUDE=%JAVA_HOME%\include;%JAVA_HOME%\include\Win32;%INCLUDE%
> set LIB=%JAVA_HOME%\lib;%LIB%
> cl HelloJni.c -Fehello.dll -MD -LD
```

And on Unix:

```
$ export JAVAHOME=/local/java   # or wherever
$ cc -I$JAVAHOME/include -I$JAVAHOME/include/solaris \
      -G HelloJni.c -o libhello.so
```

Example 24-11 is a makefile for Unix.

Example 24-11. Unix makefile

```
# Makefile for the 1.1 Java Native Methods examples for
# Java Cookbook, originally for Learning Tree International Course 471/478.
# Tested on Solaris both with "gcc" and with SunSoft "cc".
# Tested on OpenBSD with native port "devel/jdk/1.2" and cc.
# On other platforms it will certainly need some tweaking; please
# let me know how much! :-)
# Ian Darwin, http://www.darwinsys.com

# Configuration Section

CFLAGS_FOR_SO = -G # Solaris
CFLAGS_FOR_SO = -shared
CSRCS         = HelloJni.c
# JAVA_HOME should be been set in the environment
#INCLUDES     = -I$(JAVA_HOME)/include -I$(JAVAHOME)/include/solaris
#INCLUDES     = -I$(JAVA_HOME)/include -I$(JAVAHOME)/include/openbsd
INCLUDES      = -I$(JAVA_HOME)/include

all:        testhello testjavafromc

# This part of the Makefile is for C called from Java, in HelloJni
testhello:      hello.all
        @echo
```

```
        @echo "Here we test the Java code \"HelloJni\" that calls C code."
        @echo
        LD_LIBRARY_PATH=`pwd`:. java HelloJni

hello.all:      HelloJni.class libhello.so

HelloJni.class: HelloJni.java
        javac HelloJni.java

HelloJni.h:     HelloJni.class
        javah -jni HelloJni

HelloJni.o::    HelloJni.h

libhello.so:    $(CSRCS) HelloJni.h
    $(CC) $(INCLUDES) $(CFLAGS_FOR_SO) $(CSRCS) -o libhello.so

# This part of the Makefile is for Java called from C, in javafromc
testjavafromc:  javafromc.all hello.all
    @echo
    @echo "Now we test HelloJni using javafromc instead of java"
    @echo
    ./javafromc HelloJni
    @echo
    @echo "That was, in case you didn't notice, C->Java->C. And,"
    @echo "incidentally, a replacement for JDK program \"java\" itself!"
    @echo


javafromc.all:  javafromc

javafromc:  javafromc.o
    $(CC) -L$(LIBDIR) javafromc.o -ljava -o $@

javafromc.o:    javafromc.c
    $(CC) -c $(INCLUDES) javafromc.c

clean:
    rm -f core *.class *.o *.so HelloJni.h
clobber: clean
    rm -f javafromc
```

And you're done! Just run the Java interpreter on the class file containing the main program. Assuming that you've set whatever system-dependent settings are necessary (possibly including both CLASSPATH and LD_LIBRARY_PATH or its equivalent), the program should run as follows:

```
C> java jni.HelloJni
Hello from a Native Method        // from C
"myNumber" value is 42            // from C
"myNumber" value now 43           // from C
Value of myNumber now 43          // from Java
```

Congratulations! You've called a native method. However, you've given up portability; the Java class file now requires you to build a loadable object for each operating system and hardware platform. Multiply {Windows, Mac OS X, Sun Solaris, HP/UX, Linux, OpenBSD, NetBSD, FreeBSD} times {Intel, Intel-64, AMD64, SPARC, PowerPC, HP-PA} and you begin to see the portability issues.

Beware that problems with your native code can and will crash the runtime process right out from underneath the Java Virtual Machine. The JVM can do nothing to protect itself from poorly written C/C++ code. Memory must be managed by the programmer; there is no automatic garbage collection of memory obtained by the system runtime allocator. You're dealing directly with the operating system and sometimes even the hardware, so, "Be careful. Be very careful."

See Also

If you need more information on Java Native Methods, you might be interested in the comprehensive treatment found in *Essential JNI: Java Native Interface* by Rob Gordon (Prentice Hall).

24.7. Calling Java from Native Code

Problem

2416.11bYou need to "go the other way," calling Java from C/C++ code.

Solution

Use JNI again.

Discussion

JNI (Java Native Interface) provides an interface for calling Java from C, with calls to:

1. Create a JVM
2. Load a class
3. Find and call a method from that class (e.g., main)

JNI lets you add Java to legacy code. That can be useful for a variety of purposes and lets you treat Java code as an extension language (just define or find an interface or class like `Applet` or `Servlet`, and let your customers implement it or subclass it).

The code in Example 24-12 takes a class name from the command line, starts up the JVM, and calls the `main()` method in the class.

Example 24-12. Calling Java from C

```c
/*
 * This is a C program that calls Java code.
 * This could be used as a model for building Java into an
 * existing application as an extention language, for example.
 */

#include <stdio.h>
#include <jni.h>

int
main(int argc, char *argv[]) {
    int i;
    JavaVM *jvm;         /* The Java VM we will use */
    JNIEnv *myEnv;         /* pointer to native environment */
    JDK1_1InitArgs jvmArgs; /* JNI initialization arguments */
    jclass myClass, stringClass;    /* pointer to the class type */
    jmethodID myMethod;      /* pointer to the main() method */
    jarray args;         /* becomes an array of Strings */
    jthrowable tossed;     /* Exception object, if we get one. */

    JNI_GetDefaultJavaVMInitArgs(&jvmArgs);    /* set up the argument pointer */
    /* Could change values now, like: jvmArgs.classpath = ...; */

    /* initialize the JVM! */
    if (JNI_CreateJavaVM(&jvm, &myEnv, &jvmArgs) < 0) {
        fprintf(stderr, "CreateJVM failed\n");
        exit(1);
    }

    /* find the class named in argv[1] */
    if ((myClass = (*myEnv)->FindClass(myEnv, argv[1])) == NULL) {
        fprintf(stderr, "FindClass %s failed\n", argv[1]);
        exit(1);
    }

    /* find the static void main(String[]) method of that class */
    myMethod = (*myEnv)->GetStaticMethodID(
        myEnv, myClass, "main", "([Ljava/lang/String;)V");
    /* myMethod = (*myEnv)->GetMethodID(myEnv, myClass, "test", "(I)I"); */
    if (myMethod == NULL) {
        fprintf(stderr, "GetStaticMethodID failed\n");
        exit(1);
    }

    /* Since we're calling main, must pass along the command line arguments,
     * in the form of Java String array
     */
    if ((stringClass = (*myEnv)->FindClass(myEnv, "java/lang/String")) == NULL){
        fprintf(stderr, "get of String class failed!!\n");
        exit(1);
    }
```

```
    /* make an array of Strings, subtracting 1 for progname & 1 for the
     * java class name */
    if ((args = (*myEnv)->NewObjectArray(myEnv, argc-2, stringClass, NULL))==NULL) {
        fprintf(stderr, "Create array failed!\n");
        exit(1);
    }

    /* fill the array */
    for (i=2; i<argc; i++)
        (*myEnv)->SetObjectArrayElement(myEnv,
            args, i-2, (*myEnv)->NewStringUTF(myEnv, argv[i]));

    /* finally, call the method. */
    (*myEnv)->CallStaticVoidMethodA(myEnv, myClass, myMethod, &args);

    /* And check for exceptions */
    if ((tossed = (*myEnv)->ExceptionOccurred(myEnv)) != NULL) {
        fprintf(stderr, "%s: Exception detected:\n", argv[0]);
        (*myEnv)->ExceptionDescribe(myEnv);    /* writes on stderr */
        (*myEnv)->ExceptionClear(myEnv);    /* OK, we're done with it. */
    }

    (*jvm)->DestroyJavaVM(jvm);    /* no error checking as we're done anyhow */
    return 0;
}
```

Afterword

Writing—and updating—this book has been a humbling experience. It has taken far longer than I had predicted, or than I would like to admit. And, of course, it's not finished yet. Despite my best efforts and those of the technical reviewers, editors, and many other talented folks, a book this size is bound to contain errors, omissions, and passages that are less clear than they might be. Do let us know if you happen across any of these things; you can enter them at the book's errata page (*http://bit.ly/java-cookbook-3e*). Subsequent editions will incorporate changes sent in by readers just like you!

It has been said that you don't really know something until you've taught it. I have found this true of lecturing, and find it equally true of writing.

I tell my students that when Java was very young, it was possible for one person to study hard and know almost everything about Java. After a release or two, this was no longer true. Today, nobody in his or her right mind would seriously claim to "know all about Java"—if they do, it should cause your "bogosity" detector to go off at full volume. And the amount you need to know keeps growing. How can you keep up? Java books? Java magazines? Java courses? Conferences? There is no single answer; all of these are useful to some people. Oracle and others have programs that you should be aware of:

- JavaOne (*http://oracle.com/javaone*), the annual Java conference.

- The Oracle Java Technology Network (*http://bit.ly/1oieaLZ*), a free web-based service for getting the latest APIs, news, and views.

- Over Java's lifetime, the publishing industry has changed a lot. There used to be several Java-related magazines published in print, some of whose articles would appear on the Web. Today there are, so far as I know, no print magazines dedicated to Java. Oracle currently (2014) publishes the online-only *Java Magazine* every two months with technical articles on many aspects of Java; see the magazine's website (*http://bit.ly/1lqmMMX*) to download a PDF of the latest issue.

- The Java Community Process (*http://jcp.org*), the home of Java standardization and enhancement

- The OpenJDK community (*http://openjdk.java.net*) maintains and builds the open source version of the "official" JDK

- O'Reilly books (*http://java.oreilly.com*) and conferences (*http://conferences.oreilly.com*) are among the very best available!

- I keep my own list of Java Resources that I update sporadically, on my Java site (*http://darwinsys.com/java*); follow the link to Java Resources.

- The most interesting advanced topic discussions show up in Heinz Kabutz's Java Specialists Newsletter (*http://www.javaspecialists.eu*).

There is no end of Java APIs to learn about. And there are still more books to be written . . . and read.

Java Then and Now

Introduction: Always in Motion the Java Is

Java has always been a moving target for developers and writers. Some developers I meet in my commercial training programs are still not aware of some of the features of ancient Java releases, let alone Java 6 or 7. This appendix offers a look at each of the major releases of Java. For a review of the early history, see Jon Byous's Sun Microsystems article "Java Technology: An Early History" (1998) (*http://bit.ly/java-early*). You can also find a copy at the Paderborn University website (*http://bit.ly/java-early-2*).

Java Preview: HotJava

The first time that the world at large heard of Java was the May 1995 release of HotJava (*http://bit.ly/1lk5VeI*), a web browser written entirely in Java and introducing the *Java applet* for dynamic web content. The download included the first Java compiler, aimed primarily at writing applets, and the source code for much of the system. That year's SunWorld conference helped escalate this release into the public eye, with the dramatic last-minute announcement by Marc Andreessen of Netscape that Java had been licensed and would be incorporated into all Netscape browsers.

Java Arrives: 1.0

Early in 1996, Java 1.0 was "officially" released, with its API featuring the basic structure that has underpinned all the Javas that have appeared ever since (`java.lang`, `java.io`, `java.util`, and so on).

What Was New in Java 1.1

The first major revision, 1.1, was released in February 1997. It featured the new Readers/Writers classes for reading/writing text in any of the Unicode subsets or "character sets," making Java one of the first languages to support the Unicode standard for Internationalization. Supporting this was the new package java.text and some code in java.util, building upon the Readers and Writers to provide broader support for internationalization; this change introduced Calendar and GregorianCalendar, Format (DateFormat, MessageFormat, NumberFormat), and the Locale and ResourceBundle classes.

In the GUI toolkit AWT, the event model was changed from a single method to handle all events, to the now-universal event listener model used on all GUI toolkits invented since. To help support event listeners, inner classes were added to the language, which would remain the preferred way of implementing listeners up until Java 8. Two other significant additions in 1.1 were the JavaBeans conventions and packaging, and the JDBC Database Access in package java.sql, which was to become one of the cornerstones of Java Enterprise Edition (Java EE).

What Was New in Java 2 (Java SDK 1.2)

Java 1.2 was one of the two largest revisions—including Collections, Swing, and Reflection—to the Java Platform. So large was this revision that the marketing of this release introduced the term "Java 2" for the Java Platform, which was to stick around until the next of the largest releases, Java 5 and its implementation JDK 1.5. This "Java 2" name is the basis of the now long-defunct names "J2SE" and "J2EE" for the Standard and Enterprise platform editions, respectively. The Java 2 release featured the Collections framework (*http://bit.ly/1nWNfAQ*), a unified system for data structuring, introducing the basic Collections structure described in Recipe 7.3 with new implementations (and adapting older classes such as Vector and Hashtable to conform to the new interfaces).

It had become obvious that AWT was inadequate for advanced desktop GUI development, because it had been (deliberately) chosen to provide a "least common denominator" approach to GUIs on all the platforms common at the time, including Mac OS 7, OS/2, Windows 95 and Unix—if any of these platforms didn't support a feature, it was omitted. And worse—if different platforms worked differently or had bugs in a given feature, Java inherited those differences and bugs, because AWT always used the native platform components directly. Swing provided a clean break from this tradition, doing all the rendering in Java—providing consistency and full-featuredness on all platforms—and providing pluggable "look and feel" implementations to make the GUI components "look right" on each platform.

Swing's use of application rendering significantly upped the CPU load on the Java Virtual Machine, so this release also introduced the first use of "Just In Time" (JIT) in the JVM, a technique for transforming Java bytecode into native CPU (Intel, SPARC, PowerPC) code for better performance.

Although `java.lang.Class` was included in 1.0 and gained methods such as `get-Class()` in 1.1, further additions and the new package `java.lang.reflect` constituted the Reflection API (see Chapter 23), providing a standard way for classes to examine ("reflect"), instantiate, and manipulate other classes.

Finally, this release also introduced Java Interface Description Language, an interface-like definition of remote methods intended for for CORBA interoperability.

There were a few minor language changes in 1.2, most notably the inclusion of the `strictfp` keyword to allow non-`strictfp` floating-point calculations to use greater precision than the 32/64-bit IEEE-754 floating-point standard.

What Was New in Java 1.3

Released in May 2000, Java 1.3 was a smaller, more incremental release. However, it did introduce another core Enterprise API, the Java Naming and Directory Interface (JNDI).

Another of 1.3's interesting features was the Dynamic Proxy mechanism, which provided official support for dynamically generating proxy objects. To continue 1.2's gains in performance, the HotSpot JVM was included in the JDK.

Also introduced here were the first well-documented debugger mechanism, the Java Platform Debugger Architecture (JPDA), and JavaSound, an API for controlling sound devices.

What Was New in Java 1.4

This section reviews some of the changes made to Java in 1.4.

Java 1.4 Language Changes

Java SE 1.4 introduced `assert` keyword, which allows assertion testing; testing can be switched on or off dynamically without recompilation. The intention of `assert` is to encourage developers to write pre- and post-code assertions to verify correct input and output of methods; how to write unit test-like tests into your code (see Recipe 1.13).

Java 1.4 API Changes

Java SE 1.4 introduced a variety of technologies, such as a standardized Java implementation of regular expressions (see Chapter 4). Regular Expressions, while borrowed from formal language theory or theoretical computer science, found singularly powerful use in early Unix systems as the basis for almost all pattern-matching commands. Larry Wall extended them with his Perl language (see *Learning Perl* and *Perl Cookbook* [O'Reilly]); it is these extended regexes that Java implements (with a few minor changes). See Chapter 4 for plenty of details on regex.

To facilitate "exception translation" to provide tiering isolation, the platform introduced "exception chaining", the ability to wrap one exception in another; many of the standard Exception types were modified to support this. Recognizing the increasing importance of the eXtensible Markup Language, 1.4 introduced the options covered in Chapter 20 (the Java API for XML Processing, or JAXP). Finally, recognizing that applets were never going to take over the world, this release brought about Recipe 21.11, "Java Web Start".

There were a number of other features added, such as:

1. Recipe 16.10, "Network Logging with java.util.logging"
2. Recipe 7.12, "Storing Strings in Properties and Preferences"
3. Security and crypto (JCE, JSSE, JAAS)

What Was New in Java 5

Java 5 (JDK 1.5) is the other "largest" release, containing a variety of changes both in the language and in the APIs.

Java 5 Language Changes

Language changes include:

- foreach loop
- Enumeration types (`enum` keyword)
- Annotations (metadata; see Recipe 23.9)
- Generic Types
- `printf`, scanners, and the `Scanner` classes
- Variable arguments (varargs)
- Improved semantics for the Java Memory Model

- `static import`

Java 5 foreach loop

You want a convenient means of accessing all the elements of an array or collection. The Java 5 `foreach` loop syntax is as follows:

```
for (Type localVar : IterableOfThatType) {
    ...
}
```

For example:

```
for (String s : myListOfStrings) {
        // use s here
}
```

This form of `for` is pronounced as "for each" and is referred to that way in the documentation and the compiler messages; the colon (:) is pronounced as "in" so that the statement is read as "foreach String s in myListOfStrings." The `String` named s will be given each value from `myListOfStrings` for one pass through the loop. How is `myListOfStrings` declared? The `foreach` construction can be used on Java arrays, on `Collection` classes, and on anything that implements the `Iterable` interface. The compiler turns it into an iteration, typically using an `Iterator` object where `Collection` classes are involved. Example A-1 shows using foreach to iterate through an array and a `List`.

Example A-1. ForeachDemo.java

```
String[] data = { "Toronto", "Stockholm" };
for (String s : data) {
    System.out.println(s);
}

// Show the Java 5 foreach loop - do not modernize to Java 8
List<String> list = Arrays.asList(data);
for (String s : list) {
    System.out.println(s);
}
```

In modern Java, the `foreach` loop is used more commonly than the prior `for` loop. The main times when the older style would be used are:

- When you need the number of each element for calculation or indexing a target array or arrays
- When you are creating new data using a numeric index
- When the control involves floating point calculations rather than integer

- When you want to remove items from the collection during iteration, so you need explicit access to the iterator

Java 5 enums

Enumerations implement the Typesafe Enumeration Pattern described in Josh Bloch's book *Effective Java*. Bloch worked at Sun to implement this language feature, among others. The basic idea is that where you have a small, rarely changing set of values, it makes sense to list them and have them known at compile time. For example, the colors at a stoplight are red, amber, and green; we might code this as in Example A-2, at a bare minimum.

Example A-2. Color.java

```
public enum Color {
        RED, AMBER, GREEN
}
```

Enums are covered in Recipe 8.8.

Java 5 annotations

Java Annotations are metadata-like "sticky notes" that you can attach to various places in your Java code to provide extra information beyond normal Java syntax and semantics. Some (such as `java.lang.Override`) are only used at compile time; others—the majority—are consulted at runtime. They are described, with examples, in Recipe 23.9.

Java 5 generic types

One of the most notable additions to Java 5 is "generic types," such as collections, that are defined to hold objects of a certain type rather than just `Object` (obviating the downcast otherwise needed each time you get an object back from a collection). For example, with a List of `Strings`, prior to 1.5 you might have written the code in Example A-3.

Example A-3. ListsOldAndNew.java

```
    List myList = new ArrayList();
    myList.add("hello");
    myList.add("goodbye");

    // myList.add(new Date()); This would compile but cause failures later

    for (int i = 0; i < myList.size(); i++) {
            String s = (String)myList.get(i);
            System.out.println(s);
    }
```

In Java 5, you would be more likely to write this as:

```
List<String> myList = new ArrayList<>(); // Java 6: new ArrayList<String>();
myList.add("hello");
myList.add("goodbye");

// myList.add(new Date()); This would not compile!

for (String s : myList) {    // Look Ma, no downcast!
      System.out.println(s);
}
```

This mechanism is called "generics" because it allows you to write generic classes, the arguments and return types of methods of which are specified when the class is instantiated.

Although the original definition of the List interface and the ArrayList class had methods dealing in java.lang.Object, in 1.5 these types have been changed to a Generic type or "type parameter" so that you can declare and instantiate them with any object type (String, Customer, Integer), and get the benefits of stronger type checking and elimination of downcasts.

Not just these types, but all of the Collections API and most of the other parts of the standard Java API in 1.5 have been updated to be generic types. If you write your own multipurpose classes, you can fairly easily change them to be generics in the same fashion.

The notation <type> is used to specify the particular type with which the class is to be instantiated. Java developers had better get comfortable with this notation, because it is used extensively in the 1.5 javadoc!

These additions related to data structuring are all covered in Chapter 7. Also see *Java Generics and Collections*.

Variable argument lists

Java 5 introduced method declarations with variable-length argument lists, commonly called "varargs." This allows you to write a method that can be called with any number of arguments of the given type. For example, a method mySum to be called with a variable number of int arguments can be written as:

```
static int mySum(int... args) {
    int total = 0;
    for (int a : args) {
        total += a;
    }
    return total;
}
```

Note that there can only be one variable-length argument list in the parameter list of a method, and that it must be last; there can be other arguments before it, but not after.

Any of the following would be a valid call to this method:

```
System.out.println(mySum(5, 7, 9));
System.out.println(mySum(5));
System.out.println(mySum());
int[] nums = {5, 7, 9};
System.out.println(mySum(nums));
```

That last one may be a bit surprising. When you think about it, the "…" in a method declaration is a kind of syntactic sugar for "array of," so you can pass an explicit array. This does not mean that arrays and … are interchangeable; if you declare the method parameter as, say, `int[] args`, then you will be required to pass an array, not use a variable-length argument list.

The objects can be of any type; see the file *lang/VarArgsDemo.java* for examples of other types, and argument lists with other arguments before the varargs in the method declaration.

Java 1.5 API Changes

This section lists some of the changes made to Java with the Java 5 (JDK 1.5) release.

Java 5 threading: Concurrency utilities

Java was the first mainstream language with explicit support for multithreading. It has always been possible to write Java applications that run multiple sections of code more or less concurrently. In fact, even the simplest Java application creates at least one thread —Java's memory allocation garbage collection runs in a background thread, started by the Java runtime before you can say "Hello World."

However, the code required has sometimes been slightly convoluted. In Java 1.5, the API has been significantly expanded to provide a series of utility classes that make it much easier to support multithreaded applications. Even such complex operations as various types of locking, and creation of thread pools, have been addressed. This work is an outgrowth of an open source library developed by Doug Lea, author of the book *Concurrent Programming in Java* (Addison-Wesley) and a computer science professor at State University of New York in Oswego, New York. This code was contributed to the Java Community Process where it has been extensively worked over by a multitasking committee of multithreading experts. The package `java.util.concurrent` and its subpackages contain all of the new classes, and there are quite a few of them.

One of the key differences from traditional Java synchronization is that the new classes really are concurrent. In other words, while a synchronized class such as `Vector` or `Hashtable` uses the object's monitor lock to block all but a single thread from running any synchronized method at a time, the new concurrent classes will allow multiple threads to access them at the same time, yet still provide "thread-safe" access. For example, the new `ConcurrentHashMap` class allows an unlimited number of concurrent reading threads and a (settable) maximum number of writes. This will generally lead to much better scalability and faster performance, both of which become important when designing enterprise-scale application services. What's also nice about the `ConcurrentHashMap` is that, because it still implements the `Map` interface from `java.util`, it is a drop-in replacement for the older synchronized `Hashtable` class (in most cases, but do refer to the documentation for some edge cases that need consideration). Using it where suitable is as simple as adding an import and changing:

```
Map myMap = new Hashtable();
```

to

```
Map myMap = new ConcurrentHashMap();
```

Of course, because you read the section on Generics (see "Java 5 generic types" on page 834), you'll know that you probably want to use it in a typesafe way, so if your `Map` were hashing from a `String` to a `CustomerAddress` object, you'd actually write:

```
Map<String,CustomerAddress> myMap =
    new ConcurrentHashMap<String,CustomerAddress>();
```

I did say you have to get used to that `<type>` notation. Note that in 1.5, the `Map` interface is now declared as `Map<K, V>` (for Keys and Values); the iteration methods are declared in the interface as `Enumeration<K> keys()` and `Collection<V> values()`. So in this example you would get `Enumeration<String> keys()` and `Collection<CustomerAddress> values` from the "keys" and "values" methods, respectively.

Since you give the type for the keys and values when you instantiate a class implementing `Map`, you get back the iterators with the correct types built in, meaning no downcast needed when you extract the elements.

printf is back

In the early days of Java, it was common for people to try to bring the C-language `printf` functionality to Java. Most of these attempts worked only for certain cases, and were not really object-oriented approaches. After much prodding from developers and much internal debate, Sun relented and included printf functionality into Java 5.

The functionality is contained in the new `java.util.Formatter` class (not to be confused with the existing `DateFormat`, `NumberFormat`, etc., classes) and is also available in convenience routines in `System.out` (actually, in the `PrintStream` and `PrintWriter` classes). The format codes are more comprehensive than the original C `printf`, but the basic idea is the same: you pass a format string and one or more objects to be formatted according to the format string. For example, you might write:

```
System.out.printf("Pi is approximately %6.4f\n", Math.PI);
```

The % is the lead-in to the format code, and the 6.4f is (as it was in printf and in Fortran before that) the code to print a floating-point value with a field-width of six characters and four digits after the decimal place. So the program prints:

```
Pi is approximately 3.1416
```

There is much more to this, with support for date formatting, localization, and more. See the documentation for java.util.Formatter for details.

There is also scanf-like functionality, in the Recipe 10.6. This does not use % format codes, but uses a variety of next() methods, such as next(String), next(Pattern), nextInteger, nextDouble, and so on, plus all of the corresponding hasNext() methods. See the documentation for java.util.Scanner. printf, and the scanning utilities are covered in "Discussion" on page 313.

Bibliographic note/full disclosure

Some of the Java 5 material in this section originally appeared in an article (*http://bit.ly/1oYegV1*) I wrote on O'Reilly Web back in the day.

What Was New in Java 6

By contrast to Java 5, December 2006's Java 6 release was more incremental. Though there were no radical changes to the language, there were changes to the underlying JVM, including performance improvements, upgrades to garbage collection, faster application start-up, and a handful of new APIs.

Java 6 API Changes

The API changes included:

- Swing improvements include SwingWorker, table sorting and filtering, and Swing double-buffering for performance;
- Scripting Engines Support (see Recipe 24.3) provides a formal structure for invoking external scripting languages from within Java;
- Java Compiler API lets a Java program compile code on the fly;
- JAX-WS mini-server javax.xml.ws.Endpoint in the JDK;
- JDBC upgraded to JDBC 4;
- Version 2 of JAXB (Java API for XML Binding);
- Support for pluggable annotations.

What Was New in Java 7

This section lists the main changes added in Java 7.

Java 7 Language/JVM Changes

The Java 7 language introduces a small variety of useful features, including:

- Multicatch (see the following section)
- Type Inference for Generics (see "Type Inference for Generics (Diamond Operator, <>)" on page 840)
- String Switch (see "Java 7 String Switch" on page 840)
- Binary constants, like `int delta = 011001b;`
- Use of "_" as numeric group separator, like `long ageOfOldestFossil = 4_000_000_000L;` (but note that these are not used or verified, they're just for readability)
- try-with-resource (see "Try With Resources" on page 840)
- JVM `invokedynamic` instruction
- JVM performance improvements
- JVM garbage collection (GC) improvements

The first few of these are detailed starting at "Multicatch" on page 839.

The Java Virtual Machine has always had `InvokeVirtual` as a JVM instruction for support of possibly overridden methods. Java 7 introduces a related new JVM machine instruction called `InvokeDynamic`, which is intended for use by language developers to provide better support for dynamically typed languages such as JRuby, Jython (Java Python), and Clojure, some of which are discussed in Chapter 24. As this book focuses on Java, and because the changes will only result in better performance, not linguistic change, for these languages, I don't discuss it here.

Also on the JVM side, the default garbage collection algorithm has changed to "Garbage First" (G1GC). The G1GC is a server-style garbage collector targeted at MP apps with large amounts of real memory. Further, it meets a soft real-time goal with high probability—meaning better response for most apps. Although this is not the last word in GC, it is the long-term planned replacement for the widely used Concurrent Mark-and-Sweep Collector (CMS) GC.

Multicatch

You can now list multiple exception types in one catch:

```
Object newbie = null;
try {
        Class.forName(clazzName).newInstance();
} catch (InstantiationException|IllegalAccessException|
   ClassNotFoundException e) {
        // app-defined handler
        handleError("Could not create instance of " + clazzName, e);
}
```

In previous versions of Java you'd have needed three catch clauses with a lot of copy-and-paste, error-prone error handling, or, have something like catch (Exception e), which might be more than you want to catch.

Try With Resources

Another great simplification for proper error handling! You can now create resources (I/O Streams/Writers, JDBC Connections, …) as the argument of a try statement and have them closed automatically. The resource must implement the (new for this purpose) AutoCloseable interface. Many standard classes have been modified to implement AutoCloseable to support this.

```
try (BufferedReader is = new BufferedReader(new FileReader(fileName))) {
        String line;
        while ((line = is.readLine()) != null) {
                System.out.println(line); }
} catch (IOException e) {
        handleError("Problem reading " + fileName, e);
} // No finally needed, no close needed - it's all done automatically!
```

Type Inference for Generics (Diamond Operator, <>)

Java 5 introduced Generic Types, as described in "Java 5 generic types" on page 834. For example, to create a List of Strings without any warning messages, you might write:

```
List<String> names = new ArrayList<String>();
```

Java 7 brings "Type Inference" for Generic Types. Instead of having to repeat the type parameter from the declaration in the definition, omit it and just put <>. The preceding list of strings can be rewritten as:

```
List<String> names = new ArrayList<>();
```

Java 7 String Switch

This long-awaited feature lets you replace a series of if statements using string comparisons, by a single switch statement; i.e., you can now use Strings as case labels:

```
String input = getStringFromSomewhere();
switch(input) {
        case "red":
                System.out.println("Stop!");
```

```
                break;
    case "amber": case "yellow":
            System.out.println("Caution!");
            break;
    case "green":
            System.out.println("Go (placidly among the haste)");
            break;
    default:
            handleError("Invalid input: " + input);
            break;
    }
```

Obviously the strings have to be compile-time constants, either string literals or strings marked final. In fact, in real code, you would probably want to define final String variables for the cases. This should lead you to wonder why you're not using a Java 5 Enum (see "Java 5 enums" on page 834). The String Switch has a place where long strings are in use, but it needs care for issues like case sensitivity (convert to lowercase first, see "Problem" on page 89).

Java 7 API Changes

Released in July of 2011, Java 7 includes considerable support for concurrency, including the new fork/join framework (see Recipe 22.9).

Large parts of the standard API including I/O and JDBC were updated to implement AutoCloseable for use in try-with-resource. Closeable now extends AutoCloseable:

```
public interface java.lang.AutoCloseable {
  public abstract void close() throws java.lang.Exception;
}
public interface java.io.Closeable extends java.lang.AutoCloseable {
  public abstract void close() throws java.io.IOException;
}
```

URLClassLoader implements Closeable, and gains a close() method, which allows for updating of external JAR files being classloaded (on MS Windows, files can't be overwritten while open). This is aimed at, and very useful for, development of web apps.

NIO2—new Filesystem API—includes more filesystem support and operators, and a new java.io.Path class intended to replace most uses of java.io.File (see Recipe 11.10).

Version 4.1 of JDBC updated the RowSet API to version 1.1, which includes support for creating online or detached rowsets, and removed the older unsupported com.sun.rowset implementations.

A new package, java.lang.invoke, was added in support of the InvokeDynamic JVM changes for dynamically typed languages; it has classes such as MethodHandle and CallSite for use mainly by language developers.

Numerous small changes made to graphics rendering/fonts, Swing, networking, desktop, I18N, and more—see Oracle's website (*http://bit.ly/1iCCdkk*).

What Is New in Java 8

Java 8 Language Changes

The biggest new feature in the Java 8 language is lambda expressions! After a decade of debate on how to implement them, "closures" or "lambda expressions" arrived with Java 8. This is such a vast topic that it gets an entire chapter in this edition; see Chapter 9.

Annotations can now be placed on structured types.

Java 8 API Changes

Java 8 brings in the new date/time API from JSR-310. This provides a more consistent and sensible set of classes and routines for dealing with time. Chapter 6 has been completely rewritten to use the new API, ending with a recipe showing various conversions between the "old" and new APIs.

Java 8 introduced "functional programming" techniques such as closures and parallel collections, which we discuss in Chapter 9.

In support of `Streams`, there are new methods in interfaces such as `List`, `Map`, and `Set`, which have been largely unchanged since the long-gone days of Java 1.1. Fortunately the Java 8 language support adds a `default` method type in interfaces, so your custom implementations of these interfaces are not required to change (as long as you make sure you change your IDE settings to Java 8 Compiler Compliance).

As one example of `default` methods in action, `Iterable` gets a new `default` method called `forEach()`, which lets you write code like this:

```
myList.forEach(o -> /* do something with o here... */);
```

This is discussed further in "Iterable.forEach method (Java 8)" on page 204.

A new JavaScript implementation codenamed *Nashorn* is available via `javax.script` (see Recipe 24.3) and can also be run from the command line.

Javadoc (see Recipe 21.2) extended to `javax.tools` API.

Annotations can be repeated, obviating the need for "wrapper" annotations like `javax.persistence.NamedQueries`, which is just a container for a list of `javax.persistence.NamedQuery` annotations.

Finally, Java provides support for Base 64 encoding/decoding in the form of `java.util.Base64` with two nested classes for encoding and decoding.

Dozens of other small changes, such as those covered by OpenJDK (*http://bit.ly/1j9FYgJ*).

Look Away Beyond the Blue Horizon...

There are no official announcements yet for Java 9 or beyond. It is anticipated that a release, probably called Java 9, may appear around 2016 and may include more JVM optimization ("self-tuning VM"), better support for larger memory in the multi-gigabyte range, improvements for native code users, and more. Announcements of these plans typically appear at the usually annual Java World conference. Given the huge investment in Java by Oracle and Java users large and small, it is likely that there will be a Java 10, and more. There is no end in sight.

The Evolution of Client-Side Java: Applets, Browser Wars, Swing, JavaFX

While you can infer some of this from the per-JDK revision notes given in the rest of this appendix, it seems fitting to provide a unified narrative on the role of Java in the desktop.

Java began its public life as a vehicle for embedding flashy dynamic content in web pages via Java applets. Applets got off to a flying start with their incorporation in the Netscape line of browsers in 1995–96. Incidentally, part of the cross-licensing agreement between Sun and Netscape was that Netscape could use the term "JavaScript" for what was then its "LiveScript" web scripting language.

Applets, alas, never took over the world for a variety of reasons, including the fact that Microsoft never allowed Java applets to become a full player in Internet Explorer, users' fear of security issues (some of which surfaced from time to time), difficulties of installing and updating, and the increasing capabilities of CSS and JavaScript, and later HTML5.

There were some large users—for example, the *Blackboard* product (*http://blackboard.com*) used for student-instructor communication in hundreds of colleges and universities. However, even these have had issues of compatibility, sometimes requiring students to load a particular update like "JDK 1.6 Update 42" in order to be supported on a given release of BlackBoard.

Along the way, the original AWT GUI package was supplanted by Swing, a newer and better Graphical User Interface package. Around this time, the `Applet` class was supplemented with the `JApplet` class to allow `Applets` to be full users of Swing GUI classes.

Yet Java was never without competition on the desktop. Adobe Flash came along soon after Java, and because it was single-sourced, came from the home of Illustrator and Photoshop, which the web's graphic designers loved, and Flash prospered.

More recently, the browsers themselves have become competitors to both Java and Flash. The HTML5 standard introduces a large number of technologies such as increased JavaScript, the Canvas object for graphics, access to some local devices, and much more. Many new projects today are starting with HTML5. Though JavaScript is not as nice a programming environment as Java, its familiarity to the large number of web developers in circulation has helped it dominate large areas of desktop development.

One of Sun's responses was to target a new technogogy that is now called JavaFX to the desktop. JavaFX can be used in browsers or in desktop applications. It does provide considerable benefits to GUI and graphics developers. There is information on JavaFX in Chapter 14.

Also in the area of "client-side" technologies, Sun insisted from the beginning that mobile phone developers use the Java Micro Edition (ME), based on a severely cut-down JVM and a totally different user interface package. Fortunately for Sun, BlackBerry (then called Research In Motion, or RIM), agreed to this. At the time, it made sense—when the early versions of BlackBerry OS came out, mobile CPUs were slow, and memory was limited, so a tiny "LCDUI" made sense.

When Google wanted to expand into the mobile space to expand the reach of its advertising business, it soon found—and bought—a company called Android that had a Linux-based OS with a rewritten Java implementation. Android's developers had tried to reason with Sun about using more complete Java on mobile, given how mobile device CPU and memory was growing, but were rebuffed. So they went off and built the Android user interface, which has since become the most widely used Java platform. But during this time, Sun was acquired by Oracle.

Live on stage at the first JavaOne conference after the acquisition, Larry Ellison welcomed Android as part of the Java ecosystem. But when Android continued its meteoric rise, Oracle's lawyers thought they could muscle in on this, and Oracle sued Google for a billion dollars, alleging copyright, trademark, and trade secret violations. The suit was very complex, but one of the most important aspects was Oracle's claim that it could copyright the API, separately from the code. Thus, anybody ever wanting to write a class called String with the methods described in the String class' javadoc page would have to apply for permission from Oracle. Needless to say, several old-line software companies like Microsoft lined up with Oracle, while the entire open source world lined up with Google, fearing the "chilling effects" this would have on the entire open source world. And, fortunately for Android and for the open source world, so did the judge. This suit was won by Google, but Oracle has since launched an appeal, which is moving through the courts as this book goes to press.

Oh, and back to BlackBerry. Unfortunately for BlackBerry, as time and Moore's Law marched on in tandem, Java ME did not keep in step, and was left behind. BlackBerry, obligated to stay on the ME platform, and unable to modify the Java ME classes, had to spend billions of dollars in R&D through the late 1990s and the 2000s building a parallel package structure to provide modern GUI and device capabilities, which it did all through OS versions 5, 6, and 7. When it finally dawned on RIM management that the

JVM+OS combination itself was the bottleneck, they first tried to make their current JVM run on QNX, a Unix-based operating system from a company of the same name, which RIM acquired. This was doomed to failure, but a skunkworks project within the company took the open source Android and made that run in a matter of weeks. Managment decided to abandon JavaME, and to abandon Java as their main app development language, but to allow Java-based Android apps to run as almost-first-class citizens in the BB10 environment. Alas, then the company took a year and a half to get QNX working well enough on its new "BlackBerry 10" devices so that it could release it. During this time of uncertainty its sales tanked. BB10 is now available, and works well enough (and runs most Android 4.2 apps). But again, the jury is still out on whether BlackBerry can recover its destroyed market share, or will fade away or be absorbed into another stream of development.

Java continues to be used on the desktop (although the market for desktop apps is steadily losing ground to mobile devices), in the browser (decreasingly), and in mobile (particularly on Android devices and in the Android Runtime on BlackBerry 10—this is a good deal for Java developers who want to build mobile apps). Java also continues to be heavily used in enterprise environments using packages like Java EE servers, JSP/JSF pages, Spring Framework, Hibernate, and more.

Index

We'd like to hear your suggestions for improving our indexes. Send email to index@oreilly.com.

Application Bundles, 706
ArrayList, 197
    arrays vs., 196–199
    multidimensional, 234–236
arrays, 192
    ArrayList vs., 196–199
    multidimensional, 234–236
    of objects, 192
    of primitive types, 192
    resizing, 193–195
    using for data structures, 192
assert keyword, 35
assertion mechanism, 35
audio, 405
awk, 810
AWT
    ActionListener interface, 278
    Custom Layout Manager program, 510–516

B

Bachmann, Erik, 610
background threads, 754
bean containers, 699
BeanShell, 810
Bell Laboratories, 127
big-endian machines, 339
BigDecimal object, 172
BigInteger object, 172
binary data
    as input/output, 336
    reading/writing over networks, 430–431
    returning over sockets, 542–545
binary numbers, 154
bison, 316
BlackBerry, 444
Bloch, Joshua, 239, 260
BorderLayout manager, 462
BoxLayout manager, 462
bridging, 200
BufferedReader, 298–300
    StreamTokenizer and, 308–312
build tools, 1
built-in types, 139
Burke, Bill, 443
BusCard program, 533–537
buttons, 465–467

C

C programs, data streams from, 338–340
CachedRowSet subinterface, 631
callback functions, 279
callbacks, 251–255
CANON_EQ flag, 125
capture groups, 118
CardLayout manager, 462
CASE_INSENSITIVE flag, 125
cast, 143
casting, 141
CDI (Context and Dependency Injection), 48, 269
CDI Beans, 699
CDN (Content Distribution Network), 443
characters, 81
    comparing, 536
    strings of, 67
charAt() method (String), 76
Chat Client program, 450–454
checked exceptions, 266
checksum, 77
chooser operating methods, 490
chunk size, 754
CI (continuous integration), 41–45
    servers, 42
ClassCastExceptions, 344
classes
    ClassLoader, constructing with, 774
    coupling between, 267–270
    dependency injection, 267–270
    documenting, 689–693
    listing, in package, 782–784
    loading/instantiating dynamically, 772–774
    plug-in-like, 789–791
    preparing as JavaBeans, 699–702
    printing information of, 780
    reflection and, 766, 772–774
ClassLoader, 774
CLASSPATH, 14–17, 58
    benefits of using, 58
    JAR files, adding, 58
clients, 558
Clojure, 276, 801
clone command (git), 19
clone() method
    alternatives to, 248
    arguments against, 239
closures vs. inner classes, 278–281

extensions and runtime environment, 58

F

Factory pattern, 239, 241
FieldPosition, 158
fields
    private, accessing via reflection, 771
    reflection and, 767–770
File class (java.io), 365–385
    createNewFile() method, 368
    createTempFile() method, 372
    delete() method, 370
    deleteOnExit() method, 372
    list() method, 375–377
    listFiles() method, 375–377
    listRoots() method, 377
    mkdir() method, 378
    Path vs., 379
    renameTo() method, 369
file descriptors, 298
file properties, 56
files, 365–385
    attributes, changing, 373
    continued lines, reading, 332–335
    converting character sets of, 329
    copying, 318–325
    creating, 368
    creating transient, 372
    deleting, 370
    end-of-line characters, 330
    finding, 349–351
    getResource() method and, 349–351
    getResourceAsStream() method and, 349–
        351
    getting information about, 365–368
    input/output, 317–325
    opening by name, 317
    parsing, with grammatical structures, 316
    platform-independent, 331
    reading into strings, 325
    renaming, 369
    seeking, 337
    update notifications for, 380–382
    user data, saving to disk, 357–360
FileWatcherService, 380–382
FilteredRowSet subinterface, 631
final keyword, 34
Find program, 382–385
find() method, 117

Finnegan, Ken, 270
flex, 316
floats
    comparing, 149–151
    dividing integers without, 146
    ensuring accuracy of, 147–149
    rounding, 151
FlowLayout manager, 462
fluent programming, 283
FOP (Formatting Objects Processor), 664
for loops, 155
fork/join framework, 750–754
formatter format codes, 305
formatting codes for dates and times, 306
FrameMarkers MIF, 661
frameworks
    in Java, 46–49
    libraries vs., 47
FreeGeoIP service, 442
Friedl, Jeffrey, 107
functional interfaces, custom, 286–288
functional programming, 275–294
    closures, 278–281
    custom interfaces, 286–288
    lambdas, 278–281
    legacy code and, 289–293
    method references, 289–293
    mixins, 293–294
    parallel streams, 285
    streams and, 283
    throughput, improving, 285
FUSE, 295

G

Gang of Four (GoF), 241
General Markup Language (GML), 661
generic collections, 199
    avoiding typecasting with, 200–203
Generic Collections, 805
generic types mechanism, 197
getAvailableLocals() (Locale), 520
getenv() (method), 52
getImage() routine, 400
getInputStream() methods, 542
getInstance() (Locale), 527
getopt method, 59
getOutputStream() methods, 542
getResource() method, 349–351
getResourceAsStream() method, 349–351

About the Author

Ian F. Darwin has worked in the computer industry for three decades. He wrote the freeware file(1) command used on Linux and BSD, and is the author of *Checking C Programs with Lint*, *Java Cookbook*, and more than 100 articles and courses on C and Unix. In addition to programming and consulting, Ian teaches Unix, C, and Java for Learning Tree International, one of the world's largest technical training companies.

Colophon

The animal on the cover of *Java Cookbook*, Third Edition, is a domestic chicken (*Gallus domesticus*). Domestic chickens are descended from the wild red jungle fowl of India. Domesticated over 8,000 years ago in the area that is now Vietnam and Thailand, chickens are raised for meat and eggs, and the males for sport as well (although cock-fighting is currently illegal in many places).

With their big, heavy bodies and small wings, these birds are well suited to living on the ground, and they can fly only short distances. Their four-toed feet are designed for scratching in the dirt, where they find the elements of their usual diet: worms, bugs, seeds, and various plant matter.

A male chicken is called a rooster or cock, and a female is known as a hen. The incubation period for a chicken egg is about three weeks; newly hatched chickens are precocial, meaning they have downy feathers and can walk around on their own right after emerging from the egg. They're also not dependent on their mothers for food; not only can they procure their own, but they also can live for up to a week after hatching on egg yolk that remains in their abdomen after birth.

The topic of chickens comes up frequently in ancient writings. Chinese documents date their introduction to China to 1400 B.C., Babylonian carvings mention them in 600 B.C., and Aristophanes wrote about them in 400 B.C. The rooster has long symbolized courage: the Romans thought chickens were sacred to Mars, god of war, and the first French Republic chose the rooster as its emblem.

The cover image is a 19th-century engraving from the Dover Pictorial Archive. The cover fonts are URW Typewriter and Guardian Sans. The text font is Adobe Minion Pro; the heading font is Adobe Myriad Condensed; and the code font is Dalton Maag's Ubuntu Mono.

Get even more for your money.

Join the O'Reilly Community, and register the O'Reilly books you own. It's free, and you'll get:

- $4.99 ebook upgrade offer
- 40% upgrade offer on O'Reilly print books
- Membership discounts on books and events
- Free lifetime updates to ebooks and videos
- Multiple ebook formats, DRM FREE
- Participation in the O'Reilly community
- Newsletters
- Account management
- 100% Satisfaction Guarantee

Signing up is easy:

1. Go to: oreilly.com/go/register
2. Create an O'Reilly login.
3. Provide your address.
4. Register your books.

Note: English-language books only

To order books online:
oreilly.com/store

For questions about products or an order:
orders@oreilly.com

To sign up to get topic-specific email announcements and/or news about upcoming books, conferences, special offers, and new technologies:
elists@oreilly.com

For technical questions about book content:
booktech@oreilly.com

To submit new book proposals to our editors:
proposals@oreilly.com

O'Reilly books are available in multiple DRM-free ebook formats. For more information:
oreilly.com/ebooks

©2014 O'Reilly Media, Inc. O'Reilly logo is a registered trademark of O'Reilly Media, Inc. 14373